Rethinking Society

in the 21st Century

Rethinking Society in the 21st Century

CRITICAL READINGS IN SOCIOLOGY

SECOND EDITION

Edited by

Michelle Webber and

Kate Bezanson

Canadian Scholars' Press Inc.
Toronto

Rethinking Society in the 21st Century: Critical Readings in Sociology
Second Edition
edited by Michelle Webber and Kate Bezanson

Second edition published in 2008 by
Canadian Scholars' Press Inc.
180 Bloor Street West, Suite 801
Toronto, Ontario
M5S 2V6

www.cspi.org

Canadian Scholars' Press Inc. gratefully acknowledges financial support for our publishing activities from the Government of Canada through the Book Publishing Industry Development Program (BPIDP).

Library and Archives Canada Cataloguing in Publication

Rethinking society in the 21st century : critical readings in sociology / edited by Michelle Webber and Kate Bezanson. — 2nd ed.

Includes bibliographical references.
ISBN 978-1-55130-342-0

1. Sociology—Textbooks. 2. Canada—Social conditions—1991–
— Textbooks. I. Webber, Michelle II. Bezanson, Kate

HM586.R48 2008   301   C2007-906403-5

Book design: Susan MacGregor/Digital Zone
Cover art: Fran GC, "235778 Underground," from *Stock Xchng*

08 09 10 11 12   5 4 3 2 1

Printed and bound in Canada by Marquis Book Printing Inc.

Table of Contents

v

Preface

Originally faced with the double cohort, as instructors of introductory sociology, we struggled to pull together readings, for the first edition, that were at once accessible, critical, and engaging. We decided to prepare a reader that we would want to use in our classes. We sought to weave feminist, class-conscious, and anti-racist approaches to the study of sociology. This reader reflects our various interests and strengths, but also aims to broaden the traditional theoretical and political approaches found in many sociology readers. It incorporates considerable Canadian material, drawing on the contributions of scholars from a range of disciplines. The reader balances classical theoretical approaches to sociology with contemporary approaches to theory and social issues.

We are pleased to present this second edition of *Rethinking Society in the 21st Century*. We have expanded the total number of readings as well as included more Canadian content. We hope that the readings herein provoke substantive debate and discussion.

Acknowledgements

We would like to thank the students who assisted in putting this edition together, Robin Spinks and Shannon McHugh. Thanks to Canadian Scholars' Press Inc., and Megan Mueller in particular.

A Note from the Publisher

Thank you for selecting the second edition of *Rethinking Society in the 21st Century: Critical Readings in Sociology*, edited by Michelle Webber and Kate Bezanson. The editors and publisher have devoted considerable time and careful development (including meticulous peer reviews) to this book. We appreciate your recognition of this effort and accomplishment.

Teaching Features

In the busy and well-developed market of introductory sociology in Canada, this progressive volume distinguishes itself in many ways. One key feature is the book's well-written and comprehensive section openers, which help to make the readings all the more accessible to introductory students of sociology. These openers add cohesion to the sections and to the whole book. The themes of the book are very clearly presented in these section openers. The general editors have also greatly enhanced the book by adding part-closing pedagogy such as chapter-specific critical thinking questions, glossary terms, relevant Web sites, and annotated further readings.

This book also comes with a Test Bank, available on the CSPI Web site at www.cspi.org. The components of the Test Bank are as follows, per reading: 20 multiple-choice questions, 10 true/false questions, 10 short-answer questions, and 10–15 discussion or essay questions.

Introduction to Sociology

The Readings

The opening section of this book introduces students to key classical pieces in the discipline of sociology, by Emile Durkheim, Karl Marx, Friedrich Engels, and C. Wright Mills. All of these pieces appear in their original form; the editors of this anthology have not changed the author's language so as to preserve the historical authenticity of these pieces. Students should note that these classics (and some of the other older selections) utilize male pronouns instead of non-sexist alternatives. We encourage faculty and students while reading and discussing these classic pieces to consider the importance of shifts in language over time.

The first piece is Emile Durkheim's "What Is a Social Fact?" Durkheim is considered the founder of modern sociology and an influential thinker in the functionalist paradigm in sociology. Durkheim argues that sociology is a science of society. In order to explain human actions we must look at the level of society, not at the level of individuals' behaviours and motivations. He describes a "category of facts" that exerts control over individuals in aspects such as ways of acting, being, and thinking. These facts are seen as external to individuals yet affect people's behaviours. Durkheim understands these facts as being distinct from biological and psychological phenomena.

The second selection is from Karl Marx and Friedrich Engels's classic piece, *The Communist Manifesto*. Their writing on capitalism as a global economic, social, and cultural system, although written in the mid-1800s, remains incisive. Their piece asserts that all societies in history are divided on a class basis. All human relationships are understood as being organized along capitalist lines (including the structure of families). Countries enter markets to become successful capitalist societies. If this success is not realized, these countries risk humiliation and colonization. Marx and Engels assert that the working class, those whose labour creates the wealth of capitalism, will organize to end their exploitation and the domination of the bourgeoisie, those who own the means of production. The ideas of Marx and Engels have been central in the development of the social-conflict paradigm in sociology.

The last piece in the classical theory section is written by another social-conflict theorist, C. Wright Mills. Mills was writing in postwar North American society (1950s and 1960s). Mills was critical of tendencies of sociologists, especially those working in the functionalist tradition, to develop concepts devoid of political meaning. He was critical of broad and abstract concepts (such as "functional imperatives") that were completely removed from public and political concerns, historical change, and people's lives. This selection is from Mills's book *The Sociological Imagination*. Here Mills captures the meaning of the sociological perspective with his term *sociological imagination* as a way of thinking that allows people to understand how problems they experience in their own lives can be linked to public issues. These public issues are the result of broad historical and social forces. If one can understand these broad forces, then, Mills argues, one can alter these forces.

Our first contemporary theory piece is a pioneering feminist consideration of epistemology (theory of knowledge). Dorothy Smith exposes gender-biased assumptions within sociology itself. Smith argues that women have been excluded from the production of sociological knowledge. Even though there are attempts to present knowledge as universal and objective, knowledge cannot be separated from the context in which that knowledge is generated. Members of dominant groups have the power to describe and define the world around them. Smith argues that members of dominant groups have historically been unable to see how their view of the world has depended on the often invisible yet essential work of women and members of the working class. Smith explores how sociology might be transformed by women's perspectives.

The next contemporary theory piece is from a French scholar who transformed modern social theory, Michel Foucault. Like Durkheim, Foucault focuses on acts of deviance that appear to be individual and shows how these seemingly individual behaviours can best be understood by analyzing predominating cultural formations. In this excerpt from *Discipline and Punish*, Foucault utilizes the metaphor of the "panopticon" to illustrate modern society as an imaginary institution of continual surveillance. The gaze rests on the inmates continuously, leading to eventual self-surveillance. While Durkheim saw modern structures of normative regulation as more merciful than old ones, Foucault sees them as simply new forms of control.

Antonio Gramsci, a neo-Marxist scholar, forms the content for the next contemporary theoretical piece. His work is explored here by Diana Coben. Following a brief biography, Coben outlines one of Gramsci's main contributions to theoretical debate, his concept of hegemony. Unlike traditional Marxists, Gramsci argues that the state cannot rule by coercion alone; rather, there must be some form of consent to domination by the oppressed class. Hegemony accounts for the subtle, negotiated consent that the dominant class is able to secure over the oppressed class. It is important to understand that this hegemony is never fully reached; it is constantly in motion, always in negotiation.

Our last piece for the theory section is by an influential Canadian scholar in the area of anti-racism education, George Sefa Dei. This chapter forms an introduction anti-racism discourse. Dei carefully argues how race, class, and gender are all necessarily implicated in an anti-racism discourse. To do this, Dei introduces the notion of "integrative anti-racism studies" to provide a way to explore how categories of social difference (race, class, gender, sexualities, and so forth) mediate our lived experiences.

Margrit Eichler's work on non-sexist research methods represents a feminist critique of how research is designed, carried out, analyzed, and written up. Eichler points to seven forms of sexism and shows how sexism is multidimensional. The seven forms of sexism are tools to help us recognize and correct sexism in research.

Karen Potts and Leslie Brown introduce us to anti-oppressive research. They discuss what it means to engage in anti-oppressive research and how this political engagement permeates all aspects of the research process. They recognize that all knowledge is socially constructed and is implicated in relations of power and discuss ways to highlight these relations and still work productively for change.

CHAPTER 1

What Is a Social Fact?

Emile Durkheim

Before beginning the search for the method appropriate to the study of social facts it is important to know what are the facts termed "social."

The question is all the more necessary because the term is used without much precision. It is commonly used to designate almost all the phenomena that occur within society, however little social interest of some generality they present. Yet under this heading there is, so to speak, no human occurrence that cannot be called social. Every individual drinks, sleeps, eats, or employs his reason, and society has every interest in seeing that these functions are regularly exercised. If therefore these facts were social ones, sociology would possess no subject matter peculiarly its own, and its domain would be confused with that of biology and psychology.

However, in reality there is in every society a clearly determined group of phenomena separable, because of their distinct characteristics, from those that form the subject matter of other sciences of nature.

When I perform my duties as a brother, a husband or a citizen and carry out the commitments I have entered into, I fulfil obligations which are defined in law and custom and which are external to myself and my actions. Even when they conform to my own sentiments and when I feel their reality within me, that reality does not cease to be objective, for it is not I who have prescribed these duties; I have received them through education. Moreover, how often does it happen that we are ignorant of the details of the obligations that we must assume, and that, to know them, we must consult the legal code and its authorised interpreters! Similarly the believer has discovered from birth, ready fashioned, the beliefs and practices of his religious life; if they existed before he did, it follows that they exist outside him. The system of signs that I employ to express my thoughts, the monetary system I use to pay my debts, the credit instruments I utilise in my commercial relationships, the practices I follow in my profession, etc., all function independently of the use I make of them. Considering in turn each member of society, the foregoing remarks can be repeated for each single one of them. Thus there are ways of acting, thinking and feeling which possess the remarkable property of existing outside the consciousness of the individual.

Not only are these types of behaviour and thinking external to the individual, but they are endued with a compelling and coercive power by virtue of which, whether he wishes it or not, they impose themselves upon him. Undoubtedly when I conform to them of my own free will, this coercion is not felt or felt hardly at all, since it is unnecessary. None the less it is intrinsically a characteristic of these facts; the proof of this is that it asserts itself as soon as I try to resist. If I attempt to violate the rules of law they react against me so as to forestall my action, if there is still time. Alternatively, they annul it or make my action conform to the norm if it is already accomplished but capable of being reversed; or they cause me to pay the penalty for it if it is irreparable. If purely moral rules are at stake, the public conscience restricts any act which infringes them by the surveillance it exercises over the conduct of citizens and by the special punishments it has at its disposal. In other cases the constraint is less violent; nevertheless, it does not cease to exist. If I do not conform to ordinary conventions, if in my mode of dress I pay no heed to what is customary in my country and in my social class, the laughter I provoke, the social distance at which I am kept, produce, although in a more mitigated form, the same results as any real penalty. In other cases, although it may be indirect, constraint is no less effective. I am not forced to speak French with my compatriots, nor to use the legal currency, but it is impossible for me to do otherwise. If I tried to escape the necessity, my attempt would fail miserably. As an industrialist nothing prevents me from working with the processes and methods of the previous century, but if I do I will most certainly ruin myself. Even when in fact I can struggle free from these rules and successfully break them, it is never without being forced to fight against them. Even if in the end they are overcome, they make their constraining power sufficiently felt in the resistance that they afford. There is no innovator, even a fortunate one, whose ventures do not encounter opposition of this kind.

Social facts

Here, then, is a category of facts which present very special characteristics: they consist of manners of acting, thinking and feeling external to the individual, which are invested with a coercive power by virtue of which they exercise control over him. Consequently, since they consist of representations and actions, they cannot be confused with organic phenomena, nor with psychical phenomena, which have no existence save in and through the individual consciousness. Thus they constitute a new species and to them must be exclusively assigned the term social. It is appropriate, since it is clear that, not having the individual as their substratum, they can have none other than society, either political society in its entirety or one of the partial groups that it includes—religious denominations, political and literary schools, occupational corporations, etc. Moreover, it is for such as these alone that the term is fitting, for the word "social" has the sole meaning of designating those phenomena which fall into none of the categories of facts already constituted and labelled. They are consequently the proper field of sociology. It is true that this word "constraint," in terms of which we define them, is in danger of infuriating those who zealously uphold out-and-out individualism. Since they maintain that the individual is completely autonomous, it seems to them that he is diminished every time he is made aware that he is not dependent on himself alone. Yet since it is indisputable today that most of our ideas and tendencies are not developed by ourselves, but come to us from outside, they can only penetrate us by imposing themselves upon us. This is all that our definition implies. Moreover, we know that all social constraints do not necessarily exclude the individual personality.[1]

Yet since the examples just cited (legal and moral rules, religious dogmas, financial systems, etc.) consist wholly of beliefs and practices already well established, in view of what has been said it might be maintained that no social fact can exist except where there is a well-defined social organisation. But there are other facts which do not present themselves in this already crystallised form but which also possess the same objectivity and ascendancy over the individual. These are what are called social "currents." Thus in a public gathering the great waves of enthusiasm, indignation and pity that are produced have their seat in no one individual consciousness. They come to each one of us from outside and can sweep us along in spite of ourselves. If perhaps I abandon myself to them I may not be conscious of the pressure that they are exerting upon me, but that pressure makes its presence felt immediately I attempt to struggle against them. If an individual tries to pit himself against one of these collective manifestations, the sentiments that he is rejecting will be turned against him. Now if this external coercive power asserts itself so acutely in cases of resistance, it must be because it exists in the other instances cited above without our being conscious of it. Hence we are the victims of an illusion which leads us to believe we have ourselves produced

what has been imposed upon us externally. But if the willingness with which we let ourselves be carried along disguises the pressure we have undergone, it does not eradicate it. Thus air does not cease to have weight, although we no longer feel that weight. Even when we have individually and spontaneously shared in the common emotion, the impression we have experienced is utterly different from what we would have felt if we had been alone. Once the assembly has broken up and these social influences have ceased to act upon us, and we are once more on our own, the emotions we have felt seem an alien phenomenon, one in which we no longer recognise ourselves. It is then we perceive that we have undergone the emotions much more than generated them. These emotions may even perhaps fill us with horror, so much do they go against the grain. Thus individuals who are normally perfectly harmless may, when gathered together in a crowd, let themselves be drawn into acts of atrocity. And what we assert about these transitory outbreaks likewise applies to those more lasting movements of opinion which relate to religious, political, literary and artistic matters, etc., and which are constantly being produced around us, whether throughout society or in a more limited sphere.

Moreover, this definition of a social fact can be verified by examining an experience that is characteristic. It is sufficient to observe how children are brought up. If one views the facts as they are and indeed as they have always been, it is patently obvious that all education consists of a continual effort to impose upon the child ways of seeing, thinking and acting which he himself would not have arrived at spontaneously. From his earliest years we oblige him to eat, drink and sleep at regular hours, and to observe cleanliness, calm and obedience; later we force him to learn how to be mindful of others, to respect customs and conventions, and to work, etc. If this constraint in time ceases to be felt it is because it gradually gives rise to habits, to inner tendencies which render it superfluous; but they supplant the constraint only because they are derived from it. It is true that, in Spencer's view, a rational education should shun such means and allow the child complete freedom to do what he will. Yet as this educational theory has never been put into practice among any known people, it can only be the personal expression of a desideratum and not a fact which can be established in contradiction to the other facts given above. What renders these latter facts particularly illuminating is that education sets out precisely with the object of creating a social being. Thus there can be seen, as in an abbreviated form, how the social being has been fashioned historically. The pressure to which the child is subjected unremittingly is the same pressure of the social environment which seeks to shape him in its own image, and in which parents and teachers are only the representatives and intermediaries.

Thus it is not the fact that they are general which can serve to characterise sociological phenomena. Thoughts to be found in the consciousness of each individual and movements which are repeated by all individuals are not for this reason social facts. If some have been content with using this characteristic in order to define them it is because they have been confused, wrongly, with what might be termed their individual incarnations. What constitutes social facts are the beliefs, tendencies and practices of the group taken collectively. But the forms that these collective states may assume when they are "refracted" through individuals are things of a different kind. What irrefutably demonstrates this duality of kind is that these two categories of facts frequently are manifested dissociated from each other. Indeed some of these ways of acting or thinking acquire, by dint of repetition, a sort of consistency which, so to speak, separates them out, isolating them from the particular events which reflect them. Thus they assume a shape, a tangible form peculiar to them and constitute a reality sui generis vastly distinct from the individual facts which manifest that reality. Collective custom does not exist only in a state of immanence in the successive actions which it determines, but, by a privilege without example in the biological kingdom, expresses itself once and for all in a formula repeated by word of mouth, transmitted by education and even enshrined in the written word. Such are the origins and nature of legal and moral rules, aphorisms and popular sayings, articles of faith in which religious or political sects epitomise their beliefs, and standards of taste drawn up by literary schools, etc. None of these modes of acting and thinking are to be found wholly in the application made of them by individuals, since they can even exist without being applied at the time.

Undoubtedly this state of dissociation does not always present itself with equal distinctiveness. It is sufficient for dissociation to exist unquestionably in the numerous important instances cited, for us to prove that the social fact exists separately from its individual effects. Moreover, even when the dissociation is not immediately observable, it can often be made so with the help of certain methodological devices. Indeed it is essential to embark on such procedures if one wishes to refine out the social fact from any amalgam and so observe it in its pure state. Thus certain currents of opinion, whose intensity varies according to the time and country in which they occur, impel us, for example, towards marriage or suicide, towards higher or lower birth-rates, etc. Such currents are plainly social facts. At first sight they seem inseparable from the forms they assume in individual cases. But statistics afford us a means of isolating them. They are indeed not inaccurately represented by rates of births, marriages and suicides, that is, by the result obtained after dividing the average annual total of marriages, births, and voluntary homicides by the number of persons of an age to marry, produce children, or commit suicide.[2] Since each one of these statistics includes without distinction all individual cases, the individual circumstances which may have played some part in producing the phenomenon cancel each other out and consequently do not contribute to determining the nature of the phenomenon. What it expresses is a certain state of the collective mind.

That is what social phenomena are when stripped of all extraneous elements. As regards their private manifestations, these do indeed having something social about them, since in part they reproduce the collective model. But to a large extent each one depends also upon the psychical and organic constitution of the individual, and on the particular circumstances in which he is placed. Therefore they are not phenomena which are in the strict sense sociological. They depend on both domains at the same time, and could be termed socio-psychical. They are of interest to the sociologist without constituting the immediate content of sociology. The same characteristic is to be found in the organisms of those mixed phenomena of nature studied in the combined sciences such as biochemistry.

It may be objected that a phenomenon can only be collective if it is common to all the members of society, or at the very least to a majority, and consequently, if it is general. This is doubtless the case, but if it is general it is because it is collective (that is, more or less obligatory); but it is very far from being collective because it is general. It is a condition of the group repeated in individuals because it imposes itself upon them. It is in each part because it is in the whole, but far from being in the whole because it is in the parts. This is supremely evident in those beliefs and practices which are handed down to us ready fashioned by previous generations. We accept and adopt them because, since they are the work of the collectivity and one that is centuries old, they are invested with a special authority that our education has taught us to recognise and respect. It is worthy of note that the vast majority of social phenomena come to us in this way. But even when the social fact is partly due to our direct co-operation, it is no different in nature. An outburst of collective emotion in a gathering does not merely express the sum total of what individual feelings share in common, but is something of a very different order, as we have demonstrated. It is a product of shared existence, of actions and reactions called into play between the consciousnesses of individuals. If it is echoed in each one of them it is precisely by virtue of the special energy derived from its collective origins. If all hearts beat in unison, this is not as a consequence of a spontaneous, preestablished harmony; it is because one and the same force is propelling them in the same direction. Each one is borne along by the rest.

We have therefore succeeded in delineating for ourselves the exact field of sociology. It embraces one single, well-defined group of phenomena. A social fact is identifiable through the power of external coercion which it exerts or is capable of exerting upon individuals. The presence of this power is in turn recognisable because of the existence of some pre-determined sanction, or through the resistance that the fact opposes to any individual action that may threaten it. However, it can also be defined by ascertaining how widespread it is within the group, provided that, as noted above, one is careful to add a second essential characteristic; this is, that it exists independently of the particular forms that it may assume in the process of spreading itself within the group. In certain cases this latter criterion can even be more easily applied than the former one. The presence of constraint is easily ascertainable when it is manifested externally through some direct reaction of society, as in the case of law, morality, beliefs, customs and even fashions. But when constraint is merely indirect, as with that exerted by an economic organization, it is not always so clearly discernible. Generality combined with objectivity may then be easier to establish. Moreover, this second definition is simply another formulation of the first one: if a mode of behaviour existing outside the consciousnesses of individuals becomes general, it can only do so by exerting pressure upon them.[3]

However, one may well ask whether this definition is complete. Indeed the facts which have provided us with its basis are all ways of functioning: they are "physiological" in nature. But there are also collective ways of being, namely, social facts of an "anatomical" or morphological nature. Sociology cannot dissociate itself from what concerns the substratum of collective life. Yet the number and nature of the elementary parts which constitute society, the way in which they are articulated, the degree of coalescence they have attained, the distribution of population over the earth's surface, the extent and nature of the network of communications, the design of dwellings, etc., do not at first sight seem relatable to ways of acting, feeling or thinking.

Yet, first and foremost, these various phenomena present the same characteristic which has served us in defining the others. These ways of being impose themselves upon the individual just as do the ways of acting we have dealt with. In fact, when we wish to learn how a society is divided up politically, in what its divisions consist and the degree of solidarity that exists between them, it is not through physical inspection and geographical observation that we may come to find this out: such divisions are social, although they may have some physical basis. It is only through public law that we can study such political organisation, because this law is what determines its nature, just as it determines our domestic and civic relationships. The organisation is no less a form of compulsion. If the population clusters together in our cities instead of being scattered over the rural areas, it is because there exists a trend of opinion, a collective drive which imposes this concentration upon individuals. We can no more choose the design of our houses than the cut of our clothes—at least, the one is as much obligatory as the other. The communication network forcibly

prescribes the direction of internal migrations or commercial exchanges, etc., and even their intensity. Consequently, at the most there are grounds for adding one further category to the list of phenomena already enumerated as bearing the distinctive stamp of a social fact. But as that enumeration was in no wise strictly exhaustive, this addition would not be indispensable.

Moreover, it does not even serve a purpose, for these ways of being are only ways of acting that have been consolidated. A society's political structure is only the way in which its various component segments have become accustomed to living with each other. If relationships between them are traditionally close, the segments tend to merge together; if the contrary, they tend to remain distinct. The type of dwelling imposed upon us is merely the way in which everyone around us and, in part, previous generations, have customarily built their houses. The communication network is only the channel which has been cut by the regular current of commerce and migrations, etc., flowing in the same direction. Doubtless if phenomena of a morphological kind were the only ones that displayed this rigidity, it might be thought that they constituted a separate species. But a legal rule is no less permanent an arrangement than an architectural style, and yet it is a "physiological" fact. A simple moral maxim is certainly more malleable, yet it is cast in forms much more rigid than a mere professional custom or fashion. Thus there exists a whole range of gradations which, without any break in continuity, join the most clearly delineated structural facts to those free currents of social life which are not yet caught in any definite mould. This therefore signifies that the differences between them concern only the degree to which they have become consolidated. Both are forms of life at varying stages of crystallisation. It would undoubtedly be advantageous to reserve the term "morphological" for those social facts which relate to the social substratum, but only on condition that one is aware that they are of the same nature as the others.

Our definition will therefore subsume all that has to be defined it if states:

A social fact is any way of acting, whether fixed or not, capable of exerting over the individual an external constraint;

or:

which is general over the whole of a given society whilst having an existence of its own, independent of its individual manifestations.[4]

Notes

1 Moreover, this is not to say that all constraint is normal. We shall return to this point later.

2 Suicides do not occur at any age, nor do they occur at all ages of life with the same frequency.

3 It can be seen how far removed this definition of the social fact is from that which serves as the basis for the ingenious system of Tarde. We must first state that our research has nowhere led us to corroboration of the preponderant influence that Tarde attributes to imitation in the genesis of collective facts. Moreover, from this definition, which is not a theory but a mere resume of the immediate data observed, it seems clearly to follow that imitation does not always express, indeed never expresses, what is essential and characteristic in the social fact. Doubtless every social fact is imitated and has, as we have just shown, a tendency to become generalised, but this is because it is social, i.e., obligatory. Its capacity for expansion is not the cause but the consequence of its sociological character. If social facts were unique in bringing about this effect, imitation might serve, if not to explain them, at least to define them. But an individual state which impacts on others none the less remains individual. Moreover, one may speculate whether the term "imitation" is indeed appropriate to designate a proliferation which occurs through some coercive influence. In such a single term very different phenomena, which need to be distinguished, are confused.

4 This close affinity of life and structure, organ and function, can be readily established in sociology because there exists between these two extremes a whole series of intermediate stages, immediately observable, which reveal the link between them. Biology lacks this methodological resource. But one may believe legitimately that sociological inductions on this subject are applicable to biology and that, in organisms as in societies, between these two categories of facts only differences in degree exist.

CHAPTER 2
Manifesto of the Communist Party

KARL MARX AND FRIEDRICH ENGELS

self-sufficient guilds couldn't supply the demand of the growing market

* * * * *

Bourgeois and Proletarians[1]

The history of all hitherto existing society[2] is the history of class struggles.

Freeman and slave, patrician and plebian, lord and serf, guild-master[3] and journeyman, in a word, oppressor and oppressed, stood in constant opposition to one another, carried on an uninterrupted, now hidden, now open fight, a fight that each time ended either in a revolutionary re-constitution of society at large, or in the common ruin of the contending classes.

In the earlier epochs of history we find almost everywhere a complicated arrangement of society into various orders, a manifold gradation of social rank. In ancient Rome we have patricians, knights, plebians, slaves; in the middle ages, feudal lords, vassals, guildmasters, journeymen, apprentices, serfs; in almost all of these classes, again, subordinate gradations.

The modern bourgeois society that has sprouted from the ruins of feudal society has not done away with class antagonisms. It has only established new classes, new conditions of oppression, new forms of struggle in place of the old ones.

Our epoch, the epoch of the bourgeoisie, possesses, however, this distinctive feature: it has simplified the class antagonism. Society as a whole is more and more splitting up into two great hostile camps, into two great classes directly facing each other: bourgeoisie and proletariat.

From the serfs of the middle ages sprang the chartered burghers[4] of the earliest towns. From these burgesses the first elements of the bourgeoisie were developed.

increased capital flowing into Europe

The discovery of America, the rounding of the Cape, opened up fresh ground for the rising bourgeoisie. The East-Indian and Chinese markets, the colonization of America, trade with the colonies, the increase in the means of exchange and in commodities generally, gave to commerce, to navigation, to industry, an impulse never before known, and thereby gave rapid development to the revolutionary element in the tottering feudal society.

The feudal system of industry, under which industrial production was monopolized by closed guilds, now no longer sufficed for the growing wants of the new markets. The manufacturing system took its place. The guildmasters were pushed on one side by the manufacturing middle class[5]; division of labour between the different corporate guilds vanished in the face of the division of labour in each single workshop.

Meantime the markets kept ever growing, the demand ever rising. Even manufacture[6] no longer sufficed. Thereupon steam and machinery revolutionized industrial production. The place of manufacture was taken by the giant, modern industry, the place of the industrial middle class, by industrial millionaires, the leaders of whole industrial armies, the modern bourgeois.

Modern industry has established the world market, for which the discovery of America paved the way. This market has given an immense development to commerce, to navigation, to communication by land. This development has, in its turn, reacted on the extension of industry; and in proportion as industry, commerce, navigation, railways extended, in the same proportion the bourgeoisie developed, increased its capital, and pushed into the background every class handed down from the Middle Ages.

We see, therefore, how the modern bourgeoisie is itself the product of a long course of development, of a series of revolutions in the modes of production and of exchange.

Each step in the development of the bourgeoisie was accompanied by a corresponding political advance of that class. An oppressed class under the sway of the feudal nobility, an armed and self-governing association in the medieval commune[7]; here independent urban republic (as in Italy and Germany), there taxable "third estate"[8] of the monarchy (as in France), afterwards, in the period of manufacture proper, serving either the semi-feudal or the absolutist monarchy as a counterpoise against the nobility, and, in fact, corner-stone of the great monarchies in general, the bourgeoisie has at last, since the establishment of modern industry and of the world market, conquered for itself, in a modern representative state, exclusive political sway. The executive of the modern state is but a committee for managing the common affairs of the whole bourgeoisie.

The bourgeoisie, historically, has played a most revolutionary part.

The bourgeoisie, wherever it has got the upper hand,

has put an end to all feudal, patriarchal, idyllic relations. It has pitilessly torn asunder the motley feudal ties that bound man to his "natural superiors," and has left remaining no other nexus between man and man than naked self-interest, than callous "cash payment." It has drowned the most heavenly ecstasies of religious fervour, of chivalrous enthusiasm, of philistine sentimentalism, in the icy water of egotistical calculation. It has resolved personal worth into exchange value, and in place of the numberless indefeasible chartered freedoms, has set up that single, unconscionable freedom—free trade. In one word, for exploitation veiled by religious and political illusions it has substituted naked, shameless, direct, brutal exploitation.

The bourgeoisie has stripped of its halo every occupation hitherto honoured and looked up to with reverent awe. It has converted the physician, the lawyer, the priest, the poet, the man of science, into its paid wage labourers.

The bourgeoisie has torn away from the family its sentimental veil, and has reduced the family relation to a mere money relation.

The bourgeoisie has disclosed how it came to pass that the brutal display of vigour in the Middle Ages, which reactionists so much admire, found its fitting complement in the most slothful indolence. It has been the first to show what man's activity can bring about. It has accomplished wonders far surpassing Egyptian pyramids, Roman aqueducts, and Gothic cathedrals; it has conducted expeditions that put in the shade all former exoduses of nations and crusades.

The bourgeoisie cannot exist without constantly revolutionizing the instruments of production, and thereby the relations of production, and with them the whole relations of society. Conservation of the old modes of production in unaltered form, was, on the contrary, the first condition of existence for all earlier industrial classes. All fixed, fast-frozen relations, with their train of ancient and venerable prejudices and opinions are swept away, all new-formed ones become antiquated before they can ossify. All that is solid melts into air, all that is holy is profaned, and man is at last compelled to face with sober senses his real conditions of life, and his relations with his kind.

The need for a constantly expanding market for its products chases the bourgeoisie over the whole surface of the globe. It must nestle everywhere, settle everywhere, establish connections everywhere.

The bourgeoisie has through its exploitation of the world-market given a cosmopolitan character to production and consumption in every country. To the great chagrin of reactionists, it has drawn from under the feet of industry the national ground on which it stood. All old-established national industries have been destroyed or are daily being destroyed. They are dislodged by new industries, whose introduction becomes a life and death question for all civilized nations, by industries that no longer work up indigenous raw material, but raw material drawn from the remotest zones; industries whose products are consumed , not only at home, but in every quarter

of the globe. In place of the old wants, satisfied by the productions of the country we find new wants, requiring for their satisfaction the products of distant lands and climes. In place of the old local and national seclusion and self-sufficiency, we have intercourse in every direction, universal interdependence of nations. And as in material, so also in intellectual production. The intellectual creations of individual nations become common property. National one-sidedness and narrow-mindedness become more and more impossible, and from the numerous national and local literatures there arises a world literature.

The bourgeoisie, by the rapid improvement of all instruments of production, by the immensely facilitated means of communication, draws all, even the most barbarian, nations into civilization. The cheap prices of commodities are the heavy artillery with which it batters down all Chinese walls, with which it forces the barbarians' intensely obstinate hatred of foreigners to capitulate. It compels all nations, on pain of extinction, to adopt the bourgeois mode of production; it compels them to introduce what it calls civilization into their midst, *i.e.*, to become bourgeois themselves. In one word, it creates a world after its own image.

[handwritten margin note:] Become like us or you will be left behind

The bourgeoisie has subjected the country to the rule of the towns. It has created enormous cities, has greatly increased the urban population as compared with the rural, and has thus rescued a considerable part of the population from the idiocy of rural life. Just as it has made the country dependent on the towns, so it has made the barbarian and semi-barbarian countries dependent on the civilized ones, nations of peasants on nations of bourgeois, the East on the West.

The bourgeoisie keeps more and more doing away with the scattered state of the population, of the means of production, and of property. It has agglomerated population, centralized means of production, and has concentrated property in a few hands. The necessary consequence of this was political centralization. Independent, or but loosely connected provinces, with separate interests, laws, governments, and systems of taxation became lumped together into one nation, with one government, one code of laws, one national class-interest, one frontier, and one customs-tariff.

The bourgeoisie, during its rule of scarce one hundred years, has created more massive and more colossal productive forces than have all preceding generations together. Subjection of Nature's forces to man, machinery, application of chemistry to industry and agriculture, steam-navigation, railways, electric telegraphs, clearing of whole continents far cultivation, canalization of rivers, whole populations conjured out of the ground—what earlier century had even a presentiment that such productive forces slumbered in the lap of social labour?

We see then: the means of production and exchange, on whose foundation the bourgeoisie built itself up, were generated in feudal society. At a certain stage in the development of these means of production and exchange, the conditions under which feudal society produced and

PP are turned into a commodity

exchanged, the feudal organization of agriculture and manufacturing industry, in one word, the feudal relations of property became no longer compatible with the already developed productive forces; they became so many fetters. They had to be burst asunder; they were burst asunder.

Into their place stepped free competition, accompanied by a social and political constitution adapted to it, and by the economic and political sway of the bourgeois class.

A similar movement is going on before our own eyes. Modern bourgeois society with its relations of production, of exchange, and of property, a society that has conjured up such gigantic means of production and exchange, is like the sorcerer, who is no longer able to control the powers of the nether world whom he has called up by his spells. For many a decade past the history of industry and commerce is but the history of revolt of modern productive forces against modern conditions of production, against property relations that are the conditions for the existence of the bourgeoisie and of its rule. It is enough to mention that the commercial crises by their periodical return put on its trial, each time more threateningly, the existence of the entire bourgeois society. (In these crises a great part not only of the existing products, but also of the previously-created productive forces, are periodically destroyed. In these crises there breaks out an epidemic that, in all earlier epochs, would have seemed an absurdity—the epidemic of over-production. Society suddenly finds itself put back into a state of momentary barbarism; it appears as if famine, a universal war of devastation had cut off the supply of every means of subsistence; industry and commerce seem to be destroyed; and why? Because there is too much civilization, too much means of subsistence, too much industry, too much commerce. The productive forces at the disposal of society no longer tend to further the development of the conditions of bourgeois property; on the contrary, they have become too powerful for these conditions, by which they are fettered, and so soon as they overcome these fetters, they bring disorder into the whole of bourgeois society, endanger the existence of bourgeois property. The conditions of bourgeois society are too narrow to comprise the wealth created by them. And how does the bourgeoisie get over these crises? On the one hand by enforced destruction of a mass of productive forces; on the other, by the conquest of new markets, and by the more through exploitation of the old ones. That is to say, by paving the way for more extensive and more destructive crises, and by diminishing the means whereby crises are prevented.

The weapons with which the bourgeoisie felled feudalism to the ground are now turned against the bourgeoisie itself.

But not only has the bourgeoisie forged the weapons that bring death to itself; it has also called into existence the men who are to wield those weapons—the modern working class—the proletarians.

In proportion as the bourgeoisie, *i.e.*, capital, is developed, in the same proportion is the proletariat, the modern working class, developed—a class of labourers, who live only so long as they find work, and who find work only so long as their labour increases capital. These labourers, who must sell themselves piecemeal, are a commodity,[9] like every other article of commerce, and are consequently exposed to all the vicissitudes of competition, to all the fluctuations of the market.

Owing to the extensive use of machinery and to division of labour, the work of the proletarians has lost all individual character, and, consequently, all charm for the workman. He becomes an appendage of the machine, and it is only the most simple, most monotonous, and most easily acquired knack, that is required of him. Hence, the cost of production of a workman is restricted, almost entirely, to the means of subsistence that he requires for his maintenance, and for the propagation of his race. But the price of a commodity, and therefore also of labour, is equal to its cost of production. In proportion, therefore, as the repulsiveness of the work increases, the wage decreases. Nay more, in the same proportion the burden of toil also increases, whether by prolongation of the working hours, by increase of the work exacted in a given time or by increased speed of the machinery, etc.

Modern industry has converted the little workshop of the patriarchal master into the great factory of the industrial capitalist. Masses of labourers, crowded into the factory, are organized like soldiers. As privates of the industrial army they are placed under the command of a perfect hierarchy of officers and sergeants. Not only are they slaves of the bourgeois class, and of the bourgeois state; they are daily and hourly enslaved by the machine, by the over-looker, and, above all, by the individual bourgeois manufacturer himself. The more openly this despotism proclaims gain to be its end and aim, the more petty, the more hateful and the more embittering it is.

The less the skill and the exertion of strength implied in manual labour, in other words, the more modern industry becomes developed, the more is the labour of men superseded by that of women. Differences of age and sex no longer have any distinctive social validity for the working class. All are instruments of labour, more or less expensive to use, according to their age and sex.

No sooner is the exploitation of the labour by the manufacturer, so far, at an end, than he receives his wages in cash, than he is set upon by the other portions of the bourgeoisie, the landlord, the shopkeeper, the pawnbroker, etc.

The lower strata of the middle class—the small tradespeople, shopkeepers, and retired tradesmen generally, the handicraftsmen and peasants—all these sink gradually into the proletariat, partly because their diminutive capital does not suffice for the scale on which modern industry is carried on, and is swamped in the competition with the large capitalists, partly because their specialized skill is rendered worthless by new methods of production. Thus the proletariat is recruited from all classes of the population.

The proletariat goes through various stages of development. With its birth begins its struggle with the bourgeoisie. At first the contest is carried on by individual labourers, then by the workpeople of a factory, then by the operatives of one trade, in one locality, against the individual bourgeois who directly exploits them. They direct their attacks not against the bourgeois conditions of production, but against the instruments of production themselves; they destroy imported wares that compete with their labour, they smash pieces of machinery, they set factories ablaze, they seek to restore by force the vanished status of the workman of the Middle Ages.

At this stage the labourers still form an incoherent mass scattered over the whole country, and broken up by their mutual competition. If anywhere they unite to form more compact bodies, this is not yet the consequence of their own active union, but of the union of the bourgeoisie, which class, in order to attain its own political ends, is compelled to set the whole proletariat in motion, and is moreover yet, for a time, able to do so. At this stage, therefore, the proletarians do not fight their enemies, but the enemies of their enemies, the remnants of the absolute monarchy, the landowners, the non-industrial bourgeois, the petty bourgeoisie. Thus the whole historical movement is concentrated in the hands of the bourgeoisie; every victory so attained is a victory for the bourgeoisie.

But with the development of industry the proletariat not only increases in number, it becomes concentrated in greater masses, its strength grows, and it feels that strength more. The various interests and conditions of life within the ranks of the proletariat are more and more equalized, in proportion as machinery obliterates all distinctions of labour, and nearly everywhere reduces wages to the same low level. The growing competition of the bourgeois, and the resulting commercial crises, make the wages of the workers ever more fluctuating. The unceasing improvement of machinery, ever more rapidly developing, makes their livelihood more and more precarious; the collisions between individual workmen and individual bourgeois take more and more of the character of collisions between two classes. Thereupon the workers begin to form combinations (trades' unions) against the bourgeois; they club together in order to keep up the rate of wages; they found permanent associations in order to make provision beforehand for these occasional revolts. Here and there the contest breaks out into riots.

Now and then the workers are victorious, but only for a time. The real fruit of their battle lies, not in the immediate result, but in the ever-expanding union of the workers. This union is helped on by the improved means of communication that are created by modern industry and that place workers of different localities in contact with one another. It was just this contact that was needed to centralize the numerous local struggles, all of the same character, into one national struggle between classes. But every class struggle is a political struggle. And that union, to attain which the burghers of the Middle Ages, with their miserable highways, required centuries, the modern proletarians, thanks to railways, achieve in a few years.

This organization of the proletarians into a class, and consequently into a political party, is continually being upset again by the competition between the workers themselves. But it ever rises up again, stronger, firmer, mightier. It compels legislative recognition of particular interests of the workers, by taking advantage of the divisions among the bourgeoisie itself. Thus the ten-hour[10] bill in England was carried.

Altogether, collisions between the classes of the old society further, in many ways, the course of development of the proletariat. The bourgeoisie finds itself involved in a constant battle. At first with the aristocracy; later on, with those portions of the bourgeoisie itself, whose interests have become antagonistic to the progress of industry; at all times, with the bourgeoisie of foreign countries. In all these battles it sees itself compelled to appeal to the proletariat, to ask for its help, and thus, to drag it into the political arena. The bourgeoisie itself, therefore, supplies the proletariat with its own elements of political and general education; in other words, it furnishes the proletariat with weapons for fighting the bourgeoisie.

Further, as we have already seen, entire sections of the ruling classes are, by the advance of industry, precipitated into the proletariat, or are at least threatened in their conditions of existence. These also supply the proletariat with fresh elements of enlightenment and progress.

Finally, in times when the class struggle nears the decisive hour, the process of dissolution going on within the ruling class, in fact within the whole range of old society, assumes such a violent, glaring character, that a small section of the ruling class cuts itself adrift, and joins the revolutionary class, the class that holds the future in its hands. Just as, therefore, at an earlier period, a section of the nobility went over to the bourgeoisie, so now a portion of the bourgeoisie goes over to the proletariat, and in particular, a portion of the bourgeois ideologists, who have raised themselves to a level of comprehending theoretically the historical movement as a whole.

Of all the classes that stand face to face with the bourgeoisie today, the proletariat alone is a really revolutionary class. The other classes decay and finally disappear in the face of modern industry; the proletariat is its special and essential product.

The lower middle class, the small manufacturer, the shopkeeper, the artisan, the peasant, all these fight against the bourgeoisie, to save from extinction their existence as fractions of the middle class. They are therefore not revolutionary, but conservative. Nay more, they are reactionary, for they try to roll back the wheel of history. If by chance they are revolutionary, they are so only in view of their impending transfer into the proletariat, they thus defend not their present, but their future interests, they desert their own standpoint to place themselves at that of the proletariat.

The "dangerous class," the social scum, that passively rotting mass thrown off by the lowest layers of old society, may, here and there, be swept into the movement by a proletarian revolution; its conditions of life, however, prepare it far more for the part of a bribed tool of reactionary intrigue.

In the conditions of the proletariat, those of old society at large are already virtually swamped. The proletarian is without property; his relation to his wife and children has no longer anything in common with the bourgeois family relations; modern industrial labour, modern subjection to capital, the same in England as in France, in America as in Germany, has stripped him of every trace of national character. Law, morality, religion, are to him so many bourgeois prejudices, behind which lurk in ambush just as many bourgeois interests.

All the preceding classes that got the upper hand, sought to fortify their already acquired status by subjecting society at large to their conditions of appropriation. The proletarians cannot become masters of the productive forces of society, except by abolishing their own previous mode of appropriation, and thereby every other previous mode of appropriation. They have nothing of their own to secure and to fortify; their mission is to destroy all previous securities for, and insurances of, individual property.

All previous historical movements were movements of minorities, or in the interests of minorities. The proletarian movement is the self-conscious, independent movement of the immense majority, in the interests of the immense majority. The proletariat, the lowest stratum of our present society, cannot stir, cannot raise itself up, without the whole superincumbent strata of official society being sprung into the air.

Though not in substance, yet in form, the struggle of the proletariat with the bourgeoisie is at first a national struggle. The proletariat of each country must, of course, first of all settle matters with its own bourgeoisie.

In depicting the most general phases of the development of the proletariat, we traced the more or less veiled civil war, raging within existing society, up to the point where that war breaks out into open revolution, and where the violent overthrow of the bourgeoisie lays the foundation for the sway of the proletariat.

Hitherto every form of society has been based, as we have already seen, on the antagonism of oppressing and oppressed classes. But in order to oppress a class, certain conditions must be assured to it under which it can, at least, continue its slavish existence. The serf, in the period of serfdom, raised himself to membership in the commune, just as the petty bourgeois, under the yoke of feudal absolutism, managed to develop into a bourgeois. The modern labourer, on the contrary, instead of rising with the progress of industry, sinks deeper and deeper below the conditions of existence of his own class. He becomes a pauper, and pauperism develops more rapidly than population and wealth. And here it becomes evident that the bourgeoisie is unfit any longer to be the ruling class in society, and to impose its conditions of existence upon society as an over-riding law. It is unfit to rule because it is incompetent to assure an existence to its slave within his slavery, because it cannot help letting him sink into such a state, that it has to feed him, instead of being fed by him. Society can no longer live under this bourgeoisie; in other words, its existence is no longer compatible with society.

The essential condition for the existence, and for the sway of the bourgeois class, is the formation and augmentation of capital; the condition for capital is wage labour. Wage labour rests exclusively on the competition between the labourers. The advance of industry, whose involuntary promoter is the bourgeoisie, replaces the isolation of the labourers, due to competition, by their revolutionary combination, due to association. The development of modern industry, therefore, cuts from under its feet the very foundation on which the bourgeoisie produces and appropriates products. What the bourgeoisie, therefore, produces, above all, is its own grave-diggers. Its fall and the victory of the proletariat are equally inevitable.

* * * * *

Notes

1 By bourgeoisie is meant the class of modern capitalists, owners of the means of social production and employers of wage-labour. By proletariat, the class of modern wage-labourers who, having no means of production of their own, are reduced to selling their labour-power in order to live. [Engels]

2 That is, all written history. In 1847, the pre-history of society, the social organization existing previous to recorded history, was all but unknown .... With the dissolution of these primaeval communities society begins to be differentiated into separate and finally antagonistic classes. I have attempted to retrace this process of dissolution in *The Origin of the Family, Private Property and the State*. [Engels] Engels's *The Origin of the Family, Private Property and the State* was first published in 1884. [JW]

3 Guild-master, that is, a full member of a guild, a master within, not a head of a guild. [Engels]

4 A burgher was a citizen of a town. In the Middle Ages serfs sometimes attempted to escape bondage by fleeing to the towns. In late feudalism, in the epoch of the great absolutist states, the monarch gave charters to the towns, making them legal corporations. The term "burgess" in the following sentence is used interchangeably with the term "burgher" by Marx and Engels. [JW]

5 In *The Condition of the Working Class in England*, first published in 1845, Engels amplified his use of the term "middle class." "The English word middle class ... [l]ike the French word *bourgeoisie* ... means the possessing class, specifically that possessing class which is differentiated from the so-called aristocracy ...." (p. 15) [JW]

6 In *Capital*, Volume 1, Part III, Chapter XIV, Marx distinguishes between the period of manufacture, which extends from about 1550 to about 1780, and the period of modern industry, which follows it. During the period of manufacture capitalists employed wage

labourers in their workshops to produce commodities by hand, using a division of labour among the workers to operate more economically than the craftsman and his apprentices. In the period of modern industry the tools of manual production were replaced by machines. "Manufacture" is thus understood literally, as the process of making by hand. [JW]

7 "Commune" was the name taken, in France, by the nascent towns even before they had conquered local self-government and political rights as the "third estate" from their feudal lords and masters. Generally speaking, for the economic development of the bourgeoisie, England is here taken as the typical country; for its political development, France. [Engels]

8 The clergy and the nobility were the first two estates. [JW]

9 Marx was later to argue that it was labour-power, the capacity to labour, and not labour itself which the worker sold to the capitalist. This enabled Marx to distinguish between the slave mode of production, in which the slave was a commodity and could be bought and sold, and capitalism, in which the labourer remained free, but was forced to sell his or her labour-power in order to live. [JW]

10 The British Factory Act of 1847 specified that on May 1st, 1848, the working day would be reduced to ten hours from the twelve hours that had become common in the preceding decade. For a more elaborate analysis by Marx on the struggle of the workers for a shorter working day see *Capital*, Vol. 1, Part III, Section 6. [JW]

CHAPTER 3
The Promise

C. Wright Mills

Nowadays men often feel that their private lives are a series of traps. They sense that within their everyday worlds, they cannot overcome their troubles, and in this feeling, they are often quite correct: What ordinary men are directly aware of and what they try to do are bounded by the private orbits in which they live; their visions and their powers are limited to the close-up scenes of job, family, neighborhood; in other milieux, they move vicariously and remain spectators. And the more aware they become, however vaguely, of ambitions and of threats which transcend their immediate locales, the more trapped they seem to feel.

Underlying this sense of being trapped are seemingly impersonal changes in the very structure of continent-wide societies. The facts of contemporary history are also facts about the success and the failure of individual men and women. When a society is industrialized, a peasant becomes a worker; a feudal lord is liquidated or becomes a businessman. When classes rise or fall, a man is employed or unemployed; when the rate of investment goes up or down, a man takes new heart or goes broke. When wars happen, an insurance salesman becomes a rocket launcher; a store clerk, a radar man; a wife lives alone; a child grows up without a father. Neither the life of an individual nor the history of a society can be understood without understanding both.

Yet men do not usually define the troubles they endure in terms of historical change and institutional contradiction. The well-being they enjoy, they do not usually impute to the big ups and downs of the societies in which they live. Seldom aware of the intricate connection between the patterns of their own lives and the course of world history, ordinary men do not usually know what this connection means for the kinds of men they are becoming and for the kinds of history-making in which they might take part. They do not possess the quality of mind essential to grasp the interplay of man and society, of biography and history, of self and world. They cannot cope with their personal troubles in such ways as to control the structural transformations that usually lie behind them.

Surely it is no wonder. In what period have so many men been so totally exposed at so fast a pace to such earthquakes of change? That Americans have not known

such catastrophic changes as have the men and women of other societies is due to historical facts that are now quickly becoming "merely history." The history that now affects every man is world history. Within this scene and this period, in the course of a single generation, one sixth of mankind is transformed from all that is feudal and backward into all that is modern, advanced, and fearful. Political colonies are freed; new and less visible forms of imperialism installed. Revolutions occur; men feel the intimate grip of new kinds of authority. Totalitarian societies rise, and are smashed to bits—or succeed fabulously. After two centuries of ascendancy, capitalism is shown up as only one way to make society into an industrial apparatus. After two centuries of hope, even formal democracy is restricted to a quite small portion of mankind. Everywhere in the underdeveloped world, ancient ways of life are broken up and vague expectations become urgent demands. Everywhere in the overdeveloped world, the means of authority and of violence become total in scope and bureaucratic in form. Humanity itself now lies before us, the super-nation at either pole concentrating its most co-ordinated and massive efforts upon the preparation of World War Three.

The very shaping of history now outpaces the ability of men to orient themselves in accordance with cherished values. And which values? Even when they do not panic, men often sense that older ways of feeling and thinking have collapsed and that newer beginnings are ambiguous to the point of moral stasis. Is it any wonder that ordinary men feel they cannot cope with the larger worlds with which they are so suddenly confronted? That they cannot understand the meaning of their epoch for their own lives? That—in defense of selfhood—they become morally insensible, trying to remain altogether private men? Is it any wonder that they come to be possessed by a sense of the trap?

It is not only information that they need—in this Age of Fact, information often dominates their attention and overwhelms their capacities to assimilate it. It is not only the skills of reason that they need—although their struggles to acquire these often exhaust their limited moral energy.

What they need, and what they feel they need, is a quality of mind that will help them to use information and to develop reason in order to achieve lucid summations of what is going on in the world and of what may be happening within themselves. It is this quality, I am going to contend, that journalists and scholars, artists and publics, scientists and editors are coming to expect of what may be called the sociological imagination.

The sociological imagination enables its possessor to understand the larger historical scene in terms of its meaning for the inner life and the external career of a variety of individuals. It enables him to take into account how individuals, in the welter of their daily experience, often become falsely conscious of their social positions. Within that welter, the framework of modern society is sought, and within that framework the psychologies of a variety of men and women are formulated. By such means the personal uneasiness of individuals is focused upon explicit troubles and the indifference of publics is transformed into involvement with public issues.

The first fruit of this imagination—and the first lesson of the social science that embodies it—is the idea that the individual can understand his own experience and gauge his own fate only by locating himself within his period, that he can know his own chances in life only by becoming aware of those of all individuals in his circumstances. In many ways it is a terrible lesson; in many ways a magnificent one. We do not know the limits of man's capacities for supreme effort or willing degradation, for agony or glee, for pleasurable brutality or the sweetness of reason. But in our time we have come to know that the limits of "human nature" are frighteningly broad. We have come to know that every individual lives, from one generation to the next, in some society; that he lives out a biography, and that he lives it out within some historical sequence. By the fact of his living he contributes, however minutely, to the shaping of this society and to the course of its history, even as he is made by society and by its historical push and shove.

The sociological imagination enables us to grasp history and biography and the relations between the two within society. That is its task and its promise. To recognize this task and this promise is the mark of the classic social analyst. It is characteristic of Herbert Spencer—turgid, polysyllabic, comprehensive; of E.A. Ross—graceful, muckraking, upright; of Auguste Comte and Emile Durkheim; of the intricate and subtle Karl Mannheim. It is the quality of all that is intellectually excellent in Karl Marx; it is the clue to Thorstein Veblen's brilliant and ironic insight, to Joseph Schumpeter's many-sided constructions of reality; it is the basis of the psychological sweep of W.E.H. Lecky no less than of the profundity and clarity of Max Weber. And it is the signal of what is best in contemporary studies of man and society.

No social study that does not come back to the problems of biography, of history and of their intersections within a society has completed its intellectual journey. Whatever the specific problems of the classic social analysts, however limited or however broad the features of social reality they have examined, those who have been imaginatively aware of the promise of their work have consistently asked three sorts of questions:

(1) What is the structure of this particular society as a whole? What are its essential components, and how are they related to one another? How does it differ from other varieties of social order? Within it, what is the meaning of any particular feature for its continuance and for its change?

(2) Where does this society stand in human history? What are the mechanics by which it is changing? What is its place within and its meaning for the development of humanity as a whole? How does any particular feature we are examining affect, and how is it affected by, the historical period in which it moves? And this period—what are its essential features? How does it differ from other periods? What are its characteristic ways of history-making?

(3) What varieties of men and women now prevail in this society and in this period? And what varieties are coming to prevail? In what ways are they selected and formed, liberated and repressed, made sensitive and blunted? What kinds of "human nature" are revealed in the conduct and character we observe in this society in this period? And what is the meaning for "human nature" of each and every feature of the society we are examining?

Whether the point of interest is a great power state or a minor literary mood, a family, a prison, a creed—these are the kinds of questions the best social analysts have asked. They are the intellectual pivots of classic studies of man in society—and they are the questions inevitably raised by any mind possessing the sociological imagination. For that imagination is the capacity to shift from one perspective to another—from the political to the psychological; from examination of a single family to comparative assessment of the national budgets of the work, from the theological school to the military establishment; from considerations of an oil industry to studies of contemporary poetry. It is the capacity to range from the most impersonal and remote transformations to the most intimate features of the human self—and to see the relations between the two. Back of its use there is always the urge to know the social and historical meaning of the individual in the society and in the period in which he has his quality and his being.

That, in brief, is why it is by means of the sociological imagination that men now hope to grasp what is going on in the world, and to understand what is happening in themselves as minute points of the intersections of biography and history within society. In large part, contemporary man's self-conscious view of himself as at least an outsider, if not a permanent stranger, rests upon an absorbed realization of social relativity and of the transformative power of history. The sociological imagination is the most fruitful form of this self-consciousness. By its use men whose mentalities have swept only a series of limited orbits often come to feel as if suddenly awakened in a house with which they had only supposed themselves to be familiar. Correctly or incorrectly, they often come to feel that they can now provide themselves with adequate summations, cohesive assessments, comprehensive orientations. Older decisions that once appeared sound now seem to them products of a mind unaccountably dense. Their capacity for astonishment is made lively again. They acquire a new way of thinking, they experience a transvaluation of values: in a word, by their reflection and by their sensibility, they realize the cultural meaning of the social sciences.

Perhaps the most fruitful distinction with which the sociological imagination works is between "the personal troubles of milieu" and "the public issues of social structure." This distinction is an essential tool of the sociological imagination and a feature of all classic work in social science.

Troubles occur within the character of the individual and within the range of his immediate relations with others; they have to do with his self and with those limited areas of social life of which he is directly and personally aware. Accordingly, the statement and the resolution of troubles properly lie within the individual as a biographical entity and within the scope of his immediate milieu— the social setting that is directly open to his personal experience and to some extent his willful activity. A trouble is a private matter: values cherished by an individual are felt by him to be threatened.

Issues have to do with matters that transcend these local environments of the individual and the range of his inner life. They have to do with the organization of many such milieux into the institutions of an historical society as a whole, with the ways in which various milieux overlap and interpenetrate to form the larger structure of social and historical life. An issue is a public matter: some value cherished by publics is felt to be threatened. Often there is a debate about what that value really is and about what it is that really threatens it. This debate is often without focus if only because it is the very nature of an issue, unlike even widespread trouble, that it cannot very well be defined in terms of the immediate and everyday environments of ordinary men. An issue, in fact, often involves a crisis in institutional arrangements, and often too it involves what Marxists call "contradictions" or "antagonisms."

In these terms, consider unemployment. When, in a city of 100,000, only one man is unemployed, that is his personal trouble, and for its relief we properly look to the character of the man, his skills, and his immediate opportunities. But when in a nation of 50 million employees, 15 million men are unemployed, that is an issue, and we may not hope to find its solution within the range of opportunities open to any one individual. The very structure of opportunities has collapsed. Both the correct statement of the problem and the range of possible solutions require us to consider the economic and political institutions of the society, and not merely the personal situation and character of a scatter of individuals.

Consider war. The personal problem of war, when it occurs, may be how to survive it or how to die in it with honor; how to make money out of it; how to climb into the higher safety of the military apparatus; or how to contribute to the war's termination. In short, according to one's values, to find a set of milieux and within it to survive the war or make one's death in it meaningful. But the structural issues of war have to do with its causes; with what types of men it throws up into command; with its effects upon economic and political, family and religious institutions, with the unorganized irresponsibility of a world of nation-states.

Consider marriage. Inside a marriage a man and a woman may experience personal troubles, but when the divorce rate during the first four years of marriage is 250 out of every 1,000 attempts, this is an indication of a structural issue having to do with the institutions of marriage and the family and other institutions that bear upon them.

Or consider the metropolis—the horrible, beautiful, ugly, magnificent sprawl of the great city. For many upper-class people, the personal solution to "the problem of the city" is to have an apartment with private garage under it in the heart of the city, and forty miles out, a house by Henry Hill, garden by Garrett Eckbo, on a hundred acres of private land. In these two controlled environments—with a small staff at each end and a private helicopter connection—most people could solve many of the problems of personal milieux caused by the facts of the city. But all this, however splendid, does not solve the public issues that the structural fact of the city poses. What should be done with this wonderful monstrosity? Break it all up into scattered units, combining residence and work? Refurbish it as it stands? Or, after evacuation, dynamite it and build new cities according to new plans in new places? What should those plans be? And who is to decide and to accomplish whatever choice is made? These are structural issues; to confront them and to solve them requires us to consider political and economic issues that affect innumerable milieux.

In so far as an economy is so arranged that slumps occur, the problem of unemployment becomes incapable of personal solution. In so far as war is inherent in the nation-state system and in the uneven industrialization of the world, the ordinary individual in his restricted milieu will be powerless—with or without psychiatric aid—to solve the troubles this system or lack of system imposes upon him. In so far as the family as an institution turns women into darling little slaves and men into their chief providers and unweaned dependents, the problem of a satisfactory marriage remains incapable of purely private solution. In so far as the overdeveloped megalopolis and the overdeveloped automobile are built-in features of the overdeveloped society, the issues of urban living will not be solved by personal ingenuity and private wealth.

What we experience in various and specific milieux, I have noted, is often caused by structural changes. Accordingly, to understand the changes of many personal milieux we are required to look beyond them. And the number and variety of such structural changes increase as the institutions within which we live become more embracing and more intricately connected with one another. To be aware of the idea of social structure and to use it with sensibility is to be capable of tracing such linkages among a great variety of milieux. To be able to do that is to possess the sociological imagination.

* * * * *

CHAPTER 4

Women's Perspective as a Radical Critique of Sociology[1]

DOROTHY E. SMITH

The women's movement has given us a sense of our right to have women's interests represented in sociology, rather than just receiving as authoritative the interests traditionally represented in a sociology put together by men. What can we make of this access to a social reality that was previously unavailable, was indeed repressed? What happens as we begin to relate to it in the terms of our discipline? We can of course think as many do merely of the addition of courses to the existing repertoire—courses on sex roles, on the women's movement, on women at work, on the social psychology of women and perhaps somewhat different versions of the sociology of the family. But thinking more boldly or perhaps just thinking the whole thing through a little further might bring us to ask first how a sociology might look if it began from the point of view of women's traditional place in it and what happens to a sociology which attempts to deal seriously with that. Following this line of thought, I have found, has consequences larger than they seem at first.

From this point of view of "women's place" the values assigned to different aspects of the world are changed. Some come into prominence while other standard sociological enterprises diminish [....]

But it is not enough to supplement an established sociology by addressing ourselves to what has been left out, overlooked, or by making sociological issues of the relevances of the world of women. That merely extends the authority of the existing sociological procedures and makes of a women's sociology an addendum. We cannot rest at that because it does not account for the separation between the two worlds and it does not account for or analyze for us the relation between them [....]

* * * * *

The sociologist enters the conceptually ordered society when he goes to work. He enters it as a member and he enters it also as a mode in which he investigates it. He observes, analyzes, explains and examines as if there were no problem in how that world becomes observable to him. He moves among the doings of organizations, governmental processes, bureaucracies, etc., as a person who is at home in that medium. The nature of

that world itself, how it is known to him and the conditions of existence or his relation to it are not called into question. His methods of observation and inquiry extend into it as procedures which are essentially of the same order as those which bring about the phenomena with which he is concerned, or which he is concerned to bring under the jurisdiction of that order. His perspectives and interests may differ, but the substance is the same. He works with facts and information which have been worked up from actualities and appear in the form of documents which are themselves the product of organizational processes, whether his own or administered by him, or of some other agency. He fits that information back into a framework of entities and organizational processes which he takes for granted as known, without asking how it is that he knows them or what are the social processes by which the phenomena which correspond to or provide the empirical events, acts, decisions, etc., of that world, may be recognized. He passes beyond the particular and immediate setting in which he is always located in the body (the office he writes in, the libraries he consults, the streets he travels, the home he returns to) without any sense of having made a transition. He works in the same medium as he studies.

But like everyone else he also exists in the body in the place in which it is. This is also then the place of his sensory organization of immediate experience, then place where his coordinates of here and now before and after are organized around himself as centre; the place where he confronts people face to face in the physical mode in which he expresses himself to them and they to him as more and other than either can speak. It is in this place that things smell. The irrelevant birds fly away in front of the window. Here he has indigestion. It is a place he dies in. Into this space must come as actual material events, whether as the sounds of speech, the scratchings on the surface of paper which he constitutes as document, or directly anything he knows of the world. It has to happen here somehow if he is to experience it at all.

Entering the governing mode of our kind of society lifts the actor out of the immediate local and particular place in which he is in the body. He uses what becomes present to him in this place as a means to pass beyond it to the conceptual order. This mode of action creates then a bifurcation of consciousness, a bifurcation of course which is there for all those who participate in this mode of action. It establishes two modes of knowing and experiencing and doing, one located in the body and in the space which it occupies and moves into, the other which passes beyond it. Sociology is written in and aims at this second mode. Vide Bierstedt

Sociology can liberate the mind from time and space themselves and remove it to a new and transcendental realm where it no longer depends upon these Aristotelian categories. (1966)

Women are outside and subservient to this structure. They have a very specific relation to it which anchors them into the local and particular phase of the bifurcated world. For both traditionally and as a matter of occupational practices in our society, the governing conceptual mode is appropriated by men and the world organized in the natural attitude, the home, is appropriated by (or assigned to) women (Smith, 1973).

It is a condition of a man's being able to enter and become absorbed in the conceptual mode that he does not have to focus his activities and interests upon his bodily existence. If he is to participate fully in the abstract mode of action, then he must be liberated also from having to attend to his needs, etc., in the concrete and particular. The organization of work and expectations in managerial and professional circles both constitutes and depends upon the alienation of man from his bodily and local existence. The structure of work and the structure of career take for granted that these matters are provided for in such a way that they will not interfere with his action and participation in that world. Providing for the liberation from the Aristotelian categories of which Bierstedt speaks, is a woman who keeps house for him, bears and cares for his children, washes his clothes, looks after him when his is sick and generally provides for the logistics of his bodily existence.

The place of women then in relation to this mode of action is that where the work is done to create conditions which facilitate his occupation of the conceptual mode of consciousness. The meeting of a man's physical needs, the organization of his daily life, even the consistency of expressive background, are made maximally congruent with his commitment. A similar relation exists for women who work in and around the professional and managerial scene. They do those things which give concrete form to the conceptual activities. They do the clerical work, the computer programming, the interviewing for the survey, the nursing, the secretarial work. At almost every point women mediate for men the relation between the conceptual mode of action and the actual concrete forms in which it is and must be realized, and the actual material conditions upon which it depends.

Marx's concept of alienation is applicable here in a modified form. The simplest formulation of alienation posits a relation between the work an individual does and an external order which oppresses her, such that the harder she works the more she strengthens the order which oppresses her. This is the situation of women in this relation. The more successful women are in mediating the world of concrete particulars so that men do not have to become engaged with (and therefore conscious of) that world as a condition to their abstract activities, the more complete man's absorption in it, the more effective the authority of that world and the more total women's subservience to it. And also the more complete the dichotomy between the two worlds, and the estrangement between them.

Women sociologists stand at the centre of a contradiction in the relation of our discipline to our experience of the world. Transcending that contradiction means setting up a different kind of relation than that which we discover in the routine practice of our worlds.

The theories, concepts and methods of our discipline claim to account for, or to be capable of accounting for and analyzing the same world as that which we experience directly. But these theories, concepts and methods have been organizing around and built up out of a way of knowing the world which takes for granted the boundaries of an experience in the same medium which it is constituted. It therefore takes for granted and subsumes without examining the conditions of its existence. It is not capable of analyzing its own relation to its conditions because the sociologist as actual person in an actual concrete setting has been cancelled in the procedures which objectify and separate him from his knowledge. Thus the linkage which points back to its conditions is lacking.

For women those conditions are central as a direct practical matter, to be somehow solved in the decision to take up a sociological career. The relation between ourselves as practicing sociologists and ourselves as working women is continually visible to us, a central feature of experience of the world, so that the bifurcation of consciousness becomes for us a daily chasm which is to be crossed, on the one side of which is this special conceptual activity of thought, research, teaching, administration and on the other the world of concrete practical activities in keeping things clean, managing somehow the house and household and the children a world in which the particularities of persons in their full organic immediacy (cleaning up the vomit, changing the diapers, as well as feeding) are inescapable. Even if we don't have that as a direct contingency in our lives, we are aware of that as something that our becoming may be inserted into as a possible predicate.

It is also present for us to discover that the discipline is not one which we enter and occupy on the same terms as men enter and occupy it. We do not fully appropriate its authority, i.e., the right to author and authorize the acts and knowing and thinking which are the acts and knowing and thinking of the discipline as it is thought. We cannot therefore command the inner principles of our action. That remains lodged outside us. The frames of reference which order the terms upon which inquiry and discussion are conducted originate with men. The subjects of sociological sentences (if they have a subject) are male. The sociologist is "he." And even before we become conscious of our sex as the basis of an exclusion (*they* are not talking about *us*), we nonetheless do not fully enter ourselves as the subjects of its statements, since we must suspend our sex, and suspend our knowledge of who we are as well as who it is that in fact is speaking and of whom. Therefore we do not fully participate in the declarations and formulations of its mode of consciousness. The externalization of sociology as a profession which I have described above becomes for women a double estrangement.

There is then for women a basic organization of their experience which displays for them the structure of the bifurcated consciousness. At the same time it attenuates their commitment to a sociology which aims at an externalized body of knowledge based on an organization of experience which excludes their and excludes them expect in a subordinate relation.

[...] Women's perspective, as I have analyzed it here, discredits sociology's claim to constitute an objective knowledge independent of the sociologist's situation. Its conceptual procedures, methods and relevances are seen to organize its subject matter from a determinate position in society. This critical disclosure becomes then the basis for an alternative way of thinking sociology. If sociology cannot avoid being situated, then sociology should take that as its beginning and build it into its methodological and theoretical strategies. As it is now, these separate a sociologically constructed world from that which is known in direct experience and it is precisely that separation which must be undone.

I am not proposing an immediate and radical transformation of the subject matter and methods of the discipline nor the junking of everything that has gone before. What I am suggesting is more in the nature of a re-organization which changes the relation of the sociologist to the object of her knowledge and changes also her problematic. This re-organization involves first placing the sociologist where she is actually situated, namely at the beginning of those acts by which she knows or will come to know; and second, making her direct experience of the everyday world the primary ground of her knowledge.

* * * * *

The only way of knowing a socially constructed world is knowing it from within. We can never stand outside it. A relation in which sociological phenomena are objectified and presented as external to and independent of the observer is itself a special social practice also known from within. The relation of observer and object of observation, of sociologist to "subject," is a specialized social relationship. Even to be a stranger is to enter a world constituted from within as strange. The strangeness itself is the mode in which it is experienced.

[...] An alternative sociology must be reflexive (Gouldner, 1971), i.e., one that preserves in it the presence, concerns and experience of the sociologist as knower and discoverer.

To begin from direct experience and to return to it as a constraint or "test" of the adequacy of a systematic knowledge is to begin from where we are located bodily. The actualities of our everyday world are already socially organized. Settings, equipment, "environment," schedules, occasions, etc., as well as the enterprises and routines of actors are socially produced and concretely and symbolically organized prior to our practice. By beginning from her original and immediate knowledge of her world, sociology offers a way of making its socially organized properties first observable and then problematic.

Let me make it clear that when I speak of "experience" I do not use the term as a synonym for "perspective." Nor in proposing a sociology grounded in the sociologist's actual experience, am I recommending the self-indulgence of inner exploration or any other enterprise with self as sole focus and object. Such subjectivist interpretations of "experience" are themselves an aspect of that organization of consciousness which bifurcates it and transports us into mind country while stashing away the concrete conditions and practices upon which it depends. We can never escape the circles of our own heads if we accept that as our territory. Rather the sociologist's investigation of our directly experienced world as a problem is a mode of discovering or rediscovering the society from within. She begins from her own original but tacit knowledge and from within the acts by which she brings it into her grasp in making it observable and in understanding how it works. She aims not at a reiteration of what she already (tacitly) knows, but at an exploration through that of what passes beyond it and is deeply implicated in how it is.

* * * * *

Women's situation in sociology discloses to her a typical bifurcate structure with the abstracted conceptual practices on the one hand and the concrete realizations, the maintenance routines, etc., on the other. Taking each for granted depends upon being fully situated in one or the other so that the other does not appear in contradiction to it. Women's direct experience places her a step back where we can recognize the uneasiness that comes in sociology from its claim to be about the world we live in and its failure to account for or even describe its actual features as we find them in living them. The aim of an alternative sociology would be to develop precisely that capacity from that beginning so that it might be a means to anyone of understanding how the world comes about for her and how it is organized so that it happens to her as it does in her experience.

Though such a sociology would not be exclusively for or done by women it does begin from the analysis and critique originating in their situation. Its elaboration therefore depends upon a grasp of that which is prior to and fuller than its formulation. It is a little like the problem of making a formal description of the grammar of a language. The linguist depends and always refers back to the competent speakers' sense of what is correct usage, what makes sense, etc. In her own language she depends to a large extent upon her own competence. Women are native speakers of this situation and in explicating it or its implications and realizing them conceptually, they have that relation to it of knowing it before it has been said.

The incomprehensibility of the determinations of our immediate local world is for women a particularly striking metaphor. It recovers an inner organization in common with their typical relation to the world. For women's activities and existence are determined outside them and beyond the world which is their "place." They are oriented by their training and by the daily practices which confirm it, towards the demands and initiations and authority of others. But more than that, the very organization of the world which has been assigned to them as the primary locus of their being is determined by and subordinate to the corporate organization of society (Smith, 1973). Thus as I have expressed her relation to sociology, its logic lies elsewhere. She lacks the inner principle of her own activity. She does not grasp how it is put together because it is determined elsewhere than where she is. As a sociologist then the grasp and exploration of her own experience as a method of discovering society restores to her a centre which in this enterprise at least is wholly hers.

Note

1   This paper was originally prepared for the meetings of the American Academy for the Advancement of Science (Pacific Division) Eugene, Oregon, June, 1972. The original draft of this paper was typed by Jane Lemke and the final version by Mildred Brown. I am indebted to both of them.

References

Bierstedt, Robert. 1966. "Sociology and General Education." In Charles H. Page (ed.), *Sociology and Contemporary Education*. New York: Random House.

Briggs, Jean L. 1970. *Never in Anger*. Cambridge, Mass.: Harvard University Press.

Gouldner, Alvin. 1971. *The Coming Crisis in Western Sociology*. London: Heinemann Educational Books.

Smith, Dorothy E. 1973. "Women, the Family and Corporate Capitalism." In M.L. Stephenson (ed.), *Women in Canada*. Toronto: Newpress.

CHAPTER 5
Panopticism

Michel Foucault

* * * * *

Bentham's *Panopticon* is the architectural figure of this composition. We know the principle on which it was based: at the periphery, an annular building; at the centre, a tower; this tower is pierced with wide windows that open onto the inner side of the ring; the peripheric building is, divided into cells, each of which extends the whole width of the building; they have two windows, one on the inside, corresponding to the windows of the tower; the other, on the outside, allows the light to cross the cell from one end to the other. All that is needed, then, is to place a supervisor in a central tower and to shut up in each cell a madman, a patient, a condemned man, a worker or a schoolboy. By the effect of backlighting, one can observe from the tower, standing out precisely against the light, the small captive shadows in the cells of the periphery. They are like so many cages, so many small theatres, in which each actor is alone, perfectly individualized and constantly visible. The panoptic mechanism arranges spatial unities that make it possible to see constantly and to recognize immediately. In short, it reverses the principle of the dungeon; or rather of its three functions—to enclose, to deprive of light and to hide—it preserves only the first and eliminates the other two. Full lighting and the eye of a supervisor capture better than darkness, which ultimately protected. Visibility is a trap.

To begin with, this made it possible—as a negative effect—to avoid those compact, swarming, howling masses that were to be found in places of confinement, those painted by Goya or described by Howard. Each individual, in his place, is securely confined to a cell from which he is seen from the front by the supervisor; but the side walls prevent him from coming into contact with his companions. He is seen, but he does not see; he is the object of information, never a subject in communication. The arrangement of his room, opposite the central tower, imposes on him an axial visibility; but the divisions of the ring, those separated cells, imply a lateral invisibility. And this invisibility is a guarantee of order. If the inmates are convicts, there is no danger of a plot, an attempt at collective escape, the planning of new crimes for the future, bad reciprocal influences; if they are patients, there is no danger of contagion; if they are madmen there is no risk of their committing violence upon one another; if they are schoolchildren, there is no copying, no noise, no chatter, no waste of time; if they are workers, there are no disorders, no theft, no coalitions, none of those distractions that slow down the rate of work, make it less perfect or cause accidents. The crowd, a compact mass, a locus of multiple exchanges, individualities merging together, a collective effect, is abolished and replaced by a collection of separated individualities. From the point of view of the guardian, it is replaced by a multiplicity that can be numbered and supervised; from the point of view of the inmates, by a sequestered and observed solitude (Bentham, 60–64).

Hence the major effect of the Panopticon: to induce in the inmate a state of conscious and permanent visibility that assures the automatic functioning of power. So to arrange things that the surveillance is permanent in its effects, even if it is discontinuous in its action; that the perfection of power should tend to render its actual exercise unnecessary; that this architectural apparatus should be a machine for creating and sustaining a power relation independent of the person who exercises it; in short, that the inmates should be caught up in a power situation of which they are themselves the bearers. To achieve this, it is at once too much and too little that the prisoner should be constantly observed by an inspector: too little, for what matters is that he knows himself to be observed; too much, because he has no need in fact of being so. In view of this, Bentham laid down the principle that power should be visible and unverifiable. Visible: the inmate will constantly have before his eyes the tall outline of the central tower from which he is spied upon. Unverifiable: the inmate must never know whether he is being looked at any one moment; but he must be sure that he may always be so. In order to make the presence or absence of the inspector unverifiable, so that the prisoners, in their cells, cannot even see a shadow, Bentham envisaged not only Venetian blinds on the windows of the central observation hall, but, on the inside, partitions that intersected the hall at right angles and, in order to pass from one quarter to the other, not doors but zig-zag openings; for the slightest noise, a gleam of light, a brightness in a half-opened door would betray the presence of the guardian.[1] The Panopticon is a machine for dissociating the see/being seen dyad: in the peripheric ring, one is totally seen, without ever seeing; in the central tower, one sees everything without ever being seen.[2]

It is an important mechanism, for it automatizes and disindividualizes power. Power has its principle not so much in a person as in a certain concerted distribution of bodies, surfaces, lights, gazes; in an arrangement whose internal mechanisms produce the relation in which individuals are caught up. The ceremonies, the rituals, the marks by which the sovereign's surplus power was manifested are useless. There is a machinery that assures dissymmetry, disequilibrium, difference. Consequently, it does not matter who exercises power. Any individual, taken almost at random, can operate the machine: in the absence of the director, his family, his friends, his visitors, even his servants (Bentham, 45). Similarly, it does not matter what motive animates him: the curiosity of the indiscreet, the malice of a child, the thirst for knowledge of a philosopher who wishes to visit this museum of human nature, or the perversity of those who take pleasure in spying and punishing. The more numerous those anonymous and temporary observers are, the greater the risk for the inmate of being surprised and the greater his anxious awareness of being observed. The Panopticon is a marvellous machine which, whatever use one may wish to put it to, produces homogeneous effects of power.

A real subjection is born mechanically from a fictitious relation. So it is not necessary to use force to constrain the convict to good behaviour, the madman to calm, the worker to work, the schoolboy to application, the patient to the observation of the regulations. Bentham was surprised that panoptic institutions could be so light: there were no more bars, no more chains, no more heavy locks; all that was needed was that the separations should be clear and the openings well arranged. The heaviness of the old "houses of security," with their fortress-like architecture, could be replaced by the simple, economic geometry of a "house of certainty." The efficiency of power, its constraining force have, in a sense, passed over to the other side—to the side of its surface of application. He who is subjected to a field of visibility, and who knows it, assumes responsibility for the constraints of power; he makes them play spontaneously upon himself; he inscribes in himself the power relation in which he simultaneously plays both roles; he becomes the principle of his own subjection. By this very fact, the external power may throw off its physical weight; it tends to the non-corporal; and, the more it approaches this limit, the more constant, profound and permanent are its effects: it is a perpetual victory that avoids any physical confrontation and which is always decided in advance.

Bentham does not say whether he was inspired, in his project, by Le Vaux's menagerie at Versailles: the first menagerie in which the different elements are not, as they traditionally were, distributed in a park (Loisel, 104–107). At the centre was an octagonal pavilion which, on the first floor, consisted of only a single room, the king's *salon*; on every side large windows looked out onto seven cages (the eighth side was reserved for the entrance), containing different species of animals. By Bentham's time, this menagerie had disappeared. But one finds in the programme of the Panopticon a similar concern with individualizing observation, with characterization and classification, with the analytical arrangement of space. The Panopticon is a royal menagerie; the animal is replaced by man, individual distribution by specific grouping and the king by the machinery of a furtive power. With this exception, the Panopticon also does the work of a naturalist. It makes it possible to draw up differences: among patients, to observe the symptoms of each individual, without the proximity of beds, the circulation of miasmas, the effects of contagion confusing the clinical tables; among school-children, it makes it possible to observe performances (without there being any imitation or copying), to map aptitudes, to assess characters, to draw up rigorous classifications and, in relation to normal development, to distinguish "laziness and stubbornness" from "incurable imbecility"; among workers, it makes it possible to note the aptitudes of each worker, compare the time he takes to perform a task, and if they are paid by the day, to calculate their wages (Bentham, 60–64).

So much for the question of observation. But the Panopticon was also a laboratory; it could be used as a machine to carry out experiments, to alter behaviour, to train or correct individuals. To experiment with medicines and monitor their effects. To try out different punishments on prisoners, according to their crimes and character, and to seek the most effective ones. To teach different techniques simultaneously to the workers, to decide which is the best. To try out pedagogical experiments—and in particular to take up once again the well-debated problem of secluded education, by using orphans. One would see what would happen when, in their sixteenth or eighteenth year, they were presented with other boys or girls; one could verify whether, as Helvetius thought, anyone could learn anything; one would follow "the genealogy of every observable idea"; one could bring up different children according to different systems of thought, making certain children believe that two and two do not make four or that the moon is a cheese, then put them together when they are twenty or twenty-five years old; one would then have discussions that would be worth a great deal more than the sermons or lectures on which so much money is spent; one would have at least an opportunity of making discoveries in the domain of metaphysics. The Panopticon is a privileged place for experiments on men, and for analysing with complete certainty the transformations that may be obtained from them. The Panopticon may even provide an apparatus for supervising its own mechanisms. In this central tower, the director may spy on all the employees that he has under his orders: nurses, doctors, foremen, teachers, warders; he will be able to judge them continuously, alter their behaviour, impose upon them the methods he thinks best; and it will even be possible to observe the director himself. An inspector arriving unexpectedly at the centre of the Panopticon will be able to judge at a glance, without anything being concealed from him, how the entire establishment is functioning. And, in any case, enclosed as he is in the middle of this architectural mechanism, is not the director's own fate entirely bound up with it? The incompetent physician who has allowed contagion to spread, the incompetent prison governor or workshop manager will be the first victims of an epidemic or a revolt."'By every tie I could devise," said the master of the Panopticon, 'my own fate had been bound up by me with theirs'" (Bentham, 177). The Panopticon functions as a kind of laboratory of power. Thanks to its mechanisms of observation, it gains in efficiency and in the ability to penetrate into men's behaviour; knowledge follows the advances of power, discovering new objects of knowledge over all the surfaces on which power is exercised.

The plague-stricken town, the panoptic establishment—the differences are important. They mark, at a distance of a century and a half, the transformations of the disciplinary programme. In the first case, there is an exceptional situation: against an extraordinary evil, power is mobilized; it makes itself everywhere present and visible; it invents new mechanisms; it separates, it immobilizes, it partitions; it constructs for a time what is both a counter-city and the perfect society; it imposes an ideal functioning, but one that is reduced, in the final analysis, like the evil that it combats, to a simple dualism of life and death: that which moves brings death, and one kills that which moves. The Panopticon, on the other hand, must be understood as a generalizable model of functioning; a way of defining power relations in terms of the everyday life of men. No doubt Bentham presents it as a particular institution, closed in upon itself. Utopias, perfectly closed in upon themselves, are common enough. As opposed to the ruined prisons, littered with mechanisms of torture, to be seen in Piranese's engravings, the Panopticon presents a cruel, ingenious cage. The fact that it should have given rise, even in our own time, to so many variations, projected or realized, is evidence of the imaginary intensity that it has possessed for almost two hundred years. But the Panopticon must not be understood as a dream building: it is the diagram of a mechanism of power reduced to its ideal form; its functioning, abstracted from any obstacle, resistance or friction, must be represented as a pure architectural and optical system: it is in fact a figure of political technology that may and must be detached from any specific use.

It is polyvalent in its applications; it serves to reform prisoners, but also to treat patients, to instruct schoolchildren, to confine the insane, to supervise workers, to put beggars and idlers to work. It is a type of location of bodies in space, of distribution of individuals in relation to one another, of hierarchical organization, of disposition of centres and channels of power, of definition of the instruments and modes of intervention of power, which can be implemented in hospitals, workshops, schools, prisons. Whenever one is dealing with a multiplicity of individuals on whom a task or a particular form of behaviour must be imposed, the panoptic schema may be used. It is—necessary modifications apart—applicable "to all establishments whatsoever, in which, within a space not too large to be covered or commanded by buildings, a number of persons are meant to be kept under inspection" (Bentham, 40; although Bentham takes the penitentiary house as his prime example, it is because it has many different functions to fulfill—safe custody, confinement, solitude, forced labour and instruction).

In each of its applications, it makes it possible to perfect the exercise of power. It does this in several ways: because it can reduce the number of those who exercise it, while increasing the number of those on whom it is exercised. Because it is possible to intervene at any moment and because the constant pressure acts even before the offences, mistakes or crimes have been committed. Because, in these conditions, its strength is that it never intervenes, it is exercised spontaneously and without noise, it constitutes a mechanism whose effects follow from one another. Because, without any physical instrument other than architecture and geometry, it acts directly on individuals; it gives "power of mind over mind." The panoptic schema makes any apparatus of power more intense: it assures its economy (in material, in personnel, in time); it assures its efficacity by its preventative character, its continuous functioning and its automatic mechanisms. It is a way of obtaining from power "in hitherto unexampled quantity," "a great and new instrument of government ... ; its great excellence consists in the great strength it is capable of giving to any institution it may be thought proper to apply it to" (Bentham, 66).

It's a case of "it's easy once you've thought of it" in the political sphere. It can in fact be integrated into any function (education, medical treatment, production, punishment); it can increase the effect of this function, by being linked closely with it; it can constitute a mixed mechanism in which relations of power (and of knowledge) may be precisely adjusted, in the smallest detail, to the processes that are to be supervised; it can establish a direct proportion between "surplus power" and "surplus production." In short, it arranges things in such a way that the exercise of power is not added on from the outside, like a rigid, heavy constraint, to the functions it invests, but is so subtly present in them as to increase their efficiency by itself increasing its own points of contact. The panoptic mechanism is not simply a hinge, a point of exchange between a mechanism of power and a function; it is a way of making power relations function in a function, and of making a function function through these power relations. Bentham's Preface to Panopticon opens with a list of the benefits to be obtained from his "inspection-house": "Morals reformed—health preserved—industry invigorated—instruction diffused—public burthens lightened—Economy seated, as it were, upon a rock—the gordian knot of the Poor-Laws not cut, but untied—all by a simple idea in architecture!" (Bentham, 39).

Furthermore, the arrangement of this machine is such that its enclosed nature does not preclude a permanent presence from the outside: we have seen that anyone may come and exercise in the central tower the functions of surveillance, and that, this being the case, he can gain a clear idea of the way in which the surveillance is practised. In fact, any panoptic institution, even if it is as rigorously closed as a penitentiary, may without difficulty be subjected to such irregular and constant inspections: and not only by the appointed inspectors, but also by the public; any member of society will have the right to come and see with his own eyes how the schools, hospitals, factories, prisons function. There is no risk, therefore, that the increase of power created by the panoptic machine may degenerate into tyranny; the disciplinary mechanism will be democratically controlled, since it will be constantly accessible "to the great tribunal committee of the world."[3] This Panopticon, subtly arranged so that an observer may observe, at a glance, so many different individuals, also enables everyone to come and observe any of the observers. The seeing machine was once a sort of dark room into which individuals spied; it has become a transparent building in which the exercise of power may be supervised by society as a whole.

The panoptic schema, without disappearing as such or losing any of its properties, was destined to spread throughout the social body; its vocation was to become a generalized function. The plague-stricken town provided an exceptional disciplinary model: perfect, but absolutely violent; to the disease that brought death, power opposed its perpetual threat of death; life inside it was reduced to its simplest expression; it was, against the power of death, the meticulous exercise of the right of the sword. The Panopticon, on the other hand, has a role of amplification; although it arranges power, although it is intended to make it more economic and more effective, it does so not for power itself, nor for the immediate salvation of a threatened society: its aim is to strengthen the social forces—to increase production, to develop the economy, spread education, raise the level of public morality; to increase and multiply.

How is power to be strengthened in such a way that, far from impeding progress, far from weighing upon it with its rules and regulations, it actually facilitates such progress? What intensificator of power will be able at the same time to be a multiplicator of production? How will power, by increasing its forces, be able to increase those of society instead of confiscating them or impeding them? The Panopticon's solution to this problem is that the productive increase of power can be assured only if, on the one hand, it can be exercised continuously in the very foundations of society, in the subtlest possible way, and if, on the other hand, it functions outside these sudden, violent, discontinuous forms that are bound up with the exercise of sovereignty. The body of the king, with its strange material and physical presence, with the force that he himself deploys or transmits to some few others, is at the opposite extreme of this new physics of power represented by panopticism; the domain of panopticism is, on the contrary, that whole lower region, that region of irregular bodies, with their details, their multiple movements, their heterogeneous forces, their spatial relations; what are required are mechanisms that analyse distributions, gaps, series, combinations, and which use instruments that render visible, record, differentiate and compare: a physics of a relational and multiple power, which has its maximum intensity not in the person of the king, but in the bodies that can be individualized by these relations. At the theoretical level, Bentham defines another way of analysing the social body and the power relations that traverse it; in terms of practice, he defines a procedure of subordination of bodies and forces that must increase the utility of power while practising the economy of the prince. Panopticism is the general principle of a new "political anatomy" whose object and end are not the relations of sovereignty but the relations of discipline.

The celebrated, transparent, circular cage, with its high tower, powerful and knowing, may have been for Bentham a project of a perfect disciplinary institution; but he also set out to show how one may "unlock" the disciplines and get them to function in a diffused, multiple, polyvalent way throughout the whole social body. These disciplines, which the classical age had elaborated in specific, relatively enclosed places—barracks, schools, workshops—and whose total implementation had been imagined only at the limited and temporary scale of a plague-stricken town, Bentham dreamt of transforming into a network of mechanisms that would be everywhere and always alert, running through society without interruption in space or in time. The panoptic arrangement provides the formula for this generalization. It programmes, at the level of an elementary and easily transferable mechanism, the basic functioning of a society penetrated through and through with disciplinary mechanisms.

There are two images, then, of discipline. At one extreme, the discipline-blockade, the enclosed institution, established on the edges of society, turned inwards towards negative functions: arresting evil, breaking communications, suspending time. At the other extreme, with panopticism, is the discipline-mechanism: a functional mechanism that must improve the exercise of power by making it lighter, more rapid, more effective, a design of subtle coercion for a society to come. The movement from one project to the other, from a schema of exceptional discipline to one of a generalized surveillance, rests on a historical transformation: the gradual extension of the mechanisms of discipline throughout the seventeenth and eighteenth centuries, their spread throughout the whole social body, the formation of what might be called in general the disciplinary society.

* * * * *

Notes

[1] In the *Postscript to the Panopticon*, 1791, Bentham adds dark inspection galleries painted in black around the inspector's lodge, each making it possible to observe two storeys of cells.

[2] In his first version of the *Panopticon*, Bentham had also imagined an acoustic surveillance, operated by means of pipes leading from the cells to the central tower. In the Postscript, he abandoned the idea, perhaps because he could not introduce into it the principle of dissymmetry and prevent the prisoners from hearing the inspec-tor as well as the inspector hearing them. Julius tried to develop a system of dissymmetrical listening (Julius, 18).

[3] Imagining this continuous flow of visitors entering the central tower of the Panopticon, was Bentham aware of the Panoramas that Barker was constructing at exactly the same period (the first seems to have dated from 1787) and in which the visitors, occupying the central place, saw unfolding around them a landscape, a city or a battle. The visitors occupied exactly the place of the sovereign gaze.

References

Bentham, J. 1843. *Works*, ed. Bowring IV.

Julius, N.H. 1831. *Leçons sur les prisons*, I. (Fr. trans.)

Loisel, G. 1912. *Histoire des menagaeries*.

CHAPTER 6
Revisiting Gramsci

Diana Coben

The problem for would-be radical adult educators in the 1990s—those who want change "from the root" and who see the education of adults as having the potential for progressive social purpose—is to envisage the directions that change from the root might take and the nature of those progressive social purposes, at a time when the very construction of the social and of the self is being called into question (McRobbie, 1994).

In these uncertain times I want to suggest that we should revisit the ideas of a Marxist revolutionary and victim of fascism who featured posthumously as a "radical hero" in the literature of adult education in the 1980s: Antonio Gramsci (1891–1937).[1]

Why Gramsci? The uncertainty of our times makes reading Gramsci, who struggled to make sense of what were to become catastrophic uncertainties in his own life and times, particularly apposite. Gramsci teaches us to see the education of adults as part of a wider political strategy requiring organisation and direction (for Gramsci, through the political party of the working class) as well as enthusiasm, commitment and hard work; to analyse the relations of power in a particular political conjuncture pertaining at a precise historical moment; to see the state and civil society as a complex set of institutions and forces, rather than as a monolithic entity.

I believe we can learn much from his notion of politics as a moral as well as a practico-political struggle to create and maintain hegemony among disparate groups; his is a politics of difference which presages many of the current debates within postmodernism and engages with adult educators' concern to respect the subjecthood of adult learners—and adult educators. His conceptualisation of the role of intellectuals offers a way of theorising what it means to teach a fellow adult which breaks with sterile debates about elitism. As Ireland shows in his analysis of popular education in Brazil (1987), Gramsci offers us analytical tools to understand the purpose and content of the education of adults in a wider political context. Furthermore, Gramsci's conception of politics as educative is attractive to radical adult educators who see their professional practice as a form of political activity. His broad interpretation of education as a lifelong process makes his ideas particularly interesting to adult educators, while his theory of intellectuals expresses the belief that is arguably the defining characteristic of the committed adult educator: the belief that everyone is an intellectual, that everyone can and does learn throughout life.

So who was Gramsci? He was born in Sardinia and grew up in poverty and in poor health. Despite his difficulties he won a scholarship for poor students to the University of Turin and there cut his political teeth as a leader of the Factory Council movement, organising occupations of the factories by the Turin proletariat in 1919. He was a founder-member and became leader of the Italian communist party and a prolific political journalist whose interests spanned the theatre, language, literature, education and folklore as well as the more usual, concerns of a communist leader with political tactics and strategy. Imprisoned by the fascist government for the last eleven years of his life, Gramsci struggled to develop his thought against a background of political defeat, censorship of his writing and his own physical deterioration. In his prison writings and in his political journalism, Gramsci advocates a revolutionary politics, organised through the revolutionary party of the working class and informed by rigorous study within an historical and dialectical framework, constantly relating theory and practice. His is an open, questioning Marxism, not at all of the "grand narrative" type.

However, this is just one among many different "Gramscis" which have emerged since his death: there is also Gramsci the Leninist; Gramsci the Eurocommunist; Gramsci the culturalist—to name but a few (see Forgacs, 1989, for a discussion of Gramsci's posthumous "career" in relation to Marxism in Britain). With the rise of interest in the ideas of Michel Foucault and other postmodernists in the 1990s, Gramsci has emerged as a precursor of post-Marxism (Laclau with Mouffe, 1990: 121) of postmodernist and feminist critical theory (Holub, 1992) and as the theorist of a new, post-liberal form of democracy (Golding, 1992).

This proliferation of interpretations has been encouraged by the fact that the Prison Notebooks, on which Gramsci's reputation as a major twentieth-century Marxist theorist largely rest, are peculiarly open to interpretation. Gramsci died before he was able to edit and organize his notes, which are fragmentary and often cryptic, written partly in code to deceive the prison censor. As a result, political, cultural and educational theorists and politicians of the left are still arguing over his legacy.

Gramsci's Concept of Hegemony

Gramsci's first mention of hegemony comes in the essay he was writing at the time of his arrest in 1926: "Some Aspects of the Southern Question" (SPW II: 441–462) about the relationship between the south and the north in Italy (an unresolved issue which has resurfaced recently with the emergence of the Northern League). Gramsci regarded the essay as short and superficial (LP: 79) and Ernesto Laclau and Chantal Mouffe point out that its logic is "still only of preconstituted sectoral interests" (Laclau and Mouffe, 1985: 66).

Gramsci developed the concept of hegemony in the Prison Notebooks (SPN: 52–120) as part of his elaboration of a strategy for revolution in situations where the state holds power in reserve, through the institutions of civil society, rather than through force alone. This strategy he calls "war of position," by contrast with the "war of movement" or direct assault on the state. The war of position entails a process of the establishment of hegemony during what might be a long period before the seizure of state power by the revolutionaries.

Gramsci was not the first Marxist to use the term hegemony, which was in common use by Russian Marxists from the early 1880s to denote a strategy through which a proletariat-led alliance, including intellectuals and peasants, would overthrow Tsarism. Lenin developed the notion in *What Is to Be Done?* in 1902, stressing the role of the revolutionary vanguard in developing leadership based on the most advanced theory (Lenin, 1947). Gramsci was certainly aware of Lenin's usage, which, he said, "gave new importance to the front of cultural struggle and constructed the doctrine of hegemony as the complement to the theory of the state as force" (Gramsci quoted by Buci-Glucksmann, 1980: 390).

In Gramsci's expanded usage in the Prison Notebooks, hegemony comprises the:

"spontaneous" consent given by the great masses of the population to the general direction imposed on social life by the dominant fundamental group [i.e., class]; this consent is "historically" caused by the prestige (and consequently confidence) which the dominant group enjoys because of its position and function in the world of production. (SPN: 12)

However, Gramsci was no economic determinist and he rejects the simplistic idea of a purely instrumental class state. Instead, the state successfully maintains hegemony in so far as it succeeds in presenting dominant class interests as if they were universal:

It is true that the state is seen as the organ of one particular class, destined to create favourable conditions for the latter's maximum expansion. But the development and expansion of the particular group are conceived of and presented, as being the motor force of a universal expansion, of a development of all the "national" energies. (SPN: 182)

For Gramsci, hegemonic leadership is always contested, never merely an automatic function of power. As Green points out, "A hegemonic order represents a temporary settlement, the ideological balance in favour of the ruling class, not the homogeneous substance of an imposed class ideology" (Green, 1990: 94). Hegemony must be actively maintained and in seeking to maintain hegemony, the state exercises an active, ethical function, an idea Gramsci borrowed from Benedetto Croce and which, ironically, was also used by Mussolini (SPN: 258f). For Gramsci, therefore,

every relationship of "hegemony" is necessarily an educational relationship [and] every State is ethical in as much as one of its most important functions is to raise the great mass of the population to a particular cultural and moral level, a level (or type) which corresponds to the needs of the productive forces for development, and hence to the interests of the ruling classes. (SPN: 350)

Gramsci describes the parliamentary regime as a classical example of the normal exercise of hegemony

characterised by the combination of force and consent, which balance each other reciprocally, without force predominating excessively over consent. Indeed, the attempt is always made to ensure that force will appear to be based on the consent of the majority, expressed by the so-called organs of public opinion—newspapers and associations (SPN: 80 n49).

In his exploration of ways in which an alternative, working-class hegemony could be established, Gramsci, for the first time, described the ways in which the ideas of the ruling class come to hold sway over subordinate classes to such an extent that they constitute the limits of common sense for most people most of the time—a situation described by Raymond Williams as "saturating the consciousness of a society" (Williams, 1973). Gramsci's concept of hegemony thus appears to echo Marx' and Engels' statement in *The German Ideology*:

The ideas of the ruling class are in every epoch the ruling ideas, i.e., the class which is the ruling material force of society, is at the same time its ruling intellectual force (Marx and Engels, 1974: 64).

However, *The German Ideology* remained unpublished until 1932, six years into Gramsci's term of imprisonment, and there is no evidence that he knew of it.

Instead, as Forgacs (SCW: 164) reports, Lo Piparo has argued that Gramsci's lifelong interest in historical linguistics may have been an important influence on his conception of hegemony. Lo Piparo's persuasive thesis is that Gramsci extended into the political sphere concepts developed to explain the process by which speakers of a language affect speakers of other languages with whom they come into contact. In other words, as Germino points out (1990: 30), Gramsci's theory of hegemony "had its roots prior to his intellectual encounter with Marx." Perhaps the truth is that Gramsci's concept of hegemony is so rich and multi-faceted precisely because it draws on more than one source.

For Gramsci, the antithesis of hegemony, "political government" or "direct domination," comes into play when consent is lacking. It is the

apparatus of State coercive power which "legally" enforces discipline on those groups who do not "consent" either actively or passively. This apparatus is, however, constituted for the whole of society in anticipation of moments of crisis of command and direction when spontaneous consent has failed. (SPN: 12)

For a revolution to be successful necessitates victory in both the spheres of hegemony and direct domination and Gramsci is thus able to see the revolutionary process as an intellectual, moral and educational phenomenon, as well as a matter of practical politics. Indeed, Gramsci's expansion of the political, placing it, as Golding (1992: 131) says, "at the heart of all meaning," means precisely that intellectual, moral and educational phenomena are political phenomena.

* * * * *

Note

1 This article is based on extracts from my PhD thesis: "Radical Heroes: Gramsci, Freire and the Liberal Tradition in Adult Education" (Coben, 1992). The thesis is to be published in an abridged form by Garland Publishing, New York. See Davidson (1977) for an excellent intellectual biography of Gramsci.

References

List of Abbreviations of Works Cited

LP

Letters from Prison by Antonio Gramsci, selected, translated and introduced by Lynne Lawner, Lawrence and Wishart, 1975

SCW

Selections from Cultural Writings by Antonio Gramsci, edited by David Forgacs and Geoffrey Nowell Smith, translated by William Boelhower, Lawrence and Wishart, 1985

SPN

Selections from the Prison Notebooks of Antonio Gramsci, edited and translated by Quintin Hoare and Geoffrey Nowell Smith, Lawrence and Wishart, 1971. Referred to throughout this article as the Prison Notebooks

SPW II

Selections from Political Writings (1921–26) by Antonio Gramsci, translated and edited by Quintin Hoare, Lawrence and Wishart, 1978

Other Works Cited

Buci-Glucksmann, C. (1980). *Gramsci and the State*, translated by David Fernbach, Lawrence and Wishart

Coben, D. (1992). "Radical Heroes: Gramsci, Freire and the Liberal Tradition in Adult Education" unpublished PhD thesis, University of Kent at Canterbury

Davidson, A. (1977). *Antonio Gramsci: Towards an Intellectual Biography*, Merlin Press

Forgacs, D. (1989). "Gramsci and Marxism in Britain," *New Left Review* No. 176 July/August 1989, pp 70–88

Germino, D. (1990). *Antonio Gramsci: Architect of a New Politics*, Baton Rouge and London: Louisiana State University

Golding, S. (1992). *Gramsci's Democratic Theory: Contributions to a Post-Liberal Democracy*, Toronto: University of Toronto Press

Green, A. (1990). *Education and State Formation*, Macmillan

Holub, R. (1992). *Antonio Gramsci: Beyond Marxism and Postmodernism*, Routledge

Ireland, T. D. (1987). *Antonio Gramsci and Adult Education: Reflections on the Brazilian Experience* (Manchester Monographs), Manchester: The Centre for Adult and Higher Education, University of Manchester

Laclau, E. with Mouffe, C. (1990), "Post-Marxism without Apologies" in E. Laclau, *New Reflections on the Revolution of Our Time*, Verso

Laclau, E. and Mouffe, C. (1985). *Hegemony and Socialist Strategy: Towards a Radical Democratic Politics*, Verso

Lenin, V.I. (1947). *What Is to Be Done?* Moscow: Progress Publishers

McRobbie, A. (1994). "Feminism, Postmodernism and the Real Me" in M. Perryman (ed.), *Altered States. Postmodernism, Politics, Culture*, Lawrence and Wishart, pp. 113–132

Marx, K. and Engels, F. (1974). *The German Ideology*, (2nd ed.), edited and introduced by C.J. Arthur, Lawrence and Wishart

Williams, R. (1973). "Base and Superstructure in Marxist Theory," *New Left Review* No. 82, December 1973, pp. 3–16

CHAPTER 7
The Intersections of Race, Class, and Gender in the Anti-racism Discourse

GEORGE SEFA DEI

In this chapter I develop a case for why the analysis of race and racism cannot stand alone in the intellectual and political pursuit of an educational transformation which undermines social oppression. King (1994: 18) asserts the need for a new theoretical synthesis to rewrite knowledge in the academy. This is in part because of the incapacity of existing theory to provide a more complete account of human and social development. Legitimate concerns are being raised, particularly by marginalized and minority groups in society, about how conventional discourses do not adequately inform knowledge producers and consumers about the totality of human experiences. We need to reject "essences/totalizing discourses" (King 1994) and work to articulate comprehensive forms of knowledge that reveal an understanding of how our multiple identities and subject positions affect our very existence. Russo (1991: 303) quotes Evelyn Glenn in a poignant remark that our individualities, "histories and experiences are not just diverse, they are intertwined and interdependent."

I am introducing the notion of *integrative anti-racism studies* to address the problem of discussing the social constructs of race, class, gender and sexuality as exclusive and independent categories. Elsewhere (Dei 1994), I have defined integrative anti-racism as the study of how the dynamics of social difference (race, class, gender, sexual orientation, physical ability, language and religion) are mediated in people's daily experiences. Integrative anti-racism is also an activist theory and analysis that must always be consciously linked to struggles against oppression. Integrative anti-racism acknowledges our multiple, shifting and often contradictory identities and subject positions. Borrowing from postmodernism, integrative anti-racism rejects meta-narratives or grand theories. Integrative anti-racism, in effect, calls for multiplicative, rather than additive, analyses of social oppression. It is conceded that an additive analysis denies the complexity of experiences that can, and must, be examined, explained and addressed.

Integrative anti-racism provides an understanding of how different forms of social oppression and privilege have been historically constituted. It identifies how forms of social marginality and structured dominance intersect

and shift with changing conditions in society. Since one of the key objectives of the transformative project of anti-racism is to critique and deal with human injustice, all the different forms of oppression, defined along racial, ethnic, class and sexual lines, must be problematized. We cannot hope to transform society by removing only one form of oppression. There is a common link between all oppressions in the material production of society; all forms of oppression establish material and symbolic advantages for the oppressor. Any resistance to bringing the diverse and varied forms of social oppression into the anti-racism debate should be exposed both for its myopic focus and its capacity to politically paralyze social movement building. It is also destructive to fight against one form of oppression while using patterns of another to do so. An example would be a White male adult using the strap on a White child to teach the child not to be racist against a Black child. This tactic may punish racist behaviour, but it leaves physical violence as a method of controlling others and adult authority over children solidly in place.

An understanding of how race, class, gender and sexuality are interconnected in our lives will work against the construction of hierarchies of social oppression. Such hierarchies can take the form of a naive relativism and divide and fragment a movement. Racism, sexism, heterosexism and classism function in myriad forms. Integrative anti-racism therefore seeks a non-hierarchical discussion of social oppressions without assuming that all forms of oppression are unified, consistent and necessarily equal in their social effects (see Burbules and Rice 1991). This understanding follows from a recognition of the theoretical inadequacy of singular, exclusive constructs when it comes to explaining the diversity of human experiences of oppression. There is also an awareness of the need to reject "dichotomous logic ... [that] oversimplifies and limits the scope of analysis" (Sullivan 1995: 3; see also Stasiulis 1990; Brewer 1993; Grewal and Kaplan 1994). These critiques arise out of an analytical context in which the complexity of people's historical and daily experiences are continuously distorted. For example, too often intellectual discourses conflate race with black(ness) and gender with women (Carby 1982). At times too, the "conflation of race and class has been found to engender anti-Semitism by obscuring the range of class positions occupied by Jews in North America" (Sullivan 1995: 4; cf. Nestel 1993: 71).

Brewer (1993: 16) critiques dichotomous/binary oppositional modes of thought which employ *either/or* categorizations rather than *both/and* perspectives when theorizing the simultaneity, embeddedness and connectedness of myriad oppressions. An integrative anti-racism approach is based on the principle that myriad forms of oppressions are interlocked and that a study of one such system, racism, necessarily entails a study of class, gender, sexual inequalities, homophobia and ableism (see Mercer and Julien 1988). The complex nature of oppressions, and the interchangeability of the roles of "oppressor" and "oppressed" in different situations, necessitate the use of an integrative anti-racism approach to understanding social oppression. This approach is informed by the knowledge that individual subjectivities are constituted differently by the relations of race, class, gender, age, disability, sexuality, nationality, religion, language and culture.

The following discussion of integrative anti-racism primarily (but not exclusively) focuses on the three basic categories/constructs of race, class and gender. Belkhir and Ball make the interesting argument that, while "religion, sexual or political preference, [and] physical ability" are important issues affecting the human experience and condition, they "are often the result of the primary ascribed statuses" of race, class and gender. They add that the complex mixture of these social constructs "above all else influences our socialization, emotions, thought process, ideology, self-concept and our social identity." The authors further point out that "issues like religion, sexual or political preference and physical ability may certainly be examined more thoroughly through the interactive and triadic relation of race, [gender] and class" (1993: 4). But I would argue that sexual orientation, ability and religion can play primary roles in a person's lived experiences, particularly given the prevalence of heterosexism, homophobia and anti-Semitism which are particularly significant in, but not exclusive to, Euro-Western influenced societies (see also Fanon 1967).

The study of integrative anti-racism raises some important questions about social inequality: How are class divisions maintained and produced in the face of emerging and complex social identities? What qualifies as "difference" among the factors which shape and define human relations in racialized, classed and gendered contexts? How will a conception of interlocking systems of oppression, that reinforce each other and have multiple effects on individuals, avoid points of conflict? How can we prevent differences from becoming sites of competition for the primacy of one subordination or oppression over another? How do we challenge discursively imposed social identities? Perhaps most of these questions will only be answered in the actual process of doing educational and political work.

In order to respond effectively to some of these questions it is important that we view integrative anti-racism as a critical study of the social and material relations of the production of social oppressions. We must understand the material conditions for the persistence and reproduction of racism, sexism, classism, homophobia, ableism and other forms of social oppression. The political and academic goal of integrative anti-racism is to address all oppressive relations constructed along lines of difference. An integrative approach to understanding social oppressions must thus examine closely the *politics of difference*, recognizing the materiality of human existence, that is, the material consequences of myriad social identities and subjectivities. The roots of social oppression lie in material conditions and the access to property, privilege and power (see Joyce 1995; Ng, Stanton and Scane 1995). All social relations are firmly embedded in material relations. All social relations have material consequences. The politics of integrative anti-racism arise from the collective position of material disadvantage that many people find themselves locked into, and the desire to work for a just redistribution of material means.

Notwithstanding the possible tensions between bland talk about diversity and the real question of power asymmetries around the notion of difference, it is important that the social categories of race, class, gender and sexuality are not seen as competing for primacy. There is a natural contestation that must be accepted and struggled with and against if the fight against oppression is to be successful. The study of race, class, gender and sexuality in critical anti-racism work should be pursued as an integrated approach to understanding the lived (social and material) realities of people. A foregrounding of race in the integrative anti-racism approach should not mean the exclusion of class, gender and sexual orientation. Integrative anti-racism has to address the intersectionality of class, gender and sexual orientation (sexuality). Classism, sexism and homophobia do not disappear because race has become the central focus. The lived experience of those who face racism daily from others is one where they must also face inter/intra-racial classism, sexism and homophobia. I have more to say about this later in this chapter.

How do the complex politics of social difference articulate with material-economic interests? Rizvi (1995) rightly calls on educators to avoid a celebratory approach to social difference which may only serve the hegemonic interests of industrial capital. For example, the state's approach to multiculturalism adopts a superficial definition and treatment of culture, as reflected in the celebratory practices of the "saris, samosas and steel-bands syndrome" (Donald and Rattansi 1992: 2). Events like international cultural days can constitute opportune times for big business to make huge profits without any fundamental challenge to power relations in society. For example, the initial movement to bring multiculturalism into the classroom did not address the lived experiences of peoples of colour; rather, such a move focused on the more simplistic "getting to know you" move of consuming and observing "ethnic foods," dancing and dress. As we examine how difference is perceived in society, Rizvi (1995) suggests certain fundamental questions should be asked. For example, why the focus on difference? In whose interests is difference being presented and for what material purposes and consequences? We might also ask about the timing and sequencing of the uses and constructions of social difference. What qualifies as difference? No doubt there are some powerful academic and political forces more than ready to co-opt the language of difference and diversity to serve their own material needs and concerns.

bell hooks cautions against constructing a politics of difference in the academy to serve the intellectual interests of an emerging post-modern discourse. She argues that post-modern theory should not simply appropriate the experience of otherness to enhance the intellectual discourse of post-modernity. Post-modern theory should not separate the "politics of difference from the politics of racism" (hooks 1990: 26). Integrative anti-racism must be critical of how current articulations of multiple identities are/can be manipulated in the space of dominant, hegemonic discourses, particularly in academia (see Carty 1991a; Bannerji 1991a; Fumia 1995: 9).

An integrative approach to anti-racism must examine conventional understandings of the politics of identity. Hall offers one such critique when he references Marxian theory on identity; he talks about the fact that there are always "conditions to identity which the subject cannot construct" (1979: 16; see also Hall 1991). Bhabha also writes about the fact that "the visibility of the racial/cultural 'other' is at once a point of identity" (1994: 81). Hall and Bhabha make different but connected points. On the one hand, identity construction is a point of power and, therefore, difference. To claim difference is to have the power to claim one's difference as identity. On the other hand, as Hall points out, one is never entirely in control of the mechanisms of identity construction, like language, for example. However, one is not entirely controlled by the identity construction of others either. Bhabha is suggesting that the identification of others is also the moment of self-identification. Identities are not static, we are forever negotiating who and what we are. Social identities are constructed beyond notions of race, class, gender, sexuality, language and culture to the actual practices engaged in by people in the course of daily social interactions. It is crucial to a progressive politics of identity to understand that identity is not entirely dependent on categories of difference because social practice transgresses these boundaries all the time. We are not entirely constrained by the categories of race, class and gender. They are coercive and resilient structures in our lives, but they do not define the limits of social action. Our identities, then, are made in social interaction in concert with and using categories of difference and identity. In order to effectively organize for political change, we first have to recognize and understand that identity is defined by who the individual is, how the individual self is understood in relation to others, and

how such constructions of social identities match or do not match what people actually do in their daily lives.

Of equal importance, a politics of identity involves politicizing identity. It moves beyond the mere recognition and acknowledgment of identities to engage in effective political action. Identity must provide the basis for political struggle, but as others have pointed out, identity itself is not political action (Bourne 1987: 22; Train 1995). The conventional "identity politics" prioritized an essentialized, ahistorical and nonmaterialist identity (Fuss 1989). Train (1995) argues that "identity politics" eliminated the political by focusing too much on the personal. It is important for a distinction to be made between "who am I?" and "what is to be done" (Bourne 1987: 1)? These two questions are connected. One needs to know the self in order to engage in political action. But change cannot happen simply from knowing oneself. We have to find answers to the questions, "what is to be done and how?"

Thus, in a sense, the importance of adopting an integrative approach to anti-racism studies is captured in the intersections between issues of identity and social practices. The study of the concept of race is a study of representation as defined by identity, identification and social practices. Racism, as a set of material practices, is about unequal power relations. It is also about how people relate to each other on the basis of defined social identities and identifications. These reasonings implicate how we organize politically for change; they move us beyond questions about *who we are* to discussions about *what we do*. We must search for connections between identity and social practices (see Britzman 1993). Our everyday local social networks are increasingly structuring and governing our daily experiences.

Below I will explore this topic further in the context of six interrelated key issues underlying integrative anti-racism studies. The first is an understanding of the *process of articulation* of social difference. Integrative anti-racism speaks to the need to examine the social categories of difference in order to understand their points of "articulation" and connection with each other. The articulations of race, class, gender and sexuality produce sites of complex human social differences, rather than sites and sources of a celebratory approach to diversity. They are "rupturing these social categories"; thus, we need to recognize, understand and engage our multiple subject positions and to work for alternative futures. Feminist writers such as Carby (1982), Mohanty (1990), Collins (1990), hooks (1990), Carty (1991a, b), Bannerji (1991a, b) and Mullings (1992), among many others, have articulated varying ideas about multiple subjectivities to illustrate the intersections of oppressions in the everyday experiences of so-called women of colour. Many, if not all, of these authors speak from their embodied selves while making the connections between their individual and collective identities and their own experiences.

Integrative anti-racism is a critical analysis of how current understandings of the dynamics of social difference relate to issues of identity and subjectivity. It moves away from establishing a hierarchy of difference and an exclusive and problematic concern with the "other." Integrative anti-racism does not see the *self* as that which *other* is not. Human experiences are dialectically shaped by questions of social difference, by history and by socio-political contexts. The existence of multiple identities has some significance for how individuals live their lives and relate to each other in society, and how individuals come to understand society and work collectively for change.

Belkhir and Ball (1993), in their interesting discussion of the dynamics of social difference, point out the complex mixture of race, class and gender, and how these categories influence everything we do as humans. Our social world is structured by power relations of race, ethnicity, class, gender and sexuality (see also Collins 1993; Roscigno 1994). Individuals do not simply and solely fit into one specified category as an oppressor or the oppressed. One can be oppressed and an oppressor at the same time and at different times.

For example, as an anti-racist educator, I must acknowledge my own privileged middle-class background when speaking to students about "oppression." There is the question of the relational aspect of oppression (Freire 1990), there is the "nonsynchrony of oppression" (McCarthy 1988), and there is the problematic of a discourse of "humanization as a universal without considering the various definitions this term may [acquire]" from individuals of different positionalities and from diverse social groups (Weiler 1991: 53). I have to be aware of how my views as I present them in the classroom, by way of instruction or through interaction with students, could be maintaining social privilege and power. My power as a Black, middle-class, heterosexual male teacher may often work to make me forget that, while I am debating and struggling against race oppression, I might be marginalizing women and other peoples oppressed by reason of, for example, their class or sexuality. Such understandings are fundamental to any attempt to theorize the connections between social differences and oppression in the integrative anti-racism discourse.

Each individual goes through a variety of experiences in a lifetime and theoretical articulations of social reality have to reflect the intersections of such various experiences. For example, when a Southeast Asian male executive living in Canada loses his job and eventually goes on welfare, his lifetime experiences, relating to all his subject positions, come into play. We cannot essentialize race, class and gender categories. These are socially constructed categories whose social meanings and actualities in the daily experiences of peoples not only overlap but also shift in time and space. We need to understand the systemic and structural character of these social categories and how they function as social ideologies (see King 1994: 10).

* * * * *

It is thus important for an integrative approach to social oppression to disaggregate social categories such as race, class, gender and sexuality along multiple dimensions to see, for example, how race articulates with other forms of oppression. Joyce (1995: 7) posits that, as a White person, she has unearned privileges and material advantages because of the physical characteristics that Euro-Canadian/American society deems as "racially white and of highest value." But she argues that the material consequences of being a woman is the absence of power and a lack of resources that one collectively shares with other women. Women, she points out, experience a "relative position of structurally and materially less power and privilege" than men in a particularly sexist, patriarchal society (ibid.: 4). However, to be a woman of racial minority background is to have even relatively less material power and privilege in a patriarchal, White-dominated society. But even among women of racial minority backgrounds, class differences can be apparent. For example, there are differences in terms of those occupying relative positions of wealth and influence (e.g., a bank executive or university professor) and those who are employed in jobs with lower status and are paid barely enough to support the household they head.

* * * * *

As Zinn (1991: 6) has shown, it is not simply that gender cannot be understood outside of race and class. Gender is experienced differently within each racial framework and class group. Subordinate racial groups of all classes are subject to racial oppression and, while members of dominant racial groups may be oppressed by means of gender oppression, their membership in a racial group is not a source of oppression. Furthermore, class and gender differences in society are complicated by the harsh realities of intra-group oppression among members of the same socially constructed racial framework.[1] The exploitative working conditions of many "immigrant women" working in the homes of middle-class families in Canada are a well-documented case (see Ng and Ramirez 1981; Ng 1988). The task of integrative anti-racism is to unravel these interlocking systems of oppression in order to be able to intellectually articulate and engage in meaningful and progressive political action to address social injustice and oppression.

The *second* and related issue of interest in integrative anti-racism studies is the relevance of *personal experiential knowledge* and the specific ways our multiple subject positions and identities affect our ways of creating knowledge. Knowledge is produced out of a series of socio-political arrangements, such as the particular intersections of social oppressions. Lived, personal experience is central to the formulation of any social knowledge. Matsuda (1989) discusses the importance and relevance of seeing the world as experienced by the oppressed if we are to achieve effective political action and change. However, as Burbules and Rice (1991: 405) caution, we must guard against an over-valorization of personal experiential knowledge in which "external" forces mediating and/or impinging upon such knowledge are considered "coercive and imperialistic." We must also resist the temptation of presenting ourselves as not-to-be-questioned voices of authority merely because we are speaking from experience.

* * * * *

Collins (1990) and Russo (1991) also argue that experience and practice are the contextual bases of integrative anti-racism knowledge; they link this practice and experience to theory. Both authors call for a self-reflective critique and validation of personal experiences of the relational aspects of difference as part of the process of creating theoretical and practical knowledge for social transformation. Individuals must be able to articulate and critically reflect upon their own experiences and their accumulated personal knowledge about the workings of the inner self and questions of identity, in order to work collectively for change (see also hooks 1993, 1994).

The *third* issue concerns developing an understanding of how *differential power and privilege* work in society. The study of the dynamics of social difference is also a study of differential power relations. Power relations are embedded in social relations of difference. Thus, an understanding of the intersections of difference is more than a preparedness to hear each other out. It involves more than providing the means and opportunities for subordinated groups to empower themselves and find creative solutions to their own concerns. It is about ensuring that all social groups have decision-making power; safety provisions and equitable access to, and control over, the valued goods and services of society with which to attain human dignity and individual and collective survival.

Therefore, an integrative approach to anti-racism studies explores the use of power to differentiate, discriminate and establish material advantage and disadvantage among and between peoples and groups. Social power and economic advantage are intertwined. Understanding the relational aspects of social difference means delving into the critique of micro and macro structures of power and how these structures mediate people's daily experiences. It draws attention to the larger socio-political contexts in which the fragmented categories of race, class, gender and sexuality intersect in daily social practices. Attention is paid to the material needs of individuals and groups in society and how these needs are sanctioned and stratified through social relations of domination and subordination. For example, it is about understanding how the hegemony of the market economy affects the schooling experiences of minority youth. How this is manifested in schools can be attested to in the differential positions that students occupy according to their race, ethnicity, class, gender and sexual orientation. Many studies demonstrate a clearly disproportionate representation of African-Canadian/American students from working-class backgrounds in vocational courses rather than in the "academic" courses which lead students into universities

(Oakes 1985; Brown 1993; see also Fine 1991).

Integrative anti-racism examines the power of subordinated groups to resist positions of marginality through individual agency and collective will. It interrogates how groups positioned differently in society can nevertheless come together on the basis of a common abhorrence of social oppression and fight the prevailing culture of dominance. While recognizing the power of human agency, an integrative anti-racism approach also locates significant responsibility for change in the arena of those who control the structural means to effecting fundamental change in society, that is, those who control the apparatus of the state. This is an example of where the intersections of social class become important. Social power is generally in the hands of the ruling class, which comprises mostly White heterosexual males. It is thus difficult to speak about power and not highlight class. The bourgeoisie will not give up power easily since it will not be in their interest to do so. This means it will take the collective effort of the relatively powerless groups to work and bring this change about.

The *fourth* issue of concern relates to the *saliency of race* in an integrative anti-racism discourse. In recognizing the centrality of race and its "immediacy in everyday experience" (Omi and Winant 1994), integrative anti-racism also acknowledges the co-determinant status of race, class and gender dynamics. Integrative anti-racism is based on the understanding that race relations in society are actually interactions between raced, classed and gendered subjects. Thus, in theorizing integrative anti-racism, race becomes the main point of entry through which the varied forms of social oppression can and must be understood.

While it is true that we live in a society structured by relations of race, ethnicity, class, gender, sexuality and ability, among others, we nevertheless make political choices every moment and every day of our lives. Giving saliency and centrality to race and racial oppression in a critical anti-racism educational practice should not be seen as an attempt to hierarchize and/or privilege one form of social oppression over another. It is a *political decision*. Admittedly, selecting one form of human experience as a point of entry may render another experience invisible. Yet, we cannot adequately simultaneously explore all experiences with the same vigour and intensity. Therefore, we should attempt to capture, as much as possible, from the points where they intersect with one particular form of social oppression the diversity and multiplicity of human experiences. Racism should neither be subsumed nor separated from all forms of oppression. Bannerji's (1993) work is exemplary in this regard when she discusses racist sexism and sexist racism. The fight for equity should not be seen as a zero sum game that pits Blacks against Whites, women against men, heterosexuals against homosexuals, Christians against non-Christians, Canadian immigrants against First Nations peoples.

But, as we recognize the matrix of domination and subordination and conceptualize racism, sexism and classism as interactive, interlocking and mutually reinforcing systems of oppression, we must also validate the saliency and visibility of certain forms of oppression (see Collins 1993). For how can we understand and transform social reality without recognizing or acknowledging that certain forms/systems of domination and oppression are more salient and visible than others for different groups in different contexts? How do we explain the situational and contextual variations and intensities of different forms of oppression? For example, how do we account for the fact that a single, Black middle-class woman is kept out of a White neighbourhood when trying to rent or buy a house, because of her race and gender? Are we not trivializing social oppression by claiming that we are all oppressors and oppressed?

The answer to this last question is complex and deserves further comment. As Bunch (1987: 88–9) has pointed out, when individuals identify themselves according to their victimization as a member of an oppressed group, there is less ability for them to see their own agency and power to effect change. Others may also begin to identify themselves as "victims of oppression" and fail to see the severity of other forms of oppression because they are so narrowly focused on their own victimization. This is problematic, particularly when that form of oppression may not have a material basis but is experienced more as a hurtful, restrictive practice. For example, Black students can use discriminatory words or engage in discriminatory actions (such as telling White students that they cannot join in a basketball game because they cannot slam dunk) which may not have material consequences for White students. My point is that Black racism does not deny material wealth to Whites.

Nevertheless, the concept of oppression may be helpful for those who are highly privileged in society and are just beginning to learn what social oppression really is. It helps these individuals to place their own grounded experiences of oppression, no matter how comparatively trivial in relation to more widespread and sustained forms of oppression that marginalized groups regularly experience, in a webbed system of domination/subjugation. To find one's place in the web, these individuals must begin to see the whole web and how various oppressions are played off each other horizontally to keep the systems of oppression in place. It is thus a useful beginning to allow each individual to talk about his or her own oppressions. It provides an opportunity to make that first crucial step which is to enter into the discussion about oppression. Issues about the location of multiple identities, and analysis of the implications, intersections and variable degrees of material consequences of different oppressions can be pursued once the concept of oppression is connected to one's personal experience and that experience is located in the total web of systemic oppressions.

* * * * *

A conceptual and analytical distinction must be made between anti-oppression and anti-racism studies. While there are broad similarities and points of connection between "*integrative anti-racism*" and "*anti-oppression*" studies, there are important distinctions between the two. The integrative anti-racism approach sees race as both the first point of entry and a point which does not lose its position of centrality during subsequent analyses of intersecting oppression. Joyce argues that "anti-oppression education does not presume a single central point of entry nor a central point of analysis … it presumes multiple positions of identity by which an individual enters the discourse on social oppression [and] … some of those identities are individually experienced as central, and some are marginal" (1995: 6). As individuals, we possess diverse identities that variously describe who and what we are, and what we politically and consciously choose as our points of entry into discussions about oppression. In anti-oppression studies, race is one of many entry points. But it is important we also recognize that "some forms of oppression have a particularly substantial material base" when compared to others (ibid.: 6). For example, the impact of institutionalized racism on the job opportunities and wages of marginalized racial groups has a material impact that is different from the impact of racist language. In deciding on our entry points, we must make explicit our subject locations and the relative power, privileges and disadvantages, as well as the experiential knowledge and the political assumptions that we bring to the discussion. What is important in this discussion is the convergence and alliance between integrative anti-racism and anti-oppression studies. We must speak of and act on the alliances in these struggles if successful change is to happen.

Social oppression is a topic that elicits pain, anger, shame, guilt, fear and uneasiness in people. People are likely to engage the subject from diverse vantage points. For me, the experience of racism, while not diminishing its connections with other forms of oppression, runs deep. I know more about racism, perhaps, than I do about other forms of oppression, not simply because I have chosen to take the time to learn about racism, but more so because it has been a very significant part of my experience, particularly in North America (see also hooks 1984: 11). There is a prior personal and collective history that cannot be ignored. We have to deal with the historical fact that, in past academic discussions about myriad oppressions and other "isms," the topic of racism has often been pushed to the background or omitted altogether. This is what informs Enid Lee when she strongly recommends that we put "racism at the foreground, and then include the others by example and analysis" (*Rethinking Schools* 1991: 3) to illustrate the powerful connections to other forms of oppression.

The foregoing discussion also indicates that while educators stress integrative and relational aspects of difference (race, class, gender and sexuality), they must be critical of post-modern discourse that will deny the saliency of racial oppression in the anti-racism political project. Racism is what most educators and many other people are either afraid to talk about or continually and conveniently choose to ignore. While the integrative anti-racism strategy is to ensure that race is not given an exclusive pre-eminence, it must also avoid a "political paralysis" (Roman 1993) in the struggle for change. As educators, we can make pragmatic choices as to how to take up and centre race analysis for political education and for educational advocacy. It should also be possible for educators and members of society to engage in a theoretical discussion of race issues that speak foremost and most appropriately to social reality and economic materiality.

The *fifth* concern involves extending discussions about integrative anti-racism to include *global political economic* issues. Central to this is building an understanding of how current processes of globalization relate to questions of identity and social practice in Euro-Canadian/American contexts. My objective is not to re-engage in any detail the classical debates about whether or not race, gender and sexuality can be understood in terms of the analytical approach of historical materialism, or whether race, gender and sexuality must be accorded an analytical status separate and distinct from class (Marx 1853; Simmel 1950; Gabriel and Ben-Tovim 1979; see also Miles 1980). I am more interested in showing how global political economy issues (Stasiulis 1990; Satzewich 1990) relate to the integrative anti-racism dialogue and the political struggle for social change. […] [A] biological-genetic explanation of race (and gender) emerged prior to the institutionalization of capitalism and slavery. This fact neither denies the centrality of slavery in the development of capitalism, nor the significant role of capitalism in institutionalizing racism (see Cox 1948, 1976; Williams 1964).

Neo-Marxist analysis of society may inform the progressive politics of integrative anti-racism change. All current forms of social oppressions are the products of a system of capitalist insurgence and domination. In fact, many scholars have pointed to the need for the critical analysis of race, class and gender intersections to be placed in the context of global capitalism (see, for example, Bannerji 1991a; Carty 1993; Ng 1993a, b). Local problems of race, class and gender relations have their global dimensions. It is for these reasons that a narrow conception of integrative anti-racism politics must be rejected. Ongoing processes of restructuring capital at global, regional and national levels are having a deleterious impact on the ability of many individuals and groups to meet basic economic and material needs. A consequence of modern capital flows and exchanges, particularly the globalization of capital, is the growing feminization of poverty and the racialization of working-class politics. Working-class politics is now "race sensitive." Much work is currently being done to address racism within working-class groups, and some ruling groups are using race and racism as a way to divide working-class movements. There are mounting antagonisms and competitions between and among groups,

communities and nations over access to, and control over, drastically maldistributed economic and productive resources.

Undoubtedly, globalization, defined as a process of increased social, political and economic international integration, driven primarily (but not exclusively) by the interests and dictates of modern industrial and transnational capital, has produced some challenges that need to be addressed by anti-racism education. Globalization is the new justification used by Euro-Canadian/American society for asserting its political and economic dominance over indigenous and colonized peoples. Globalization has resulted in a crisis of knowledge about human society, a crisis manifested in the contradictions and tensions of a competitive knowledge economy, the internationalization of labour and the concomitant struggles over power-sharing among social groups. Globalization has also accelerated the flow of cultures across geographical, political and cultural borders. Cultural borders can be marked by a language or concentrations of one racial or ethnic group within a diverse population, or by more malleable cultural forms like dress and music. Cultural borders are not necessarily materially or geographically constrained. Any agenda for educational and social transformation must be able to deal with the dilemmas and contradictions inherent in the trend towards cultural homogenization, cultural differentiation and cultural revitalization in our societies.[2]

* * * * *

The harsh economic lessons of globalization clearly point to the urgent need for a new approach to education that responds appropriately to the challenge of difference and diversity in communities internationally. In Euro-Canadian/American circles, current academic and political projects of rupturing hegemonic social science paradigms have added fuel to the demand of marginalized communities for education to respond to the pressing concerns of racism, sexism, classism and other forms of oppressive and discriminatory practices that diminish our basic humanity. In fact, anti-racism education emerged as a consequence of the ongoing transformations in social science epistemologies to offer alternative readings of how, as social beings, we live our lives in multi-racial, multi-ethnic, pluralistic communities.

Each individual in society lives and experiences different material realities. Nevertheless, we are all governed by a set of socio-political and structural conditionalities. There must be some awareness on the part of anti-racism educators and practitioners of the structures, constraints, limitations and possibilities embedded in the wider social contexts. This awareness is fundamental to political work for an alternative society (see Brewer 1993: 15). For example, the practice of integrative anti-racism education needs to recognize at all levels the forces of political rigidity and economic constraints that obstruct the envisioning and actualization of alternative social formations.

* * * * *

The current ultra-conservative rhetoric, utilizing racist code words to blame racial minorities and women for the most recent economic problems, has an appeal to many lower middle- and working-class Whites (particularly males) in Euro-Canadian/American society. But there are clear examples in the apportioning of blame of the intersections of class, race and gender. Many White women do not accept the blame, just as some Black men may accept the rhetoric blaming women for some societal problems. This is because of the prevailing economic climate of diminishing wages, increasing unemployment and economic insecurity (see Apple 1993). In particular, dominant group members of middle-class backgrounds see their privileges under assault and their class positions weakening in the face of globalization and the downward trends in national economies. This may, in part, explain the election of the Progressive Conservatives in the 1995 Ontario provincial election as they basically promised to punish the poor and protect the "beleaguered middle-class" in their election campaign.

Within the Canadian context, many people, irrespective of class, racial and gender backgrounds, are threatened by national and international economic insecurity. Whites, particularly men, have more to lose since economic disparities rely upon racist and patriarchal power structures which provide unequal access to opportunities and resources. In a context of political and economic insecurity, those with the highest vested interest in maintaining material advantage are the most likely to feel threatened by further destabilizing forces that question their advantage. They speak up to protect the status quo.

In the Euro-Canadian/American context this is made apparent by voices of criticism over such issues as employment equity and affirmative action policies. Agents of oppression become very defensive about being exposed and will use whatever (considerable) means in their power and influence to bury, hide and deflect their agency. Examples of such strategies appear in the "take the offensive," blame someone or scapegoat the poor, Blacks, women and feminism's attitude in order to avoid responsibility for agency as part of the "oppressor" group. Others deny the inequality or divest themselves from membership in the oppressing group and instead focus on individual agency. Other strategies include shifting the frame of reference of debate completely to nullify or stymie the argument so as to maintain control of the agenda. Sometimes too, those who wield power and have the means to do so will attempt to silence opponents or critics or even have someone else speak on their "behalf." Others will plead the cause of "fairness" or "reasonableness" in order to fall back into normalcy and the familiarity of existing conditions. My argument is that, rather than question the Canadian government's economic policies and the activities of private and corporate organizations, some Canadians, especially those feeling most threatened, decide to vent their anger on "immigrants," racial minorities, the working poor, those who are not employed and women.

Therefore, discussions of racism and public discourses which blame marginal and disempowered groups for economic problems must recognize institutionalized poverty through bringing class issues seriously into the anti-racism debate (see Troyna 1993: 11). Integrative anti-racism cannot sufficiently deal with the problem of racial oppression without simultaneously confronting the structural problems of economic poverty, cultural sexism,[3] and capitalist patriarchy. Integrative anti-racism must interrogate how current social formations continue to reproduce conditions of abject poverty in the midst of affluence and plenty for a few. In doing so, it must guard against reductionistic arguments that pit class against race. Such arguments fit well with the ideological position that class inequality is the fundamental problem of human social relations. And the neo-conservatives would argue that, through paid labour and hard work, people can overcome racial subordination. But, class relations are not only sustained by material (economic) relations. Class is also a social identity constructed through ideological and symbolic practices.

Race, class, gender and sexuality mutually affect each other. An integrative anti-racism approach must reject analyses which reduce racial subordination to economics. Rather, it must examine how people relate to the processes and struggles over the control of the means of production and reproduction. Such an inquiry reveals the exploitative character of the current social formation and the nature of individual and collective action developed around questions of individual and collective identity and social practice. No doubt, economic relations and imperatives influence the production of racial and gender ideologies, just as gender and racial structures can be understood only in the context of a historically constituted set of economic formations. Integrative anti-racism must speak to working-class concerns (e.g., equity, poverty, class bias in institutional structures and educational practices) in a way that recognizes the intersections of difference.

* * * * *

Admittedly, the mode of reproduction of racism, sexism, homophobia and so forth cannot be explained with reference to capitalism alone. While all social formations have been good at maintaining subordinate and dominant relations, it appears, however, that post-industrial economies have systematically cultivated relations of domination between and among social groups to serve particular material and ideological interests. West (1987) has asked for an understanding of how racist beliefs form part of the common-sense knowledge of various social formations, how racist ideologies operate in everyday practices and constructions of identities, how state bureaucratic structures continually regulate the lives of racial minorities in particular, and how those minorities resist state repression, domination and class exploitation. To respond to these questions, we have to examine how racism, capitalist patriarchy and other forms of gender and sexual oppression work jointly in the lived experiences of people (see Stasiulis 1990). We must be able to articulate an alternative form of global education that connects issues of global economic oppression, capitalist patriarchy, human rights, environmental racism and international development, and respond to the urgent need to build coalitions across national borders to deal with global social injustice. Such global education will stress the mutual interdependence and interconnections among nations and peoples in a common struggle for change.

The question today is not whether capitalist social formations need racism and other oppressions to reproduce wealth and material advantage for their most privileged members. It is a question of *how* and *why*. Racism and patriarchy continue to be powerful ideologies and social practices that serve the interests of modern industrial capital (see Williams 1964). Racism, sexism and other forms of oppression, constituted along the lines of difference, function as effective social barriers. These practices help segment the labour force. As others have repeatedly argued, racism and sexism regulate the labour force not only by consigning people to particular roles and responsibilities in production relations, but also by the very practice of systemic exclusion from sharing in the material and social goods of society. But, above everything else, racism and other forms of oppression serve to maintain and reproduce the capitalist system.

Finally, the related *sixth* issue concerns how educators, students and community workers can engage in a progressive politics for *social transformation*, utilizing the integrative anti-racism approach. A more genuinely integrative anti-racism approach to social change requires focusing on the utilization of the relative power and privilege constituted around notions of race, class, gender and sexuality, and prioritizing *all* forms of oppression. Privilege and oppression, as Dahan (1992: 48) points out, co-exist in our individual and collective lives. By virtue of one's race, social class, gender and sexual orientation, it is easier or more difficult to access the dominant culture and the associated economic and political capital in Euro-Canadian/American contexts.

In the struggle for social transformation, public policy must not be confused with political action and, conversely, action should be seen as a precursor to effective change. For change to take place, integrative anti-racism discourse and practice must be grounded in people's actual material conditions. The political, communicative and educational practices of integrative anti-racism call for people to work together to develop a "community of differences"; that is, a community in which our differences help to strengthen us collectively to develop some degree of a shared commitment to justice and social transformation. Social transformation

is possible when solidarity is understood to mean constructing coalitions among and between difference, and coalitions come to be openly defined in terms of relations of power (see Joyce 1995). Without a doubt, struggles against race, class, gender and sexuality discrimination generate distinct versions of what justice should look like (see Troyna and Vincent 1995). But the goal of coalition building is to educate each other so that there is, or can be, a common view of justice. The struggle against injustice implies a struggle for justice. We cannot, as a society, choose to ignore injustice.

As we struggle for change through the politics of an integrative anti-racism approach, we must continually guard against what Mohanty has observed as the "erosion of the politics of collectivity through the reformulation of race and difference in individualistic terms" (1990: 204). This means that definitions of identity should extend beyond references to personal experience and make connections with the wider community. We cannot reject the politics of identity and difference. And, we cannot simply engage in what can be called "politics of the moment" or situational politics. Integrative anti-racism must ground the new politics of change in an understanding of the history of colonialism and recolonization, as well as of how global capital (through processes of economic domination) continually produce definitions of "valid" knowledge about ourselves and society.

The politics of integrative anti-racism change can start in the classroom, in the home, in the workplace and in community actions and groups. There are some pedagogical and communicative challenges to the pursuit of an integrative anti-racist perspective. As already discussed, there is always the temptation to prioritize race and overlook the embedded inequalities which flow from class, ethnicity, culture, gender, sexuality and religious and language disparities, many of which are refracted through the official and hidden curriculum of the school and society. Since anti-racism education has to deal simultaneously with race, class, gender and sexual orientation, the anti-racist pedagogue, trainer and/or activist should necessarily be anti-classist, anti-sexist and anti-homophobic in her or his social practices. For anti-racism teachers, an awareness of the link between personal identity, experience and authority is crucial.

There must be congruence between the theory and practice engaged by anti-racism educators and practitioners. For example, the teacher's theoretical viewpoint of anti-racism education and the classroom atmosphere (e.g., that of an anti-authoritarian, democratic environment) that is nurtured should be closely aligned in order to make change happen. This is particularly true in the context of an anti-racist pedagogy that questions privilege, attempts to create a critical and powerful voice for students and develops their sense of critical judgement, while at the same time attempting to provide an openness to teaching that is non-universalizing.

Notes

1 See the film, *My Beautiful Launderette*, for a representation of these complex relations.

2 As groups are formulated and reformulated within different relations and categories there is an inevitable homogenizing of groups of people. Larger groups of people are grouped under broad terms. "The Global Economy" is one such term. This epithet constructs us all as being involved in a seamless world economy; all sharing and producing the material goods of our collective labour. Cultural differentiation is a concomitant social process. While we may all be part of "the global economy," certain factions of our society get singled out for not contributing to this world of plenty. Racist, sexist and classist ideologies mobilize popular sentiment against these "troublemakers" and every other group scrambles for a moral high ground. This is the negative side of cultural differentiation. There are also processes of cultural differentiation that serve to empower marginalized groups as they claim space in the public consciousness.

3 By "cultural sexism" I am referring to patriarchal tendencies and practices embedded in upholding certain cultural traditions that are disempowering to women.

References

Apple, Michael. 1993. "Rebuilding Hegemony: Education, Equality, and the New Right." In Dennis Dworkin and Leslie Roman (eds.), *Views beyond the Border Country*. New York: Routledge, pp. 91–114.

Bannerji, Himani. 1991a. "But Who Speaks for Us?: Experience and Agency in Conventional Feminist Paradigms." In Himani Bannerji, Linda Carty, Ken Dehli, Susan Heald and Kate McKenna (eds.), *Unsettling Relations: The University as a Site of Feminist Struggles*. Toronto: Women's Press, pp. 67–108.

———. 1991b. "Racism, Sexism, Knowledge and the Academy." *Resources for Feminist Research* 20(3/4): 5–12.

——— (ed.). 1993. *Returning the Gaze: Essays on Racism, Feminism and Politics*. Toronto: Sister Vision Press.

Belkhir, Jean and Michael Ball. 1993. "Editor's Introduction: Integrating Race, Sex and Class in Our Disciplines." *Race, Sex and Class* 1(1): 3–11.

Bhabha, Homi. 1994. *The Location of Culture*. London: Routledge.

Bourne, Jenny. 1987. *Homelands of the Mind: Jewish Feminism and Identity Politics*. London: The Institute of Race Relations, Race and Class Pamphlet No. 11.

Brewer, Rose M. 1993. "Theorizing Race, Class and Gender: The New Scholarship of Black Feminist Intellectuals and Black Women's Labour." In Stanlie James and Abena Busia (eds.), *Theorizing Black Feminisms*. New York: Routledge, pp. 13–30.

Britzman, Deborah. 1993. "The Ordeal of Knowledge: Rethinking the Possibilities of Multicultural Education." *Review of Education* 15: 123–35.

Brown, Robert. 1993. A Follow-up of the Grade 9 Cohort of 1987 Every Secondary Student Survey Participants. Toronto Board of Education, Research Report #207.

Bunch, C. 1987. *Passionate Politics: Feminist Theory and Action*. New York: St. Martin's Press.

Burbules, N.C. and S. Rice. 1991. "Dialogue across Difference: Continuing the Conversation." *Harvard Educational Review* 61(4): 393–416.

Carby, Hazel. 1982. "White Women Listen! Black Feminism and the Boundaries of Sisterhood." In Paul Gilroy/Centre for Contemporary Cultural Studies (ed.), *The Empire Strikes Back* London: Hutchinson, pp. 212–35.

Carty, Linda. 1991a. "Black Women in Academia." In Himani Bannerji, Linda Carty, Kari Dehli, Susan Heald and Kate McKenna (eds.), *Unsettling Relations*. Toronto: Women's Press, pp. 13–44.

———. 1991b. "Women's Studies in Canada: A Discourse and Praxis of Exclusion." *Resources for Feminist Research* 20(3/4): 12–18.

———. 1993. "Introduction: Combining Our Efforts: Making Feminism Relevant to the Changing Sociality." In Linda Carty (ed.), *And Still We Rise: Feminist Political Mobilizing in Contemporary Canada*. Toronto: Women's Press, pp. 7–21.

Collins, Patricia Hill. 1990. *Black Feminist Thought*. London: Harper Collins.

———. 1993. "Toward a New Vision: Race, Class and Gender as Categories of Analysis and Connection." *Race, Sex and Class* 1(1): 25–45.

Cox, Oliver. 1948. *Caste, Class and Race: A Study in Social Dynamics*. New York: Monthly Review Press.

———. 1976. *Race Relations: Elements and Social Dynamics*. Detroit: Wayne State University Press.

Dahan, Carole. 1992. "Spheres of Identity: Feminism and Difference: Notes by a Sephardic Jewess." *Fireweed* 35: 46–50.

Dei, George J.S. 1994. "Reflections of an Anti-racist Pedagogue." In Lorna Erwin and David MacLennan (eds.), *The Sociology of Education in Canada*. Toronto: Copp Clark Pitman, pp. 290–310.

Donald, James and Ali Rattansi (eds.). 1992. *Race, Culture and Difference*. Newbury Park, CA: Sage.

Fanon, Frantz. 1967. *Black Skin, White Masks*. New York: Grove.

Fine, Michelle. 1991. *Framing Dropouts: Notes on the Politics of Urban Public High School*. New York: State University of New York Press.

Freire, Paulo. 1990. *Pedagogy of the Oppressed*. New York: Continuum.

Fumia, Doreen. 1995. "Identifying Sites of Anti-racism Education. Everyday Lived Experiences Seen as the Micropolitics of Institutionalized Racialized Practices." Unpublished paper, Department of Sociology in Education, Ontario Institute for Studies in Education, Toronto.

Fuss, Diana. 1989. *Essentially Speaking: Feminism, Nature and Difference*. New York: Routledge.

Gabriel, John and Gideon Ben-Tovim. 1979. "The Conceptualization of Race Relations in Sociological Theory." *Ethnic and Racial Studies* 2(2): 190–212.

Grewal, Inderpal and Caren Kaplan. 1994. "Introduction: Transnational/Feminist Practices and Questions of Postmodernity." In Inderpal Grewal and Caren Kaplan (eds.), *Scattered Hegemonies*. Minneapolis: University of Minnesota Press.

Hall, Stuart. 1979. "Ethnicity: Identity and Experience." *Radical America* Summer (1979): 9–20.

———. 1991. "Old and New Identities: Old and New Ethnicities." In A. King (ed.), *Culture, Globalization and the World System*. New York: State University Press, pp. 41–68.

hooks, bell. 1984. *Feminist Theory: From Margin to Centre*. Boston: South End Press.

———. 1990. *Yearning: Race, Gender, and Cultural Politics*. Boston: South End Press.

———. 1993. *Sisters of the Yam: Black Women and Self-Recovery*. Toronto: Between the Lines.

———. 1994. *Teaching to Transgress: Education as the Practice of Freedom*. New York: Routledge.

Joyce, Moon V. 1995. "Approaches to Anti-racist/Anti-oppression Education: Implications for Employment Equity Interventions." Unpublished paper, Department of Sociology in Education, Ontario Institute for Studies in Education, Toronto.

King, Joyce E. 1994. "Perceiving Reality in a New Way: Rethinking the Black/White Duality of Our Time." Paper presented at the Annual Meeting of the American Educational Research Association, New Orleans, LA, April 4–9.

Marx, Karl. 1853. "The Future Results of British Rule in India." *New York Daily Tribune* August 8.

Matsuda, Marie. 1989. "When the First Quail Calls: Multiple Consciousness as Jurisprudential Method." *Women Rights Law Reporter* 11(1): 7–10.

McCarthy, Cameron. 1988. "Rethinking Liberal and Radical Perspectives on Racial Inequality in Schooling: Making the Case for Nonsynchrony." *Harvard Educational Review* 58(3): 265–79.

Mercer, Kobena and I. Julien. 1988. "Race, Sexual Politics and Black Masculinity: A Dossier." In Rowena Chapman and Jonathan Rutherford (eds.), *Male Order: Unwrapping Masculinity*. London: Lawrence Wishart, pp. 97–164.

Miles, Robert. 1980. "Class, Race and Ethnicity: A Critique of Cox's Theory." *Ethnic and Racial Studies* 3(2): 169–81.

Mohanty, Chandra Talpade. 1990. "On Race and Voice: Challenges for Liberal Education in the 90s." *Cultural Critique* 14: 179–208.

Mullings, Leith. 1992. *Race, Class and Gender: Representations and Reality*. Memphis, TN: Center for Research on Women, Memphis State University.

Nestel, A. 1993. "Facing Foreclosure: A Jew in the Classroom." Department of Adult Education, Ontario Institute for Studies in Education, Toronto, Ontario.

Ng, Roxana. 1988. *The Politics of Community Services: Immigrant Women, Class and the State*. Toronto: Garamond Press.

———. 1993a. "Racism, Sexism and Nation Building in Canada." In Cameron McCarthy and Warren Crichlow (eds.), *Race, Identity and Representation in Education*. New York: Routledge, pp. 50–59.

———. 1993b. "Sexism, Racism, Canadian Nationalism." In Himani Bannerji (ed.), *Returning the Gaze: Essays on Racism, Feminism and Politics*. Toronto: Sister Vision Press, pp. 182–96.

——— and J. Ramirez. 1981. *Immigrant Housewives in Canada*. Toronto: Immigrant Women's Centre.

———, P. Staton and J. Scane (eds.). 1995. *Anti-racism, Feminism and Critical Approaches to Education*. Toronto: OISE Press.

Oakes, Jeannie. 1985. *Keeping Track: How Schools Structure Inequality*. New Harlem, CT: Yale University Press.

Omi, Michael and Howard Winant. 1993. 2nd edition. *Racial Formation in the United States*. New York: Routledge.

Rethinking Schools. 1991. "An Interview with Educator Enid Lee: Taking Multicultural, Anti-Racist Education Seriously." *Rethinking Schools* 6(1) October–November: 1–4.

Rizvi, Fazal. 1995. "Commentary on Panel Session: 'Equity Issues in Education.'" Annual Meeting of the American Educational Research Association, San Francisco, April 18–22.

Roman, Leslie. 1993. "White Is Colour! White Defensiveness, Postmodernism and Anti-racist Pedagogy." In Cameron McCarthy and Warren Crichlow (eds.), *Race, Identity and Representation in Education*. New York: Routledge, pp. 71–88.

Roscigno, Vincent. 1994. "Social Movement Struggle and Race, Gender, Class Inequality." *Race, Sex and Class* 2(1): 109–26.

Russo, Ann. 1991. "We Cannot Live without Our Lives." In Chandra Mohanty, Ann Russo and Lourdes Torres (eds.), *Third World Women and the Politics of Feminism*. Bloomington: Indiana University Press, pp. 297–313.

Satzewich, Vic. 1990. "The Political Economy of Race and Ethnicity." In Peter Li (ed.), *Race and Ethnic Relations in Canada*. Toronto: Oxford University Press, pp. 209–30.

Simmel, Georg. 1950. "The Stranger." In K.H. Wolf (ed.), *The Sociology of George Simmel*. New York: The Free Press, pp. 92–96.

Stasiulis, Daiva. K. 1990. "Theorizing Connections: Gender, Race, Ethnicity and Class." In P.S. Li (ed.), *Race and Ethnic Relations in Canada*. Toronto: Oxford University Press, pp. 269–305.

Sullivan, Ann. 1995. "Realizing Successful Integrative Anti-racist Education." Unpublished paper, Department of Sociology in Education, Ontario Institute for Studies in Education, Toronto.

Train, Kelly. 1995. "De-homogenizing 'Jewish Women': Essentialism and Exclusion within Jewish Feminist Thought." MA thesis, Department of Education, University of Toronto, Toronto.

Troyna, Barry (ed.). 1993. *Racism and Education: Research Perspectives*. Toronto: OISE Press.

——— and Carol Vincent. 1995. "Equity and Education: The Discourses of Social Justice." Paper read at the Annual Meeting of the American Educational Research Association, San Francisco, CA, April 18–22.

Weiler, Kathleen. 1991. "Freire and a Feminist Pedagogy of Difference." *Harvard Educational Review* 6(4): 449–74.

West, Cornel. 1987. "Race and Social Theory." In M. Davis (ed.), *The Year Left*. New York: Verso, pp. 73–89.

Williams, Eric. 1964. *Capitalism and Slavery*. London: Deutsch.

Zinn, M.B. 1991. *Race and the Reconstruction of Gender*. Memphis, TN: Center for Research on Women, Memphis State University, Research Paper Number 14.

Research Methods

CHAPTER 8
Sexism in Research

MARGRIT EICHLER

Introduction

Over a century ago, a schoolmaster named Edwin A. Abbott wrote an amusing "Romance of Many Dimensions," entitled *Flatland*,[1] in which he described the adventures of the Square, a being from a two-dimensional universe (Flatland), who explores a one-dimensional universe (Lineland) and a three-dimensional universe (Spaceland). The Square describes the inability of the King of Lineland, a one-dimensional being, to grasp the essence of a two-dimensional universe, and then describes his own incapacity to believe in the existence of a three-dimensional universe. It is only when he is physically lifted out of his own universe and sees it from above (a dimension that is nonexistent in his own Flatland) that he becomes capable of intellectually grasping the existence of three-dimensional space.

When the Square returns to his own country, he eagerly tries to spread the Gospel of Three Dimensions, but is predictably put into prison as a dangerous lunatic, where he languishes at the end of the novel, "absolutely destitute of converts."

The following is an excerpt in which our hero, the Square, tries to convince the King of Lineland that there are, in fact, two dimensions. He argues that, in addition to Lineland's motions of Northward and Southward, which are the only directions in which lines can move in Lineland, there is another motion, which he calls from right to left:

King: Exhibit to me, if you please, this motion from left to right.

I: Nay, that I cannot do, unless you could step out of your Line altogether.

King: Out of my Line? Do you mean out of the world? Out of Space?

I: Well, yes. Out of your Space. For your Space is not the true Space. True Space is a Plane; but your Space is only a Line.

King: If you cannot indicate this motion from left to right by yourself moving in it, then I beg you to describe it to me in words.

I: If I cannot tell your right side from your left, I fear that no words of mine can make my meaning clear

to you. But surely you cannot be ignorant of so simple a distinction.

King: I do not in the least understand you. (Abbott, 1952:62)

Like the King of Lineland, we have been brought up in an intellectually limited universe. Our dilemma is that all our major concepts, our way of seeing reality, our willingness to accept proof, have been shaped by one dimension—one sex—rather than by two. For as long as we remain within this intellectual universe, we are incapable of comprehending its limitations, believing it to be the only world that exists. In order to truly understand our universe, we must create a vantage point that allows us to observe it both for what it is and for what it is not. Not an easy task, as the Square found out when he tried to explain the existence of left and right to a person who had never experienced them.

Similarly, none of us has ever lived in a nonsexist society: moving toward nonsexist scholarship is comparable to trying to comprehend a dimension that we have not materially experienced. We can describe it in theoretical terms, but we cannot fully appreciate its nature until we are able to lift ourselves out of our current confining parameters. This involves becoming aware of sexism in research and starting to eliminate it.

Sexism in research was first recognized as a major problem around the mid-1970s. While books and articles that pointed out the problem existed before that time,[2] it is only since the mid-1970s that critiques have appeared with some regularity and in more mainstream outlets.

In the early 1970s and continuing into the 1980s, various organizations, publishers, and publication outlets began adopting rules about the use of nonsexist language,[3] and recently, about nonsexist content.[4] Nevertheless, sexism in research is still badly understood. Even less well understood is how to conduct research in a nonsexist manner.

* * * * *

Sexism in Research

Most analyses of sexism in research focus either on one discipline or subject area or else on one type of sexism.[5] Indeed, we do not tend to speak of "types of sexism," but of "sexism," pure and simple.[6] The term "sexism" suggests that we are dealing with one problem that may manifest itself in different areas differently, but which nevertheless is a single basic problem—what one might call the "big blob" theory of sexism.

This book takes a different approach. Sexism is here broken down into seven different types. Of these seven types, four are primary and three are derived. Primary problems are those that cannot be reduced one to the other, although they coexist and often overlap. Derived problems are problems that are not logically distinct from the primary problems but which appear so frequently that they warrant being identified by a special label. The primary problems are: (1) androcentricity, (2) overgeneralization, (3) gender insensitivity, and (4) double standards. Derived problems are: (5) sex appropriateness, (6) familism, and (7) sexual dichotomism. There is a certain arbitrariness about identifying seven, rather than, say, six or five or eight sexist problems in research.[7] There is also a certain arbitrariness in the manner in which the boundaries have been drawn. The seven problems presented here have emerged through many attempts to order the otherwise diverse materials concerning critiques of sexism. The success of the approach presented here does not depend on acceptance of this categorization as the best possible or on correctly pigeonholing empirical problems under their appropriate theoretical labels, however. Instead, what is important is recognizing that sexism is multidimensional rather than unidimensional, identifying a sexist problem as such, and rectifying it. In other words, the seven problems are intended to serve as tools to facilitate the recognition and correction of sexism in research, rather than as an ultimate system of categorization.

It is helpful to think of the four primary problems as a set of movable circles. They all have a different core, and sometimes they overlap very heavily, sometimes only at the periphery, sometimes not at all. Occasionally, all four circles may overlap. Thus there may be more than one correct classification of a problem. The three derived problems, in contrast, can be thought of as constituting inner rings that are strongly defined within two of those larger circles.

* * * * *

The Seven Sexist Problems
Androcentricity

Androcentricity is essentially a view of the world from a male perspective. It manifests itself when ego is constructed as male rather than female, such as when "intergroup warfare" is defined as a "means of gaining women and slaves." In this case, the "group" is defined as consisting only of males, since the women are what is "gained." From an androcentric perspective, women are seen as passive objects rather than subjects in history, as acted upon rather than actors; androcentricity prevents us from understanding that both males and females are always acted upon as well as acting, although often in very different ways. Two extreme forms of androcentricity are gynopia (female invisibility) and misogyny (hatred of women).

This definition raises a difficulty that must be acknowledged. Theoretically speaking, problems of perspective could come in two versions: one female, one male. The female version would be gynocentricity, or a view of the world from a female perspective. I have labeled this problem androcentricity rather than, for instance, andro-gyno-centricity for two reasons. First, the problem is so overwhelmingly biased in the male direction that to accord a female version of the problem equal status would be inappropriate. I have, however, included the few examples of incipient gynocentricity that I found in my search of the literature. Second, it is not really possible to find a form of gynocentricity that is in any way comparable to androcentricity, for the simple reason that we live in an androcentric social, political, and intellectual environment. Thus even when we attempt to take a consciously female perspective, this attempt occurs within an overall intellectual environment in which both our vehicle for thought (language) and the content of thought (concepts) are colored by thousands of years of overwhelmingly androcentric thinking. It is therefore both misleading and inaccurate to treat possible gynocentricity as comparable to actual androcentricity. However, it is important to acknowledge that sexism can theoretically come in two forms, and to remind ourselves that neither is acceptable in scholarship.

Overgeneralization/Overspecificity

Overgeneralization occurs when a study deals with only one sex but presents itself as if it were applicable to both sexes. Its flip side is overspecificity, which occurs when a study is reported in such a manner that it is impossible to determine whether or not it applies to one or both sexes. Using a sample of male workers and calling it a study of social class is an instance of overgeneralization; the same problem arises when one uses the term "parents" to refer exclusively to mothers (ignoring fathers). Overspecificity occurs when single-sex terms are used when members of both sexes are involved (e.g., "the doctor ... he, or "man is a mammal"). Many (but not all) of the problems involving sexist language belong in this category.

There is considerable overlap between overgeneralization/overspecificity and androcentricity. Nevertheless, one cannot be equated to the other. A study may be androcentric without being overgeneral, such as when male violence against women is dismissed as trivial or unimportant (thus maintaining male over female interests) although the actors are correctly identified by their sex. A study may also be overgeneral or overspecific without being necessarily androcentric, such as when a study uses all male subjects (e.g., male students) or all female subjects (e.g., mothers) but presents the findings in general terms ("students" respond well to ability grouping, or "parents" tend to teach their children concepts through ostensive definitions).

Gender Insensitivity

Gender insensitivity is a simple problem: it consists of ignoring sex as a socially important variable. It sometimes overlaps with overgeneralization/overspecificity, but the two are not identical: In the case of general insensitivity, sex is ignored to such a degree that the presence of overgeneralization or androcentricity cannot even be identified. If a study simply fails to report the sex of its respondents, or if a policy study completely ignores the different effects of, let us say, a particular unemployment insurance policy on the two sexes, then we cannot identify whether male or female subjects were included or whether males or females would differentially profit from or be hurt by a particular policy. In a completely gender-insensitive study, it would be impossible to identify other problems because information necessary to do so is missing.

Double Standards

The use of double standards involves evaluating, treating, or measuring identical behaviors, traits, or situations by different means. A double standard is by no means easy to identify, although it may sound easy: it involves recognizing behaviors, traits, or situations as identical when they bear different labels or are described in different terms. For instance, some psychological disorders occur only in one sex. To find out whether or not a given example is an instance of the application of a double standard, one must (1) identify a larger category for the disorder; (2) determine whether there is a complementary disorder for the other sex; (3) identify whether the two are equivalent; and (4) determine whether they are evaluated in different ways. Only when all these preconditions obtain are we dealing with a double standard. If the disorder appears in only one sex, no double standard is involved.

Identification is not made easier by the fact that a researcher may have used different instruments to measure identical attributes of the sexes. For example, social status is currently derived by using different measures for the sexes. [...] However, this different measurement coincides with an actual difference in social standing between the sexes, a difference that we are incapable of measuring adequately because we have no sex-free instrument at our disposal. Identification of a double standard thus involves distancing oneself to some degree from the social context

as it is presented—not a simple thing to do, and never perfectly achieved.

A double standard is likely to be inspired by, or lead to, androcentricity, but it need not necessarily do so. Using female-derived categories of social status for women and male-derived categories for men is an instance of a double standard in the use of instruments, but it is neither gender insensitive nor androcentric nor overgeneral/overspecific.

Sex Appropriateness

Sex appropriateness, our first "derived" category, is nothing but a particular instance of a double standard, one that is so accepted within the relevant literature that it is proudly acknowledged with special terms: for example, "appropriate sex roles," or "appropriate gender identity." The absence of appropriate gender identity is called dysphoria, and it is classed as a psychological disorder. Sex appropriateness becomes a problem when human traits or attributes are assigned only to one sex or the other and are treated as more important for the sex to which they have been assigned. It is not a problem when we are dealing with a truly sex-specific attribute, such as the capacity to ejaculate or to give birth to children. It is a problem when it is applied to such human capacities as child rearing (as opposed to child bearing).

This particular example of a double standard has been singled out from the overall discussion of double standards because sex appropriateness is still widely accepted within the social science literature as a legitimate concept.

Familism

Familism is a particular instance of gender insensitivity. It consists of treating the family as the smallest unit of analysis in instances in which it is, in fact, individuals within families (or households) who engage in certain actions, have certain experiences, and so on. It is not a problem of sexism when no such attribution occurs. Another manifestation of familism occurs when the family is assumed to be uniformly affected (positively or negatively) in instances in which the same event may have different effects on various family members.

This problem has been singled out from the general discussion of gender insensitivity for the same reason that sex appropriateness has been singled out from the discussion of double standards: It is a very well-accepted practice within the social sciences to engage in familism, and is, at present, still considered to be entirely legitimate.

Sexual Dichotomism

Sexual dichotomism is another subaspect of the use of double standards. It involves the treatment of the sexes as two entirely discrete social, as well as biological, groups, rather than as two groups with overlapping characteristics. It leads to an exaggeration of sex differences of all types at the expense of recognizing both the differences and the similarities between the sexes. It is particularly important to recognize sexual dichotomism as a form of sexism because it is sometimes used as a "cure" for gender insensitivity. When this occurs, it is simply a case of substituting one form of sexism for another; and it is doubly misleading because it creates the illusion of having achieved a solution.

* * * * *

Sexism and Scientific Objectivity

One spinoff from the various critiques of sexism in research has been a renewed doubt about the possibility of objectivity in the social sciences. While academicians have traditionally assumed that objectivity is a hallmark of their work, feminist scholars have challenged this assumption. Some feminist researchers even maintain that objectivity is, in principle, impossible to achieve, and that the most we can do is to admit to an unabashed subjectivity, our own as well as everybody else's.[8] However, the logical consequence of such a principled stance is that research, including the implied cumulative knowledge it generates, is impossible.

This seems rather like throwing out the baby with the bathwater. Instead, it is more useful to identify the various components commonly included under the heading of objectivity and look at them separately, in order to eliminate the problematic aspects of objectivity while maintaining the useful ones. One scholar who engages in such a process of separating useful from harmful components of objectivity is Elizabeth Fee.[9] She suggests that the following "aspects of scientific objectivity ... should be preserved and defended":

> The concept of creating knowledge through a constant process of practical interaction with nature, the willingness to consider all assumptions and methods as open to question and the expectation that ideas will be subjected to the most unfettered critical evaluation.[10]

Fee also rejects certain aspects of "objectivity" in research. For example, she rejects as not helpful the notion that objectivity requires a distancing of the researcher from the subject matter, and of the production of knowledge from its uses. Likewise, she rejects as unnecessary the divorce between scientific rationality and emotional or social commitment; she also rejects the assumption that knowledge must flow only from the expert to the nonexpert and thus that a dialogue is not possible. She deplores the prevailing split between subject and object, in which the knowing mind is active and the object of knowledge entirely passive. Such a structure of knowledge results in a depersonalized voice of abstract authority that legitimizes domination. Finally, she rejects

as impossible the complete freedom of research from its sociopolitical environment.

Though she focuses on the concept of the "scientific process" and not on "objectivity" per se, Karen Messing argues that "the ideology and the background of the researcher" can influence the research process at eleven different stages[11]:

> the selection of the scientists,
> their access to facilities for scientific work,
> the choice of research topic,
> the wording of the hypothesis,
> the choice of experimental subjects,
> the choice of appropriate controls,
> the method of observation,
> data analysis,
> interpretation of data,
> the publication of results,
> and the popularization of results.[12]

Jill McCalla Vickers list as one of her methodological rebellions "the rebellion against objectivity,"[13] which she sees as (a) "treating those you study as objects and objectifying their pains in words which hide the identity of their oppressors," or (b) "being detached from that which is studied."[14] She accepts objectivity as "the rules which are designed to facilitate intersubjective transmissibility, testing, replication, etc."[15]

Finally, Evelyn Fox Keller has beautifully demonstrated that objectivity has been largely equated with masculinity.[16] She discusses particularly the misconception that objectivity requires detachment of the knower, both in emotional as well as in intellectual terms. Moreover, she argues that

> the disengagement of our thinking about science from our notions of what is masculine could lead to a freeing of both from some of the rigidities to which they have been bound, with profound ramifications for both. Not only, for example, might science become more accessible to women, but, far more importantly, our very conception of "objective" could be freed from inappropriate constraints. As we begin to understand the ways in which science itself has been influenced by its unconscious mythology, we can begin to perceive the possibilities for a science not bound by such mythology.[17]

It seems, then, that it is possible to be critical of the way in which objectivity has been defined without having to abandon the concept and sink into the morass of complete cultural subjectivism. We need to separate clearly objectivity from detachment and from the myth that research is value-free. Neither of the latter two conditions is, in principle, possible for any researcher (or anybody else). Our values will always intrude in a number of ways into the research process, beginning with the choice of the research question; and we will necessarily always be informed by a particular perspective. Nor is there any need to detach ourselves emotionally from the research process—in fact, this is impossible, and what appears as scholarly detachment is in reality only a matter of careful disguise.

Objectivity remains a useful and important goal for research in the following ways:

(1) a commitment to look at contrary evidence;
(2) a determination to aim at maximum replicability of any study (which implies accurate reporting of all processes employed and separation between simple reporting and interpretation, to the degree that these are possible);
(3) a commitment to "truth-finding" (what Kenneth Boulding has called veracity),[18] and
(4) a clarification and classification of values underlying the research: nonsexist research, for instance, is, based on the value judgment that the sexes are of equal worth, while androcentric research grows out of the belief that men are of higher worth (and therefore more important) than women.

I find it useful to think of objectivity as an asymptotically approachable but unreachable goal, with the elimination of sexism in research as a station along the way.

Solving the Problem of Sexism in Research

When we regard a problem as simple, a single solution often seems appropriate. Once we begin to differentiate among different and distinct components of a problem, however, different and distinct solutions become a necessity. When we fail to make the proper distinctions, we may—unwittingly and despite the very best intentions— replace one problem of sexism with another.

The analysis of sexism in language provides a case in point. Early and incisive studies of sexism in language convinced a number of organizations and individuals that sexist language was unacceptable in scholarly research (or elsewhere, for that matter!).[19] Typically, these analyses pointed out the use of so-called generic male terms as sexist, and often they included reference to such demeaning terms as "girls" for "women," or nonparallel terms (Mrs. John Smith but not Mr. Anne Smith, or the use of Mrs. or Miss, which indicate marital status, versus Mr., which does not).

As a consequence of these critiques, guides were published that replaced so-called generic male terms with truly generic terms: policeman became police officer; fireman, fire fighter; postman, mail carrier; workman, worker; chairman, chairperson; mankind, humanity; and so on. In effect, occupational and other terms were "desexed." The generic "he" was replaced with "he or she," or "s/he," or "they," or "one," or "people," and so on. Guides of this type continue to be important and useful, but unless care is taken as to how and when and in what context these gender-neutral terms are used, another form of sexism may inadvertently enter the picture.

The use of male (or sex-specific) terms for generic situations is one form of overgeneralization, one of our sexist problems. However, there is another aspect to the same problem: the use of generic terms for sex-specific situations, which is just as problematic as is the first manifestation. For example, if researchers talk about workers in general while only having studied male workers (constantly and cautiously using "they," "people," "the individual," "the person," and so on, with nary a female in sight), they simply replace one sexist problem with another in the manner in which language is used.[20] Language that employs "nonsexist" generic terms for sex-specific situations creates the same problem in reverse and constitutes at one and the same time an example of both overgeneralization and gender insensitivity.[21] In other words, when the content is sex specific, the language used should also be sex specific.

Sexism takes more than one form, and therefore ways to combat it may also take more than one form. The trick is to develop criteria that help us determine which solution is appropriate when. [...]

Notes

1 Edwin A. Abbott, *Flatland: A Romance of Many Dimensions* (New York: Dover, 1952).

2 See, for instance, Ruth Hershberger, *Adam's Rib* (New York: Harper & Row, 1970), first published in 1948; or the special issue on sexism in family studies of the *Journal of Marriage and the Family* 33: 3, 4 (1971).

3 An early example are the guidelines by Scott, Foresman and Co., "Guidelines for improving the image of women in textbooks" (Glenview, IL, 1972); see also "Guidelines for equal treatment of the sexes in McGraw-Hill Book Company publications" (n.d.); "Guidelines for nonsexist use of language," prepared by the American Psychological Association Task Force on Issues of Sexual Bias in Graduate Education, American Psychologist (June 1975): 682–684; "Guidelines for nonsexist use of language in National Council of Teachers of English publications" (March 1976).

4 For example, the Canadian Psychological Association approved a set of nonsexist guidelines in 1983; see Cannie Stark-Adamec and Meredith Kimball, "Science free of sexism: A psychologist's guide to the conduct of nonsexist research," *Canadian Psychology* 25: 1 (1984): 23–34. The Canadian Sociology and Anthropology Association passed a motion at its general annual meeting in 1984 that all official publications must be nonsexist in language and content; see Margrit Eichler, "And the work never ends: Feminist

contributions," Canadian Review of Sociology and Anthropology 22, 5 (1985): 619–644, esp. p. 633; "AERA guidelines for eliminating race and sex bias in educational research and evaluation," *Educational Researcher* 14, 6 (1985). The American Sociological Association published a set of guidelines in one of its publications; see "Sexist biases in sociological research: Problems and issues," *ASA Footnotes* (January 1980): 8–9, but its major journal, the *American Sociological Review*, does not require that articles be nonsexist in language and content. The Social Sciences and Humanities Research Council in Canada published a booklet suggesting that sexist research is bad research; see Margrit Eichler and Jeanne Lapointe, "On the treatment of the sexes in research" (Ottawa: Social Sciences and Humanities Research Council of Canada, Minister of Supply and Services, 1985); however, the assessment forms for projects do not include a criterion that the research be nonsexist. For an overview of strategies adopted by Canadian professional social science organizations and scholarly journals, see Linda Christiansen-Ruffman et al., "Sex bias in research: Current awareness and strategies to eliminate bias within Canadian social science" (Report of the Task Force on the Elimination of Sexist Bias in Research to the Social Science Federation of Canada, 1986).

5 See, for instance, Shulamit Reinharz, Marti Bombyk, and Janet Wright, "Methodological issues in feminist research: A bibliography of literature in women's studies, sociology and psychology," *Women's Studies International Forum* 6, 4 (1983): 437–454; and Margrit Eichler with the assistance of Rhonda Lenton, Somer Brodribb, Jane Haddad, and Becki Ross, "A selected annotated bibliography on sexism in research" (Ottawa: Social Sciences and Humanities Research Council of Canada, 1985).

6 This is not always true. Sexism is occasionally broken down into different ways in which it manifests itself, but such different manifestations are usually not seen as logically distinct. As an example, see Kathryn B. Ward and Linda Grant, "The feminist critique and a decade of published research in sociology journals," *Sociological Quarterly* 26, 2 (1985): 139–157.

7 Indeed, my first attempt to identify a set of superordinate sexist problems involved six, rather than seven problems; see Margrit Eichler, "Les six peches capitaux sexistes," in Huguette Dagenais (ed.), *Approches et methodes de la recherche feministe. Actes du colloque organise par le Groupe de recherché multidisciplinaire feministe*, Mai 1985. (Université Laval: Maquettiste, 1968): 17–29.

8 This is, for instance, the position taken by Liz Stanley and Sue Wise in *Breaking Out: Feminist Consciousness and Feminist Research* (London: Routledge &. Kegan Paul, 1983). They argue:

> We don't believe that "science" exists in the way that many people still claim it does. We don't see it as the single-minded objective pursuit of truth. "Truth" is a social construct, in the same way that "objectivity" is; and both are constructed out of experiences which are, for all practical purposes, the same as "lies" and "subjectivity." And so we sell all research as "fiction" in the sense that it views and so constructs "reality" through the eyes of one person. (p. 174)

9 Elizabeth Fee, "Women's nature and scientific objectivity," in Marian Lowe and Ruth Hubbard (eds.), *Women's Nature: Rationalizations of Inequality* (New York: Pergamon, 1983): 9–27.

10 Ibid., p. 16.

11 Karen Messing, "The scientific mystique: Can a white lab coat guarantee purity in the search for knowledge about the nature of women?" in Marian Lowe and Ruth Hubbard (eds.), *Women's Nature: Rationalizations of Inequality* (New York: Pergamon, 1983): 75–88.

12 Ibid., p. 76.

13 Jill McCalla Vickers, "Memoirs of an ontological exile: The methodological rebellions of feminist research," in Angela Miles and Geraldine Finn (eds.), *Feminism in Canada: from Pressure to Politics* (Montreal: Black Rose, 1982): 27–46.

14 Ibid., p. 40.

15 Ibid. In a more recent article, Vickers pushes toward a new epistemology; see Jill Vickers, "So then what? Issues in feminist epistemology." Unpublished paper presented at the 4th annual meeting of the Canadian Women's Studies Association, Winnipeg, 1986.

16 Evelyn Fox Keller, *Reflections on Gender and Science* (New Haven: Yale University Press, 1985).

17 Ibid., pp. 92–93.

18 Kenneth E. Boulding, "Learning by simplifying complexity: How to turn data into knowledge," in *The Science and Praxis of Complexity*, contributions to the symposium held at Montpellier, France, 1984 (Tokyo: United Nations University, 1985): 31.1 would like to thank Ursula Franklin for drawing my attention to this quote.

19 Some of the early studies include Virginia Kidd, "A study of images produced through the use of a male pronoun as the generic," *Movements: Contemporary Rhetoric and Communication* (Fall 1971): 25–30; Joseph W. Schneider and Sally L. Hacker, "Sex role imagery and the use of generic man in introductory texts," *American Sociologist* 8 (1973): 12–18; some of the later studies include Jeannette Silveira, "Generic masculine words and thinking," *Women's Studies International Quarterly* 3, 2/3 (1980): 165–178; Janice Moulton, George M. Robinson, and Cherin Elias, "Sex bias in language use: 'Neutral' pronouns that aren't," *American Psychologist* 33, 11 (1978): 1032–1036; Mary Vetterling-Braggin (ed.), *Sexist Language: A Modern Philosophical Analysis* (Totowa, NJ: Littlefield, Adams, 1981); John Briere and Cheryl Lanktree, "Sex-role related effects of sex bias in language," *Sex Roles* 9, 5 (1983): 625–632.

20 There is one exception to this general rule. When a communication is intended to solicit the representation of both sexes, even though only one is represented at a given point in time, it may be appropriate to use nonsexist language, as in announcements advertising jobs so far held only by men (for example, fire fighters, police officers, or chairpersons).

21 Another instance in which an attempt to avoid sexism may inadvertently lead to another type of sexism occurs when researchers trying to avoid gender insensitivity fall into the error of sexual dichotomism by treating sex as a categorical variable for all sorts of social phenomena.

Becoming an Anti-oppressive Researcher

KAREN POTTS AND LESLIE BROWN

Beginning with Choices, Assumptions, and Tenets

Given a simple choice between being an oppressive and an anti-oppressive researcher, hopefully we would all choose the latter. However, the choice is not really that simple or straightforward. Committing ourselves to anti-oppressive work means committing to social change and to taking an active role in that change. Being an anti-oppressive researcher means that there is political purpose and action to your research work. Whether that purpose is on a broad societal level or about personal growth, by choosing to be an anti-oppressive researcher, one is making an explicit, personal commitment to social justice. Anti-oppressive research involves making explicit the political practices of creating knowledge. It means making a commitment to the people you are working with personally and professionally in order to mutually foster conditions for social justice and research. It is about paying attention to, and shifting, how power relations work in and through the processes of doing research.

* * * * *

Three Emerging Tenets of Anti-oppressive Research

We propose three tenets of anti-oppressive research. These are not discrete; rather, they are fully interrelated and our articulation of them reflects how they inform one another. When we want to reflect on whether our research work is actually anti-oppressive research, we refer to these principles to assess our topic, our methods, our relationships, our analysis, our action, and the overall evaluation of our research work.

Anti-oppressive Research Is Social Justice and Resistance in Process and in Outcome

Research can be a powerful tool for social change. It also can, and has been, just as powerful in maintaining the status quo and supporting the evolution of societies that reward some people and inhibit others. Research

can be used to suppress ideas, people, and social justice just as easily—maybe even more easily—than it can be used to respect, empower, and liberate. Good intentions are never enough to produce anti-oppressive processes or outcomes.

Choosing to be an anti-oppressive researcher is not for the faint of heart. Being [...] a competent researcher is not enough. As anti-oppressive workers, we are social justice[1] activists, not only in the placard-waving sense, but also in the sense of making a personal commitment to action, of purposefully working to make change for individuals, communities, and institutions. As anti-oppressive researchers, we recognize that usually the first target of change is ourselves.

* * * * *

Choosing to be an anti-oppressive researcher means choosing to do research and support research that challenges the status quo in its *processes* as well as its outcomes. It seeks to resist oppression embedded in our selves, our work, and our world. bell hooks talks about the challenges of "teaching to transgress," of creating an environment in which we continually reflect on our processes in order to transform the enterprise of teaching and learning (hooks, 1994). Similarly, anti-oppressive researchers have the challenge of continually reflecting, critiquing, challenging, and supporting their own and others' efforts in the process of research and knowledge production to transform the enterprise of research [...] and ultimately the world in which we live.

Anti-oppressive Research Recognizes That All Knowledge Is Socially Constructed[2] and Political

Science and empiricism offer no more an "objective" explanation of the world and reality than, for example, ancient myths. (Chambon, Irving, and Epstein, 1999, p. 34)

So how do we know what we know? This is a question of epistemology, and it is key for understanding an anti-oppressive approach to research. From an anti-oppressive perspective, knowledge does not exist in and of itself, isolated from people. Rather, it is produced through the interactions of people, and as all people are socially located (in their race, gender, ability, class identities, and so on) with biases, privileges, and differing power relations, so too is the creation of knowledge socially located, socially constructed. Recognizing that knowledge is socially constructed means understanding that knowledge doesn't exist "out there" but is embedded in people and the power relations between us. It recognizes that "truth" is a verb; it is created, it is multiple: truth does not exist, it is made. Therefore, in anti-oppressive research, we are not looking for a "truth"; we are looking for meaning, for understanding, for the power to change.

Having accepted that there are many "truths," each socially constructed, whose knowledge is constructed through our research projects? Knowledge has become a commodity in the new "knowledge economy." Patents and copyrights protect the elite ownership of knowledge and such ownership can then be bought and sold. This puts the power of knowledge into the hands of the elite, the wealthy, and the privileged. Anti-oppressive research puts the ownership of knowledge back into the hands of those who experience it, who need it.

Picking up on the notion of how power and knowledge are inherently interrelated, anti-oppressive researchers recognize that knowledge is political; it is not benign as it is created in the power relations between people. Knowledge can be oppressive in how it is constructed and utilized and/or it can be a means of resistance. Often, it is a complex combination of both. Anti-oppressive practice is about resistance and therefore research processes can also become acts of resistance.

Anti-oppressive researchers are aware of the dynamics involved in the social construction of knowledge, and use this awareness to further the goals of social justice. Therefore, anti-oppressive research is not a process to discover knowledge, but a political process to co-create and rediscover knowledge. Through anti-oppressive research, we construct emancipatory, liberatory knowledge that can be acted on, by, and in the interests of the marginalized and oppressed.

The Anti-oppressive Research Process Is All about Power and Relationships

If power is cunning and pervasive enough, it will co-opt freedom; if freedom is resistant and persistent enough, it will cause power to tremble. (Caputo, 2000, p. 33)

So what is power and what does it have to do with the research process? Power is a concept that has been taken up in many different ways by many different theorists. [...] [W]e use a conceptualization proposed by Elias:

Instead of power being a "thing" which persons, groups, or institutions possess to a greater or lesser degree, Elias argued that we should think in terms of power relations, with ever-changing "balances" or "ratios" of power between individuals and social units ... and that all human relationships are essentially relations of power. (van Krieken, 2003, p. 118)

To apply Elias's idea of power relations, consider the relationship in positivist research between the researcher and those being "researched." In positivism, the researcher is the expert and is seen as the primary, and often only, person with the power and ability to create knowledge, to act on that knowledge, and to profit from its "creation." Those who are being studied, although they are not necessarily treated badly, are nevertheless objects; they are acted upon and have no input or real involvement or control in the process. In positivist research, those being researched rarely have any interpersonal relationship with the researcher, and there is usually no recognition of these hierarchical and distant power relations or any attempt to change them.

Even in many qualitative or what are termed "empowerment"[3] approaches to research, the relationship between researchers and the researched is often paternalistic. "Participatory" approaches often have members of the researched group conducting interviews or surveys, but with little substantive control over the research process. "Giving" people voice and hearing their stories can be exploitative/paternalistic or empowering or a confusing mix of power relations. Attending to issues of power in the relationships between people involved in research is complex.

* * * * *

Rethinking the Researching Process: Anti-oppressive Practice in the Process of Inquiry

Anti-oppressive research requires an attitude that accepts ambivalence and uncertainty, thereby enabling us to question that which appears "normal" and taken for granted to (re)negotiate processes and create spaces for ourselves and others who are commonly excluded from the creation of knowledge. We have found that the work of becoming anti-oppressive researchers has challenged us to reflect upon our sense of self, history, our context(s), and our actions with others. It has highlighted the need for skills in thinking critically, listening carefully, and analyzing relations of power of which we are a part so that we can identify and unpack assumptions, unearth patterns of thinking and acting, and recognize their effects.

In most social research texts, the research process is described as a problem-solving process. You are likely familiar with this linear process: (1) pose a question; (2) design a plan to study it; (3) collect some information;

(4) analyze the information; (5) draw some conclusions and pose new questions. We contend that research is not as linear as this model implies. In fact, this linear problem-solving model reproduces the dominant Western scientific method(ology) of constructing knowledge. As well this model leaves out some key research processes, like taking action on the knowledge that our work constructs.

[...] [T]here are alternative ways of interpreting and engaging within the (research) process that is produced by and reproduces power relations that do not oppress anyone or reinforce relations of domination. Therefore, we decided to organize our discussion of rethinking the research process within this problematic problem-solving structure [...] to demonstrate our epistemological assumption that we work from where we are, not from where we would rather be.

Questioning

Learning is really remembering, found by asking the right questions.

—Plato

Questioning is the "mess-finding" stage in the research process as well as the one that opens us up to possibilities. What are the issues? What do we know already? What is our relationship to the issues and questions? What do other people know about it? What do we want to find out?

Anti-oppressive research involves paying attention to power relations, beginning with asking, "Who says this is a question that needs to be studied anyway?" We also find ourselves constantly negotiating our position along a continuum of insider/outsider relations. On the insider pole of the continuum is epistemic privilege; that is, the privilege insiders have since they have lived experience of the issue under study. The outsider end of the continuum is a more traditional, positivist researcher role. You position yourself as outside the situation and in a position of studying "Others." Most of us on the journey of becoming anti-oppressive researchers find ourselves somewhere in the middle of the continuum. In practice, negotiating and positioning ourselves as researchers is seldom as simple as declaring which position we hold. In some instances, we may think we are insiders only to find that others involved in the project (especially those providing data) see us as set apart, as outsiders. There are insider/outsider tensions in all research relationships.

*　*　*　*　*

Outsider relations are established in the very declaration that a question is "research" with all its formal connotations. There is an inherent power in naming the issue to be studied and why it is worthy of study. The

research topic and question(s) guide the research by articulating what is, and therefore what isn't, to be explored. Anti-oppressive researchers pay attention to the ways a research topic is produced and pose various questions to ascertain what is happening and uncover assumptions. Who is involved in shaping the topic? What is and what is not explored? Anti-oppressive researchers continually wrestle with whose interests are being served (and not being served) by the study of this question.

For example, consider these questions in analyzing the politics of the following questions: Is there funding available for certain topics? Who determines those topics and why? Is an issue "hot" because it is topical in the newspaper? If so, who decides what gets to be newsworthy and why? Is an agency requesting the research? If so, what are their reasons, explicit and implicit, for doing so? Is it to justify future funding? Is it to rationalize actions already committed to? Is it for reflecting on practice in order to change processes? Has an instructor requested it? Is it developed by participants and, if so, why? It is important to acknowledge who is involved, or to be involved, in any way in the research. There are a myriad of reasons and interests to be served in any piece of research.

A topic may be readily converted into a research question with little regard for the political and epistemological implications of posing such a question in a particular way. In anti-oppressive research, we closely examine our process of creating topics and questions. We work to avoid jumping thoughtlessly from what "we" interpret is happening to the development of a topic, and then to a question. Instead, we contemplate the possible effects of asking a particular question as opposed to other questions, and strive to unearth our assumptions about people, relationship, power, and knowledge that are embedded in each of the ways that we might construct the question. As our individual perspectives are limited, we do so in concert with others. Then we can make more informed choices about which topic and question we really want to pursue.

*　*　*　*　*

This initial stage of questioning involves finding out what others know about the topic. Traditionally, this means checking the academic literature. Being an anti-oppressive researcher means critically reading existing knowledge to understand how it was constructed, by whom and for whose benefit, and therefore how it will affect our construction of research about the issue. Anti-oppressive researchers recognize "knowledge" other than what is published in academic books and articles. For instance, lived experience of self and others can also provide a valid point of departure for a research topic. Popular knowledge found in magazines and on TV may also supplement data. We each have to ask ourselves how we determine the trustworthiness or validity of knowledge. Are we more persuaded by what our professor says or what our mom says about our topic? Critical assessment of the various sources of knowledge on a topic and the authority each source brings to that knowledge is part of an anti-oppressive approach to the first stage of the research process.

As important as it is to have a clear starting place, the initial clarity of the research question is tenuously held. When it comes down to it, finding "the question" is seldom that simple. Sometimes the question finds us. Sometimes questions are more like hunches, experienced tensions, or disjunctures sensed in our own lives. Going from clarity to fuzziness can be okay. Questions usually change as the inquiry proceeds. And sometimes the question that was answered is not clearly revealed until the end of the process. We have often found that throughout the process, we learn more about what it was we really wanted to know. The art of the question is in the re-researching, the willingness to look again.

Designing and Redesigning a Plan to Study the Questions

Anti-oppressive research must be anti-oppressive in terms of both purpose and process. [...] Significant thought and relationship building are integral to the designing and planning of emancipatory methods. The research journey must be purposeful (goals) and intentional (process).

When you are on a planned road trip, you often run across opportunities and obstacles that didn't exist on your map. Modifications to the plan are made within the context of your purpose, who is on the trip, how much time and money you have, and so on. Similarly, a research design is a dynamic plan that gets tweaked and altered along the way. The process is shaped by the design, which reflects the goals of the research. The intention or purpose of the research is interrogated and made clearer as one considers the topic and question. It is revisited throughout the research journey. As the topic, questions, and purpose become clearer, ideas about data, data sources, and ways to gather and think about data begin to emerge. This feeds the development of a research design.

There are many questions that an anti-oppressive researcher asks in the ongoing process of articulating a design. These questions arise out of an epistemological understanding of the nature of the relationship between the researcher and the researched. Who has an interest or stake in the research? Who are we going to involve, and how? What are the ethical considerations in the research? How are we going to collect data and, once collected, how are we going to interpret it? Who owns the data? What constraints are there to the research design? What criteria will we use to judge the quality of our research? Exploring these questions is integral to the process of designing a research study.

The first question posed asks us to consider how the various interests/power relations construct the research process. Just as there are stakeholders in the construction of the research question, there are stakeholders in the research design, and they may not be the same people. For example, if perchance we are doing a research project as part of a university course, then we have to be aware of how the requirements of the assignment and the ethical review processes of the university construct the research and constrain the possibilities. Or, if our purpose is to secure future funding for an addictions support program and we know that the funders want to know the extent of the problem, who needs to be served, and what alternative programs cost, we would not likely design a research project that interviewed one client in great depth about her experience as a drug user. If we happened to be receiving pay from a government department, we also have to recognize how the interests of government will affect our relations with participants we may be working with in the research. Conversely, if we didn't have external funding but were working collectively with others to explore an issue common to all of us all, we would want to ensure that our design included the collective participation of everyone in the group rather than being controlled by one designated researcher. Regardless of the project, there are always interests that shape the conduct of the research and ultimately the construction of knowledge produced.

There are also interests that will affect the utility of the research. It is therefore useful to develop relationships with our potential audience and with those whom we are targeting for change. Politically, we have to consider when is the best time to engage this stakeholder group. There may be some merit to engaging this group throughout the research process in order to build rapport and possible support. There are a variety of ways one might consider, from developing an advisory group made up of representatives of all stakeholders to connecting the marginalized with the dominant through the actual research processes. [...] Whatever the approach, the intention is that the actual process of the research becomes an intervention for change rather than relying only on the impact of the research outcome, or product.

At some points decisions will need to be made regarding who to involve in some or all of the research process. This is what positivist researchers may call developing a "sampling strategy." However, the goals for anti-oppressive research are very different as involving people is done more for community building, empowerment, and a better understanding than for goals of representativeness or validity. "Sampling" in anti-oppressive research is seldom random. Sampling is a power-laden decision and seen as one of many political acts in research. In this, ideally, an outsider researcher is never the sole source of invitations to participate. Ideally it is a community of participants/insider researchers who do the inviting/including.

Ethical questions affect every research design. The ethics of anti-oppressive research reflect a commitment to and respect for people and relationships as well as for action and social justice. The use of "informed consent" is one example. Constant renegotiation regarding a process of informed consent is important as this highlights our commitments to the community, about our relationship to them, the data, and the process. Although most "informed consent" processes have become institutionalized for purposes of avoiding liability, we have reclaimed the concept of "informed consent" to be a formal contract of our obligations to research participants, and a declaration of their ownership of the data, their right to a transparent research process, and their right to as much involvement or control as they choose. Certainly this way of working has led to some interesting situations for us (e.g., a community deciding to withdraw its data toward the end of a study) and as logistically difficult as these situations have and can be, revisiting the ethics of anti-oppressive research guides one's decision making.

Respecting people and relationships also guide our response to questions of the ownership of data. The term "data" in its origins means "gift." From an anti-oppressive perspective, we see data as a gift that participants bestow and we work to respect those gifts and treat them ethically. This means we must ask who owns the data, and what does ownership mean? If "we" (researchers) agree that participants own the data, and if after the research is completed the participants decide they don't like what we, the researchers, have said, what happens then?4 Or if we hear the story of a participant that is compelling but filled with tangential comments and expressions that we feel are distracting to what the research is saying, do we have the right to edit their story? Once edited, whose story is it? There are at least three voices in interpreting data: the participant who gives the story, the writer/researcher who records and retells it, and the reader who interprets it (Marcotte, 1995). "How are all these voices attended to?" is a question we ask ourselves. Developing and attending to relationships, including those to data and data sources, is critical in anti-oppressive research.

Identifying the constraints to any design is important so that an anti-oppressive researcher can then identify the spaces within those constraints that can make the research less oppressive in its process, and ultimately in its outcome. The types of constraints you will encounter will differ and change in every inquiry. However, there are some constraints that you can usually anticipate, such as time, resources, and institutional/organizational structures. For example, if your research is connected with a university, you will be expected to submit your study for approval to an ethics review committee. In general, the policies of these committees have been designed to address the issues of ethics in positivist research. Therefore, you might anticipate having to mould your presentation of an anti-oppressive research design to fit these institutional regulations. In another example, suppose you have been asked by government

to do some research. You will likely have a limited time frame and budget and may face the constraints of having the research questions predetermined, and possibly the design as well. Just because we may be confined to doing a standardized survey questionnaire doesn't mean that we can't think about how to involve participants in the research, its process, and its outcome. Rather than designing the questionnaire yourself in isolation, it is possible to give up or share control with those being "researched" to design the questions and the process. Rather than administer a questionnaire "to" participants, for example, we could complete it "with" participants. This should be more than just semantics; this shift in language produces a different relationship among the people involved in the research. It is also important that we never ask questions of others that we are not willing to answer and share ourselves. Whatever the challenges and constraints, we have a responsibility to work with what we have, to not give up.

* * * * *

Within the design, it is also important to be clear about the criteria by which we want the quality of our research work to be evaluated so that we can ensure that there are methods in place to achieve them. It is the operationalization of "quality" that will make your research credible, publishable, actionable, and worth listening to. Without quality assurance strategies, research can be dismissed as an opinion essay with no relevance for being acted upon. So what criteria are appropriate to judge the quality of anti-oppressive research? And who gets to decide this? Figuring this out requires attention to the perspectives of those who have an interest in the research, all within the framework of tenets and ethics of anti-oppressive research. So, for example, you may know that statistical data will be important for having your research taken seriously by a certain policy maker, so you will need "valid and reliable" data-gathering and analysis procedures. Yet, you will also be cognizant that such procedures are designed to be consistent with the tenets and ethics of anti-oppressive research.

Collecting Data: Seeking, Listening, Learning

In a perfect world, everything we have planned in our design goes exactly as predicted. However, we live in an imperfect world. Collecting data is not a process in the research journey that is isolated from the other processes. As anti-oppressive researchers, we strive to be perceptive, to pay attention to what we are in the midst of. By paying attention, we gradually enhance our abilities to perceive, describe, analyze, and assess our reality. This increased perceptivity produces expanded experience and enables us to recognize and respond to opportunities as they arise throughout the research process.

In order to undertake the work of collecting data, we have to develop our listening and critical reflecting skills. By paying attention, a unique approach to listening emerges, one that we call political listening. We listen not for what we expected to hear or for what fits with what we already think, but for assumptions made both by ourselves as listeners and by speakers while attending to the dance of power. It involves being open and perceptive, interpreting, and judging. [...] Through political listening, one becomes aware of the construction of multiple interpretations and multiple truths. Listening not only affects the relationship between researcher and participant, but facilitates analysis and the opportunities for anti-oppressive actions. By listening to participants, we begin to interpret the data, refine our research question, and rethink our design. By articulating their experience and thoughts, the participants make meaning of their lives. By paying attention and listening, we become increasingly aware of contexts, histories, and social dynamics. We can discover new opportunities for acting that we had not foreseen or planned, and come to know only through critical and detailed reflection on practice. Through paying attention and listening, research is reconceptualized and becomes an emergent, unfolding process rather than a trip to a predetermined destination.

*   *   *   *   *

Making Meaning

Making meaning is often thought of as "analyzing data." When doing anti-oppressive research, we assume that meaning making is not restricted to any one part of the research process but happens throughout the research process. As such, we pay attention to our processes of interpretation, reflection, and construction of meaning as the research journey unfolds.

While meaning making is ongoing, we do have "data" to compile and make sense of, which is the focus of this next part of the discussion. In practice, we have found that it is useful, as we begin to review our data, to revisit our research questions and design and consider how they have evolved and shifted from the original plan. By rearticulating our research design, we can open ourselves to understanding more specifically what we want to know and thus ask of the data. We also can become more aware of the kinds of data and data sources we have and our positioning in relation to the data. This clarity grounds our interpretations and analysis of the data. Our way of gathering and working with data has probably been modified as the research process unfolds. All these shifts and changes influence and determine what data we actually have and how we make sense of the data.

There are a number of questions that we reflect upon as we plan for and engage in making meaning. These include issues of power and who does the analysis as well as issues of what concepts frame the analysis, who

benefits from the meaning making, and what analytic tools are appropriate.

Power lurks in all our reflections and decisions. Just figuring out who gets the privilege of making meaning is laden with issues of power. For us, research is a social process and therefore the more positivist notion of one or two designated researchers who are responsible for analyzing the data is not our reality. Yet, even though we work collaboratively with participant-researchers, potential users of the research, and others in making meaning of our data, we are often challenged with the underlying hierarchy inherent in our relationships. The analysis stage presents an opportunity for the social construction of knowledge to be facilitated in an intentionally liberatory way. Some people in the process are seen as experts in the topic of study while others are seen as experts in particular data analysis techniques or in the lived experience of the data. Our collaborative meaning-making processes are influenced by the perceived and exercised power that we each bring to the process. These differences often become visible when there are disagreements about meanings or the importance of meanings. Further, while it may be ideal to have everyone possible involved in the meaning making, the reality often is that not everyone has the time or interest in participating. Figuring out how to enable individuals to participate as they would wish is challenging.

Another point of reflection in planning and engaging in meaning making concerns the conceptual framework that informs the research. Kirby and McKenna (1989) challenge us to articulate our "conceptual baggage"—that is, the concepts, beliefs, metaphors, and frameworks that inform our perspective on, and relationship to, the research topic. The term "baggage" has somewhat of a negative connotation, so we like to think about our "luggage." We carry our framework, which is not inherently good or bad, around with us and it is through this framework that we view the data. Making visible the luggage is an individual and collective process. Ensuring that everyone has had the opportunity to discuss the concepts that inform our perspectives helps to alleviate conflicts that can arise during the analysis of different perceptions of meaning and can expose contradictions in helpful ways. The conceptual framework that informed the project at the outset evolves during the project and new or additional concepts, metaphors, and frameworks emerge. Winnowing through minutes of meetings about the topic or trying to explain to your friends what the research is about are often fruitful ways to discern the emergent frameworks. Discussing these frameworks with research-participants can illuminate contradictions in concepts that may be held. It is illuminating to consider how different concepts, metaphors, and frameworks produce different meanings and the production of different knowledge. Such discussions often bring up questions about which interpretation(s) is seen as more valuable or believable than another and why.

As researchers we have found it particularly helpful to revisit the topic and questions to think through the fit between our approaches to analysis with what we really want to know. This revisiting is vital and informs the ability to make meaning and to extend the findings into conclusions and action.

The other point of reflection in the meaning-making process is thinking about who benefits from the chosen research process. What (whose) purpose does the research serve? There is an old saying that "figures don't lie, but liars can figure." The techniques of analysis, of making meaning of data, contribute to the meaning made. What is the intended outcome, and how is the data analysis, whether statistical or not, being constructed? What data are included in the analysis and what are left out? Why? If using interview data, who decides which quotes from participants to include and who to exclude? Again, knowledge is constructed, and paying attention to why and how it is constructed is an ongoing challenge for anti-oppressive researchers.

* * * * *

What kind of approach should be taken? Some options include involving participants or those ultimately affected by the research (who may not be the participants) in analyzing the data. What about having an advisory group for our research and having them conduct the analysis? Or finding a way to involve the people who will be responsible for making change as a result of the research? Whichever approach is used, consider how it will affect the "results" of the research and how those results could be used.

Posing Conclusions and New Questions, and Taking More Action

One continuously thinks about new questions, new realizations, and applications of ideas as one travels through the research process. Yet at some point along the journey, there is the time to capture them as "conclusions" to the trip. Tied to these conclusions are new questions as any research study usually raises more questions than answers. This circular process, a research process, reflects the lifelong learning process we are all in.

Conclusions have a particular power because they are the construction of knowledge that leads to recommendations and actions. As well, the conclusions are often the "sound bites" in the research that an audience listens for. Sometimes these consumers of our research are interested in our trip, in the story of our process, but more often they are interested in what we have "found." How conclusions are constructed, therefore, has particular impact on how consumers will take up the research in their own lives. We have found it challenging to construct conclusions that give the context of our journey to our findings. We have had to remind ourselves that posing

conclusions is useful for us individually and collectively as researchers, as well as other potential audiences. Once again, questions regarding who gets to articulate the conclusions and questions and how this is done arise for us. These ideas may guide future research studies, so we ask ourselves whose interests are, or may be, served in these questions.

The manner and form in which we present our conclusions and questions also affects how they may be taken up. Formal written report form is commonplace and although useful, it is almost inherently classist, exclusionary, and appropriative in that it requires translating marginal knowledges into the language of the elite. A written report may be appropriate for our purpose, but as the way we present our research contributes to the meaning and significance attached to conclusions, other options are worthy of consideration. Brainstorming with co-researchers for options that could facilitate goals of empowerment and social justice then becomes a key part of the work. For instance, would it be better to hold a community workshop to discuss the research, or produce a journal article, or write a letter to the editor, or put the findings into a popular theatre presentation, or convene a session of strategic planning, or produce a video or a web site? Whose interests are served by each of the options available?

[…] [R]esearch […] is a site for practising democracy. Recognizing our "agency," our ability to make a choice in how something will be done, enables us to be purposeful in our anti-oppressive actions. Reframing research as practice that produces radical democracy has helped us as researchers to move beyond the trap of oppositional thinking within anti-oppressive research. How we pose conclusions and devise actions is yet another opportunity to practise democracy and thereby make real our beliefs about power relations and social justice. Posing conclusions brings us to ask the critical question, so what? How will the research be used, and by whom? Who else could make use of it, and how? What uses could it have that were not intended? Remember that producing a product that sits on a shelf does not mean that the research, or the research report, does not fill a purpose. Too often research is used to delay decision making or distract attention from an issue. What is the professional obligation of the researcher in ensuring that the research is used for social change, not only throughout the process of conducting the research but after the research is concluded? We have found that by returning to our original discussions about the issues and what we wanted to know, we discover many possibilities about what to do with the findings and who will use them and how they will or could be used. Anti-oppressive action in the research process means taking up the processes and tools of research in ways that are congruent with the principles and values of empowerment and social justice wherever and whenever possible.

Credibility, Action-Ability, and Trustworthiness: Reclaiming Reliability and Validity

Assessing how well we did, how we know if our research is credible, actionable, and trustworthy, is important in anti-oppressive research. However, in contrast to most positivist work, this assessment is a theoretical, principled question as opposed to a technical concern. Anti-oppressive research is not so much concerned with the ability of our research instruments to "measure" accurately; rather, our concerns relate to whether we adhered to our research principles.

Some of the questions we ask include: Can participants see themselves in the study? Does the analysis "ring true" to participants? "Yes" answers to both these questions are most easily assured by having the participants of any research study determine the questions and do the analysis. We ask ourselves if we can see our own limitations as researchers and participants. Can we see where our conceptual luggage and our biases affected the process and outcome? We ask if we have been transparent in our biases and in the power relations and decisions that were made regarding the research process. Did we make any effort to include multiple perspectives? Did we take enough time for authentic relationships to be built and did we give people the time and respect to be truly honest? Finally, did we just skim the surface or did we strive for a critical understanding of an issue—that is, does our research have "soul"? And, we ask, did this research matter? Did it leave participants better off?

* * * * *

Notes

[1] For us, social justice means transforming the way resources and relationships are produced and distributed so that all people can live dignified lives in a way that is ecologically sustainable. Our critical view of social justice includes social sustainability, intergenerational equity, global justice, and eco-centric justice (Ife, 2002, pp. 75–78). It takes direct aim at the sources that reproduce structural disadvantage, whether those are through institutions, like income security, or through human relations, such as racism. It is also about creating new ways of thinking and being, not only criticizing the status quo. Social justice means acting from a standpoint of those who have the least power and influence, relying on the wisdom of the oppressed (Ife, 2002, p. 88).

[2] Social constructionism speaks to theories that relate to the socially created nature of life. These theories are first associated with the 1966 book, *The Social Construction of Reality* (Berger and Luckmann, 1966).

[3] "Empowerment" is a problematic term because it is often used with varied meanings. In this chapter, when "empowerment" appears in quotations, it is being contested as a term that often implies a feeling without real power, upward mobility, individual self-confidence, or it is an illusion of real power. When we as authors speak of real empowerment, we are using the term as Lather does, "drawing on Gramsci's (1971) ideas of counter-hegemony ... empowerment to mean analyzing ideas about the causes of powerlessness, recognizing systemic oppressive forces, and acting both individually and collectively to change the conditions of our lives" (Lather, 1991, pp. 3–4).

[4] Cultivating co-researchers is one way that many who try to be more anti-oppressive in their research engage the tenets of anti-oppressive work. As knowledge is socially constructed and what is created through coming together as knowers is more than what each co-researcher knew before coming together, co-researching can become a way of producing knowledge and producing knowers. Yet such an approach is not without its own power issues. Too often, we have seen projects where insiders are co-researchers who are marginalized or given a token position within the research design. It begs the question, to what extent can research truly be anti-oppressive unless the people experiencing the issue under study *are* the researchers and are in control of the research decisions?

References

Berger, P., and Luckmann, T. (1966). *The social construction of reality*. Toronto: Random House of Canada Limited.

Caputo, J.D. (2000). *More radical hermeneutics: On not knowing who we are*. Bloomington: Indiana University Press.

Chambon, A.S., Irving, A., and Epstein, L. (1999). *Reading Foucault for social work*. New York: Columbia University Press.

hooks, b. (1994). *Teaching to transgress: Education as the practice of freedom*. New York: Routledge.

Ife, J. (2002). *Community development: Community-based alternatives in an age of globalization* (2nd edition). Frenchs Forest, NSW: Pearson Education Australia.

Kirby, S.L., and McKenna, K. (1989). *Experience, research, social change: Methods from the margins*. Toronto: Garamond Press.

Lather, P. (1991). *Getting smart: Feminist research and pedagogy within the postmodern*. New York: Routledge.

Marcotte, G. (1995). Metis c'est may nation. "Your Own People," comme on dit: Life histories from Eva, Evelyn, Priscilla, and Jennifer Richard. Paper prepared for the Royal Commission on Aboriginal Peoples.

Narayan, U. (1988). Working together across difference: Some considerations on emotions and political practice. *Hypatia* 3 (2), 31–47.

van Krieken, R. (2003). Norbert Elias. In A. Elliott and L. Ray (Eds.), *Key contemporary social theorists*. Oxford: Blackwell Publishing.

Rethinking Section 1:
INTRODUCTION TO SOCIOLOGY

Critical Thinking Questions

Section 1A: Classical Theory

Emile Durkheim

1. Are duties we perform as social actors external to individuals?
2. According to Durkheim, what is a social current?
3. How can we identify social facts?
4. What is the connection between power and social facts?

Karl Marx and Friedrich Engels

1. Why do Marx and Engels assert that understanding one's present society requires an investigation into societies of the past?
2. What is class conflict? How is class conflict different from other forms of conflict (between individual people or nations)?

C. Wright Mills

1. Why do people tend to view how society works in individual terms?
2. According to Mills, what are the benefits of employing one's sociological imagination?
3. Can you think of an example from your own life that you once thought of as an individual or private trouble that you now see is a public issue?

Section 1B: Contemporary Theory

Dorothy E. Smith

1. Who is generally considered the subject of sociology? How is a woman's world bifurcated?
2. How does the organization of public work depend upon men's alienation from their bodily and local existences? What does Smith argue this means for women?
3. Explain Smith's image of an alternative sociology. Where must the sociologist be situated?

Michel Foucault

1. Can power be both productive and repressive?
2. Why does Foucault place such an emphasis on surveillance? What does it have to do with power, if anything at all?
3. Do you believe that you are disciplined into obedience? Why or why not? Provide examples.
4. Who has the power to decide if language, actions, and so forth are racist? Who ought to be able to decide such things?

Diana Coben

1. How is the notion of consent important for hegemony?
2. What is the role of the dominant class in Gramsci's concept of hegemony?
3. Can you think of current applications for Gramsci's concept beyond class dynamics?

George Sefa Dei

1. What is meant by intersectionality?
2. How do race, class, and gender intersect?
3. Discuss the role of education in integrative anti-racism.
4. What is meant by the politics of identity?
5. How does globalization fuel racism?

Section 1C: Research Methods

Margrit Eichler

1. What is the difference between primary sexist problems and the derived problems?
2. Provide examples for the seven sexist problems in research identified by Eichler. What are the implications of sexist research?
3. Can you think of other ways to apply Eichler's seven sexist problems beyond research?

Karen Potts and Leslie Brown

1. How is social location important to anti-oppressive research? What social location(s) do you occupy, and how does this affect your claim to being anti-oppressive (should you choose to make this claim)?
2. Discuss the differences between positivist research and anti-oppressive research.
3. What are outsider/insider relations? How are power relations integral to these relations? What causes insider/outsider tensions? Can they be alleviated?

Glossary Terms

Section 1A: Classical Theory

Emile Durkheim

social facts: Patterned ways of thinking, acting, and feeling that exist outside of any one individual but exert control.

Karl Marx and Friedrich Engels

bourgeoisie: Those who own the means of production.

capitalism: An economic system characterized by a competitive market, private ownership of the means of production, and the pursuit of profit.

epoch: Period of time.

means of production: Tools, factories, land, and investment capital used to produce wealth.

proletariat: Those who sell their labour power for a wage.

C. Wright Mills

imperialism: Practices and attitudes of those who rule in places away from home that initiate and justify that rule.

milieux: Setting.

personal troubles: These occur within the character of the individual person and within the range of his or her immediate relations with others.

public issues: Matters that transcend the local environment or immediate social relations.

Dorothy E. Smith

alienation: A Marxist term for a worker's lack of connection to the product of his or her labour.

bifurcation: A split into two parts.

experience: Not just a tacit understanding of what happens to us but delving beyond to understand how our worlds are shaped by relations that extend beyond our immediate settings.

Michel Foucault

disciplinary society: A society based on surveillance.

panopticon: A prison structure (design by J. Bentham) in which inmates are always on display but never know when they are being watched.

Diana Coben

hegemony: Spontaneous consent of the masses to the general direction imposed on social life by the dominant group.

war of movement: Direct assault on the state.

war of position: The establishment of hegemony over a long period before revolutionaries seize state power.

George Sefa Dei

integrative anti-racism: Understanding how the dynamics of social difference (race, class, gender, and so forth) are mediated in daily life.

saliency of race: Race as a central analytic unit; importance of race in daily experiences.

Margrit Eichler

androcentricity: A view of the world from a male perspective.

gender insensitivity: Ignoring sex as a socially important variable.

gynocentricity: A view of the world from a female perspective.

Karen Potts and Leslie Brown

agency: An individual holds a sense of agency when he or she has the capacity to act in response to relations of oppression, and ultimately seeks to change these relations; ability to make choices.

anti-oppressive researcher: A researcher with political purpose and action; a researcher who commits to social change and social justice, paying careful attention to shifting power relations.

epistemology: Attempts to answer the question "How do we know what we know?"; ways of knowing.

Relevant Web sites

http://www.mcmaster.ca/socscidocs/w3virtsoclib/theoriest.htm

This site serves as a link to multiple sociological theory Web sites. The site covers theorists such as Bourdieu, Durkheim, Goffman, Gramsci, Marx, Weber, and so forth.

http://www.italnet.nd.edu/gramsci/

This is the international Gramsci society Web site. It contains resources on the life and work of Antonio Gramsci.

http://www.iwp.uni-linz.ac.at/lxe/sektktf/bb/HyperBourdieu.html

This site is the HyperBourdieu World Catalogue. The site provides a comprehensive bibliography and mediagraphy of written works and public addresses by Pierre Bourdieu.

http://www.relst.uiuc.edu/durkheim/

A presentation of information concerning the French sociologist Emile Durkheim can be found on this site.

http://bobcat.cc.oxy.edu/~maeda/crtlinks.html

Here you will find many helpful links for critical race theory.

http://www.brocku.ca/english/courses/4F70/postcol.html

This site takes the viewer through some issues in post-colonial theory.

http://www.emory.edu/ENGLISH/Bahri/orientalism.html

This site provides an overview of Edward Said's Orientalism. There are also links to other related sites.

http://www.bc.edu/schools/cas/sociology/vss/smith

An article written about Canadian sociologist Dorothy Smith and her concepts of "voice, standpoint, and power."

http://www.cddc.vt.edu/feminism/enin.html

This is a feminist theory Web site that offers research materials and general information for people interested in women's social conditions and struggles.

http://csf.colorado.edu/isa/sections/ftgs

This is the feminist theory and gender studies section of the International Studies Association. The site offers a listserv that people may join and other relevant links.

Further Reading

Bourdieu, Pierre. (1999). "Structures, *Habitus*, Practices." In Anthony Elliott (ed.), *Contemporary Social Theory*, pp. 107–118. Oxford: Blackwell Publishers.
A key piece by the French theorist Pierre Bourdieu.

Butler, Judith. (1990). *Gender Trouble: Feminism and the Subversion of Identity*. London: Routledge.
Explores gender theoretically arguing that there is no "authentic" femininity or masculinity located in male and female bodies or in our inner selves.

Campbell, Marie, and Ann Manicom (eds.). (1995). *Knowledge, Experience, and Ruling Relations*. Toronto: University of Toronto Press.
A collection of papers by people engaged with the writings of Dorothy Smith.

hooks, bell. (1981). *Ain't I a Woman: Black Women and Feminism*. Boston: South End Press.
Examines the impact of sexism on Black women.

Reay, Diane. (2000). "'They Employ Cleaners to Do That': Habitus in the Primary Classroom." *British Journal of Sociology of Education, 16*(3), pp. 353–371.
An empirical example of Bourdieu's habitus.

Said, Edward. (1978). *Orientalism*. New York: Pantheon Books.
A key piece in post-colonial theory.

Seidman, Steven. (2001). "From Identity to Queer Politics: Shifts in Normative Heterosexuality." In Steven Seidman and Jeffrey Alexander (eds.), *The New Social Theory Reader*, pp. 352–360. London: Routledge.
An introductory piece to queer theory.

Selwyn, Neil. (2000). "The National Grid for Learning: Panacea or Panopticon?" *British Journal of Sociology of Education, 21*(2), pp. 243–255.
An empirical piece utilizing Foucault's work on the panopticon.

Smith, Dorothy. (1999). *Writing the Social*. Toronto: University of Toronto Press.
Dorothy Smith's most recent collection of papers published in book format.

Van Den Hoonaard, Will. (2001). "Is Research-Ethics Review a Moral Panic?" *Canadian Review of Sociology and Anthropology, 38*(1), pp. 19–36.
Explores the research ethics review procedure and outlines these reviews are organized with quantitative studies in mind.

Foundations of Society

The Readings

Our first piece in this section takes up child socialization by examining how children come to learn the concept of "bloody revenge" and the implications of such socialization for violence and aggression among children and youth. Antoinette Errante illustrates that violence is not isolated to just military activities; rather, violence is embedded in our cultural practices. In making arguments about violent masculinities, Errante draws on responses from the United States to the attack of September 11, 2001, on the World Trade Center.

Next in this section, utilizing a symbolic interactionist approach, Kent Sandstrom weaves first-hand accounts of men living with AIDS with theoretical insights about identity. While the interview accounts illustrate how men with AIDS think and feel about their lives, their inevitable deaths and post-mortal reality, the strength of the piece is its theoretical demonstration of how the construction of the self is an active and social process.

The importance and fluidity of culture are explored in our next three selections. We begin with Michael Atkinson's article on the body projects of women's tattooing. Atkinson draws on feminist post-structuralist work to illustrate how women's tattoos are "embodied signifiers of gender." Through interviews with women, Atkinson argues that women's tattoo practices are an active example of women negotiating deeply embedded cultural notions of femininity.

In the past few years, we have started to see an academic body of literature emerge that takes up "trans" issues (issues of transgendered people). The piece presented here is an interview with Viviane Namaste on the political project of rendering transsexual people "visible." The piece is an accessible introduction to trans issues. Namaste comments on institutional forms of discrimination that trans people experience. She ends the interview by encouraging people to learn about the history of trans people in Canada and to think through how issues that affect trans people also link to issues that other marginalized people experience.

The last selection examining culture takes up Canadian teenage identities. Stephen Gennaro argues that a "perpetual adolescence" has emerged. He links the development of this state to new information and communication technologies. Gennaro also takes up the theoretical question of identity (teenage identity) formation, exploring the connection between Canadian identity formation and American media and advertising. He explores how people come to define themselves through cultural commodity consumption.

CHAPTER 10

Where in the World Do Children Learn "Bloody Revenge"?: Cults of Terror and Counter-terror and Their Implications for Child Socialisation

Antoinette Errante

*   *   *   *   *

Global Matters in Learning Bloody Revenge

Conflict-based solidarities should concern educators and child advocates worldwide because they are the "schools" wherein children learn bloody revenge, the idea that bloody, violent retaliation against a group or individual is *justified* and, generally, speaking, a defensive posture. The "us-against-them in the war-on-terror" ethos that has taken root in the USA as a result of the devastating losses sustained by the September 11, 2001, attack on the World Trade Center is an obvious example of conflict-based solidarity. Yet conflict-based solidarities insinuate themselves in the lives of children in many forms and with varying degrees of implicit or explicit violence. Gangs, hate groups, family feuds, playground cliques are all examples of potential conflict-based solidarities to the extent that the communion and sense of belonging that makes group membership so appealing requires the construction and maintenance of an enemy. Social scientists and psychologists have become fond of turning "other" into a verb; "othering" refers to the psychological, social and political phenomenon whereby we distinguish whom we are and with whom we are aligned by defining all outsiders as others. Conflict-based solidarities take this one step further because they require not only othering but a process of demonisation or dehumanisation of the groups that they define as "not us." Thus, some churches may distinguish members of their congregation from others based upon liturgy or beliefs, but this othering does not require them to take violent action upon others in order for their congregation to remain intact. Moreover, this form of othering is based upon a positive cultivation of in-group attitudes, values, belief and dispositions that gives the congregation a sense of pride and communion. Hate groups, on the other hand, maintain their bonds and their sense of pride on the basis of the violence they perpetrate against those they define as others as well as

the amount of energy they expend in constructing narratives that dehumanise, demonise or that otherwise place outsiders in an inferior position to themselves. Conflict-based groups' sense of identity and solidarity is actually an illusion, an empty narrative reflecting the displacement of their low sense of cohesiveness and belonging onto narratives regarding what *others* are and are not, rather than based on the positive cultivation of traits related to the "meaning of us."

Conflict-based solidarities impress themselves in the daily lives of children to the degree they dominate three different kinds of experiences: (1) modelled solidarity experiences are solidarities and discursive practices children observe in high status adults, including parents, teachers, political leaders, community leaders and sports or cultural icons; (2) lived solidarity experiences refer to the solidarities and discursive practices in which children personally engage in their daily lives, from their interactions in family systems, to interactions on school busses, at school, in the playground and during other extra-curricular activities; and (3) vicarious solidarity experiences include all situations and circumstances whereby children experience solidarities indirectly. Vicarious experiences occur through empathic identification or self-projection such as when we witness first-hand the real-life experience of others (e.g., South African children watching apartheid police brutality against adult Blacks) or when we identify with real-life or fictional experiences typically mediated by media and popular culture (e.g., an American youngster watching apartheid brutality on television or video games where "the hero" destroys dark, Arab-looking, enemies). Children's vicarious experiences through fantasy play enable them to project themselves into imagined scenarios. In an age of global technology, internet, video games, and MTV, children also experience vicariously through simulated play. Since children's play is also the ground where they often work out real-life conflicts and scenes, though, the content and schemata of fantasy and simulated play may actually attract children because they constitute more of a hyper-reality than the fiction we suppose them to.

Taken together, these three kinds of experiences frame the values, attitudes, ideals, dispositions and behaviours of solidarity that parents, communities, social movement leaders and the adults behind global information and cultural production offer up to children. When our collective energies offer children modelled, lived, and vicarious solidarity experiences in which doing bloody revenge trumps reconciliation and doing peace, then our daily practices become spaces for the generational transmission of hatred and revenge (Harkness, 1993; Post, 2000). Every modelled, lived, and vicarious solidarity experience we offer our children, in other words, is either teaching children to proliferate violence or to proliferate peace.

As feminist social critics might observe, the everyday experiences we offer to children is one important way in which the "personal becomes political." But the personal is also increasingly global: the personal standpoints which shape our political and social cognitions regarding violence and its proliferation have taken on a global dimension because the stage on which our modelled, lived and vicarious solidarity experiences are produced and disseminated is increasingly a global one. Globalisation is like a transport system defined by its capacity to rapidly shift and move the "sites" of people, identities, borders, ideologies, media, and commodities. Whether globalisation contributes to learning bloody revenge or learning peace depends upon the types of people, identities, borders, ideologies, media, commodities it is rapidly transporting.

But globalisation is not a neutral transport system, for its very dynamics reflect a host of hegemonic political, social, cultural, and economic forces that are contested at many "local" points on the global superhighway. For instance, borders are the symbolic and material means by which we delimit and construct identities of "us" versus "them" (Comaroff & Comaroff, 1992). In an increasingly globalised world order, where these borders are constantly shifting, our identities reveal themselves to be not only multiple and nested but also, inter-, intra- and transnational. Moreover, thanks to globalisation, bloody conflicts—and the meanings attributed to these—are no longer contained geographically; they can easily become inscribed in the people, ideas, movements that globalisation transports. Bloody conflicts worldwide therefore increasingly influence the identity borders children and youth construct for themselves, in terms of who they are, whom they are like and who their enemies are.

* * * * *

In the remaining portion of this paper, I will explore some of these questions with specific reference to cults of terror and counter-terror and their impact on the subsequent socialisation of children for violent conflict. Based upon an examination of the cross-national literature regarding the socialisation of children during protracted conflicts marked by cults of terror, I propose that the global-local dimensions of learning bloody revenge require that we understand the following: (1) the role that culture and psychology plays in learning bloody revenge; (2) the ways in which the socialisation context created by terror makes making up so hard to do; and (3) the persistent and global link between all forms of violence and gender socialisation, particularly prevailing conceptions of masculinity. Since global/local cultural dynamics tend to be mutually constitutive, the cross-cultural dynamics of gender socialisation and violent masculinities also illustrate the influence of an increasingly globalised media and youth culture on learning bloody revenge. Throughout, I will examine what the above literature suggests might be some of the long-term impact of the September 11, 2001, attack on the World Trade Center on the socialisation of children with respect to non-violent conflict resolution.

How and Why We Fight and Reconcile: The Role of Culture and Psychology in Learning Bloody Revenge

[...] Violence and the will to violence is not solely, or perhaps even primarily, perpetuated and reproduced in military manoeuvres, but in the cultural practices that constitute the quotidian (Wolfe, 1996; Krohn Hansen, 1997). If all our practices and dispositions are cultural acts, in the sense that they give expression to our underlying normative frameworks (Bourdieu, 1977; Cohen, 1985; Bruner, 1996), what could be more powerful as sources of our "world-of-meaning" (Avruch, Black, *et al.*, 1991) regarding violence than our practices of daily life? Through these practices, we become agents as well as objects of history, culture, and society.

As expressions of a community's normative framework, the practices of daily life can tell us a great deal regarding the conditions under which communities and individuals come to perceive the existence of a conflict, the values, attitudes, behaviours and dispositions they bring to the resolution of conflicts, and the degree and conditions under which they privilege peaceful or violent resolutions (Avruch, Black, et al., 1991; Wolfe & Yang, 1996). In the case of the September 11, 2001 attack on the World Trade Center, President Bush and his administration very early on delineated the grounds for the existence of a conflict by framing the incident as an attack designed to annihilate US civilisation. From this perspective, the conflict clock began ticking the moment the planes hit the towers. From this follows the belief that the incident was unprovoked and that therefore the US's military response was a defensive one or a counter-terrorist response. In contrast, parties not aligned with this perspective (subsequently framed in official discourse as enemies of the USA) hold very different notions regarding when the conflict clock began ticking and subsequently the justness or defensive nature of the US response. In either case, social movement leaders helped their followers make sense of the global/local, national/international forces surrounding this event in culturally meaningful terms. (e.g., "The enemy is a coward who wishes to destroy our civilisation of freedom and justice" versus "The attack was a strong response to counter US imperialism, which has for decades oppressed peoples around the world.") And just about "every side" argued that "God is on our side." Of course, cultural meaning systems are neither closed, nor monolithic; however, they do privilege certain narratives of conflict over others. Any group's narrative of conflict subsequently also tells us what that group believes is worth fighting for.

Whether to resolve a perceived conflict through violence or peaceful negotiation is also a matter of cultural practices, or what Ross (1993) calls a group's "socialisation templates"—that is, the historical and contemporary repertoire of attitudes, values, behaviours and dispositions available to a group regarding conflict and its resolution. Youth do not arbitrarily manifest certain responses to conflict and not others; rather, these are shaped by the discursive practices and behaviours inscribed in the modelled, lived and vicarious experiences of their daily lives. Youth will tend to adopt outlooks and dispositions that they view as status-conferring (Ember & Ember, 1994). Although these socialisation templates may change or privilege different values and dispositions regarding conflict at different moments in time, what these templates suggest is that beliefs, dispositions and responses to conflicts are socially constructed and the result of learned behaviour.

Culture-bound frameworks notwithstanding, if we compare the discursive practices of social movement leaders in the USA with those of social movement leaders sympathetic to Osama Bin Laden and Al-Qaeda, the message to their followers (and to the children and youth whom they might soon need to recruit) is eerily similar: (1) There is an enemy out there who wishes your annihilation and the annihilation of our way of life; (2) We are blameless victims of this evil perpetrator; (3) Because we are blameless, we must defend ourselves; (4) It is justifiable when we are blameless to retaliate violently against our enemy.

Constructed in culturally and socially meaningful ways, this kind of blamespeak is typical of discursive practices and normative frameworks that protract and justify violence (Bandura, 1990; Beattie & Doherty, 1995). Blamespeak may also derive from historical specificities. Nesbitt and Cohen (1996), for example, use a variety of historical, archival and experimental data to show how the southern "culture of honour" in the US has left a historical legacy of violent socialisation templates wherein violence is viewed as justifiable in response to an insult, to protect home and property, or to aid in socialising children. Across cultures, wherever there is blamespeak, there are likely to be socialisation templates that justify violence in certain contexts.

Blamespeak affects socialisation templates in two ways. First, it creates a conceptual category of "justifiable violence." In addition, where blamespeak is used,

it will influence children's burgeoning sense of themselves in relation to their in-groups and their outgroups. Blamespeak contributes to children formulating grandiose self-concepts in relation to their own identity and the groups with which they identify. Blamespeak will also influence the degree to which children formulate demonised dehumanised images of specific others.

Blamespeak thus tends to dominate discursive practices related to cults of terror and counter-terror. Unfortunately, these kinds of socialisation templates do not provide any party involved in a conflict with discursive practices or dispositions that would facilitate their resolving the violence. In order to not socialise the next generation to protract a violent conflict, blamespeak and its socialisation templates have to be somehow "overridden" by all parties and across children's modelled, lived and vicarious solidarity experiences. This requires that alternative high-status conciliatory socialisation templates exist and that the discursive practices of blamespeak are not prolonged. Unfortunately, as I will illustrate in a moment, the more the protracted the violence, the more likely it is that such conciliatory templates have had their status eroded, and in some cases, their very existence forgotten.

The reasons why blamespeak contributes to socialisation templates that tend to protract and proliferate violence become clearer if we examine the social and psychological dynamics of violent conflict. We cannot understand either peace or conflict without giving the study of social bonds their due, and for this the literature on the dynamics of shame is most helpful in explaining why—when under siege—we tend to form the bonds that we do. Shame comprises a family of emotions that are evoked when we perceive that acceptable social distances have been compromised (Retzinger, 1991). Although shame signals may be culture-bound, across cultures shame is evoked by feelings of disrespect or threats to one's dignity; threats to ideals that are important for one's self-definition are more shame-inducing than those that are not. Since shame enables us to assess when bonds are threatened, when acknowledged, it can be a mechanism for repairing social bonds, and therefore crucial to the peaceful resolution of conflict. This is what Braithwaite (1989) refers to as "reintegrative shame." By acknowledging our shame, we express our sense of loss, vulnerability or fallibility. When this manifestation of humanity occurs between conflicting individuals or groups, it can draw them closer by creating an atmosphere of negotiation which does not threaten the dignity of reconciling parties. Peace and reconciliation cannot occur without some form of reintegrative shame (Scheff, 1994; Errante, 1999).

The problem lies in the fact that we are mostly desperate to conceal our individual and collective shame precisely because it reveals these vulnerabilities. It is this unacknowledged shame that is at the base of most protracted conflicts (Coleman, 1985; Scheff & Retzinger, 1991). In these instances, shame is "by-passed" or transformed into more tolerable emotions such as anger, guilt or envy or is concealed under masks of defiance, indignance or superiority. When by-passed shame within individuals or groups begets by-passed shame between individuals or groups, it can quickly escalate from anger to rage to violence or "shame-rage spirals" (Scheff & Retzinger, 1991) where escalating levels of shame lead to escalating levels of rage. Blamespeak between conflicting parties is a good (if tame) example of a shame-rage spiral. In this sense, therefore, all conflict resolution strategies constitute shame management strategies.

If culture tells us when and how to get angry, shame dynamics tell us why individuals and groups get angry in the first place. Shame dynamics suggest that, rather than being opposites, violence and peace are ultimately both ways through which individuals and/or groups affirm their right to exist. Whether we choose violent or peaceful alternatives depends upon the repertoire of conflict resolution strategies available to us and the degree to which the context facilitates or puts a premium on some strategies and not others. In this sense, harmony is not necessarily synonymous with peace, nor is conflict necessarily synonymous with violence or even the lack of peace (Merry, 1987; Harrington & Merry, 1988; Nader, 1991). Rather, peace requires the existence of sanctioned forms of non-violent conflict resolution, for as the anti-apartheid struggle in South Africa demonstrated, when all peaceful means of protest are criminalised, oppressed groups are likely to turn to violent strategies (Ndebele, 1995).

Shame dynamics also underscore the relationship between the types of existing social bonds and the likelihood that conflict will erupt and be resolved violently. According to shame theories, peace is the cause and result of attunement, that is a healthy balance between individual identity and identification with group(s) (Scheff & Retzinger, 1991). Alienation can result from either under or over-identification with a group, or both. When individuals are too little attuned to groups, they experience alienation through isolation. But they can also experience alienation through hypersolidarity. While it may appear that one can never get enough of a seemingly good thing such as solidarity, hypersolidarity is actually the cause and result of engulfed bonds and fosters "bimodal alienation" (Scheff, 1994), whereby solidarity within a group is maintained by under-identification with all outgroups. The price of group membership is that members sacrifice any parts of themselves that do not conform to the values, attitudes, behaviours and dispositions of the group. Hypersolidarity, therefore, does not tolerate multiple group affiliations.

Hypersolidarity can help us understand the local/global dimensions of violent conflict. Weakened social bonds, which are experienced as alienation precede rather than follow conflict (Scheff, 1994): the greater the level of alienation/weak bonds, the greater the potential for violent protracted conflict. This is how we have traditionally explained interpersonal as well as international

conflicts. Campbell (1996) suggests how insecure bonds within communities can provoke conflict between communities; that is, how local conflicts turn global: "intolerance displayed in some communities which appear strongly bound together against a common adversary is evidence of an insecure base, which relies on mistrust and projection to keep boundaries intact" (p. 104). The greater the level of weakened social bonds within communities, the likelier they will respond to external threats to group cohesion (which subsequently are perceived by the group as constituting a "situation of conflict") through violent means. This is in part because, over time, the existing low levels of group cohesion have tended to privilege violent conflict resolution strategies within the community.

* * * * *

The historicity and evolution of a conflict subsequently affect the socialisation patterns passed down to children and youth. Most existing studies regarding the socialising causes and consequences of violence and war assume the existence of a pre-conflict society, with pre-conflict cultural and psychological dispositions. The "violent period" is constructed as an extraordinary incident in the total life of a community; this allows us to treat a violent period as a pathological event, and behaviours and dispositions under these circumstances as abnormal.

If we consider silent impasses as integral parts of extended conflicts, identifying a pre-conflict period may be difficult. In many societies worldwide, violence has been an integral part of their existence for generations. The nature of the conflicts may change (e.g., within groups/between groups) but the socialisation templates regarding conflict and its resolution appear relatively constant. We cannot, in other words, assume violence as an abnormal context for many children across the globe; rather violence has become normalised across children's modelled, lived and vicarious experiences of daily life. It is difficult to transmit non-violent socialisation templates once a group has forgotten what those are.

The challenge, then, is not only to understand how violence-based socialisation templates, and their concomitant cultures and psychologies, are normalised over time, but also how these might potentially manifest themselves over time. For instance, how is child and youth socialisation in moments of active conflict related to socialisation during silent impasses? Do silent impasses represent periods in which children learn alternative non-violent conflict resolution strategies or are they periods where violent behaviour normally directed toward the enemy is now displaced onto other contexts (such as family violence, drug abuse or criminality)? The cross-national evidence suggests the latter. I will illustrate this when I explore the local/global dimensions of gender socialisation and violent masculinities.

These, then, are the cultural and psychological factors that influence generally the socialisation contexts for violence or reconciliation across cultures. They are subsequently the socialisation templates communities pass on to their youth. Terrorism and cults of terror influence these socialisation contexts in specific ways.

The World That Terror Creates: Bloody Revenge and Why Making Up Is So Hard to Do

One of the distinguishing features of protracted conflicts, particularly those characterised by cults of terror, is that the very nature of these conflicts makes communities susceptible to social disintegration. As Kimmel (1988) notes citing Robert Jay Lifton's work, terror does this by "[severing] filaments of identity" by destabilising the daily practices and beliefs through which such identities are developed and sustained. Our sense of well-being and pride derives from our capacity to perform culturally sanctioned and status-conferring roles as parents, children, siblings, and citizens (Csikszentmihalyi, 1990). These roles do not exist in isolation but are part of a web of social networks through which a community expresses solidarity in daily life. The more cults of terror threaten these daily practices, the more acute our sense of alienation. Life becomes meaningless precisely because terrorism and cults of terror threaten our capacity to engage in the practices through which we make sense of our lives.

Communities will tend to defend themselves against external threats such as those presented by war or cults of terror by idealising their own community and vilifying and de-humanising outgroups or their so-called enemies. Such "splitting" helps communities and individuals mask the terror of group annihilation by providing a new cultural and psychological ground upon which to reconstruct the self and the group. Given that alienation precedes conflict, however, we can predict that community responses to cults of terror, that is, the degree to which acts of terror are interpreted as ones constituting a threat that requires violent retaliation, will also vary according to existing levels of social discord within communities, and the degree and manner in which this has influenced socialisation templates regarding the resolution of conflict.

* * * * *

In the case of communities already experiencing feelings of anomie before an external threat, these may even find the solidarity that splitting produces compelling and positive. Under hypersolidarity, even "acting normal" becomes a form of resistance to terror; it thus imbues a "normal" life that has perhaps lost meaning with a purpose. In the United States, for instance, public messages have been ubiquitous that charge: "don't let the terrorists win. Go on with your life." Even buying a car or going to the launderette, in this context, becomes a form of resistance to an external enemy.

The greater the sense of existing social disintegration, therefore, the more susceptible a group to hypersolidarity. Communities marked by weak bonds within may be more receptive to interpretative frameworks based on the construction and maintenance of an external enemy (Volkan, 1988). Consider, for instance, that US leaders framed the World Trade Center attack of September 11 as a battle and described an enemy even before they knew what or whom was involved. President Bush's remarks on September 12, 2001, framed the incident most explicitly and in a manner largely unquestioned by either media or public:

The deliberate and deadly attacks which were carried out yesterday against our country were more than acts of terror. They were acts of war. This will require our country to unite in steadfast determination and resolve. Freedom and democracy are under attack.

The American people need to know that we're facing a different enemy than we have ever faced. This enemy hides in shadows, and has no regard for human life. This is an enemy who preys on innocent and unsuspecting people, then runs for cover. But it won't be able to run for cover forever. This is an enemy that tries to hide. But it won't be able to hide forever. This is an enemy that thinks its harbours are safe. But they won't be safe forever.

This enemy attacked not just our people, but all freedom-loving people everywhere in the world. The United States of America will use all our resources to conquer this enemy. We will rally the world. We will be patient, we will be focused, and we will be steadfast in our determination.

This battle will take time and resolve. But make no mistake about it: we will win.

Thus, the initial templates offered to Americans for making sense of the overwhelming devastation and sense of loss they felt regarding the events of September 11 framed the incident as a conflict, a *battle*, in which "we"/Americans were the heroes and "they" and their allies/supporters were our enemies (whoever they were for we did not know who they were nor what they wanted when President Bush made this address). My point is neither to affirm nor contradict this framing of the incident. My point is to highlight the causes and consequences of framing events in this manner on the proliferation of violence.

US responses to this human tragedy and Americans' sense of external threat apparently produced pro-social responses typical of solidarity: Americans and their allies (the "we" in this case) lit candles and found a new font of spirituality. We brought food to strangers. We hugged one another, cried together, and saluted the flag together. Patriotic songs filled our airwaves and when we sang "I'm proud to be an American," we sang it with a new sense of conviction. In the midst of such tragedy, these acts were inspiring, perhaps even intoxicating.

These moments of solidarity and helping behaviours are not without precedent worldwide nor in the USA. They are frequently manifest after natural disasters (Eränen & Liebkind, 1993). And they were also behaviours

Americans exhibited after the Oklahoma City bombing by Timothy McVeigh. One might say that this kind of helping behaviour and solidarity is part of the US "cultural toolkit" (Swidler, 1986) and a socialisation template for responding to crisis.

What makes the responses to September 11, 2001, different is that these templates were engaged in a significantly different way. The framing of the events of September 11 as the result of a battle with an enemy produced a series of responses based upon hypersolidarity that should concern us precisely because they are so intoxicating even as they defend against the fear of annihilation. Authentic pride and attunement with one another in relation to a series of national values is only at the surface similar to terror-induced hypersolidarity, which is actually a mask for existing weak social bonds within communities. Hypersolidarity is, in other words, how cults of terror insinuate themselves into the cultural practices of daily life in countries throughout the world, and it is also how cults of terror are born and reproduced.

How Terror-Induced Hypersolidarity Undermines Reconciliation and the End of Terror

There are two factors that distinguish hypersolidarity from attunement, and they have as much to do with what conflict-based interpretative frameworks *leave out* as they do with what they *leave in*. One of the allures of hypersolidarity is its promise of the lack of ambivalence in unstable times: not only are there "good guys" and "bad guys," but they have already been identified for us. We need look no further for an explanation and a solution. Moreover, the explanation is one that counts "you" clearly amongst "the good guys." It is for this reason that people looking for connection and meaning, and an exalted sense of purpose that will alleviate their sense of alienation and aimlessness—such as those who joins gangs, cults, fundamentalist religious groups, and fraternities/sororities—are most vulnerable to hypersolidarity's allure (Hazani, 1993; Levine, 1999; Blazak, 2001). The greater our sense of aimlessness, the greater our intolerance of ambiguity and the more susceptible we are to charismatic leaders offering solutions, harmony, and a sense of purpose. The greater our intolerance of ambiguity, the greater our general distaste for dissent.

This intolerance of dissent is what distinguishes hypersolidarity from attunement. Hypersolidarity and its insistence on conformity requires and promotes amnesia. It makes us uncritical regarding the ways in which we frame our conflict-related experiences. Consider the ways in which hypersolidarity has affected the manner and degree to which the US or its allies have challenged the US leadership's framing of the events of September 11, 2001. On September 12, Secretary Rumsfeld announced that the terrorist attacks show a "new battlefield.... A different kind of conflict...." Let us for a moment suspend all that we believe about September 11. Why and how did we

come to frame the events of September 11 as an "act of war" which required a military response? What alternative ways of framing this incident were subsequently discarded? Although in the US, there were initial media reports regarding lapses in US intelligence, for instance, it would be a full year before any serious discussion was given to understanding/constructing the attack also as a case of malfeasance on the part of US intelligence. Moreover, we could challenge pro-Al-Qaeda groups with the same questions regarding their framing of the incident.

* * * * *

The allure of hypersolidarity during periods of conflict is precisely what makes it detrimental to conflict resolution and the consolidation of peace. Peace would require concessions, a loosening of our symbolic and material borders. Peace requires we give up our war-time idealised constructions of ourselves and the dehumanised constructions of our enemies. We would have to be willing to tolerate dissent, as well as accept group members with multiple and nested identities. We would have to be willing to give up our enemies, but this means also giving up the conflict-based identities that have come to define "us" as much as they have defined "them." Everything that made "us" "us" must now become undone.

* * * * *

If we engage in patterns of social interaction that encourage bi modal alienation, the transition from war to peace is not only painful—it amounts to a kind of individual and collective psychological suicide—for both us and our enemies. The danger is not only that we will not want these feelings of hypersolidarity to go away. The danger is that the psychological, cultural and economic underpinnings of hypersolidarity make it difficult to subvert—violence and conflict become both self-perpetuating and self-sustaining.

And so protracted violent conflict is sustained by weak social bonds within countries and between them—so that one responds to a situation which provokes shame with rage or humiliated fury, which provokes shame in the other, by-passed as rage or humiliated fury and so on. But if these shame-rage spirals represent the bare bones of violent and protracted conflict, they are supported by and articulated through the cultural practices and socialisation templates that are transformed/reconceptualised/and conceived in order to give dynamic expression to them. These would be the myriad practices and templates through which we express fury, grandiosity, indignation and pride, to name a few.

One of the most pervasive of these practices is masculinity itself. This takes us back to the beginning and to the question of existing normative frameworks and practices underlying the proliferation of violence across cultures. Increasingly, the cross-national literature suggests that if we want to teach peace, we are going to have to fundamentally rethink how we socialise boys and girls. Worldwide and at every level of social interaction there seems to be a dangerous fusion of violence with notions of masculinity. Violence as hypermasculinity has been further eroticised in popular culture. We socialise both boys and girls to be producers and consumers of violent masculinities (Grieg, Kimmel & Lang, 2000).

Boys Who Kill Turn Us On: Violence as Power in Hypermasculinities

Robin Morgan (1989/2001) documents the fascination worldwide with "the demon lover." She argues that we have eroticised war and killing to such a degree that the hypermasculine armed male who kills is "the man" that boys across cultures aspire to be, as well as the "the man" that most women secretly (or not) admire and are attracted to. In the weeks following the September 11, 2001, attack on the World Trade Center, if I had to classify the linguistic and paralinguistic cues of the state leaders and media commentators regarding the prospects of war, in the way that I do in my oral history work (Errante, 2000), my first "read" would have to be that their expressions were characterised by arousal. The media report that women consider Secretary Rumsfeld a sex symbol. *Vanity Fair* (2001) dedicated a front cover and an extensive portion of an issue to centrefold-like portraits of the "The War Room" in the White House. The US Republican party tried to use for fundraising purposes a glamorised picture of President Bush dealing with the aftermath of the September 11, 2001, attack on the World Trade Centre. Media commentators noted how "lucky" President Bush was to "get a war" during his Presidency as that would secure his legacy. If we hate war so much, why this fascination?

Certainly, if we consider the images of masculinity portrayed in blockbuster films made in the US and exported worldwide along with other forms of popular culture, the "demon lover" is well-represented (Donald, 1992; Gibson, 1994; Savran, 1996; Sparks, 1996; Hatty, 2000; Neroni, 2000; Scharer, 2001). Moreover, Hollywood has fulfilled its post-September 11, 2001, promise to contribute to the war against terrorism by releasing a series of war movies, which, movie moguls claim, Americans are "hungry for."

This response is noteworthy on two grounds. First, it is noteworthy for the direction Hollywood, as a representative/producer/transmitter of popular culture and thus potent agent of socialisation templates, did not take. For instance, Hollywood film executives chose not to contribute to the war on terrorism by contributing movies presenting alternative socialisation templates, such as movies about peace processes, or instances where violence was somehow averted. However, Hollywood's responses to the war on terrorism probably do indeed constitute responses to what Hollywood perceives the US (and by extension international) market is "hungry for"; that is, current socialisation templates regarding conflict and its

resolution. These movies might also defend against a collective masculinity wounded by the sense of vulnerability the September 11, 2001, attack on the World Trade Center provoked. By contrast, these movies tend to celebrate masculinity and heroic agency (Sparks, 1996) or in other ways portray heroic violence as a hallmark of manhood (Donald, 1992). What is troubling is that we know such media exposure to violence is increasingly linked directly to violent behaviours in boys (Hatty, 2000; Scharer, 2001). To the degree that power has been linked to violence in popular culture, this phenomenon is now spreading to violence in girls, although it tends to be a violence that is cultivated by the gender dynamics that hypermasculinities create (Arntz, 1998).

Popular culture thus not only represents but also further cultivates socialisation templates that conflate power, violence and masculinity worldwide. The dynamics regarding the role of popular cultures in the worldwide socialisation of youth for proliferation violent conflict are complex, and I am certainly not suggesting they are deterministic. Nevertheless, local and global popular cultural trends contribute to (or mitigate) the existing collective energies invested in teaching children bloody revenge. Violent behaviour is not the cause and result of one factor but of a broader "ecology" that supports it (Gilligan, 1996; Garbarino, 1999).

Worldwide, the personality traits leading to violent behaviour tend to be shame-based and more prevalent in boys and men (Gilligan, 1996; Garbarino, 1999). Their prevalence among boys and men can be traced to the ways in which we socialise boys (and, by extension, girls, see Gilligan, 1982 and Real, 2002). Whenever boys are raised in socialisation contexts that punish them for displaying emotions that do not conform to socially constructed notions of "manliness" (such as fear, shame, sadness, vulnerability), over time boys suppress these emotions before feeling their affects (Kaufman, 1992; Real, 2002). The result is psychic numbing and low empathy, which, when combined with other violence-prone socialisation factors, can prime males for brutality and violence (Bowker, 1998; Gilligan, 1996; Errante, 1999).

One of the main emotions that is defended against with hypermasculine violent behaviours is the fear of not being considered masculine enough (Bowker, 1998; Messerschmidt, 2000; Ramphele, 2000). Whenever men lose control or access to the material and symbolic goods through which they can affirm their (culturally and socially constructed) masculinities, if no alternative nonviolent and high-status templates of masculinities are offered to them, they may resort to violent behaviour.

Across cultures, economic and material well-being are particularly stable criteria of high-status masculinity. The globalising trends in media and popular culture have tended to converge images of the "manly man" with consumerist culture. Not surprisingly, therefore, across cultures we find that men defend against emasculation resulting from unemployment or their inability to purchase high-status material goods (that affirm their masculinities) by displaying and displacing power on to the bodies of women and children (Campbell, 1996; Anderson & Umberson, 2001). Indeed, male unemployment and gender-based violence has become a major focus of gender and development policy worldwide (Mokwena, 1991; Cornwall & White, 2000; Ramphele, 2000). That this link between material well-being and violence is gendered can be seen in the fact that chronic stress due to physical abuse in children is linked only to unemployment in fathers (Martinez & Richters, 1993).

In addition to unemployment, other challenges to masculinity have also been expressed directly as sexual violence in the American schoolyard (Messerschmidt, 2000); amongst former militarised South African youths who were unable to make the post-apartheid transition (Mokwena, 1991); in Serbian nationalism (Bracewell, 2000) and Irish nationalism (Aretxaga, 1998).

Violent masculinities have also more broadly been linked with nationalist ideologies in the former Yugoslavia (Papic, 1994; Sofo-Sypros, 1996), "masculine Hinduism" among the Shiv Sena in India (Banerjee, 1999), Sikhs (Mahmood, 1996), Northern Ireland (Bairner, 2001), South Africa (Ramphele, 2000) and in conflicts between Israelis and Palestinians (Peteet, 1994). Gender-related anomie can also create the kind of apocalyptic thinking that we are increasingly beginning to identify with suicidal terrorism (Hazani, 1993; Hoffman, 1995; Jurgensmeyer, 2000). In this world of suicidal terrorism, all revenge is just and preferably bloody. Conflicts are not resolved but eliminated.

* * * * *

The fusion of violence and masculinity enables us to glimpse at the links across terrorism, political violence and structural violence, that is, inequality across and within nations. Violent conflict reproduces and is reproduced by conceptions of masculinity that sanction, ennoble and eroticise bloody revenge in domestic quarrels and international disputes alike. What we need are culturally and socially constructed socialisation templates that put a premium on non-violent masculinities.

Conclusion: Where in the World Do Children Learn Bloody Revenge?

The danger of engaging in violent conflicts is that the cultural, social and psychological templates such conflicts create often survive long after conflicts apparently subside. These templates become part of the "cultural toolkit" (Swidler, 1986) from which societies pull their conflict resolution strategies. And so, even if we could "win" our war against terrorism tomorrow, the kinds of internal practices and beliefs that have begun to take root as a result—such as xenophobia, exhalation of the military, tolerance for the suppression of civil liberties, intolerance for ambivalence and a righteous attitude toward responding to violence with violence—will linger. These behaviours, dispositions and practices constitute some of the societal challenges to post-war transitions. For the child who was born and raised in a situation of high conflict—what constitutes normal? For a child soldier who has secured all his basic needs with his gun and his willingness to use it—what skills does he bring to the post-conflict transition?

And lest we not see American children in this scenario, consider the proliferation of war movies and the rhetoric of the use of violence for a "just cause," stir in the military heroes placed before them, and add all this to the existing practices and artefacts of violence: guns and video games. Hypersolidarity's intolerance of dissent makes us less likely to challenge the erosion of non-violent strategies and their importance for child socialisation.

Perhaps we have tended not to look at the impact of bloody conflict on the subsequent socialisation of children as a global issue because we want to believe that if the cause is just, children will learn about justice and not violence. But every society believes that their part in a bloody conflict is just; children growing up in cultures marked by violence do not escape unscathed in terms of what they learn about violence as a source of power over others simply because the society in which they live believes their cause to be just. This perception ignores the fact that growing up in a context of bloody revenge tends to teach children that violence is a just and power-full response to conflict in the global order. Moreover, the degree to which international conflicts influence children's perceptions that violence is a highly sanctioned form of conflict resolution also affect and can be affected by the degrees to which violent conflict resolution is already sanctioned within societies. In the end, whether we feel "our causes" are just or not, whether "we" started "it" first or not, all violent conflicts tend to foster attitudes, values and behaviours in youth that tend to protract rather than resolve violent conflict. Cumulatively these trends normalise terror. And cumulatively, in the USA and other apparently "peaceful" societies, they are contributing to the formation of our own brand of militarised youth.

References

Anderson, K. L. & Umberson, D. (2001). Gendering Violence: Masculinity and Power in Men's Accounts of Domestic Violence. *Gender and Society*, 15(3), pp. 358–380.

Aretxaga, B. (1998) What the Border Hides: Partition and the Gender Politics of Irish Nationalism. *Social Analysis*, 42(1), 16–32.

Arntz, S. (1998) *Sex, Power and the Violent School Girl*. New York: Teachers College Press.

Avruch, K., Black, P. *et al.* (Eds.) (1991) *Conflict Resolution: Cross-cultural Perspectives*. New York: Greenwood Press.

Bairner, A. (2001) Gender, Class and Nation. *Peace Review* 13(1), pp. 21–26.

Bandura, A. (1990) Mechanisms of Moral Disengagement, in: W. Reich (Ed.) *Origins of Terrorism: Psychologies, Ideologies, Theologies, States of Mind*. New York: Cambridge University Press, pp. 161–191.

Banerjee, S. (1999) Warriors in Politics: Religious Nationalism, Masculine Hinduism and the Shiv Sena in Bombay. *Women in Politics*, 20(3), pp. 1–26.

Beattie, G. & Doherty, K. (1995) "I Saw What Really Happened": The Discursive Construction of Victims and Perpetrators in Firsthand Accounts of Paramilitary Violence in Northern Ireland. *Journal of Language and Social Psychology*, 14(4), pp. 408–433.

Blazak, R. (2001) White Boys to Terrorist Men: Target Recruitment of Nazi Skinheads. *American Behavioral Scientist*, 44(6), pp. 982–1000.

Bourdieu, P. (1977) *Outline of a Theory of Practice*. Cambridge: Cambridge University Press.

Bowker, L. H. (Ed.) (1998) *Masculinities and Violence*. Thousand Oaks, CA: Sage.

Bracewell, W. (2000) Rape in Kosovo: Masculinity and Serbian Nationalism. *Nations and Nationalism*, 6(4), pp. 563–590.

Braithwaite, J. (1989) *Crime, Shame and Reintegration*. Cambridge: Cambridge University Press.

Bruner, J. (1986) *Actual Minds, Possible Worlds*. Cambridge, MA: Harvard University Press.

Bruner, J. (1996) *The Culture of Education*. Cambridge, MA: Harvard University Press.

Campbell, B. (1996) Gender Crisis and Community, in: S. Kraemer & J. Roberts (Eds.) *The Politics of Attachment: Towards a Secure Society*. New York: Free Association Books, pp. 102–109.

Cohen, A.P. (1985) *The Symbolic Construction of Community*. London: Routledge.

Coleman, M. (1985) Shame: A Powerful Underlying Factor in War and Violence. *Journal of Psychoanalytic Anthropology*, 8(Winter), pp. 67–79.

Comaroff, J. & Comaroff, J. (1992) *Ethnography and the Historical Imagination*. Boulder, CO: Westview Press.

Cornwall, A. & White, S.C. (2000) Men, Masculinities and Development: Politics, Policies and Practice. *IDS Bulletin*, 31(2), pp. 1–6.

Csikszentmihalyi, M. (1990) *Flow: The Psychology of Optimal Experience*. New York: Harper & Row.

Donald, R. (1992) Masculinity and Machismo in Hollywood's War Films, in: S. Craig (Ed.) *Men, Masculinity and the Media*. Thousand Oaks, CA: Sage, pp. 124–136.

Ember, C. & Ember, M. (1994) War, Socialization and Interpersonal Violence: A Cross-Cultural Study. *The Journal of Conflict Resolution*, 38(4), pp. 620–646.

Eränen, L. & Liebkind, K. (1993) Coping with Disaster: The Helping Behavior of Communities and Individuals, in: J.P. Wilson & B. Raphael (Eds.) *International Handbook of Traumatic Stress Syndromes*. New York: Plenum Press, pp. 957–964.

Errante, A. (1999) Peace Work as Grief Work in Mozambique and South Africa: Post-conflict Communities as Context for Child and Youth Socialization. *Peace and Conflict: Journal of Peace Psychology*, 5(3), pp. 261–279.

Errante, A. (2000) But Sometimes You're Not Part of the Story: Oral Histories and Ways of Remembering and Telling. *Educational Researcher*, 29(2), pp. 16–27.

Garbarino, J. (1999) Lost Boys: *Why Our Sons Turn Violent and How We Can Save Them*. New York: Free Press.

Gibson, J.W. (1994) *Warrior Dreams: Violence and Manhood in Post-Vietnam America*. New York: Hill & Wang.

Gilligan, C. (1982) *In a Different Voice: Psychological Theory and Women's Development*. Cambridge: Harvard University Press.

Gilligan, J. (1996) *Violence: Our Deadly Epidemic and Its Causes*. New York: Grosset/Putnam Books.

Greig, A., Kimmel, M. & Lang, J. (2000). *Men, Masculinities and Development: Broadening Our Work towards Gender Equality* (Gender in Development Monograph Series #10): UNDP.

Harkness, L.L. (1993) Transgenerational Transmission of War-Related Trauma, in: J.P. Wilson & B. Raphael (Eds.) *International Handbook of Traumatic Stress Syndromes*. New York: Plenum Press, pp. 635–643.

Harrington, C. & Merry, S. (1988) Ideological Production: The Making of Community Mediation. *Law and Society Review*, 22, pp. 709–735.

Hatty, S. (2000) *Masculinities, Violence and Culture*. Thousand Oaks, CA: Sage.

Hazani, M. (1993) Sacrificial Immortality: Toward a Theory of Suicidal Terrorism and Related Phenomenon, in: L.B. Boyer & R.M. Boyer (Eds.) *The Psychoanalytic Study of Society, Vol. 18: Essays in Honor of Alan Dundes*. Hillsdale, NJ: Analytic Press, pp. 415–442.

Hoffman, B. (1995) "Holy Terror": The Implications of Terrorism Motivated by a Religious Imperative. *Studies in Conflict and Terrorism*, 18(4), pp. 271–284.

Jurgensmeyer, M. (2000) *Terror in the Mind of God: The Global Rise of Religious Violence*. Berkeley: University of California Press.

Kaufman, G. (1992) *Shame: The Power of Caring*. Rochester, Vermont: Schenkman Books.

Kimmel, M.S. (1988) Prophet of Survival. *Psychology Today*, June, pp. 45–48.

Krohn Hansen, C. (1997) The Anthropology and Ethnography of Political Violence. *Journal of Peace Research*, 34(2), pp. 233–240.

Levine, S. (1999) Youth in Terrorist Groups, Gangs and Cults: The Allure, the Animus, and the Alienation. *Psychiatric Annals*, 29(6), pp. 342–349.

Mahmood, C.K. (1996) Why Sikhs Fight, in: A.W. Wolfe & H. Yang (Eds.) *Anthropological Contributions to Conflict Resolution*. Athens: University of Georgia Press, pp. 11–30.

Martinez, P. & Righters, J.E. (1993) The NIMH Community Violence Project: II. Children's Distress Symptoms Associated with Violence Exposure. *Psychiatry*, 56(February), pp. 22–35.

Merry, S. (1987) Disputing without Culture. *Harvard Law Review* 100, pp. 2057–2073.

Messerschmidt, J.W. (2000) Becoming "Real Men": Adolescent Masculinity Challenges and Sexual Violence. *Men and Masculinities* 2(3), pp. 286–307.

Mokwena, S. (1991) *The Era of Jackrollers: Contextualising the Rise of Youth Gangs in Soweto.* Johannesburg: Center for the Study of Violence and Reconciliation.

Morgan, R. (1989/2001) *The Demon Lover: The Roots of Terrorism.* New York: Washington Square Press.

Nader, L. (1991) Harmony Models and the Construction of the Law, in: K. Avruch, P. Black & J. Scimecca (Eds.) *Conflict Resolution: Cross-cultural Perspectives.* New York: Greenwood Press, pp. 41–59.

Ndebele, N. (1995) Recovering Childhood: Children in South African National Reconstruction. *Children and the Politics of Culture.* Princeton, New Jersey: Princeton University Press, pp. 321–334.

Neroni, H. L. (2000) The Men of Columbine: Violence and Masculinity in American Culture and Film. *Journal for the Psychoanalysis of Culture and Society,* 5(2), pp. 256–263.

Nesbitt, R.E. & Cohen, D. (1996) *Culture of Honor: The Psychology of Violence in the South.* Boulder, CO: Westview Press.

Papic, Z. (1994) Nationalism, Patriarchy and War in ex-Yugoslavia. *Women's History Review,* 3(1), pp. 115–117.

Peteet, J. (1994) Male Gender and Rituals of Resistance in the Palestinian Intifada: A Cultural Politics of Violence. *American Ethnologist,* 21, pp. 31–49.

Post, J.M. (2000) Terrorist on Trial: The Context of Political Crime. *Journal of the American Academy of Psychiatry and the Law,* 28(2), pp. 171–178.

Ramphele, M. (2000) Teach Me How to Be a Man: An Exploration of the Definition of Masculinity, in: V. Das, A. Kleinman, M. Ramphele & P. Reynolds (Eds.) *Violence and Subjectivity.* Berkeley, CA: University of California Press, pp. 102–130.

Real, T. (2002) *How Can I Get through to You?* New York: Scribner.

Retzinger, M.S. (1991) *Violent Emotions: Shame and Rage in Marital Quarrels.* Newbury Park, CA: Sage.

Ross, M.H. (1993) *The Culture of Conflict: Interpretations and Interests in Comparative Perspective.* New Haven, CT: Yale University Press.

Savran, D. (1996) The Sadomasochist in the Closet: White Masculinity and the Culture of Victimization. *Differences,* 8(2), pp. 127–152.

Scharer, E. (2001) Men, Muscles and Machismo: The Relationship between Television Violence Exposure and Aggression and Hostility in the Presence of Hypermasculinity. *Media Psychology,* 3(2), pp. 159–188.

Scheff, T. (1994) *Bloody Revenge: Emotions, Nationalism and War.* Boulder, CO: Westview Press.

Scheff, T.J. & Retzinger, S.M. (1991) *Emotions and Violence: Shame and Rage in Destructive Conflicts.* Lexington, MA: Lexington Books.

Sofos-Spyros, A. (1996) Inter-ethnic Violence and Gendered Constructions of Ethnicity in Former Yugoslavia. *Social Identities,* 2(1), pp. 73–91.

Sparks, R. (1996) Masculinity and Heroism in the Hollywood "Blockbuster": The Culture Industry and Contemporary Images of Crime and Law Enforcement. *British Journal of Criminology,* 36(3), pp. 348–360.

Swidler, A. (1986) Culture in Action: Symbols and Strategies. *American Sociological Review,* 51, pp. 273–286.

Volkan, V.D. (1988) The Need to Have Enemies and Allies: From Clinical Practice to International Relationship. New York: James Aronson.

Wolfe, A.W. (1996) Contributions of Anthropology to Conflict Resolution, in: A.W. Wolfe and H. Yang (Eds.) *Anthropological Contributions to Conflict Resolution.* Athens: University of Georgia Press, pp. 1–10.

Wolfe, A.W. & Yang, H. (Eds.) (1996) *Anthropological Contributions to Conflict Resolution.* Athens: University of Georgia Press.

CHAPTER 11
Preserving a Vital and Valued Self in the Face of AIDS

KENT L. SANDSTROM

During the past decade sociologists have focused increased attention on the lived experience of HIV disease. Much of their research has concentrated on how persons with HIV disease cope with and counteract stigma (Sandstrom, 1990; Siegel and Krauss, 1991; Weitz, 1991), experience and manage uncertainty (Weitz, 1989), negotiate sexual relationships (Sandstrom, 1996a), utilize doctors and medical resources (Kayal, 1993; Weitz, 1991), build support networks (Sandstrom, 1996b), and, more generally, reconstruct their lives and selves (Adam, 1996; Kotarba and Lang, 1986; Sandstrom, 1990, 1996a, 1998; Weitz, 1991). In addressing these themes, sociologists have insightfully revealed many of the central challenges confronted by persons with HIV disease. However, they have not yet delineated the distinctive challenges to self encountered by people with HIV in the twilight of their moral career—that is, when developing serious AIDS-related complications and facing the prospects of profound debilitation and impending death.

This paper attempts to address this gap in the literature by examining the existential challenges that men with AIDS experience during the final phases of their illness career. These challenges include (1) how to come to terms with debilitating symptoms and a diminishing future; (2) how to offset the threats posed by suffering, dependence, and dying; and (3) how to construct and solidify identities that extend beyond death.

In exploring these issues, this paper extends the sociological literature on illness, death, and dying in a couple of important ways. First, it illustrates some of the most prominent identity dilemmas encountered by men grappling with advanced symptoms of a terminal illness. As Kathy Charmaz (1994, p. 269) has noted, identity dilemmas "include the knotty problems and hard decisions" that emerge as seriously ill people "experience trials, tribulations, and transitions that affect who they are and who they can become." In accord with Charmaz's emphases, this paper highlights the trials, tribulations, and transitions that shape the self-images and identity constructions of men with AIDS, particularly as they come to grips with dying and death.

In addition to this, the paper reveals how men with AIDS construct post-mortal identities and sustain a sense of symbolic immortality (Lifton, 1978) as they enter the

final period of their lives. Through focusing on this phenomenon, the paper offers insight into how people with terminal illnesses fashion enduring selves and futures and, in this process, gain a sense of control and transcendence over death as an ultimate limit. This is an important aspect of their unfolding "moral experience" (Goffman, 1961).

Along with contributing to the sociological literature in the above ways, this paper illustrates and extends the theoretical insights of symbolic interactionism. Symbolic interactionism provides an especially illuminating framework for examining how men with AIDS define themselves and their illness, because it accentuates the processual, interactive, and interpretive dimensions of human experience and selfhood. Following Mead (1934) and Blumer (1969), interactionists assume that (1) people act toward things, including things like AIDS, based on the meanings that those things have for them; (2) the meanings of things are not inherent but rather derive from processes of social and self-interaction (Denzin, 1983, 1989a; Durig, 1996); (3) meanings have a fluid and mutable quality; and (4) people construct lines of action not only in terms of the meanings they give to objects or events around them or to their internal experiences but also in terms of the meanings they give to themselves. In fact, in fashioning ongoing social acts, the "self" is often the most central and meaningful social object that they take into account (Blumer, 1969; Stryker, 1980).

Guided by these assumptions, a symbolic interactionist analysis of the experience of men with AIDS focuses significant attention on how they construct meanings for self in light of the unfolding implications of their illness. In a related vein, it also emphasizes how these men's images of self are affected by their visions of and expectations for the future, and vice versa. As implied in the writings of many interactionists, people construct images of self not only in terms of the past and present, but also in terms of their anticipation of the future (Charmaz, 1991; Corbin and Strauss, 1987; Mead, 1934; Markus and Nurius, 1986; Strauss, 1993). Building upon this premise, this paper examines and portrays how the self-images and identity constructions of men with AIDS both influence and become influenced by their visions of the future, particularly as their illness enters its latter stages.

Finally, in adopting a symbolic interactionist perspective, this paper accentuates how men with AIDS, like all human beings, are actors rather than reactors; that is, they are active agents who, because of their ability to use symbols and engage in self-interaction, do not merely react to the physical and social ramifications of their illness. Instead, they have the capacity to creatively act toward their health situation, to negotiate and transform the meanings attributed to it, and, correspondingly, to exercise a measure of control over its consequences for self (Sandstrom 1990).

Methodology

This study draws on interview data from an availability sample of twenty-one men diagnosed with AIDS [....]

The men interviewed in this study ranged in age from 20 to 56; six were in their 20s; eight were in their 30s; six were in their 40s; and one was in his 50s. The vast majority were White; the only two non-Whites were African American. Fifteen of the twenty-one men had become infected with HIV through having sex with other men. Thirteen of these men identified themselves as gay, while the other two described themselves as bisexual. Among the remaining six men, three had contracted HIV through injection drug use, two had contracted it through sex with infected women, and one had contracted it through blood products he received as a hemophiliac.

All of the men in this study had developed AIDS-related opportunistic infections, such as Kaposi's sarcoma (KS), pneumocystic carinii pneumonia (PCI), oytomegalovirus (CMV), toxoplasmosis, neuropathy, tuberculosis, or dementia. Eighteen of the twenty-one men were suffering from advanced and disabling AIDS-related symptoms during the time that they were interviewed. The remaining three men were comparatively healthy, but they had experienced debilitating and potentially fatal AIDS symptoms in the past.

Everyone in the study was interviewed on at least two occasions, because the interview process was lengthy (an average of four hours), and illness or fatigue made it difficult to talk for more than a couple of hours at a time [....]

All of the interviews were audiotaped and transcribed. In analyzing the interview transcripts, I employed the "grounded theory" approach elaborated by Charmaz (1990) and Glaser and Strauss (1967). In accord with this approach, I began to analyze transcript data during the early stages of interviewing, identifying the central themes and categories which emerged from respondents' statements. After each interview, I adjusted the interview schedule to focus more closely on these emerging themes and categories. When the interview process was completed, I utilized, reorganized, and further developed these themes and categories to form the structure of this paper. Most importantly, throughout the process of data collection and analysis, I tried to stay close to the meanings of the individuals interviewed while also framing these meanings within the theoretical perspective of symbolic interactionism.

Challenges to Self Encountered in the Twilight of the AIDS Career

In the earlier phases of their illness, men with HIV/AIDS struggle most centrally with issues of stigma and uncertainty (Sandstrom, 1990, 1996a; Weitz, 1989, 1991). They worry about how, whether, or when to disclose their health status and how to address or counteract the threat of devaluation it poses. They also worry about the unpredictable aspects of their HIV infection, such as when it will provoke serious symptoms, what specific symptoms will arise, what treatments will be available for these symptoms, and how both the symptoms and treatments will disrupt their everyday lives.

As their illness unfolds and advances to its latter stages, the concerns of men with HIV/AIDS begin to change. Stigma becomes a less salient issue for them as their social contacts become more restricted and they surround themselves with a trusted and supportive network of others. In addition to this, their struggles with uncertainty diminish. In fact, men with AIDS feel as anguished about the certainties that accompany their advancing illness as the uncertainties, particularly certainties such as debilitating symptoms and a rapidly diminishing future.

Coming to Terms with Debilitation and a Shrinking Future

As they grapple with advanced health complications, men with AIDS find it increasingly difficult to manage their illness and preserve an identity apart from it. They discover that they can no longer contain the disease, as they had in the past, by closely monitoring their health practices and reducing their social involvements. Instead, AIDS becomes a defining feature of their lives—it fills their days and compels them to reorder their priorities, activities, and self-conceptions.

In many cases, AIDS triggers or exacerbates symptoms of unyielding fatigue, pain, indigestion, or diarrhea. These symptoms, in turn, evoke feelings of frustration and demoralization in affected men, as highlighted by one of my informants, Peter,[1] when he remarked: "I'm sick and tired of being sick and tired! I really am. I'm sick and tired all the time, you know. That's the hard part about this damn disease—there's such a constancy to it."

As time passes, men with AIDS no longer experience many good days, or periods of restored health, that offer them respite and renewal. Their lives become a litany of bad days—periods marked by continuous sickness and a profound sense of devitalization.[2] As Neil, who had lived with AIDS for over five years, described: "I just feel kind of dragged out. I have a lot of days like that now ... I just feel dragged out, tired, and icky. I don't even have those real good days that I used to have in the middle of bad ones. It's just fatigue, fatigue, fatigue all the time!"

In addition to being plagued by debilitating physical symptoms, men with AIDS may suffer from impaired mental functioning, such as disorientation, memory loss, dementia, and a general slowing of cognitive processes (see also Weitz 1989). These manifestations of their illness, of course, also limit their activities and disrupt their images of self and the future.

In light of the bodily changes they experience, men with AIDS often feel as if they have grown old prematurely. They recognize that they must deal with the same types of symptoms, feelings, and challenges as their aging relatives. As Peter observed:

I feel like it [life with AIDS] is similar to being old! My grandmother and I—we are on the same physical level. She's seventy-nine and I'm thirty-nine but it's like we're dealing with the same kind of problems. You know, I could very, very easily be treated as a geriatric patient and it would be proper care. And when my grandmother complains to me, my final line is "Yeah, look at it, I have all the same problems you do and I'm forty years younger ...." I really do feel more related to being old in that sense—more than to having AIDS actually. Because all the symptoms just make you old! And you even look old! ... Looking at me is the same as looking at my grandmother, but she's seventy-eight years old! And she's got these aches and pains and ... bad days, just like me.

*　　*　　*　　*　　*

Generally speaking, as their health worsens, men with AIDS—like many elderly people—struggle to come to terms with the threats posed by their diminishing capacities and futures. In addressing these threats, they find it difficult to rely upon the strategies they had adopted in previous phases of their illness, such as maintaining a positive outlook and accentuating the empowering ramifications of life with HIV (Kayal, 1993; Sandstrom, 1990; Weitz, 1991). Instead, these men develop and utilize other adaptive strategies which help them to sustain a sense of control, vitality, and self-value in their daily bouts with advanced illness. One of these strategies is to stop thinking much about the future, as Neil revealed:

I don't look into the future very much anymore because even though I know some good things will come along I anticipate that it's going to get harder and worse. I don't know, from what I've been able to see with other people it doesn't get better. Or, it stays the same, which doesn't offer me much to look forward to either.

As they wrestle with severe manifestations of their illness, men with AIDS become absorbed in the present and try to suppress thoughts of their prospective health situation.

When asked, "What do you see as you think about your health in the future?" the men I interviewed typically gave a variation of the following response: "I don't really see much. I try not to think about it. I guess I'm probably going to get even more sick and die .... So, I just live day to day."

By choosing to "live one day at a time," men with AIDS derive a greater sense of control in the present and find new sources of personal satisfaction and fulfillment. Many start to notice and appreciate the beauty of little things happening around them and vivid feelings arising within them. Most crucially, through anchoring themselves in an intense present (Charmaz, 1991), these men discover a rejuvenating sense of joy, vitality, and transcendence, as reflected in the following excerpts:

You know, I just feel blessed for each day, really—for the sun, the trees, everything. I just feel like I have a more intense experience of life. Yeah, there's times for me when it even comes off as feeling high—like a high from drugs or something like that, except it's not from that. It's just from being so immersed in life—there's a high in that for me .... When I got really sick and truly realized that I had a limited amount of time left to live, I started to look at things differently. All of a sudden each new day was precious to me—it was a gift that offered special surprises. I started to see and experience each moment as sacred, at least in some respects.

When living in the intense present, men with AIDS experience not only a revitalizing sense of joy and transcendence, but also a heightened sense of urgency—urgency to act, take risks, experience things, build new or stronger relationships, and, in their own words, "make the most of the opportunity each new day presents." In addition to this, these men often feel an urgency to complete unfinished business. Given their health situation, they realize that they have a limited future, and they feel motivated to achieve something meaningful while they still can. For example, when reflecting upon how his ongoing health problems affected the goals he set for self, Greg asserted:

I have this kind of, like, drive underneath about, you know, accomplishing something .... I feel like, "Yeah, I should be doing this, I should be doing that." ... There's still other things, more things I want to accomplish— like, I have a couple of research and writing projects I want to get finished and published. Although I, you know, make sure I do things to build my self-esteem and take care of myself daily, there are still like some big things that I would like to do.

*　　*　　*　　*　　*

Nevertheless, while advancing illness and a heightened sense of finitude give men with AIDS greater incentive to make and pursue plans for their future, this becomes extremely challenging when they suffer from debilitating (and sometimes erratic) symptoms. These symptoms make it virtually impossible for them to formulate and follow through on long-range plans. The plans they do make are usually tentative or short-term in nature and hinge upon how they feel on a given day, as Vic observed when discussing how he plans for the future:

I kind of wait till the last minute. I'll say, "Well, I don't know if I can handle that or not. We'll see." Like, there's, um, well, someone's doing a campout at the end of May [about four weeks away]. And I think I'm just going to wait till the last minute to decide. I'll see how my energy level is. Maybe I can do that, maybe not. We'll see. So in a sense, in a general sense, my plans for the future are a little more uncertain and ... a little more immediate.

In an effort to maximize their flexibility in planning, many men with AIDS work out tacit agreements with lovers, friends, or family members which allow them to easily change or cancel any plans that they make. They rely upon these intimate others to understand that plans or outings depend upon their fluctuating health situation.

Along with limiting the abilities of men with AIDS to plan, seriously debilitating symptoms alter their goals for self. As their health deteriorates and they become more disabled, these men have much greater difficulty imagining themselves pursuing new ambitions, roles, or identities. In light of this, they begin to set more immediate and tangible goals. Through attaining these goals, they can sustain a sense of accomplishment and self-worth. Kirby alluded to this when he reported:

I try to set goals that I can deal with physically. Right now I'm finishing my basement—putting up some Sheetrock. And I just say, "I'll get a couple of pieces of Sheetrock on the wall today. And then I'll sit back and enjoy that—enjoy having some kind of accomplishment.

Overall, the men who suffer from severe AIDS-related complications orient themselves toward attaining smaller-scale goals, such as exercising regularly, going on outings with friends, attending special parties or events, working on household projects, and, more generally, "taking time to do and appreciate little things." By pursuing and attaining these modest goals, they sustain a sense of mastery and control in their daily battles with debilitating symptoms. In doing so, they experience the self-worth that derives from engaging in efficacious action—action that gives one a sense of being "on top of" rather than merely "up to" the challenges that life poses (Brissett, 1972).

Confronting the Threats of Suffering, Dependence, and Dying

As their illness advances and their symptoms become more ominous, men with AIDS struggle to come to grips with their prospective mortality. Yet the threat of mortality is not usually the source of their greatest concerns. When reflecting upon the future, they commonly stress the pain, suffering, and debilitation they are likely to endure as they near the end of their lives. In fact, the men I interviewed felt far more afraid of the dying process than of death itself. When describing their anxieties regarding the future, they shared comments such as the following:

I'm not afraid of death and what happens after death, I'm more afraid of the transition—it's going from here to there, dying, that's the scary part .... The fears that I have connected with it [the future] are to physical pain. I mean death hasn't and doesn't particularly scare me. It's the pain leading up to death that scares me .... I've been fairly close to death, but it just doesn't bother me .... I guess if anything bothers me it's having to go back to the hospital and go through all those procedures—like having a lung biopsy without anesthesia. That's not fun .... Stuff like that is what I don't want to go through again—the pain and discomfort.

In addition to fearing the prospect of pain and suffering, men with AIDS feel concerned about the possibility of losing many of their mental capacities, especially those capacities that are integral to their sense of self. As Lenny remarked:

It worries me that I might lose my full faculties—my mental faculties. That is one of my major worries. Because I pride myself in being intelligent and rational—and being in control. Yeah, so that is a scary thing for me. And, um, I know it could happen. I mean, I've gone from having an excellent memory to only having an okay memory and things like that. That's been hard to deal with.

Of course, those men who have already experienced symptoms of disorientation or dementia feel particularly anxious about further deterioration of their mental abilities.

At the same time that they grapple with these fears, men with AIDS worry about the prospect of losing valued physical capacities, such as their ability to walk or move around easily. They also feel troubled about losing their sexual capabilities and dealing with the changes this will evoke in their intimate relationships and identities.[3] As Neil indicated:

As I've gotten more sick I've wondered about how much longer I'll be able to be sexual. I mean, over the last few months my sexual functioning has just gone downhill. It's hard for me to get excited and, uh, to have sex, especially with my chronic fatigue. Sex takes a lot of energy—it wipes me out for a couple of days. And that doesn't feel very satisfying! But I know it's still important for [my lover]. I just worry about what's going to happen when I get even more sick. I mean, it's gonna get to the point where I'm not going to be able to have sex with him. So then what will happen? How will I feel about that? And how will he react?

As they come to terms with the decline taking place in their bodies and minds, men with AIDS feel especially concerned about the challenges they will face when they become more dependent on others. On one level, they worry about how they will preserve a sense of autonomy, masculinity, and self when they suffer from serious debilitation and have to give others more control over their lives. As Ron observed:

I was thinking lately that if I become an invalid and have to be taken care of all the time, uh, I'd rather kill myself. That's part of dealing with getting really sick—dealing with how am I going to be taken care of or take care of myself. I mean, you know, it's like a progression of giving up your independence, which is, uh, an important part of your manhood. I mean, first of all, you deal with the humility about being sick and then the humility of having to depend on other people .... And then when you talk about becoming an invalid, it's like a process of giving up control—giving up control of, uh ... your identity.

On another level, men with AIDS worry about the burdens they will impose upon their caregivers in the last phases of the disease. Some men hope that they can avoid having relatives, particularly older parents, serve as their primary caregivers. [...]

* * * * *

In an effort to deal with these concerns and gain a greater sense of control over their future, men with AIDS usually make arrangements that specify who will care for them and how they should be cared for if or when they become incapacitated. Some make plans for their lovers, spouses, or close relatives to serve as key caregivers because they are most likely or willing persons to serve in this role. Other men, however, make arrangements to receive caregiving assistance from a variety of others—friends, partners, parents, siblings, hospice volunteers, visiting nurses, and other medical specialists—so that they will not overly burden any one person. These men hope to delegate the responsibilities of caregiving so that no one will feel overwhelmed by and resentful about the tasks involved. Dennis reflected the sentiments of those adopting this approach when he remarked, "It's a major burden for one person to have to do—to have to go through—being a primary caregiver. So you have to spread the load out a little bit."

Along with planning for their future care, men with AIDS make arrangements which are designed to enhance their control over the process of dying. For instance, Rick planned to end his life when his symptoms progressed to the point where he had no real hope for recovery. He expected to make this choice in the near future because of the dramatic loss of vision and energy he had recently suffered. When reflecting upon the future, he stated:

I am a firm believer in self-deliverance, or in what some people call voluntary death .... You know, there's a time when you've just got to say "good-bye," and when that time comes for me, I'll be ready to do it. Other people might try to hang on and hang on, you know, [through] life support and artificial resuscitation. I think that's ridiculous .... I don't want to just hang on and depend on someone else to make decisions for me. I want to have some control over the process. So when the time comes and I've become debilitated and my quality of life has diminished, you know, to an extremely low point, then I'll be ready to perform self-deliverance.

More commonly, men with AIDS exercise control over their dying process by arranging to die a natural death rather than relying upon doctors to make decisions about their health care. They do this in a variety of ways, including filling out living wills which prevent physicians from taking extraordinary measures to prolong their lives (Weitz, 1991) and assigning durable power of attorney to loved ones who agree to let them "die with dignity" if they become incapacitated and lose the ability to make their own decisions.

Finally, another way that men with AIDS gain a greater measure of control over their dying and future is through making advanced funeral and burial arrangements, and indicating what types of rituals, memorials, or celebrations they want friends and family to observe.

While discovering ways to gain control over their dying and death is important for men with AIDS, they also devote their energies to sustaining a sense of hope for the future. Some do this by making plans to fulfill lifelong dreams such as finishing treasured projects or traveling to places they had always wanted to see. Others remain hopeful through focusing on the dramatic resurgences of health that they (or their friends) have experienced in the past. Still others derive ongoing hope from the possibility that a medical cure will arrive on the scene before their health deteriorates further. In support of this possibility, they point to the major advances that have taken place in HIV-related medical knowledge and treatments during the past decade. As Alan suggested when discussing his hopes for ongoing survival:

Well, they have come up with medicines, more helpful medicines, you know ... And as they come up with better combinations, maybe they can treat me in time. Because I'm still physically intact, you know—my hearing is good, my eyesight is good, and, um, you know, some of the worst things that happen to people I haven't experienced yet. So it's kind of like if they could arrest the virus right now, I could get back into being a normal, healthy person.

In addition to these strategies, men with AIDS often find hope for the future through prayer and spirituality. As a result of their prayers and spiritual beliefs, they feel better able to cope with their suffering and prospective death. Although their spirituality does not always offer immediate benefits, it helps them to feel more hopeful in coming to terms with the future, as Hal revealed:

My spirituality gives me hope. I don't know if it sustains me all the time. There's times when it doesn't feel like it's doing a damn bit of good. But that's okay, it doesn't have to. I don't think that's what spirituality is about. Um, it's just kind of something that helps me in getting through, you know, getting through the days and what lies ahead.

Yet another strategy that men with AIDS use to sustain hope is focusing on the possibility that they will die a relatively painless and serene death. Usually, they recognize this possibility after seeing a friend or lover have such an experience. For instance, Stuart emphasized how a number of his friends with AIDS had "felt a sense of peace and serenity as their lives drew to a close" and "had come to accept and welcome death." In turn, he anticipated that he could have a similar experience as he underwent the last stages of the dying process.

Transcending Death: Building a Post-mortal Self

As symbolic interactionist theorists have emphasized, individuals coming to terms with terminal illnesses face the task of making sense of their dying and making sense of themselves as dying persons (Lofland, 1978; Marshall, 1975, 1980). In doing so, they commonly try to give redemptive meaning to their lives and to sustain a sense of personal continuity, often by "accentuating portions of their personal histories for which they wish to be remembered" (Unruh, 1983, p. 342). They also strive to gain a measure of control over the final chapters of their lives and over their post-mortal future. This struggle for control becomes integrally related to their struggle for meaning and continuity. By effectively legitimating or making sense of their unfolding biographies and prospective deaths, terminally ill individuals can gain an enhanced sense of control (Marshall, 1980). In fact, through giving redemptive meaning to their lives and deaths, and through defining death as a positive transition for self rather than as a cessation of self, they can gain mastery over it as an ultimate limit. In essence, they can transcend death, at least symbolically (Becker, 1975).

As they become increasingly cognizant of their prospective deaths, people with terminal illnesses often experience an "epiphany" (Denzin, 1989b)—an existential crisis that challenges or disrupts their fundamental meaning structures and self-understandings. In turn, they begin to reshape their sense of self, linking and anchoring it to what comes after death (Charmaz, 1991). In many cases this involves them in efforts to construct or experience an immortal self, or what some analysts call the "postself" (Lifton, 1967; Schmidt and Leonard, 1986). Through building and becoming anchored in a viable postself, dying individuals find a way to sustain a sense of hope and vitality in their daily lives. They also solidify and preserve important identities and assure themselves that their lives have had or will have an enduring meaning and purpose.

As they come to terms with their prospective deaths, men with AIDS, like others dealing with terminal illness, engage in efforts to anchor their sense of self in a post-mortal future. Those struggling with life-threatening symptoms, such as the men in this study, are especially inclined to devote themselves to the construction of a post-self. They do this in a number of ways. (See Table 11.1 for a summary of the various strategies these men use to fashion postselves.)

In some cases, men with AIDS focus their energies on maintaining close and caring personal relationships in the hope that after dying they will "be remembered as someone who reached out and did little things for other people." They may also dedicate themselves to collecting artifacts or to writing journals that will be passed on to friends, family, or the wider public. They hope that this will allow their experiences or "stories" to live on in the memories of others.

In addition to using these strategies, many of the men I interviewed anchored a postself, or sense of symbolic immortality (Lifton, 1978), in the enduring contributions they had made through their work as artists, writers, teachers, carpenters, businesspeople, or medical specialists. Several also stressed the "legacy" they would leave as a result of their efforts as HIV/AIDS educators and volunteers or as leaders of the gay community. For instance, Hal and Lee emphasized the significant impact they had made through combating homophobia and promoting HIV-related education and support programs in the small towns where they had lived. Others, such as Bob, Dave, and Jay, accentuated how they made a lasting difference through speaking publicly about HIV-related issues, as highlighted in the following excerpt:

I get up in front of crowds of people and say, "Hey I'm a human being and I have feelings just like you. And I hope that you never find yourself in the same position that I'm in .... I talk about all the things that have happened to me—about getting fired from my job and watching my friends die. And I do it in a way that moves them—that gets them to think more deeply about things and, um, that helps them to focus on their common humanness with me—with us, with people with HIV."

As they come to terms with their finitude, men with AIDS not only construct an enduring self in terms of the legacies they will leave behind, they also anchor a sense of continuity in beliefs that they will live on spiritually after dying. In discussing their future and prospective death, my informants shared remarks that illustrated how their religious beliefs, or spiritual outlooks, provided them with a basis for building and sustaining an immortal self. As Curtis remarked:

Table 11.1: **Strategies Used to Construct Valued Post-Selves**	
Strategies	**No. of interviewees utilizing[a]**
Sustaining close personal relationships to be remembered as a caring person	9
Passing on personal mementos or journals	6
Highlighting enduring vocational accomplishments	12
Stressing significant volunteer accomplishments (especially AIDS-related education and advocacy)	11
Embracing visions of a spiritual afterlife	16[b]
Linking the AIDS self to enduring social and historical dramas	4

[a] Many of the men I interviewed used more than one of these strategies in building and sustaining a post-self. As a result, the sum total of the numbers listed in the right column of the table is larger than the sample size of twenty-one men.

[b] The men in this study embraced three different types of visions of a spiritual afterlife. Four men believed in reincarnation, three men believed in traditional Christian visions of bodily resurrection, and nine men believed that their spirit or "life force" would continue on in some way after they died.

I think my spirituality is very tied to that—to giving me a sense of living on. I don't think there would be any religion or spirituality if people didn't die, you know. And personally, yeah, it's important in coming to terms with that, um, with living on and what that means.

Drawing upon religious or spiritual frameworks, the men I interviewed often saw death as a transition to a new realm of being rather than as an ending to their personal existence. Although some accepted traditional Christian views of the afterlife, most espoused alternative views because of the anti-gay, anti-drug, or anti-sex messages conveyed by many variants of Christian theology. Rather than thinking of the afterlife in terms of Heaven and Hell, they typically embraced philosophies that emphasize how one's life force continues on in a never ending spiritual journey.

Overall, belief in an afterlife offers men with AIDS an important basis of hope and continuity regarding their present and future. By drawing upon these beliefs, they can solidify and preserve their sense of "real self" (Turner, 1976) and anchor it in a future beyond death. This makes the prospect of death less ominous and frightening. Moreover, rather than viewing death as the ultimate loss of self, they redefine it as an opening to new experiences and, implicitly, to an enhanced or transformed self. This conception of death is reflected in the following remarks shared by Trent:

Death is the very thing that makes it possible for us to transcend—the means by which we transcend. It just opens up more and more possibilities and opportunities for wholeness and for unity with God or the Godhead, whatever we might identify as that.

Given their sense of being trapped in a devitalizing present, men with AIDS who embrace this view even look forward to death, at least on one level, because of the new life they anticipate having afterward. Although they feel somewhat fearful of the dying process, they also feel, as Dennis noted, "excited to move on to the new adventure and wonderful possibilities offered in the hereafter."

Yet, while belief in an afterlife can foster feelings of hope and anticipation regarding the future, it can also evoke feelings of anxiety and uncertainty. For instance, Matt and Vic, who accepted traditional Christian conceptions of the afterlife, worried about what would happen after they died. As Matt remarked, "I wonder whether I'll be shoveling coal in one place or pushing clouds in the other." In a related vein, those men who believed in reincarnation also wondered whether their future lives would be more or less rewarding than their present ones. [...]

*　　*　　*　　*　　*

As noted above, the men I interviewed rarely embraced or expressed traditional Christian views when it came to their images of the afterlife and of a post-mortal self. At times, however, they drew upon variants of Christianity in their efforts to immortalize the self and to give both redemptive meaning and social significance to their experiences as persons living with AIDS. For instance, Jay utilized Catholic imagery in defining people with AIDS as part of a "litany of saints" who, in suffering, embodied Christ. As he explained:

I believe, like Mother Teresa says, that those who suffer the most—they're like Jesus. The more you suffer, the closer you are to the face of Jesus. She talks about that imagery—how when she reaches to the beggar, the leper, the dying person in the street, that that is Jesus .... She says, "That person is Jesus in a distressing disguise." And I believe that people with AIDS, in the quality of suffering they endure, become—like others who suffer—most like Christ.

By defining the experience of people with AIDS (and, implicitly, his own experience) in this way, Jay not only gave it a redemptive and transcendent meaning, he also connected it to an overarching legacy and an unfolding sociohistorical drama. In fact, he suggested that people with AIDS had a prophetic historical role to play. They were being "called or chosen to convey a message to others about what was happening around them." In elaborating, Jay asserted:

> I think that people with AIDS have an amazing role to play in history. There's so many messages that have been conveyed and arc yet to be conveyed—about the disease and what it means for the planet and how we live. There's so much we can learn from this, and I think people with AIDS can be like modern-day prophets. That doesn't mean other people can't be prophetic, too. There are many people in other situations who have that ability as well, but I think AIDS is, uh, is prophetic just because of its connection with sexuality and, um, life-giving things. It reflects the whole paradigm of planetary illness and how Mother Earth is hurting—and when any living, breathing organism is hurting, what happens sooner or later is disease results. And AIDS is an example of that.

Most importantly, by connecting the experience of people with AIDS to larger religious themes and social dramas, Jay legitimized his own illness experience and gained a sense that it had a redeeming, significant, and enduring purpose.

Discussion

This paper has focused on the identity dilemmas and changes that men with AIDS experience in the twilight of their moral career. In so doing, it has revealed the strategies these men use to sustain a sense of control, value, and continuity in the face of the threats posed by their advancing illness. In addressing these themes, this paper has highlighted how men with AIDS construct goats for and images of self in terms of their expectations for the future. For instance, as their immediate future looks more ominous, men with AIDS typically engage in efforts to build and affirm post-mortal selves. In many cases, they do this by emphasizing the legacies they will leave behind through their community involvements, job accomplishments, creative activities, or personal relationships. In addition to this, men with AIDS frequently anchor post-mortal selves in visions of an afterlife—a life where they will be freed from current constraints and will experience a transformed or enhanced self. Ultimately, regardless of how they construct and embrace post-mortal

selves, men with AIDS gain a measure of control and transcendence over their prospective deaths by doing so. They also derive a sense of hope, vitality, and continuity that helps them in their ongoing struggles to cope with the implications of their advanced illness.

In exploring these dynamics, this paper has illustrated the merits of the symbolic interactionist premise that coming to terms with the future is a central aspect of the experience of chronically and terminally ill persons (Charmaz, 1991; Corbin and Strauss, 1987). At the same time, this paper has refined and extended the insights of symbolic interactionism by demonstrating how terminally ill people construct identities and lines of action not only in terms of their prospective earthly future but also in terms of a post-mortal future. Through making this contribution, the paper has highlighted an important but relatively neglected aspect of the identity work and moral experience of people with serious illnesses. In the process, it has shared findings and analyses that broaden previous interactionist-oriented approaches to identity work and moral experience—including the approach formulated by Erving Goffman.

In examining the social dynamics that surround mental illness and stigma, Goffman (1961, 1963) revealed the moral nature of the events and relationships that blend together to form a unifying theme of lived experience for discredited individuals. However, he did this in a way that emphasized the institutional and relational, rather than phenomenological, features of moral experience. Goffman stressed how specific contexts and interactions produce stigmatized individuals and influence their ongoing identity negotiations and enactments. In his related analyses, Goffman rarely included the words or self-understandings of the people he studied and, thus, did not provide an "insider's view" into their identity constructions or moral experience (Sandstrom 1996a). This paper, on the other hand, accentuates the interpretations and self-understandings of the individuals who serve as the focus of its analyses—that is, men living with AIDS. The paper draws heavily upon the words and voices of these men to reveal how they define themselves and their futures in the face of their advancing illness, how they fashion related identities, and how these identities enable them to sustain a sense of social value and symbolic continuity. Through highlighting these themes, this paper extends Goffman's conception of moral experience, focusing greater attention on the phenomenological dimensions of this experience, especially those dimensions that go beyond issues of stigma, information control, and interactional tension.

Notes

This article is a revised version of a paper presented at the 1997 meeting of the Midwest Sociological Society, held in Des Moines, Iowa. The research was supported in part by grants from the Graduate School and the College of Social and Behavioral Sciences at the University of Northern Iowa. The author wishes to thank Sampson Lee Blair, Dennis Brissett, Alexander Durig, Gary Alar Fine, Bob Fulton, Vicki Kessler, Ron Roberts, and the anonymous reviewers of *Sociological Inquiry* for their helpful comments.

1 All of the names used in this paper are pseudonyms.

2 This discussion draws upon the cogent observations offered by Kathy Charmaz (1991) in her analyses of the lived experience of persons with serious chronic illness.

3 For a more detailed discussion of the sexual self-changes and challenges evoked by AIDS, see Sandstrom 1996a.

References

Adam, Barry. 1996. *Experiencing HIV*. New York: Columbia University Press.

Becker, Ernest. 1975. *The Denial of Death*. New York: Free Press.

Blumer, Herbert 1969. *Symbolic Interactionism*. Englewood Cliffs, NJ: Prentice-Hall.

Brissett, Dennis. 1972. "Toward a Clarification of Self-Esteem." *Psychiatry* 35:255–63. Charmaz, Kathy. 1994. "Identity Dilemmas of Chronically Ill Men." *Sociological Quarterly* 35:269–88.

_____. 1991. *Good Days, Bad Days: The Self in Chronic Illness and Time*. New Brunswick, NJ Rutgers University Press.

_____. 1990. "'Discovering' Chronic Illness: Using Grounded Theory." *Social Science and Medicine* 30:1161–72.

Corbin, Juliet, and Anselm Strauss. 1987. "Accompaniments of Chronic Illness: Changes in Body Self, Biography and Biographical Time." Pp. 249–82 in *Research in the Sociology of Health Care*, vol. 6 (The Experience and Management of Chronic Illness), edited by J. Roth and P. Conrad. Greenwich, CT: JAI Press.

Denzin, Norman. 1989a. *Interpretive Interactionism*. Beverly Hills, CA: Sage.

_____. 1989b. *Interpretive Biography*. Beverly Hills, CA: Sage.

_____. 1983. "A Note on Emotionality, Self, and Interaction." *American Journal of Sociology* 89:402–8.

Durig, Alexander. 1996. *Autism and the Crisis of Meaning*. Sarasota Springs, NY: SUNY Press.

Glaser, Barney, and Anselm Strauss. 1967. *The Discovery of Grounded Theory*. Chicago: Aldine.

Goffman, Erving. 1963. *Stigma*. Englewood Cliffs, NJ: Prentice-Hall.

_____. 1961. *Asylums*. Garden City, NY: Anchor Books.

Kayal, Philip. 1993. *Bearing Witness: Gay Men's Health Crisis and the Politics of AIDS*. Boulder, CO: Westview Press.

Kotarba, Joseph, and Norris Lang. 1986. "Gay Lifestyle Change and AIDS Preventive Health Care. Pp. 127–43 in *The Social Dimensions of AIDS: Method and Theory*, edited by D. Feldman and T. Johnson. New York: Praeger.

Liflon, Robert Jay. 1978. *The Broken Connection*. New York: Basic Books.

_____. 1967. *Death in Life: Survivors of Hiroshima*. New York: Random House.

Lofland, Lyn. 1978. *The Craft of Dying: The Modern Face of Death*. Beverly Hills, CA: Sage.

Markus, Hazel, and P. Nurius. 1986. "Possible Selves." *American Psychologist* 41:954–69.

Marshall, Victor. 1980. *Last Chapters: A Sociology of Aging and Dying*. Monterey, CA: Brooks/Cole.

_____. 1975. "Age and Awareness of Finitude in Developmental Gerontology." *Omega* 6:113–21.

Mead, George Herbert. 1934. *Mind, Self, and Society*. Chicago: University of Chicago Press.

Sandstrom, Kent. 1998. "Coming to Terms with Bodily Losses and Disruptions Evoked by AIDS." *Illness, Crisis, and Loss* 48:17–31.

_____. 1996a. "Redefining Sex and Intimacy: The Sexual Self-images, Outlooks, and Relationships of Gay Men Living with HIV Disease." *Symbolic Interaction* 19:241–62.

_____. 1996b. "Searching for Information, Understanding, and Self-Value: The Utilization of Peer Support Groups by Gay Men Living with HIV/AIDS." *Social Work in Health Care* 23:51–74.

_____. 1990. "Confronting Deadly Disease: The Drama of Identity Construction among Gay Men with AIDS." *Journal of Contemporary Ethnography* 19:271–94.

Schmidt, Raymond, and W. Leonard II. 1986. "Immortalizing the Self through Sport." *American Journal of Sociology* 91:1088–111.

Siegel, K., and B. Krauss. 1991. "Living with HIV Infection: Adaptive Tasks of Seropositive Gay men." *Journal of Health and Social Behavior* 32:17–31.

Strauss, Anselm. 1993. *Continuing Permutations of Action*. New York: Aldine de Gruyter.

Stryker, Sheldon. 1980. *Symbolic Interactionism: A Social Structural Version*. Menlo Park, CA: Benjamin Publications.

Turner, Ralph. 1976. "The Real Self: From Institution to Impulse." *American Journal of Sociology* 81:989–1016.

Unruh, David. 1983. "Death and Personal History: Strategies of Identity Preservation." *Social Problems* 30:340–51.

Weitz, Rose. 1991. *Life with AIDS*. New Brunswick, NJ: Rutgers University Press.

_____. 1989. "Uncertainty and the Lives of Persons with AIDS." *Journal of Health and Social Behavior* 30:270–81.

SECTION
2B Culture

CHAPTER 12
Pretty in Ink:
Conformity, Resistance, and Negotiation in Women's Tattooing

MICHAEL ATKINSON

Introduction

In this article, tattoos are analyzed as embodied signifiers of gender. More specifically, I tap into critical feminist and profeminist research on the body, and Elias and Scotson's theory of established/outsider social relationships (Elias & Scotson, 1965), to argue that women's tattoos are layered with culturally established, resistant, and negotiated images of femininity. Through the examination of 40 Canadian women's tattoo narratives, a critical investigation of how bodies are encoded with cultural messages about femininity is offered. Emphasis is given to both the intended (encoded) messages about gender embedded in tattoos by female wearers and the established cultural codes about "appropriate" gender display that influence how tattoos are decoded by audiences.

Theoretical Underpinnings

*   *   *   *   *

One of the most neglected areas within research on tattooing is women's involvement in the practice. As tattooing has long been associated with masculinity, only a handful of researchers have attended to issues in the cultural construction and expression of femininity through tattooing (Atkinson, 2001; DeMello, 2000; Mifflin, 1997; Sanders, 1991; Wroblewski, 1992). When issues related to femininity have figured into analyses of tattooing, emphasis is principally directed toward how acquiring tattoos can significantly jeopardise a woman's femininity. For example, Steward (1990, p. 127) classified North American women who have participated in tattooing as "tramps," "dykes," and "farm wives." Adopting the position that women who choose to mark their bodies with tattoos wilfully violate existing norms about gender, links have been made between tattooing and the "fallen" or overtly masculine woman (Gray, 1994). In a similar way, recent research has focussed on (and perhaps overemphasized) the liberating nature of tattoos for women, as marking the body with tattoos immediately connotes a significant violation of feminine body practice (cf. DeMello, 2000; Mifflin, 1997; Vale & Juno, 1989).

Although information gleaned from existing research illuminates a series of relevant questions pertinent to women's tattooing, we ultimately know very little about how tattoos are actively constructed and experienced by women—especially in the Canadian context, as no empirical research has been conducted on Canadian women's experiences with tattoos save for the partial analyses provided by Atkinson (2001), and Atkinson and Young (2001). In order to pursue a more theoretically stimulating and empirically informed account of Canadian women's tattooing experiences (as theoretical understandings of tattooing have been largely constructed around men's experiences with the body project), several concepts central in feminist and profeminist research on the body are worth (re)consideration.

Feminisms, Bodies, and Tattooing

Building largely upon the works of Foucault (1977, 1979, 1980) and other poststructuralists, feminist researchers have illustrated how hegemonic masculine authority in Western cultures is partly maintained through the active biological (i.e., medical) and social (i.e., norms, values, beliefs) control of women's bodies (Balsamo, 1996; Davis, 1994; Haug, 1987; Nicholson, 1990). In these processes, women's bodies become socially constructed, monitored, and regulated in accordance with a dominant image of the "feminine body" as thin yet curvy, placid yet playful, sexy yet wholesome. In describing the female body as a "text of culture," Bordo (1989) wrote:

Through the pursuit of an ever-changing, homogenising, elusive ideal of femininity—a pursuit without a terminus, a resting point, requiring that women constantly attend to minute and often whimsical changes in fashion—bodies become what Foucault calls "docile bodies"—bodies whose forces and energies are habituated to external regulation, subjection, transformation, and improvement. (p. 14)

Bordo (1989) maintained that socially accepted women's body projects such as breast augmentation or excessive dieting are best viewed as caricatured expressions of dominant ideals of the female body, because these body projects express traditional images of the female body (and women's marginalized positions within social structures that produce them) in excess (Bordo, 1989, 1993; Davis, 1997; Miller & Penz, 1991). Central in the feminist literature is, then, the relationship between body modification and social structures of power/authority:

> It is no coincidence that this sexual ideal (of the slim, soft, innocent body) is an image which connotes powerlessness. Admittedly, the actual ideal is not of a demure, classically "feminine" girl per se, but a vigorous and immature adolescent … it is not a shape which suggests power. (Coward, 1985, p. 41)

In order to conceptually synthesise the pioneering work of feminist scholars in this area, we may draw upon Elias and Scotson's process-sociological understanding of "established" and "outsider" figurational relationships (Elias & Scotson, 1965). Elias and Scotson (1965) principally argued that community life is moulded around the relationships between established and outsider social groups. Elias and Scotson (1965) inferred a model of figurational dynamics that takes into account the distribution of power chances between and within a series of mutually identified social groups. Established social groups are those that are more deeply embedded in both the base and superstructural segments of a figuration—typically because they have a longer history there, and/or greater access to resources (e.g., material, cultural, political, and educational) in the figuration—and consequently control key ideological state apparatuses (Elias & Scotson, 1965). Established groups have considerable ability to influence the construction of social laws, promulgate cultural norms, and promote collective ways of interpreting social rituals, such as body modification practices.

Conversely, outsider groups are more marginal members of a figuration, less embedded in power positions, and socially/culturally dominated (in varying degrees) on the basis of their marginalized statuses and associated roles. Outsiders are generally excluded from participation in socially influential power structures within a figuration, and as a result, their social opportunities and cultural experiences are often "given" to them (or interpretively configured) by members of established groups. Thus, what is deemed to be acceptable for an outsider to participate in as a form of social interchange or cultural expression is restricted in accordance with established conventions and practices (including, e.g., how to modify one's body). To break established rank and violate cultural idiom within a figuration by transgressing established norms can be risky social practice for an outsider, as it may warrant social contempt or some other control response (Elias & Scotson, 1965).

Jibing, then, with the more central principles of Elias' work on civilizing processes in Western cultures (Elias, 1983, 1991, 1994, 1996)—and feminist research on body projects more generally—Elias and Scotson (1965) revealed how social standards (including norms of acceptable bodily display) protect the vested interests of established groups, such as a figurational patriarchy.

Feminist and process-sociological researchers have argued that body projects can accomplish more than the simple reproduction of established gender codes. That is, although many have inspected body projects that reaffirm and reproduce established images of the beautiful female body, the study of how body projects can be used by outsiders to resist established cultural ideology is equally germane. For example, Maguire and Mansfield (1998) suggested that the "unnatural" strength cultivated by women who participate in aerobic exercise breeds both a physical and a social power that challenges the established masculine hegemony. By poaching an established male body practice (i.e., athletic exercise) women challenge the gender order. Through the study of radical forms of cosmetic manipulation, Davis (1997) illustrated how women contest established cultural codes by engaging in certain types of "gender appropriate" plastic surgery to the extreme, and in the process, excessively embrace the images and practices of the socially marginalized. These theatrical body modifications are vulgar or "grotesque" (Bakhtin, 1984) in comparison to established images of the beautiful woman.

* * * * *

Method

Data were collected during a 3-year participant observation-based study of tattoo enthusiasm in Canada. During the research, I spent over 400 hours "hanging out" with tattoo artists and their clients in various tattoo studios—mainly in the cities of Calgary (AB) and Toronto (ON). Through the research process I interacted with hundreds of tattoo enthusiasts, and eventually approached 92 of them to ask if they would be willing to be interviewed. Although both men and women were interviewed in the study, data discussed here pertain to the women I interviewed about their tattoo body projects.

* * * * *

In total, 40 women were interviewed. Although the group of interviewees initially developed as a convenience sample, I eventually targeted several categories of tattoo enthusiasts for interview purposes, including women with different socioeconomic backgrounds, ethnic affiliations, religious beliefs, and sexual or lifestyle preferences. Furthermore, I sought out women with assorted levels of involvement in the practice—in reference to how long they had been tattooed (in years); how many tattoos they had acquired (total number); how many times they had been tattooed (number of sittings or total number of hours); and, how extensively they had been tattooed (amount of skin covered by tattoos and locations of tattoos on the body).

* * * * *

It is interesting that my being a male researcher seemed to stimulate a heightened degree of exchange about the subject of gender and tattooing. I found that in sharing stories about our social experiences with tattoos, the interviews became lively discussions geared toward dissecting how gender is central in framing one's interpretations of tattoos. Being able to relate to the women as fellow tattoo enthusiasts, but discussing our lived experiences with tattooed skin from different gender standpoints, became central in developing a grounded understanding of how tattoos are constructed along gender lines. Stories about, and theoretical interpretations of, women's tattooing presented in this article have been assembled as a result of these "active" conversations. Although a degree of theoretical and conceptual abstraction is undertaken in order to cull the women's tattoo narratives around the theme of gender, my overarching goal is to present their gendered understandings of tattooing by using their own terms and categories.

Results

* * * * *

Established Conformity and Women's Tattooing

As critical feminists have suggested (Sanford, 1992; Wolf, 1990), established North American standards of feminine beauty tend to produce passive female bodies. The established female form is not a physical shape (i.e., we may think of the quintessential runway model or beauty pageant contestant as the ideal-type) that demands social attention for its foreboding, powerful, or authoritarian stature. Whereas masculinity is partially achieved through the corporeal display of strength, aggression, risk-taking, and the ability to withstand pain and injury (cf. Sabo, 1986; Young, 1993; Young & White, 1995), preferred understandings of femininity consider such display among women as repugnant. As a result, established feminine body projects (which, ironically, are often rife with pain) highlight the docility of women's bodies.

For many of the women I interviewed, attending to the body as a communicative symbol of established femininity is everyday ritual. Common body projects such as applying make-up; blow-drying, colouring, or fixing one's hair; wearing dresses or skirts; exercising at the gym; dieting; and of course, shopping for body modification projects, are clearly ingrained in the gendered habitus (Elias, 1994). In the process of linking body

ritual to one's social status as a feminine woman, many women's tattooing projects are performances of established femininity. In this study, almost two-thirds (25, 62%) of the women I interviewed conformed to established constructions of femininity through their tattooing projects. This was initially evident in portions of their tattoo narratives that detailed the "pre-tattoo enthusiast stage," in which the women were debating whether or not to partake in the body project:

I couldn't decide whether or not I was going to get tattooed. One of the main reasons was that, I dunno, I guess I never thought it looked lady-like. And all the guys I knew, were like, "you want to do *what*?" They looked at me like I was crazy … But then I started talking about getting a string of roses tattooed across my lower back, right at the top of my butt. I think it looks sexy, and so do all my male friends. Like, when you go out with a high-cut t-shirt on, and low-rise jeans, you can see it really well, and it looks great. I've got a pretty flat stomach too, and when I'm dressed up in the right clothes it makes my body look killer. (Janine, age 22)

As confirmed by Janine and 16 (40%) of the other women I interviewed, by taking into account how men would decode the tattooing project as a signifier of femininity, some women enter into the process only if it will homologically complement their established feminine body projects.

On these grounds and others, established female body projects are not simply the embodiment of diffuse cultural constructions of femininity, they are acts of consent to the underlying structures of figurational power distribution that help create such established images of femininity (cf. Bordo, 1993; Ellman, 1993; Gillespie, 1996). The ongoing self-monitoring of one's daily physical regimen and preferences for body modification, as part of "doing gender," help reproduce relational structures of authority and power between established and outsider gender groups. As a vital part of social organization within a figuration, these seemingly banal cultural rituals translate into justifications for and confirmations of the ways in which social statuses and roles are hierarchically divided along gender lines (Chernin, 1983; Sanford, 1992). This was clearly evidenced in Celeste's (age 24) narrative about her decision to be tattooed:

My boyfriend always said that he didn't want me to get tattooed … but I harped at him for about a year and then he finally agreed that it was okay. He wanted to help me decide what to get exactly and where. He seemed really happy when I said that I wanted a tattoo on the front of my stomach, right under my bikini-line. He thought it would be special if only he and I could share it, well, you know when, right? I want him to be attracted to me, and appreciate how I look, and I don't want a tattoo to ruin that … He threatened to leave me a couple of times when I said I wanted to cut all my hair off and go real short. He hates short hair, and said "no way." I thought if he liked the tattoo, and so did I, then everybody would be happy.

In Celeste's case, and that of 9 (23%) other women I interviewed, her desire was to enhance her body aesthetically through tattooing. As with many other mainstay forms of female body modification such as liposuction or excessive dieting, the underlying act is not simply a process of beautifying the female form, it is also an act of self-imposed gender stratification. Celeste's tattoo project is an embodied reproduction of the established cultural standard that women conform to men's desires and sexual interests—to the extent that a woman will radically modify her body in the process of such conformity. Akin to the process of breast augmentation, then, tattooing the body for these reasons symbolically justifies women's (and femininity's) cultural position as the outsider, as the Other.

As suggested in Celeste's and others' tattoo narratives, although women have historically shunned widespread participation in tattooing, newly established sensibilities about female sexuality have incorporated this body practice into the mix. Reminiscent of the "carnival era" of tattooing in North America (ca. 1920–50) in which scantily clad tattooed women were paraded through side-shows to titillate male audiences, women's current tattoo practices are often constructed as a sexual curiosity by men (DeMello, 2000; Mifflin, 1997). Women's participation in this traditionally masculine body practice is often mediated by the ways in which it can be sexualized. Once more, the body project becomes an act of corporeal beautification if undertaken with reverence to established constructions of femininity. For example, Ashlyn (age 28) stated:

Some girls get big boobs [implants] and others get their lips or hips done. I chose tattooing because it makes me look great, and it draws attention to my body. When I'm out at a club, I know guys will see my tattoo [on her upper right breast] and come over and talk to me. Not a lot of women have them, and I know it sets me apart from the crowd … guys are really cool about my tattoo, and no one has ever said that I look like less of a woman for having it. I mean, as long as I don't go out and tattoo a snake across my neck.

We must be careful not to reduce the manners by which women conform to gender codes through tattooing into such a neatly packaged process. Although the narratives above strongly suggest that pursuing established standards of femininity through body work may motivate one's involvement in the practice, it does not capture the myriad ways in which established constructions of femininity are (re)produced through tattooing.

As I have argued elsewhere (Atkinson, 2001), for example, another learned motivation that underscores how tattooing is undertaken in the process of conform-

ing to established femininity centres on the manners by which a tattoo body project can be generically cast as a tool for "exploring femininity" in a culturally fragmented, postmodern world. Given that emotionality and introspection conform well with established interpretations of femininity, it makes sense that tattooing (if done as an expression of emotionality or self-exploration) can be reconciled in some cases as a feminine practice. Wrapped in discourses of empowerment, identity-exploration, and personal meaning, some women offer elaborate justifications for their involvement in tattooing as a "woman's" form of expression. For at least 7 (18%) of the women I interviewed, these quests for individuality, as personally emancipating as they may be conceived, concern established ideas about femininity:

Women are a lot freer to be who we want to be nowadays. I'm not like my mom, right, who looks and dresses exactly like the men in her life always expected her to. I love my mom, but she has an outdated way of thinking about how women should look. All prim and proper like a little schoolgirl. If you want to get a tattoo, get a tattoo. That's what I say … be careful, though, and don't go attracting all kinds of unwanted criticism you don't need … I decided to have my lower back tattooed [a sun and moon] about 10 months ago, and my friends all love it; especially my close girl friends. But I didn't do it for anybody else other than me. It's my own way of personalising my body. (Heather, age 21)

Even though these projects tend to be whitewashed with nouveau-hip sentimentalities about "girl power" and the freedom of choice (vis-à-vis the dismantling of established gender codes), they almost invariably *reproduce* established ideas about femininity and the feminine body. This is plainly evidenced by the specific images chosen by the women, the location/placement on their bodies, and the actual sizes of the tattoos selected.

First, among women who are exceedingly sensitive about jeopardizing their established femininity through the tattooing process, the design of the tattoo is normally the principal concern. As tattooing is precarious social practice if undertaken with reckless abandon (re: one's gender status), the image selected must resound with established images of femininity:

I love the butterflies that I have done around my ankle. I know it's not cool to say it these days, but it looks cute and girly. Sometimes women like to look pretty, and I think that tattoo makes my leg look really pretty. That's why I asked Phil [tattoo artist] to colour them pink and yellow, because I want my butterflies to look beautiful. (Selena, age 29)

Floral imagery (e.g., roses, orchids, lilies, or abstract vine work), animals or insects (e.g., birds, dolphins, turtles, cats, butterflies, beetles, or ladybugs), celestial motifs (e.g., suns, moons, or stars), and cartoon characters (e.g., Minnie

Mouse, Hello Kitty, Snoopy) are commonly chosen as they immediately connote established feminine qualities and attributes such as being gentle, nurturing, playful, and delicate. They are deemed less gruesome or violent than "typical" men's tattoos, and thus they become feminized. As Lenskyj (1999) described in her research efforts on female athletes, women who encroach onto a traditionally male terrain like sport must engage in a certain degree of "apologizing" for their conduct. In the case of tattooing, the only way the practice is acceptable for women in some social circles is to feminize the project overtly in accordance with established gender codes.

Second, the strategic placement of some women's tattoos brims with conformity to established constructions of femininity. For instance, the overarching "rule of placement" for more conforming women is concealability. Fearing reprimand or scorn from others, these women do not publicly flaunt their dalliances into tattooing, and thus the lower back, the hips, and the upper back are the most common locations for their tattoo projects:

The only thing that kept going through my mind was, "what about my wedding dress." There was no way in hell that I could see myself standing at the altar, right beside my future husband, right in front of the whole congregation, with a fat tattoo of a heart stuck up there on my bare arm. That would look so tacky, and it would ruin the whole experience of being a bride. Brides in their lace gowns with huge tattoos showing don't paint a very attractive picture … My tattoo is on my lower back, where no one has to ever see it except me. (Devon, age 26)

However, regularly concealed parts of the female body are also those that tend to be highly sexualized. As a fringe benefit of concealing her tattoos, Trina (age 30) explained that by having them on her lower back (traced around the contours of her upper buttocks, and around the front of her pelvis), she had received "positive feedback" from her sexual partners:

There's quite an aesthetic pleasure that comes from seeing a naked body with elegant markings around its sensuous parts. We've all seen dozens of naked bodies in our lives, and when you are having sex with a partner, it's always exciting to experience difference … I remember one man I dated became immediately aroused when I told him about the tattoo across the top of my ass. When we eventually had sex, he couldn't wait to find out what it looked like. It's funny because he only wanted to have sex from behind so he could see it the whole time. He's not the only guy that I've slept with who has said that I have the most beautiful ass ever, and that they would have never guessed that I would be someone who was into tattooing.

In a conceptually related way, if the tattoo is placed "out in the open" (e.g., the ankle or lower leg), it can be discursively configured as a form of feminine/sexual ornamentation akin to a piece of jewellery. If viewed by the tattoo enthusiasts and their social networks as an act of compliance to established femininity, then, tattooing and femininity may become closely related.

Third, concerns about jeopardizing one's femininity will bear on the size of the tattooing project. Describing extensively, or "heavily" in the common parlance, tattooed bodies as "disgustingly unfeminine," Cora (age 28) articulated her thoughts about the size of her tattoo in the following way:

There's a fine line between something that is dignified and understated, and something that is boorish and ugly. When I see a woman with a lot of really large tattoos, I think, that doesn't become her at all. I can't see a heavily tattooed woman and say to myself, wow, that's really feminine. Aesthetically, it doesn't work.

Heavily influenced by the locations on the body preferred by these women for their tattoo projects, the size of their tattoos are relatively dictated by dominant understandings of how femininity and tattooing are related. On the basis of the narratives of 32 (80%) of the enthusiasts I interviewed, there is little to suggest that a "large" tattoo is consistent with established constructions of femininity.

In sum, the desire to maintain a culturally established feminine status is either explicit or implicit in many Canadian women's tattooing body projects. In some cases, the women readily acknowledged the nature of their compliance; others were more reluctant to acknowledge any conformity. In either case, it became evident through the exploration of their tattoo narratives that the interpretive resource provided by one's gender mediates most aspects of the tattoo body project—from the selection of a tattoo, to the way it is displayed, to the way tattooed skin is socially experienced. It is this mediation that is key for understanding the processes of cultural conformity in women's tattooing. As suggested below, however, it is similarly crucial for interpreting processes of cultural resistance and negotiation in women's tattooing.

Cultural Resistance and Women's Tattooing

Even a cursory review of the sociological literature reveals a meta-narrative that suggests that tattooing is undertaken by North American women as acts of cultural rebellion. It is argued that North American women pursue alternative cultural constructions of femininity and the feminine form (Atkinson, 2001; Atkinson & Young, 2001) by wilfully violating established body idiom through tattooing. Rejecting the idea that women's bodies are passive and best unscathed, women tattoo enthusiasts express different standards for what they consider to be feminine through their tattoo projects. This version of femininity starkly contrasts established gender ideologies and traditionally feminine forms. As Caroline (age 31) described,

I've never heard anybody say, I think women are all about bows, daisies, sunny days, and tattoos. When you say the word "tattoo," I mean, you think of a guy right away ... Women nowadays believe that whatever men can do women can do better, and that includes tattooing. We're taking over the whole business [laughs].

For Caroline and likeminded women tattoo enthusiasts, indelibly marking the skin with tattoos is a social crusade into a historically masculine body practice. Among the women I interviewed, 15 (38%) stated that one of their main interests in tattooing projects is derivative of the extent to which a woman's tattooed flesh is a breach of established body convention. Inferring the body as a communicative text of culture, emphasis is given to the ways in which the marked body resists established constructions of the "body beautiful," a body that is recognizable in its docility and attractive for its fleshy curves, shapes, and contours. By cleverly using a profane body modification project to disrupt entrenched cultural images of the beautiful female body, some Canadian women are drawing alternative images of femininity through their body work.

As body projects are typically expressions of conformity to established gender ideologies, modifying the skin to wage cultural resistance is an act of cultural subversion. The bricolage (Levi-Strauss, 1966, 1969) involved in the tattooing process bespeaks of a conscious attempt to expand the cultural boundaries of women's body projects. Rather than passively partaking in ritualized, mass-marketed, and painful body projects in the pursuit of ideal-type feminine forms, some Canadian women promote individuality and alternate constructions of femininity through body play:

Squeezing your breasts into a tight bra doesn't feel comfortable. Neither does pasting fake eyelashes to your eyelids, or going hungry all day just to stay a size 4. Pushing, pulling, stretching, or binding your body to look good for a man isn't my idea of fun ... So when people tell me that I'm nuts for getting tattooed [because it's painful], I respond by telling them that I'm not the one who mutilates my body every day to look like the fashion models in magazines. Punishing your body to appease somebody else is psychotic, and most of the women I know don't get that. But they still have the nerve to stare at me and think I'm less of a "woman" for choosing this [tattooing]. (Laura, age 24)

Just as some women have learned to inscribe cultural conformity upon their bodies through ritual projects of identity construction, other women have equally learned to confront the established gender order through body modification. A "flesh journey" (cf. Atkinson & Young, 2001) such as tattooing can, then, disturb the established order as it creates a certain amount of cultural "noise" (Hebdige, 1979) as a nonstandard body project.

* * * * *

In the process of engaging in cultural resistance through tattooing, the idea that women are symbolically liberated via this "liminal rite of passage" (Pitts, 1998) is often promoted through situated narratives. Associating one's tattooing projects with gender discrimination and social stratification (i.e., as a method of struggling against such marginalization), the body project is inserted into collective identity politics. Exploring the ways tattooing can serve a mimetic function (cf. Atkinson, 2001) for social outsiders in patriarchal figurations, Canadian women reveal their tattoos as a means of exhibiting their gender wounds:

I participate in a women's group that meets once a month. About a year and a half ago one of the women mentioned she received a tattoo a couple of days prior to our meeting. All of the women in the group are very middle-class and we were pretty startled by this. We all clamoured around her, poking and prodding to see if we could guess where it was placed. After about 5 minutes of persistent badgering she lifted up the back of her shirt and showed us a tattoo of an angel with broken wings. I couldn't get over how beautiful it looked, and it made me gasp when she told us how it helped her manage her feelings about being raped when she was a teenager ... We talked about her tattoo for hours and how she felt as a woman about being sexually abused. By the end of the session, 5 of us decided we were going to have tattoos done as well. I mean, the way it helped Sandy deal with her victimization was incredible. I think most women have been abused like that at some point in our lives ... Ten of the women in the group now have tattoos, and each one of us has taken a turn writing a story about our tattoo and what it means. We present them at group meetings and go over how tattooing helps women feel in control of our bodies. It's absolutely exhilarating to hear the stories, and to be friends with such strong women. (Marion, age 29)

The resulting narratives become widely circulated scripts for decoding the significance of tattooing as acts of personal reclamation, self-definition, and gender empowerment. In this way, gender resistance through tattooing becomes discursively configured as an interdependent and intersubjective enterprise among Canadian women.

Not only are discourses shared among some Canadian women in the process of "doing" resistance to established gender ideologies, certain tattoo designs are also commonly worn. Rather than inscribing roses, butterflies, or moons onto the body, traditionally masculine tattoo designs are strategically chosen by some women. For instance, skulls and crossbones, hearts and daggers, eagles, or tribal (e.g., Polynesian, Melanesian, or African) motifs are often utilized to disassemble established cultural associations between femininity and weakness:

Why should men get to wear all the really cool "traditional" tattoos? All of the really boss designs that I like are from the old school days, like all the sailor tattoos … I'm not stupid, and I know tattooing is this macho thing, and that's why girlies have worn little rainbows or baby pandas or whatever, and dance around saying "Ooh, look at my cute little tattooed ass." More of the girls I hang out with don't care about that crap, and don't buy into a tattoo because it's what looks right on a woman. I have these tattoos [heart and banner, navy ship] to show I'm strong-willed, just like the tradition of tattooing in our culture. (Jenna, age 19)

Similarly, by tattooing "pin-up girls" on her body, Clarice (age 26) sought to reclaim and redefine the naked/partially nude body as a symbol of femininity. As an avid tattoo "collector" (cf. Vail, 1999), she described her pin-up girl tattoos in the following way:

Every time I go into Chapters or some other bookstore and pick up magazines, all I see are half-naked women. Turn on the t.v., and it's exactly the same. All men know about women are their naked bodies, and usually it's men who get to control how many naked women are in a film or whatever … Guys flip out when they see the two pin-up girls I have tattooed on my arm. Some of them, right, the first question they ask me, or want to ask me, is, "Are you a dyke?" Guys are so predictable. But that is the reaction I want from men. I want a guy to look at me, look at my tattoos, and have everything he thinks about women screwed up.

In these cases, the tattooed body is literally designed to fracture established gender ideologies by inverting typical masculine or feminine icons and attributing alternative cultural meanings to them through a process of bricolage. The strategic placement of the symbol on the body is also central in women's tattoo projects that are motivated by cultural resistance. Choosing parts of the body that tend to be exposed or exposable in everyday life situations, some Canadian women offer their bodies to be decoded as confrontational or different. By tattooing arms/forearms, hands, lower legs/calves, upper chests, and necks, women consciously breach established body idiom (Goffman, 1959, 1963) as part of their rejection of established cultural understandings of femininity. The designs tend to be larger than those selected by more conforming tattoo enthusiasts and encompass greater portions of body space. Even though the tattoos are concealable in most cases, enthusiasts often believe that tattoo body projects intended for social resistance must be visible to be effective. As a segment of Karen's (age 25) tattoo narrative described,

When it comes to tattooing, bold is beautiful. I hate women who talk tough about their tattoos, pretending like they've done something rebellious with their bodies just because they have an ant dot [tattoo] on their hip.

What's the point in even getting tattooed if people aren't going to see it? For young women it's important that we aren't embarrassed about having tattoos, and we can't let what's expected of us "girls" restrict our involvement … People don't respect half-stepping. If we're going to bother saying something through our tattoos, make everybody listen or the message gets lost.

According to Karen and her peers, without actually confronting others in the process of "being confrontational," no discernable challenge to established understandings of the body can be initiated.

To imply, however, that all forms of resistance to established constructions of the female body through tattooing are similar to those described above would be patently false. Although the strategies outlined above seem to be the standards for interpreting when and how resistance through women's tattooing and other radical forms of body modification is undertaken (cf. DeMello, 2000; Pitts, 1998; Vale & Juno, 1989), they simply do not capture the full range of resistance expressed by women through this type of body work.

In this study, 6 (15%) of the women I interviewed stated that their resistance to established gender codes is more subtle and private than the wildly spectacular variation displayed by, what they perceive to be, more "radical" feminists. These women are astutely aware of the ways in which tattooing a "feminine" body undermines established body codes, and have become drawn into the recent popularity of women's tattooing in Canada for this reason. Many of these women have also become privy, in one context or another, to tattooing narratives that detail the liberating nature of the body project for women. Hence, some Canadian women are fascinated by the possibilities of using the body in a popularly rebellious way. At the same time, they are not eager to be labelled a "deviant female" through their participation in tattooing.

The pragmatic position that some Canadian women adopt toward tattooing is, then, founded upon a desire to engage in resistance to established gender codes while maintaining a semblance of conformity to such edicts. The contestation of established cultural body images and practices (and relationships of social inequality that produce them) is crucial here, but is not undertaken with social/cultural recklessness. The negotiated centre-point between outright conformity and unapologetic resistance allows a tattoo enthusiast to be compliant or rebellious in situated contexts of interaction. Assessing when the marks might be stigmatizing (i.e., involving an unbearable loss to identity, status, or role-set), or socially rewarding (i.e., having one's resistance to gender codes respected and appreciated, or receiving kudos from others about one's tattoos), is central in the negotiation process and can shape a woman's involvement in tattooing.

The main rationale for negotiating one's involvement in resistant forms of tattooing articulated by the women I interviewed hinged upon the idea that tattooing should be a private customization of the female body. For these women, resistance to gendered ways of thinking and acting is accomplished through subtle acts of protest rather than overt and easily targeted forms of gender "bending." The tattooed body does not necessarily have to be publicly displayed to others in this process, as a tattoo body project reflects a deeper and more symbolic dialogue with the self. The tattooed body is an illustrative diary of one's innermost thoughts and feelings about established constructions of femininity and established gender ideologies:

> To change Descartes' terms slightly, "I tattoo, therefore I am." Personally, I didn't do any of this [points to tattoos on her arms] for anyone other than myself. When it comes to my body, I make the decisions. If I want to look different than I'm supposed to [as a woman], because that's how I feel, then I can deal with that through my tattoos. I don't have to stand on the top of buildings and scream out that I lived as an anorexic, or that I have been taught to hate the way my body looks—or, I should say, how it *used* to look … It wasn't until I started to express myself though tattooing, and figured out how I wanted to look as a woman, that I had a grip on my identity and a strong sense of who I am. I don't see any reason why I should include anyone else in that either. A tattoo is something that is supposed to be personally satisfying and meaningful … for me, it's not about the public consumption of my identity anymore. (Chasey, age 22)

As McRobbie (1994) and Muggleton (2000) have pointed out, negotiated forms of social resistance can be injected into a gamut of private, personal practices that are never given to audiences for consumption. In the case of tattooing, there is an inner satisfaction derived from simply expressing anger, frustration, or depression about established constructions of femininity through a tattoo body project.

* * * * *

Rena (age 23) stated that her inclinations to be tattooed were tempered by the fear that her modified flesh would meet with significant disapproval from her family:

> I wanted to get tattooed so badly. But my dad always said that he thought women with tattoos look like whores. And, he said that if people look at you like a whore, they will treat you like one. But that was the point for me, right … not looking like a good little girl, or always doing what I was told. My mom always agreed with him, and even my brother asked me why I wanted to do it. I have this friend named Marcy, and she has a devil girl tattooed on her shoulder. My dad won't even talk to her anymore when she comes by the house, and has basically told me he doesn't want me to hang around with her … So, I finally screwed up enough courage to be tattooed with the Chinese symbol of eternity and took

the plunge. I thought my butt would be the best place because even when I am in a bikini, my dad would never see it. He's never seen it to this day, and I don't think I could ever bring myself to even tell him.

In Rena's case, she interpreted her family members' negative sentiments about tattooing as a form of social protection. By condemning the body project as outside the established gender norm, family members impress upon the budding enthusiast the importance of following established cultural practices. By selecting locations on the body for the project that are regularly covered by clothing, however, these tattoo enthusiasts are able to negotiate their involvement and "pass" as norm abiding (Goffman, 1959, 1963).

The reactions to tattooing body projects (experienced or anticipated) expressed by employers and coworkers can be even more tenuous than those provided by family members or friends. A primary concern for women tattoo enthusiasts, especially in neo-conservative business environments, is that negative reactions from coworkers will interfere with their achieved statuses at work. For the most part, they come to view their tattoo projects as a form of "intolerable deviance" (Stebbins, 1996) in the workplace—a profane form of representation that carries immediate career ramifications:

> When I go to work I'm not there completely on my own terms. I feel like the company pays my salary, and gets to tell me how to behave. That's the price you pay to get paid … I work in an office as a personal assistant and if you come in looking bizarre in front of all the stuffed shirts who hit on you all day, you catch hell. You have to maintain a business persona at work, and apparently you can't have a tattoo and be professional … especially if you are a woman. At work, I can't bring my [gender] politics there everyday, and I have to cover it up. I've had nightmares about going to work naked—not because everyone can see my breasts, but because everyone could see the tattoos on my breasts. [The company] gives off this image like they're hip and young and urban, but we'd see how hip they are if I came in with a low-cut top on. I'd be the hippest girl on the unemployment line. (Laura, age 24)

In recognizing that one's attitudes about gender resistance through tattooing may not be intersubjectively appreciated in the workplace, enthusiasts may negotiate their involvement in tattooing as personal necessity; that is, women enthusiasts are not oblivious to their economic interdependencies and curtail their body modification projects accordingly.

The impetus to negotiate one's involvement in this form of self-expression can, however, create internal tensions for women who perceive their conformity to established body politics as a character deficiency. Five (13%) of the women I interviewed used the term "selling out" to describe their sense of public inauthenticity:

I made the conscious choice to tattoo my body, and I'll never regret it. It was probably the defining moment in my life so far ... it was the only time I did anything solely for myself, to display who I am as an individual. Still, I'm not indifferent to ridicule from other people about my tattoos, so I keep them under wraps most of the time. I go home at night and cry sometimes because I don't have the brass to stand up and ask people to accept me for how I look. I had this vision of how tattooing was going to change my life for the better, and make me more socially confident. And when I sell out by hiding my body under the clothes I wear, I feel like a shy little girl again, peeking around my mother's skirt to see who's talking to me. (Adele, age 23)

Complying with pressures created by established gender codes and supported in institutional contexts such as the family, school, or workplace, some women enthusiasts believe that they compromise a part of their resistant philosophies by putting on a conforming front (Goffman, 1959, 1963). In socially presenting a disingenuous persona in the front regions of everyday settings, these women experience an unsettling bifurcation of identity. By undertaking a series of body management techniques in order to hide their tattooed flesh when in the presence of others, some Canadian women come to view their negotiation as an act of cowardice.

In brief, the decision to engage in cultural dissent through body projects such as tattooing appears to be mediated by one's purpose or motivation for the project and the degree to which the resulting body modification jeopardizes one's achieved/ascribed cultural statuses. Although the central purpose of the body project may be to challenge the very basis of such statuses and associated roles (i.e., as they support established constructions of femininity), Canadian women are not impervious to established cultural norms about gender and its representation. Resistance, therefore, to established social constructions of gender through tattooing exists on a sliding scale. Although some women's tattoo body projects are flagrant violations of established body play and dominant images of masculinity/femininity, others are privately negotiated acts of dissent.

Discussion

* * * * *

Canadian women who actively comply with established constructions of femininity through their body work deftly mould their tattooing projects into acts of gender conformity. Caught up in the current popularity of tattooing among the younger generations, and the ways in which it has been fashionably inserted into the mainstream (Atkinson & Young, 2001; DeMello, 1995; Irwin, 2000), these women narratively and physically construct the projects with deference to established gender expectations.

By drawing attention to the beautiful/sexual feminine body and highlighting the docility of the female form, these women's tattoo projects are conceptually equivalent to other body projects such as liposuction, breast enlargement, excessive dieting, and corseting in that each reinforce the established feminine form as the cultural norm (Davis, 1994; Gillespie, 1996; Wolf, 1990). Furthermore, such tattoo projects garner favourable attention from others (e.g., parents, peers, boyfriends, husbands) as they are explicitly assembled as acts of consent to established constructions of femininity. As a result, these body projects symbolically reproduce women's outsider social status in Canada, and *physically* illustrate the ways women's bodies are sexualized, objectified, regulated, and monitored in accordance with established cultural constructions.

However, other women tattoo enthusiasts reject the oppressive outsider social standing that established femininity carries in Canada, and they challenge such depictions of femininity through their body projects. Subverting established reasons for engaging in body projects (i.e., the pursuit of an ideal-type femininity), these women utilize the tattooed body as a billboard for political protest. Instead of consenting to masculinist preferences for the female body through painful processes of body manipulation, these women seek to dismantle established ideologies and the structures of gender stratification they buttress. In de Certeau's terms (de Certeau, 1984), they use "what they have" in order to wage resistance. As the body is one of the most socially recognized signifiers of one's gender, immediate confrontations to the established patriarchal hegemony in Canada can be initiated through bold and highly visible tattoo projects.

We must question, however, whether or not these acts of cultural defiance are merely "magical solutions" (Cohen, 1972/1999) to common problems of status adjustment among women in Canada. Because the flamboyantly tattooed woman's body tends to elicit negative responses from established others (i.e., as a "freakish," "unattractive," or "deviant" body), does the campaign of resistance through tattooing further entrench these women into the status of the outsider? Just as Punk Rockers solidified their marginalized social class positions by adopting radical physical styles to express their collective sense of alienation and disenfranchisement (Hall & Jefferson, 1976; Hebdige, 1979), these women may very well be reinforcing the sanctity of established images of femininity (and related established body practices) as the cultural norm.

It is not surprising, then, that many of the women I interviewed preferred to negotiate their involvement in tattooing. Neither accepting nor consenting to established constructions of femininity in Canada (yet not ignoring their cultural saliency), some women tactically engage in tattooing as a form of negotiated resistance to dominant gender codes. Established and outsider social relationships (vis-à-vis gender) are partially maintained in this process of negotiation, but the women nonetheless derive an inner satisfaction from their negotiated cultural transgressions. The negotiation is justified by women as social necessity in most cases—as an overt tattooing body project may jeopardize key interdependencies one shares with conforming others. It is further justified as a deeply personal form of self-expression, and the tattoo designs or symbols represent an individual's unique biography. In all cases, the negotiation permits women to explore tattooing as a self-directed "flesh journey" (Atkinson & Young, 2001) of self-discovery without raising the ire of, or stirring unwanted critique from, "unenlightened" (Stebbins, 1996) audiences.

In conclusion, the discussion presented in this article is not a totalizing, static, or definitive account of women's experiences with tattooing in Canada or elsewhere. We must recognize that women's tattooing experiences are highly varied, culturally contextual, and temporally bound. In this respect, there is a pressing need for extended and concatenated research (Stebbins 1992) on women's tattooing—both within Canada and elsewhere. Within this lacuna, we would immediately benefit from in-depth empirical analyses of the ongoing social construction of tattooing as an intersubjectively meaningful body project among women, the long-term and unintended impacts of women's participation in the body project on men's involvement in tattooing, and of course, the stylistic changes in North American tattooing as a result of the increasing "feminization" of the tattoo business (Atkinson, 2001). Future researchers should strive to enrich our knowledge about women's involvement in tattooing through theoretical innovation, methodological experimentation, and substantive exploration. As women's participation in the body project continues to expand and diversify, so must our sociological understanding of women's tattooing.

References

Atkinson, M. (2001). Miscreants, malcontents, and mimesis: Sociogenic and psychogenic transformation in the Canadian tattoo figuration. Unpublished doctoral dissertation, the University of Calgary, Calgary, Alberta, Canada.

Atkinson, M., & Young, K. (2001). Flesh journeys: Neo primitives and the rediscovery of radical body modification. *Deviant Behavior*, 22, 117–146.

Balsamo, A. (1996). *Technologies of the gendered body: Reading cyborg women*. Durham: Duke University Press.

Bakhtin, M. (1984). *Rabelais and his world*. Bloomington: Indiana University Press.

Bordo, S. (1989). The body and the reproduction of femininity: A feminist appropriation of Foucault. In S. Bordo & A. Jaggar (Eds.), *Gender/body/knowledge: Feminist reconstructions of being and knowing* (pp. 13–33). New Brunswick: Rutgers University Press.

Bordo, S. (1993). *Unbearable weight: Feminism, western culture, and the body*. Berkeley: University of California Press.

Chernin, K. (1983). *Womansize: The tyranny of slenderness*. London: The Women's Press.

Cohen, P. (1999). Subcultural conflict and working-class communities. In P. Cohen (Ed.), *Rethinking the youth question: Education, labour and cultural studies*, (pp. 48–65). Durham: Duke University Press. (Original work published 1972.)

Coward, R. (1985). *Female desires*. London: Paladin Books.

Davis, K. (1994). *Reshaping the female body: The dilemmas of cosmetic surgery*. London: Routledge.

Davis, K. (1997). "My body is my art: Cosmetic surgery as feminist utopia?" *The European Journal of Women's Studies*, 4, 23–37.

de Certeau, M. (1984). *The practice of everyday life*. Berkeley: University of California Press.

DeMello, M. (1995). Not just for bikers anymore: Popular representations of American tattooing. *Journal of Popular Culture*, 29, 37–52.

DeMello, M. (2000). *Bodies of inscription: A cultural history of the modern tattoo community*. Durham: Duke University Press.

Elias, N. (1983). *The court society*. Oxford: Basil Blackwell.

Elias, N. (1991). *The society of individuals*. Oxford: Basil Blackwell.

Elias, N. (1994). *The civilizing process*. Oxford: Basil Blackwell.

Elias, N. (1996). *The Germans: Studies of power struggles and the development of habitus in the nineteenth and twentieth centuries*. Oxford: Basil Blackwell.

Elias, N., & Scotson, J. (1965). *The established and the outsiders*. London: Sage.

Ellman, M. (1993). *The hunger artists: Starving, writing, and imprisonment*. London: Virago.

Foucault, M. (1977). *Discipline and punish: The birth of the prison*. London: Penguin Books.

Foucault, M. (1979). *The history of sexuality: vol. 1. An introduction*. London: Allen Lane/Penguin.

Foucault, M. (1980). *Power/knowledge: Selected interviews and other writings 1972–1977*. Brighton: Harvester Press.

Gillespie, R. (1996). Women, the body and brand extension in medicine: Cosmetic surgery and the paradox of choice. *Women and Health*, 24, 69–85.

Goffman, E. (1959). *Presentation of self in everyday life*. Garden City: Doubleday.

Goffman, E. (1963). *Stigma*. Englewood Cliffs: Spectrum.

Gray, J. (1994). *I love mom: An irreverent history of the tattoo*. Toronto: Key Porter.

Hall, S., & Jefferson, T. (1976). *Resistance through rituals: Youth subcultures in post war Britain*. London: Routledge.

Haug, F. (1987). *Critique of commodity aesthetics: Appearance, sexuality, and advertising in capitalist society*. Minneapolis: University of Minnesota Press.

Hebdige, D. (1979). *Subculture: The meaning of style*. New York: Methuen and Company.

Irwin, K. (2000). Negotiating the tattoo. In P. Adler & P. Adler (Eds.), *Constructions of deviance* (pp. 459–470). Belmont: Wadsworth.

Lenskyj, H. (1999). Women, sport, and sexualities: Breaking the silences. In P. White & K. Young (Eds.), *Sport and gender in Canada* (pp. 170–181). New York: Oxford University Press.

Levi-Strauss, C. (1966). *The savage mind*. London: Weidenfeld and Nicolson.

Levi-Strauss, C. (1969). *The raw and the cooked*. Chicago: University of Chicago Press.

Maguire, J., & Mansfield, L. (1998). No-body's perfect: Women, aerobics and the body-beautiful. *Sociology of Sport Journal, 15*, 109–137.

McRobbie, A. (1994). *Postmodernism and popular culture*. London: Routledge.

Mifflin, M. (1997). *Bodies of subversion: A secret history of women and tattoo*. New York: Juno Books.

Miller, L., & Penz, O. (1991). Talking bodies: Female body-builders colonize a male preserve. *Quest, 43*, 148–163.

Muggleton, D. (2000). *Inside subculture: The postmodern meaning of style*. Oxford: Berg.

Nicholson, L. (1990). *Feminism/postmodernism*. New York: Routledge.

Pitts, V. (1998). Reclaiming the female body: Embodied identity work, resistance and the grotesque. *Body and Society, 4*, 67–84.

Sabo, D. (1986). Pigskin, patriarchy and pain. *Changing men: Issues in gender, sex, and politics, 16*, 24–25.

Sanders, C. (1991). Memorial decoration: Women, tattooing, and the meanings of body alteration. *Michigan Quarterly Review, 30*, 146–157.

Sanford, W. (1992). Body image. In the Boston Women's Health Book Collective (Eds.), *The new our bodies, ourselves* (pp. 23–30). New York: Touchstone.

Stebbins, R. (1992). Concatenated exploration. *Quality and Quantity, 26*, 435–442.

Stebbins, R. (1996). *Tolerable differences: Living with deviance*. Whitby: McGraw-Hill.

Steward, S. (1990). *Bad boys and tough tattoos: A social history of the tattoo with gangs, sailors, and street corner punks 1950–1965*. New York: The Haworth Press.

Vail, A. (1999). Tattoos are like potato chips … you can't have just one: The process of becoming a tattoo collector. *Deviant Behavior, 20*, 253–273.

Vale, V., & Juno, A. (1989). *Modern primitives: An investigation of contemporary adornment and ritual*. San Francisco: Re/Search Publications.

Wolf, N. (1990). *The beauty myth*. London: Chatto and Windus.

Woodward, K. (1997). *Identity and difference*. London: Sage.

Wroblewski, C. (1992). *Tattooed women*. London: Virgin.

Young, K. (1993). Violence, risk, and liability in male sports culture. *Sociology of Sport Journal, 10*, 373–396.

Young, K., & White, P. (1995). Sport, physical danger and injury: The experiences of elite women athletes. *Journal of Sport and Social Issues, 19*, 45–61.

CHAPTER 13
Making the Lives of Transsexual People Visible: Addressing the Politics of Social Erasure

VIVIANE NAMASTE

The following interview with Viviane Namaste was conducted by Clarice Kuhling and Gary Kinsman and published in New Socialist *39 (January/February 2003): 31–34. The format here is slightly different from that of the published interview.*

Q: Can you briefly describe for our readers what "transsexual" and "transgender" mean?
A: The term transsexual refers to individuals who are born in one sex—male or female—but who identify as members of the "opposite" sex. They take hormones and undergo surgical intervention, usually including the genitals, to live as members of their chosen sex. Transsexuals are both male-to-female and female-to-male.

The term transgender is really popular in Anglo-American communities, and is used as an umbrella term to include all kinds of people who do not fit into normative relations between sex and gender. This would include, for instance, transsexuals, drag queens (men who perform as women on stage only, usually in a gay male club or social environment), intersexed individuals (people who are born with genitals that cannot be easily classified as "male" or "female"), drag kings (females who perform as men on the stage in lesbian cultural spaces), transvestites (heterosexual males who cross-dress in "women's" clothes and who receive sexual gratification from this act), as well as people who do not identify with either of the categories "male" or "female."

While the term transgender is currently one of the most popular, it needs to be pointed out at this stage in history that increasingly, transsexuals object to being included under a catch-all phrase of transgender. They argue that the health care and social service needs of transsexuals are quite specific, and that this specificity is lost when people use a vague term like transgender. Furthermore, the popularity of the term transgender emerges from the Anglo-American lesbian and gay community. While this discourse may have meaning for some transsexuals who understand their lives in these terms, it does not speak to the transsexuals who do not make sense of their lives, and their political struggles, within the confines of a lesbian/gay framework. It is important to point this out, because most of the Anglo-American writers and self-designated activists on "transgender" issues come out of the lesbian/gay community and express themselves in those terms. My empirical research contradicts this underlying assumption, since most of the transsexuals I have interviewed do not articulate their needs according to a lesbian/gay framework.

All of this to say that questions of language are deeply political!

Q: Why did you title your book *Invisible Lives: The Erasure of Transsexual and Transgendered People*?
A: Most of the academic approaches to transsexuality argue that transsexuals are produced by the medical and the psychiatric establishment. Alternatively, they use the case of transsexuality to illustrate the social construction of gender. There are all kinds of examples of this type of scholarship, and unfortunately, it does not appear that things are about to change in the near future.

There are a couple of things that need to be unpacked in this type of work. First, this work is always, and only, about identity. It limits itself to how and why transsexuals decide to live as members of the opposite sex. Or it uses transsexuals to speak about the relations between social norms and gender identity. What is left out of these accounts is any real understanding of what everyday life is like for transsexuals. So while critics are churning out books, articles, and essays on transsexuals and the transgendered, they have nothing to say about the very real circumstances in which transsexuals live. They cannot offer us even a tiny piece of information about transsexuals and the law, or access to health care, or the struggles that transsexuals have with employment, or the situation of transsexuals in prison.

So my book begins with a critique of this kind of intellectual work. And I argue that, if we actually do some empirical research on some of the matters most pressing for transsexuals—civil status, access to health care, the decriminalization of prostitution, abusive police practices—we discover that transsexuals are quite literally shut out and excluded from the institutional world. They do not have access to many kinds of services, such as shelters for battered women. And so then I begin with this empirical data and I raise two questions with respect to theory. In the first instance, I argue that the theories concerned with the production of transsexuality have got it wrong: transsexuals are not, in point of fact, produced by the medical and psychiatric institution. Rather, they are continually erased from the institutional world—shut out from its programs, excluded from its terms of reference. And the second question I raise comes out of this reflection: I inquire about the relevance of writing theory that cannot make sense of the everyday world, and that actually contributes to the very invisibility of transsexuality that a critical theory needs to expose. This is part of a much broader debate in the university, especially within the social sciences, about the role and function of an intellectual. And I argue that if theory and university scholarship erase transsexuals in much the same way as do different institutional practices, then they are really part of the problem that needs to be understood, and not at all critical inquiry.

Q: What are some of the institutional forms of discrimination and oppression that transsexual and transgendered people face in patriarchal capitalist societies?
A: There are a variety of forms of discrimination. Access to services is one of the major barriers: detoxification programs especially, state funding for surgery, access to hormones in prison, access to emergency shelter. Much of this access is dependent on the individual attitudes of service providers. So when someone is uneducated about transsexuals and transvestites, they may refuse access to services based on misinformation or prejudice. Another type of discrimination comes out of a total lack of institutional policies for transsexuals. This is especially true for female-to-male transsexuals. In these instances, some people cannot get services because bureaucrats do not have a clear written directive.

Access to the media is a whole other form of institutional discrimination. Transsexuals are often required to give their autobiography on demand: How long have you known? Are you operated? How did your family take the news? These kinds of personal questions can provide some insight into the lives of transsexuals, but they are also, in a sense, quite invasive and rude. It is astounding to me that within 15 seconds of knowing an individual is transsexual, some [interviewers] feel comfortable enough to ask transsexual individuals to describe the physical appearance and sexual function of their genitals. How is it that cultural taboos regarding speaking openly about sexuality and genitalia with people you do not know well, go out the window when it comes to transsexuals? One of the effects of this demand is that it is difficult for transsexuals to address the real issues: cops who harass street prostitutes and escorts, access to health care and social services, changing one's name and sex.

The other issue with respect to access to the media is the whole affiliation with lesbian/gay and feminist communities. As I mentioned earlier, most of the self-designated activists emerge from lesbian/gay and/or feminist communities, and they frame the issues in these terms. This means that transsexuals who do not make sense of their lives according to lesbian/gay discourse have no voice. And I reiterate here that based on my empirical research and observations within the milieu for more than 10 years, the majority of transsexuals do not make sense of their lives in lesbian/gay terms. Yet we never hear these voices. And even though we have some empirical research that challenges an equation amongst transsexuals and lesbians/gays—I refer here to my research as well as that of Henry Rubin, whose book on female-to-male transsexuals, *Self-Made Men*, has just been published by Vanderbilt University Press in 2003—our research and observations are ignored both by critics in queer theory as well as by transgender activists who align themselves with queer politics. So to return to the notion of institutions, transsexuals experience discrimination to the extent that they cannot express themselves in their own terms.

The last institutional barrier I want to cite is that of consultation. So often, the government develops policies without consulting transsexuals at all. Or in certain cases, consultation happens with middle-class non-prostitute transsexuals, who represent their unique interests without ensuring that the broader needs of transsexuals are addressed.

Q: Could you tell us a bit about the struggles of transsexuals in Québec and the institutional relations they are up against when trying to get their "sex" changed on official documents?
A: Legally, Québec is a civil code jurisdiction, and within civil code jurisdictions, the body is legally inscribed as a matter of public order. This is quite different than the legal situation within a common law jurisdiction. What this means practically, in terms of name and sex change, is that transsexuals can only change their name after surgical intervention on the genitals. This legal framework is quite specific to civil code countries, and goes back to a long legacy of the Napoleonic Code. In terms of everyday life, this creates all kinds of problems: a female individual begins to take hormones, lives as a man without detection, but their identity documents remain in the female name. Employment, access to health care, and everyday situations like picking up a registered letter from the post office become very problematic.

The situation is especially complicated for female-to-male transsexuals. The Direction de l'état civil (Office of Civil Status) clearly states that a male-to-female transsexual must undergo a vaginoplasty—the construction of the vagina—in order to change name and sex. Yet in the case of female-to-male transsexuals, in at least 1997 and 1998 the Office invoked a rather vague criterion of structurally changing the genital organs. It did not say if this meant a phalloplasty (the construction of a penis), or if it referred to removing the uterus and the ovaries alongside undergoing a double mastectomy and taking male hormones. So things are not always clear, and my research indicates that at certain times there is no standardized policy in this area. However, on a more positive note, it appears that since the late 1990s, the Direction de l'état civil is more clear with respect to the surgeries and procedures required for change of name and sex in the case of female-to-male transsexuals (hysterectomy, double mastectomy, hormone therapy).

In recent times, a court ruled that a male-to-female transgendered person in Québec can add a female name to their birth certificate.[1] It will be interesting to see what kind of impact this has for transsexuals in Québec, and if the access will be universal. The ruling specifies, for instance, that this modification can be made if the individual can demonstrate that they have lived as a woman for five years. Certainly, for transsexuals who "transition" and are able to keep their jobs, providing such evidence is not difficult. But for individuals who do not work in any kind of legal economy, and who do not go to school, the proof of such an identity, established through official documents—pay stubs, school transcripts, credit cards—is less certain. In this regard, while the ability to change one's name after five years is a definite improvement over not being able to do so at all before genital surgery, it is important to reflect on whether the administrative procedures favour middle-class transsexuals.

Q: What is the significance of the challenge to the two-gender dichotomous (male/female) system that transgendered and transsexual people raise? How can radical activists who are not transsexual or transgendered take up this critique of gender relations in the daily work that they do?

A: This question comes up again and again on the left. I am happy to have the opportunity to answer it, in a sense to undo this question, because it helps to illustrate some of the issues that I have raised in my previous answers.

Let me begin by briefly summarizing some of the underlying assumptions of this question. The question follows a line advanced by some self-designated transgender activists and repeated over and over again by queer theorists in the university. It argues that the binary sex/gender system, the exclusive division of the world into "men" and "women," is oppressive. And this argument further contends that this is oppressive not only to transsexuals, but indeed to men and women who consider themselves "properly" sexed and gendered. And having made this critique of the binary sex/gender system, this position then goes on to state that social change can happen through some kind of disruption or displacement of the sex/gender system. That's where transgendered people come in, located within this framework as those who successfully challenge the status quo and point out a new way of going forward.

Now, having given a brief overview of what I see as some of the underlying assumptions of the question, let me return to the division I made earlier between "trans-

sexual" and "transgendered." I said that more and more, a lot of transsexuals take a critical distance from the term transgendered. And this question allows us an opportunity to think through why. The question assumes that "transgendered" people will see their bodies, identities, and lives as part of a broader process of social change, of disrupting the sex/gender binary. Now many transgendered people make such an argument: you can read it in the works of Leslie Feinberg, Riki Ann Wilchins, or Kate Bornstein.[2] But many transsexuals do not see themselves in these terms. They would situate themselves as "men" and as "women," not as "gender radicals" or "gender revolutionaries" or "boyzzz" or "grrrrrrls."

Most transsexuals I know, and most I have interviewed, describe themselves as men or women. And there is a sense in which this position cannot be understood in relation to the question posed, "What is the significance of the challenge to the two-gendered dichotomous system that transsexual/transgendered people raise?" Because transsexuals seek to have a different embodied position within that system. I hope it is clear here what I am trying to do—I hope to show how asking the question in this way forces transsexuals to speak a language that is foreign to us. And while it may have meaning and relevance for transgendered people, it has very little to do with the everyday lives of transsexuals.

Now it is usually assumed, in the university and even in progressive movements for social change, that people who adopt "essentialist" positions are not politically progressive. But you know, I think that the interest in social constructionism in the Anglo-American university is in danger of blinding people to the very good political work that one can do from an essentialist position. And I will go out on a limb here—because to be a good thinker and activist and teacher means taking some risks—and I will say that in the case of transsexuals, essentialism has such a bad name!

Let me cite an example to help illustrate my case. It is so often assumed, as the question posed to me does, that in disrupting a binary sex/gender system, transgendered people are in the forefront of social change. I cited the works of Leslie Feinberg and Riki Ann Wilchins earlier. Both of these writers are located within this framework: they advocate a "transgender" revolution. Now, this is supposed to be a position that is so much more sophisticated than those "terrible" essentialist transsexuals. And the position advocated by Feinberg and Wilchins is the one cited by critics in queer theory. These are the authors who make it onto the course outlines of university studies. And it is all done by well-intentioned, well-meaning teachers who would situate themselves as allies of transsexuals.

But let us examine in more depth some of the political work of Feinberg and Wilchins. Wilchins has been not only active, but instrumental, in lobbying for the delisting of gender identity disorder from the manual of psychiatrists, the Diagnostic and Statistical Manual of Mental Disorders IV. And Feinberg also supports such a position, notably in publishing the "International Bill of Gender Rights" in her book.3 This Bill also contends that gender identity disorder has no place in the psychiatric diagnostic manual. If such a lobby is successful, it will mean that it will be impossible to pay for sex-reassignment surgery either through a private insurance company or through state/provincial health insurance. In this light, the activism of Wilchins and Feinberg supports the privatization of health care. (Feinberg represents herself as a Marxist activist, which is the biggest irony of all!) So here we have a case of some transgender activists, influenced by social constructionist theory, who argue that they are the cutting edge of social change. Yet they are involved in political work that is deeply conservative.

Now let us contrast this with the work of some transsexuals like Margaret O'Hartigan, who has been instrumental in ensuring that sex-reassignment surgery is paid for through state health insurance in Minnesota, and who has offered a trenchant critique of the funding of health care services in Oregon, including services for transsexuals. Now, O'Hartigan is an essentialist: she is not making any claims to disrupting the sex/gender binary, she is not hailing herself as the new vanguard of third-wave feminism. What she is doing, is the highly unglamorous work of research, lobbying, and activism to ensure that all transsexuals can have access to health care, regardless of their economic or financial resources. So here we have an example of an essentialist (gasp!) who is, in my opinion, doing some excellent political work.

Yet I want to go even further. In certain discussions in a university context, there is an acknowledgment that essentialism can be useful politically. Judith Butler, for example, recognizes that while her theoretical work interrogates the sign of "woman," it is at times necessary to invoke the category "woman" in order to make political gains.4 This argument, of course, could easily be extended to the case of transsexuality: that one needs an identity of "transsexual" in order to advance things politically. I can accept the terms of this argument. However, what I am saying today also goes far beyond this idea. I think that academics and activists set a very dangerous precedent if we maintain that people's identities are acceptable only if and when they can prove that they are politically useful. Who gets to decide what constitutes "politically useful" anyway? To my mind, this still reinforces a dynamic in which transsexuals have to prove themselves: you see, we're really all right because we use our transsexual identity for some good law reform. I refuse to accept these terms.

I cited the case of Margaret Deidre O'Hartigan earlier, arguing that she was involved in some critical health care activism. Now, in very specific and practical terms, she and other activists in Portland, Oregon, engaged in a very detailed reading of the kinds of state coverage offered to its citizens.5 And they found significant gender differences with respect to the ranking of different procedures for reimbursement. So for instance, state coverage paid for testicular implants in the case of a male who has lost his testicles, but did not allow for breast implants in the case of a woman who loses her breasts. This kind of activism, then, shows a clear gender bias in social policy. And in point of fact, the activism is not particularly premised on any kind of transsexual identity. So my earlier statement that this was good work being done by an essentialist is a bit unfair. The work is good, period. And whether or not O'Hartigan is an essentialist is irrelevant. So that is one of the points I am happy to make here today. In many university and activist contexts, essentialist identities can only be accepted to the extent that they clearly satisfy some unspecified political agenda. And I am saying something quite different, albeit perhaps unpopular in social constructionist circles. Accepting transsexuality means accepting that people live and identify as men and women, although they were not born in male or female bodies. And that this needs to be kept separate from political work. Some transsexuals situate themselves on the left, and do their political work from this perspective. Others are moderate, or deeply conservative politically. I want to say that if we accept transsexuality in and of itself, then we don't need to make it conditional on a particular political agenda.

So I hope it is clear, then, how the question posed to me contains all kinds of assumptions that I do not accept. And so one of the things I hope to do is to encourage people to be deeply critical of the kinds of information and knowledge available on transsexuals, perhaps especially the knowledge advocated by "transgendered" people. In practical terms, this means reading more than Leslie Feinberg, Riki Ann Wilchins, Kate Bornstein, or Judith Butler.

That being said, and in a critical spirit of solidarity, I would encourage people in the labour movement and in progressive circles to openly critique the "party line" when it comes to transsexuals and transgendered people. Feinberg and Wilchins and many others like them are invested and implicated in precisely the forms of economic and global capitalism that progressive people seek to understand and transform. You know, I think in the past five years, transgendered people have become so trendy. And sometimes I have a feeling that in part because of this trendiness, people are afraid to criticize what transgendered people say because they don't want to be called "trans-phobic." Don't get stuck there: some transgendered people are involved in regressive political work and it needs to be denounced.

I want to say two more things before concluding. Firstly, I want to encourage people to learn about what is going on here in Canada. Transsexuals have such a rich history in Canada, and prostitutes have been the first ones to organize to get services for transsexuals—in Montréal, in Vancouver, and in Toronto. Yet so much of the writing in English on transgendered people is produced by Americans. By studying how transsexuals have organized here in Canada, we can reframe some of the questions that people ask. Of course, since I live in Québec, I would also encourage English Canadians to learn French, since it would allow them a whole other way to see and understand the world. But that's another interview!

I think it is most useful to think about these questions not in terms of the individual rights of transsexuals, but in terms of how these issues link with those of other marginalized populations, or with the functioning of the state in general. And I think that leftists can play a very important role in this regard. I am thinking, for instance, of a panel that Trish Salah organized around labour and prostitution at the Sexin' Change conference in October 2001 in Toronto. Prostitute activist Kara Gillis actually noted that this was one of the first times she had been invited to a specifically union/labour context, despite the fact that her activism frames prostitution as work. So organizing these kinds of events allows people to make broader connections and shifts the focus from a narrow one of "transsexual rights." Prostitute activist Mirha-Soleil Ross argued that day, for instance, that the decriminalization of prostitution would have a more positive impact on the lives of most transsexuals than any kind of human rights legislation. So that is something progressive people can do: integrate transsexual activists into your work not to speak about gender and transsexuality, but to make broader links concerning the regulation of marginalized people.

Notes

1 The background and ruling of this case are available online at www.micheline.ca/page034-1-etat-civil.htm.
2 Leslie Feinberg, *Transgender Warriors: Making History from Joan of Arc to Dennis Rodman* (Boston: Beacon, 1996); Riki Ann Wilchins, *Read My Lips: Sexual Subversion and the End of Gender* (Ithaca: Firebrand Books, 1997); Kate Bornstein, *Gender Outlaw: On Men, Women, and the Rest of Us* (New York: Vintage Books, 1994).
3 Feinberg, *Transgender Warriors*.
4 Butler, "Gender Insubordination," in Diana Fuss, ed. *Inside/Out: Lesbian Theories, Gay Theories* (New York: Routledge, 1991): 13–31.
5 Filisa Vistima Foundation, "Re-prioritization of Coverage for Transexualism through the Oregon Medical Assistance Program," (February 28, 1998). Available from Filisa Vistima Foundation, PO Box 82447, Portland, Oregon, 97282, USA.

CHAPTER 14
Purchasing the Canadian Teenage Identity: ICTs, American Media, and Brand-Name Consumption

Stephen Gennaro

Introduction

In 1973, anthropologist Clifford Geertz stated:

> We live ... in an "information gap." Between what our body tells us and what we have to know in order to function, there is a vacuum we must fill ourselves, and we fill it with information (or misinformation) provided by our culture.[1]

Less than a decade later sociologist Raymond Williams wrote that the information provided by our culture (to borrow a term from Geertz) was "Advertising: The Magic System." For Williams, advertising is not simply a means of selling but also "a true part of the culture of a confused society."[2] Today, information and communication technologies (ICTs) along with the merger between the culture industries and big business have produced individuals with fragmented identities who are oversaturated with images, relationships, and information: in short, saturated selves.[3] This dislocates the individual from conventional forms of identifying "who they are." As such, the saturated self is a displaced individual who is also part of a larger Technological Diaspora, that is, those who search to redefine themselves in light of new ICTs and return to their homeland, their consumption-constructed nation, or the imagined community of youth.

The idea of an imagined community was first conceived in 1983, when Benedict Anderson, a former Professor of International Studies at Cornell University, published *Imagined Communities: Reflections on the Origin and Spread of Nationalism*. In his work, Anderson chronicles how language formed nationalism and how nations were mere artificial constructs that bound people together—even when geographically disparate—through the idea of sharing similar cultural patterns (namely, language).[4] The reconstruction of Anderson's "imagined community" in the new millennium is produced by the culture industries of the media through the privileging of youth culture, which allows people from all geographic areas, age brackets, racial backgrounds, and economic conditions to share similar cultural patterns of consumption (or, at minimum, the desire for consumption) of products that make a person feel young. Whether listening to a popular radio station, skimming the pages of a fashion magazine, watching a television sitcom, or simply walking down a city street, the culture industries' message is simple: (1) to be young is to be happy; (2) youth is "hip"; and, (3) the way to be young is to buy products that give you that youthful feeling.

As youth search for acceptance during adolescence and continually look for a sense of identity and community, they rely (either consciously or unconsciously) on the culture industries for guidance. Young people find their identity in the mythical media creation of the imagined community of youth. The desire to be a citizen in the imagined community of youth, however, is not restricted to young people since the line between adulthood and adolescence has been blurred by the culture industries. As a consequence, the processes that have been attributed by psychologists to the stage of development in the individual's life referred to as adolescence are now life-long processes which leave that individual in a state of perpetual adolescence.

This article examines the emergence of perpetual adolescence as a growing concern in North American society. It looks at the ways in which American popular music, popular culture, and advertising influence and disturb the identity formation of teenagers by linking the rise of American big business and advertising over the last 150 years with developments in ICTs to illustrate how and why a distinctly youth focus arose in the media. While much has been written about young people and their relationship to the media, and, more recently, the phenomenon of childhood disappearing, no one has yet noted that what is really happening is that the media is extending adolescence forever. Childhood has now replaced adulthood as individuals find themselves in a state of perpetual adolescence. Everyone enters childhood with their first purchase of a commodity, but now no one ever leaves it. [...] In this perpetual state of extended adolescence, there is no longer the "in-between period" separating infancy from adulthood; it is now the "in-between period" separating birth from death. Perpetual adolescence allows one to understand why fifty-year-old men buy Harley Davidsons and why thirteen-year-old girls wear thongs. It makes sense of the recent home renovation phenomenon and the brand-name craze of cultural commodities. In short, it helps one understand today's postmodern-globalized society.

This article is also interested in the formation of a Canadian Teenage Identity, and how it is influenced consciously and unconsciously by American media and advertising. As a nation, Canada's dependency on the United States for cultural artifacts, goods, services, and identities leaves the country in a precarious position. In many ways, the culture, cultural production, and the culture industries in Canada are merely local reproductions of larger American currents of thoughts, images, and actions. What then makes the Canadian Teenage Identity different from its American counterpart? Nothing. Previously, one might have argued Canadians have not become "American" because of their focus on issues of social justice, social welfare, and social responsibility. However, recent trends in Canadian society stemming from the country's own period of adolescence, desire for definition, and push towards an active role in the global economy have placed Canada in a position where the difference between the two countries is disappearing rapidly.

In an era of global markets and the decline of the nation-state, the question arises, why study Canada as a nation and why discuss its search for national identity? Arguably one could say that Canada is no different than many countries that experience the push of American cultural industries. Two quick points need to be made here to explain why Canadian identity matters. First, even as the world is getting infinitely bigger (or smaller depending on one's choice of metaphor) due to globalization and ICTs, the argument that the nation-state has been or is being replaced by international corporations only works on a political level. From a cultural standpoint, the nation-state, as a form of identifying one's self, shows no signs of decline. Whether using the American president or the golden arches as an example, American culture is always on display around the world. Microsoft, Starbucks, Nike, and Coca-Cola are all international corporations with no connection to the political governance of the United States, but it would be ludicrous to suggest that every time a person sees the logo or hears the jingle of these companies that America, and the ideals it promotes (freedom, democracy, liberty), are somehow not connected. The only thing globalization has done to change the role between nations and culture is perhaps to illuminate that the Nike swoosh and American flag are as connected to images of child labor, consumerism, and questionable foreign policy decisions (i.e., invading Iraq) as they are to rags to riches stories. Globalization has forced a re-examination of relationships between nations without dismissing the idea of nations, nationhood, or national identity. Second, it is precisely because the lines between nationhood and national identity have become blurred between Canada and the United States that Canada can be used as an example of an adolescent nation. While many nations have experienced a heavy influence from U.S. industries, no country has had to endure it like Canada. [...] The two countries share an economy, a border, a media, and except for healthcare, same-sex marriage, Cuban policy, tolerance of marijuana, and Iraq, they also share a culture.

*　*　*　*　*

The Imagined Community of Youth

Benedict Anderson asserts that the nation can be considered an imagined political community, and he linked this idea to the rise of, first, the printing press, and then, print as commodity, which allowed for ideas surrounding the nation to be circulated and exchanged. The availability of knowledge through print as commodity and the accompanying rise in literacy challenged (a) ideas surrounding divine monarchs and social hierarchies, (b) the notion of privileged access to truth in script language, and (c) the idea that history and cosmology were the same. The possibility of imagining the nation only arose once these three previously held "givens" in society had been undermined by the arrival of print as commodity.

In much the same way that the imagined nation arose out of the technological advancements in printing and the mass availability of print as commodity, so too did the possibility of imagining a community of youth arise from advancements in technology in the late nineteenth and early twentieth centuries. Beginning with the railroad and telegraph, technological advancements fueled the rise of American big business. This led to advancements in mass-produced brand-name goods for consumption and an advertising business to sell them. The advertising business of the twentieth century would use additional technological advancements—from print as commodity to television—to segment the marketplace and create distinct consumers for distinct brand-name products. By the mid-twentieth century, the culture industries had produced a distinct youth culture, an "imagined community," through which all young people could find a common identity. As Anderson observes, "it is imagined because the members ... will never know most of their fellow members, meet them, or even hear of them, yet in the minds of each lives the image of their communion." Brand-name recognition thus became the passport to an imagined community of youth.

New literacies are required to deal with advancements in ICTs. [...] In response to the new ICTs of the twentieth century, sociologists of education note that: "popular culture ... helps children develop their own language, through which they are able to develop their own sense of identity and connection to the world ... [it] has become a method of communication that enhances their idea of community."[5] In response to advertisements, individuals shared the common language of purchasing and developed a consumption ethic that made the first imaging of a youth culture possible.

The Technological Diaspora

Technology has increased the number of relationships individuals engage in, the variety of those relationships, and the intensity at which they are engaged. When a person reaches the point of saturation, they become part of a larger group of unstable people, all suffering from the same ill effects of new technologies. According to social psychologist Kenneth Gergen

> [n]ew technologies make it possible to sustain relationships—either directly or indirectly—with an ever-expanding range of other persons. Changes of this magnitude are seldom self-contained. They reverberate throughout culture, slowly accumulating until one day we are shocked to realize that we've been **dislocated**—and can't recover what has been lost.[6]

As a displaced peoples, dislocated from their conventional identification of the self by ICTs, North Americans in the new millennium are members of the Technological Diaspora. Unable to properly define who they are in the current ICT age, they struggle to return to their homeland. That homeland is the false nationhood of the imagined community of youth which is created by the culture industries to sell commodities.

Communications theorist and media critic Neil Postman correctly notes that: "American adults want to be parents of children less than they want to be children themselves."[7] Adults, too, have been displaced from their homeland. Adults, too, are now more than ever a part of the Technological Diaspora, where those who are displaced yearn to return to the imagined community of youth which is created through the media's privileging of youth culture. Every person in America lives within the marketplace. Each individual is a consumer and a purchaser of commodities. The American re-creation of the Athenian agora runs from coast to coast and some would even argue that it crosses the seas as an imperial force in foreign markets. The walls surrounding the marketplace are nonexistent as there is no real danger to the marketplace's existence because everyone lives and interacts within it. [...] Stay young, stay hip, stay cool are the messages of the cultural industries. [...]

Could one imagine middle-aged men with ponytails and earrings in the 1950s? Today, young and old consumers buy Prada purses, Nike shoes, or Tommy Jeans because the culture industries make commodities to suit every price range. However, stop for a moment and examine a convertible car or a motorcycle, both advancements of technology that the media has associated with the youth market. As witnessed in the 1950s rock 'n' roll music, James Dean, early Marlon Brando movie characters, or the all-leathered Elvis in his 1968 comeback special, the biker and the rebel are young, indestructible, cool, and always drive a fast car. But who buys cars and motorcycles as commodities for consumption? Who purchases durable goods to signify their identity? Only those who can afford to, and that is why, with rare exception, the person driving the convertible is a balding, middle-aged man, not a sixteen-year-old cheerleader, or why the person cruising on the Harley-Davidson is, with rare exception, not a part of a biker gang but a middle-class, corporate executive. The message is simple: Buy a Hummer ... stay young.

Yes, North America today is a society of perpetual adolescents and nowhere is this more evident than in the emerging subculture of corporate chronics.[8] The drug culture has always been associated with youth culture. Often, popular memory originates this relationship between youth and drugs to the 1960s hippie culture. However, President Franklin D. Roosevelt in the 1930s spoke of "reefer madness" as a problem with youth and incorporated educational and vocational training into his New Deal programs in an effort to occupy youth with more productive activities than taking drugs.[9] Furthermore, as social ecologist Mike Males notes, statistics indicate that drug use is not higher among young people. Yes, just as "some teenagers try to master the tasks of adolescence through escape—for instance through drug use or alcohol abuse," many adults partake in this same exercise.[10] This can explain why so many corporate chronics, that is, young professionals, work from 9–5 and then smoke dope and play Playstation throughout the remainder of the day. It is no coincidence that the main demographic of video game consumers is the mid-twenties single male. Indeed, over eighty percent of the video game consoles purchased in North America in 2004 were bought by consumers over the age of eighteen. The average age of video game players was twenty-nine, and almost seventy percent of the market was male consumers.[11] The corporate chronics represent the same market value to the culture industries that teenagers in the 1950s did with rock 'n' roll in that they are willing to spend money to consume because they have disposable income and leisure time. The rigors of trying to cope with assimilation into society have led corporate chronics, as dislocated individuals, to search for an escape. The result is the rise of a multi-billion-dollar video game industry.

The Saturated Self

Kenneth Gergen's thesis on the "saturated self" is perhaps one of the best ways to understand how the need for an imagined community of youth, a Technological Diaspora, and perpetual adolescence have arisen in today's society. Gergen claims that the rapid development of new ICTs over the last century "immerses us ever more deeply in the social world, and exposes us more and more to the opinions, values, and lifestyles of others."[12] Gergen calls this process social saturation. "[A]s social saturation proceeds we become pastiches, imitative assemblages of each other. In memory we carry others' patterns of being with us."[13] In short, new ICTs (the telephone, television, and Internet) allow an individual to interact with more people, cultures, events, and places than ever before. According to psychologists, this poses a problem for adolescent development and identity formation since, "[o]ne expression of a successful mastery of adolescent issues is the formation of a viable and coherent sense of personal identity."[14]

[T]he result of oversaturation is perhaps best described as the Hallmark syndrome, where an individual possesses preprogrammed social responses to the actions of others. Individuals know when to act happy or when to react sad. They know that they respond to death with grief and to a promotion at work with celebration. Advertisers and the media have taught us to buy a Hallmark card for every occasion lest we forget how to respond to every possible scenario. What began as oversaturation has resulted, arguably, in a loss of free will. Moreover, for psychologists, "[i]dentity is the bridge between the self and his [or her] society. A coherent and viable identity allows the individual to realize drives and longings in societally [sic] approved ways, while giving the individual a sense of meaningfulness and self-continuity."[15] What problem does this pose for individuals—both young and old—when the societally approved ways in which they deal with their drives are simply pastiches of media and social imagery?

Gergen's ideas are perhaps most useful in describing the fragmenting of identity through a process which he terms "multiphrenia," or "the splitting of the individual into a multiplicity of self-investments."[16] [T]his fragmented and multiphrenic condition is encouraged upon our youth by dumping phrases like "extra-curricular" into their minds. Witness the large number of Canadian youth who work part-time or volunteer while attending school. According to Statistics Canada, in 2001, forty-four percent of all teenagers ages fifteen to nineteen had jobs, and in 2000, thirty-seven percent of the total youth population volunteered time to a charity or non-profit organization.[17] Young people are told that universities do not simply look at their marks but at their "extra-curricular" activities as well, that employers look for well-rounded individuals, and that success is based on being multi-skilled and capable of multi-tasking.

As a result of society's push for young people to become multi-skilled "multi-taskers" adolescents define themselves by identity fragmentations. They are no longer simply: son, brother, student. Now they are: son, brother, student, cashier, volunteer, football player, swim team member, debater, chess enthusiast, Microsoft proficient, HTML knowledgeable, recreational softball player, group member, team player, television watcher, and commodity purchaser. A résumé is nothing more than an expression of multiphrenia, with the most impressive résumés coming from, and the best jobs going to, those who can best fragment their "selves." We thus find ourselves in a society that values, privileges, and rewards fragmented identity.

This scenario is forced upon older people as well: "diversify your portfolio" is no longer a term that refers only to playing the stock market or economic interests. In today's world, individuals are encouraged to "diversify their identity" by managing their identity as a broker

would manage a portfolio. Here adulthood parallels adolescence in that "[a]dolescence is a time of trying out new roles, discarding old roles, and establishing a sense of coherence."[18] Thus, the multiphrenic condition of identity formation in the ICT age is just one way in which the adult acts like an adolescent.

One result of the multiphrenic condition is that an individual now requires "continual learning." Continual learning is often a response to advancements in ICTs, a "re-skilling" to offset the "de-skilling" effects of technology.

* * * * *

A recent example of the de-skilling effects of technology has been the change in the role of secretaries or executive assistants, who now require advanced computer skills in Microsoft Office in addition to the ability to type, or "take a letter" short hand. Or, what about the recent rage of Research in Motion's cellular phone/web browser technology "the Blackberry," which in addition to being an electronic day-timer (or PDA) allows an individual to receive phone calls or e-mails anywhere at anytime, virtually eliminating any need for a secretary or executive assistant. Marxist economist/sociologist Harry Braverman spoke to the changes in labor patterns when discussing how mechanization changed the work force in the first half of the twentieth century. For Braverman, an increase in workplace technology and mechanization produced a need for skilled labor to perform those same tasks. Instead of requiring the skill to work a lathe, a company could now hire someone to push a button or supervise a machine performing the same task. Workers required a re-skilling, but one which was not empowering to the worker in that it only trained the worker in how to assist the machine as a passive supervisor rather than as an active worker.[19] In North America in the twenty-first century, being a productive citizen, consumer, or employee requires an education on how to speak the digital language and the culture industries teach the lingo. The goal is to increase the amount of people need to know by oversaturating them with images and information.

Since most people no longer spend their entire working lives with the same company, being employable requires that individuals continually develop new skills through education and re-education.

More and more, workers and businesses are finding themselves **displaced** by technology. Their salvation lies in ongoing education so that their skills remain relevant to the current environment of rapidly changing technology and skill requirements especially due to computers.[20]

Learning becomes a life-long practice; it is no longer an activity confined to school. Learning the new literacies of the new technology becomes the ticket to better opportunities, both socially and economically, in the new millennium. Or, as sociologist Karen Sternheimer notes: "critical media literacy skills are a contemporary necessity for living in our media saturated culture."[21] A focus on learning and developing tools through education, with which to use to create a "self" and integrate into society is just one more way in which adult and adolescent lives are now one in the same.

Less than two centuries ago, few people had any formal education. During the course of the twentieth century in North America public education was extended to the entire public, but only while they were young. Eventually, that was not enough education, and society required individuals to get a high school diploma. As Braverman describes in the last chapter of Labor and Monopoly Capital, individuals with high school diplomas got better jobs and thus it became a social requirement, a rite of passage.[22] But that book was written in 1974, and it was only a matter of time before the high school diploma was not enough education and society required that individuals get a university degree. Again, individuals were led to believe that the university degree was a guarantor of a better standard of living. Yet in 2005, getting an education now means getting a second degree, an MBA, a law degree, a Master's degree, or even attending a college program for a trade skill after finishing university. While Braverman suggested that the trend for extending the mandatory school age (that is how long society made its youth go to school) emerged out of World War II as a way to keep unemployment down by keeping a large portion of the population busy, it has had an even more staggering effect. Raising the age at which people finish school has now created a scenario in the new millennium where continual learning is required and therefore no amount of education is ever enough to properly prepare an individual for a life in the workforce. It is never a good enough time to graduate; education has made everyone unemployable. The only type of education necessary today is how to be a consumer and lessons regarding how to make purchases are taught at a very early age.

As such, the processes attributed by psychologists to the stage of development in the individual's life referred to as adolescence—a desire for increased intimacy, emotional trial and turbulence, separation from parents and authority, and the formation of a positive self-identity—are now life-long processes. Furthermore, what had previously been seen as the symbols of the completion of adolescence—the ability to maintain a healthy, mature relationship with a member of the opposite sex, the ability to control sexual and violent urges, the ability to rationally distinguish between fact and fiction, and the ability to balance out the competing "selves" of an individual's identity—are now life-long struggles.

The American Agora

Central to any discussion of perpetual adolescence is an understanding of the role of American big business and advertising in its creation. By connecting the rise of American big business to advertising in the second half of the nineteenth century and highlighting the importance of the establishment of brand-name products in the early to mid-1900s, the rise of rock 'n' roll music at mid-century, and the emergence of media convergence at the end of the millennium, one can see how the culture industries created the imagined community of youth.

By the second half of the nineteenth century, technological development in America had made mass production of consumer goods possible. The newly mass-produced goods needed consumers and advertising emerged as the bridge between mass-produced goods and mass purchasing. Business historian Alfred D. Chandler, Jr., described the period before railways as a time of local markets and the general store that provided a small selection of goods; there were no branded, packaged goods.[23] The transition from many small- or medium-sized companies to big businesses was made possible by the technological advancements of the railroad, telegraph, and radio, as well as changes in systems, such as the emergence of middle management and advertising. The goal of advertisers in the last half of the nineteenth century was to establish markets for goods by turning geographically separated cities into one unified marketplace.

Advertisers in the early twentieth century tried to carve out a market share of this unified marketplace by tailoring products and advertisements to consumers on the basis of gender, class, race, age, and other categories, such as the marketing of household appliances to housewives on the basis that they would "make their lives easier." To distinguish and differentiate their product in the marketplace, companies began to aim for brand-name recognition. In fact, "brands that ranked first in their product lines in the 1920s and were still number one in their product lines at the end of the [twentieth] century included Ivory soap, Wrigley's chewing gum, Coca-Cola soft drinks, Kodak cameras and film, Goodyear tires, Gillette razors, Campbell's soup, Nabisco crackers, and Del Monte canned fruit."[24] The longevity of popularity enjoyed by some of the early twentieth century's brand names gives further credence to the marketing ideas of the companies at this time, that brand-name packaging of items for individual purchase would drive commodities from the marketplace, in that, "once a brand gains a strong foothold, an unbranded product cannot compete as long as the branded item is maintained at high quality and reasonable cost."[25] As brands pushed commodities out of the marketplace, the brand names themselves, and later culture, became the commodities for sale.

As brand-name products emerged, brand-name recognition became the focus of advertising. The goal of brand-name advertising was not to create a direct link between the product and the consumer but to create a relationship of comfort between the consumer and the brand name. "That's why most of us would feel more comfortable brushing our teeth with Crest toothpaste than a generic tube. We think we know something about Crest based on experience and advertising."[26] Brand-name awareness reaches its pinnacle once consumers can no longer separate a brand name from the product itself: witness Kleenex tissues or Scotch tape. Here the brand-name relation has become so ingrained in the consumers' psyche that they refer to the product itself by the brand name of a company.

With the rise of branding, the focus of advertising was no longer on short-term sales but rather long-term customer loyalty.

＊　＊　＊　＊　＊

Imagine the surprise and delight of the advertising and big business world when it realized that they did not have to make commercials that even remotely spoke to their product anymore because brand-name recognition proved a better sales pitch than forced selling. The movement of the advertisers from a focus on immediate sales to a focus on brand-name recognition [...] falls in line with Adorno's ideas concerning mass culture:

All mass culture is fundamentally adaptation. However, this adaptive character, the monopolistic filter which protects it from any external rays of influence which have not already been safely accommodated with it reified schema, represents an adjustment to the consumers as well. The pre-digested quality of the product prevails, justifies itself and establishes itself all the more firmly so far as it constantly refers to those who cannot digest anything not already pre-digested. It is baby food.[27]

Ah, the sweet taste of pabulum for the masses!

One of the areas of academic writing that Adorno is best known for is his work on the sociology of popular music. Here, too, Adorno believed that the culture industries were turning what were previously areas of artistic expression into nothing more than avenues for consumption. Popular music in the twentieth century, especially rock 'n' roll, has always been a site for identity formation, commodity consumption, and youthful expression. With the emergence of rock 'n' roll, advertisers were able to successfully target a specific demographic (youth) and create a brand-name relationship between young people and a brand of rock 'n' roll. Regardless of what adults had to say about rock 'n' roll, the music industry only cared about record sales. The newly segmented youth market became a mainstay in the American economic marketplace as seen in the rise of the annual gross revenue of the U.S. recording industry from $109 million in 1945 to $603 million by 1959, an increase of almost 600% over fifteen years, thanks in large part to Elvis-mania and *American Bandstand*.[28] Rock 'n' roll's emergence in society following World War II was a case of "the right place at the right time" if ever there was one. Yet, rock 'n' roll's survival was based on the rapid emergence of excessive advertising to and a positive response from a distinct teenaged market.

Elvis Presley's early success was, in many ways, the result of the industry's commodification of Elvis and direct marketing to a distinct youth market. As such, the resulting youth market and rock 'n' roll music industry, which have been co-dependents ever since, owe much of their "rise to power" to their success in marketing Elvis. From the moment Elvis Presley's music was first heard on American radio (July 7, 1954),[29] Elvis was targeted to and welcomed by youth (mainly young girls), and became a symbol of sexual rebellion. However, the early strategy of "selling Elvis" was different from anything prior in the music industry. The strategy behind Elvis's marketing employed by his manager, Colonel Tom Parker, was described by one of the Colonel's employees as follows:

The Colonel doesn't sell Elvis to the public, dig? He sells Elvis to the people who sell to the public, and those are the media people—the television and motion picture personalities, the executives, and businessmen who control the networks, the important radio people. It is an endless trip for the Colonel. Elvis, as a product, always in the state of being sold.[30]

Elvis, not his music, was the commodity. The music was simply one of many venues through which "Elvis" the product was sold to the public.

Elvis's stature in the American youth market in the early years grew not simply through radio play and record sales (like most major artists at this time) but through a combination of radio play, record sales, television appearances (especially those on *The Ed Sullivan Show*), movies, and brand-name products, including socks, sweaters, lipstick, pencils, sodas, and pajamas. Elvis's brand products were being produced by all the culture industries and purchased in record numbers. "All told, the fan could buy seventy-eight different Elvis Presley products that grossed about $55 million by December 1957."[31] Elvis thus became the first brand-name cultural commodity and the first example of media convergence.

American Bandstand continued the industry trend of the commodification of culture that had erupted with Elvis. On August 5, 1957, *American Bandstand* first appeared on American television to more than eight million viewers.[32] The show relied on financing secured through an advertising contract with Beechnut Spearmint Gum, which was intent on targeting the potential teenage audience. In the words of host Dick Clark, "teenagers have nine billion dollars a year to spend" and hence the show was focused, like its sponsors, on tapping into this new resource.[33]

The response to *American Bandstand* was overwhelming; it swept across American teenagers like an epidemic. *American Bandstand* received 45,000 letters a week, grossed $500,000 a year, and generated higher television ratings than the telecasts of its two major network competitors combined. It not only informed teenagers as to what songs, singers, and albums were cool but also initiated all the latest dance crazes, from the Twist to the

Mash Potato.[34] Teenagers used this knowledge to purchase the newest records and learn the latest dances thereby asserting their distinct identity. "In the absence of major rock stars, and working within the new medium of television, the far-sighted Clark had created a rock 'n' roll that emphasized the audience as much as the music."[35] The music industry had followed the trend of advertising in the twentieth century, which shifted from product-centered ads to consumer-centered ads. In the same way, Dick Clark and American Bandstand, looking to segment the music market and generate sales with a new youth market, advertised not product-centered music but an audience-centered music instead.

The privileging of youth culture and its connection to rock 'n' roll can best be summarized as created by advertising and validated by purchasing. In other words, the privileging of youth culture arose in the 1950s as advertisers looked to tap into a vast resource of money that resided with a growing youth population. As a segment of society, youth became validated as more than simply a subculture through consumption and purchasing as perhaps best evident by the survival of rock 'n' roll. Despite widespread adult disdain for the new music, it survived because of youth purchases of rock 'n' roll records.

Rock 'n' roll music offers an excellent introduction into the phenomenon of convergence and synergy. By discussing Elvis as the first example of media convergence, it has been suggested that Elvis used his television appearances to sell his music, his music to sell his movies, and his movies to sell brand-name products. Convergence describes how media corporations purchase stakes in multiple medias, while synergy describes how once they own multiple medias, corporations use one product to sell another. Much like Elvis or American Bandstand, the media conglomerates of the second half of the twentieth century also work using convergence and synergy. For example, while watching a television show on one particular cable channel, viewers are being sold products owned by other companies within that cable channel's "im-media-te" family.[36]

At the turn of the millennium, the bulk of power of the culture industries lay in the hands of five multinational media companies: Disney, News Corp, Viacom, Vivendi Universal, and AOL-Time Warner. In 2000, AOL-Time Warner, for example, owned magazines like Time, People, Sports Illustrated, cable stations like CNN and HBO, Warner Brothers Studio (film), Atlantic and Elecktra music labels, Warner Brooks, AOL (Internet), three professional sports franchises (NBA, NHL, and MLB), and much more.[37] One does not have to be a conspiracy theorist to see the magnitude of convergence that controls the media. Under these circumstances, it's often difficult to know where journalism leaves off and self-promotion begins.[38] The magnitude of convergence in North American society is best illustrated by the amount of television young people watch. A study performed by the Canadian government in 1996 discovered that by the age twelve the average child had watched over 12,000 hours of television, double the time they had spent in school by that age.[39]

A recent study in the Toronto Star shows the extent to which adults are also influenced by television. The article looks at several issues, most notably the rise in home improvement reality shows, from Trading Spaces to Debbie Travis's Facelift. According to the article, Canadian homeowners, in 2002, spent $23.4 billion on repairs and renovations, eleven percent more than in 2001 and nearly seventy-five percent more than in 1996.[40] The drastic rise in home renovations over the last decade highlights both the extent to which the television shows influenced the desire of its viewers to renovate and the extent to which adults look to television and media for ideas and identity. "Children's play with particular toys or knowing about the latest fad is a way of creating a shared culture. Adults use consumption in the same way, of course, buying cars, gadgets, and clothes that indicate we are members of various groups."[41] Little kids, little purchases; big kids, big purchases.

It would be naïve to suggest that television and advertising have created passive consumers, uneducated, uninfluenced by outside sources, and apathetic to anything other than shopping. Family and friends play a pivotal role in informing young people about integrating into society. It is not only the media but family and peer groups that are influencing young people's purchasing patterns and identity formation. As young people look to break their familial ties during adolescence, peers replace parents as the dominant source of information on how to manage one's own identity. "Teenagers reach out to and are heavily focused upon others in their age group. As a result, much of their self-formation occurs in the context of relationships with other teenagers. They imitate and learn from one another."[42] Children identify themselves within their peer community through purchasing patterns. "Consumption is a social act; buying may be an individual activity, but the types of purchases we make can create a sense of shared identity."[43] The shared identity through purchasing is not an isolated phenomenon solely experienced by youth. Brand-name recognition is the pabulum of the electronic age, feeding the culture of perpetual adolescents as if they were perpetual infants. Adorno elaborates on this point when he states, "[i]t is no coincidence that cynical American film producers are heard to say that their pictures must take into consideration the level of eleven year olds. In doing so they would very much like to make adults into eleven year olds."[44]

What exists today then is a fragmented marketplace which focuses primarily on selling images and identities of "youth" to both young and old people alike. Although the advertising company benefits from the fragmented marketplace it always dreams of a unified, universal market, where all consumer demographics can be reached simultaneously. The ideal target audience of advertisers and big business is youth sensibilities with an adult wallet, the perpetual adolescent.

* * * * *

Canada as Adolescent?

Nowhere are the ideas of the saturated self, the Technological Diaspora, and the perpetual adolescent more applicable today than in Canada. In much the same way that an adolescent looks for separation from its parents and acceptance from its peers, Canada appeared to be in a similar position throughout the twentieth century as it tried to define itself through separation from mother Britain and approbation from the United States. Canada can be viewed as an adolescent country since it experiences the same anxieties, stresses, changes, and quest for identity as adolescents.

Much like adolescents, Canada has always struggled with its in-between identity: not quite British dependent but not quite independent; not quite American yet not distinctly Canadian. Provincially, Quebec is not wholly French, but certainly not English. Globally, Canada is an "in-between" nation as well; not a powerful country in world politics, but still a "first world" country. Every year the United Nations ranks Canada one of the best places to live in the world and yet Canadians flock at the opportunity to move south of the 49th parallel. Lastly, Canada was a good enough friend to house all of the displaced Americans and those traveling on flights to and from the United States on September 11, 2001, and the days that followed but it was not a good enough friend to warrant any mention from President George W. Bush as he thanked America's allies for their support four months later in his State of the Union address. Being "in-between" in so many different ways, Canada itself appears to house a multiphrenic identity.

This final section examines a case study, albeit a reified one, by applying the concept of what psychologists refer to as role change, to ask the question, does Canada represent a country in a state of perpetual adolescence on the global scale? Role change contains three stages: (1) role conflict, (2) role discontinuity, and (3) role incongruence. The continual struggle of Canadian governments, academics, and artists with their "many Canadian selves" in an endless search for a Canadian identity would suggest that this is the case.

Role change refers to the nature of adolescence as an "in-between period," but also speaks to the way in which an adolescent tries to make sense of the many competing "selves" and the sexual and violent tendencies they are experiencing. Often, adolescents make sense of these changes either through imitation or role playing. This usually involves the examples put forth at home by their parents or in society, either through mass media icons or societal role models of teachers and educators. For Canada, the adolescent country, the example comes from its neighbor, the United States. It is not that Canada lacks a popular culture, rather it is that Canadians do not want Canadian popular cultural artifacts. It is not that Canadians do not have access to a Canadian identity, it is that they do not want one; they would rather purchase the American identity.

One component of adolescent role change is what psychologists characterize as role conflict. As discussed earlier, the saturated self takes on many roles, such as son, brother, boyfriend, and student. An unavoidable series of circumstances that all adolescents encounter is when two or more of these roles come into conflict with one another. For the adolescent individual, this usually involves a struggle between the competing interests of familial duty and peer pressure. For the adolescent country, the ongoing struggle sees Canada attempting to protect its own interests while trying to satisfy those of its American neighbors. As historian J.L. Granatstein notes, "Canadians ... have been obliged to wrestle with their vastly richer and more powerful neighbor, so much so that they have come to define themselves not as they were and are, but in contradistinction from that great and grasping neighbor."[45] On a national level, Canadians struggle with role conflict, between neighbor and sovereign country and not only in an economic sense.

Another component of role change is discontinuity. This refers to a lack of order in the transition from one role to the next. With regard to perpetual adolescence, this is exactly the difficulty in identity formation being discussed. For the adolescent individual, this transition could refer to the recent graduate who learns that a university degree does not guarantee him/her a job in the marketplace. Adolescent country discontinuity can best be seen through the vast amount of money spent to maintain Canadian television programming even though it is more cost effective to carry simulcast American sitcoms, which generate higher ratings. "The top 20 programs in the Toronto market (audience share) in the spring 1998 were all big ticket American shows ... and at least 2/3 of all shows watched by English Canadians are American."[46] This begs the question, in what way is the Canadian Teenage Identity shaped by media, if most of its media influences are American?

The third component of role change is incongruence. Here the adolescent is placed in a position that he/she is not properly suited for or is placed in a position that he/she would not have chosen for him/herself. For the adolescent individual, an example of incongruence would be when parents place unrealistic expectations on their children. For the adolescent country, incongruence can be seen through Canadian dependency on American cultural goods. Canadians are trained to be consumers and citizens through American media, but they are asked to be consumers with Canadian currency. The only remaining debate then is do Canadians choose to be the cultural dependent to the United States or are they simply passive consumers of American media messages and cultural imperialism?

As Canadians enter the new millennium and an era of technological advancement, globalization, and American corporate imperialism, understanding its relationship to these larger issues might help to explain

Canada's identity confusion. On the one hand, Canada appears open to lighter marijuana laws, same-sex marriage, free health care, and non-participation in the war in Iraq, but at the same time Canadians insist on shopping at the Gap or Walmart, buying coffee from Starbucks, watching American television, listening to American music, drinking Coca-Cola, eating at McDonald's, and wearing Nike sneakers. Being a Canadian and being a teenager thus have a lot in common. This begs the question: Is Canada, as a nation, lost in an abyss of perpetual adolescence in the same way that its citizens are?

* * * * *

Notes

1   Clifford Geertz, "The Impact of the Concept of Culture on the Concept of Man," in *The Interpretation of Cultures: Selected Essays* by Clifford Geertz (New York: Basic Books, Inc., 1973), 50.

2   Raymond Williams, "Advertising: The Magic System," in *Problems of Materialism and Culture: Selected Essays* (London: Verso, 1980), 191.

3   The term "self-saturated" is taken from Kenneth J. Gergen, *The Saturated Self: Dilemma of Identity in Contemporary Life* (New York: Basic Books, Inc., 1991).

4   Benedict Anderson, *Imagined Communities: Reflections on the Origin and Spread of Nationalism* (London: Verso, 1993).

5   Cameron White and Carole Basile, "Hearts and Minds: Schools and the Battle of Pokemon and Harry Potter," in *True Confessions: Social Efficacy, Popular Culture, and the Struggle in Schools*, ed. Cameron White (Cresskill, NJ: Hampton Press, 2003), 81.

6   Gergen, *The Saturated Self*, 3 [emphasis added].

7   Neil Postman, *The Disappearance of Childhood* (New York: Vintage Books, 1994), 138.

8   "Corporate Chronic" is the author's own term.

9   Mike Males, *The Scapegoat Generation: America's War on Adolescents* (Monroe, ME: Common Courage Press, 1996), 177.

10 "Adolescents: Self and Culture," in Daniel Offer, Eric Ostrow, Kenneth Howard, and Robert Atkinson, *The Teenage World: Adolescents' Self-Image in Ten Countries* (New York: Plenum Medical Book Company, 1988), 13.

11 "Video games shoot to record on popular titles," *The Globe and Mail* (Toronto), March 3, 2005, B10.

12 Gergen, *The Saturated Self*, 49.

13 Ibid., 71.

14 Erik Erikson quoted in Offer, Ostrow, Howard, and Atkinson, *The Teenage World*, 13.

15 Ibid.

16 Gergen, *The Saturated Self*, 74. Certainly there is a play on words here with schizophrenia.

17 Statistics Canada, *Youth in Canada*, 3rd ed. (Ottawa, Ontario: Minister of Industry, 202), 59–66.

18 "Adolescents: Self and Culture," in Offer, Ostrow, Howard, and Atkinson, *The Teenage World*, 11.

19 "The more science is incorporated into the labor process, the less the worker understands of the process; the more sophisticated an intellectual product the machine becomes, the less control and comprehension of the machine the worker has. In other words, the more the worker needs to know in order to remain a human being at work, the less does he or she know." Harry Braverman, *Labor and Monopoly Capital: The Degradation of Work in the Twentieth Century* (New York: Monthly Review Press, 1974), 425.

20 Robert K. Logan, *The Sixth Language: Learning a Living in the Internet Age* (Toronto: Stoddart, 2000), 203 [emphasis mine].

21 Karen Sternheimer, *It's Not the Media: The Truth about Pop Culture's Influence on Children* (Boulder, CO: Westview Press, 2003), 215.

22 Braverman, *Labor and Monopoly Capital*, 424–49.

23 For more information on the role of railroads and the telegraph in the rise of American big business and the change in roles for the advertiser, producer, seller, and purchaser of goods in the nineteenth and early twentieth centuries, see Alfred D. Chandler, Jr., *The Visible Hand: The Managerial Revolution in American Business* (Cambridge, MA: Belknap Press, 1977).

24 Thomas K. McCraw, *American Business, 1920–2000: How It Worked* (Wheeling, IL: Harlan Davidson, Inc., 2000), 55.

25 Ibid., 54.

26 Sternheimer, *It's Not the Media*, 152.

27 Theodor Adorno, "The Schema of Mass Culture," in *The Culture Industry: Selected Essays on Mass Culture*, ed. J.M. Bernstein (London: Routledge, 1991), 58.

28 Ethnomusicologist, Grammy Award winner, and Staxx Records biographer Rob Bowman, Lecture, York University, Toronto, January 6, 2003. See also David Taras, "Swimming against the Current: American Mass Entertainment and Canadian Identity," in *Canada and the United States: Differences That Count*, ed. David M. Thomas, 2nd ed. (Peterborough, Ontario: Broadview Press, 2000), 193, 194, 200.

29 David Szatmary, *Rockin' in Time: A Social History of Rock-and-Roll*, 4th ed. (Englewood Cliffs, NJ: Prentice-Hall, 2000), 43.

30 Jon Hartmann, an employee of Colonel Parker, quoted in ibid., 44.

31 Ibid., 47.

32 Ibid., 55.

33 Ibid.

34 Ibid.

35 Ibid.

36 This is a play on words between convergence and immediate family.

37 Taras, "Swimming against the Current," 200.

38 Ibid.

39 David Taras, "The CBC and Canadian Television in the New Media Age," in *A Passion for Identity: An Introduction to Canadian Studies*, ed. David Taras, 3rd ed. (Scarborough, Ontario: ITP Nelson, 1997), 265.

40 "Surfing the new you: TV shows sell the idea that we can transform ourselves. Why are so many people buying?" *Toronto Star*, January 10, 2004, L1, L4.

41 Sternheimer, *It's Not the Media*, 164.

42 "Adolescents: Self and Culture," in Offer, Ostrow, Howard, and Atkinson, *The Teenage World*, 15.

43 Sternheimer, *It's Not the Media*, 164.

44 Adorno, "The Culture Industry Revisited," 237.

45 J.L. Granatstein, Yankee Go Home? Canadians and Anti-Americanism (Toronto: Harper Collins Publishers, 1996), 4–5.

46 Taras, "Swimming against the Current," 199.

Rethinking Section 2:
FOUNDATIONS OF SOCIETY

Critical Thinking Questions

Section 2A: Socialization and Social Interaction

Antoinette Errante

1. What is meant by conflict-based solidarity? Identify and describe the three different kinds of solidarity experiences.
2. Errante argues that "the everyday experiences we offer to children is one important way in which the 'personal becomes political.'" What is meant by this phrase? How is the personal becoming increasingly global?
3. How does Errante link violence and masculinity?

Kent L. Sandstrom

1. What are the implications of this article for our understanding of identity, or what does it tell us about identity (who we think we are)? Why might this be important?
2. An important theme in social theory is the debate/tension between two concepts: (a) structure and (b) agency. Define these two concepts. How does symbolic interactionism manage this debate and why is it significant? How does Sandstrom handle this debate?
3. Think about and give examples of how meaning might be fluid. How might meanings help promote or hinder social life?

Section 2B: Culture

Michael Atkinson

1. How are women's bodies socially constructed? How is femininity part of this construction?
2. What reasons did the women give for tattooing? How is tattooing a form of established femininity?
3. How can tattooing be understood as a practice of cultural resistance?
4. Do all tattoos carry the same symbolic significance? Explain.

Viviane Namaste

1. Explain Namaste's distinction between transsexual and transgender.
2. What is the significance of "identity" in this piece?
3. How do institutions exclude transsexual people?
4. How are transgendered people marginalized in society?

Stephen Gennaro

1. What are the main messages of the culture industry? How are they exemplified through media?
2. In a brand-name and consumption-based culture, how does socio-economic status affect/influence the creation of identities?
3. How is language an important part of an imagined community of youth?
4. Gennaro poses the question: "Is Canada, as a nation, lost in an abyss of perpetual adolescence in the same way that citizens are?" Discuss possible answers to this question. Is this portion of the article convincing?

Glossary Terms

Section 2A: Socialization and Social Interaction

Antoinette Errante

conflict-based solidarities: Solidarity groups bound by imagining a common enemy that is constructed as a demonized, de-humanized other.

lived solidarity experiences: Solidarities and practices that children engage with in daily life.

modelled solidarity experiences: Solidarities and practices of high-status adults observed by children.

vicarious solidarity experiences: Situations and circumstances that children indirectly experience.

Kent L. Sandstrom

grounded theory: A qualitative approach to analyzing data; developing theory from data.

mutable: Can be changed.

post-mortal self: Constructions of self that will transcend death.

Section 2B: Culture

Michael Atkinson

established groups: Long-standing social groups with access to resources.

outsider group: Marginal group that stands outside of key power positions.

Viviane Namaste

transgender: Umbrella term to include a range of people who fall outside normative relations of sex and gender. Includes but is not limited to transsexuals, drag queens, intersexed individuals, drag kings, transvestites, and so forth.

transsexual: Individuals who are born as one sex (male or female), but identify as members of the "opposite" sex.

Stephen Gennaro

imagined community of youth: A consumption-constructed nation created through a privileging of a youth culture via the media through which all youth can find a common identity.

perpetual adolescence: The disappearance of boundaries surrounding a set time period around the developmental stage of adolescence, now a lifelong process.

saturated selves: People with fragmented selves; oversaturated with images, information, and relationships.

Relevant Web sites

http://www.bbc.co/uk/society

This site illustrates British culture and social relationships through pictures, message boards, and articles.

http://www.culturecanada.gc.ca/culture.nsf

This French and English site is the government of Canada's "one-stop Web access to government culture, heritage, and recreation services."

http://www.mcdc.org

This site informs the public about cultural diversity in an effort to make workplaces more understanding spaces.

http://www.culture.ca/canada/

This is "Canada's cultural gateway." The mandate of the site is to engage Canadians in cultural life, and to educate and entertain.

http://racerelations.about.com

Run by About, this site offers many links to information on affirmative action, White privilege, stereotyping, hate crimes, and so forth.

http://www.wadsworth.com/sociology_d/special_features/popups/virtual/03.html

This site offers many links to other sites concerned with socialization. There is also an online quiz to test your knowledge.

http://faculty.plattsburgh.edu/robert.harsh/socializa.htm

Outlines the contributions of George Herbert Mead and Erving Goffman.

http://www.childdevelopmentinfo.com/parenting/socialization.shtml

Provides a "how-to" of socialization for parents, offered by the Child Development Institute.

http://mud.5341.com/msg/1292.htm

Here you will find several articles discussing social interaction online. The articles explore the ways in which traditional social interaction is challenged by online communities.

http://learninfreedom.org/socialization.html

This Web site provides examples of home-school socialization. The authors argue that the age segregation characteristic of traditional schools leads to poor socialization.

Further Reading

Bibby, Reginald. (2001). *Canada's Teens: Today, Yesterday, and Tomorrow.* Toronto: Stoddart.
An analysis drawing from Canada-wide surveys of both teens and adults.

Eder, Donna, with Catherine Colleen Evans and Stephen Parker. (1995). *School Talk: Gender and Adolescent Culture.* New Brunswick: Rutgers University Press.
A comprehensive and engaging qualitative analysis of modern adolescents.

Gerbner, George. (1995). "Television Violence: The Power and the Peril." In Gail Dines and Jean Humez (eds.), *Gender, Race, and Class in Media: A Text-Reader*, pp. 547–557. Thousand Oaks: Sage.
An article that outlines how television violence can affect both adults' and children's attitudes and behaviours.

Goffman, Erving. (1959). *The Presentation of Self in Everyday Life.* New York: Anchor Books.
A classic piece in symbolic interactionist theory.

Kanter, Rosabeth Moss. (1977). *Men and Women of the Corporation.* New York: Basic Books.
A key study of gender operating in corporations illustrating the interaction between social interaction and social organizations.

Mead, George Herbert. (1934). *Mind, Self and Society.* Chicago: University of Chicago Press.
A classic theoretical address concerning symbolic interactionism.

Neal, Mark Anthony. (1999). *What the Music Said: Black Popular Music and Black Public Culture.* New York: Routledge.
An analysis of the various social forces shaping Black popular music over the past 50 years.

Reay, Diane. (2001). "'Spice Girls,' 'Nice Girls,' 'Girlies,' and 'Tomboys'": Gender Discourses, Girls' Cultures, and Femininities in the Primary Classroom." *Gender and Education, 13*(2), pp. 153–166.
Explores contemporary gendered power relations in primary school.

Stanley, Liz, and Sue Wise. (1983). *Breaking Out.* London: Routledge.
The authors offer a critique of the concept of socialization.

Thorne, Barrie. (1993). *Gender Play.* Buckingham: Open University Press.
The author explores whether girls and boys occupy different gendered cultures.

Major Social Institutions

The Readings

Section 3A: Family

CHAPTER 15
The Way We Weren't: The Myth and Reality of the "Traditional" Family, *Stephanie Coontz*

CHAPTER 16
Family Responsibilities: The Politics of Love and Care, *Meg Luxton*

CHAPTER 17
Will & Grace: Negotiating (Gay) Marriage on Prime-Time Television, *Karin Quimby*

Section 3B: The Economy and Labour

CHAPTER 18
Serving the McCustomer: Fast Food Is Not about Food, *Ester Reiter*

CHAPTER 19
The Discarded Factory: Degraded Production in the Age of the Superbrand, *Naomi Klein*

Section 3C: Education

CHAPTER 20
Enchanting McUniversity: Toward a Spectacularly Irrational University Quotidian, *George Ritzer*

CHAPTER 21
Keeping the Ivory Tower White: Discourses of Racial Domination, *Carol Schick*

Section 3D: Health and Health Care

CHAPTER 22
Gender, Race, and Health Inequalities, *Ann Pederson and Dennis Raphael*

In Canadian society, there are many building blocks to social life. In this section, we consider the central institutions of families, the economy, education, and health. For each topic, we trouble the idea that there is something "natural" or functional about these social entities.

"Family" is often considered to be the key site of our collective social life. It is within this social institution that children are usually first socialized, and within this social grouping that many of our norms and values are learned. But families—however they are defined and whatever their makeup—do not exist in isolation from other social institutions. Political forces and practices, trends in the macro-economy, and conditions of paid and unpaid work also affect and shape individuals. The social institutions in Canadian society exert profound positive and negative influences over our daily lives and, depending on one's social location, can be agents that liberate or oppress. One of the central tasks of sociological inquiry is to move beneath the surface of social relations to reveal the structure and consequences of "common sense" ideas about society. "Family" is a subject that provokes heated debate as it is at once deeply personal and politically charged. The readings about family in this section challenge the idea of the male breadwinner model and suggest that families must be seen as both places of nurturing and care as well as places of subordination and inequality. They underline that there is no one family form, but rather that families come in many configurations and none should be prioritized over another.

Stephanie Coontz contrasts the ideal that many North Americans have about family life (often a happy, White, middle-class nuclear family with Dad working for pay and Mum at home with the kids) with historical evidence of the functions of marriage for society and gender divisions of labour within families. She asserts that the "revival" of a romanticized ideal of the "traditional" family form is narrow and serves few people. Coontz shows that while women are more autonomous and have greater equality today, families are not sites of equal sharing of work and responsibility. She argues that the challenge is to build social institutions and values that meet the needs and realities of contemporary families. Meg Luxton's research shows an alarming trend toward the burden of caregiving work being shifted to families in the late 1990s. Changes in state-level funding for caregiving supports translate into increased unpaid work for mostly women in households at a time when labour market demands are also intense and conditions of work deteriorating for many. Luxton introduces us to the concept of neo-liberalism, which involves favouring little government involvement in social policy and thus greater private market and family provision of social services. Luxton's research confirms that families are not isolated social institutions; rather, they are often fragile and require support and investment. She points out that as neo-liberal states retreat from social service provision, they often assume that women in families will make up for service cuts. This assumption has dramatic and sometimes tragic consequences for many families. Karin Quimby presents an analysis of the television sit-com *Will & Grace*. She suggests that the very definition of marriage is challenged on this show and, by extension, in many people's lived experiences. The intimacy of a gay man and his best friend (a single woman) responds to straight women's disappointment with traditional heterosexual relationships. Moreover, she asserts that the nature of the relationship between the two main characters forces a deeper discussion of what constitutes family and marriage.

The readings on the economy and labour in this section go to the heart of the disconnect between global capitalism and citizenship. Ester Reiter's compelling examination of the fast-food industry underlines the fallacy of the appearance of greater freedom emanating from global "McWorld" capitalism: collective protections afforded to people on the basis of citizenship are increasingly replaced with the hollow individual freedom to be customers. She considers the nature of the work relationship in the fast-food world, and speculates on the bleakness of a future modelled on fast-food corporatism. Exploring a similar theme, Naomi Klein examines the corporate practices behind big-name logos like Nike, Disney, and the Gap, foregrounding the lived experiences of workers in export-processing zones. The hyper-value placed on creating brand affiliation comes at the excruciating expense of the people who do the work of production. Manufacturers, in the age of the "discarded factory," are less and less responsible to their own workforces. These readings on the economy and work are blunt in their assessment of the social anesthetic of a consumption-driven economy: The search for satiety based on consumption is endless because the quest itself is porous, and its costs in human, environmental, and social terms are high for producers and for consumers alike.

Education is not neutral and is increasingly organized by corporatist practices of rationalization while carrying with it a legacy of exclusion and elitism. George Ritzer considers the McDonaldization of higher education. He asserts that the escalating culture of consumerism has transformed the university into a site of consumption, making students and their parents into customers. Yet the low-cost and efficiency models demanded by customers cannot produce the individualized consumption experience many expect; the nature of the relationship between student and university is profoundly altered by a charade of attracting consumers rather than seeking intellectual excellence. Carol Shick's chapter considers the university as a site of racial privilege. Based on interviews with White, pre-service education students attending a cross-cultural course, she explores the processes through which students affirm their sense of entitled, racially based occupancy of university space.

Finally, this section explores health and health care in Canada, attending to questions of gender and race in particular. Ann Pederson *and* Dennis Raphael consider the complexity of understanding the *social* determinants of health. While being sick and getting care might appear to be an equal-opportunity experience, they make plain that social and economic vulnerability predispose particular populations, especially Aboriginal people and women, to significant risk.

CHAPTER 15

The Way We Weren't:
The Myth and Reality of the "Traditional" Family

Stephanie Coontz

Families face serious problems today, but proposals to solve them by reviving "traditional" family forms and values miss two points. First, no single traditional family existed to which we could return, and none of the many varieties of families in our past has had any magic formula for protecting its members from the vicissitudes of socioeconomic change, the inequities of class, race, and gender, or the consequences of interpersonal conflict. Violence, child abuse, poverty, and the unequal distribution of resources to women and children have occurred in every period and every type of family.

Second, the strengths that we also find in many families of the past were rooted in different social, cultural, and economic circumstances from those that prevail today. Attempts to reproduce any type of family outside of its original socioeconomic context are doomed to fail.

Colonial Families

American families always have been diverse, and the male breadwinner-female homemaker, nuclear ideal that most people associate with "the" traditional family has predominated for only a small portion of our history. In colonial America, several types of families coexisted or competed. Native American kinship systems subordinated the nuclear family to a much larger network of marital alliances and kin obligations, ensuring that no single family was forced to go it alone. Wealthy settler families from Europe, by contrast, formed independent households that pulled in labor from poorer neighbors and relatives, building their extended family solidarities on the backs of truncated families among indentured servants, slaves, and the poor. Even wealthy families, though, often were disrupted by death; a majority of colonial Americans probably spent some time in a stepfamily. Meanwhile, African Americans, denied the legal protection of marriage and parenthood, built extensive kinship networks and obligations through fictive kin ties, ritual co-parenting or godparenting, adoption of orphans, and complex naming patterns designed to preserve family links across space and time.

The dominant family values of colonial days left no room for sentimentalizing childhood. Colonial mothers, for example, spent far less time doing child care than do modern working women, typically delegating this task to servants or older siblings. Among white families, patriarchal authority was so absolute that disobedience by a wife or child was seen as a small form of treason, theoretically punishable by death, and family relations were based on power, not love.

The Nineteenth-Century Family

With the emergence of a wage-labor system and a *national* market in the first third of the nineteenth century, white middle-class families became less patriarchal and more child-centered. The ideal of the male breadwinner and the nurturing mother now appeared. But the emergence of domesticity for middle-class women and children depended on its absence among the immigrant, working class, and African American women or children who worked as servants, grew the cotton, or toiled in the textile mills to free middle-class wives from the chores that had occupied their time previously.

Even in the minority of nineteenth-century families who could afford domesticity, though, emotional arrangements were quite different from nostalgic images of "traditional" families. Rigid insistence on separate spheres for men and women made male-female relations extremely stilted, so that women commonly turned to other women, not their husbands, for their most intimate relations. The idea that all of one's passionate feelings should go toward a member of the opposite sex was a twentieth-century invention—closely associated with the emergence of a mass consumer society and promulgated by the very film industry that "traditionalists" now blame for undermining such values.

Early Twentieth-Century Families

Throughout the nineteenth century, at least as much divergence and disruption in the experience of family life existed as does today, even though divorce and unwed motherhood were less common. Indeed, couples who marry today have a better chance of celebrating a fortieth wedding anniversary than at any previous time in history. The life cycles of nineteenth-century youth (in job entry, completion of schooling, age at marriage, and establishment of separate residence) were far more diverse than they became in the early twentieth century. At the turn of the century a higher proportion of people remained single for their entire lives than at any period since. Not until the 1920s did a bare majority of children come to live in a male breadwinner-female homemaker family, and even at the height of this family form in the 1950s, only 60 percent of American children spent their entire childhoods in such a family.

From about 1900 to the 1920s, the growth of mass production and emergence of a public policy aimed at establishing a family wage led to new ideas about family self-sufficiency, especially in the white middle class and a privileged sector of the working class. The resulting families lost their organic connection to intermediary units in society such as local shops, neighborhood work cultures and churches, ethnic associations, and mutual-aid organizations.

As families related more directly to the state, the market, and the mass media, they also developed a new cult of privacy, along with heightened expectations about the family's role in fostering individual fulfillment. New family values stressed the early independence of children and the romantic coupling of husband and wife, repudiating the intense same-sex ties and mother-infant bonding of earlier years as unhealthy. From this family we get the idea that women are sexual, that youth is attractive, and that marriage should be the center of our emotional fulfillment.

Even aside from its lack of relevance to the lives of most immigrants, Mexican Americans, African Americans, rural families, and the urban poor, big contradictions existed between image and reality in the middle-class family ideal of the early twentieth century. This is the period when many Americans first accepted the idea that the family should be sacred from outside intervention; yet the development of the private, self-sufficient family depended on state intervention in the economy, government regulation of parent-child relations, and state-directed destruction of class and community institutions that hindered the development of family privacy. Acceptance of a youth and leisure culture sanctioned early marriage and raised expectations about the quality of married life, but also introduced new tensions between the generations and new conflicts between husband and wife over what were adequate levels of financial and emotional support.

The nineteenth-century middle-class ideal of the family as a refuge from the world of work was surprisingly modest compared with emerging twentieth-century demands that the family provide a whole alternative world of satisfaction and intimacy to that of work and neighborhood. Where a family succeeded in doing so, people might find pleasures in the home never before imagined. But the new ideals also increased the possibilities for failure: America has had the highest divorce rate in the world since the turn of the century.

In the 1920s, these contradictions created a sense of foreboding about "the future of the family" that was every bit as widespread and intense as today's. Social scientists and popular commentators of the time hearkened back to the "good old days," bemoaning the sexual revolution, the fragility of nuclear family ties, the cult of youthful romance, the decline of respect for grandparents, and the threat of the "New Woman." But such criticism was sidetracked by the stock-market crash, the Great Depression of the 1930s, and the advent of World War II.

Domestic violence escalated during the Depression, while murder rates were as high in the 1930s as in the 1980s. Divorce rates fell, but desertion increased and fertility plummeted. The war stimulated a marriage boom, but by the late 1940s one in every three marriages was ending in divorce.

The 1950s Family

At the end of the 1940s, after the hardships of the Depression and war, many Americans revived the nuclear family ideals that had so disturbed commentators during the 1920s. The unprecedented postwar prosperity allowed young families to achieve consumer satisfactions and socioeconomic mobility that would have been inconceivable in earlier days. The 1950s family that resulted from these economic and cultural trends, however, was hardly "traditional." Indeed, it is best seen as a historical aberration. For the first time in 100 years, divorce rates dropped, fertility soared, the gap between men's and women's job and educational prospects widened (making middle-class women more dependent on marriage), and the age of marriage fell—to the point that teenage birth rates were almost double what they are today.

Admirers of these very nontraditional 1950s family forms and values point out that household arrangements and gender roles were less diverse in the 1950s than today, and marriages more stable. But this was partly because diversity was ruthlessly suppressed and partly because economic and political support systems for socially sanctioned families were far more generous than they are today. Real wages rose more in any single year of the 1950s than they did in the entire decade of the 1980s; the average thirty-year-old man could buy a median-priced home on 15 to 18 percent of his income. The government-funded public investment, home ownership, and job creation at a rate more than triple that of the past two decades, while 40 percent of young men were eligible for veteran's benefits. Forming and maintaining families was far easier than it is today.

Yet the stability of these 1950s families did not guarantee good outcomes for their members. Even though most births occurred within wedlock, almost a third of

American children lived in poverty during the 1950s, a higher figure than today. More than 50 percent of black married-couple families were poor. Women were often refused the right to serve on juries, sign contracts, take out credit cards in their own names, or establish legal residence. Wife-battering rates were low, but that was because wife-beating was seldom counted as a crime. Most victims of incest, such as Miss America of 1958, kept the secret of their fathers' abuse until the 1970s or 1980s, when the women's movement became powerful enough to offer them the support denied them in the 1950s.

The Post-1950s Family

In the 1960s, the civil rights, antiwar, and women's liberation movements exposed the racial, economic, and sexual injustices that had been papered over by the Ozzie and Harriet images on television. Their activism made older kinds of public and private oppression unacceptable and helped create the incomplete, flawed, but much-needed reforms of the Great Society. Contrary to the big lie of the past decade that such programs caused our current family dilemmas, those antipoverty and social justice reforms helped overcome many of the family problems that prevailed in the 1950s.

In 1964, after fourteen years of unrivaled family stability and economic prosperity, the poverty rate was still 19 percent; in 1969, after five years of civil rights activism, the rebirth of feminism, and the institution of nontraditional if relatively modest government welfare programs, it was down to 12 percent, a low that has not been seen again since the social welfare cutbacks began in the late 1970s. In 1965, 20 percent of American children still lived in poverty; within five years, that had fallen to 15 percent. Infant mortality was cut in half between 1965 and 1980. The gap in nutrition between low-income Americans and other Americans narrowed significantly, as a direct result of food stamp and school lunch programs. In 1963, 20 percent of Americans living below the poverty line had never been examined by a physician; by 1970 this was true of only 8 percent of the poor.

Since 1973, however, real wages have been falling for most Americans. Attempts to counter this through tax revolts and spending freezes have led to drastic cutbacks in government investment programs. Corporations also spend far less on research and job creation than they did in the 1950s and 1960s, though the average compensation to executives has soared. The gap between rich and poor, according to the April 17, 1995, *New York Times*, is higher in the United States than in any other industrial nation.

Family Stress

These inequities are not driven by changes in family forms, contrary to ideologues who persist in confusing correlations with causes; but they certainly exacerbate such changes, and they tend to bring out the worst in all families. The result has been an accumulation of stresses on families, alongside some important expansions of personal options. Working couples with children try to balance three full-time jobs, as employers and schools cling to policies that assume every employee has a "wife" at home to take care of family matters. Divorce and remarriage have allowed many adults and children to escape from toxic family environments, yet our lack of social support networks and failure to forge new values for sustaining intergenerational obligations have let many children fall through the cracks in the process.

Meanwhile, young people find it harder and harder to form or sustain families. According to an Associated Press report of April 25, 1995, the median income of men aged twenty-five to thirty-four fell by 26 percent between 1972 and 1994, while the proportion of such men with earnings below the poverty level for a family of four more than doubled to 32 percent. The figures are even worse for African American and Latino men. Poor individuals are twice as likely to divorce as more affluent ones, three to four times less likely to marry in the first place, and five to seven times more likely to have a child out of wedlock.

As conservatives insist, there is a moral crisis as well as an economic one in modern America: a pervasive sense of social alienation, new levels of violence, and a decreasing willingness to make sacrifices for others. But romanticizing "traditional" families and gender roles will not produce the changes in job structures, work policies, child care, medical practice, educational preparation, political discourse, and gender inequities that would permit families to develop moral and ethical systems relevant to 1990s realities.

America needs more than a revival of the narrow family obligations of the 1950s, whose (greatly exaggerated) protection for white, middle-class children was achieved only at tremendous cost to the women in those families and to all those who could not or would not aspire to the Ozzie and Harriet ideal. We need a concern for children that goes beyond the question of whether a mother is waiting with cookies when her kids come home from school. We need a moral language that allows us to address something besides people's sexual habits. We need to build values and social institutions that can reconcile people's needs for independence with their equally important rights to dependence, and surely we must reject older solutions that involved balancing these needs on the backs of women. We will not find our answers in nostalgia for a mythical "traditional family."

CHAPTER 16
Family Responsibilities:
The Politics of Love and Care

MEG LUXTON

*   *   *   *   *

The Importance of Social Responsibilities

A defining feature of capitalism is the separation of the production of commodities from the production and reproduction of people. Capitalist economics only recognizes as economically valuable activities of the market, taking for granted the existence of people available as workers and consumers. And while wages are recognized as a cost of production they are not directly tied to the costs of social reproduction—all the activities that ensure the day to day and generational survival of people, from having babies, raising children, provisioning household members by cooking, cleaning, maintaining the home, and caring for those who are ill or elderly (Fox and Luxton, 2001: 26). Two spheres, the state and family household, act to mediate the gap between earnings and costs of living. The state through its regulations, by redistributing wealth and providing services, plays a role in ensuring certain standards of living (Ursel, 1992). Families, and particularly women, through the unpaid work they do in their own homes, taking care of themselves and the people they love, make up the difference (Luxton and Corman, 2001).

One of the major contributions of the women's movement has been its insistence that the caregiving activities that go on in our homes are important, economically valuable work. Feminists have challenged prevailing economic theories and the policies informed by them, insisting that the labours of love central to domestic labour and caregiving are necessary for capitalist economics and for the survival of all of us, as individuals and as a people or a species (Waring, 1988). The women's movement also argues that the duty and self-sacrifice required by those providing caregiving are often oppressive. Feminists call for a reorganization of society so that love and care can flourish as creative social forces. The on-going struggles of the women's movement have focussed on efforts to win social recognition and support for interpersonal caregiving (Luxton, 1997). However, the neo-liberal political agenda that has come to dominate international economics and governing practices is creating a climate in which [feminist] demands seem outdated and impractical, and opposition to them is increasing.

Neo-liberalism and the Privatization of Caregiving

A neo-liberal agenda has dominated policy making in Canada for about two decades now. As these policies have been implemented, the central tenets of neo-liberalism have become increasingly clear. Most obvious is its commitment to expanding the unfettered investment of capital and a growing reliance on markets and private profit making. Key to this is the emphasis on reducing the role of the state in providing services and protections for the population as a whole, while strengthening its activities in support of business interests and private profit making. One of the main assumptions motivating this agenda is that "private choice is better than public regulation as a mechanism for allocating resources and ordering social affairs" (Philipps, 2000: 1).

This neo-liberal agenda argues that changing international realities put roughly the same demands on all governments (Brodie 1996: 4). Representing the interests of the business or corporate sector, it calls on governments to adopt as priorities: the creation of free markets and the pursuit of free trade policies (such as NAFTA) to maximize exports and enable market forces to restructure national economies as parts of transnational or regional trading blocs; the reduction of government regulation of the economy to free business from "oppressive" government controls, especially by weakening labour market regulation (such as anti-scab legislation, or pay and employment equity policies); reducing taxes on corporations; reducing government spending on social programs; and privatizing public services (Brodie, 1995: 16).

These changes in economic and social policy have both required and produced a change in the dominant assumptions about social life. Part of what fuelled the emergence of neo-liberalism, and especially its most conservative wing, the new right, was the revitalization of existing and emergence of new activist, equality, and liberation movements in the 1960s and 1970s. These movements organized collectively to challenge the inequalities and discriminations faced by members of socially recognized groups: women, Aboriginal peoples, visible minorities, immigrants, people with disabilities, low income, lesbian, gay, bisexual and transgendered peoples. Activists from these movements revealed that existing welfare policies and practices sustained and reproduced prevailing assumptions about class, gender, race, disability, and sexuality, actively reproducing the subordinate and marginalized status of these and a range of other social constituencies. What the new right attacked was not just the existing welfare state social security net already in place, but what it might have become in response to the expansionist and transformative demands of what are called the "equity seeking groups."

That attack has had significant success. As Marjorie Cohen has argued, it was a shift from a period in which "the deep contradictions in capitalism were modified by a system of social welfare based on the assumption that the well-being of the economy depended on the well-being of the people in it" to a situation in which "social and economic well-being for people is subordinate to the well-being of the corporate sector" (Cohen, 1997: 5). There has also been a strong move away from collective responsibility to individual initiative with a concomitant acceptance of greater insecurity and inequality, as government's practice moves from a redistributive state to one that more openly justifies and reinforces market outcomes by rewarding those who place the least demand on public social programmes and to cajoling the rest of us to follow their example (Philipps, 2002).

Central to this is a claim that individuals and their families should take more responsibility for their own care, that government provision of services is inefficient and costly, that reliance on state services weakens individual initiative and undermines family and community ties, and that caregiving is best arranged through voluntary familial and community networks. In almost all welfare economies, family caregiving, and particularly women's unpaid labour, is a crucial but unrecognized part of welfare provision. State policies have assumed that families have always been the main provider of welfare: family members are left to work out their own solutions to the problems of combining paid employment and unpaid domestic labour, and women typically have had the primary responsibility for implementing those solutions (Luxton and Corman, 2001). The women's movement has challenged such arrangements, called for state support for women's economic independence (through equal work and pay legislation and the provision of childcare services, maternity and parental leaves, for example), and for public recognition and valuing of the activities Sorokin identified: love, service, sacrifice, mutual aid and duty, that are so central to unpaid work in the home (Armstrong and Armstrong, 1994; Maroney and Luxton, 1997). Yet the success of neo-liberalism rests on widespread acceptance that households must absorb more of the work necessary to ensure their subsistence and the livelihoods of their members.

In neo-liberalist discourse, support for privatization carries a double meaning, implying both the private sector of the economy and the private realm of the family. A whole range of developments have reduced or eliminated government services, enforcing "self-reliance," that is, compelling people to rely on earnings, support from friends and family and voluntary organizations and privatized services [....]

Advocates of neo-liberal policies tend to argue either that economic developments in recent years prove their efficacy or that there is no other choice. They point to government surpluses, to increased trade, to the growing profits of so many major banks and corporations, and to the increased personal wealth enjoyed by many as evidence of success. They note that globalization means that if Canada is to remain competitive, Canadian governments must comply. In the words of Margaret Thatcher, a leading implementer of neo-liberalism, "There is no alternative" (Harvey, 2000: 17). When confronted with evidence that many people are not benefiting from the current regime, they tend to attribute such problems to personal failure, a lack of initiative, or an inability to adapt to changing circumstances.

＊　　＊　　＊　　＊　　＊

The impact of changes in international investment and trade, national labour market practices and regulations, the consequences of cuts to government social services and transfer payments to health and education, and the effects of income inequalities have all been well-documented by both advocates and opponents. Contending assessments have been extensively debated but one outcome is clear. There is growing inequality as the income differences between the wealthiest and poorest groups in Canada have increased dramatically (Yalnizyan, 1998; *The Globe and Mail* 16/3/01: A3). This class inequality is also deeply gendered and racialized as women, and particularly aboriginal and immigrant women and women of color, are more likely to be poor than men, in part because of their major responsibility for caregiving (Statistics Canada 2000: 137, 205, 259). What is less well documented, and to date, less subject to discussion, is the impact of the changing economic order on individual and family responsibility for caregiving, changes which, like poverty, have disproportionately affected women.

According to the United Nations statistics on poverty in industrialised nations, 11.7 per cent of people living in Canada have incomes below 50 per cent of its median income (compared to 5–7 per cent in European countries and 19.1 per cent in the USA) (Townson, 2000: 14). Not only has the number of people with low incomes risen since the early 1980s, but the degree of poverty experienced by those living on low incomes has dramatically deepened.[1] The National Council of Welfare in its 1999 *Poverty Profile* reports that the number of individuals and families living at less than half the poverty line has also grown. Women, discriminated against in the paid labour force, typically earn less than men (Drolet, 1999) and have been responsible for providing unpaid, family-based caregiving, which has kept many out of the paid labour force for significant periods of time (Armstrong and Armstrong, 1994). As a result, women more than men have relied on social services and have been disproportionately affected by government cuts (Day and Brodsky, 1998).

Increases in the numbers of people living with low incomes are obviously related to changes in the kinds of jobs available and their rates of pay, hours, and benefits. Restructuring in manufacturing and government downsizing have significantly reduced the numbers of full year, full-time unionized jobs that pay a living wage and benefits. More and more new jobs are part time, pay low wages and offer few or no benefits. These labour market changes affected men, especially young men who in previous generations would have been able to get industrial and manufacturing employment, undermining their ability to support families. They have also significantly reduced the numbers of "good jobs" available to women especially in the public sector (Luxton and Reiter, 1997: 213). That labour market tendency was reinforced by government policies that backed away from employment and pay equity measures, allowing the historic discrimination in access to jobs and gender differences in pay rates to continue (Drolet, 1999: 32). Over the past decade the growth of low paid, temporary jobs has created a female-dominated contingent workforce of people who rarely earn a living wage (Vosko, 2000).

Changing government policies, especially cuts to unemployment/employment insurance, social services and welfare, have had a disproportionately negative impact on women. The federal government's 1990 cap on the Canada Assistance Plan (CAP), which cut federal support to Ontario, Alberta, and British Columbia, and then its 1996 decision to eliminate CAP and replace it with the Canada Health and Social Transfer (CHST), forced provinces and territories to cut welfare funding. But many provincial and territorial governments were already making eligibility for welfare more stringent and its recipients subject to demeaning scrutiny and control [....] Changes to the federal (un)employment insurance benefits in 1997 have meant that proportionately, fewer women than men are eligible, in part because more women have part-time jobs where it is harder to get enough qualifying hours and it became more difficult to qualify after time out of the labour force (*The Globe and Mail* 23/3/00: A1, A6).

Over the past two decades, the percentage of women living in poverty has steadily increased. In 1980, 1.8 million women had low incomes; now, about 2.2 million adult women have low incomes. Almost 19 per cent of adult women are poor. When women have low incomes, their children live in poverty too. About 20 per cent of low-income women are mothers raising their children on their own; another 51 per cent are co-parents in low-income families (Townson, 2000: 12). The National Council of Welfare estimates that the total welfare income for a single parent with one child ranged from a low of 50 per cent of the poverty level in Alberta to a high of 69 per cent in Newfoundland. For couples with two children, welfare incomes averaged around 50–55 per cent of the poverty level (National Council of Welfare, 1999).

While poverty rates and levels offer one measure of the impact of current policies on social life, we know less about the impact of the changing economic order on individual and family responsibility for caregiving. Precisely because family life is private and individualized, what happens to individuals and in individual family households is often difficult to assess. Motivated by the Harris government's assertion that people should rely less on government services and more on family, friends, neighbours, and community, I did a study, based on in-depth interviews with 117 people, of various class and ethnic backgrounds, living in the greater Toronto region. The study asked, in the context of changing job markets and government cutbacks to social services, what caregiving people provide for and accept from others in their households, extended family, friendship or neighbourhood networks, or their communities? What prompts people to give support and aid? What reduces their sense of responsibility to each other? What strengthens it? How are caregiving exchanges negotiated and what principles underlie such negotiations?[2]

Here I want to report on two themes which shed light on the impact of neo-liberalism on the way love and care are practiced: the constraints that force people to depend on others while making it difficult for people to provide the kind of care they value, and the way people's tendency to contribute to caregiving increases when these responsibilities are shared and supported by government services, while the lack of other supporting services often causes people to withdraw from caregiving, often at the expense of important personal relationships.

The majority of people I interviewed described how their ability to provide care was constrained by their material circumstances, many of which had become more limiting as a result of neo-liberal policies. For example, in twenty-two out of twenty-five households, where adult children were cohabiting with their parents, the two generations were living together only because at least one party could not afford the alternative, either because they had lost their job or their income was insufficient. Even those who willingly accepted the arrangement said there were problematic consequences for their relationships. A man explained that he had readily converted part of his house so his son, daughter-in-law, and their two children could have an apartment. He enjoyed living with them and willingly looked after the children after school each day, relishing his intimacy with the grandchildren. He described the costs of their arrangement:

It seems like it's a success but it is actually not. We all know I am helping them out, because they can't manage on their own. We know we wouldn't live like this if we didn't have to, so every day we have to struggle with that knowledge. They feel inadequate and I feel noble. Neither is healthy. I catch myself watching how they spend their money and resenting it. I think I have a right to tell them how to live. After all, I'm making sacrifices for them. It is not good for my relationship with my son and his wife (M A#36).

Many people reported that cutbacks to social services had forced them to pick up more unpaid work or left them struggling to cope with new demands. A mother of two school-aged children described what she faced:

My kids' school used to have a great after school programme. For just a dollar per day per kid, there were things to do every afternoon—sports, chess club, drama, arts and crafts, you name it. Then it got cut. So now, for my youngest, I have this deal with three other parents. We hire a high school student who comes to the school everyday and picks the kids up. We arranged for a taxi to pick the student and the three kids up and drive them to the community centre where there is a drop in, but kids have to have their own babysitter or parent. Then we pick the kids up from there. It is endlessly complicated. If the student gets sick, or has exams or whatever, or just last week, one kid was sick for a week so her parents didn't want to pay the sitter or taxi, so my budget was shot. Sometimes things get very tense (F A#31).

A woman whose husband was hospitalized for three weeks said that her employer allowed her to have one week paid "emergency" leave and two weeks unpaid leave. She was grateful and made full use of both:

It was so wonderful I could just stay at the hospital and not have to even think about work. My company was really good to me (F A#21).

However, her husband's illness lasted longer than the time allowed her. She had to go back to work just when he was sent home, still too ill to care for himself. Like so many others in her situation, she found existing policies insufficient:

I was in a state of panic for weeks. It was so difficult. I went to work, but how could I concentrate? I was frantic with worry about what was happening at home (F M#21).

Another woman described the new responsibilities and new stress she acquired when her husband was injured:

So on top of my regular job I now have almost a second job, at home, looking after him. I have to get up with him at night, sometimes three or four times. I have to make sure he gets his medication at the right time. Sometimes if I get stuck in traffic on the way home I get so scared because he has to get his injections right on

time and if I'm late, it's just so much a problem (F M#16).

New insecurities in the workplace created problems for many. People reported having difficulties ensuring satisfactory care, even when they could afford it. A highly paid lawyer described what happened when her mother required constant care after a serious illness:

For the first few days, she came to my home and I hired round the clock nursing care. But it was very unsatisfactory. I couldn't rely on them. They kept phoning me to ask questions and I didn't really trust them around the house. So I contacted one of these services and got them to locate a good nursing home. It costs the earth, but I don't have to worry (F M#15).

However, while she was satisfied with the quality of care her mother received, she regretted her lack of personal involvement, a lack imposed by her need to work long hours in order to make enough money to pay for the care:

I could afford it. That wasn't the problem. But I felt terrible. I want to be more involved, you know. If she could have stayed at home I could have seen her more often and been much more involved in her care every day. As it is, I go to visit early in the morning on the way to work and I pop in briefly at night. But it's not the same (F M#15).

She approached the senior partner in her firm to ask if she could cut back her hours for a few months:

I guess I was naïve or something. A few years ago, it was nothing for people to get time off, or go part time. The firm was renowned for its flexibility and openness. Well, was I in for a shock. He didn't just say "no." He actually asked me if I were really cut out for this job! He said this is a new era. Things are more competitive now. Firms that want to survive have to be tough, and this firm, he said, expected everyone who works for it to be tough. He said he was sorry my mother was ill and he knew I would make the right decision (F M#15).

She recognized that if she stopped practicing law to care for her mother all her wealth and skills would be diminished and she could risk poverty.

Other people reported difficulties paid caregivers faced as their workplaces changes. A paid care provider reported that changes in the organization of her work undermined the quality of care she and her coworkers could offer:

I used to work for a government agency as a home care provider. They privatized the agency, so I lost my job. Later I got another job in a private agency but it wasn't unionized and I make about half what I made before. And all they care about is making their money so we actually don't provide care to people any more. We go in and get out as fast as we can. I feel terrible about it (F A#13).

These examples illustrate the way neo-liberal economic policies reduce standards of living for many and impose even more unpaid work on private family households, relying on families, typically women, to absorb the social costs of caregiving. But families' resources are not infinite and women's ability to increase their unpaid work can only stretch so far. While most people were loathe to talk about their breaking points, a few described the devastating effects of overload. The lawyer, unable to get time off work to spend with her mother, described her sense of loss:

> For a brief moment, my mother and I reached a new level of intimacy. We were the closest we've ever been, and we were starting to talk about our relationship, to heal old hurts. But then I wasn't there very much She never said anything but I know she felt hurt. And I felt guilty and couldn't talk about it. So the barriers went back up (F M#15).

A mother described the difficult choices she made when restructuring at her factory meant her employer changed the time she had to start work:

> My shift used to start at 10 a.m. That was very good. I got the children up and took them to the daycare. We had a lot of time. We could sing and tell stories and I didn't have to rush them. Mornings were a very good time. Now I have to be at work at 7 a.m. I let the children sleep until 5:30. Then I must wake them. It is very hard. They are so tired and do not want to get up and then I have to rush, rush, rush. My employer, he says if we are late three times we get fired, so I am very mean to my children in the morning now. It makes me very sad (F A#28).

People are reluctant to talk about family situations that were not supportive but a few indicated some of the tensions and dangers they faced when forced to rely on families. A woman, aged thirty-four, described how she and her two young children had moved into her parents' home after her partner died. She had left that home at fifteen to escape her father's sexual abuse. She returned because the authorities had threatened to take her children away unless she found a home, something she had failed to do in the Toronto housing market on her income from welfare. Feeling trapped, she was frightened that her decision might put her children at risk:

> I've told him not to go anywhere near my kids or I'll kill him. And I never leave them alone with him, ever. It's a hell of a life (F A#31).

She went on to offer a trenchant critique of neo-liberalism, referring to the slogan of the Tory government, the "commonsense revolution":

> When I was a kid and ran away from home, the welfare at least kept me out of my Dad's way and off the streets.

I was on it about three years. I finished school, got a job, and had a good life. That seems like a good return on the investment, I think. Then [my husband] gets killed, I apply but now it's not enough for me and my kids to live on. All we need is a bit of help for a couple of years till I can get on my feet—a place to live, daycare, a job I can support us on. Instead, we're here and trapped, just so someone can enjoy a nice tax cut, but there are big costs for me and my kids—some commonsense way to do things! (F A#31).

The conflicts many people felt between what they aspired to offer or receive, in the way of care, and what they were able to give, or likely to get, are central to the negotiations they enter into when determining the extent to which they get involved, and the quality of care provided. The closer the relationship is (with respect to both kin ties and history), the more likely people are to help each other, but nothing is automatic. People always negotiate (Finch 1989; Finch and Mason 1993). While there were significant differences, particularly based on ethnic background, in how readily people assumed they had the right to expect care from others or accepted the obligation to provide caregiving to others, especially family members, most people acknowledged that such negotiations were complex and emotionally difficult. A daughter described the tensions between her and her mother, produced by her sense that she could not cope alone:

> We Chinese people expect family to take care of family. My mother is old and needs care. She just assumes I will look after her. And so do all the people I talk to when I try to get help—her doctor just tells me what a good daughter I am. The social worker was more understanding but she said there was nothing she could do. What would she say if I weren't here, I wonder? And I believe that is right, that I should look after my mother. But in the old days, I would have others to help me, my aunts and sisters, and my brothers and their wives. There would be several sisters and brothers and aunts to help. And I would not have to go to work at a job, but would work at home. My mother doesn't understand that if I look after her I will do it all alone and I will have my job too. It is too much for me. I need help. But who is there to help me? (F M#23).

There was a clear relationship between the extent of the potential dependence of the care receiver and the willingness of potential caregivers to commit themselves. The more caregivers anticipated that, once they expressed a willingness to provide care, they would be expected to take on full responsibility, the more hesitant they were to make the commitment. A recurring theme was that most professionals and officials associated with government institutions and agencies assumed that family members, and especially women, would provide care and exerted considerable pressure to force families to accept that decision regardless of their actual circumstances and ability to provide care. Such pressures easily evoked anguish or guilt for those who wanted to provide care but couldn't:

My husband was injured at work. He was in hospital for weeks and we thought he was going to die. So I took time off work to stay with him. Then I had to go back to work. When he got out of the hospital, he needed full-time care. Everyone—the doctors, the social workers, the nurses—they all assumed I would take care of him. When I said I couldn't, they acted like I was a monster! Surely if I was a good wife I would do anything for him. Like who was going to pay the bills? I said, he needs care, he should get it. That's what health care is for. Or, he was injured at work, the company should pay someone to care for him. It was a big struggle. I spent hours fighting to get him the care he needed. They really tried to make me do everything but I said I can't, I have to work. I felt terrible, but he understood (F M#16).

Such decisions can have painful and disruptive effects on important relationships. A man had been actively involved in looking after his mother for several years. He visited her daily, ran errands for her, paid her bills, helped with household maintenance, and offered her extensive emotional support. As her mobility decreased, it became clear she would need full-time care. She described their negotiations:

He was stretched to the limit already. We both knew he could keep up what he was doing but he couldn't handle more. But we were all under such pressure for him to move me in with him. And we talked about it and finally we agreed he should take a job he was offered in another city. That way they couldn't force him to do more and he wouldn't feel totally guilty. It was so sad because if I could have got the support I get when he isn't around, he'd still be here. Instead he comes once a month but it's not the same (F M#28).

Official policies about limits to state support when family support is available, may act to block or reduce such support. A mother explained her hesitation about agreeing to have her son and his child move in with her:

You know, I feel like the wicked witch of the west, but I keep saying, "No, you can't move in here." I am afraid that once they move in, they will lose their welfare benefits and the daycare subsidy, and I will be expected to support them for the rest of my life. I just have my pension. It doesn't go far. If I could just have them move in here, that would be very nice. I love my son. He is a lovely man to live with and my grandchild is a joy. I would be happy to help look after him. But I can't take on the whole responsibility. It is too much (F A#27).

Official assumptions that family members will provide care sometimes violate the recipient's desire for independence or evoke their fears of obligation to loved ones.

A daughter described her father's position:

When my father was ready to leave hospital, everyone, his doctor, the social worker, they all assumed I would bring him home to my house. My father was very clear. He said, "No, I do not live with my daughter. You have to get me help." It was quite a struggle because it was obvious I was a simple solution for them (F M#31).

Official assumptions that family should provide care sometimes created painful situations for those needing care:

There I was. They were ready to send me home and I couldn't even stand up by myself. The hospital social worker walked in all cheery to ask when my family was coming to get me. I had to say I had no one to come and get me. Do you have any idea how painful that was to say? Then, it was like I was a bad person because I didn't have someone to look after me and I was such a problem because they had to find services for me! (M M#32).

In contrast, when people had a sense that they could make a helpful contribution to someone's well-being without getting overwhelmed by demands, they were often happy to volunteer.

When my daughter lost her daycare subsidy, she was desperate for childcare and asked if I would do it. I wasn't sure at first, but when I heard she had made an arrangement with another mother for two days a week, I agreed to take [the child] the other three. It works out really well (F A#32).

What emerged from these interviews most clearly is that these people are coping with the erosion of their standards of living, but at significant cost, both economic and interpersonal. They continue to provide care for each other but recognize the wear and tear that increased stress imposes on their relationship. As one man put it:

The bonds of love are strong so we use them to keep us afloat. But there's always the risk those same bonds may strangle us when we have to pull hard on them (M A#28).

Many of the people interviewed expressed a strong sense that the circumstances they found themselves in offered few choices. Repeatedly, stories about increased stress and interpersonal strain were concluded with a shrug and a resigned "but what can you do?" This response is perhaps not surprising in the face of widespread claims that neo-liberal policies are the only option, that there is no alternative. One thing that came out in the interviews was that, while most people did not know how to make changes to improve their circumstances, they had clear ideas about what would improve their situations. What people identified most clearly will come as no surprise. They wanted a living income, decent housing, good health care, time freed from employment to provide care, and access to quality care from reliable sources when they were unable to provide it themselves.

This is where historical memory is so important. For despite all the claims that this is a new world order and that globalization is new, as the term "neo" implies, these are actually a revival of old policies. The assumption that individuals and their families must be self-reliant, bearing as much of the cost of social reproduction as possible, is actually as old as 18th century liberalism itself, and has been central to the organization of capitalist economic relations since their inception (Picchio, 1992). There has also been a long tradition of opposition with well-developed visions of alternatives: a living income, access to education, jobs and training, effective health and safety protections on the job, a safe environment, a shorter working day, week and year, access to housing, health care, child care, elder care, and support for people with disabilities. These are old demands, demands that the labour movement, the women's movement, the left and other progressive movements have put forward for decades (Heron 1996, Carroll, 1997). They are demands that put a decent standard of living for everyone ahead of capitalist profit making, that refuse to subordinate love and care to economic factors. And, contrary to the assertions of neo-liberal proponents, there is extensive historical evidence available to support claims that such alternatives are indeed viable and that the social world they produce is more equitable. That historical record fuels the current challenge to neo-liberalism (*The Globe and Mail* 24/1/01: A15).

*   *   *   *   *

Notes

[1] Statistics Canada identifies people as low income if they need to spend more than 55 per cent on their before-tax income on food, shelter, and clothing. Actual figures are calculated each year and vary by the number of people in a family, and by the number of people living in a region. This approach has been used for over thirty years in Canada (National Council of Welfare 1997).

[2] This study was funded by a grant from the Social Sciences and Humanities Research Council of Canada. I thank that organization for its support and the people who participated in the study. I also thank Ann Eyerman who, as the research associate on the project, conducted many of the interviews and managed the project.

References

Armstrong, Pat, and Hugh Armstrong. 1994. *The Double Ghetto: Canadian Women and Their Segregated Work*, 3rd ed. Toronto: McClelland & Stewart.

Barlow, Maude. 1998. *The Fight of My Life: Confessions of an Unrepentant Canadian*. Toronto: HarperCollins.

Brodie, Janine. 1995. *Politics on the Margins: Restructuring and the Canadian Women's Movement*. Halifax: Fernwood.

Brodie, Janine. 1996. "Canadian Women, Changing State Forms, and Public Policy," in Janine Brodie (ed.), *Women and Canadian Public Policy*. Toronto: Harcourt Brace and Co.

Carroll, William (ed.). 1997. *Organizing Dissent: Contemporary Social Movements in Theory and Practice*, 2nd ed. Toronto: Garamond.

Che-Alford, Janet, and Brian Hamm. Summer 1999. "Under One Roof: Three Generations Living Together," *Social Trends*. Statistics Canada, Catalogue No. 11-008, 6–9.

Cohen, Marjorie. Spring/Summer 1997. "What Women Should Know about Economic Fundamentalism," *Atlantis: A Women's Studies Journal* Vol. 21.2.

Day, Shelagh, and Gwen Brodsky. 1998. *Women and the Equality Deficit: The Impact of Restructuring Canada's Social Programs*. Ottawa: Status of Women.

Drolet, Marie. December 1999. *The Persistent Gap: New Evidence on the Canadian Gender Wage Gap*, Income Statistics Division, Statistics Canada, Catalogue No. 75F0002MIE-99008. Ottawa: Minister of Industry.

Finch, Janet. 1989. *Family Obligations and Social Change*. Cambridge: Polity Press.

Finch, Janet, and Jennifer Mason. 1993. *Negotiating Family Responsibilities*. London: Routledge.

Finestone, Sheila. January 1992–April 1995. *Women's Equality in Canada: Progress in Implementing the Nairobi Forward-Looking Strategies for the Advancement of Women*. Ottawa: Secretary of State, Government of Canada.

Fischer, Charles. April 1994. "The Valuation of Household Production: Divorce, Wrongful Injury and Death Litigation," *American Journal of Economics and Sociology*, Vol. 53, No. 2, 187–201.

Fox, Bonnie, and Meg Luxton. 2001. "Conceptualizing Family," in Bonnie Fox (ed.), *Family Patterns, Gender Relations*. Toronto: Oxford University Press.

The Globe and Mail. 23 March 2000. "UI Fraud Suspected as Sickness Claims Soar" by Daniel Leblanc. A1, A6.

The Globe and Mail. 24 January 2001. "The Battle of the Global Gatherings" by Naomi Klein. A15.

The Globe and Mail. 16 March 2001. "Wealth Gap Grew Wider, Statscan Study Finds" by Heather Scoffield. A3.

Hansard, Ontario. 30 April 1998. "Throne Speech Debate," www.on.ca/hansard/36-parl/session/L005a-3.htm-101K.

Harvey, David. 2000. *Spaces of Hope*. Berkeley, Los Angeles: The University of California Press.

Heron, Craig. 1996. *The Canadian Labour Movement: A Short History*. Toronto: Lorimer and Company.

Janigan, Mary. 13 November 2000. "Towards a Two-Tier System," *Maclean's Canada's Weekly Newsmagazine*, 22.

Luxton, Meg (ed.). 1997. *Feminism and Families: Critical Policies and Changing Practices*. Halifax: Fernwood.

Luxton, Meg, and June Corman. 2001. *Getting by in Hard Times: Gendered Labour at Home and on the Job*. Toronto: University of Toronto Press.

Luxton, Meg, and Ester Reiter. 1997. "Double, Double, Toil and Trouble ... Women's Experience of Work and Family 1980–1995," in Patricia Evans and Gerda Wekerle (eds.), *Women and the Canadian Welfare State: Challenges and Change*. Toronto: University of Toronto Press, 197–221.

Maroney, Heather Jon, and Meg Luxton. 1997. "Gender at Work: Canadian Feminist Political Economy Since 1988," in Wallace Clement (ed.), *Understanding Canada: Building on the New Canadian Political Economy*. Montreal and Kingston: McGill-Queen's University Press, 85–117.

National Council of Welfare. 1997. *Poverty Profile 1995* (authors Richard Shillington and Clare Lochead). Ottawa.

National Council of Welfare. 1999. *Poverty Profile 1997*. Ottawa.

Philipps, Lisa. July 2000. "Tax Law and Social Reproduction: The Gender of Fiscal Policy in an Age of Privatization," unpublished paper from the SSHRC-funded project on "Feminism, Law and the Challenge of Privatization," Osgoode Hall Law School, York University.

Picchio, Antonella. 1992. *Social Reproduction: The Political Economy of the Labour Market*. Cambridge: Cambridge University Press.

Rebick, Judy. 2000. *Imagine Democracy*. Toronto: Stoddart.

Sorokin, Pitrim. 1956. *Fads and Foibles in Modern Sociology*. Chicago: Henry Regnery.

Statistics Canada. 2000. *Women in Canada 2000: A Gender-Based Statistical Report*. Ottawa: Minister of Industry.

Status of Women Canada. August 1994. *Canada's National Report to the United Nations for the Fourth World Conference on Women*. Ottawa: Status of Women Canada.

The Toronto Star. 27 September 1995. "Find Job to Feed Kids, Tsubouchi Urges" by Kelly Toughill.

The Toronto Star. 28 September 1995. "Welfare Not Set Up to Feed Kids: Harris" by Kelly Toughill. A14.

The Toronto Star. 16 April 1998. "Pregnant WomenLose Benefit" by Patricia Orwen and Laurie Mousebraaten. A2.

Townson, Monica. May 2000. "Women in Canada Remain among 'Poorest of the Poor,'" *The CPPA Monitor*, Vol. 7, No. 1, The Canadian Centre for Policy Alternatives.

Ursel, Jane. 1992. *Private Lives, Public Policy: One Hundred Years of State Intervention in the Family*. Toronto: The Women's Press.

Vosko, Leah. 2000. *Temporary Work: The Gendered Rise of Contingent Work*. Toronto: University of Toronto Press.

Waring, Marilyn. 1988. *If Women Counted: A New Feminist Economics*. New York: Harper & Row.

Yalnizyan, Armine. 1998. *The Growing Gap: A Report on Growing Inequality between the Rich and Poor in Canada*. Toronto: The Centre for Social Justice.

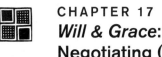

CHAPTER 17
Will & Grace:
Negotiating (Gay) Marriage on Prime-Time Television

KARIN QUIMBY

[…] [T]he situation comedy's "humor relies upon, and is in response to, issues and problems found within the social structure" (Means Coleman, 4). While most would agree that *Will & Grace* is the first successful *gay* sitcom on network television, it is, ironically, the question of marriage—and, more specifically, the form and function of male-female intimacy—that fuels the primary anxiety or problem that this show attempts to negotiate. That is, *Will & Grace* has not yet directly addressed the issue of gay marriage (as the title to this article might seem to suggest), but the show's construction of the relationship between its title characters, Will and Grace (Eric McCormack and Debra Messing), reveals the pressure that the gay marriage issue has brought to bear on the "definition" of marriage, which is currently under hot debate in living rooms and rooms of Congress alike. By acknowledging the significance and primacy of those common and consequential intimacies developed between straight women and gay men, *Will & Grace* responds in part to straight women's dissatisfactions with traditional—marital—definitions of male-female love, commitment, and desire. Because such nontraditional relationships as Will and Grace's often go unrecognized in straight culture and are dismissed at times in gay culture with the "fag hag" appellation, the significant cultural and political work that this television comedy undertakes is the taking seriously of this form of queer affiliation. […]

That conventional marriage is under some attack in this sitcom is no more apparent than in the outrageous attitudes of supporting character Karen Walker (Megan Mullally), the only character in the show actually to be wedded during the first four seasons. We learn that Karen has married a rich man exclusively for his money and that she performs the requisite sexual trade-off in a way that defines marriage as merely a sex-for-money contract. This husband never appears on screen, which suggests his utter dispensability except for his role as a source of money. Moreover, Karen is not the least bit interested in the young children who came along with the marriage, and is constantly devising ways to avoid coming into any contact with them. By showing such disrespect for traditional attitudes toward marriage and parenthood, her character delivers the most direct challenge that the

show issues to those sacred institutions. Although some have described her as a "diva-bitch," one might also understand Karen as representing a woman who audaciously turns the tables on women's usually subordinated position in marriage, and enthusiastically exploits this institution for her own gain.

In contrast to the unqualified denigration of marriage traditions that the character of Karen Walker offers up, the relationship between Will and Grace acknowledges the loving and supportive intimacies that people of different sexual orientations can form. Right from the start of the pilot episode, Will and Grace—although "only" friends—are represented as being so connected that they finish each other's sentences and draw from a wealth of quirky prior references when playing charades, which suggests the longevity of their relationship and its unique and fundamentally compatible temper. In an appearance on the 2002 Emmy Awards show, Eric McCormack, who plays Will Truman, described the show's intent: "It's about a friendship between a straight woman and a gay man. It's not boyfriend/girlfriend. It's not girlfriend/girlfriend. It's something deliciously in between." Indeed, the primary characters, Will and Grace, represent two people who are navigating their way through a relationship that has no prescribed model in our culture. In this sense, they (or the scriptwriters) are inventing the shape and trajectory of their "in-between" relationship as they go. Michael Warner reminds us that "because gay social life is not as ritualized and institutionalized as straight life, each relation is an adventure in nearly uncharted territory—whether it is between two gay men, or two lesbians, or a gay man and a lesbian, or among three or more queers, or between gay men and the straight women whose commitment to queer culture brings them the punishment of the 'fag hag' label" (115–16).[1] By developing its popular narrative around the latter form of queer relationship, *Will & Grace* extends the recent trend in film and television narratives that addresses straight women's desire for relationships with men that exist outside the norms proscribed by the heterosexual contract. In the last few years, films such as *My Best Friend's Wedding* (1997), *The Next Best Thing* (2000), and, more recently, the cable show *Sex in the City*, feature the involved desires that straight women and gay men often develop.[2] Could it be that these films and cable TV show, along with the network hit *Will & Grace*, signal the most recent manifestation of straight women's dissatisfaction with the norms of masculinity and the kinds of relationships that such gendered conventions demand?

Early reviews of the show suggest how this new (to television) form of relationship that Will and Grace dramatize may serve to question normative forms of heterosexual union. Alyssa Katz suggests that Will and Grace's relationship acknowledges "the value of friendship between men and women that doesn't lock them into their ordained roles … Whatever it is that Grace finds in Will makes him the most important man in her life; his ability to look at her as something other than a sexual conquest can't be the least of it." Other reviews of *Will & Grace*, in their attempt to make sense out of the dynamics present in the straight woman/gay man relationship, do so by questioning marriage definitions. Robert Laurence ponders a hypothetical: "If marriage is largely friendship, Grace might be better off married to Will, clearly her true kindred spirit. But there's that other part of marriage, the sex part, and in that regard they have nothing in common" (E1). Of course, they do have much in common in most other arenas, including their shared attraction to men—but that shared desire is, needless to say, not coherent to a heterosexual paradigm. Also concerned with what position sex occupies in a relationship between a man and a woman, Simon Dumenco from *Us* magazine plugs the comedy as being about "the kind of friendship that's possible between a man and a woman when sex doesn't get in the way" (50). Dumenco intimates that the kind of friendship Will and Grace have is one, presumably, that relatively few straight men would be interested in having, as if having sex with a woman precludes a man from sharing other more "feminine" pleasures with her. Will and Grace's friendship is the kind that shares the excitement of counting the days until the Barney's sale, the kind that shares gossip and fashion tips, and, most important, the kind that attends closely to the emotional life of each "partner." To have such a friendship idealized on prime-time television highlights some of the very qualities straight women often complain are lacking in their relationships with men, qualities of care and nurturing that, when expressed by men in patriarchal culture, are typically denigrated. The popularity of the show suggests just how important to some women such intimate relationships with men are.

One of the perplexing questions that *Will & Grace* raises is that although one of the primary audiences for the show is the young, hip, college-educated urban woman (the very kind of woman Grace embodies), the sitcom still must appeal to a wider and presumably more conservative audience to explain its numerous Emmy awards (including best comedy) and its seventh season on NBC's prime-time line-up. How can a show that seems to issue such a biting critique of marriage and celebrate gay men as the ideal partners for straight women be so popular with a wide audience of presumably straight-identified spectators who have a certain stake in maintaining the status quo? The answer loudly pronounces itself in the pilot episode.

While it is true that *Will & Grace*'s weekly narratives critique normative social and personal relationships, they simultaneously support a form of relationship that can be interpreted as satisfying narrative and social conventions. To assert this paradox, the writers and producers of the show manipulate representations of Will and Grace's already ambiguous in-between relationship in a way to make this show palatable to a more conservative audience by "visualizing" what in fact is a queer relationship as a decidedly heterosexual one. [...] [T]o be popular, television texts must be both polysemic and flexible—that is, they must appeal to more than one kind of audience. [...] The pilot episode to the *Will & Grace* series establishes the precise nature of this struggle as one founded in the conflict over the definition of Will and Grace's relationship specifically, and of the possible shapes of male-female desire more generally.

One of the devices that open up a text to polysemic readings is contradiction, which helps ensure that a show will be popular with a wider variety of audiences. In most cases, the dominant ideology works to smooth out those contradictions "by constructing a 'consensus' around its point of view which represses the contradictions in a text and thus militates against social change" (Fiske 88). This consensus is often accomplished by way of the episode's conclusion, which returns to normality the conflict driving the episode's narrative. The obvious contradiction present in many of the scenes between Will and Grace is the ability to read them simultaneously as a gay man/straight woman dyad *and* as an ideal heterosexual couple. This contradiction surely is resolved by some straight-identifying audiences through the psychic mechanism routinely invoked in response to gay people and gay culture: disavowal. Disavowal, which might be understood through the phrase "I know … but all the same," allows some audience members both to acknowledge gay male difference (which is most often represented in the show through the hyperbolic discourse of camp and is enacted through the figure and comedic routines of supporting character "Just Jack" [Sean Hayes]) and to disavow this difference through the heterosexual fantasy that visualizes Will and Grace's eventual coupling. Thus, whereas audiences "know" that Will is gay, many still will choose to believe, to see, or to "know" him to be really heterosexual. [...]

Understanding the importance of such a dynamic (to know Will simultaneously as gay and as not gay) to attract and keep audiences who may be somewhat uncomfortable (if also fascinated) with representations of gay life, the writers and producers of the show situate this very dynamic of contradiction or disavowal as central to the narrative, and play it out several times in the pilot episode. In the scene that occupies the final minutes of the pilot episode, we find that Grace has just run out on her wedding and, still clad in her wedding gown, ends up nursing her wounds with Will in a straight bar. Assuming that Will and Grace themselves have just been married, the patrons at the bar call for a toast by the happy couple, and a kiss. This final scene literally mimics one of the possible reading positions for this show; the straight audience in the bar serves to express all of the normal assumptions attending the glorious moment of marriage. Unable to read the admittedly subtle codes of Will's homosexuality (many have commented on Will's "straight" appearance as one of the most obvious ways of making him "safe" for a more conservative audience), the bar patrons loudly demand the enactment of the heterosexual rituals associated with marriage, and we can observe how easy it is made for audiences to comfortably recuperate Will's gay identity into a heterosexual narrative.

One male bar patron says to Will, "Hey, what about a toast to your lovely new bride?!" The chorus of voices in the background concurs *in unison* with an energetic, "Yea!" Will and Grace look apprehensively at each other for a moment until Will concedes to the demand, apparently deciding that it is easier to go along with the crowd's assumption than to explain the queer nature of their relationship and face the possible repercussions of coming out in a bar full of drunken straight people. So instead, Will raises his glass and says with bravado, "Here's to the ball and chain. If she makes it through the night ... Ba Bing, I think I'll keep her!" The bar audience laughs in simple, rowdy appreciation, completely unaware of Will's gross parody of heterosexual manhood. Indeed, only by reading Will as gay (which the straight bar patrons clearly do not) can one understand his toast to Grace as a critique of a certain version of straight maleness and not as a humorous endorsement of it. In fact, as we learn earlier in the show, Will urges Grace to reject this very kind of straight man (the kind who high-fives after sex) by advising her to refuse the marriage proposal. Grace's rejection of the straight man at the altar indicates that she does indeed want something different from a man than adolescent sports gestures during sex. Will's toast returns us to this earlier critique of hetero masculinity, and audiences at home (those who choose to) further recognize Will's toast as directly contradicting his real feelings toward Grace; he has no intention of having sex with her, of course, nor does he see her as his property to keep or not. Indeed, his toast serves to contrast those very qualities that Grace finds so appealing in him—his sensitivity and attention to details about her emotional life not the least of them.

Beyond the critique of prosaic hetero masculinity uttered by Will, the nature of Grace's desire for a man like Will is precisely what fuels her subsequent toast to him. When Grace stands up to toast Will, the tone changes entirely from one of raucous, raunchy heterosex to one that plainly reveals the depth and breadth of her affection for Will. "To my Will" she says, "You are my hero and my soul mate and I'm a better woman for loving you." Like Will's toast, this declaration can be read simultaneously in at least two ways. The straight bar audience responds to it, as no doubt some audiences at home do, with the requisite expression of "Aww ..." What Grace is in fact expressing, however, is not the standard form of heterosexual marital love, but the intricate desire of a straight woman for a gay man. The use of the term "soul mate" is an attempt to express the profound inferiority and "delicious" scope of that love. For those who recognize the complexity of such a relationship (largely the gay men and straight women who love one another), Grace's sentiments give voice and shape to one of the "lived arrangements of queer life."

The complexity of this moment and their relationship is, however, quickly vaporized by the force of the friendly but all too insistent pressure of heterosexual expectation chanted again in unison by the bar audience: "kiss, kiss, kiss, kiss, kiss ..." At this forceful insistence, Grace grabs Will's face and plants a rather long kiss on him. When she finishes, she looks at him and asks, "Nothing? Anything?" Although Will immediately indicates to Grace that the kiss has done nothing to change his sexual orientation (as if it could!), to the straight audience in the bar, as to straight audiences in their living rooms, the possibility (and, as many of my students have claimed, the *probability*) of Will and Grace's eventual coupling is precisely what makes the contradictions and complexities of their queer relationship coherent to a traditional straight-identified audience, and the gay content of the show permissible on prime-time American television.

But the audience for *Will & Grace* that has catapulted it into Emmy award status and renewed seasons cannot be, it seems, as naïve as the straight bar audience presented in the show's pilot episode. To characterize the audience as monolithically straight or gay does not do justice to the far more queer spectator positions that the show actually encourages. It is indeed outside such banal hetero/homo moments that much of the show operates. *Will & Grace*, one might say, exaggerates the usually more coded or subtextual forms of queer desires and pleasures that exist in most, if not all, mass culture productions, as Alexander Doty has convincingly argued. He proposed that "queer positions, queer readings, and queer pleasures are part of a reception space that stands simultaneously beside and within that created by heterosexual and straight positions" (15). Moreover, "not only can basically heterocentrist texts contain queer elements, but basically heterosexual, straight-identifying people can experience queer moments" (3).[3] Although many self-defined lesbian and gay audiences are devoted to the show especially for its "out" representation of white gay male culture, Doty's theory helps explain how this show (among others) may appeal to straight-identified audiences, especially straight women audiences, who, I am arguing, have much at stake in the show's redefinitions of male-female relationships. Doty articulates the kind of liberation possible when shows like *Will & Grace* produce such queer narratives: "When cultural texts encourage straight-identified audience members to express a less-censored range of queer desire and pleasure than is possible in daily life, this 'regression' has positive gender- and sexuality-destabilizing effects" (4). The audiences for *Will & Grace* seem especially inclined, given the overtly queer nature of much of the material, toward experiencing pleasure through a range of impulses and cultural expressions that are not straight, but at the same time, they may not be strictly gay or lesbian. This dynamic is most obviously represented through the relationships of the straight women (Grace and Karen) to the gay men (Will and Jack) on the show. Indeed, the very popularity of *Will & Grace* emphasizes "just how much everyone's pleasures in mass culture are part of this contra-straight, rather than strictly anti-straight, space—just how queer our responses to cultural texts are so much of the time" (15).

Love Will Keep Us Together

That *Will & Grace* explores the contra-straight space of heterosexual women's relationships to gay men as one of its narrative foci is apparent in most episodes, but is addressed specifically in an episode that aired in the second season. In this episode, Grace suffers the anxiety regularly faced by those whose relationships are not socially sanctioned. That it takes until the second season for Grace finally to confront her unconventional relationship with Will in a direct way underscores the show's reliance on the fiction of Will and Grace's "heterosexual" possibilities discussed above.

This second-season episode produces some of the more thoughtful meditations on what relationships between women and men mean if they are not the sanctified ones privileged and supported through the institution of marriage. At the beginning of the episode, Grace runs into an old friend who, like her, had a primary relationship with a gay man when they were in college. Here is how their conversation proceeds:

Grace: It's been so long! How are you? How's Charlie?

Heidi: Oh, ya know, I don't know. We kind of drifted apart. He moved to San Francisco a couple of years ago, met a guy at a Pottery Barn, had a glass of Chardonnay and … poof, instant couple.

Grace: What? You guys were best friends. You did everything together … What happened?

Heidi: Nothing happened. You know—gay man, straight woman—it's not like we had anything holding us together, you know like a house or kids. You must have been through something like that with Will?

Grace: Uh, no. We're still together. Roommates, having fun, doing stuff. No offense, sweetie, but I know how to keep my gay man (with bravado).

Heidi: Well, good for you. I guess you and Will are the exception.

Grace: I guess …

This brief encounter suggests, first of all, the commonality of the gay man/straight woman relationship in our culture today.[4] In this episode, however, Will does not seem to have the same investment as Grace in maintaining the relationship as an exclusive one, and is planning travels and bar nights out with his gay male friends. Grace becomes increasingly panicked that their relationship means nothing within the dominant cultural order (which of course is true) because they do not have the signifiers of institutionalized heterosexuality holding them together—a house and kids. This rather bald rendering of what does hold heterosexual (and, increasingly, homosexual) couples together does nothing less than expose the materialist basis of marriage. But Grace literally buys into this version of commitment and responds to her increasing anxiety over losing Will by having them purchase a piano together which, she explains to him, is designed to help them establish a sense of family.

Grace's panic over losing Will increases as the episode progresses, and the most interesting scene comes by way of the parallel story, starring Karen and Jack, through which Grace's "queer" desire for Will is represented hyperbolically through Karen's queer desire for the gay pornography that Jack has been writing. It is important to note that both Jack and Karen, as supporting characters, operate in the space of excess or hyperbole; they exaggerate the often more mundane characteristics of the lead characters. That is, if Grace's desire for Will in this episode can be read as queer in terms of it existing outside normative structures of a heterosexually defined male-female relationship, Karen's pleasure in the gay porn that Jack is writing exaggerates—and thus makes perfectly queer—this tangle of straight-gay desire. Just as the heterosexual audience in the bar mimicked the very behavior and response necessary for some straight people's pleasure in understanding the nature of Will and Grace's relationship, Karen's excessively erotic response to gay male pornography virtually enacts the kinds of queer spectatorial desires also produced by this show, and thus opens up a space for audiences—especially straight audiences—to identify and desire queerly themselves.

In the following scene, Karen is reading some of Jack's gay porn when Grace arrives and asks to process "the piano situation" with her. It is clear in the scene that Karen is entirely engrossed in reading and responding to the pornography and is not in fact responding to Grace at all, yet Karen's erotic outbursts offer humorous but salient responses to Grace's serious questions about commitment. The scene opens with Karen reading the pornography out loud while "working" in Grace's office:

Karen: "Like some fantastic farm animal he grunted and whispered: 'Tonight, my love, you will see the face of God.' Christian closed his eyes and received him hungrily." Lord, this is hot.

Grace (arriving at the office): Hi, Kar. Do you know if Joe Zavaldi happened to call to say what he thought of my design of the breakfast nook?

Karen: "He shuddered and screamed out, 'I am reborn!'"

Grace: I knew the marble countertop would be a big splash. (Pause) Karen, can I ask you something?

Karen: "Oh, yea, give it to me."

Grace: Well, Will and I bought this piano together and for the first couple of days it was great, but now it just seems like he's bored with it.

Karen: "Oooh. Ouch."

Grace: Like last night, he just up and walked out in the middle of our sing-along.

Karen: "Filthy beast!"

Grace: Well, that's a little strong.

Karen: "Give it right back to him."

Grace: You know what? I will! You know he doesn't understand how important this piano is.

Karen: (with the tempo of their exchange now in crescendo): "That's it! That's the stuff!"

Grace: If you're going to bring something into your life, you have to invest some time into it.

Karen: "Yes!"

Grace: It's a commitment. And that means both people have to be committed to it, right?

Karen: "Yes. Yes!"

Grace: I mean, I'm not going to just let him walk away from this. I'm going to protect what's important in my life!

Karen: "Yes!"

Grace: Yes!

Karen: "Yes!"

Grace: Yes!

Grace: Thanks for your support, Karen. I feel better.

Karen (lighting up a postcoital cigarette): Oh. Grace. When did you get here?

This scene's dialogic structure situates the voices on dual registers, which forces the audience to read Grace and Karen's contrary desires simultaneously—for commitment on the one hand, and pleasure and sex on the other. Together, these two voices represent a range of possible desires that straight women may manifest for or about gay men, from raunchy sexual fantasy to devoted companionship. This scene is choreographed in such a way that these contrary desires mix and mingle unpredictably as they rise to orgasmic pitch. Grace's final pronouncement, "I'm going to protect what's important in my life," reveals the depth of her love and commitment to Will, but such a traditionally possessive statement of relationship is simultaneously undermined by Karen's commitment to queer sexual pleasure and her utter obliviousness to Grace's presence. So Karen, as the hyperbolic representative of pleasure for pleasure's sake, gets the last word and the last laugh.

This same dialogic pattern returns at the end of the episode, when Grace and Will finally reconcile their own seemingly conflicted desires. By representing Will and Grace's voices on dual registers (one talks while one responds by singing lyrics from a Captain and Tennille song), the narrative again produces an occasion to disrupt and critique dominant ideologies of male-female relationship and desire. To lead up to this scene, Grace plans an "old-fashioned piano party," inviting friends over to their apartment so that Will won't feel like he needs to go out to the bar with his gay friends. Things do not go well in general, and when Will accidentally spills the root beer floats (signifiers of old-fashioned family gatherings and values) on the piano (the signifier of wanting to reinvent these same values in this "family"), Grace finally explodes.

Grace: Oh my God. Oh my God. Look what you did. You ruined it. You ruined everything.

Will: Grace I'm sorry, but it's just a piano.

Grace: No it's not. It's more than that, but you don't realize it. Just forget it, just go, just move to San Francisco, and go scuba diving for cute guys in underpants because obviously there's nothing keeping you here.

Will: Have you been gargling with bong water?

Grace: We're drifting apart, Will. People do. It happened to Heidi and Charlie. They don't even talk anymore.

Will: Oh my God, is that what this is all about? Grace, we are always going to be in each other's lives.

Grace: How do you know that? Huh? Things change. You're going to get a boyfriend. I'm going to get a boyfriend …

Will: … Hopefully not the same boyfriend.

Grace: We're not a couple. We're not married. We don't have kids. What do we have to keep us together?

Will: (playing the piano now and singing softly) Love, love will keep us together.

Grace: Don't do that. There are a million things that can pull us in a million different directions.

Will: Think of me, babe, whenever …

Grace: And then we'll end up talking less and less.

Will: Some sweet talking guy comes along, singing his song …

Grace: Don't do this. We're talking about our friendship here.

Will: Don't mess around, you've just got to be strong …

Grace: You know doing this stupid song is not going to take away my concerns, okay?

Will: Just stop.

Grace: Stop!

Will: 'Cause I really love you. Stop.

Grace: Stop!

Will: I've been thinking of you.

Grace and Will (singing together): Look in my heart and let love keep us together.

This musical conclusion serves to quell Grace's anxiety over the definition of their relationship in a way that seems to wrap up the episode neatly and return the narrative to a position of stasis. However, this conclusion in fact produces several contradictory discourses, effectively maintaining the text's polysemic openness, even at the end, to allow for multiple interpretations. Similar to the dynamic present at the end of the pilot episode, the "love" discourse expressed by Will and Grace seated together on the piano bench and gazing into each other's eyes can be read in a very conventional way: as the romantic love between a man and a woman, a love that would, in its normal trajectory, be expressed ultimately in the decision to marry. In this sense, the ending calls up the embattled definition of marriage, a debate that has swept the country over the last several years in the form of state amendments and federal acts such as DOMA (Defense of Marriage Act), which insist on defining marriage as that which exists exclusively between one man and one woman. If one ignores the rest of the episode's narrative, one might easily read Will and Grace's final declaration of love for each other as precisely that of a normal heterosexual couple. On the other hand, the notion of love alone keeping a relationship together challenges the definition of relationship that was defined earlier in the show through materialist, or state-certified means—a marriage certificate, a house and a child, or in this case, a piano.

However, that this sentiment is conveyed in the year 1999 through a decades-old Captain and Tennille song situates this conclusion most conspicuously within the discourse of camp. Because camp operates through hyperbole, this song itself works through a double articulation that is capable of bearing both the dominant ideology and a simultaneous critique of it. Camp allows for a subversive, or at least parodic, subtext to run counter to the main text, and both "texts" can be read simultaneously by the viewer and her or his disunited subjectivity. Thus, Will and Grace's final, musical declaration of love for one another can be read simultaneously as voicing a heteroromantic love *and* a queer love that exists outside that exclusive and exclusionary frame. Still, the question remains at the end: what kind of love will keep Will and Grace together as the unified chanting forces of compulsory heterosexuality attempt to muster all nonconforming forms of love and desire into the circumscribed frame of marriage? What makes the *Will & Grace* sitcom a significant critique of the marriage contract and other normative heterosexual structures is that it often constructs these moments of semiotic excess in which there is too much contradictory desire to be controlled fully by the dominant ideology. It is here in these excessive, contested sites of meaning that heteronormative discourses can be disavowed—for a change.

*   *   *   *   *

Notes

1 In arguing that the gay marriage agenda forecloses the wider possibilities of understanding human relationships and disciplines them into the kind of sanctified dyads that are privileged (economically, politically, emotionally) at the expense of others who do not fit into the licensed form, Warner rightly proposes that straight culture has much to learn from the "welter of intimacies" developed and nurtured by those who fall outside the norm. "Queers should be insisting on teaching these lessons" he says, but "instead, the marriage issue, as currently framed, seems to be a way of denying recognition to these relations, of streamlining queer relations into the much less troubling division of couples from friends" (116).

2 The plots for these films themselves reveal fascinating and different forms of straight female–gay male desire that are too complex to discuss at length here. *My Best Friend's Wedding* (1997), directed by P.J. Hogan, stars Julia Roberts and Rupert Everett as her gay best friend whose friendship both models the kind of intimacy and understanding straight women desire from men, and helps her sort through her love for a straight male friend who is almost beyond her grasp. *The Next Best Thing* (2000), directed by John Schlesinger, stars Madonna as Abbie, who is tired of failed relationships with straight men and has a one-night stand with her gay friend. When she turns up pregnant, they agree to raise the baby together. Five years later, Abbie falls in love with a straight man and wants to move away with her and Robert's little boy, Sam, and a nasty custody battle ensues. *Sex in the City* features a regularly appearing gay man as Sarah Jessica Parker's best friend, with whom she can explore various kinds of queer desires.

3 Doty defines queer as well as anyone: "Queerness … is a quality related to any expression that can be marked as contra-, non-, or anti-straight" (xv).

4 Indeed, I would propose that most gay men have had, at one time or another, a significant other who is a straight woman.

Works Cited

Becker, Ron. "Prime-Time Television in the Gay Nineties: Network Television, Quality Audiences, and Gay Politics." *The Velvet Light Trap* 42 (1998): 36–47.

Doty, Alexander. *Making Things Perfectly Queer: Interpreting Mass Culture.* Minneapolis: U of Minnesota P, 1993.

Dumenco, Simon. "*Will & Grace & Love & Sex.*" *Us Weekly* 16 Oct. 2000: 50.

Feuer, Jane. "The Situation Comedy, Part 2." *The Television Genre Book.* Ed. Glen Creeber. London: British Film Institute Publishing, 2001. 67–70.

———. "Will and Grace." *The Television Genre Book.* Ed. Glen Creeber. London: British Film Institute Publishing, 2001. 72.

Fiske, John. *Television Culture.* London: Routledge, 1999. 84.

Katz, Alyssa. "Beyond Ellen." *The Nation* [New York] 2 Nov. 1998: 32–34.

Laurence, Robert P. "*Bloom* Likely to Wilt, but There's Wit in *Will & Grace.*" *San Diego Union Tribune* 12 Sept. 1998: E1.

Means Coleman, Robin R. *African American Viewers and the Black Situation Comedy: Situating Racial Humor.* New York: Garland, 2000.

Warner, Michael. *The Trouble with Normal: Sex, Politics, and the Ethics of Queer Life.* New York: Free Press, 1999.

CHAPTER 18
Serving the McCustomer: Fast Food Is Not about Food

ESTER REITER

Citizen into Customer: Cultural and Ideological Implications

People are hungry—for community, for nurturance. Young and old, we need and want to be cared for, cared about, loved. Our lives are difficult, and so we need some escape to a place where we will be valued, where our needs will matter, where we can play. For many families/households, gathering around a table to share a meal has been an occasion where emotional connections are affirmed. The soul as well as the belly needs feeding. It is no accident that the feast has often been at the centre of community events. However, in the past half century, the search to satisfy our needs has been fed increasingly by mass consumption of consumer goods. *We are on a treadmill and we know something is missing.* The more we need, the more we buy, but the more we buy the hungrier we are for something that will really satisfy, so the more we need. In this age of non-standardized work, where family members all have part-time jobs, one custom that has contributed to our well-being has become a special event rather than a regular occurrence—the family meal. We are now a society that grazes and snacks rather than a society that sits down with our families each evening. How and when did the commercialization of the family dinner occur?

During the Second World War, more people than ever frequented restaurants. Following the war, Canadian restaurant owners faced the end of their prosperous years, because eating at home was once again an option for families. Restaurateurs no longer had a ready clientele of people working odd hours and whose spouses were overseas. Some restaurant owners thought about how and where they could create a market for their food to keep themselves in business. Luring the average family into buying ready-made food held the promise of a new market that looked "like magic ... It's a magic that enables any restaurant to be as big as a city, to gather profits as big as the operator's imagination and to do these without major capital outlay." This, however, was no small challenge as it meant stiff competition with Mom. After all, "she puts love into her cooking."[1]

We can trace to the 1920s the attempt not just to sell what people want but to create a market by convincing people of what they need. As washing machines, dryers, televisions and dishwashers became available, the focus became selling one to each individual family. Individual women were encouraged to make themselves attractive through the consumption of cosmetics, the right shampoo, undergarments, seasonal fashion. These luxuries soon became essential. For example, the mass production of automobiles, the growth of suburbs and the lack of easily accessible public transportation made buying a car a necessity. During the Second World War women entered the paid workforce in greater numbers, but after the war, they were encouraged, even compelled, to leave their blue-collar jobs and return to their homes where they were encouraged to buy more consumer goods. However, the stay-at-home mom and the breadwinner dad became an economic impossibility for more and more families. From the 1960s to the present, women increasingly entered the labour force, and now, the income-earning wife and mother is more common than not.

These days, Mom is tired—she's working outside the home for pay and may have little or no time to cook. So she, like the rest of her family, needs a taste of the good life, the feeling of being taken care of. The call to "give yourself a treat today" is seductive and the affordability makes it possible. People flock to fast-food outlets—McDonald's, A&W, Burger King—for the golden fries boiled in oil, the brown bun (sweetened and nicely browned by the caramelized sugar it is dusted with), the hamburger. For many people, eating meat once constituted a rare treat. At one time only available to the wealthy on a regular basis, today meat is widely available as fast food, which itself has become comfort food—easy to eat, fun and, as the ads tell us, satisfying. There's the rub. This bargain-basement instant solution that promises to fill our needs still leaves us hungry. So we buy more food, more things, hoping somehow to satisfy this need of ours. McDonald's, for example, promotes itself as a "fast, hassle-free solution" to satisfying hunger, which simultaneously provides "value" that includes alignment with "community events, entertainment promotions and personalities that are important to our customers." Thus the purchased meal promises to provide something that "no one else can—the total McDonald's experience."[2]

McDonald's is one of the biggest success stories in recent history, having had its beginnings in the post–Second World War boom. In the 1960s, Ray Kroc took over the profitable hamburger stand in California and turned McDonald's into a global corporation. In 1997, it reported over US$33 billion in sales in 111 countries around the world. McDonald's employees worldwide number more than one million, in 23,000 restaurants. The long-term prospects look brightest outside the US, where there are already 12,000 restaurants, with plans to add a few thousand more each year.[3] McDonald's is committed to expansion. In their words:

> McDonald's vision is to dominate the global foodservices industry. Global dominance means setting the performance standards for customer satisfaction while increasing market share and profitability through our Convenience, Value and Execution Strategies.
> —McDonald's Annual Report, 1995

As an example of this global expansion, McDonald's recently announced a one-billion-dollar investment in Latin America, where it plans to double the number of restaurants to two thousand by the end of the year 2000. Expansions into Bolivia, Lebanon and Sri Lanka are also heralded. According to McDonald's senior vice-president, Ed Sanchez, this is McDonald's contribution to economic development.[4]

Who benefits from this development? The World Bank defines the poverty line as the equivalent of US$370 a year. In the eight-year period from 1985 to 1993, while McDonald's became richer, the number of poor people in the world increased by 20 percent, to 1.2 billion. While poverty has increased, so has wealth. From 1960–1991, the share of the world's income for the richest fifth of the world *rose* from 70 percent to 85 percent, while the share of income for the poorest fifth *dropped* from 2.3 percent to 1.4 percent. These figures become even more dramatic when broken down by gender. The Human Development Report of the United Nations Development Program found that over 70 percent of the people now living in absolute poverty are women.[5]

As the consumer society has developed, freedom has come to mean the freedom to buy. We are led to believe that the more we consume, the freer we are. We are asked to see ourselves as private, individual and solitary, where there is no "we" only a "me." Our dreams, we are told by the banks, have no limits. Multinationals such as Nike tell us to "Just do it," as long as our imaginations stay within the confines of what can be bought. At work, we are downsized, re-engineered, organized into teams to enable even more intensification of work, and this is called empowerment. We are freer then we have ever

been, but within a range that empowers individuals in their decisions of which brand of running shoes to buy— as long as we don't ask the bigger questions, as long as we don't challenge the all-powerful primacy of the market and the corporations which run it. In the process of gaining all these new choices, collective action to defend public interests—such as environmental protection, social safety nets, health, education and the public sector—are becoming wildly unrealistic fantasies. And anyway, we are told they are infringements on our freedom, defined as an individual's right to choose. As privatization, deregulation and the rule of the "bottom line" deplete the resources available to the public sector in Canada, we see private fast-food companies moving in to fill the gap. At the same time, corporations promise to expand our freedom through offering us greater choice of different name brands. What gets lost in this brave new "McWorld" is the respect for what Ursula Franklin calls the "indivisible benefits" that form the basis of civil society.[6] Our sense of ourselves as citizens—with justice, fairness and equity as operating principles—is replaced by the "freedom" to become customers.

Fast-food companies present themselves as charitable, community-minded citizens (and perhaps sincerely believe it). They have tapped lucrative markets in schools, hospitals and other publicly funded resources such as zoos and sports arenas. For example, marketing gimmicks such as Pizza Hut's and McDonald's literacy programs reward first graders' achievements with fast-food certificates, promoting their product and their charitable image simultaneously. While the marketing image may be benign, the ideology is not. The fast-food industry does not much care about the health of either growing children or the environment. Nor does it concern itself with the poverty and hunger in the countries that provide the meat for the hamburgers North Americans consume. This benign and charitable image is a technique to reach the newest consumer—children.

Servicing customers under five years old is only profitable if they are targeted in selective ways. As John Hawkes, McDonald's chief marketing officer in the United Kingdom acknowledges, two-to-eight-year-olds are the age group to which hamburger ads are geared because it is among children as young as two that brand loyalty can be effectively created.[7] Promoting the well-being of this age group involves support for institutions such as affordable daycare and junior kindergarten. This kind of support, however, doesn't provide the same bottom-line advantage, so corporations such as McDonald's are not supportive of public funding that provides the resources children need.

Corporate sponsorship is spreading into other educational settings. In the US, Burger King has opened "Burger King Academies," fully accredited quasi-private high schools in fourteen cities. There are plans to do the same in London, England. In this new entrepreneurial model, with a voucher system where parents are given money and choices as to how to use it, schools don't teach so much as sell. They also shape a way of looking at the world, which engenders what education critic Jonathan Kozol calls "predictability instead of critical capacities."[8] Children are described as future "assets" or "productive units"; the child becomes "the product." This approach is also spreading into other sectors, such as healthcare. Can you distinguish which of the following quotes is about running a healthcare service and which is about hamburgers?

As an *industry leader*, we provide *cost effective* services of *premier quality* in an environment which values our *people and partnerships* while focusing on our *customers* within a *profitable, innovative* organization positioned for the future.[9]

... we work together to take advantage of enhanced skills, attitudes, and behaviours of all our people and to share knowledge across geographic and organizational borders ... As the industry leader, we're embracing change from a position of strength, challenging ourselves to reach even higher levels of excellence in understanding and meeting the needs and expectations of our customers.[10]

The first is MDS laboratory services, a for-profit healthcare company based in Ontario, which has healthcare investments in many previously publicly run facilities, such as hospital laboratory services. The second is from McDonald's 1994 Annual Report.

In the management literature, there is much talk of "serving the customer," obscuring the relationship between employer and employee and foregrounding the employee's responsibility to satisfy the consumer. The focus is not on equality and justice for the employee, but on satisfaction for the customer. This is touted as the road to good government.[11] It seems there is a new religion and it is called corporate self-interest, which benefits corporations with support from the state. In their very popular book *Reengineering the Corporation*, Michael Hammer and James Champy talk about the "shift of power from producers to consumers." According to them, it is the customer who now calls the shots and we are told individual customers—whether consumers or industrial firms—demand that they be treated individually.[12] Similarly, in *Reinventing Government: How the Entrepreneurial Spirit Is Transforming the Public Sector*, David Osborne and Ted Gaebler praise competition that will give us "more bang for the buck." In the process, the citizen has become the customer and public interest is reduced to the needs of individual customers, and democracy is equated with cost efficiency.[13]

What does this discourse of democracy, of meeting people's needs through consumption, really mean? US critic Noam Chomsky describes democracy as really meaning "a system of governance in which elite elements based in the business community control the state by virtue of their dominance of the private society while the population observes quietly." In Chomsky's view, the key aim of democracy, US style, is not the freedom of speech and worship and the freedom from want and fear articulated by Franklin Delano Roosevelt, but the fifth unmentioned and well-documented "freedom to rob and to exploit."[14]

Working at McDonald's: Exploited Worker or "The Perfect Job"?[15]

McDonald's expects to expand its employees by the year 2000: the number of employees will increase 150 percent from one million at the end of 1997 to nearly two and one half million. The promotional pamphlet used by McDonald's Canada for hiring targets the young, who are out for a first job, and retirees. In the past, about 70 percent of the crew have consisted of young people. More than 50,000 employees have been through McDonald's international management training facility in Oak Brook, Illinois.[16]

Common to most fast-food training programs, managers drill their employees with "democratic" rhetoric: the employees are a team, the manager is the coach and their function is to work together to better serve the customer. "Counter hostesses" (cashiers) are to treat customers as guests and make them "happy." As one employee pamphlet says, "Your job is a sort of social occasion. You meet people—you want these people to like you."[17] These counter jobs are most often assigned to the female employees. The fast-food industry capitalizes on a gender ideology that takes the traditional division of labour in the home and locates it in a for-profit workplace. Thus women who are expected to care for others in the non-market sphere of the family are called upon to produce these feelings in their minimum-wage jobs. Such an approach works in a setting where the customer is always visible while the real boss is an abstract concept located in some head office far away. The omnipresent managers supervise the workers closely, ensuring that each micro step is performed according to the manual, but they have no real power over important issues such as wages or working conditions. The real decision-makers are nowhere in sight. Serving the "customer" is an effective management strategy, using the service aspect of a job to control labour and dependent on exploiting the good will of workers. It was pioneered in fast food but is now commonly found in many management manuals. It comes in some variant through other management strategies such as team concept, total quality management and continuous quality improvement. Meeting the "needs" of the customer are harnessed to the profit motives of management to make sure that surveillance of the worker is complete.

In what Arlie Hochschild calls the "managed heart," the fast-food companies attempt to harness human emotions for a dual purpose.[18] On the one hand, the "customer first" strategy is a good way to expand the market, and on the other hand, it is a very effective technique for monitoring workers' acquiescence to the very restrictive work practices imposed. Anyone who has worked in fast food or has been to a fast-food outlet has some idea of how the system operates. Virtually no cooking is done on the premises; rather each outlet is an assembly plant. Even the lettuce comes pre-shredded, and the eggs pre-scrambled in a carton. Each motion is timed to the second, and a labour schedule prepared in advance for each hour (half hour during the rushes), so that workers, rushing around at full speed, can serve the customer within the allotted time. Everything has been considered and preplanned—from the assembly of the food to getting it to the customer. All details are predetermined, such as the number of pickles (four, not three and two halves) on a burger, the amount and placement of the mustard, the number of fries that the scoop will hold (too much is cheating the store; too few, cheating the customer). The employees must follow the rules with not even the most minor of variations.

The "people skills" that managers must have make it their responsibility to ensure that morale remains high in an outlet. All kinds of social activities and the training system are designed to create the illusion that "McDonald's is a great place to work."[19] This special "experience" is meant to stimulate the notion of McDonald's as a family where one will be looked after. What remains unarticulated is that one may not unionize in one's family, although plenty of exploitation may exist. However, workers become aware that McDonald's is not their family, and that the working conditions leave something to be desired, the pay is low and the company does not really care about them. Thus, even though unionization in this industry is strongly resisted, organizing drives have occurred and continue to occur regularly. The goal is not so much monetary. Sarah Inglis, who led the almost-successful organizing drive of a McDonald's in Orangeville, Ontario, in 1994, explained that having a union can offer workers things such as dignity and self-respect, something she feels young workers are also entitled to.

In February 1998, over 82 percent of workers at the McDonald's outlet in St. Hubert, Quebec, decided that they needed a union to improve their deteriorating working conditions, so they signed up with the Brotherhood of Teamsters. In response, McDonald's Canada and the franchise owners suddenly decided that, after seventeen years in operation, the outlet was unprofitable and would have to be closed. The Quebec Federation of Labour (QFL) stepped in and offered to buy up this newly unprofitable franchise. Nothing doing. McDonald's refused to negotiate. The QFL and the Canadian Labour Congress considered a boycott of the chain and decided to engage in a major organizing drive in Quebec.[20]

In Montreal, the Brotherhood of Teamsters is applying for certification to represent workers at a McDonald's outlet. Montreal's labour commissioner has ruled in favour of the union by finding that the outlet had tried to tamper with its employee list by adding more anti-union workers to its crew to fend off certification. Accreditation hearings for this outlet and several other restaurants in the Montreal area continue. In Squamish, British Columbia, Jennifer Wiebe and Tessa Lowinger, Grade Twelve students, succeeded in organizing the only McDonald's outlet in the town with the Canadian Auto Workers (CAW). The union was certified by the British Columbia Labour Relations Board on August 19, 1998. These young women define their top bargaining priority to be a workplace with decent and safe working conditions, where employees will be treated with respect. (The CAW has organized eleven Starbucks and forty Kentucky Fried Chicken outlets in the province.)[21]

Taking on the Giant

Not only unionization but public outcry has presented serious challenges to McDonald's. Indeed, McDonald's guards its image as a company that gives to the community as basic to its functioning, and thus public criticisms are treated very seriously. In June 1997, the McLibel Trial concluded—this was the longest running trial in English history, representing a battle between the fast-food giant and Helen Steel and Dave Morris of North London. At issue was a pamphlet entitled "What's Wrong with McDonald's?" produced in 1986 by the London Greenpeace group. The pamphlet criticized McDonald's for promoting unhealthy food, exploiting workers, robbing the poor, damaging the environment, exploiting children through its advertising and murdering animals—not exactly previously unheard of charges. Eleven years after the pamphlet was first distributed, and two and one half years of trial testimony and many tens of millions of dollars in legal fees later, McDonald's made history. They had what one commentator called "the most expensive and disastrous public relations exercise ever mounted by a multinational company."[22]

The two defendants, who provided their own defence, faced the most high-powered lawyers money could buy. A technicality left the defendants having to prove not only that what their pamphlet claimed—that multinationals and the food industry do not promote health—but also that McDonald's itself directly caused conditions such as rainforest destruction and hunger in the Third World. The text in the pamphlet had to be treated as statements of fact to be proven with primary sources of evidence. The McLibel two did quite well despite this handicap. Although the high court judge, Mr. Justice Roger Bell, ordered the penniless defendants to pay £60,000 in damages, he found as a fact that McDonald's makes "considerable use of susceptible young children" in their advertising, is "culpably responsible" for cruelty to animals and pays low wages to its workers. The food was also found to have high salt and fat content and did not have the positive nutritional benefit claimed in advertisements and promotions.[23]

An Internet Website (www.mcspotlight.org) set up in the course of the trial was accessed over 24 million times in the first eighteen months of its existence by people from all over the world, and it continues posting news in cyberspace about anti-McDonald's struggles throughout the world. (This is an example of how the Internet can be an important tool for cross-border organizing. In this instance, it was very successful in mobilizing international solidarity.)

As well, Mr. Justice Bell pointed out, "McDonald's is strongly antithetic to the idea of unionisation of crews in their restaurants." UK McDonald's vice-president Sid Nicholson indicated that for an employee "to inform the union about conditions inside the stores" would be a breach of the employee's contract and considered "gross misconduct," and therefore a "summary sociable offence." According to Robert Beavers, the US senior vice-president of McDonald's, since the 1970s a "flying squad of experienced managers was dispatched to a store whenever word came of an attempt to organise it."[24]

Wal-Mart, with whom McDonald's has a retail partnership, is also working hard to oppose unionization. Wal-Mart offers McDonald's food "to go" in over eight hundred front check-out counters. The Ontario provincial labour board ruled that Wal-Mart had engaged in unfair labour practices in its Windsor store by threatening to shut down the store if employees voted for a union. As it was not legally possible to keep a union out, the conservative Harris government proceeded to change the labour law in Ontario by introducing a new labour bill called the "Wal-Mart bill," which made a certification vote mandatory. Judith McCormack, the former chair of the Ontario Labour Relations Board, called the bill an invitation to employers to engage in unfair labour practices by enhancing their ability to "jeopardize the credibility and authority of the law."[25]

The struggles to unionize McDonald's challenge us to look behind the scenes and to ask questions about the world of production, and they challenge the wisdom of accepting the marketplace as the determinant of how we should live. For unions, fast food employees represent the new labour force—vulnerable workers, primarily women and young people in part-time jobs, working in small outlets for very large employers. Organizing in this sector requires some leadership. It is a time-consuming and expensive process. But we have enough examples of organizing attempts to know that it can be done. The majority of consumers eat fast food, and almost everyone has a relative or friend who has had firsthand experience with the labour process. There are growing alliances between all who have an interest in challenging fast food—workers, women's groups, environmental groups. Together we can redefine the nature of democracy to make it mean what we think it should. Why should corporations who make wealth immorally and unethically have the right to subordinate communities and their goals to individual private interests? Living in a civilized society means providing all members, waged and unwaged, with access to basic needs. Indeed it could be argued that one of the great achievements of

this century is the creation of a public sector, flawed though it is, that will defend and protect our interests not only as separate individuals but as members of a community.

Is Our Future Fried?

I think Marx described it best of all:

> The need for a constantly expanding market for its products chases the bourgeoisie over the whole surface of the globe. It must nestle everywhere, settle everywhere, establish connections everywhere … In place of the old wants, satisfied by the production of the country, we find new wants, requiring for their satisfaction the products of distant lands and climes …
>
> It compels all nations, on pain of extinction, to adopt the bourgeois mode of production; it compels them to introduce what it calls "civilization" into their midst, i.e., to become bourgeois themselves. In one word, it creates a world after its own image.
>
> All that is solid melts into air, all that is holy is profane, and man [sic] is at last compelled to face with sober senses his real conditions of life, and his relation with his kind.[26]

It should be clear that fast food is not about food. Rather, the idea behind fast-food corporations is to promote consumer consumption and allegiance to what, without the hype, could be seen as relatively dull, undifferentiated products. As blind tastings have proven, it is easier to tell a Whopper, a Big Mac or a Wendy's Single apart in television commercials than it is when you are eating them.[27]

The labour process in fast food, then, is not about the quality of the food produced, nor is it about how best to serve customers. It is about creating an illusion of participation in an authoritarian workplace. Carole Patemen refers to the difference between the psychological feel-good effects of what she calls "pseudo participation" and real involvement in one's workplace. Is a workplace where workers feel good an adequate substitution for one where workers have a say in how their jobs are organized? Democratization requires full participation at a higher level where important decisions are made. Rhetoric about empowerment, about workers and managers sharing a common goal in serving the customer, is not a replacement for the real thing. The real thing is an authority structure where the workers' role is not just to obey orders from on high, but one where workers will share in all the rewards of doing business well, including gain (profits), knowledge and power.[28]

Is fast-food corporatism our future? Perhaps it is. But we need to understand that there is nothing inevitable about a future based on the bottom line. And as a measure for future planning, for the survival of the planet and the peoples of the globe, this top-down approach to feeding the world has not worked very well. The proliferation of the golden arches has occurred in a world where over one billion people, 70 percent of whom are women, live in poverty; where neo-natal deaths due to maternal malnutrition number in the millions; where child labour proliferates; and where inequalities between the rich and the poor continue to increase. What is our responsibility? Perhaps we need to reconsider the effi-cacy of the consumer model used to sell hamburgers. How do we begin to build a more humane society in which we do not subordinate the goods of the community and the well-being of people to maximize gain for some individuals? How can we reclaim our place as active citizens rather than passive consumers?

Notes

1   *Canadian Hotel and Restaurant*, 15 September 1955, 23.

2   McDonald's Corporation Annual Report, 1996, 9, 100.

3   McDonald's Corporation Annual Report, 1997. McDonald's posts financial results on a regular basis on its Website. These figures are constantly changing. See "Press Releases. Financial." *McDonald's*. <http://www.Mcdonalds.com>.

4   "Press Releases. Financial." *McDonald's*. <http://www.Mcdonalds.com>. April 1998.

5   United Nations Fourth World Conference on Women, Platform for Action, Beijing, 1995.

6   Ursula Franklin, *The Real World of Technology* (Toronto: CBC Enterprises, 1990; reprint, Concord, ON: House of Anansi Press, 1992).

7   John Vidal, *McLibel: Burger Culture on Trial* (New York: New Press, 1997), 141.

8   Jonathan Kozol, "The Sharks Move In," *New Internationalist* (October 1993), 8–10.

9   Emphasis in original. Vision '96. Press release from MDS announcing the "Clinical Laboratory Management Association (CLMA) 1995 Quality Management Award," 1995.

10 "Management Editorial," McDonald's Corporation Annual Report, 1994.

11 John Ralston Saul, *The Unconscious Civilization* (Concord, ON: House of Anansi Press, 1995), 96.

12 Michael Hammer and James Champy, *Reengineering the Corporation* (New York: HarperCollins, 1994), 18.

13 David Osborne and Ted Gaebler. *Reinventing Government* (New York: Plume Books, 1993), 80.

14 Noam Chomsky, *On Power and Ideology* (Montreal: Black Rose Books, 1987), 6–7.

15 "Come Join Our McDonald's Team," Pamphlet from McDonald's Canada.

16 "International McFacts," McDonald's Canada Promotional Package, 1998.

17 This was a handout given to employees at Burger King. Quoted in *Ester Reiter, Making Fast Food: From Frying Pan to Fryer* (Montreal: McGill Queen's, 1991), 86.

18 Arlie Hochshild, *The Commercialization of Human Feeling* (Berkeley: University of California Press, 1983).

19 Quoted from a McDonald's mini-application for employment.

20 Tu Chanh Ha, "McDonald's Closes, Workers' Union Bid Dies," *The Globe and Mail*, 13 February 1998, A3.

21 Dene Moore, "McChicken? Not These Two," *The Toronto Star*, 24 August 1998, A1.

22 Channel 4 News (UK), quoted in posting on the Website of the McLibel Support Campaign. "The McLibel Trial Story." McSpotlight. <http://www.mcspotlight.org>. September 1997. The Website provides a full history of the trial and updates on the 1999 McLibel Appeal.

23 Madelaine Droran, "Burger Chain Wins McLibel Suit," *The Globe and Mail*, 20 June 1997, A1.

24 Vidal, McLibel, 231.

25 Judith McCormack, "Bill Weakens Deterrent to Unfair Labour Practices," *The Toronto Star*, 23 June 1998, A19.

26 Karl Marx, *Communist Manifesto* (Toronto: Canadian Scholars' Press, 1987), 24.

27 *Nation's Restaurant News*, August 1984, 3.

28 Carole Patemen, *Participation and Democratic Theory* (New York: Cambridge, 1970), 77.

CHAPTER 19

The Discarded Factory:
Degraded Production in the Age of the Superbrand

Naomi Klein

Our strategic plan in North America is to focus intensely on brand management, marketing and product design as a means to meet the casual clothing wants and needs of consumers. Shifting a significant portion of our manufacturing from the U.S. and Canadian markets to contractors throughout the world will give the company greater flexibility to allocate resources and capital to its brands. These steps are crucial if we are to remain competitive.

—John Ermatinger, president of Levi Strauss Americas division, explains the company's decision to shut down twenty-two plants and lay off 13,000 North American workers between November 1997 and February 1999

Many brand-name multinationals [...] are in the process of transcending the need to identify with their earthbound products. They dream instead about their brands' deep inner meanings—the way they capture the spirit of individuality, athleticism, wilderness or community. In this context of strut over stuff, marketing departments charged with the managing of brand identities have begun to see their work as something that occurs not in conjunction with factory production but in direct competition with it. "Products are made in the factory," says Walter Landor, president of the Landor branding agency, "but brands are made in the mind."[1] Peter Schweitzer, president of the advertising giant J. Walter Thompson, reiterates the same thought: "The difference between products and brands is fundamental. A product is something that is made in a factory; a brand is something that is bought by a customer."[2] Savvy ad agencies have all moved away from the idea that they are flogging a product made by someone else, and have come to think of themselves instead as brand factories, hammering out what is of true value: the idea, the lifestyle, the attitude. Brand builders are the new primary producers in our so-called knowledge economy.

This novel idea has done more than bring us cutting-edge ad campaigns, ecclesiastic superstores and utopian corporate campuses. It is changing the very face of global employment. After establishing the "soul" of their corporations, the superbrand companies have gone on to rid themselves of their cumbersome bodies, and there is nothing that seems more cumbersome, more loathsomely corporeal, than the factories that produce their products. The reason for this shift is simple: building a superbrand is an extraordinarily costly project, needing constant managing, tending and replenishing. Most of all, superbrands need lots of space on which to stamp their logos. For a business to be cost-effective, however, there is a finite amount of money it can spend on all of its expenses—materials, manufacturing, overhead *and* branding—before retail prices on its products shoot up too high. After the multimillion-dollar sponsorships have been signed, and the cool hunters and marketing mavens have received their checks, there may not be all that much money left over. So it becomes, as always, a matter of priorities; but those priorities are changing. As Hector Liang, former chairman of United Biscuits, has explained: "Machines wear out. Cars rust. People die. But what lives on are the brands."[3]

According to this logic, corporations should not expend their finite resources on factories that will demand physical upkeep, on machines that will corrode or on employees who will certainly age and die. Instead, they should concentrate those resources in the virtual brick and mortar used to build their brands; that is, on sponsorships, packaging, expansion and advertising. They should also spend them on synergies: on buying up distribution and retail channels to get their brands to the people.

This slow but decisive shift in corporate priorities has left yesterday's non-virtual producers—the factory workers and craftspeople—in a precarious position. The lavish spending in the 1990s on marketing, mergers and brand extensions has been matched by a never-before-seen resistance to investing in production facilities and labor. Companies that were traditionally satisfied with a 100 percent markup between the cost of factory production and the retail price have been scouring the globe for factories that can make their products so inexpensively that the markup is closer to 400 percent.[4] And as a 1997 UN report notes, even in countries where wages were already low, labor costs are getting a shrinking slice of corporate budgets. "In four developing countries out of five, the share of wages in manufacturing value-added today is considerably below what it was in the 1970s and early 1980s."5 The timing of these trends reflects not only branding's status as the perceived economic cure-all, but also a corresponding devaluation of the production process and of producers in general. Branding, in other words, has been hogging all the "value-added."

When the actual manufacturing process is so devalued, it stands to reason that the people doing the work of production are likely to be treated like detritus—the stuff left behind. The idea has a certain symmetry: ever since mass production created the need for branding in the first place, its role has slowly been expanding in importance until, more than a century and a half after the Industrial Revolution, it occurred to these companies that maybe branding could replace production entirely. As tennis pro Andre Agassi said in a 1992 Canon camera commercial, "Image is everything."

Agassi may have been pitching for Canon at the time but he is first and foremost a member of Team Nike, the company that pioneered the business philosophy of no-limits spending on branding, coupled with a near-total divestment of the contract workers that make its shoes in tucked-away factories. As Phil Knight has said, "There is no value in making things any more. The value is added by careful research, by innovation and by marketing."6 For Phil Knight, production is not the building block of his branded empire, but is instead a tedious, marginal chore.

Which is why many companies now bypass production completely. Instead of making the products themselves, in their own factories, they "source" them, much as corporations in the natural-resource industries source uranium, copper or logs. They close existing factories, shifting to contracted-out, mostly offshore, manufacturing. And as the old jobs fly offshore, something else is flying away with them: the old-fashioned idea that a manufacturer is responsible for its own workforce. Disney spokesman Ken Green gave an indication of the depth of this shift when he became publicly frustrated that his company was being taken to task for the desperate conditions in a Haitian factory that produces Disney clothes. "We don't employ anyone in Haiti," he said, referring to the fact that the factory is owned by a contractor. "With the newsprint you use, do you have any idea of the labour conditions involved to produce it?" Green demanded of Cathy Majtenyi of the *Catholic Register*.7

From El Paso to Beijing, San Francisco to Jakarta, Munich to Tijuana, the global brands are sloughing the responsibility of production onto their contractors; they just tell them to make the damn thing, and make it cheap, so there's lots of money left over for branding. Make it *really* cheap.

Exporting the Nike Model

Nike, which began as an import/export scheme of made-in-Japan running shoes and does not own any of its factories, has become a prototype for the product-free brand. Inspired by the swoosh's staggering success, many more traditionally run companies ("vertically integrated," as the phrase goes) are busy imitating Nike's model, not only copying the company's marketing approach, [...] but also its on-the-cheap outsourced production structure. In the mid-nineties, for instance, the Vans running-shoe company pulled up stakes in the old-fashioned realm of manufacturing and converted to the Nike way. In a prospectus for an initial public stock offering, the company lays out how it "recently repositioned itself from a domestic manufacturer to a market-driven company" by sponsoring hundreds of athletes as well as high-profile extreme sporting events such as the Vans Warped Tour. The company's "expenditure of significant funds to create consumer demand" was financed by closing an existing factory in California and contracting production in South Korea to "third party manufacturers."8

Adidas followed a similar trajectory, turning over its operation in 1993 to Robert Louis-Dreyfus, formerly a chief executive at advertising giant Saatchi & Saatchi. Announcing that he wanted to capture the heart of the "global teenager," Louis-Dreyfus promptly shut down the company-owned factories in Germany, and moved to contracting-out in Asia.9 Freed from the chains of production, the company had newfound time and money to create a Nike-style brand image. "We closed down everything," Adidas spokesperson Peter Csanadi says proudly. "We only kept one small factory which is our global technology centre and makes about 1 percent of total output."10

Though they don't draw the headlines they once did, more factory closures are announced in North America and Europe each week [...].11 That sector's job-flight patterns have been equally dramatic around the globe. [...] Though plant closures themselves have barely slowed down since the darkest days of the late-eighties/early-nineties recession, there has been a marked shift in the reason given for these "reorganizations." Mass layoffs were previously presented as an unfortunate necessity, tied to disappointing company performance. Today they are simply savvy shifts in corporate strategy, a "strategic redirection," to use the Vans term. More and more, these layoffs are announced in conjunction with pledges to increase revenue through advertising spending, with executives vowing to refocus on the needs of their brands, as opposed to the needs of their workers.

Consider the case of Sara Lee Corp., an old-style conglomerate that encompasses not only its frozen-food namesake but also such "unintegrated" brands as Hanes underwear, Wonderbra, Coach leather goods, Champion sports apparel, Kiwi shoe polish and Ball Park Franks. Despite the fact that Sara Lee enjoyed solid growth, healthy profits, good stock return and no debt, by the mid-nineties Wall Street had become disenchanted with the company and was undervaluing its stock. Its profits had risen 10 percent in the 1996–97 fiscal year, hitting $1 billion, but Wall Street, as we have seen, is guided by spiritual goals as well as economic ones.[12] And Sara Lee, driven by the corporeal stuff of real-world products, as opposed to the sleek ideas of brand identity, was simply out of economic fashion. "Lumpy-object purveyors," as Tom Peters might say.[13]

To correct the situation, in September 1997 the company announced a $1.6 billion restructuring plan to get out of the "stuff" business by purging its manufacturing base. Thirteen of its factories, beginning with yarn and textile plants, would be sold to contractors who would become Sara Lee's suppliers. The company would be able to dip into the money saved to double its ad spending. "It's passé for us to be as vertically integrated as we were," explained Sara Lee CEO John H. Bryan.[14] Wall Street and the business press loved the new marketing-driven Sara Lee, rewarding the company with a 15 percent jump in stock price and flattering profiles of its bold and imaginative CEO. "Bryan's shift away from manufacturing to focus on brand marketing recognizes that the future belongs to companies—like Coca-Cola Co.—that own little but sell much," enthused one article in *Business Week*.[15] Even more telling was the analogy chosen by *Crain's Chicago Business*: "Sara Lee's goal is to become more like Oregon-based Nike Inc., which outsources its manufacturing and focuses primarily on product development and brand management."[16]

In November 1997, Levi Strauss announced a similarly motivated shake-up. Company revenue had dropped between 1996 and 1997, from $7.1 billion to $6.8 billion. But a 4 percent dip hardly seems to explain the company's decision to shut eleven plants. The closures resulted in 6,395 workers being laid off, one-third of its already downsized North American workforce. In this process, the company shut down three of its four factories in El Paso, Texas, a city where Levi's was the single largest private employer. Still unsatisfied with the results, the following year Levi's announced another round of closures in Europe and North America. Eleven more of its North American factories would be shut down and the total toll of laid-off workers rose to 16,310 in only two years.[17]

John Ermatinger, president of Levi's Americas division, had a familiar explanation. "Our strategic plan in North America is to focus intensely on brand management, marketing and product design as a means to meet the casual clothing wants and needs of consumers," he said.[18] Levi's chairman, Robert Haas, who on the same day received an award from the UN for making life better for his employees, told *The Wall Street Journal* that the closures reflected not just "overcapacity" but also "our own desire to refocus marketing, to inject more quality and distinctiveness into the brand."[19] In 1997, this quality and distinctiveness came in the form of a particularly funky international ad campaign rumored to have cost $90 million, Levi's most expensive campaign ever, and more than the company spent advertising the brand in all of 1996.

"This Is Not a Job-Flight Story"

In explaining the plant closures as a decision to turn Levi's into "a marketing company," Robert Haas was careful to tell the press that the jobs that were eliminated were not "leaving," they were just sort of evaporating. "This is not a job-flight story," he said after the first round of layoffs. The statement is technically true. Seeing Levi's as a job-flight story would miss the more fundamental—and more damaging—shift that the closures represent. As far as the company is concerned, those 16,310 jobs are off the payrolls for good, replaced, according to Ermatinger, by "contractors throughout the world." Those contractors will perform the same tasks as the old Levi's-owned factories—but the workers inside will never be employed by Levi Strauss.

For some companies a plant closure is still a straightforward decision to move the same facility to a cheaper locale. But for others—particularly those with strong brand identities like Levi Strauss and Hanes—layoffs are only the most visible manifestation of a much more fundamental shift: one that is less about where to produce than how. Unlike factories that hop from one place to another, these factories will never rematerialize. Mid-flight, they morph into something else entirely: "orders" to be placed with a contractor, who may well turn over those orders to as many as ten subcontractors, who—particularly in the garment sector—may in turn pass a portion of the subcontracts on to a network of home workers who will complete the jobs in basements and living rooms. Sure enough, only five months after the first round of plant closures was announced, Levi's made another public statement: it would resume manufacturing in China. The company had pulled out of China in 1993, citing concerns about human-rights violations. Now it has returned, not to build its own factories, but to place orders with three contractors that the company vows to closely monitor for violations of labor law.[20]

This shift in attitude toward production is so profound that where a previous era of consumer goods corporations displayed their logos on the façades of their factories, many of today's brand-based multinationals now maintain that the location of their production operations is a "trade secret," to be guarded at all costs. When asked by human-rights groups in April 1999 to disclose the names and addresses of its contract factories, Peggy Carter, a vice president at Champion clothing, replied: "We have no interest in our competition learning where we are located and taking advantage of what has taken us years to build."[21]

Increasingly, brand-name multinationals—Levi's, Nike, Champion, Wal-Mart, Reebok, the Gap, IBM and General Motors—insist that they are just like any one of us: bargain hunters in search of the best deal in the global mall. They are very picky customers, with specific instructions about made-to-order design, materials, delivery dates and, most important, the need for rock-bottom prices. But what they are *not* interested in is the burdensome logistics of how those prices fall so low; building factories, buying machinery and budgeting for labor have all been lobbed squarely into somebody else's court.

And the real job-flight story is that a growing number of the most high-profile and profitable corporations in the world are fleeing the jobs business altogether.

The Unbearable Lightness of Cavite: Inside the Free-Trade Zones

Despite the conceptual brilliance of the "brands, not products" strategy, production has a pesky way of never quite being transcended entirely: *somebody* has to get down and dirty and make the products the global brands will hang their meaning on. And that's where the free-trade zones come in. In Indonesia, China, Mexico, Vietnam, the Philippines and elsewhere, export processing zones (as these areas are also called) are emerging as leading producers of garments, toys, shoes, electronics, machinery, even cars.

If Nike Town and the other superstores are the glittering new gateways to the branded dreamworlds, then the Cavite Export Processing Zone, located ninety miles south of Manila in the town of Rosario, is the branding broom closet. After a month visiting similar industrial areas in Indonesia, I arrived in Rosario in early September 1997, at the tail end of monsoon season and the beginning of the Asian economic storm. I'd come to spend a week in Cavite because it is the largest free-trade zone in the Philippines, a 682-acre walled-in industrial area housing 207 factories that produce goods strictly for the export market. Rosario's population of 60,000 all seemed to be on the move; the town's busy, sweltering streets were packed with army jeeps converted into minibuses and with motorcycle taxis with precarious sidecars, its sidewalks lined with stalls selling fried rice, Coke and soap. Most of this commercial activity serves the 50,000 workers who rush through Rosario on their way to and from work in the zone, whose gated entrance is located smack in the middle of town.

Inside the gates, factory workers assemble the finished products of our branded world: Nike running shoes, Gap pajamas, IBM computer screens, Old Navy jeans. But despite the presence of such illustrious multinationals, Cavite—and the exploding number of export processing zones like it throughout the developing world—could well be the only places left on earth where the super-brands actually keep a low profile. Indeed, they are positively self-effacing. Their names and logos aren't splashed on the façades of the factories in the industrial zone. And here, competing labels aren't segregated each in its own superstore; they are often produced side by side in the same factories, glued by the very same workers, stitched and soldered on the very same machines. It was in Cavite that I finally found a piece of unswooshed space, and I found it, oddly enough, in a Nike shoe factory.

I was only permitted one visit inside the zone's gates to interview officials—individual factories, I was told, are off limits to anyone but potential importers or exporters. But a few days later, with the help of an eighteen-year-old worker who had been laid off from his job in an electronics factory, I managed to sneak back to get the unofficial tour. In the rows of virtually identical giant shed-like structures, one factory stood out: the name on the white rectangular building said "Philips," but through its surrounding fence I could see mountains of Nike shoes piled high. It seems that in Cavite, production has been banished to our age's most worthless status: its factories are unbrandable, unswooshworthy; producers are the industrial untouchables. Is this what Phil Knight meant, I wondered, when he said his company wasn't about the sneakers?

Manufacturing is concentrated and isolated inside the zone as if it were toxic waste: pure, 100 percent production at low, low prices. Cavite, like the rest of the zones that compete with it, presents itself as the buy-in-bulk Price Club for multinationals on the lookout for bargains—grab a really big shopping cart. Inside, it's obvious that the row of factories, each with its own gate and guard, has been carefully planned to squeeze the maximum amount of production out of this swath of land. Windowless workshops made of cheap plastic and aluminum siding are crammed in next to each other, only feet apart. Racks of time cards bake in the sun, making sure the maximum amount of work is extracted from each worker, the maximum number of working hours extracted from each day. The streets in the zone are eerily empty, and open doors—the ventilation system for most factories—reveal lines of young women hunched in silence over clamoring machines.

In other parts of the world, workers live inside the economic zones, but not in Cavite: this is a place of pure work. All the bustle and color of Rosario abruptly stops at the gates, where workers must show their ID cards to armed guards in order to get inside. Visitors are rarely permitted in the zone and little or no internal commerce takes place on its orderly streets, not even candy and drink vending. Buses and taxicabs must drop their speed and silence their horns when they get into the zone. [...] If all of this makes Cavite feel as if it's in a different country, that's because, in a way, it is. The zone is a tax-free economy, sealed off from the local government of both town and province—a miniature military state inside a democracy.

As a concept, free-trade zones are as old as commerce itself, and were all the more relevant in ancient times when the transportation of goods required multiple holdovers and rest stops. Pre–Roman Empire city-states, including Tyre, Carthage and Utica, encouraged trade by declaring themselves "free cities," where goods in transit could be stored without tax, and merchants would be protected from harm. These tax-free areas developed further economic significance during colonial times, when entire cities—including Hong Kong, Singapore and Gibraltar—were designated as "free ports" from which the loot of colonialism could be safely shipped back to England, Europe or America with low import tariffs.[22] Today, the globe is dotted with variations on these tax-free pockets, from duty-free shops in airports and the free banking zones of the Cayman Islands to bonded warehouses and ports where goods in transit are held, sorted and packaged.

Though it has plenty in common with these other tax havens, the export processing zone is really in a class of its own. Less holding tank than sovereign territory, the EPZ is an area where goods don't just pass through but are actually manufactured, an area, furthermore, where there are no import and export duties, and often no income or property taxes either. The idea that EPZs could help Third World economies first gained currency in 1964 when the United Nations Economic and Social Council adopted a resolution endorsing the zones as a means of promoting trade with developing nations. The idea didn't really get off the ground, however, until the early eighties, when India introduced a five-year tax break for companies manufacturing in its low-wage zones.

Since then, the free-trade-zone industry has exploded. There are fifty-two economic zones in the Philippines alone, employing 459,000 people—that's up from only 23,000 zone workers in 1986 and 229,000 as recently as 1994. The largest zone economy is China, where by conservative estimates there are 18 million people in 124 export processing zones.[23] In total, the International Labor Organization says that there are at least 850 EPZs in the world, but that number is likely much closer to 1,000, spread through seventy countries and employing roughly 27 million workers.[24] The World Trade Organization estimates that between $200 and $250 billion worth of trade flows through the zones.[25] The number of individual factories housed inside these industrial parks is also expanding. In fact, the free-trade factories along the U.S.–Mexico border—in Spanish, *maquiladoras* (from *maquillar*, "to make up, or assemble")—are probably the only structures that proliferate as quickly as Wal-Mart outlets: there were 789 maquiladoras in 1985. In 1995, there were 2,747. By 1997, there were 3,508 employing about 900,000 workers.[26]

Regardless of where the EPZs are located, the workers' stories have a certain mesmerizing sameness: the workday is long—fourteen hours in Sri Lanka, twelve hours in Indonesia, sixteen in Southern China, twelve in the Philippines. The vast majority of the workers are women, always young, always working for contractors or subcontractors from Korea, Taiwan or Hong Kong. The contractors are usually filling orders for companies based in the U.S., Britain, Japan, Germany or Canada. The management is military-style, the supervisors often abusive, the wages below subsistence and the work low-skill and tedious. As an economic model, today's export processing zones have more in common with fast-food franchises than sustainable developments, so removed are they from the countries that host them. These pockets of pure industry hide behind a cloak of transience: the contracts come and go with little notice; the workers are predominantly migrants, far from home and with

little connection to the city or province where zones are located; the work itself is short-term, often not renewed.

As I walk along the blank streets of Cavite, I can feel the threatening impermanence, the underlying instability of the zone. The shed-like factories are connected so tenuously to the surrounding country, to the adjacent town, to the very earth they are perched upon, that it feels as if the jobs that flew here from the North could fly away again just as quickly. The factories are cheaply constructed and tossed together on land that is rented, not owned. When I climb up the water tower on the edge of the zone and look down at the hundreds of factories, it seems as if the whole cardboard complex could lift up and blow away, like Dorothy's house in *The Wizard of Oz*. No wonder the EPZ factories in Guatemala are called "swallows."

Fear pervades the zones. The governments are afraid of losing their foreign factories; the factories are afraid of losing their brand-name buyers; and the workers are afraid of losing their unstable jobs. These are factories built not on land but on air.

"It Should Have Been a Different Rosario"

The air the export processing zones are built upon is the promise of industrialization. The theory behind EPZs is that they will attract foreign investors, who, if all goes well, will decide to stay in the country, and the zones' segregated assembly lines will turn into lasting development: technology transfers and domestic industries. To lure the swallows into this clever trap, the governments of poor countries offer tax breaks, lax regulations and the services of a military willing and able to crush labor unrest. To sweeten the pot further, they put their own people on the auction block, falling over each other to offer up the lowest minimum wage, allowing workers to be paid less than the real cost of living.

In Cavite, the economic zone is designed as a fantasyland for foreign investors. Golf courses, executive clubs and private schools have been built on the outskirts of Rosario to ease the discomforts of Third World life. Rent for factories is dirt cheap: 11 pesos per square foot—less than a cent. For the first five years of their stay, corporations are treated to an all-expenses-paid "tax holiday" during which they pay no income tax and no property tax. It's a good deal, no doubt, but it's nothing compared to Sri Lanka, where EPZ investors stay for ten years before having to pay any tax.[27]

The phrase "tax holiday" is oddly fitting. For the investors, free-trade zones are a sort of corporate Club Med, where the hotel pays for everything and the guests live free, and where integration with the local culture and economy is kept to a bare minimum. As one International Labor Organization report puts it, the EPZ "is to the inexperienced foreign investor what the package holiday is to the cautious tourist." Zero-risk globalization. Companies just ship in the pieces of cloth or computer parts—free of import tax—and the cheap, non-union workforce assembles it for them. Then the finished garments or electronics are shipped back out, with no export tax.

The rationale goes something like this: *of course* companies must pay taxes and strictly abide by national laws, but just in this one case, on this one specific piece of land, for just a little while, an exception will be made—for the cause of future prosperity. The EPZs, therefore, exist within a kind of legal and economic set of brackets, apart from the rest of their countries—the Cavite zone, for example, is under the sole jurisdiction of the Philippines' federal Department of Trade and Industry; the local police and municipal government have no right even to cross the threshold. The layers of blockades serve a dual purpose: to keep the hordes away from the costly goods being manufactured inside the zone, but also, and perhaps more important, to shield the country from what is going on inside the zone.

Because such sweet deals have been laid out to entice the swallows, the barriers around the zone serve to reinforce the idea that what is happening inside is only temporary, or is not really happening at all. This collective denial is particularly important in Communist countries where zones house the most Wild West forms of capitalism this side of Moscow: this is *definitely* not really happening, *certainly* not here where the government in power maintains that capital is the devil and workers reign supreme. In her book *Losing Control?*, Saskia Sassen writes that the zones are a part of a process of carving up nations so that "an actual piece of land becomes denationalized...."[28] Never mind that the boundaries of these only-temporary, not-really-happening, denationalized spaces keep expanding to engulf more and more of their actual nations. Twenty-seven million people worldwide are now living and working in brackets, and the brackets, instead of being slowly removed, just keep getting wider.

It is one of the zones' many cruel ironies that every incentive the governments throw in to attract the multinationals only reinforces the sense that the companies are economic tourists rather than long-term investors. It's a classic vicious cycle: in an attempt to alleviate poverty, the governments offer more and more incentives; but then the EPZs must be cordoned off like leper colonies, and the more they are cordoned off, the more the factories appear to exist in a world entirely separate from the host country, and outside the zone the poverty only grows more desperate. In Cavite, the zone is a kind of futuristic industrial suburbia where everything is ordered; the workers are uniformed, the grass manicured, the factories regimented. There are cute signs all around the grounds instructing workers to "Keep Our Zone Clean" and "Promote Peace and Progress of the Philippines." But walk out of the gate and the bubble bursts. Aside from the swarms of workers at the start and end of shifts, you'd never know that the town of Rosario is home to more than two hundred factories.

The roads are a mess, running water is scarce and garbage is overflowing.

Many of the workers live in shantytowns on the outskirts of town and in neighboring villages. Others, particularly the youngest workers, live in the dormitories, a hodgepodge of concrete bunkers separated from the zone enclave by only a thick wall. The structure is actually a converted farm, and some rooms, the workers tell me, are really pigpens with roofs slapped on them.

The Philippines' experience of "industrialization in brackets" is by no means unique. The current mania for the EPZ model is based on the successes of the so-called Asian Tiger economies, in particular the economies of South Korea and Taiwan. When only a few countries had the zones, including South Korea and Taiwan, wages rose steadily, technology transfers occurred and taxes were gradually introduced. But as critics of EPZs are quick to point out, the global economy has become much more competitive since those countries made the transition from low-wage industries to higher-skill ones. Today, with seventy countries competing for the export-processing-zone dollar, the incentives to lure investors are increasing and the wages and standards are being held hostage to the threat of departure. The upshot is that entire countries are being turned into industrial slums and low-wage labor ghettos, with no end in sight. As Cuban president Fidel Castro thundered to the assembled world leaders at the World Trade Organization's fiftieth-birthday celebration in May 1998, "What are we going to live on? ... What industrial production will be left for us? Only low-tech, labor-intensive and highly contaminating ones? Do they perhaps want to turn a large part of the Third World into a huge free trade zone full of assembly plants which don't even pay taxes?"[29]

As bad as the situation is in Cavite, it doesn't begin to compare with Sri Lanka, where extended tax holidays mean that towns can't even provide public transportation for EPZ workers. The roads they walk to and from the factories are dark and dangerous, since there is no money for streetlights. Dormitory rooms are so overcrowded that they have white lines painted on the floor to mark where each worker sleeps—they "look like car parks," as one journalist observed.[30]

Jose Ricafrente has the dubious honor of being mayor of Rosario. I met with him in his small office, while a lineup of needy people waited outside. A once-modest fishing village, his town today has the highest per capita investment in all of the Philippines—thanks to the Cavite zone—but it lacks even the basic resources to clean up the mess that the factories create in the community. Rosario has all the problems of industrialization—pollution, an exploding population of migrant workers, increased crime, rivers of sewage—without any of the benefits. The federal government estimates that only 30 of the zone's 207 factories pay any taxes at all, but everybody else questions even that low figure. The mayor says that many companies are granted extensions of their tax holiday, or they close and reopen under another name, then take the free ride all over again. "They fold up before the tax holiday expires, then they incorporate to another company, just to avoid payment of taxes. They don't pay anything to the government, so we're in a dilemma right now," Ricafrente told me. A small man with a deep and powerful voice, Ricafrente is loved by his constituents for the outspoken positions he took on human rights and democracy during Ferdinand Marcos's brutal rule. But the day I met him, the mayor seemed exhausted, worn down by his powerlessness to affect the situation in his own backyard.[31] "We cannot even provide the basic services that our people expect from us," he said, with a sort of matter-of-fact rage. "We need water, we need roads, we need medical services, education. They expect us to deliver all of them at the same time, expecting that we've got money from taxes from the places inside the zone."

The mayor is convinced that there will always be a country—whether Vietnam, China, Sri Lanka or Mexico—that is willing to bid lower. And in the process, towns like Rosario will have sold out their people, compromised their education system and polluted their natural resources. "It should be a symbiotic relationship," Ricafrente says of foreign investment. "They derive income from us, so the government should also derive income from them…. It should have been a different Rosario."

Working in Brackets

So, if it's clear by now that the factories don't bring in taxes or create local infrastructures, and that the goods produced are all exported, why do countries like the Philippines still bend over backward to lure them inside their borders? The official reason is a trickle-down theory: these zones are job-creation programs and the income the workers earn will eventually fuel sustainable growth in the local economy.

The problem with this theory is that the zone wages are so low that workers spend most of their pay on shared dorm rooms and transportation; the rest goes to noodles and fried rice from vendors lined up outside the gate. Zone workers certainly cannot dream of affording the consumer goods they produce. These low wages are partly a result of the fierce competition for factories coming from other developing countries. But, above all, the government is extremely reluctant to enforce its own labor laws for fear of scaring away the swallows. So labor rights are under such severe assault inside the zones that there is little chance of workers earning enough to adequately feed themselves, let alone stimulate the local economy.

The Philippine government denies this, of course. It says that the zones are subject to the same labor standards as the rest of Philippine society: workers must be paid the minimum wage, receive social security benefits, have some measure of job security, be dismissed only with just cause and be paid extra for overtime, and they have the right to form independent trade unions. But in reality, the government views working conditions in the export factories as a matter of foreign trade policy, not a labor-rights issue. And since the government attracted the foreign investors with promises of a cheap and docile workforce, it intends to deliver. For this reason, labor department officials turn a blind eye to violations in the zone or even facilitate them.

Many of the zone factories are run according to iron-fist rules that systematically break Philippine labor law. Some employers, for instance, keep bathrooms padlocked except during two fifteen-minute breaks, during which time all the workers have to sign in and out so management can keep track of their nonproductive time. Seamstresses at a factory sewing garments for the Gap, Guess and Old Navy told me that they sometimes have to resort to urinating in plastic bags under their machines. There are rules against talking, and at the Ju Young electronics factory, a rule against smiling. One factory shames those who disobey by posting a list of "The Most Talkative Workers."

Factories regularly cheat on their workers' social security payments and gather illegal "donations" from workers for everything from cleaning materials to factory Christmas parties. At a factory that makes IBM computer screens, the "bonus" for working hours of overtime isn't a higher hourly wage but doughnuts and a pen. Some owners expect workers to pull weeds from the ground on their way into the factory; others must clean the floors and the washrooms after their shifts end. Ventilation is poor and protective gear scarce.

Then there is the matter of wages. In the Cavite zone, the minimum wage is regarded more as a loose guideline than as a rigid law. If $6 a day is too onerous, investors can apply to the government for a waiver on that too. So while some zone workers earn the minimum wage, most—thanks to the waivers—earn less.[32]

* * * * *

The Shoppers Take Flight

The fear that the flighty multinationals will once again pull their orders and migrate to more favorable conditions underlies everything that takes place in the zones. It makes for an odd dissonance: despite the fact that they have no local physical holdings—they don't own the buildings, land or equipment—brands like Nike, the Gap and IBM are omnipresent, invisibly pulling all the strings. They are so powerful as buyers that the hands-on involvement owning the factories would entail has come to look, from their perspective, like needless micro-management. And because the actual owners and factory managers are completely dependent on their large contracts to make the machines run, workers are left in a uniquely weak bargaining position: you can't sit down and bargain with an order form. So even the classic Marxist division between workers and owners doesn't quite work in the zone, since the brand-name multinationals have divested the "means of production," to use Marx's phrase, unwilling to encumber themselves with the responsibilities of actually owning and managing the factories, and employing a labor force.

If anything, the multinationals have more power over production by not owning the factories. Like most committed shoppers, they see no need to concern themselves with how their bargains were produced—they simply pounce on them, keeping the suppliers on their toes by taking bids from slews of other contractors. One contractor, Young Il Kim of Guatemala, whose Sam Lucas factory produces clothing for Wal-Mart and J.C. Penney, says of his big-brand clients, "They're interested in a high-quality garment, fast delivery, and cheap sewing charges—and that's all."[33] In this cutthroat context, each contractor swears he could deliver the goods cheaper if the brands would only start producing in Africa, Vietnam or Bangladesh, or if they would shift to homeworkers.

More blatantly, the power of the brands may occasionally be invoked to affect public policy in the countries where export zones are located. Companies or their emissaries may make public statements about how a raise in the legal minimum wage could price a certain Asian country "out of the market," as Nike's and Reebok's contractors have been quick to tell the Indonesian government whenever strikes get out of hand.[34] Calling a strike at a Nike factory "intolerable," Anton Supit, chairman of the Indonesian Footwear Association, which represents contractors for Nike, Reebok and Adidas, called on the Indonesian military to intervene. "If the authorities don't handle strikes, especially ones leading to violence and brutality, we will lose our foreign buyers. The government's income from exports will decrease and unemployment will worsen."[35] The corporate shoppers may also help draft international trade agreements to reduce quotas and tariffs, or even lobby a government directly to loosen regulations. In describing the conditions under which Nike decided to begin "sourcing" its shoes in China, for instance, company vice president David Chang explained that "one of the first things we told the Chinese was that their prices had to be more competitive with our other Far East sources because the cost of doing business in China was so enormous…. The hope is for a 20 percent price advantage over Korea."[36] After all, what price-conscious consumer doesn't comparison shop? And if a shift to a more "competitive" country causes mass layoffs somewhere else in the world, that is somebody else's blood on somebody else's hands. As Levi's CEO Robert Haas said, "This is not a job-flight story."

Multinational corporations have vehemently defended themselves against the accusation that they are orchestrating a "race to the bottom" by claiming that their presence has helped to raise the standard of living in underdeveloped countries. As Nike CEO Phil Knight said in 1996, "For the past 25 years, Nike has provided good jobs, improved labor practices and raised standards of living wherever we operate."[37] Confronted with the starvation wages in Haiti, a Disney spokesperson told *The Globe and Mail*, "it's a process all developing countries go through, like Japan and Korea, who were at this stage decades ago."[38] And there is no shortage of economists to spin the mounting revelations of corporate abuse, claiming that sweatshops are not a sign of eroded rights but a signal that prosperity is just around the corner. "My concern," said famed Harvard economist Jeffrey D. Sachs, "is not that there are too many sweatshops but that there are too few … those are precisely the jobs that were the stepping stones for Singapore and Hong Kong and those are the jobs that have to come to Africa to get them out of back-breaking rural poverty."[39] Sachs's colleague Paul Krugman concurred, arguing that in the developing world the choice is not between bad jobs and good jobs but between bad jobs and no jobs. "The overwhelming mainstream view among economists is that the growth of this kind of employment is tremendous good news for the world's poor."[40]

The no-pain-no-gain defense of sweatshops, however, took a severe beating when the currencies of those very countries supposedly benefiting most from this development model began crashing like cheap plates. First in Mexico, then Thailand, South Korea, the Philippines and Indonesia, workers were, and in many cases still are, bringing home minimum-wage paychecks worth less than when the "economic miracle" first came to bless their nations years ago. Nike's public-relations director, Vada Manager, used to claim that "the job opportunities that we have provided to women and men in developing economies like Vietnam and Indonesia have provided a bridge of opportunity for these individuals to have a much better quality of life,"[41] but by the winter of 1998, nobody knew better than Nike that that bridge had collapsed. With currency devaluation and soaring inflation, real wages in Nike's Indonesian factories fell by 45 percent in 1998.[42] In July of that year, Indonesian president B.J. Habibie urged his 200 million citizens to do their part to conserve the country's dwindling rice supply by fasting for two days out of each week, from dawn until dusk. Development built on starvation wages, far from kick-starting a steady improvement in conditions, has proved to be a case of one step forward, three steps back. And by early 1998 there were no more shining Asian Tigers to point to, and those corporations and economists that had mounted such a singular defense of sweatshops had had their arguments entirely discredited.

The fear of flying has been looming large in Cavite of late. The currency began its downward spiral a few weeks before I arrived, and since then conditions have only worsened. By early 1999, the price of basic commodities like cooking oil, sugar, chicken and soap had increased by as much as 36 percent from the year before. Paychecks that barely made ends meet now no longer accomplish even that. Workers who had begun to find the courage to stand up to management are now living not only under the threat of mass layoffs and factory flight but with the reality. In 1998, 3,072 businesses in the Philippines either closed down or scaled back operation—a 166 percent increase over the year before.[43] For its part, Nike has laid off 268 workers at the Philips factory, where I had seen, through the surrounding fence, the shoes lying in great piles. A few months later, in February 1999, Nike pulled out of two other Philippine factories as well, these ones located in the nearby Bataan export zone; 1,505 workers were affected by the closures.[44] But Phil Knight didn't have to do the dirty work himself—he just cut the orders and left the rest to the contractors. Like the factories themselves, these job losses went unswooshed.

The transience woven into the fabric of free-trade zones is an extreme manifestation of the corporate divestment of the world of work, which is taking place at all levels of industry. Cavite may be capitalism's dream vacation, but casualization is a game that can be played at home, and contracting out, as *Business Week* reporter Aaron Bernstein has written, is trickling up. "While outsourcing started in manufacturing in the early 1980s, it has expanded through virtually every industry as companies rush to shed staff in everything from human resources to computer systems."[45] The same impetus that lies behind the brands-versus-products and contracts-versus-jobs conflict is fueling the move to temp, part-time, freelance and homework in North America and Europe. [...]

This is not a job-flight story. It is a flight-from-jobs story.

Notes

1 Landor Web site.
2 "People Buy Products Not Brands," by Peter Schweitzer (J. Walter Thompson White Papers series, undated).
3 "Big Brand Firms Know the Name Is Everything," *Irish Times*, 27 February 1998.
4 Bob Ortega, *In Sam We Trust* (New York: Times Books, 1998), 342.
5 "Trade and Development Report, 1997," United Nations Conference on Trade and Economic Development.
6 Doanld Katz, *Just Do It: The Nike Spirit in the Corporate World* (Hollbrook: Adams Media Corporation, 1994), 204.
7 Cathy Majtenyi, "Were Disney Dogs Treated Better Than Workers?" *Catholic Register*, 23–30 December 1996, 9.
8 "Extreme Spreadsheet Dude," *Baffler* no. 9, 79, and *Wall Street Journal*, 16 April 1998 (on-line).
9 John Gilardi, "Adidas Share Offer Set to Win Gold Medal," *Reuters*, 26 October 1995.
10 *Globe and Mail*, 26 September 1997.
11 Charles Kernaghan, "Behind the Label: 'Made in China,'" prepared for the National Labor Committee, March 1998.
12 *Los Angeles Times*, 16 September 1997, D5. Furthermore, Sara Lee's investors had been getting a solid return on their investment but the stock "had gained 25 per cent over the prior 12 months, lagging the 35 per cent increase of the benchmark Standard & Poor's 500-stock index."
13 Tom Peters, *The Circle of Innovation* (New York: Alfred A. Knopf, 1997), 16.
14 David Leonhardt, "Sara Lee: Playing with the Recipe," *Business Week*, 27 April 1998, 114.
15 Ibid.
16 Jennifer Waters, "After Euphoria, Can Sara Lee Be Like Nike?" *Crain's Chicago Business*, 22 September 1997, 3.
17 Nina Munk, "How Levi's Trashed a Great American Brand," *Fortune*, 12 April 1999, 83.
18 "Levi Strauss & Co. to Close 11 of Its North American Plants," *Business Wire*, 22 February 1999, B1.
19 *Wall Street Journal*, 4 November 1997, B1.
20 Joanna Ramey, "Levi's Will Resume Production in China after 5-Year Absence," *Women's Wear Daily*, 9 April 1998, 1.
21 "Anti-Sweatshop Activists Score in Campaign Targeting Athletic Retailers," *Boston Globe*, 18 April 1999.
22 Richard S. Thoman, *Free Ports and Foreign Trade Zones* (Cambridge: Cornell Maritime Press, 1956).
23 These are International Labor Organization figures as of May 1998 but in "Behind the Label: 'Made in China,'" by Charles Kernaghan, March 1998, the figures on China's zone are much higher. Kernaghan estimates that there are 30 million inside the zones, and that there are 400—as opposed to 124—special economic zones inside China.
24 The International Labor Organization's Special Action Program on Export Processing Zones. Source: Auret Van Heerden.
25 This estimate was provided by Michael Finger at the World Trade Organization in a personal correspondence. No official figures are available.
26 Figures for 1985 and 1995 provided by the WTO. Figures for 1997 supplied by the Maquila Solidarity Network/Labor behind the Label Coalition, Toronto.
27 World Accounting Report, July 1992.
28 Saskia Sassen, *Losing Control? Sovereignty in an Age of Globalization* (New York: Columbia University Press, 1996), 8–9.
29 "Castro Dampens WTO Party," *Globe and Mail*, 20 May 1998.
30 Martin Cottingham, "Cut to the Bone," *New Statesman & Society*, 12 March 1993, 12.
31 Personal interview, 2 September 1997.
32 The Workers' Assistance Center, Rosario.
33 Ortega, *In Sam We Trust*, 250.
34 "South Korea Will Leave Indonesia if Strikes Continue," *Straits Times* (Singapore), 30 April 1997, 18. The article reported that Reebok's Indonesian executive Scott Thomas had met with South Korean officials, saying that if the worker strikes continued in Indonesia, the company might relocate again, saying Reebok "could place its orders easily with other countries if the situation persisted."
35 *Jakarta Post*, 30 April 1997.
36 "Nike in China" (abridged), Harvard Business School, 9-390-092, 12 August 1993.
37 "Nike Joins President Clinton's Fair Labor Coalition," *PR NewsWire*, 2 August 1996.
38 Christopher Reed, "Sweatshop Jobs Don't Put Food on Table," *Globe and Mail*, 9 May 1997.
39 Allen R. Myerson, "In Principle, a Case for More 'Sweatshops,'" *New York Times*, 22 June 1997, 4–5.
40 Ibid.
41 "Labour-Women Say Nike Supports Women in Ads, But Not in Factories," Inter Press Service, 29 October 1997.
42 "Raising Wages a Penny an Hour," National Labor Committee press release, 29 March 1999. Wages fell from 27 cents an hour to 15 cents an hour, even after Nike announced a 6 percent raise.

43 "High Unemployment, Higher Prices and Lower Wages," Ibon press release, 15 March 1999.

44 "Two Shoe Firms Close RP Shops," *Philippine Daily Enquirer*, 22 February 1999. The two factories were P.K. Export, which laid off 300 workers in 1998 and employed another 767 when the closure was announced, and Lotus Footwear, which employed 438 workers when it filed a notice of factory closure.

45 Aaron Bernstein, "Outsourced—and out of Luck," *Business Week*, 17 July 1995, 60–61.

CHAPTER 20

Enchanting McUniversity:
Toward a Spectacularly Irrational University Quotidian

GEORGE RITZER

The McDonaldization of the university—the creation of McUniversity (Ritzer 1998)—is not only a reality, but the process continues to expand and accelerate—that is, the university operates in an increasingly efficient manner, its operations are more and more predictable, it relies more than ever before on quantifiable measures (often to the detriment of quality), and it utilizes an increasing number of nonhuman technologies that control and even replace professors. Furthermore, the acceleration of these processes, as well as of McDonaldization in general, brings with it a series of irrationalities of rationality, especially a decline in the quality of education.

Given the ever-increasing reality of McUniversity, the purpose of this chapter is to discuss what can be done about problems caused by excessive rationalization. The analysis follows the logic not only of *The McDonaldization of Society* (Ritzer, 2000), but also of *Enchanting a Disenchanted World: Revolutionizing the Means of Consumption* (Ritzer 1999). While the rationale for relying on *McDonaldization* is obvious, the utilization of the approach derived from the latter work is based on the assumption that the university is a means of consumption—that is, it is a setting that makes it possible for customers (in this case, students and their parents) to consume education. This, of course, presumes that there has been a change in the relationship between students (and their parents) and the university. They increasingly see themselves as consumers of education in much the same way as they are consumers of what the mall (including the cybermall) and Disney World have to offer. This, in turn, has altered the way in which the university and its staff relate to them. Instead of viewing them as reliable, long-term clients, the university must now treat students as fickle customers who may be difficult to attract and retain.

This leads to many different kinds of changes in the university, but those focused on here are the changes in the university as a setting of consumption. It is the setting that has been McDonaldized to, among other things, deliver education efficiently and at a reasonable cost. The McDonaldization of the university's setting is attractive to consumers, especially because in a McDonaldized

society they come to expect things like efficiency and low cost (e.g., the McDonald's value meal picked up at the drive-through window). However, there are limits to the attractiveness of a McDonaldized setting, especially in the university. Students are unlikely to be attracted to, and to remain long at, a bare-bones university that resembles and operates like a factory in an enterprise zone in Thailand or a no-frills warehouse store. As consumers, students have become accustomed to far more elaborate means of consumption that combine McDonaldization with spectacle[1] (in some cases McDonaldization itself can be spectacular). Thus, contemporary indoor shopping malls (and megamalls like Mall of America in Minneapolis), Las Vegas casino-hotels, cruise-ships, and theme parks (like Disney World) are clearly McDonaldized, but much of the rationalized workings of these systems is concealed beneath a spectacular surface. Masses of consumers are drawn by the spectacles and are well served by the McDonaldized operations. Students want the same things from the university and while the university has been delivering increasingly McDonaldized processes, it has not been notably successful in creating spectacles. The university needs to be *both* McDonaldized *and* spectacular.

Because they are both McDonaldized and spectacular, I have also called the new means of consumption "cathedrals of consumption." The challenge to the university is to become a cathedral for the consumption of education. Cathedrals of consumption are rationalized, but this brings with it disenchantment. To attract their clientele, cathedrals cannot remain disenchanted, and they seek to reenchant themselves by becoming more spectacular. Spectacles give cathedrals an aura of magic, of enchantment. The world's great religious cathedrals have long sought to become spectacular through their great size, high vaulted ceilings, huge stained-glass windows, and so on. However, we must remember that great rationality is required to build and operate religious cathedrals, and this exists side-by-side with the enchantment produced by spectacles. Today's great cathedrals of consumption have followed a similar course, albeit to a much greater degree than religious cathedrals—that is, they are both more rationalized and more spectacular than religious cathedrals. Consider Disney World or the Bellagio casino-hotel and the degree of rationalization required to operate these settings and to accommodate the hordes of people that pass through them each day, as well as the enormous spectacle produced by them.

As with the modern cathedrals of consumption, today's universities cannot simply McDonaldize—they must also utilize spectacles in order to make themselves seem enchanted to their consumer base. What can the modern university "learn from Las Vegas"? Are the spectacles produced by the modern cathedrals of consumption in Las Vegas (and elsewhere) of relevance to the university? Can they be used by the university to overcome the liabilities associated with a heavy reliance on McDonaldization and become a source of enchantment that allows the university to attract and keep students? Perhaps more importantly, can they be used to *improve* the quality of education? To begin to answer these questions, we must first examine, at least briefly, the ways in which the cathedrals of consumption make themselves more spectacular and enchanted.

Creating Spectacles

There are at least three broad mechanisms used by the cathedrals of consumption to create spectacles. The first is development and use of *simulations*, or elaborate fakes, designed to amaze and delight consumers. This focus on simulations is motivated by the fact that the real, the authentic, is difficult to work with, is often not in the right place, and is difficult or impossible to manipulate in ways that could make it even more spectacular. Thus, from the point of view of Las Vegas entrepreneurs, the "real" Venice in Italy is in the wrong place (it is not in Las Vegas and cannot be transported there), it is difficult to work with (those pesky Venetians might object to major changes in their city), and it is hard, to say the least, to make it more spectacular. Thus, the entrepreneurs built a simulated Venice in Las Vegas: the Venetian casino-hotel (and shopping mall). Las Vegas is increasingly defined by such simulations (e.g., New York, New York; Bellagio; Mandalay Bay), and simulations mark many other cathedrals of consumption. For example, Disney World is a world of innumerable simulations (e.g., the fake Main Street by which one enters and leaves); a new park has recently opened adjacent to Disneyland in Anaheim that is a simulation of California (in, no less, the "real" state of California). Such simulations are spectacular and magical, and they serve to enchant the settings in which they are found.

A second mechanism for the production of spectacle and enchantment is *implosion*. If explosion (often associated with modernity) involves the creation of innumerable new phenomena, implosion (usually associated with postmodernity) involves the elimination of boundaries between extant phenomena so that they collapse in on one another. The existence of two or more phenomena—once deemed as necessarily distinct—in the same setting creates a sense of spectacle and magic for consumers. Thus, malls and theme parks were at one time seen as distinct settings that were each spectacular in their own way. However, with the arrival of the Edmonton Mall and the Mall of America, the boundaries collapsed, and malls and theme parks came to exist under one roof.

A third technique for enchanting the new means of consumption is the manipulation of time and space. The manipulation of the latter can take the form of time compression: things that formerly took days or weeks can now be done in hours, minutes, or even nanoseconds. The spectacle associated with the fast-food restaurant, especially in its early years, was the fact that food was available in seconds or minutes. Today, the time needed to purchase stock on line has been reduced to virtually nothing. One of the ways in which space is made spectacular is to encompass enormous areas under one roof or in one setting. The modern cruise ship, sometimes as long as three football fields, encompasses a "hotel" for 3–4,000 people, a casino, a spa, restaurants, swimming pools, and so on. Universities have already made many efforts to manipulate time and space in order to seem more spectacular. For example, classes taught by closed-circuit television or online make it possible for students across the country to take courses at a given university. These courses can be taken at very different times in the several time zones, or they can be taken at any time, at the leisure of the student. And universities pour funds into building immense facilities such as stadiums and athletic centers with the intention of attracting students.

Toward a Spectacularly Irrational University Quotidian

Since it is a means of consumption, the university *could* follow the lead of the major cathedrals of consumption and seek to reenchant itself through the creation of spectacles using mechanisms like simulation, implosion, and the manipulation of time and space. However, while the university has, in various ways, taken this course of action, there are severe limitations in this regard. It simply cannot afford to grow too, to become much like a Las Vegas casino-hotel or Disney World. If it did, it would delegitimize itself and lose far more than it would gain. Furthermore, creating a spectacular physical plant and superstructure would attract students, but it would do nothing about improving the quality of education. Thus, the issue is: are there any lessons to be gained from the cathedrals of consumption that the university can use in its effort to attract and retain students *and* to improve the quality of their educational experience?

I think the answer is yes, but the university must adapt the ideas of enchantment and spectacle to its own particular characteristics and realities. (In fact, all means of consumption must do this.) What this means is that, unlike the Las Vegas casino, the university cannot focus exclusively on massive external structures (the size of its football stadium, the impressiveness and beauty of its grounds), but must, rather, devote most of its attention to the quite unspectacular day-to-day operations, the most fundamental everyday realities, that make a university a university. This is far from an astounding conclusion, but the focus of this essay on spectacle and enchantment does lead us to a somewhat counter-intuitive conclusion: what the university needs to do is to seek in various ways to *make the seemingly unspectacular spectacular*! What it needs to do is to focus on its quotidian activities and to find ways to make them spectacular and enchanting. What are those unspectacular activities? And how can they be made more spectacular, more enchanted, *and* more beneficial from an educational point of view?

Of course, the irreducible minimum of the university involves professors teaching and students learning (and, to some degree, vice versa). Perhaps the most spectacular and enchanted thing the university could do would involve a return to personal, direct, intensive contact between professor and student. Imagine what a sensation a university would make by announcing that henceforth all undergraduate (and graduate) education would involve only one-on-one tutorials and seminars involving a maximum of ten students. The news would ricochet around the world, and students would flock to that university. The spectacular reenchanted university would have done its job and attracted the clientele it needs to survive. Furthermore, that clientele would probably involve better students who are willing, and maybe even able, to pay for such an education, which, undoubtedly, would be of higher quality than that which is currently generally available in McUniversity.

There are several problems with this scenario (e.g., where are all these new professors to come from?), but the crucial stumbling block is the astronomical costs involved. A massive influx of new (and costly) faculty would be required to create such a university. The university, and especially the governmental agencies that back most universities, would need to come up with billions, perhaps trillions, of dollars to fund such a university, and/or the tuition for paying students would have to multiply manyfold. If the latter were the case, the newly enchanted university would be counterproductive and many able students attracted by the "spectacular unspectacular" would be put off by the high cost. And, if the government were asked to foot the bill, it would undoubtedly refuse. In an era in the United States of "no new taxes," and even gigantic tax cuts, there would be virtually no support for such a massive infusion of funds into higher education. This is especially likely to be the reaction since the bulk of the new money would go into hiring and paying staff. We live in an era in which the emphasis is on cutting back on personnel costs, not increasing them on a massive scale. This is especially true of hiring new faculty members, as there is already a widespread suspicion that there are now too many of them and too much money is spent on them.

So it comes as no surprise that we are *not* returning to an academia characterized by tutorials and small seminars. How, then, do we make the quotidian activities of the university more enchanting and spectacular? In answering this question, we must look forward rather than backward, although we can take our lead from the historic activities of the university. Thus, one of the things that is needed is to speculate about the use of advanced technologies, some of which may not yet be in existence, that can give the university of the future a flavor of the past. In the following section I will sketch out a few ideas that are somewhere between contemporary realities, easily envisioned technological advances, and science fiction. They all involve making the unspectacular activities of the university more spectacular. They are also based on the assumption that high-tech solutions, even though they may be costly, are far cheaper than the low-tech solution of hiring hordes of new faculty members. However, in contrast to increasing McDonaldization, these solutions involve the use of nonhuman technologies to *enhance* human technology.

The reader will no doubt notice that this involves a complete inversion of one of the basic characteristics of McDonaldization: instead of replacing human with nonhuman technology, the focus here is on the use of nonhuman technology to enhance human technology. This is of crucial importance because it leads to the broader argument that informs the rest of this chapter—in order to make its quotidian activities more spectacular and better educationally, the university must *deMcDonaldize* (Ritzer 1998) them—that is, those activities must be reconceptualized and reorganized so that they involve the obverse of each of the basic principles of McDonaldization. To put it another way, those activities must be made *spectacularly irrational*.

Nonhuman Technology That *Enhances* Human Technology

The idea of a high-tech, wired lecture hall is nothing new—indeed, many are already in existence[2] and as they currently exist, they do create something of a spectacle that is attractive to students. However, the high-tech classrooms with which I am familiar do not deal with the quotidian issues of concern here. In fact, if anything, they exacerbate the problem of a lack of personalized contact between teacher and student. If the idea is to recreate something like the personal contact that existed between students and professors, how can that be accomplished in the high-tech lecture hall? I envision something like the following: A lecture hall seating 500, even 1,000, students is fully wired; computer screens are found on each student's desk and at the podium. Students, professors, and teaching assistants bring their personal disks to class and insert them into their disk drives. Each disk has the name and some personal information on each of the participants. With a tap on the keyboard, a professor can bring up the name of any student anywhere in the class and call on that student *by name*. Or, when students want to ask questions of the professor, their names, locations in the classroom, and bits of personal information about them (e.g., major, interests, grade point average, grades in the class, attendance records, etc.) are highlighted on the professor's computer screen. (Much more personal information can even be added if the professor wishes.) Such information permits the professor to have a *more personal interaction* with each student, perhaps tailoring questions and answers to the student's interests, major, and even personality. This clearly involves the use of nonhuman technology to enhance, not control or replace, the interaction between professor and student.

As the lecture unfolds, students enter additional questions that come to mind (and that may not require class time to answer) into their computers, and these are transmitted directly to the computers of teaching assistants (TAs). The assistants can answer such questions as they come in, thereby giving students *instantaneous and personalized feedback*. Especially important questions, or those that are of general interest, can be transmitted by TAs to the professor's computer, along with the identity of the student raising the questions. The professor takes occasional (and welcome) breaks from the lecture to bring up a screen with the questions that have come in since the previous break for questions. The professor (or a designated TA) selects the best questions and/or those that are of most general interest and responds *directly and personally to the student* who asked each question.

Also during the lecture, students offer continual feedback, noting when a particular example is unclear, the point of a given slide is obscure, and so on. TAs can clarify immediately (it would be impossible for the lecturer to deal with all of these issues during the lecture), or bring up the issue with the professor later. TAs can then give students the needed clarifications via computer. In addition, assistants and professors are given the feedback they need in order to come up with better examples, clearer slides, and so forth, for the next time the lecture is given or the course is taught.

At the end of each class period, students give instant evaluations of the lecture (and the professor can offer similar evaluations of student performance during class). All involved can reassess what transpired on the basis of these instantaneous evaluations.

Of course, this kind of relationship would not stop with the end of class. Students can transmit all sorts of questions to TAs from their dorm rooms, apartments, or even the library. TAs can filter these questions, answering most and passing some on to the professor, perhaps to be dealt with in the next class.

Online chats between students, assistants, and professors are already common. An integral part of the course could be an online chat of an hour or two with the professor. Assistants could be available for longer periods of time for such chats with students.

One could go on with this, spinning out all sorts of variations on this theme. Much will emerge as the technology becomes available and all involved learn how to use it better. However, the essential point is that advanced nonhuman technology would be used in spectacular new ways to enhance the most essential of the day-to-day educational activities involving interaction between students, professors, and assistants. Of course, this would not be of the kind of interaction that takes place in one-on-one tutorials or miniseminars. However, given the fact that we are not returning to such an educational world, it is the best we can do, and it may, in some ways, even be superior to older methods. For example, students can raise questions via the computer, and they can be answered immediately by TAs, even as the lecture proceeds. In the "old days" professors had to interrupt their lectures to answer such questions. Many questions that might have gone unraised or unanswered are now more likely to be asked and answered.

However, what immediately comes to mind about this set of suggestions, and others to be discussed below, is: does this not all involve a further McDonaldization of education? And does it not bring with it a further disenchantment, not reenchantment, of education? Yes, this does involve a further McDonaldization of education. Of course, McDonaldization itself can be spectacular in various ways, but it also brings with it disenchantment. More specifically, we are here discussing one element of McDonaldization: increasing control through the substitution of nonhuman for human technology. However, it all depends on how the technology is being used. In the preceding scenario nonhuman technology is *not* being used to control humans, but, rather, to enhance their ability to interact with one another within the context of a large lecture. Furthermore, the nonhuman technology is not being used to replace human beings—as students, assistants, or professors—but to enhance their ability to function as human beings, at least in the context of the given of a large lecture. The latter may not be the ideal educational method, but given the fact that large lectures are likely to grow increasingly ubiquitous, technology can be used to allow it to function in a more human (i.e., personalized) way.

The real danger lies in using such technology to control instructors and their assistants (and students) or to replace them completely with nonhuman technologies.[3] For example, we already have classes consisting wholly of videotaped lectures by professors that can be accessed at home or in the library, or classes employing elaborate computer programs that answer student questions rather than having answers provided by TAs or professors. This is the worst of the McDonaldization of education, involving its complete dehumanization. The objective, instead, should be to use nonhuman technology to humanize education as much as possible given the realities (e.g., large lectures) of today's (and tomorrow's) university.

Technology could be used in many other ways to enhance the relationship between students and professors. For example, students could use their computers to access their professor's works in progress. Students could be given access to grant proposals under consideration, raw data sets, and articles and books in process. In terms of the latter, students could follow their professor's work as it evolves, even on a page-by-page basis. Much of the material would be beyond most students, but they would get a glimpse of the creative process. This access to the emergence of scholarly works, especially by their own teachers, would seem (and be) quite spectacular to most students, and it would certainly be beneficial from an educational point of view. Of course, it would work best when the works in question are textbooks aimed at students. Students would understand what they are reading, and they could even be allowed to make comments on the text and suggestions for improvement. The greatest spectacle from a students' point of view would be to see their own ideas integrated into the emerging text (and, hopefully, being thanked in print for them).

The reverse process would also be possible: professors—more probably, teaching assistants—could access student papers in process and even comment as they are being written. Problems could be picked up as papers are being written rather than at the end of the process, when nothing can be done about them. The best students would certainly find this quite spectacular, and the result would be better papers. Those who do their papers at the last minute or purchase term papers over the web or from other students might not be so thrilled by this possibility. Of course, students (and professors) would be free to block access to some or all of their work.

All of the ideas discussed in this section rely on the use of advanced technology, but in the following sections we focus on more human ways of making the unspectacular aspects of education more spectacular and better educationally through the inversion of the basic principles of McDonaldization.

The Unpredictable University Quotidian

The university is currently characterized by a highly predictable round of lectures, discussions, reading assignments in textbooks, exams (often in the quite routine multiple-choice format), and grades or marks at the end of the process. It would be quite a spectacle if the university sought to inject as much unpredictability as possible into the day-to-day life of the university. This builds, in part, on ideas like "mass customization" and "sneakerization"—that is, one can create considerable diversity without totally surrendering the advantages of McDonaldization. What universities need to do is to find ways of teaching large numbers of students in more customized or at least "sneakerized" ways. In the latter, they need to follow the lessons of the athletic shoe industry and its discovery that it could produce hundreds of

different varieties of shoes without sacrificing the McDonaldization of production and distribution. If the university were to find ways to "mass customize" or "sneakerize" its educational system, it would inject much more unpredictability into the process, and that unpredictability would be quite spectacular to students accustomed to an educational system where they have relatively few options. And any kind of greater customization, be it through sneakerization or mass customization, is likely to improve educational quality.

In fact, advanced technologies can be used to help to accomplish these goals. The kinds of lectures discussed in the previous section permit some degree of customization by allowing students to ask questions electronically and permitting professors to respond in a more personal way, even one that is tailored to students. However, rather than exploring the possibilities offered by technology in this realm (and there are many), I prefer to focus on what universities, departments, and professors could do to inject more unpredictability into the educational process.

Once again, let us focus on the introductory course, because it is subject to the greatest pressure to undergo McDonaldization. While many universities make use of large lectures, others use multiple sections involving, say, fifty students each. There is often much commonality in these sections; in fact, departments often impose a common textbook and curriculum. What I envision, in contrast, is a series of sections each of which is designed to be different from all the others. Each section would be clearly labeled and defined, so that its distinctive focus and its differences from all other sections would be clear to students, who would be free to choose the one that best fits their needs and interests. Below I outline a number of hypothetical "sneakerized" sections for an imagined course in introductory sociology that implements such an approach:

Introduction to sociology

1. using a basic textbook, a lecture format, and multiple-choice questions;
2. using only original works of classic and contemporary sociologists, lecture format, essay exams;
3. through the novel, discussion format, outline for a proposed novel required;
4. through motion pictures (or television programs), discussion format, story board for a proposed movie (or TV program) required;
5. through the newspaper, subscription to the *New York Times* required, discussion format, students required to write several newspaper-style articles;
6. through the Internet, all basic topics in sociology covered through visits to a wide range of websites, construction of an original website required;
7. taught by nonacademics (e.g., businesspeople, social workers, government administrators) with degrees in sociology; the focus would be on applied issues, and reading assignments would utilize applied

materials; grades would be based on an internship in the "real" world;

8. for those who plan on majoring in sociology and doing sociological research, focus is on methods and statistics, lecture and discussion, a research article required.

Clearly such a list is nearly endless, but such an array of available sections gets away from the numbing sameness of introductory sociology and offers some level of sneakerization.

While the above leads to diversity, it does not deal satisfactorily with the issue of unpredictability. That is best handled by (human) instructors and their assistants. What can be done to inject unpredictability into today's university?

1. Avoid textbooks! Instead, use a great many diverse reading assignments from many different types of sources. Better yet, have instructors create their own textual material.

2. Avoid doing the same thing from class to class. A lecture in one class period followed by a discussion in the next and then viewing a movie/videotape, some sort of field trip, and so on.

3. Consciously try to inject unpredictability into each class. Lecture for a time, invite questions, get students to speak on the issue, invite graduate assistants to add their perspective, and so on. Try to efficiently cover a given topic in one period, ramble off on a series of tangents in another, and totally refuse to stay on topic in the next one.

4. Bring in unannounced guest speakers as discussion leaders at various points during the semester.

5. Give impromptu writing assignments in class. Pop quizzes would also inject some (unwelcome to students) unpredictability.

6. Give only subjective evaluations of exams, papers, quizzes during the semester. Put off giving a letter or number grade until as late as possible.

Clearly, these suggestions do little more than scratch the surface. Each instructor is in a position to create all sorts of unpredictable events during a class and a semester. Given the great predictability of virtually everything else they encounter in the university (and in the larger society), many students will find unpredictable classes truly spectacular and educationally beneficial.

However, bear in mind that it is very possible to McDonaldize unpredictability and thereby to eliminate the very spectacle and educational advance we are trying to create. I have previously written about two imaginary chains (Ritzer 1998), "Miss Haps" and "Miss Steaks," based on the routinization of a series of mishaps and mistakes. Thus, for example, the activities of waitpersons would be choreographed so that they would occasionally engage in pratfalls or "accidentally" spill a plate of (plastic) french fries. In these and other ways, the

unpredictable would be McDonaldized. In much the same way, the university could McDonaldize the unpredictable events discussed above. This might create a spectacle, but it would not be the kind of spectacle the university needs. Such a spectacle requires more genuine unpredictability and not the kind of simulated unpredictability one might experience were Miss Haps and Miss Steaks real restaurant chains.

Quality, *Not* Quantity

Another inversion of the principles of McDonaldization—an emphasis on quality not quantity—would also help to make the day-to-day activities of the university more spectacular. Too often, the demands of mass education cause the quality of education, particularly what goes on in the classroom, to suffer. Much of what has been said in this part of this essay has to do with improving the quality of education. Beyond the things discussed thus far, I would suggest the truly radical idea of having the very best people in the university teach the most and have the greatest amount of contact with students. While this is often accorded lipservice, the fact is that in the main the university's best-known and most important professors are usually rewarded with *reduced* teaching loads, especially at the undergraduate level. Instead of concentrating on their research, graduate seminars, and international academic jetsetting, let us have our very best professors teach undergraduates, especially in lower-level, even introductory, courses. Just having some of the university's "stars" walking into such a classroom would cause a stir, if not a spectacle. Spectacle would certainly be created if they were able to integrate their own work and ideas with the traditional material taught in lower-level courses and do it all in an interesting and accessible manner.

Not all, or even most, will be able to do that, at least initially. To deal with that problem there is another revolutionary idea: let us devote considerable time, energy, and resources to teaching professors how to teach. This would involve everything from required courses in graduate school on teaching, periodic refresher courses for professors, and special tutelage for the "stars" who are to be brought into the basic courses. Improving the quality of teacher training will lead to improvements in the quality of their teaching.

Inefficiency

There is much to be said in favor of making education as inefficient as possible. Again, the clients (students), who are accustomed to efficiency in all areas of their lives, would find an inefficient educational process spectacular and often to their advantage educationally. Ordinarily, the emphasis is on efficiently covering a wide range of topics. How about courses that strive to be inefficient? Courses that pause to devote as much time as necessary to issues that catch students' attention and that elicit intense interest from them. Does it really matter whether all fifteen predesignated topics are covered in a semester? If it does, do they all have to be covered in class? Could not whatever topics are not covered in class be left to the students to cover on their own? (My most memorable college course was one in which the professor *refused* to *ever* cover *any* topic in the course. He referred us to the text and ancillary readings on each topic but devoted every class to whatever the class wanted to discuss. It was a highly stimulating class, and I learned a lot in it: it was a spectacle to me and others in the class—although still others found it frustrating and misguided. Whatever I learned about the subject—clinical psychology, as I recall—I got from readings done outside class-time.)

My thinking on spectacular inefficiency is guided by the following example from the education of small children requiring you to imagine "a cluster of excited children examining a turtle with enormous fascination and intensity. Now children, put away the turtle, the teacher insists. We're going to have our science lesson. The lesson is on crabs" (Silberman 1970:125). While it may be efficient to move from subject to subject (from turtles to crabs) according to a preset schedule, it would be better educationally to stay with one subject (turtles) until the interest in it is exhausted. It may be inefficient to spend so much time on turtles (the lesson on crabs may be delayed, shortened, or even eliminated), but the educational advantages may be enormous.

The Rationality of Irrationality

Ultimately it is quite rational—or, more accurately, reasonable—for the university to organize its quotidian activities in a highly irrational manner. The quality of education would, I believe, improve with an increase in the irrationality of education. The McDonaldization of the university's everyday educational activities produces a number of irrationalities, especially a decline in the quality of education. It behooves the university to deMcDonaldize its everyday educational activities—to increase their degree of *in*efficiency, *un*predictability, *in*calculability, and use of *human* technology—in order to improve their quality. Furthermore, such a deMcDonaldized education will seem quite spectacular to students. Thus, there is a double advantage to deMcDonaldized education: it both works better and will attract and keep larger numbers of students.

I am not suggesting that the university as a whole needs to deMcDonaldize in order to deliver deMcDonaldized education. In fact, it could be argued that a highly McDonaldized university structure and system is required to deliver such an education. Record-keeping in a deMcDonaldized educational system, for example, might be more difficult because of differentiation in educational programs. If we had more differentiated introductory sociology courses, for instance, then the university would need to keep track of which classes are prerequisites for what academic and career directions. More advisers would be needed to explain the much more complicated educational systems to prospective students, employers, and admissions directors of graduate programs at other universities. One of the ironic consequences of deMcDonaldizing the quotidian activities of the university is the further McDonaldization of the structure of the university.

Yet in a way this makes perfect sense. The problem is not McDonaldization per se, but *excessive McDonaldization* (Ritzer & Ovadia, 2000) and the *inappropriate extension of McDonaldization* to domains that ought not to be McDonaldized to any great extent. As Weber pointed out long ago, there are good reasons for large-scale organizations to be bureaucratized—that is, rationalized. And there might be good reasons to McDonaldize a factory, an army, and so on.[4] However, that does not mean that everything should be McDonaldized; and that everything gains from increases in McDonaldization. Clearly, everyday educational activity is one of those areas (another is the doctor–patient relationship) that have been overly and inappropriately McDonaldized. What a spectacle it would be if the quotidian activities of the university were truly deMcDonaldized! And just imagine how much better the educational process itself would function!

Conclusion

To survive as a means of consumption, the university must learn from the highly successful cathedrals of consumption and find ways of becoming more spectacular. However, while the cathedrals of consumption focus on grand, colossal, and superficial spectacles, the university cannot take this direction. It must, instead, focus on making more spectacular the quotidian activities that go to the heart of its educational functioning. While everything around it is growing increasingly McDonaldized, the route open to the university is to create spectacle by deMcDonaldizing its quotidian activities. Inefficient, unpredictable, incalculable education employing human technologies will seem quite spectacular to students, especially in contrast to the numbing McDonaldization that is increasingly found almost everywhere else. The spectacle of the deMcDonaldization of the university's everyday activities will not only be spectacular and attract students, but it will also serve to enhance dramatically the quality of the educational process.

Notes

[1] I am using the concept of the spectacle throughout this analysis. While it is drawn from Debord (1968) and the Situationists (Ritzer & Stillman, 2001), it is used differently here. I am simply using the idea to refer to anything that is attention-grabbing, exciting, and interesting.

2 While I will focus on large lectures, it is clearly possible (as Caroline Persell reminds me) that such technology can also be used to enhance collaborative and cooperative learning.

3 As Caroline Persell has pointed out to me, much of my discussion implies that faculty would control the introduction of new technologies and use them to enhance day-to-day education. However, the political economy of the university makes it clear that there are other powerful forces that might be inclined to adopt and deploy such technologies for very different, even antithetical, purposes.

4 If not, there are at least sound reasons to McDonaldize aspects or levels of these structures.

References

Debord, G. (1968). *The Society of the Spectacle*. London: Verso, 1994.

Ritzer, G. (1998). *The McDonaldization Thesis: Explorations and Extensions*. London & Thousand Oaks, CA: Sage.

Ritzer, G. (1999). *Enchanting a Disenchanted World: Revolutionizing the Means of Consumption*. Thousand Oaks, CA: Pine Forge Press.

Ritzer, G. (2000). *The McDonaldization of Society: New Century Edition*. Thousand Oaks, CA: Pine Forge Press.

Ritzer, G., & Ovadia, S. (2000). The process of McDonaldization is not uniform, nor are its settings, consumers, or the consumption of its goods and services. In M. Gottdiener (Ed.), *New Forms of Consumption: Consumers, Culture and Commodification*. Lanham, MD: Rowman and Littlefield (33–49).

Ritzer, G., & Stillman, T. (2001). The new means of consumption and the situationist perspective. In G. Ritzer (Ed.), *Explorations in the Sociology of Consumption: Fast Food, Credit Cards and Casinos*. London & Thousand Oaks, CA: Sage (181–202).

Silberman, C. E. (1970). *Crisis in the Classroom: The Remaking of American Education*. New York: Random House.

CHAPTER 21

Keeping the Ivory Tower White: Discourses of Racial Domination

Carol Schick

As a marker of difference and an indicator of respectability, space cannot be underestimated as a sign of personhood and legitimacy. This chapter examines a university space that remains dominated by those who identify as white. It examines how discourses in this university space function in ways that privilege whiteness, so that whiteness persists as what is worth knowing and as an identification worth performing. Ironically, the efforts to maintain the university space as white-dominated were instigated by the presence and acknowledgement of diverse populations in the university as well as a potential shift in power relations within the academy which was brought on by alternative political thought.

At the education faculty in the Canadian university in which this study is set, racial privilege was used to reconfirm the space as white in the midst of and, in part, because of the introduction of a compulsory cross-cultural course in a pre-service teacher-training program. I conducted semi-structured interviews with twenty-one white pre-service teachers who had attended this course. By applying a discourse analysis[1] to the interviews, I examined processes by which white identification is affirmed and supported by educated white participants who claim liberal values of equity and tolerance. My research indicates that racial identification processes, to which these participants have access, establish them as "rightful occupants" of university space. In many examples drawn from their discourses, participants perform themselves as belonging "in here," a place characterized by abstraction, objectivity, and rationality; quite unlike "out there," where others belong and which participants describe as political, embodied, and not necessarily rational. In their association with the university as a site of white domination, participants reinforce their identities, a process that further supports their performance of whiteness in other teaching arenas.

My understanding of how space produces subject identifications is drawn from the work of Sherene Razack,[2] whose analysis argues that space produces identities of both privilege and degeneracy. As a production of difference, the designation of space constructs and contains identities that are said to belong in a particular site. Social relations that converge in specific sites

mark out places of privilege and elite formation against contamination by an outside Other. Since spaces produce identities, continuous surveillance is necessary to prevent the loss of privilege and respectability. My research findings illustrate that the surveillance and disciplinary practices that support the production of dominant identifications also produce intellectual identities in this site. Participants from this education faculty struggle to establish themselves as legitimate occupants of this white space in which their own claims to whiteness are insecure. In describing the multicultural course, they use the intellectual discourses of the university so that the influence *of* the Other is turned into discourse *about* the Other. These participants come to know themselves as knowledgeable, innocent, and in control; and their access to privilege is measured by how they use this compulsory multicultural course to confirm their rightful place in the university.

Spatial Arrangements

In 1988, the College of Education at the University of Saskatchewan accepted the proposal of the Subcommittee on Multicultural Teacher Education, which acknowledged that newly graduated teachers could expect to meet a diverse ethnic, racial, and minority student body within the province. The proposal constituted the framework for the motion passed at Academic Affairs (University Council), which required a compulsory course in multicultural education for all pre-service teachers with a specific focus on Aboriginal culture. The proposal's rationale reflected "the changing nature of the responsibilities of teachers and teacher educators in a country in which multiculturalism and human rights have become the cornerstones of Canadian citizenship."[3]

Multicultural education, framed as an issue that was "not going to disappear," was described as "consonant with the changing balance among ethnocultural groups in this country." The rationale and philosophical ethic of the proposed course were "concerned with equality of educational opportunity and outcome," and the "creation of multiculturally literate citizens who respect and promote linguistic and cultural diversity, social equality, racial harmony, and national cohesiveness as cornerstones of Canadian society." Finally, the compulsory course would ensure that graduates would "be able to function effectively in situations requiring cross-cultural perspectives, understandings and competencies."4 After many course proposals and incarnations of the committee, a course was finally piloted in 1993–94.

In the multicultural course under discussion, over 90 per cent of students were white. Although Saskatchewan is a province made up of widely diverse ethnocultural groups, it is Aboriginal peoples whose critical mass most sharply challenges the discourses of hegemonic whiteness at all intersections of personal and institutional contact. Though the overarching view was to produce teachers who can teach "students from majority and minority backgrounds,"5 and despite the variety of populations at this particular Canadian university, a significant purpose of this course was to produce white teachers who would "know something about" Aboriginal culture.

Since 1988, the course has become a requirement without which pre-service education students cannot graduate. Each year, several sections of the course are taught by both Aboriginal and white teachers. What, then, is produced by this compulsory multicultural course in a setting where students already perform dominant subjectivities? How is the setting contained and strengthened as an elite white space through the development of a compulsory curriculum that requires multicultural, cross-cultural learning of all its students?

Desiring Whiteness

The research participants were interviewed following their completion of the course. It is hardly surprising that the participants' greatest desire is to be accepted as legitimate entrants into a professional college of education and as successful teacher candidates. Many of the students are of non-Anglo European ancestry and from working-class origins; many have direct contact with older relatives for whom English is not a first language. Gaining access to norms and values formed in the privileged space of the university allows these participants to claim a "toehold on respectability."6 The security of their white identities is dependent upon their construction of themselves as not-Other. As white-ethnic minority participants, they claim entitlement by moving closer to the centre of white norms and values by means of "dominance through difference." They need the credentials the university will give them and the ideological training to "become a teacher."

I am not assessing participants' interviews for particular racist or non-racist claims, nor suggesting that they express some essential white identity. I am examining their discursive practices for the processes they use to perform their subject identities in spite of, and perhaps because of, compulsory multicultural education. This includes tactics by which participants justify their university attendance as normal and appropriate. These discursive practices are not necessarily peculiar to a particular geographic location or a particular individual, but rather they are peculiar to a community of speakers in which the discourses are easily understood. I explore some of the discursive practices participants use to access the elite space of the university: specifically, their knowledge of how domination is organized and produced in this site.

For example, participants use discursive practices to justify their own positionings as respectable, innocent, and "well-intended." Kim pointed out that "when you see someone else getting stepped on ... your heart goes out to them because you know, hey, I've had it happen to me."7 At other times, however, his identity as defender of the oppressed conflicts with his delight in experiencing the privileges of his educated white male status. He can hardly conceal his pleasure, for example, when describing how surprised he was, on a trip to the Philippines, to be called "Sir" by elders. Even though he suggests that others are elitist, this same position has become available to him as a university-educated white male.

Because participants' own dominant identities are not yet fixed, they require the university to uphold the racial configurations of a white teaching profession. By aligning themselves with this elite space, they secure their own legitimacy and respectability. Before I address the substantive issue of how participants produce themselves as white subjects in this elite space, it is necessary to discuss the contexts in which their claims to legitimacy are considered the norm.

Threatening Ideas

Cross-cultural, multicultural initiatives—also called antiracist or oppositional—frequently meet with resistance. Difficulty in implementing and teaching such courses suggests that they pose some kind of threat in the spaces where they are introduced. Equity initiatives appear to be inevitably disruptive, no matter how carefully worded or ideologically mild the agenda. What is being endangered by a cross-cultural course in this white-dominated university of the Canadian Prairies? What are anti-oppressive courses up against? How might multicultural, cross-cultural stories implicitly undermine claims of white entitlement? What common-sense assumptions do they disturb?

From the very beginning, the compulsory nature of the cross-cultural course was considered an affront, even though it was by no means the only mandatory course in the participants' program. Margaret Wetherell and Jonathan Potter indicate that "[t]o define something as compulsory is, in terms of the liberal discourse of freedom and human rights, to define it negatively. Compulsion is automatically rhetorically bad."8 Many view cross-cultural matters as a private affair and therefore resent the suggestion that they require preparation in a public space before they can encounter their racialized Other in the classroom.

The compulsory nature is also at odds with a popular Canadian persona: the laissez-faire individual who has no particular ideology except to allow others to live with their differences. The participants treat the course as an objectifying, intellectual exercise akin to mathematics and language instruction. However, their negative responses in describing the effects of the course indicate that they actually have had very little success at maintaining objective distance, suggesting instead the extent to which the experience of the course was more of a moral and ethical issue for many participants. They attempt to distance themselves by saying: "I really felt alienated in that class," "I was taking it to be almost a form of forced reverse discrimination," and "Why is this being shoved in our face all the time?"[9] By describing the course in such negative terms, participants can dismiss any effects the course may have had on them.

Multicultural education also threatens Canadian stories of immigration in which Europeans produce a national narrative that establishes them as the "original inhabitants." Heroic tales of successful occupation by white settlers are narratives that legitimize European, especially Anglo, claims of entitlement. Another part of the national narrative, however, one which is more conveniently "forgotten," is the colonizing process that threatens Aboriginal people with geographic, cultural, and economic erasure. The notion of historic Anglo entitlement shapes Canada as a white space in which Aboriginal land claims need not be taken seriously; this spatial configuration—which is a *dis/placement*—establishes European immigration as instrumental in the founding of Canada. The claims of Aboriginal people are ignored in the celebratory heroism attached to immigration mythology, and the construction of dominant white-identified people is established through the production of Aboriginal peoples as Other. The control of space, on which domination depends, also requires a relationship with another whom it is necessary to designate as abject and Other. Lenore Keeshig-Tobias describes the necessity of the Other for the production of dominant Canadian identities in her poem "O Canada":

We have always walked on the edge/of your dreams, stalked/you as you made wild your way/through this great land/generation after generation/And, O Canada, you have always been/Afraid of us, scared, because you know/you can never live without us.[10]

In Western Canada, both degeneracy and privilege are produced as effects of spatialization. White entitlement is produced and rationalized as survey lines, deeds, boundaries, purchase prices, and mortgages—signs of ownership and belonging.[11] White entitlement is also produced relationally against the Otherness of original habitants. Production of the space as white, therefore, is never complete, and the identities that depend on the legitimacy of domination are forever insecure.

What else is challenged by a compulsory course on multicultural education? The proposal from the University of Saskatchewan refers to the recommendations of "defin-itive Canadian and international texts which implicitly critique the historical context of discrimination and racism"[12] in Canada. Canadian institutions are subject to the Canadian Charter of Rights and Freedoms, the Constitution, and the Universal Declaration of Human Rights, in which the rights of minorities are defended. Responding to diverse populations is not simply an act of conscience or a desire to "do the right thing." Mandating a multicultural course "reflects the changing nature of the responsibilities of teachers and teacher educators."[13] In an increasingly pluralist society, elite institutions can no longer maintain race, class, and gender barriers, that is, they cannot keep out the Other. Diverse populations and legal documents that protect minority interests may motivate multicultural studies, yet diverse bodies of knowledge on university campuses threaten the knowledge and space of the elite. David Sibley describes how alternate knowledge threatens established hierarchies and power structures in academia:

There are certain parallels between the exclusion of minorities, the "imperfect people" who disturb the homogenized and purified topographies of mainstream social space, and the exclusion of ideas which are seen to constitute a challenge to established hierarchies of knowledge and, thus, to power structures in academia. In both cases, there is a distaste for mixing expressed in the virtues of pure spaces and pure knowledge. In both cases, it is power—over geographical space or over the territory marked out by groups within an academic discipline—which is under threat.[14]

How is this threat to "power structures in academia" averted or at least contained? One way is to offer a multicultural course. This course may forestall demands the Other might make on white space, contain challenges of racism and discrimination brought against the white spaces, and limit accusations that the academic space is exclusionary. Being supportive of diverse bodies of knowledge is consistent with inquiry and open-mindedness, the cornerstones of white liberalism. Ironically, while the multicultural course may be threatening, it strengthens the space as liberal and as one in which whites welcome the Other. The multicultural course threatens participants because it presents symbolic reminders of the Others' demands. Participants' whiteness and "toehold on respectability" are always insecure and they rely on their exclusive access to elite spaces to produce themselves as dominant. They also rely on the university space as a site for the reaffirmation of their bourgeois, racialized identity as the not-Other.

Space as a major metaphor in participant discourses is indicated by the often-repeated expressions "fit in" and "out there." The desire to fit in is protected against the unconstrained, illogical space where unpredictable, potentially harmful, outdated, and contrary knowledge resides. Participants are very much aware that "that kind of knowledge is *out there*"; even the "real" world of teaching is contaminated space. Participants take great care to keep their knowledge and identities safe so that they themselves are not "outed." They want to "fit into" an elitist knowledge centre with its access to a "regime of truth," which is characterized by middle-class status, whiteness, ability, normative sexuality, post-secondary education, up-to-date training, possession of cross-cultural knowledge (politically correct attitudes), assumptions of moral superiority, idealism, and innocence.

In the next section, I show how participants' discourses indicate that educational institutions work to their advantage in the formation of their entitlement. In these central places of education and learning, participants attempt to distinguish themselves from "other" ways of life found "out there." What is already in place to make these discourses understandable? To which discourses do white pre-service teachers already have access in the construction of white privilege?

Securing White Entitlement
Rationality Rules

There are two techniques that participants use to secure white entitlement. The first is the identification with ideological space of rationality and objectivity. As a source of white bourgeois legitimacy, the university, like no other place, represents the establishment and practice of that most distinguishing trait of white male legitimacy: rationality.[15]

Participants use a variety of rhetorical strategies to claim this ideological space, including reporting the reactions of classmates, objectifying self- and others' reactions, making disclaimers, claiming credentials as a feminist sympathizer, offering evidence of supportive actions, and offering extensive qualification of negative remarks.[16] These strategies produce participants as utterly reasonable people, ones who understand the necessity of civility, rationality, and self-control. Participants have an interest in claiming these identities because logic and reasoning are not only highly prized in the teaching profession, they are also markers of civility and the right to govern. Their claims create a distinction between "us" and "them" around the ownership and distribution of emotions and intellect. In possession of intellectual control, participants offer their own rationality and moderation as the basis for dismissing other remarks with which they disagree; their demonstration of what is considered rational and reasonable maintains their identities as non-prejudiced supporters of tolerance.

Participants express negative remarks about the course in a variety of ways—not as biased opinions, but as statements of reasoned fact. For example, the course content is questionable because it implicates white participants in a racist history. This revised history undermines the participants' positions as neutral players; it calls into question issues of knowledge—who holds it? how is it constituted? what knowledge can be considered legitimate? Their conclusions lead them to believe that the "facts" of the course, which do not necessarily present a flattering image of racially dominant people, are merely a point of view or a particular slant; they are unfounded notions that need not be taken seriously. Participants also report that issues were forced on them, either by means of materials or by the professor's methods. Some hold that it was mildly coercive and others that it was outright manipulative: "I didn't like what the class was doing to me because it was changing how I felt and it wasn't changing it in a really positive manner." "This class was very much directed at trying to get you to believe, focus on cultural ideas and make you think those ideas."[17]

The expression "make you think those ideas" may be intellectually impossible, but does suggest that some kind of coercion is at work. Participants defend themselves against the implications of the course by describing it as something forced on them, further evidence of its emotional, irrational, and unreasonable premises. Both presentation and course material are suspect: "The Native focus was a little too Native."[18] The phrase "too Native" implies abandonment of all that is rational and civil while retaining the potential to *go Native*, a prospect that must be guarded against.

Even though the course is seen as unfairly emotional and irrational, the participants see their hostile reactions as completely justified and reasonable because they have been provoked. As Chris points out: "I really thought that [the course] was a travesty in many ways because I thought there was some really … uncalled for situations that we were placed into."[19] Justification of their emotional responses signals participants' assertion of dominance. Even though their emotional response is a deviation from reasonableness, the contradiction goes unacknowledged. Instead, their manipulation of "rationality" indicates their insider knowledge about conditions under which deviations may occur. By rejecting the course, participants declare authority or superiority over it; similarly, their performance of a credible, dominant identification includes the authority to pronounce that their own extreme actions are reasonable. Citing that other classmates were similarly affected is further evidence of credibility.

These discourses rely on the university as the home of official white rationality and knowledge—the markers by which a taxonomy of difference may be established and where "different from" means "unequal to." Here is the mythological, safe, and pure place of abstraction and objectivity; the world of knowledge and theory; a place for the "disembodied" mind. There is no awareness of the university as a site where power relations exist. The assumption is that knowledge and intellectual teachings are objective and neutral and need not be challenged. Chris expresses her dissatisfaction when issues in the classroom became political and were no longer objective:

I know there's problems that go beyond the university class. Like there's *problems with politics and things like that and I think that those are being brought into the classroom* rather than being sort of left at the door, and we were all people, looking for a better, some sort of a solution. *But those problems weren't left at the door, they were brought in.*[20]

The real-world politics of gender, culture, and classroom management are strongly resisted. When this intrusion happens—when an issue becomes too personal for comfort—participants use their indignation to re-establish their dominant identities and central positions. The space must be maintained; the identities—those who are in control and those who are not—cannot be confused. If participants' reactions are described as unreasonable, their authority and their ability to discern what is reasonable are undermined.

Taking Place

The second technique participants use to secure white entitlement is to identify themselves with the physical space and with the normative designation of who is likely to be found there. It is hardly surprising that participants desire identification with the university. The attendance of people who do not fit any of those categories does not belie the claim that the university is a white, elite, male-dominated place. Indeed, the point of interest is how these hegemonic European values are maintained in spite of the presence of others who are neither male nor European. Criticism of university elitism is typically managed by suggesting that such arguments are one sign of the university's legacy of liberalism and rationalism as evidenced in its capacity for tolerance and open debate. Pat describes one of the attractions of the university in comparison to his workplace:

If I took this class and I went back to [my trucking job], I wouldn't be able to go in and say, "You know, you can't really call the, you know, the Hispanic janitor, you know, a spic. You can't do that. That's bad." That part wouldn't go over very well in the coffee room full of, you know, huge stereotypical truck drivers. *At university you can discuss these things and talk about them....*[21]

Participants are very interested in associating themselves with the university; they look to it for the legitimating function it offers to those who do not necessarily come from the ranks of the social elite. In exchange, the speed with which participants are able to comply with the normative values and requirements determines how well they are prepared to "fit in" with university life and performance. For Pat, university is a place of privilege where learning takes place with intellectual types who are his equals: "You get spoiled at university, I find, because you're with a certain type of people all the time." The university is a rational place where differences on issues of race and gender can be discussed as intellectual topics. The social, economic, and intellectual gulf between the truckers' coffee room and the university is well marked; it is unreasonable to expect that the coffee room can accommodate what participants consider the same high standards of behaviour found in the pure space of the university. Pat, however, considers himself a liberal thinker and agrees that the ideas in the cross-cultural course should be taught to all university students, no matter what their course of study:

Actually I'm saying that every course should be happening across the disciplines but this course in particular because we're talking about it; because when you step *out in the street in Canada* you can't get away from issues of culture or gender. They're all around you so to not integrate them I think is an *injustice to the very ideas.*[22]

Pat has indicated that he is a moderate in all things, therefore he is willing to discuss "culture and gender," which he assumes are part of what he will meet "out in the street in Canada." He identifies this street venue as separate from where he now resides. This meeting on the street will not be voluntary, but forced; and in a place that lacks order and control such as the street, one will have to expect such irrationalities as "culture and gender." In the pure white space of the university, these issues can be discussed as intellectual topics so as not to do "injustice to the very ideas." In his position as a privileged insider, he can assume that these are disembodied "ideas" that do not touch him personally and are separate from the life he now lives.

This participant offers himself as innocent and naive; he is shocked to learn that his levels of self determination and rationality are not experienced by all people. Although he is perhaps even more naive in his ignorance than he would care to claim, he is proud of his arrival at liberal thought and the level of control and autonomy he describes. He finds himself in a dilemma; he says that his liberal, autonomous outlook—characterized by such qualities as "saying whatever I like"; "having common sense, being rational"; "being a strong, independent thinker"; "being in charge of one's own destiny"—is not unique but neither is it a widely held belief. Furthermore, he assumes these qualities are his personal possession, his property, and warrant him taking up his position of privilege. These are the possessions that mark his dominance and of which he is proud. His expression of surprise that these qualities are not widely circulated or in general use does not completely cover his pride that his possession of them affords him a unique and powerful status.

The dilemma he faces is in trying to appear both humble about his access to elite space and, at the same time, maintaining that his privileges are available to everyone. He resolves his dilemma by claiming innocence and naïveté as well as by referring to his associations with other people from other cultures to refute any notion that his own access is culturally enhanced. Aída Hurtado suggests that "most [whites] can detect when whiteness is being questioned and its potential privilege dismantled."[23] The response is to de-emphasize its function as a group while at the same time universalizing its privilege by saying, like Pat, that "anybody" can achieve merit,[24] pretending that the value attached to being white does not exist. The contradictions in participants' discourses are most interesting for the use participants make of them and the tension participants produce by holding these conflicts.

Pat struggles continually, through many rhetorical devices, to keep himself in a good light, which is defined by objectivity, rationality, the life of the mind, and an uninvolved stance separate from gender and culture. He is the "anti-imperialist" "seeing-man"[25] who claims to be supportive of the cross-cultural course because it fits his liberal philosophy. He has figured out the "correct way" to think about Otherness; he knows what an anti-racist stance should sound like. Maintaining this particular identity as a sympathetic white male enhances his credibility in and entitlement to this dis/embodied white space. The university site recuperates whiteness and accomplishes the very successful performance of this participant identity in a way that cannot easily be questioned.

Beings in Outer Spaces

Yet there are those in the university whose identities—such as the representative Aboriginal professor—who are perceived as being "out of place." Her embodied presence poses a dilemma for many of the participants; some of their greatest hostility is reserved for her. For, if she can be a legitimate authority in this site, and if participants' own legitimacy is dependent on their whiteness, the presence of the Aboriginal female professor undermines their entitlement. The Aboriginal professor triggers conflicting desires such as authority/subordination in the professor–student relationship. Some participants find it confusing and some reassuring that even though at a distance they reject the professor's authority, they find her agreeable one-on-one. Chris displays a distinct lack of control, however, in that she both desires the professor for her difference and is repelled by her attraction:

Before the class ... *I had respect for the Native culture* and I understood the issues.... But *after the class I felt resentful in some way.* It wasn't ... a growing experience. To me, it was a diminishing experience because I felt I became more narrow-minded. And since I've taken that class I've tried to put the class out of my mind because it wasn't a good experience. *And I think a lot of it had to do with the professor.*[26]

Chris rejects and anticipates the presence of the Aboriginal body as it is positioned to provide her with an experience of Western culture that is not otherwise available to her. For Bev, however, the smooth objectification of cultural knowledge is continually interrupted by personal relations:

The professor at the university was not liked by our class as a whole. *We didn't like her because we felt she didn't*

like us.... It wasn't enjoyable to go to class because of the instructor. We challenged what she had to say. *We didn't accept everything she said word for word. We spoke our minds* and I don't think she liked that much....[27]

Participants consider their rejection of the professor as reasonable because it is in response to the professor's unreasonableness. That participants don't accept "everything she said word for word" indicates that they are discerning and rational, not slavish believers of what anybody tells them.

Jan, who reacts to contested spaces, has portrayed herself as credible and sympathetic by means of her personal interest in cross-cultural issues as well as her voluntary enrolment in a number of Native Studies courses. She frequently refers to her "place" in her interview, speaking of "out there" and "coming back," wondering where she and others "fit in."

Jan is caught in a dilemma of her own making. She is a supporter of Aboriginal issues and of what she calls "differences." But now that Aboriginal people are claiming the sites of their children's education for themselves—by organizing more band-controlled schools and hiring more Aboriginal teachers—Jan suggests that differences don't really matter that much. At the same time that she doesn't want her whiteness to be held against her or to exclude her from a job, she continues to rely on her white privilege for access to jobs in an Aboriginal school—a space that has never belonged to her and that has only recently been denied to her. She is very confused about her "place" and finds that her question of where she fits in is her greatest concern:

Even after the information, I'm seeking it out, there's people out there that are saying well *you don't fit in.* I've had profs where I've asked that question in Native Studies or otherwise and got told well we don't want your help.... And as far as I'm concerned *I have to try to fit in,* and I mean maybe one day I'll be the minority. You know, I want to fit in. *I don't want to have no rights like you* [Natives] *had no rights.* Like, if one day I'm to come to Saskatchewan and you [Native] people make up the majority of the population, which could very well be, I'd like to know that *I'm going to fit in* somewhere. *I don't want to be treated the way you've been treated,* you know.[28]

The circle of benefits leads back to white control, even when the sense of place is not clear. The question "Where do I fit in?" must be answered so that white identity, as a condition of its privilege, will be secure. There is a strong sense of place in describing the "pure" and the "impure," but she questions how white dominant people are to "take their place" "out there" in areas where white privilege may be less secure than in the white space of the university. Even at times when sense of place may be uncertain, white participants assume that they will maintain their place as identity keepers and definers in their own lives and those of Aboriginal peoples.

An assumption that presupposes the contradictions and dilemmas of these participants is that cultures and identities are "settled," separate, and real. They rely on a realist approach when it supports their entitlement to attend the clean, well-lighted space of the university, or when they wish to secure the teaching job of their choice, or when they are granted privilege in hiring practices. In contrast, when participants explain their need for further entitlement to space to which they may not have ready access—such as teaching in Aboriginal-run schools—they eschew the notion of separate and divided identities. They assume that their privilege need not be a barrier to access because, with privilege, comes the ability to change at will the significance of their embodied status. Participants assume that they can transform their identities as required by performing themselves, in chameleon-like fashion, as "not really white." When coming up against the walls of contested space, white participants imagine they can pass through the walls by leaving their bodies behind.

These participants, as do many others, position themselves at the centre of a place-knowledge-privilege repertoire of self-definition. This repertoire occurs most often in the distinctions participants make between "here," where the participants are, and "out there." "Here" typically refers to a university environment, which is mainly white, middle-class, elite, straight, privileged, and often liberal in rhetoric if not in action. "Here" is a protected, enlightened, and enlightening place in the middle of raging storms of prejudice, unrealistic claims, and misinformation. By definition of quantity, "here" may be considered a minority position; but in these circumstances, adopting a minority position marks the exclusive rather than the excluded. This exclusive access supports participants in the performance of their roles as reliable witnesses in which they claim that various life circumstances have provided them with unique and unclouded perspectives. These unique positions are contrasted with participants' illustrations of how others have failed to be rational, moderate, knowledgeable, and fair.

When this self-referential place-knowledge-privilege cycle is interrupted by experiences such as found in the cross-cultural course, the participants struggle to re-establish their central positions. It is the disruption of the cycle that makes visible the norms that support it. Pat describes how the contested site of white privilege is neither exclusive nor secure: the "in here" place of the university is not completely pure, having among its members some aberrant character types:

The things that happened in the course, I think, are a reflection of character ... for good or for bad.... When you go into the washroom and you see somebody scrawling some racial or gender slur on the wall, I'm actually a little bit surprised about that because you think, geez, I mean, in university and they didn't even spell ... that

word right. What's going on? Oh, they didn't flush the toilet either, that doesn't surprise me. But when you get outside the walls of this institution, you're exposed to it everyday. I think I'm going to see it.[29]

That the university space has been invaded and contaminated by unreliable characters is an indication that white privilege and its power to exclude and define are continuously under siege. The contamination is an exception in this place where the walls typically act as borders between space that is rational and the space "out there" where disorder cannot be contained. Pat suggests that it is not rational to be racist and sexist, that evidence of discrimination and prejudice in the university would seem to be a problem of irrationality and an individual's bad character. Because whiteness signals innocence, it is inconceivable that this contagion could be from someone who "belongs" here.

The notion of secure spaces for the production and control of identities is a myth and an impossibility. Michel Foucault's illustration of the production of sexuality offers a good analogy of the production of racial identity.[30] He claims one is mistaken to assume that identities can be controlled or limited or that contagion is from without. In the case of sexuality, it is false to assume that everything learned about sexuality within the family is normative, proper, and "safe." On the contrary, as Ann Laura Stoler points out, the family is the site where sexuality acquires social meaning, where we begin to identify as sexual beings; as the family is the site where sexuality is learned, it is not a haven from "sexualities of a dangerous outside world, *but the site of their production.*"[31]

I suggest that the same is true regarding the production of whiteness in university spaces. Like the familial context, these white places produce identities in which codes and expectations of proper white behaviour are vigorously enforced by reiterative, normative practices and designations of what is worth knowing. It is inconceivable to Pat that white privilege and racism are what one *learns* at university. He must maintain that elite white space is safe from contamination and innocent of racism because, tautologically, university space is elite and white. It is in these ideologically coded spaces that the performance of whiteness is most thoroughly embodied and reinforced as normative, especially in the midst of a course on multicultural education. Sexuality, class, ability, and ethnicity are learned through whiteness as the embodiment of what the Other is not. Here is the site where the performativity of whiteness coheres—in the "unsettled and unsettling"[32] population of the discursively absent Other.

Self-Preservation

The division of identities into site-specific locations supports a "grid of intelligibility"[33] through which a white bourgeoisie comes to define itself. Participants' access to white-identified spaces does not necessarily follow from racist practices or confrontations or from particular events. Rather, access is gained through using "historical discourse as a strategic weapon of power."[34] For example, class-and-race-specific sites of education—such as universities that are instrumental in the production of white identities—are one tactic for maintaining distinct spaces in Canadian society.

The participants' responses are reactions to a cross-cultural studies course, as I have tried to make clear, do not represent individual racist actions per se. Yet as Stoler explains, there are ways in which current discursive practices are used to "work up" and "assemble" older forms of racism already in place. Following Foucault, Stoler provides this understanding of racism:

> [R]acism is more than an ad hoc response to crisis; it is a manifestation of *preserved possibilities*, the expression of an underlying discourse of permanent social war, nurtured by the biopolitical technologies of *"incessant purification."* Racism does not merely arise in moments of crisis, in sporadic cleansings. It is internal to the biopolitical state woven into the weft of the social body, threaded through its fabric.[35]

The assumption that society must at all times be protected from the biological dangers of its ever-present "sub-race" produces an "internal racism," requiring "incessant purification" as one of the fundamental dimensions of social normalization.[36] Participants desire "incessant purification" as a justification for their claim to innocence.

"Preserved possibilities," which remain available for reproduction of the social order, can be contrasted with the effects of university space on the construction of Aboriginal students' identities. Rick Hesch describes the process of social reproduction in a teacher-education program for Aboriginal students attending a Prairie university. Hesch states that in spite of the affirmative nature of the program, Aboriginal students' experiences are racialized, gendered, and classed in ways that contribute significantly to their overall problem of staying in the university and completing their programs. Describing students' decisions to leave as a "choice" is ironic considering the exclusionary nature of the institution. Hesch continues, however, that even the successful completion of the program—constrained as it is by a university environment—"both enables and limits the possibilities for the development of [A]boriginal teachers."[37] At the same time, the affirmation of white identities in this site continues apace in that any lack of success Aboriginal education students may have in the university system leaves those jobs and the ideological spaces they might have filled still available for prospective white teachers. Through these spatial arrangements and preserved possibilities, the entitlement and belonging of white students is affirmed.

The "preserved possibilities" of the white participants are their rights to reject or access anything they choose such as the knowledge of cross-cultural teachers, positions in Aboriginal-controlled schools, or proprietorial status at a university. These "preserved possibilities" were in place long before they participated in their cross-cultural course, which for some participants was a moment of crisis.

For most of the participants, their interactions with the course placed them in contradictory positions which they struggled to explain: they defend their dominant subjectivities against the implications of the cross-cultural course and the anger and uncertainty it arouses; they affirm their identities as non-prejudiced, liberal individuals. They support their liberal identities by claiming their responses are rational and unemotional, quite unlike the responses of anyone with whom they might disagree. Participants justify their own emotional responses by implying that it is only what reasonable people would do when provoked by the unreasonableness of others. Participants rely heavily on a particular understanding of rationality and emotional control to mark them as self-determining individuals. Regardless of their own conduct or that of others, it is their description of the events that performs participants as insiders and demonstrates their control of the definition of rationality which is, perhaps, the single, most highly prized claim of white bourgeois subjects.

In ideologically white spaces such as university campuses, identities are produced both inside and outside the specific site. The maintenance of domination is actively supported by white students, as the participants in my project demonstrate. Their grasp on bourgeois white identification relies on their allegiance to prestigious white space and their access to privilege and social respectability. They depend on university processes and make full use of a mandatory multicultural course to support white domination so that they may establish and produce their own legitimacy as "good" teaching bodies and "respectable" Canadian citizens.

Notes

1 See Margaret Wetherell and Jonathan Potter, *Mapping the Language of Racism: Discourse and the Legitimation of Exploitation.* New York: Columbia University Press, 1992.

2 See Sherene Razack, "Race, Space, and Prostitution: The Making of the Bourgeois Subject," *Canadian Journal of Women and the Law 10*, 2, (1998): 338.

3 The Subcommittee on Multicultural Teacher Education, Multicultural Teacher Education: A Proposal for a Multicultural Teacher Education Component for the Incorporation into the Program. Saskatoon, SK: University of Saskatchewan College of Education, 1988, 5.

4 Ibid., 9, 13.

5 Ibid., 9.
6 See M.L. Fellows and Sherene Razack, "The Race to Innocence: Confronting Hierarchical Relations among Women," *Iowa Law Review I*, 2 (1998): 335.
7 Kim, interview with author, 10 November 1995. All names of interviewees are pseudonyms.
8 Wetherell and Potter, *Mapping the Language of Racism*, 189.
9 Responses are drawn from interviews with participants in November 1995.
10 Lenore Keeshig-Tobias, "O Canada (bear v)," in C. Fife, ed., *The Colour of Resistance: A Contemporary Collection of Writing by Aboriginal Women*. Toronto: Sister Vision Press, 1993, 69–70.
11 C. Harris, "Whiteness as Property," *Harvard Law Review 106*, 8 (1993): 1707.
12 The Subcommittee on Multicultural Education, *Multicultural Teacher Education*, 10.
13 Ibid., 5.
14 David Sibley, *Geographies of Exclusion: Society and Difference in the West*. London: Routledge, 1995, 116.
15 See David Goldberg, *Racist Culture: Philosophy and the Politics of Meaning*. Oxford: Blackwell, 1993.
16 See Wetherell and Potter, *Mapping the Language of Racism*.
17 Drawn from interviews with participants in November 1995.
18 Ibid.
19 Chris, interview with author, 12 November 1995.
20 Ibid. Emphasis added.
21 Pat, interview with author, 15 November 1995. Emphasis added.

22 Ibid. Emphasis added.
23 Aída Hurtado, *The Color of Privilege: Three Blasphemies on Race and Feminism*. Ann Arbor: University of Michigan Press, 1996, 149.
24 See Harris, "Whiteness as Property."
25 See M.L. Pratt, *Imperial Eyes: Travel Writing and Transculturation*. London: Routledge, 1992.
26 Chris, interview with author, 4 November 1995. Emphasis added.
27 Bev, interview with author, 4 November 1995. Emphasis added.
28 Jan, interview with author, 12 November 1995. Emphasis added.
29 Pat, interview with author, 15 November 1995.
30 See Michel Foucault, *The History of Sexuality: An Introduction*, trans. R. Hurley, vol. I. New York: Vintage Books, 1990.
31 Ann Laura Stoler, *Race and the Education of Desire: Foucault's History of Sexuality and the Colonial Order of Things*. Durham, NC: Duke University Press, 11995, 110. Emphasis added.
32 See Toni Morrison, *Playing in the Dark: Whiteness and the Literary Imagination*. New York: Vintage, 1993.
33 Stoler, *Race and the Education of Desire*, 53.
34 Ibid., 54.
35 Ibid., 69. Emphasis added.
36 Ibid.
37 See Rick Hesch, "Cultural Production Cultural Reproduction in Aboriginal Service Teacher Education," in L. Erwin and D. MacLennan, eds., *Sociology of Education in Canada: Critical Perspectives in Theory, Research and Practice*. Toronto: Copp Clark Longman, 1994, 200.

Health and Health Care

CHAPTER 22

Gender, Race, and Health Inequalities

Ann Pederson and Dennis Raphael

Introduction

Whether one is a man or a woman affects one's health status, use of health services, experience of illness, and engagement in health-related activities such as caring for others or participating in sports. Health is grounded in the context of men's and women's lives: it arises from the roles we play, the expectations we encounter, and the opportunities available to us based upon whether we are women or men, girls or boys. However, while all societies are divided along the "fault lines" of sex and gender (Papanek 1984), there are other social processes and dimensions of social location that also contribute to health. Many people in Canada are disadvantaged as a result of differences in income, power, age, sexual orientation, geographic location, disability, and/or race or as a result of experiences of violence, trauma, migration, or colonization. Racialized discrimination of visible minority groups and Aboriginal peoples has contributed to serious inequalities in health. When the combined effects of gender and race are considered, Aboriginal women are among the most vulnerable members of Canadian society.

This chapter delves briefly into issues of gender, race, and health. In the first section, we consider women's and men's health comparatively but also independently, with particular emphasis on women's health given the continued need to argue for its inclusion as a separate area of study, research, and practice. We argue that gender is a marker of social and economic vulnerability that manifests itself in inequalities in access to health and health care (Standing 1997). For women, income inadequacy and caregiving responsibilities are major contributors to health. The second part of the chapter looks more closely at how race and ethnicity contribute to health in Canada. We consider how the analysis of race and health—with the exception of Aboriginal health—is in its infancy. Recent evidence suggests that while the health of recent immigrants to Canada is excellent, over time health status deteriorates, especially among immigrants of non-European descent. This may be due to the poor living conditions to which these immigrants are

subjected. Gender-based and race-related diversity analysis should be incorporated into health research and policy development to both understand and improve health.

Gender and Health
Key Concepts

It can be useful to distinguish between "sex" and "gender" in discussing men's and women's health. "Sex" refers to biological aspects of being male or female. While sex is perhaps most visible in terms of reproduction, there are underlying physiological processes and anatomical features that are typically different in males and females. "Gender," on the other hand, refers to the social attributes commonly ascribed to people who are male or female. All societies are organized in ways that reflect constructions of women and men as different kinds of people, with respective roles, responsibilities, and opportunities, including access to resources and benefits. As a social construct, the particular expressions and understandings of gender can vary over time and place and among communities. Behaviours, customs, roles, and practices are flexible and more variable across societies than the sex-related hormonal, anatomical, or physiological processes that typically characterize male and female bodies.

Gender is a relational concept and involves not only the ascribed attributes that are systematically assigned to each sex but also relations between women and men (Health Canada 2000), including gender power. For example, the legal codes that frame social relationships—such as marriage, divorce, and child custody—have important implications for relations between women and men (as well as for relations between partners of the same sex) by the ways that they shape access to or responsibility for employment, income, housing, child care, and social benefits. Such practices enshrine social norms and values and contribute to individual expectations and personal as well as social identities. These social processes, in turn, contribute to physical and mental well-being through access to resources, opportunities, and power. Thus, sex and gender interact to create health conditions, situations, and problems that are unique to one sex or which vary in terms of prevalence, severity, risk factors, or interventions for women or men (see Greaves et al. 1999). Sex and gender also interact with the other determinants of health discussed in this volume such as socio-economic status, paid and unpaid work, and disability (Janzen 1998).

Standing (1997: 2) describes gender as a marker of vulnerability in two senses in the global context:

First, women are found disproportionately among the most vulnerable population groups. They tend to be poorer than men on average, to have less access to income earning opportunities and other resources, including health care, and to be more dependent on others for their longer term security.... Second, access to and utilization of health services are importantly influenced by cultural and ideological factors, such as the embargoes on consulting male practitioners, lack of freedom to act without permission from husbands or senior kin and low valuation of the health needs of women and girls compared to that of men and boys.

In Canada, women's health and men's health similarly reflect important sex- and gender-related opportunities and vulnerabilities.

Health Status

According to Statistics Canada, average life expectancy at birth in 1999 was 79.0 years. Broken down by sex, however, women had an average life expectancy of 81.7 years while men had an average life expectancy of 76.3 (Health Canada 2002). This breakdown illustrates the value of even basic sex-disaggregation of data, as the overall figure masks the differences in life expectancy between women and men. However, [...] differences among women or men are also important to understanding the health of Canadians. Average life expectancy at birth in 1999 for First Nations people living on and off reserve was estimated to be 76.6 years for women and 68.9 years for men, sobering evidence of inequalities in Canada (Health Canada 2002).

The main causes of death among women and men in Canada are similar: coronary heart disease, cancer, and chronic lung disease; however, an analysis of potential years of life lost (PYLL) indicates that a larger number of PYLL are attributable to accidents for men as opposed to cancer for women (DesMeules, Manuel, and Cho 2003). Further, the size of the difference in PYLL between women and men in Canada varies across the lifespan, "with the largest discrepancy between men and women emerging in early and middle adulthood, where death from external causes (e.g., motor vehicle accidents) occurs at a much greater rate for men" (Janzen 1998: 21).

Women's apparent health advantage is reduced when morbidity and health care utilization are examined. For example, women report more frequent long-term disability and more chronic conditions than men (DesMeules, Turner, and Cho 2003). Ruiz and Verbrugge (1997), among others, suggest that the higher mortality rate and lower life expectancy of men compared to women have been misinterpreted to mean that women enjoy superior health, completely ignoring, they contend, the higher prevalence of chronic conditions in women, particularly in later life. Moreover, women's health status may be converging with that of men's: data suggest a narrowing of the gender gap in longevity in industrialized countries, most of it due to improvements in men's life expectancy (Trovato and Lalu 1996). Just as women's life expectancy increased dramatically in the middle of the 20th century as a result of reductions in maternal mortality, the current pattern of life expectancy observed between women and men may not hold in the future.

"Women are sicker, men die quicker" used to be an adage that supposedly summarized sex differences in health in Western industrialized countries such as Canada. Janzen (1998: ii) warns, however, that recent evidence of the complexity and variability of gender differences in health suggests that "broad generalizations about health-related gender differences are inappropriate." Let's consider at least six ways that sex and gender are important in shaping health and health care needs (Donner and Pederson 2004; Greaves et al. 1999).

First, there are sex-specific conditions, including the full spectrum of reproductive issues. These include birth control for women, pregnancy, childbirth, menstruation, menopause, and female infertility, as well as cervical cancer screening. For men, sex-specific conditions include prostate and testicular cancer and other diseases of the reproductive system, as well as male infertility and related problems. Second, there are conditions more prevalent among women or men, such as breast cancer, eating disorders, depression, and self-inflicted injuries in women and substance use, schizophrenia and HIV/AIDS in men. Third, there are conditions that appear to be sex-neutral, such as heart disease, but where the signs, symptoms, and appropriate treatment may be different in women and men (Grace 2003). Fourth, there are the ways in which women's gendered roles in our society influence their health, including: women's caregiving responsibilities; the sex-segregation of the labour force, both in general and within health care in particular; the demands of women's caregiving responsibilities; women's average lower incomes; and women's greater responsibilities for combining paid work with child care or caring for other family members.

Fifth, gender stereotypes within the health care system itself may negatively affect women's health. These include both stereotypes about women's use of care and stereotypes about women's caregiving roles. For example, women are often assumed to use health care services more than men, but there is good evidence that this is related to sex-specific care and not to male stoicism or to women's predisposition to seek help. For example, in Manitoba in 1994–1995, the per capita cost of providing females with health care services funded by the Medicare system was approximately 30 percent higher than for men. However, after the costs of sex-specific conditions were removed, and considering costs for both physicians' services and acute hospital care, the costs of insured health care services for women were about the same as for men (Mustard et al. 1998). It has also been suggested that negative stereotypes about women lead to women receiving negatively differential treatment in everything from the use of life-saving drugs during heart attacks (Grace 2003) and the secondary prevention of ischemic heart disease (Hippisley-Cox et al. 2001), to physicians being more likely to assume women's physical symptoms are psychological in origin (McKie 2000).

Finally, there is the overmedicalization of normal aspects of women's lives, including pregnancy, childbirth, and menopause. This practice of framing normal life events as medical problems has been challenged by the women's health movement for over 40 years, with some successes (for example, the reintroduction of midwifery into Canada and its organization as a licensed profession, and challenges to the view of menopause as an estrogen-deficiency disease). Recent marketing campaigns for products to manage erectile dysfunction and male-patterned hair loss suggest that men are not immune to this trend to overmedicalization either.

Some Issues Affecting Men's and Women's Health in Canada

While overall tobacco use has declined in Canada, the decline in smoking prevalence among men has been more pronounced than the decline in smoking prevalence among women, with men's prevalence having declined from 61 percent to 25 percent between 1965 and 2001, while women's smoking prevalence declined from 38 percent to 21 percent during the same time period (Kirkland, Greaves, and Devichand 2003). Moreover, smoking rates among teenaged girls are comparable to, or exceed, those of teenaged boys, and there is evidence documenting that girls start to smoke earlier than boys (Kirkland, Greaves, and Devichand 2003). Aboriginal and First Nations peoples have the highest rates of smoking in Canada (62 percent of First Nations peoples and 72 percent of Inuit were smokers in 1997 compared to 29 percent of the general Canadian population) (Reading 1999). Pearce, Schwartz, and Greaves (2005) suggest that there are important gendered patterns within these overall data that link women's tobacco use to poverty, child care responsibilities, few employment opportunities, and poor housing, among other factors.

Poverty is one of the most pressing issues for women in Canada (Box 22.1). Women are more likely than men to be poor in Canada, given current patterns of childbearing, child custody following divorce, and women's employment over the lifespan. Families headed by lone mothers are particularly vulnerable to poverty, both in terms of incidence (56 percent were poor in 1997) and depth (incomes for poor lone-mother families were, on average, $9,046 *less* than the low-income cut-off poverty line in 1997) (Ross, Scott, and Smith 2000).

The availability of child care is an important contributor to women's quality of life as it is essential for the support of their equality (Friendly 2004). It assists women in their role as primary child rearers and facilitates employment outside the home (Palacio-Quintin 2000). Similarly, home health and supportive care are important to Canadian women because women are the most

---

Box 22.1: Canadian Women, Poverty, and the Minimum Wage

Part of the reason the wage gap is as big as it is in Canada is because women make up two-thirds of the minimum-wage earners. In Canada, minimum-wage earnings do not provide people with a fair income. In fact, minimum-wage earnings fall well below the poverty line.

For example, Manitoba's minimum wage of $7.00/hour (as of April 1, 2004) falls well below both the low-income cut-off, a formula determined by Statistics Canada that often acts as Canada's unofficial poverty line, and the acceptable living level, a poverty line determined by anti-poverty organizations in Winnipeg.

	Low-Income Cut-off (urban)	*Minimum Wage Earnings	Acceptable Living Level (pre-tax) in Winnipeg
Family of one	$17,409	$14,560	$14,409
Family of two (one adult, one child)	$21,760	$14,560	n/a
Family of three (one adult, two children)	$27,063	$14,560	$30,697
Family of four (two adults, two children)	$32,238	$29,120	$38,550
Family of four (one adult, three children)	$32, 238	$14,560	$38,550

* Based on 40 hours/week, 52 weeks/year, no allowance for sick days, holidays, or periodic layoffs.

Source: The UN Platform for Action Committee, 2004. Available on-line at http://unpac.ca/economy/wompoverty4.html.

likely recipients of such care, the most likely to be employed as formal caregivers, and serve as the primary caregivers of family members (National Coordinating Group on Health Care Reform and Women nd). As such they are most likely to be affected when such care is not available or accessible (Morris, Robinson, and Simpson 1999). These two issues typify how governmental policy directions affect the quality of life of women (Fast and Keating 2000; Friendly, 2004; Raphael and Bryant 2004).

Experiences of violence differ for women and men, although they report similar rates of victimization (Statistics Canada 2001). As detailed by Eichler (1997), a man is more likely to experience violence on the street whereas a woman is more likely to experience violence from a family member in her own home. Men report higher rates of robbery and assault, but sexual assaults are more likely to be perpetrated against women (Statistics Canada 2001). The meaning of these gender differences for the physical and psychological safety of women and girls is profound because often "home" does not provide them with security. While violence does affect men in the home, it is a tiny proportion of the violence experienced by men (2.3 percent) whereas it is the single largest type of violence experienced by women (27.5 percent) (Health Canada 2003a). Responses to "family" or "domestic violence" must reflect these gendered patterns if they are to be of any value in reducing the incidence of violence against women.

Mental health and illness also offer interesting illustrations of sex and gender differences in Canada. Sex differences have been noted in the prevalence of specific mental health problems. For example, women are nearly twice as likely as men to be diagnosed with depression (Health Statistics Division 1998) and anxiety (Howell et al. 2001), particularly young women (Canadian Council on Social Development 1998). The highest prevalence of depression is found, however, among Aboriginal women, in part as a result of living in impoverished conditions (Health Canada 2003b). Men are more often diagnosed with schizophrenia, certain personality disorders, and substance abuse (Culbertson 1997). Women and men also have different patterns of access to and use of mental health services, with women accessing the system more frequently, receiving treatment more often, and having higher rates of hospitalization for psychiatric problems than men (Federal-Provincial and Territorial Advisory Committee on Population Health 1996; Rhodes and Goering 1994).

Mental illness is associated with experiences of violence and trauma, and being mentally ill puts women at risk for further abuse (Anderson and Chiocchio 1997). Poverty and homelessness are associated with serious mental illness for both men and women in Canada, but less is known about homelessness regarding women than men, in part because the patterns of being without shelter manifest differently for women. Women are more likely, for example, to "couch surf" or stay temporarily with friends and family when they are without shelter,

one effect of which is that fewer women appear in homeless shelters and in homelessness research, despite women's higher levels of poverty. Differences such as these have led analysts such as Morrow (2003) to call for a comprehensive policy response to women's mental health in Canada.

Occupational health research and practice remains largely gender-blind (Messing 1998). The labour force remains largely sex-segregated in some areas, despite the influx of women into many "traditionally" male occupations in the past 40 years. Interestingly, repetitive strain injury is reported equally by both men and women, but there is some evidence suggesting that the percentage of women affected by these problems is rising, particularly women in traditionally male-dominated occupations. Possible explanations include psychosocial aspects of the workplace as well as poorly designed workstations, deadlines, and self-reported stress. In addition, many women's occupational health issues remain hidden in the household because women's labour in this setting is not recognized as work and the health risks associated with unregulated activities in individual households are seldom the target of policy interventions.

Each of these issues illustrates the various ways that sex and gender influence patterns of health and illness among women and men in Canada. Increasing recognition of some of the gender-related differences in health call for action from policy makers, researchers, and clinicians.

*   *   *   *   *

Race, Ethnicity, and Health

Aside from a long-standing concern with the health status of Canada's Native peoples, analysis of the relationship of race and ethnicity with health is in its infancy in Canada. One reason is the relatively greater historical racial homogeneity of Canadian society as compared, for example, to the U.S. Another reason is that, until recently, health researchers have generally found few health status differences—outside of Aboriginal populations—among racial and ethnic groups in Canada. This is certainly not the case in the U.S. where extensive effort is focused—to the exclusion of social class and income issues—upon identifying racial and ethnic differences in health status.

Increasing attention in Canada is being paid to racial and ethnic issues in health as changing patterns of immigration result in increasing numbers of members of visible minority groups. These Canadian efforts—much of which are being carried out within an immigration studies focus—are directed at two issues: (a) the relationship of race and ethnicity to health status and (b) an analysis of the quality of various social determinants of health experienced by racial and ethnic groups in Canada. A particularly important form this focus is taking is that of examining the health status and economic and social conditions associated with various "racialized groups."

The focus here is upon race with emphasis on the situation of two important groups: Aboriginal peoples and immigrant groups in Canada called "visible minorities" or "racialized groups." "Racialization" is a term that considers how groups of individuals come to be treated in inferior ways compared with the dominant group (Allahar and Cote 1998).

Differences in health status between Aboriginal peoples in Canada and non-Aboriginal peoples are striking. However, differences in traditional indicators of health status between racialized immigrant groups and non-racialized groups were few until recently; frequently the health status of non-White groups is superior to that of Whites. Two recent studies find, however, that the health status of non-European immigrants in Canada appears to deteriorate over time. In addition, recent research finds profound differences in economic and social conditions among racialized—especially recently immigrating—groups. This is important as difficult economic and social conditions are frequently precursors to poor health status and these racialized immigrant groups are a significant proportion of the population in Canadian urban areas.

Race, Ethnicity, and Health

There is a well-developed sociological literature regarding the definition of race, ethnicity, and related issues (McMullin 2004). Clear consensus exists—at least among academics in the social sciences—that race and ethnicity are social constructions representing dominant groups' historical attempts to maintain control and power over those identified as members of "other" races or groups. Many health researchers and health workers do not share this view and for them race and ethnicity are indicators of biological disposition to disease or a convenient marker to identify targets for public health interventions (Cruickshank et al. 2001).

These interventions are frequently focused on modifying behavioural risk factors for disease (such as tobacco use, physical inactivity, or poor diet), or improving access to health care. Less common is a public health concern with addressing the social and economic conditions that members of different racial groups are exposed to and working to modify these risk conditions through public policy. The concern here is with two issues: (1) How has the race concept been applied to understanding health and its determinants? (2) What is known about health inequalities among members of different racial groups?

Race and Health Status: Concepts

Lee, Mountain, and Koenig (2001: 58) point out that "historically, race, genetics, and disease have been inextricably linked, producing a calculus of risk that implicates race with relative health status." Rather than view the greater incidence of a disease among a group as potentially reflecting social and economic conditions that result

from discrimination and prejudice, these associations can be attributed to genetic causes. Duster argues that when the association between race and illness is viewed through a "prism of heritability," environmental and class-related causes of illness among specific racial groups can be ignored or suppressed (Duster 2003). Similarly, Krieger (2003: 195) states: "Myriad epidemiological studies continue to treat 'race' as a purely biological (i.e., genetic) variable or seek to explain racial/ethnic disparities in health absent consideration of the effects of racism on health."

Racial differences in health status can be attributed to exposures to specific material conditions of life that result from both membership in specific social and occupational classes as well as the systematic experience of discrimination and prejudice. Members of racialized groups in Canada are overrepresented in lower-status occupations and experience greater incidence of poverty and low income (Galabuzi 2004, 2005). There is increasing evidence that such overrepresentation is due to discrimination, reflecting the presence of racism in Canadian society.

Jones outlines three forms of racism, all of which will have impacts on health (Jones 2000). *Institutionalized racism* is concerned with the structures of society and may be codified in institutions of practice, law, and governmental inaction in the face of need. *Personally mediated racism* is defined as prejudice and discrimination and can manifest itself as lack of respect, suspicion, devaluation, scapegoating, and dehumanization. *Internalized racism* is when those who are stigmatized accept these messages about their own abilities and intrinsic lack of worth. This can lead to resignation, helplessness, and lack of hope. These concepts are clearly applicable to Canadian society (Galabuzi 2004, 2006).

Race and Health Status: Aboriginal Peoples in Canada

Systematic reviews of health issues facing Canada's Aboriginal peoples are available (Health Canada First Nations and Inuit Health Branch 2003; Shah 2004). Aboriginal peoples overall show significantly greater incidence of a range of afflictions and premature death from a variety of causes. These issues result from the poor state of any number of social determinants of health (e.g., income, housing, food security, employment and working conditions, social exclusion, etc.) and reflect a history of social exclusion from Canadian society.

There is a large gap in mortality between the Aboriginal and the general Canadian population. In 1996–1997, mortality rates among First Nations and Inuit peoples from eastern and western Canada and the prairie provinces were almost 1.5 times higher than the national rate. During this same period, infant mortality rates among First Nations peoples were close to 3.5 times the national infant mortality rates. Neonatal death rates are double the general Canadian rates and post-neonatal mortality rates almost four times higher.

Further, off-reserve Aboriginal peoples rate their health status lower than the overall Canadian population (Tjepkema 2002). For every age group between 25 and 64, the proportion of Aboriginal peoples reporting fair or poor health is double that of the total population. The effect is more pronounced among Aboriginal women. For example, 41 percent of Aboriginal women aged 55–64 reported fair or poor health, compared with 19 percent of women in the same age group in the total Canadian population. Among those aged 65 and over, 45 percent of Aboriginal women reported fair or poor health, compared with 29 percent in the total female population. Poor economic and social conditions are responsible for these differences in health.

Race and Health Status: Non-Aboriginal Peoples in North America

United States

Health disparities among racial and ethnic minorities are the focus of numerous research initiatives, national and state public health agendas, and local public health activity. Indeed, the focus on racial and ethnic disparities is so great that issues of health differences related to income and wealth, social class, and gender are frequently downplayed or neglected. As a result, a great amount of evidence is available concerning racial and ethnic differences in health status among Americans (U.S. Department of Health and Human Services 2004a). The most recent information on these differences can be succinctly summarized as follows: "There are continuing disparities in the burden of illness and death experienced by African Americans, Hispanic Americans, Asian/Pacific Islanders, and American Indians/Alaska natives, as compared to the US population as a whole" (U.S. Department of Health and Human Services 2004b: 1).

In most cases, these racial/ethnic differences exist in life expectancy, infant mortality, and virtually every other indicator of health status. The predominant focus on the causes of these disparities is unduly focused on access to health care and behavioural risk factors with rather less attention paid to the economic and social conditions of these groups and the public policies that spawn these conditions. The precarious economic and social conditions under which these minority groups live are well documented, but these issues take a back seat to traditional health care and public health concerns with behaviour and lifestyle modifications (Raphael 2003).

Canada

Canada's concern with issues of race and health as it relates to immigrant groups has been spurred by changing immigration patterns over the past 20 years. While previously a large proportion of immigrants to Canada were of European descent, Galabuzi (2004: 239) points out: "There has been a significant change in the source countries with over 75% of new immigrants in the 1980s and 1990s coming from the Global South." Racialized (or visible minority) groups now constitute significant proportions of those living in many urban areas (e.g., Toronto, 36.8 percent; Vancouver, 36.9 percent; Calgary, 17.5 percent; Edmonton, 14.6 percent; Ottawa, 14.1 percent; Montreal, 13.6 percent; Winnipeg, 12.5 percent, etc.). Of particular concern is emerging evidence that the social and economic conditions under which members of racialized groups are living are distinct threats to health.

Unlike the situation in the U.S., there is little evidence—outside of studies of Native peoples—of health differences among racial groups (McMullin 2004). Much of this may be due to what has been termed the healthy immigrant effect whereby immigrants to Canada have superior health status compared to native-born Canadians (Hyman 2001). Since a significant proportion of visible-minority Canadians are recent arrivals in Canada and subject to health screening, it is not surprising that many studies find that non-White status is not associated with poorer health status. [...] [I]mmigrants—both more recently arrived and those from earlier periods—show evidence of superior health status compared to native-born Canadians (Chen, Wilkins, and Ng 1996).

However, the recent availability of both cross-sectional and longitudinal data from the National Population Health Survey (NPHS) provides compelling evidence that the health of immigrants to Canada, especially non-European immigrants, deteriorates over time as compared to Canadian-born residents and European immigrants. Newbold and Danforth (2003) found that immigrants to Canada were more likely than non-immigrants to rate their health as poor or fair and that this was especially the case for those who have been in Canada longer.

A more nuanced and recent analysis is provided by longitudinal analysis of NPHS data (Ng, Wilkins, Gendron, and Berthelot 2004). They categorized respondents into four groups: recent (10 years or less) European immigrants, recent non-European immigrants, long-term (more than 10 years) European immigrants, and long-term non-European immigrants. They then examined the likelihood that individuals reported a transition from good, very good, or excellent health to either fair or poor health.

They found that, as compared to the Canadian-born population, recent non-European immigrants were twice as likely to report a deterioration in health from 1993–1994 to 2002–2003. Long-term non-European immigrants were also more likely to report such deterioration. There was no effect for either of the two European immigrant groups. Of importance was the finding that these differences were reflected in recent non-European immigrants who were 50 percent more likely to become frequent visitors to doctors than the Canadian-born population.

The additional predictors of transition to lower health status included a number of factors best described as social determinants of health. These were low income adequacy, less education, and low support. As the authors commented, "Findings from the literature on immigrants' integration in Canada have shown that those with non-European origins to have low-paid jobs that require little education. Because immigrants with European origins share a similar culture with the Canadian born, they may encounter fewer social, economic, and lifestyle barriers than do those from non-European countries" (Ng, Wilkins, Gendron, and Berthelot 2004: 6). We now turn to these issues.

Racial and Ethnic Differences in Social Determinants of Health

Extensive scholarship is identifying profound issues related to the material conditions of life among Aboriginal and visible-minority immigrants, and non-White Canadians. These are clearly related to social determinants of health such as income, employment and working conditions, housing, education, and recreational opportunities. Indeed, these differences are so profound as to require application of the broad concept of social exclusion as both process and outcome of various societal factors driving these differences (Galabuzi 2004).

Shah provides much evidence concerning the economic and social status of Aboriginal peoples in Canada while Galabuzi (Galabuzi 2004, 2006) does so for racialized immigrant groups in Canada. Concerning the latter, these include: (a) a 30 percent income gap in 1998 between racialized and non-racialized groups; (b) higher than average unemployment, with unemployment rates two to three times higher than non-racialized groups; (c) deepening levels of poverty; (d) overrepresentation in lower-paying and lower-status jobs; (e) differential access to housing; (f) increasing racial and economic concentration in Canadian urban areas; and (g) disproportionate contact of racialized groups with the criminal justice system (Ornstein 2000; Pendakur 2000; Reitz 2001).

Statistics Canada has documented differences in income and employment status of recent and earlier immigrants to Canada (Picot 2004). There is a consistent finding that the rate of low income among immigrants (particularly recent immigrants) has been rising during the 1990s while falling for the Canadian-born. Picot attempted to identify the factors responsible for the deteriorating economic welfare of immigrants and found that the rise in low-income status affected immigrants in all education and age groups, including the university educated (Picot 2004). The study found that the economic returns to recent immigrants for their work experience and education were diminished as compared to that seen for earlier immigrants. Considering that 75 percent of these recent immigrants were members of racialized groups, the hypothesis that racism and discrimination are responsible for these diminishing returns must be considered.

As noted, to date health status differences among racialized and non-racialized groups were not consistent. There is evidence from more in-depth studies of members of racialized groups in Canada that these members are encountering significant threats to physical and mental health that are not easily detected by traditional health status measures or are mediated by the "healthy immigrant" effect (Beiser et al. 2002; Canadian Research Institute for the Advancement of Women 2002; Noh et al. 1999). However, international research indicates that exposure to adverse economic and social conditions are reliable precursors to disease. While in the past immigrants to Canada gradually reached income and employment levels comparable to the Canadian-born, this may not continue to be the case.

The pattern of increasing economic and racial concentration in Canadian urban areas suggests cause for concern (Hatfield 1997; Myles, Picot, and Pyper 2000; United Way of Greater Toronto 2004). Such concentration of visible-minority groups has been associated in the U.S. with poor health and increasing social disintegration (Ross, Nobrega, and Dunn 2001). This process may well be underway in many Canadian urban centres, but to date there is little research on the lived experience of members of racialized groups in Canada.

We also know nothing about the experience of discrimination and racism and their effects upon members of racialized groups in Canada. We would expect that such studies would replicate findings that refugees who reported the experience of racial discrimination had higher depression levels than those who did not (Noh et al. 1999). Research on the effects of discrimination in the U.S. and the U.K. suggest attention to this area is needed (Karlsen and Nazroo 2002; Krieger 2003).

* * * * *

References

Allahar, A., and J. Cote. (1998). *Richer and Poorer: The Structure of Inequality in Canada*. Toronto: Lorimer.

Anderson, C., and K. Chiocchio. (1997). "The Interface of Homelessness, Addictions and Mental Illness in the Lives of Trauma Survivors." In *Sexual Abuse in the Lives of Women Diagnosed with Serious Mental Illness*, edited by M. Harris and C. Landis, 21–38. Amsterdam: Oversees Publisher's Association.

Beiser, M., F. Hou, I. Hyman, M. Tousignant. (2002). "Poverty, Family Process, and the Mental Health of Immigrant Children in Canada." *American Journal of Public Health* 92(2): 220–227.

Canadian Council on Social Development. (1998). *The Progress of Canada's Children, Focus on Youth*. Ottawa: Canadian Council on Social Development.

Canadian Research Institute for the Advancement of Women. (2002). *Women's Experience of Racism: How Race and Gender Interact*. Ottawa: CRIAW.

Chen, J., Wilkins, R., Ng, E. (1996). "Health Expectancy by Immigrant Status, 1986 and 1991." *Health Reports* 8(3). Ottawa: Statistics Canada, Catalogue 82-003-XIE: 29-38.

Cruickshank, J., J.C. Mbanya, R. Wilks, B. Balkas, N. McFarlane-Anderson, T. Forrester. (2001). "Sick Genes, Sick Individuals or Sick Populations with Chronic Disease? The Emergence of Diabetes and High Blood Pressure in African-Origin Populations." *International Journal of Epidemiology* 30(1): 111–117.

Culbertson, F.M. (1997). "Depression and Gender: An International Review." *American Psychologist* 52(1): 25–31.

DesMeules, M., D. Manuel, and R. Cho. (2003). "Health Status of Canadian Women." *Women's Health Surveillance Report: A Multi-dimensional Look at the Health of Canadian Women*. Ottawa: Health Canada, Canadian Population Health Initiative.

DesMeules, M., L. Turner, and R. Cho. (2003). "Morbidity Experiences and Disability among Canadian Women." In *Women's Health Surveillance Report: A Multi-dimensional Look at the Health of Canadian Women, edited by M. DesMeules, D. Stewart, A. Kazanjian, H. McLean, J. Poyne, B. Vissandjée*, 19–20. Ottawa: Health Canada, Canadian Population Health Initiative.

Donner, L., and A. Pederson. (2004). "Beyond Vectors and Vessels: Women and Primary Health Care Reform in Canada," prepared for the National Workshop on Primary Care and Women, February 6–7, 2004, Winnipeg, Sponsored by the National Coordinating Group on Health Care Reform and Women and the Prairie Women's Health Centre of Excellence.

Duster, T. (2003). *Backdoor to Eugenics*. New York: Routledge.

Eichler, M. (1997). *Family Shifts: Families, Policies, and Gender Equality*. Toronto: Oxford University Press.

Fast, J., and N. Keating. (2000). *Family Caregiving and Consequences for Careers: Towards a Policy Research Agenda*. Ottawa: Canadian Policy Research Networks.

Federal-Provincial and Territorial Advisory Committee on Population Health. (1996). *Report on the Health of Canadians: Technical Appendix*. Toronto: Federal Provincial and Territorial Advisory Committee on Population Health.

Friendly, M. "Early Childhood Education and Care." In *Social Determinants of Health: Canadian Perspectives*, edited by D. Raphael, 109–124. Toronto: Canadian Scholars' Press.

Galabuzi, G.E. (2004). "Social Exclusion." In *Social Determinants of Health: Canadian Perspectives*, edited by D. Raphael, 235–252. Toronto: Canadian Scholars' Press.

_____. (2006). *Canada's Economic Apartheid: The Social Exclusion of Racialized Groups in the New Century*. Toronto: Canadian Scholars' Press.

Grace, S. (2003). "Presentation, Delay, and Contraindication to Thrombolytic Treatment in Females and Males with Myocardial Infarction." *Women's Health Issues* 13(6): 214–221.

Greaves, L., et al. (1999). *CIHR 2000: Sex, Gender and Women's Health*. Vancouver: British Columbia Centre of Excellence for Women's Health.

Hatfield, M. (1997). *Concentrations of Poverty and Distressed Neighbourhoods in Canada*. Ottawa: Applied Research Branch, Human Resources Development Canada (HRDC).

Health Canada. (2000). *Health Canada's Gender-Based Analysis Policy*. Ottawa: Minister of Public Works and Government Services Canada.

_____. (2002). *Healthy Canadians: A Federal Report on Comparable Health Indicators 2002*. Ottawa: Health Canada.

_____. (2003a). *Exploring Concepts of Gender and Health*. Ottawa: Women's Health Bureau, Health Canada.

_____. (2003b). *The Health of Aboriginal Women*. Ottawa: Health Canada.

Health Canada First Nations and Inuit Health Branch. (2003). *A Statistical Profile on the Health of First Nations in Canada*. Ottawa: Health Canada, First Nations and Inuit Health Branch.

Health Statistics Division. (1998). National Population Health Survey Overview, 1996/97. Ottawa: Statistics Canada.

Hippisley-Cox, J., M. Pringle, N. Crown, A. Beal, A. Wynn. (2001). "Sex Inequalities in Ischaemic Heart Disease in General Practice: Cross-sectional Survey." *British Medical Journal* 322: 832.

Howell, H.B., Brawman-Mintzer, J., Monier, K.A. Yonkers. (2001). "Generalized Anxiety Disorders in Women." *Psychiatric Clinics of North America* 24(1): 165–178.

Hyman, I. (2001). Immigration and Health. Working Paper Series. Ottawa: Applied Research and Analysis Directorate, Health Canada.

Janzen, B.L. (1998). *Women, Gender and Health: A Review of the Recent Literature*. Winnipeg: Prairie Women's Health Centre of Excellence.

Jones, C. (2000). "Levels of Racism: A Theoretic Framework and a Gardener's Tale." *American Journal of Public Health* 90(8): 1212–1215.

Karlsen, S., and J.Y. Nazroo. (2002). "Relation between Racial Discrimination, Social Class, and Health among Ethnic Minority Groups." *American Journal of Public Health* 92(4): 624–632.

Kirkland, S., L. Greaves, and P. Devichand. (2003). "Gender Differences in Smoking and Self-Reported Indicators of Health." In *Women's Health Surveillance Report: A Multi-dimensional Look at the Health of Canadian Women*, edited by M. DesMueles, D. Stewart, A. Kazanjian, H. McLean, J. Poyne, B. Vissandjée, 11–12. Ottawa: Health Canada, Canadian Population Health Initiative.

Krieger, N. (2003). "Does Racism Harm Health? Did Child Abuse Exist before 1962? On Explicit Questions, Critical Science, and Current Controversies: An Ecosocial Perspective." *American Journal of Public Health* 93(2): 194–199.

Krieger, N.A. (2000). "Refiguring 'Race': Epidemiology, Racialized Biology, and Biological Expressions of Race Relations." *International Journal of Health Services* 30: 211–216.

Lee, S.S., J. Mountain, and B.A. Koenig. (2001). "The Meanings of Race in the New Genomics: Implications for Health Disparities Research." *Yale Journal of Health Policy, Law and Ethics* 1: 33–75.

McKie, R. (2000). "Moaning Men Push Women to Back of Health Queue." *U.K. Observer* (May 7).

McMullin, J. (2004). *Understanding Social Inequality: Intersections of Class, Age, Gender, Ethnicity and Race in Canada.* Toronto: Oxford University Press.

Messing, K. (1998). *One-Eyed Science: Occupational Health and Women Workers.* Philadelphia: Temple University Press.

Morris, M., J. Robinson, J. Simpson. (1999). *The Changing Nature of Home Care and Its Impact on Women's Vulnerability to Poverty.* Ottawa: Status of Women Canada.

Morrow, M. (2003). *Mainstreaming Women's Mental Health: Building a Canadian Strategy.* Vancouver: British Columbia Centre of Excellence for Women's Health.

Mustard, C., et al. (1998). "Sex Differences in the Use of Health Services." *New England Journal of Medicine* 338: 1678.

Myles, J., G. Picot, and W. Pyper. (2000). *Neighbourhood Inequality in Canadian Cities.* Ottawa: Statistics Canada, Business and Labour Market Analysis Division.

National Coordinating Group on Health Care Reform and Women. (nd). *Women and Home Care: Why Does Home Care Matter to Women?* Winnipeg: National Coordinating Group on Health Care Reform and Women.

Newbold, K.B., and J. Danforth. (2003). "Health Status and Canada's Immigrant Population." *Social Science and Medicine* 57: 1981–1995.

Ng, E.R., Wilkins, F. Gendron, and J.-M. Berthelot. (2004). *Dynamics of Immigrants' Health in Canada: Evidence from the National Population Health Survey.* Ottawa: Statistics Canada.

Noh, S., M. Beiser, V. Kaspar, F. Hou, A. Rummens. (1999). "Perceived Racial Discrimination, Depression, and Coping: A Study of Southeast Asian Refugees in Canada." *Journal of Health and Social Behavior* 40: 193–207.

Ornstein, M. (2000). *Ethno-Racial Inequality in the City of Toronto: An Analysis of the 1996 Census.* Toronto: Access and Equity Unit, Strategic and Corporate Policy Division, Chief Administrator's Office.

Palacio-Quintin, E. (2000). "The Impact of Day Care on Child Development." *Isuma* 1(2): 17–22.

Papanek, H. (1984). *Women in Development and Women's Studies: Agenda for the Future.* East Lansing: Office of Women in International Development, Michigan State University.

Pearce, D., D. Schwartz, and L. Greaves. (2005). *No Gift: Tobacco Policy and Aboriginal People in Canada.* Vancouver: British Columbia Centre of Excellence for Women's Health.

Pendakur, R. (2000). *Immigrants and the Labour Force: Policy, Regulation and Impact.* Montreal: McGill-Queen's University Press.

Picot, G. (2004). *The Deteriorating Economic Welfare of Immigrants and Possible Causes.* Ottawa: Statistics Canada.

Raphael, D., T. Bryant. (2004). "The Welfare State as a Determinant of Women's Health: Support for Women's Quality of Life in Canada and Four Comparison Nations." *Health Policy* 68: 63–79.

Raphael, D. (2003). "A Society in Decline: The Social, Economic, and Political Determinants of Health Inequalities in the U.S.A." In *Health and Social Justice: A Reader on Politics, Ideology, and Inequity in the Distribution of Disease,* edited by R. Hofrichter, 59–88. San Francisco: Jossey Bass.

Reading, J. (1999). *The Tobacco Report: First Nations and Inuit Regional Health Surveys.* Winnipeg: Northern Health Research Unit, University of Manitoba.

Reitz, J.G. (2001). "Immigrant Skill Utilization in the Canadian Labour Market: Implications of Human Capital Research." *Journal of International Migration and Integration* 2: 347–378.

Rhodes, A., and P. Goering. (1994). "Gender Differences in the Use of Outpatient Mental Health Services." *Journal of Mental Health Administration* 21(4): 338–347.

Ross, D., K. Scott, and P. Smith. (2000). *The Canadian Fact Book on Poverty,* 2000. Ottawa: Canadian Council on Social Development.

Ross, N., K. Nobrega, and J.R. Dunn. (2001). "Income Segregation, Income Inequality and Mortality in North American Metropolitan Areas." *GeoJournal* 53(2): 117–124.

Ruiz, M.T., and L.M. Verbrugge. (1997). "A Two-Way View of Gender Bias in Medicine." *Journal of Epidemiology and Community Health* 51: 106–109.

Shah, C. (2004). "Aboriginal Health." *Social Determinants of Health: Canadian Perspectives,* edited by D. Raphael, 267–280. Toronto: Canadian Scholars' Press.

Standing, H. (1997). "Gender and Equity in Health Sector Reform Programmes: A Review." *Health Policy and Planning* 12(1): 1–18.

Statistics Canada. (2001). *Women in Canada. Canadian Centre for Justice Statistics Profile Series.* Ottawa: Statistics Canada.

Tjepkema, M. (2002). "The Health of the Off-reserve Aboriginal Population." *Health Reports Supplement* 13: 1–17.

Trovato, F., and N.M. Lalu. (1996). "Narrowing Sex Differentials in Life Expectancy in the Industrialized World: Early 1970s to Early 1990s." *Social Biology* 43(1–2): 20–37.

U.S. Department of Health and Human Services. (2004a). *Health, United States 2004.* Washington: U.S. Department of Health and Human Services.

U.S. Department of Health and Human Services. (2004b). *HHS Fact Sheet.* Washington, DC: U.S. Department of Health and Human Services.

United Way of Greater Toronto. (2004). *Poverty by Postal Code: The Geography of Neighbourhood Poverty, 1981–2001.* Toronto: United Way of Greater Toronto.

* * * * *

Rethinking Section 3:

MAJOR SOCIAL INSTITUTIONS

Critical Thinking Questions

Section 3A: Families

Stephanie Coontz

1. Coontz suggests that referring to "traditional" family forms and values to solve the problems experienced by families today is problematic. How is "traditional" family defined? Is it problematic to define family in this way? Is there an alternative method to alleviate families of some of the stresses they incur?
2. Discuss some of the key shifts in the dynamics of "family" over time (from colonial families to the post-1950s family).
3. How is the concept of "family" related to the state, the market, and the mass media?

Meg Luxton

1. What are the problems with relying on families to pick up the slack for cuts in social spending?
2. What assumptions does neo-liberal restructuring make about the availability and ability of families to assume caregiving work? What are the gender dimensions of these assumptions?
3. What are the consequences for family relations of increased unpaid work and caregiving burdens?

Karin Quimby

1. Quimby asserts that "television texts are always the site of a struggle for meaning." How is this apparent in *Will & Grace* (and in other television shows)? Use the notion of "closure" and "openness" to guide your answer.
2. Discuss the relationship between consensus and contradiction.
3. Based on what you have read in the article, what reasoning do you feel the show maintains for not directly addressing the issue of gay marriage?

Section 3B: The Economy and Labour

Ester Reiter

1. What role, if any, does globalization play in the creation of the "brave new 'McWorld'"?
2. Children are noted as the newest consumers. Why is it effective to market to children? What examples (other than McDonald's) illustrate the effectiveness of this marketing scheme?
3. How does the fast-food industry contribute to gendered labour organization?
4. What are some possible reasons why corporations such as McDonald's would be opposed to unionization?

Naomi Klein

1. Klein notes that in earlier years it was commonplace for corporations to display their logos on factory walls, whereas now the location of production is oftentimes viewed as a valuable secret to be kept hidden. Explain the underlying reasons behind this shift in the attitude toward production.
2. What role do governments play in this new era of production (both in the country where the product is being assembled and sold)? Is this role in need of changing? Can it be changed?
3. Discuss the paradox when Klein notes that she "finally found a piece of unswooshed space, and [...] found it, oddly enough, in a Nike shoe factory."
4. Why is there a fear of unionization in Cavite? What are the implications of union formation in factories such as those in export processing zones?

Section 3C: Education

George Ritzer

1. How is the process of McDonaldization realized in universities?

2. Can you identify aspects of McDonaldization in your own university?
3. How are universities sites of consumption?

Carol Schick

1. What is White privilege?
2. Discuss the connection between university space and White privilege.
3. Why might there be resistance to a compulsory course on multiculturalism? How would you react to such a course? Why?
4. How do experiences of Aboriginal faculty relate to relations of White privilege?

Section 3D: Health and Health Care

Ann Pederson and Dennis Raphael

1. Given the apparent sex-specific health conditions outlined in the article, what consequences could arise from ignoring sex and gender when discussing health and medicine?
2. How is socio-economic status linked to gender and race? How does this affect health? Provide specific examples.
3. Discuss the debate between the varying definitions of "race" and "ethnicity." Is it problematic to have conflicting definitions between the social sciences and the field of medicine? If so, how?

Glossary Terms

Section 3A: Families

Stephanie Coontz

male breadwinner-female homemaker family: A socially determined male role within a family where the husband (or other male head of household) will provide financially for all members of the family and the female will undertake all work pertaining to social reproduction This system encourages male financial independence, while females are forced to be dependent.

"traditional" families: A nostalgic view of the family characterized by a male breadwinner-female homemaker model, typically presented as the "appropriate" or "natural" form.

Meg Luxton

caregiving: The activities involved in looking after the needs of another person, which are often more intense in the case of a child or dependent adult. Caregiving can be organized through familial networks, community networks, paid care, or government-funded agencies and systems.

neo-liberalism: A political and economic approach that seeks, among other things, to reduce the role of the state in policy-making initiatives while emphasizing private economic growth.

social reproduction: The activities involved in the daily and generational reproduction of family members and individuals.

Karin Quimby

consensus: Is used to stifle contradictions in television, usually in a show's conclusions.

contradiction: Ensures that a show will be popular to a wider array of audiences. Will and Grace exist in contradiction as both the "ideal" heterosexual couple, but also as the gay man/straight woman pair.

disavowal: Is central to the success of *Will & Grace*; acknowledging that something is "known" while still believing in an alternate way of knowing about this particular topic. For example, audience members "know" that Will is a gay man, but many choose to believe him to be truly heterosexual.

institutional heterosexuality: The dominant cultural order where to be in a heterosexual relationship means ascribing to institutional norms such as marriage, birthing children, and owning a home.

Section 3B: The Economy and Labour

Ester Reiter

managed heart: A term coined by Arlie Hochshild identifies the method fast-food companies utilize to inspire human emotion as serving two purposes: customer satisfaction and a diligent work ethic from employees.

McWorld: A play on words using the corporation "McDonald's" to denote that we exist in a society where the freedom to consume takes precedence over core principles of citizenship such as justice, fairness, and equity.

Naomi Klein

free-trade zones: Synonymous with export-processing zones; these areas, designed to attract foreign investors, are key sites for the production of many consumer goods (toys, garments, etc.) where goods are imported, assembled, and exported, all free of tax.

Section 3C: Education

George Ritzer

cathedrals of consumption: Rationalized, disenchanted, and "spectacular" sites.

implosion: Elimination of boundaries between phenomena.

Carol Schick

rationality: A technique used by participants to secure White entitlement. Identification with ideological space of rationality and objectivity.

taking place: A technique used by participants to secure White entitlement is to identify themselves with the physical space and with the normative designation of who is likely to be found there.

White bourgeoisie: White ruling class; holds dominant position in power relations.

White spaces: Spaces like universities, which are predominantly White in attendance, faculty, and the powers of the space.

Section 3D: Health and Health Care

Ann Pederson and Dennis Raphael

gender: Socially constructed attributes assigned to men and women; "masculine" and "feminine" behaviours, customs, roles, and practices as ascribed by society.

intersectionality: The understanding of the multiple social processes (gender, race, age, religion, sexuality, etc.) underlying social experiences (access to health care, poverty, criminality, etc.).

racialization: Specific groups of individuals are racialized when treated with inferiority compared to members of the dominant group in society.

sex: Biological, anatomical, hormonal, and physiological aspects of being male or female; most visibly noted in the reproductive process.

Relevant Web sites

http://www.gov.on.ca/MBS/english/government/family.html

Government of Ontario site offers sources and information to parents on marriage, divorce, parenting, adoption, disabilities, and so forth.

http://www.afa.net

A non-profit organization's site promoting a particular set of family values. The site critiques the influence of media on family values.

http://www.cprn.org/en/network.cfm?network=/

A comprehensive site discussing the varying ways that social policy affects Canadian families. The site contains links to news articles and other publications.

http://novaonline.nv.cc.va.us/eli/spd110td/interper/relations/linksfamilystructure.html

This site examines a range of family structures. The site also provides links to information on parenting, blended families, lone-parent families, and gay and lesbian families.

http://www.cfc-efc.ca

This site is the Child and Family Canada Web site. It is a public education site that examines issues pertinent to Canadian families via articles, chat rooms, and other helpful links.

http://www.canadianeconomy.gc.ca/english/economy

A Government of Canada site offering a guide to the national economy. The site provides access to statistics and information about the federal government.

http://www.cprn.org/en/network.cfm?network=4

The mandate of this site is to create knowledge and lead public debate on social and economic issues that are important to the well-being of Canadians. The site explores the labour market and changes in the workplace.

http://www.politicswatch.com/index2.html

A site offering information on Canadian politics. This site includes a daily news review, voter resources, archival data, and legislative agenda updates.

http://www.on.hrdc-drhc.gc.ca/enghlish/lmi/welcome_e.shtml

This site provides information about the economy and occupational and social trends within Ontario.

http://142.206.72.67/r006_e.htm

A site run by Statistics Canada providing an online e-book of Canada. The site contains information on the Canadian economy, political landscape, and the labour market.

Further Reading

Acker, Sandra, and Michelle Webber. (2006). "Women in Academia: Approach with Care." In C. Skelton, B. Francis, and L. Smulyan (eds.), *The SAGE Handbook of Gender and Education*, pp. 483–496. London: Sage.
An overview of the literature on women faculty in higher education.

Barndt, Deborah (ed.). (1999). *Women, Food, and Globalization: Women Working the NAFTA Food Chain*. Toronto: Second Story Press.
Examines the interconnections between food production in the South, consumption in the North, and women's labour in both settings.

Coontz, Stephanie. (1992). *The Way We Never Were: American Families and the Nostalgia Trap*. New York: Basic Books.
A critical examination of the myths of family forms and a historical corrective to these mis-truths.

Ehrenreich, Barbara. (2001) *Nickled and Dimed: On (Not) Getting by in America*. New York: Metropolitan.
A first-hand account of working and living on minimum-wage in America.

Eichler, Margaret. (1988). *Families in Canada Today: Recent Changes and Their Policy Consequences*, 2nd ed. Toronto: Gage.
A pivotal examination of changes in Canadian families and the responses of social policies to these changes.

Fox, Bonnie. (1980). *Hidden in the Household: Women's Domestic Labour under Capitalism*. Toronto, Canadian Women's Educational Press.
Pathbreaking Canadian study theorizing women's unpaid labour in relation to capitalism.

Gupta, T.D. (1996). *Racism and Paid Work*. Toronto: Garamond Press.
Critical examination of the dynamics of racism and discrimination in paid work in Canada.

Jackson, Andrew. (2005). *Work and Labour in Canada: Critical Issues*. Toronto: Canadian Scholars' Press Inc.
Original book that examines critical issues surrounding work and labour in Canada. Integrates labour, industry, and the global economy from a Canadian perspective.

Luxton, Meg. (1980). *More Than a Labour of Love: Three Generations of Women's Work in the Home*. Toronto: Women's Press.
Major Canadian study of the importance of domestic labour to the functioning of capitalist economies.

Luxton, Meg, and June Corman. (2001). *Getting By in Hard Times: Gendered Labour at Home and on the Job*. Toronto: University of Toronto Press.
Longitudinal study of the effects on paid and unpaid work of massive industrial restructuring in Hamilton, Ontario.

O'Neill, Michel, Ann Pederson, Sophie Dupere, and Irving Rootman (eds.). (2007). *Health Promotion in Canada: Critical Perspectives*, 2nd ed. Toronto: Canadian Scholars' Press Inc.
Profile of the history and evolution of health promotion in Canada. Offers case studies from each region of Canada and examines what the future holds for health promotion worldwide.

Raphael, Dennis (ed.). (2004). *Social Determinants of Health: Canadian Perspectives*. Toronto: Canadian Scholars' Press Inc.
Summarizes how socio-economic factors affect the health of Canadians, surveys the current state of social determinants of health across Canada, and provides an analysis of how these determinants affect Canadians' health.

Raphael, Dennis, Toba Bryant, and Marcia Rioux (eds.). (2006). *Staying Alive: Critical Perspectives on Health, Illness, and Health Care*. Toronto: Canadian Scholars' Press Inc.
Provides new insights into health, illness, and disability. Offers a range of approaches for understanding health issues. Fosters critical thinking skills by applying these perspectives toward understanding contemporary health issues in Canada and the United States.

Rinehart, James. (1996). *The Tyranny of Work: Alienation and the Labour Process*, 3rd ed. Toronto: Harcourt Brace.
A pivotal account of the sociology of work with Canadian content.

Ritzer, George. (1996). "The McDonalidization Thesis: Is Expansion Inevitable?" In *International Sociology*, 11(3), pp. 291–307.
Important study in the bureaucratization and standardization of work in the late 20th century.

Webber, Michelle. (2005). "Don't Be So Feminist: Exploring Student Resistance to Feminist Approaches in a Canadian University." *Women's Studies International Forum*, 28, pp. 181–194.
An empirical investigation of the delegitimation of feminist knowledges.

Webber, Michelle. (2006). "Transgressive Pedagogies? Exploring the Difficult Realities of Enacting Feminist Pedagogies in Undergraduate Classrooms in a Canadian University." *Studies in Higher Education, 31*(4), pp. 453–467.
Discusses feminist pedagogy and student subjectivities.

Issues of Inequality

Despite important gains in some areas, Canada remains an unequal society. In this section, individual and intersecting axes of inequality are explored. None of the forms of inequality discussed here stands alone. Rather, we find that women are more likely to be poor than are men, people of colour are more likely to be over-represented in low-wage employment and among the elderly, poverty is overwhelmingly female. The readings in this section represent a snapshot of important debates and evidence in sociological examinations of stratification. We begin with social class.

Porter's classic piece on social class and power in Canada underlines a belief that recurs in Canada today: Canada is a class-less or, at best, a middle-class society. Porter's article challenges this myth and suggests that social class and power are intimately connected in Canada. Duffy and Mandell's examination of poverty in Canada offers a picture of social inequality that many Canadians would like to believe does not exist. They reveal that in the late 1990s, over 17 percent of Canadians were poor. This poverty is patterned by factors such as geographic location, age, level of education, gender, family structure, race, and ethnicity. Income inequality and disparities widen social divisions among classes and have long-term consequences for the well-being of societies. Bales, in contrast, draws attention to the persistence of slavery, despite the presence of capitalism and the wage relation. Recall that class systems are considered open, and upward or downward mobility is a possibility, while caste systems are generally closed. The presence of slavery alongside a capitalist class system poses important questions for social and economic theory as well as for political action. Bales notes that in many ways slavery today is more perilous than some historical forms of slavery. Slaves are cheaper than they have ever been. The slavery at work in much of the world today is often short-term and is usually hidden, and slavery itself is globalized. Inequalities of class, then, must also be understood in terms of involuntary, unfree labour in global capitalism.

Another central dimension of social inequality is gender. Sen, Connell, Butler, and Kelly, Pomerantz, and Currie offer different approaches to gender inequality. Nobel laureate Amartya Sen makes a powerful case for the long-term effects for individuals, societies, and economies of gender inequality. Sen notes that high female-mortality rates are among the most egregious outcomes of systemic gender inequality, but is careful to couch this inequality in an analysis of social inequalities in general. Sen sees women's empowerment and agency as important remedies. Connell's groundbreaking work on men and masculinities offers a theoretical perspective on the cult of masculinity, which binds men into rigid roles that ultimately deny them, and women, the possibilities of existing as full humans. His now famous term "hegemonic masculinity" is important in critical theories and approaches to gender relations. Like Sen, however, he forwards the idea that these gender relations can be challenged and changed. Butler takes up the issue of gender identification. Via an exploration of appropriations and performances of femininity and masculinity, she explodes the idea of an original or essential gender. Finally, Kelly, Pomerantz, and Currie consider "girlhood" as experienced by skater girls in British Columbia. They explore the extent to which skateboard culture provides alternatives to mainstream discourses of femininity. They build on the corollary of Connell's notion of hegemonic masculinity—emphasized femininity—to extrapolate on girls' resistance to sexism in skater culture.

Grace-Edward Galabuzi and Stuart Hall offer important analyses of the persistence and character of racism, while Rhoda Howard-Hassman explores the idea of a "Canadian" ethnic identity in Canada. Galabuzi offers a compelling and stark picture of the extent and depth of inequalities of race in Canada. He shows the social, economic, and political effects of the legacy of a White settler society and the persistence of these inequalities in the 21st century. Hall considers the representation of race in media, arguing that cultural belonging, race, and difference play central roles in how images of people of colour are presented and interpreted. He highlights the practice of stereotyping as central to the representation of racial difference, and power as central to stereotyping. These two readings offer a glimpse into the dynamics of racism and exclusion at play in society. Howard-Hassman takes a controversial position in her chapter on Canadian identity. She asserts that there *is* a Canadian ethnic identity, which is encouraged by a multicultural policy that prizes liberal individual identity formation. She ties liberal multiculturalism and Canadian identity to the project of national unity.

Age and sexuality are the two final axes of social stratification in this section. Grant tackles the issue of age and aging in Canadian society, while Adams, Beaver, and Namaste consider the struggles of gays, lesbians, and transsexuals. Grant examines the demographic landscape of Canada and considers the extent to which age and health are twinned in practice and in policy terms. She details changes in the Canadian health care system over the last three decades and speculates about the challenges that an aging population will place on that system. She is careful to consider the role played by other axes of inequality: elderly women are more likely to have less income and to suffer from chronic rather than fatal illnesses. The excerpt from Adams considers the construction of heterosexuality in post-World War Two North America. She traces the emergence of a rigid notion of heterosexuality as counterposed with homosexuality and argues that there is nothing "natural" or universal about heterosexuality. Sexuality, like gender and race, is socially constructed and imbued with power. Certain forms of power are "normalized," according to Adams, so that it is hard to imagine alternatives. Normalization operates at the level of the individual in limiting choices and at the level of society in creating and reinforcing social norms. Adams considers the experience of the normalization of heterosexuality for postwar youth as a social process. Beaver offers the experience of First Nations peoples in Canada, demonstrating that the normalization of heterosexual relations came with colonization and that two-spirited peoples were respected in pre-European colonization societies. Hers is a reflection on injury and pain and a call to change the future. Finally, Namaste challenges the spectacle of "looking at" transsexuals in mainstream media and considers the various ways in which transsexuals are excluded from self-representation in both mainstream and alternative media.

CHAPTER 23

The Growth of Poverty and Social Inequality: Losing Faith in Social Justice

ANN DUFFY AND NANCY MANDELL

Introduction

By the middle of the twentieth century, there was growing optimism in industrialized countries that poverty and social inequality could be simply eradicated. In the postwar boom years, many increasingly affluent families were indulging in the burgeoning consumer market, the children of working-class and immigrant parents were heading off to university, and the social possibilities seemed endless. The media speculated on how we would learn to cope with the leisure and prosperity that promised to be our destiny. The second half of the twentieth century saw much of this promise falter. Despite the "wars on poverty" launched in the 1960s by both Canada and the United States, as the new century dawns the prospect of prosperity for all seems increasingly a fool's dream (Davies, 1997). Canadian society remains marred by growing homelessness, increasing numbers of poor children, and entrenched social inequities. Rather than historical anachronisms, poverty and inequality have become centrepieces of social research and social activism and seem destined to be foundational to the history of the twenty-first century.

* * * * *

Poverty in Canada Today

This is a rich, rich, rich country. The trouble is, it's too rich at the top and too poor at the bottom. (Senator David Croll in Goar, 1990)

Any discussion of poverty inevitably must confront the contentious issues of definition and measurement. It is easy to see that homeless, starving children in nineteenth-century Montreal (or modern Somalia) were poor; it is more difficult to identify those contemporary Canadians who have too little to get by and who are unable to participate in any meaningful fashion in the social, political, educational, or spiritual life of the nation.[1] While these individuals are not (necessarily) starving or homeless, they are "relatively deprived" in the nation and community in which they live. For years, government

agencies, social researchers, and advocacy groups have struggled to arrive at meaningful standards of impoverishment—level of family income, costs of housing, food, clothing, fuel, etc.—that distinguish the poor. To date Canada has not arrived at an "official" definition of poverty and relies, uneasily, on Statistics Canada's low-income cut-offs (LICOs) to identify the poor. This resolution has been far from satisfactory and in recent years the definitional debate has greatly intensified, with, for example, some advocates weighing in with a much more restrictive conception of poverty (Sarlo, 1992; National Council of Welfare, 1999a; Toronto Star, 1999; Burman, 1996: 19–23).

In particular, "a market basket approach" is currently the centre of heated debate. In this approach, analysts determine the necessities the average Canadian family needs for economic and social existence—transportation, shelter, clothing, personal care, household needs, furniture, telephone, reading, recreation, school supplies, and so on. Families unable to afford the market basket are considered "poor." The net result has been a much more conservative approach to poverty. For example, the poverty line according to the market basket measure (1997) for a family of four in a large city is $25,647, in contrast to the low-income cut-off of $32,377 (pre-tax) (National Council of Welfare, 1999a:5). Critics argue that the market basket approach is just as arbitrary and clumsy as the LICOs. For example, in some versions of the market basket approach, tea, coffee, eyeglasses, and dental care are not included on the grounds that the former two are optional and the latter two can be obtained through private charities (Crane, 1998; National Council of Welfare, 1999a). Clearly, there are important political implications attached to definitions that produce either a more or less restrictive notion of the numbers of poor (National Council of Welfare, 1998a: 6).

Since any definition of poverty that goes beyond simple physical human survival is relative, defining poverty always involves drawing a somewhat arbitrary line below which live the "poor." As a result, definitions of poverty are always subject to political pressures and agendas. A stricter definition may, at the stroke of a pen, dramatically reduce the numbers of poor (and, of course, vice versa). For governments seeking to respond painlessly (and inexpensively) to pressures for social reform, this is always and everywhere a tempting alternative.[2]

In the midst of these definitional debates, the best-known and most widely used measure continues to be the Statistics Canada definition (adopted in 1973; reset in 1992) that establishes income cut-offs below which people are considered to live in "straitened circumstances."[3] The cut-offs are based on the notion that poor families are those whose size of income requires them to spend more than 54.7 per cent of their gross income on food, clothing, and shelter, leaving few or no funds for transportation, health, personal care, education, household operation, recreation, or insurance. These income cut-offs vary in terms of the size of the household and the size of the area of residence (more than 500,000, 100,000–499,999, and so on), resulting in 35 separate low-income cut-offs. For example, a single person living in Regina in 1998 on less than $14,468 was considered "poor" by the Statistics Canada definition (1986 base), while a two-person family living on less than $15,202 in a rural area was deemed poor (National Council of Welfare, 1999a: 109).

While the Statistics Canada parameters provide us with a revealing portrayal of poverty in Canada, this portrait has serious limitations. It leaves out all Natives living on reserves, institutional inmates, residents of Yukon, the Northwest Territories, and Nunavut, and the homeless. It tells us nothing about the duration of poverty, that is, how long any one individual is poor. There is also considerable debate about the locational adjustments. According to Statistics Canada calculations, it is 31 per cent less expensive to live in rural areas. While research does suggest that shelter costs are lower than in the city, transportation costs are, in fact, higher. Further, access to subsidized public services such as child care, health services, and education, as well as to competitively priced goods, is likely restricted in many rural areas. The Canadian Council on Social Development, for example, calculates that rural costs are probably about 88 per cent of those in large urban centres, but also points out that there are considerable differences between cities. In short, locational adjustments are likely both inaccurate and imprecise. Others argue that with the large tax bite, income cut-offs should be based on after-tax income.[4] In addition, the measures ignore differences in the actual level of need in the household. For example, severe disability and lack of access to subsidized services may significantly increase household economic needs (Ross et al., 1994: 26–31).

Finally, there are general problems attached to the Statistics Canada measures of poverty. Like many measures, they reinforce the notion that there are two kinds of people: the poor and the non-poor. This is a split that is too easily translated into "us" and "them" and sustains stereotypes of the poor as somehow different and, possibly, defective.

In fact, poverty is a very porous identity.[5] Within the course of a year or two, low-income Canadians may drift in and out of "official" poverty. Recent research examining low-income patterns between 1982 and 1993 found that most people had only one spell of low income within this time period and it lasted on average two years. Indeed, the chances of a period of low income ending after one year were better than 50 per cent and for the clear majority of individuals (60 per cent) a period of low income was a temporary setback, not a chronic and persistent problem (Laroche, 1998). Unemployment, illness, accident, or disability may, even in the course of a month, tip the balance. Similarly, in the course of a lifetime, an interplay of key factors (notably, gender, age, marital status, and number of children) may trigger a slide into low income and poverty. Given these patterns, the problem of poverty needs to be understood as encompassing a broad continuum of individuals and families both below and above the designated "poverty line."[6]

Further, the poor are far from a homogeneous group. For example, the sources of income for the poor vary considerably. Many are "welfare poor" because the social assistance they receive is below the low-income cut-offs. In 1998, basic welfare assistance for a single parent with one child ranged from $11,300 in Saskatchewan to $13,695 in Ontario, but in each instance this benefit would place the individual well below the Statistics Canada low-income cut-offs (National Council of Welfare, 1999–2000: 40–1). In British Columbia (1998), for example, total welfare income provided only 38 per cent of the poverty-line income for a single employable individual and 61 per cent for a single parent with one child (ibid., 41). Being reliant on welfare for economic survival means living in poverty.

Many poor Canadians are termed "the working poor" because, although they have paid employment, their earnings from work are below the low-income cut-offs. Of 1,108,000 poor heads of families under age 65 in 1997, 21 per cent were employed full-time and 35 per cent were employed part-time—leaving 36 per cent who did not work and 8 per cent who were unable to work (National Council of Welfare, 1999a: 86). Paid employment is no guarantee that poverty will be avoided. When the worker is a single parent, when only one parent in the family is employed, when the work is part-time, contract, short-term, irregular, low-wage, unskilled (young, immigrant, and/or poorly educated workers), and when there are dependent children in the home, employment frequently fails to provide an escape from poverty (Kazemipur and Halli, 2000; Ross et al., 1994: 76–9; Gunderson et al., 1990: 68–71).

Taken as a whole the portrait of poverty in Canada today is sobering. In 1997, 5.1 million Canadians—17.2 per cent of children, women, and men in Canada—were poor. Among unattached individuals,[7] 36.3 per cent (1,496,000 Canadians) lived below the low-income cut-offs; among families, 14.3 per cent (1,203,000 families) did so (National Council of Welfare, 1999a). Predictably, these poverty rates are patterned by a variety of social factors. For example, there is a distinct regional dimension to Canadian poverty. In 1997, only 12.9 per cent of Alberta families were poor, while poverty was a fact of life for 18.9 per cent of Newfoundland families. Youth is also a critical determinant of poverty rates. One in three (34 per cent) families (couples with children) headed by young people (under 25 years of age) is poor. Families and individuals with low levels of education[8] are more likely to be poor, as are families with only one wage-earner. Not surprisingly, participation in the paid labour force is directly related to poverty rates, with "a good job [being] the best insurance against poverty for Canadians under the age of 65" (ibid.; Lawton, 1998). Finally, as discussed in more detail below, a complex intersection of factors such as gender, age, family structure and composition, race, ethnicity, and current social policies conditions poverty rates (Kazemipur and Halli, 2000; National Council of Welfare, 1999a; Ross et al., 1994).

The Feminization of Poverty

Canadian women are particularly at risk of being poor. This "feminization of poverty" refers to the fact that women in many industrialized Western nations, as well as in developing countries, are more likely to be poor than men (Pearce, 1978; Goldberg, 1990). Though Canadian women continue to be better off than their American counterparts (as a result of lower rates of single parenthood and more expansive social policies), the poverty rate for women (1997) was 18.3 per cent and for men 14.3 per cent. As a result, women comprise 57 per cent of Canadian adults who are poor (National Council of Welfare, 1999a: 99). Further, at every age level adult women have higher poverty rates than men (National Council of Welfare, 1998a: 85, 36, 19). Nor is this a new problem; the ranks of the poor have long been populated by women who were deserted, widowed, or orphaned (Katz, 1975: 60; Simmons, 1986). Evidence suggests, too, that women figure among the poorest of the poor. For example, until recently the largest poverty gap for poor families (how far below the poverty line an individual or family lives) was found among female-headed single-parent families (under 65 with children under 18) (National Council of Welfare, 1998a: 53, 60; 1998b: 12). Their situation improved marginally in 1997, when couples under 65 with children under 18 averaged $9,822 below the poverty line and headed the list of the poorest of the poor, followed closely by single-parent mothers at $9,337 below the poverty cut-off (National Council of Welfare, 1999a).

While the reasons behind women's impoverishment are complex they have much to do with traditional gender ideologies, inequities in the labour force, and flaws in our family law and responses to marriage breakdown. For generations, women have been expected to devote their lives to their unpaid duties in marriage and motherhood. Although many wives and mothers also worked for pay, this was generally seen as undesirable. Lower pay rates for women, rules against the employment of married women, and the peripheralization and stigmatization of "women's work" all reinforced the notion that women's place was in the home (Duffy and Pupo, 1992: 13–40).

Throughout the twentieth century, however, these notions came under increasing attack. The first and second waves of the women's movement, advanced education for women, and the reduction in family size, among other factors, undermined the traditional sexual division of labour. In particular, increasing numbers of Canadians have found that they simply cannot survive on the uncertain income of a single male (or female) breadwinner. The failure of wages to keep pace with inflation, increases in taxation, high rates of unemployment, and the loss of high-paying industrial and resource-extraction jobs have made the male breadwinner family increasingly anachronistic. In 1997, 66 per cent of married women with children under age 16 and 59 per cent of women with children under age three were employed (National Council of Welfare, 1999b: 12). Indeed, the poverty rate among husband-wife families would double (to 22.1 per cent of Canadian families) if these wives and mothers were not in the paid labour force (National Council of Welfare, 1999a: 100).

While much has changed, much remains the same. Women are still encouraged to focus their energies on marriage and motherhood; women's employment is still less well paid than men's, with full-time women workers earning about 73 per cent of male wages; patterns of sexual and gender harassment continue to maintain female job ghettos (Statistics Canada, 1999: 27). Women are still occupationally segregated into work with lower wages, less prestige, and less opportunity for advancement (Statistics Canada, 1998: 53). These employment inequities are likely to be further exacerbated if a woman is a recent immigrant or disabled or a member of a visible minority. For example, only 58 per cent of recent immigrant women aged 25–44 and holding a university degree were employed in 1996, in contrast to 86 per cent of comparable non-immigrant women (Badets and Howatson-Leo, 1999: 17). Similarly, the poverty rate for disabled women over 15 years of age is 29.5 per cent (Ross et al., 1994: 41). In short, a variety of factors intersect in a complex manner to compound some women's vulnerability to impoverishment.

Finally, almost all women, regardless of race, ethnicity, or disability, are still considered responsible for most child care, family caregiving, and housework. In the absence of adequate child-care and parental leave policies, juggling the conflicting demands of child care, housework, and paid work often means costly interruptions in labour force participation and/or peripheral employment as a part-time, casual, or contract employee (Marshall, 1993; Fast and Da Pont, 1997). Being employed in "women's work" or taking several years off to care for young children can translate into disaster when marriages end in divorce, when women face long years of widowhood, or when women become single parents.

Single parenthood, typically the result of divorce, can have devastating effects on women's economic well-being. An astounding 57.1 per cent of single-parent mothers are poor (1997), in contrast to a poverty rate of 11.9 per cent for couples with children (National Council of Welfare, 1999a). Without a male breadwinner in the family and with inadequate or non-existent support payments, many women cannot provide sufficient income for their families. For example, research on low-income patterns between 1982 and 1993 found that lone-parent women were particularly susceptible to long-term impoverishment, often spending between 5.1 and 6.9 years out of 10 in low income in contrast to the average of two years (Laroche, 1998). Further, as noted above, they are likely to sink deep into poverty.

Single parenting is a particularly potent combination when combined with youthfulness or young children. Single-parent mothers under age 25 have a staggering poverty rate of 93.3 per cent and single-parent mothers with children under age seven have rates as high as 80.2 per cent (National Council of Welfare, 1999a). However, contrary to powerful stereotypes, single mothers are not primarily teenagers having numerous babies so they can live off welfare payments. Teenage mothers comprise only 3 per cent of all single parents on welfare and almost half (49 per cent) of single mothers have only one child and another one-third (31 per cent) have only two children (National Council of Welfare, 1998c: 33).

For many of these women, low income is a direct consequence of marriage breakup. The Economic Council of Canada's five-year survey of Canadian incomes found women's incomes (adjusted for family size) dropped by about 39 per cent when they separated or divorced and thereafter rose only slightly. Three years after the marriage breakup, women's incomes were still 27 per cent below their earlier level. Men's income (adjusted for family size), in contrast, increased by an average of 7 per cent. Along with the labour force inequalities discussed above, inadequate support payments produce the inequity. Only 68 per cent of divorces involving dependent children (1989) resulted in a child-support order, and those orders averaged a scant $250 per child per month (Economic Council of Canada, 1992: 49). Further, as repeatedly explored in the media, problems persist in the successful collection of child-support payments from non-custodial parents.

Despite the clear neediness of single mothers, recent social policy initiatives have tended to exacerbate their plight. For example, in Ontario, single welfare mothers of school-age children are required to sign up for workfare,[9] and these mothers, along with other welfare recipients, are now required to get by on substantially lower rates of social assistance. This push to any form of paid employment is often coupled with inadequate child-care provisions. To further compound their plight, single mothers must also confront the persistent tendency to stigmatize mothers on welfare as somehow less worthy

of social support than, for example, low-income two-parent families. Popular ideology suggests that single mothers who receive social assistance are simply being encouraged to have more children[10] and these children are perceived as growing up troubled and disruptive.

Growing old provides little promise of relief to women. While policy initiatives between 1980 and 1996 have successfully eased much of the poverty burden for the elderly, it has by no means eliminated it. Unattached elderly women (65 and over)—typically, those who are widowed, divorced, or separated—face high rates of poverty. In 1997, 42 per cent of unattached women over age 65, compared to 27.2 per cent for unattached elderly men, lived below the low-income cut-offs.[11] Another 25 per cent of unattached older women are only slightly above the poverty line (earning 100 to 125 per cent of the poverty line) (National Council of Welfare, 1999a). Increasing age exacerbates the problem. Unattached women aged 75–9 have a poverty rate of 48 per cent, and the rate rises to 53 per cent for unattached women 85 or older. Women are particularly at risk[12] because they are less likely to receive income from occupational pension plans, the Canada/Quebec Pension Plan, and investments. The traditional patterns of women's lives, with work interruptions to take care of family responsibilities, work in low-paying, poorly benefited jobs, and high rates of part-time and contractual work, contribute to high rates of female impoverishment whenever women find themselves without a spouse (McDonald, 1997).

Based on current trends in marriage, divorce, and life expectancy, an estimated 84 per cent of all Canadian women can expect to spend some portion of their adult lives without a male breadwinner in the home—as pregnant teens, single mothers, divorced middle-aged workers, and/or elderly widows (National Council of Welfare, 1990: 17). Today, as marriage is increasingly postponed, almost every woman will be self-supporting at some point. Yet, few Canadian women live with these expectations, and fewer still plan their work and marital lives to bring them financial independence and solvency (Duffy et al., 1988). In a society that perpetuates unrealistic notions of romantic love, marital life, and parenting, and in an economy premised on the peripheralized, low-wage, ghettoized work of women, many women continue to be set up for poverty.

Predictably, certain groups of women—immigrant women, the disabled, minority women, and Native Canadians—are at greater risk. Native women, for example, have lower than average labour force participation rates, lower than average earnings, and substantially higher rates of unemployment, partly because of the remote, rural areas in which many live (Federal, Provincial, and Territorial Advisory Committee, 1999: 47; Abella, 1984). Visible-minority and immigrant women frequently find that racial and ethnic discrimination, along with language difficulties and inadequate government policy, translate into long hours of low-wage work (Kazemipur and Halli, 2000; National Council of Welfare, 1990: 118–27). Foreign-born elderly women, in all marital categories, have lower average incomes than their Canadian-born counterparts. Elderly women who are recent immigrants and/or who come from less-developed countries receive particularly low incomes (Boyd, 1989). Although the majority of disabled adults live on low incomes, disabled women are, generally, worse off than their male counterparts (Ross and Shillington, 1989: 28; Barile, 1992).

The Poverty of Children

Interwoven with the impoverishment of women and families is the poverty of children. More than a million children[13] (or 19.6 per cent of Canadian children in 1997) are growing up poor (Crane, 1999). Young children (aged 0–11 years) have even higher poverty rates, with one-quarter (Ontario) to one-third (Newfoundland) living below the Statistics Canada low-income cut-offs (Cheal et al., 1997). Despite a unanimous vote in the House of Commons in 1989 to eradicate child poverty by the year 2000—the highly publicized Campaign 2000—Canadian child poverty rates grew from 1989 to 1996 and remain high today (National Council of Welfare, 1999a). Indeed, although the number of Canadian children increased by just 6 per cent between 1989 and 1997, the number of "poor" children rose by 37 per cent, and since the mid-1980s Canadian children have had a consistently higher rate of poverty than adult Canadians under age 65 (Crane, 1999; National Council of Welfare, 1999a). Children constitute more than one-quarter of our poor and the child poverty rate in Canada is, with the exception of the United States, the United Kingdom, and Australia, the highest in the industrialized world (National Council of Welfare, 1999b: 7; Hurtig, 1999: 320).

Simple explanations for the expansion of child poverty, such as the dramatic increase in single-parent families, provide only part of the puzzle. While children in families headed by single mothers have extremely high poverty rates (60.4 per cent in 1997), most (56 per cent) poor children in Canada are growing up in two-parent families (National Council of Welfare, 1999a: 91). These children are poor because their parents are poor and their parents' poverty often stems from unemployment, underemployment, inadequate minimum-wage levels, and reduced social welfare supports (ibid.; Baxter, 1993).[14]

The Changing Face of Poverty

How is it that, as our country's economy has expanded, as our gross domestic product (GDP) has increased year after year, there have been growing numbers of poor men, women and children in Canada? (Hurtig, 1999: xiii)

Poverty patterns are far from static or monochromatic. Over time there have been important changes in poverty and, depending on where you look in the population and in the country, there are significant variations in the nature of impoverishment.

In the 1960s and early 1970s, there were significant reductions in the rate and depth of poverty (Economic Council of Canada, 1992: 2). Progress slowed during the 1970s, and since 1973 the poverty rate has tended to fluctuate with the health of the economy (Ross and Shillington, 1989: 21; National Council of Welfare, 1988: 1). This is reflected, for example, in the marked decrease in the numbers of Canadians, from all types of families, living on low incomes during the 1970s. From the early 1980s to 1995, however, there was little evidence of decline in low-income rates and indications of increases of low income among some types of families (Zyblock and Lin, 1997). Most recently, poverty rates have been less inclined to mirror the ups and downs of the economy, suggesting that a more or less permanent underclass is emerging.

Among the general Canadian population, single parents are at a distinct disadvantage in terms of impoverishment, but this is also true for individuals living on their own. Among unattached (unmarried) individuals poverty rates have shown relatively little improvement. From 1980 to 1997, poverty rates for this population fluctuated from 41.4 per cent in 1980 to a low of 34.1 per cent in 1990 and back up to 36.3 per cent in 1997. Further, the depth of poverty experienced by unattached men and women under age 65 has remained alarmingly high from 1980 to the present. In 1997, unattached men and women under age 65 were earning on average only slightly more than half (54 per cent and 55 per cent respectively) of the poverty line. In other words, these individuals were living almost $7,000 below the low-income cut-offs (National Council of Welfare, 1999a).

Similarly, there has been considerable regional variation in poverty rates. Although in the last several decades Ontario and Quebec have fairly consistently held their claims to having, respectively, among the lowest and highest provincial poverty rates, other provinces have been less consistent. Prince Edward Island has moved from above to below the national average in terms of poverty rates, while Alberta and British Columbia's poverty rates moved from below the national average to above or at the national level (ibid.). Amid these changes, poverty has also increasingly become an urban phenomenon.

The Lost Generation: The Poverty of Young Adults

Among the alarming trends has been the growing vulnerability of young adults. Certainly, the appearance of food banks on campuses signalled a dismal deterioration in the lives of many Canadian university and college students (McGrath, 1998). Young people who marry and have dependants are in a particularly difficult economic position. Although in 1997 young families (those headed by someone under age 25) comprised only 4 per cent of all Canadian families, they accounted for 11 per cent of poor families, and almost half (42.8 per cent) of young families were low income (Crane, 1999). As high rates of unemployment and underemployment continue to plague young workers, not surprisingly, the rates of poverty grow among families with young parents (under age 35).

From 1973 to 1986 there was also an increase in the number of poor families with two or more earners. This reflects, in part, the failure of real family wages to keep pace with rising costs, along with a failed commitment to maintain an adequate minimum wage. In 1973 minimum-wage legislation meant that someone who worked 40 hours a week over 52 weeks could earn a yearly income 20 per cent over the poverty line. By 1991 the same worker would have to work 50 hours a week for 52 weeks simply to reach the poverty line (Kitchen et al., 1991: 36). During this same period, education has become less of a barrier to impoverishment; by 1997, 7.7 per cent of heads of poor families and 23.4 per cent of poor unattached individuals held a university degree (National Council of Welfare, 1999a). Although these rates are the lowest among all educational categories and confirm the partial protection from poverty provided by higher education, the pattern also indicates that poverty may be "more a result of lack of job opportunities rather than a lack of education (National Council of Welfare, 1997: 48; Hurtig, 1999: 133–4).

Homelessness

Another important shift in poverty patterns has been the dramatic emergence of urban homelessness in Canada and other industrialized countries. By the late 1990s, activists and analysts were pointing to homelessness as a "national disaster" and "national crisis" (James, 1999). Toronto, "a magnet for the homeless," provided shelter for an estimated 5,000 homeless each night during the winter of 1998 (Gillespie, 1998). Research on shelter patterns suggests that one-fifth of those using shelter beds are children (under 18 years of age). Shelters and hostels, once considered stop-gap solutions, seemed increasingly entrenched as a long-term response to the homeless. Yet, even as the numbers of shelters and food banks burgeoned, there were not enough available beds or services (Orwen, 1998). Toronto front-line workers estimated that two to four homeless died each week and analysts suggested that, nationally, the number of Canadian homeless was approaching 200,000 (Crowe, 1998).[15]

The Elderly: The Success Story

Despite the unrelenting advance of homelessness in our urban centres, there is nothing immutable or inevitable about poverty. As dramatically evidenced by the fight against poverty among senior Canadians, it is possible to reverse established patterns of income inequality. Policy changes, including the creation of the federal Guaranteed Income Supplement in 1967 for low-income seniors, the creation of the Canada/Quebec Pension Plan in 1966, and the implementation of provincial supplements, have meant that instead of one-third (33.6 per cent) of all seniors being poor (as in 1980), a near-record low of less than one-fifth (17.0 per cent) are now living below low-income cut-offs (1997). Similarly, the poverty rate for poor senior couples went from 22.2 per cent in 1980 to 7.0 per cent in 1997 (National Council of Welfare, 1999a: 19, 20). Although the number of Canadians aged 65 and older has increased from 2.2 million in 1980 to 3.5 million in 1997 (a 59 per cent increase), the number of seniors living in poverty has actually decreased over this time period (ibid.).

The exception to these cheery developments is the continuing plight of unattached (unmarried) seniors. As with other segments of the population, living on one's own leads to higher overall rates of poverty. This is particularly true of Canadians 65 and older. In 1980, more than two-thirds (68.7 per cent) of unattached women 65 and older and more than half (57.8 per cent) of comparable senior men were living below the low-income cut-offs. Since that time there has been marked improvement. However, much remains to be done—in 1997 almost half of senior unattached women (42 per cent) and more than one in four senior unattached men were poor (ibid., 22).

[…] [T]here are alarming signs of growing social division and the entrenchment of inequalities. As in numerous US communities, there is a noticeable trend among the well-to-do to seal themselves off from the unpleasant realities of poverty and deprivation. Gated communities, security guards and services, 24-hour concierges, and other kindred developments speak to this trend towards middle-and upper-class defensiveness. Combined with ideological campaigns portraying welfare recipients as undeserving cheats, presenting the homeless as both malevolent and lazy, and stereotyping single mothers as irresponsible drains on the economy, these developments are frightening in their implications. Instead of fighting poverty, there is a move to fight the poor.

Whether Canadians in the twenty-first century will be able to transcend our history, with its often punitive, niggardly responses to the poor and disadvantaged, and whether we will have the courage and creativity to opt for a more equitable nation remains to be seen.

Notes

1 This definitional problem is compounded by the pervasive ideology in Canadian society that we are a basically "classless society" (Allahar and Coté, 1998).

2 For example, P. Sainath, noted Indian journalist, recounts the struggles over such competing definitions of poverty. In the late 1980s, the government of India devised a very narrow definition of impoverishment that reduced the poverty rate to just over 19 per cent of the population. When a succeeding government dumped "this particular piece of dishonesty," the percentage of Indian people living in poverty soared to 39.9 per cent in 1997 (Sainath, 1996: 348–50).

3 Statistics Canada warns against the use of low-income cut-offs as a poverty line. They have also proposed an alternative, simpler measure—the low-income measure—which is 50 per cent of the median income in Canada.

4 Commencing in 1990, Statistics Canada published an appendix that included low-income cut-offs based on after-tax income. Estimating the number of people living in poverty using the after-tax method results in a reduction in the rate (for 1990) from14.6 per cent to 11.5 per cent (Ross et al., 1994: 28).

5 A recent survey of labour and income dynamics in Canada found, for example, that between 1993 and 1994 over one million Canadians fell into poverty, almost as many climbed out, and slightly more remained poor in both years (National Council of Welfare, 1998a: 9).

6 In addition, historical trends increase or decrease vulnerability to official poverty. As evidenced most dramatically during the Great Depression, impoverishment may touch any individual or family.

7 "Unattached individuals" are those who are not married and who are not living with family members.

8 Level of education, however, does not dictate likelihood of poverty. Many Canadians who have relatively little education avoid impoverishment and, conversely, there are numerous families and individuals with post-secondary education who are still poor (National Council of Welfare, 1998a: 45).

9 Workfare refers to the increasingly popular policy of requiring able-bodied recipients of social welfare benefits to take some form of state-orchestrated employment. In Ontario, for example, some welfare recipients have been deployed into phone solicitation positions. Refusal to accept such positions may result in loss of welfare benefits. Needless to say, these initiatives have resulted in strong protests from poverty activists.

10 Research indicates that single-parent mothers have fewer children on average than two-parent families (National Council of Welfare, 1998a: 41).

11 However, the poverty gap (the amount of income needed to bring the population up to the poverty line) for unattached senior women (and men) is significantly less than that experienced by other parts of the poor population, notably unattached men under age 65 and single-parent mothers (National Council of Welfare, 1998a: 52).

12 Research suggests that the death of a wife actually decreases the risk of poverty for her husband (as cited in McDonald, 1997: 557).

13 Not included in these figures are the 51 per cent of Native children who are poor (Kitchen et al., 1991: 15).

14 In 1999, the average Toronto single mother "on welfare" received $1,071.70 a month. She paid on average $680.53 in rent, which left $391.17 or $13.03 a day for food, clothing, transportation, a telephone, and other expenses (Hurtig, 1999: 292).

15 The Toronto Mayor's Task Force on Homelessness (headed by Anne Golden) found that 170,000 different individuals had used shelters for the homeless in Toronto between 1987 and 1996 (Golden, 1998).

References

Abella, R.S. 1984. *Equality in Employment: A Royal Commission Report*. Ottawa: Ministry of Supply and Services.

Allahar, Anton L., and James E. Coté. 1998. *Richer and Poorer: The Structure of Inequality in Canada*. Toronto: James Lorimer.

Armstrong, Jane. 1992. "Is Our Welfare System Being Abused?," *Toronto Star*, 1 Mar., A7, A18.

Badetsjane, and Linda Howatson-Leo. 1999. "Recent Immigrants in the Workforce," *Canadian Social Trends* 52 (Spring): 16–22.

Barile, Maria. 1992. "Dis-Abled Women: An Exploited Genderless Under-class," *Canadian Woman Studies* (Summer): 32–3.

Baxter, Sheila. 1988. *No Way to Live: Poor Women Speak Out*. Vancouver: New Star Books.

_____. 1993. *A Child Is Not a Toy: Voices of Children in Poverty*. Vancouver: New Star Books.

Beauchesne, Eric. 1991. "Income Guarantee Doesn't Discourage Work, Study Finds," *Toronto Star*, 4 July, A12.

Benner, Allan. 1998. "Report Offers Real Portrait of Poverty," *St. Catharines Standard*, 26 Nov., A7.

Blouin, Barbara. 1992. "Welfare Workers and Clients: Problems of Sexism and Paternalism," *Canadian Women's Studies* (Summer): 64–5.

Bradbury, Bettina. 1982. "The Fragmented Family: Family Strategies in the Face of Death, Illness, and Poverty, Montreal, 1860–1885," in Joy Parr, ed., *Childhood and Family in Canadian History*. Toronto: McClelland & Stewart.

_____. 1991. "Surviving as a Widow in Nineteenth Century Montreal," in Veronica Strong-Boag and Anita Clair Fellman, eds, *Rethinking Canada: The Promise of Women's History*. Toronto: Copp Clark.

Bragg, Rebecca. 1999. "Housing Top Priority for Canada's Poor," *Toronto Star*, 26 Mar., E4.

Burman, Patrick. 1988. *Killing Time, Losing Ground: Experiences of Unemployment*. Toronto: Wall & Thompson.

_____. 1996. *Poverty's Bonds: Power and Agency in the Social Relations of Welfare*. Toronto: Thompson Educational Publishing.

Carey, Elaine. 1998a. "Record-High Income Taxes Gobble Fifth of Family Pay," *Toronto Star*, 23 June, A4.

_____. 1998b. "Rich Get Richer as Wage Gap Widens," *Toronto Star*, 22 Oct., A1, A36.

Carniol, Ben. 1987. *Case Critical: The Dilemma of Social Work in Canada*. Toronto: Between the Lines.

Cheal, David, et al. 1997. "Canadian Children in the 1990s," *Canadian Social Trends* 4 (Spring): 1–9.

Copp, Terry. 1974. *The Anatomy of Poverty: The Condition of the Working Class in Montreal, 1897–1929*. Toronto: McClelland & Stewart.

Coulter, Rebecca. 1982. "The Working Young of Edmonton, 1921–1931," in Joy Parr, ed., *Childhood and Family in Canadian History*. Toronto: McClelland & Stewart.

Crane, David. 1998. "Where do we draw the line on poverty?", *Toronto Star*, 4 Nov., E2.

_____. 1999. "Children Are the 'Sound Bite' in Productivity," *Toronto Star*, 15 Apr., D2.

Crowe, Cathy. 1998. "In the Calculation of Real Disasters Homelessness Has Easily Won Its Place," *Toronto Star*, 30 Oct., A21.

Davies, Gareth. 1997. "Understanding the War on Poverty: The Advantages of a Canadian Perspective," *Journal of Policy History* 9, 4: 425–49.

Denton, Margaret, and Alfred Hunter. 1991. "Education and the Child," in Richard Barnhorst and Laura C. Johnson, eds, *The State of the Child in Ontario*. Toronto: Oxford University Press.

Duffy, Ann. 1992. "Day Care Need 'Enormous,' Study Says," *Toronto Star*, 29 Feb., A21.

Duffy, Ann, Nancy Mandell, and Norene Pupo. 1988. *Few Choices: Women, Work and Family*. Toronto: Garamond Press.

_____. 1992. *Part Time Paradox: Connecting Gender, Work, and Family*. Toronto: McClelland & Stewart.

Duncan, Kenneth. 1974. "Irish Famine Immigration and the Social Structure of Canada West," in Michiel Horn and Ronald Sabourin, eds, *Studies in Canadian Social History*. Toronto: McClelland & Stewart.

Dunphy, Catherine. 1999. "Aboriginal People Look to Leave Toronto's Mean Streets," *Toronto Star*, 27 Mar., A8.

Economic Council of Canada. 1992. *The New Face of Poverty: Income Security Needs of Canadian Families*. Ottawa: Ministry of Supply and Services.

Fast, Janet, and Moreno Da Pont. 1997. "Changes in Women's Work Continuity," *Canadian Social Trends* (Autumn): 2–7.

Federal, Provincial, and Territorial Advisory Committee on Population Health for the Meeting of Ministers of Health, Charlottetown, PEI 1999. *Toward a Healthy Future: Second Report on the Health of Canadians*. Ottawa: Minister of Public Works and Government Services.

Freid, Loren. 1998. "Are We Asking the Right Questions?," *Toronto Star*, 9 Oct., A24.

Gaffield, Chad. 1984. "Wage Labour, Industrialization and the Origins of the Modern Family," in Maureen Baker, ed, *The Family: Changing Trends in Canada*. Toronto: McGraw-Hill.

Gelles, Richard J., and Claire P. Cornell. 1990. *Intimate Violence in Families*, 2nd edn. Newbury Park, Calif.: Sage.

Gillespie, Kerry. 1998. "Civilized Society Feared at Risk," *Toronto Star*, 29 Sept., B1.

Goar, Carol. 1990. "Senator's Passionate Attack on Poverty," *Toronto Star*, 13 Jan., D4.

_____. 1995. "Unequal Shares of the American Dream," *Toronto Star*, 14 May, F5.

Goldberg, Gertrude Schaffner. 1990. "Canada: Bordering on the Feminization of Poverty," in Gertrude Goldberg and Eleanor Kremen, eds, *The Feminization of Poverty: Only in America?* New York: Praeger.

Golden, Anne. 1998. "Breaking the Cycle of Homelessness," *Toronto Star*, 30 Sept., A18.

Green, Sara Jean. 1999. "Street Youth Program Nets $1.1 million grant," *Toronto Star*, 27 Mar., A9.

Guest, Dennis. 1980. *The Emergence of Social Security in Canada*. Vancouver: University of British Columbia Press.

Gunderson, Morley, and Leon Muszynski, with Jennifer Keck. 1990. *Women and Labour Market Poverty*. Ottawa: Canadian Advisory Council on the Status of Women.

Hale, Sylvia M. 1990. *Controversies in Sociology: A Canadian Introduction*. Toronto: Copp Clark Pitman.

Houston, Susan E. 1982. "The 'Waifs and Strays' of a Late Victorian City: Juvenile Delinquents in Toronto," in Joy Parr, ed., *Childhood and Family in Canadian History*. Toronto: McClelland & Stewart.

Hudson, Kellie. 1999. "Dentists Root Out 2nd-Class Care for Welfare Children," *Toronto Star*, 28 Mar., A1, A4.

Hurtig, Mel. 1999. *Pay the Rent or Feed the Kids: The Tragedy and Disgrace of Poverty in Canada*. Toronto: McClelland & Stewart.

Hyndman, Brian. 1998a. "Being Poor Still Means Being Sicker, Dying Younger Than Rich," *Toronto Star*, 8 Jan., A15.

_____. 1998b. "Children Paying for War on Debt," *Toronto Star*, 10 July, A26.

Interfaith Social Assistance Reform Coalition. 1998. *Our Neighbours' Voices: Will We Listen?* Toronto: James Lorimer.

James, Royson. 1999. "We Can't Turn Backs on Homeless," *Toronto Star*, 31 Mar., B2.

Johnson, Leo A. 1972. *Poverty in Wealth*. Toronto: New Hogtown Press.

Katz, Michael B. 1975. *The People of Hamilton, Canada West: Family and Class in a Mid-Nineteenth-Century City*. Cambridge, Mass.: Harvard University Press.

_____. 1983. *Poverty and Policy in American History*. New York: Academic Press.

_____. 1986. *In the Shadow of the Poorhouse: A Social History of Welfare in America*. New York: Basic Books.

Kazemipur, A., and S.S. Halli. 2000. *The New Poverty in Canada: Ethnic Groups and Ghetto Neighbourhoods*. Toronto: Thompson Educational Publishing.

Kitchen, Brigitte, Andrew Mitchell, Peter Clutterbuck, and Marvyn Novick. 1991. *Unequal Futures: The Legacies of Child Poverty in Canada*. Toronto: Child Poverty Action Group and the Social Planning Council of Metropolitan Toronto.

Laroche, M. 1998. "In and Out of Low Income," *Canadian Social Trends* (Autumn): 20–4.

Lawton, Valerie. 1998. "Plight of the Long-Term Jobless," *Toronto Star*, 7 Nov., B4.

McCarthy, Shawn. 1992. "Ottawa Missing $90 Billion a Year as Cheaters Use Cash to Dodge Taxes," *Toronto Star*, 30 Apr., A1, A32.

McDonald, Lynn. 1997. "The Invisible Poor: Canada's Retired Widows," *Canadian Journal of Aging* 16, 3: 553–83.

McGrath, Paul. 1998. "Food Banks Part of Life on Campus," *Toronto Star*, 23 Feb., F1, F2.

MacLeod, Linda. 1987. *Battered But not Beaten: Preventing Wife Battering in Canada*. Ottawa: Canadian Advisory Council on the Status of Women.

Marquardt, Richard. 1998. *Enter at Your Own Risk: Canadian Youth and the Labour Market*. Toronto: Between the Lines.

Marsden, Lorna, chair. 1991. *Children in Poverty: Toward a Better Future*. Standing Senate Committee on Social Affairs, Science and Technology. Ottawa: Ministry of Supply and Services.

Marshall, Katherine. 1993. "Dual Earners: Who's Responsible for Housework?," *Canadian Social Trends* (Winter): 11–15.

Mulvany, C. Pelham. 1884. *Toronto: Past and Present*. Toronto: W.E. Caiger.

National Council of Welfare. 1988. *Poverty Profile 1988*. Ottawa: Ministry of Supply and Services.

_____. 1990. *Women and Poverty Revisited*. Ottawa: Ministry of Supply and Services.

_____. 1991. *Welfare Incomes 1990*. Ottawa: Ministry of Supply and Services.

_____. 1997. *Another Look at Welfare Reform*. Ottawa: Ministry of Supply and Services.

_____. 1998a. *Poverty Profile 1996*. Ottawa: Minister of Public Works and Government Services Canada.

_____. 1998b. *Child Benefits: Kids Are Still Hungry*. Ottawa: Minister of Public Works and Government Services Canada.

_____. 1998c. *Profiles of Welfare: Myths and Realities*. Ottawa: Minister of Public Works and Government Services Canada.

_____. 1999a. *Poverty Profile 1997*. Ottawa: Minister of Public Works and Government Services Canada.

_____. 1999b. *Preschool Children: Promises to Keep*. Ottawa: Minister of Public Works and Government Services Canada.

_____. 1999c. *Children First*. Ottawa: Minister of Public Works and Government Services Canada.

_____. 1999–2000. *Welfare Incomes: 1991 and 1998*. Ottawa: Minister of Public Works and Government Services Canada.

Nett, Emily. 1990. *Canadian Families: Past and Present*. Toronto: Butterworths.

Offord, Dan. 1991. "Growing Up Poor in Ontario," *Transition* (Vanier Institute of the Family) (June): 10–11.

Orwen, Patricia. 1998. "Food Bank Use Jumps 17% in GTA in Just One Year," *Toronto Star*, 11 Sept., A2.

Pearce, Diana. 1978. "The Feminization of Poverty: Women, Work and Welfare," *Urban and Social Change Review* 11 (Feb.): 28–36.

Pfeiffer, J. William. 1999. *Road Kill on the Information Highway: The Future of Work in Canada*. Toronto: Pfeiffer and Co.

Pupo, Norene. 1988. "Preserving Patriarchy: Women, the Family and the State," in Nancy Mandell and Ann Duffy, eds, *Reconstructing the Canadian Family: Feminist Perspectives*. Toronto: Butterworths.

Rashid, Abdul. 1989. *Family Income*. Ottawa: Ministry of Supply and Services.

_____. 1998. "Family Income Inequality: 1970–1995," *Perspectives on Labour and Income* 10, 4 (Winter): 12–17.

_____. 1999. "Family Income: 25 Years of Stability and Change," *Perspectives on Labour and Income* 11, 1 (Spring): 9–15.

Reitsma-Street, Marge, Richard Carriere, Adje Van de Sande, and Carol Hein. 1993. "Three Perspectives on Child Poverty in Canada," *The Social Worker* 61, 1 (Spring): 6–13.

Robinson, Patricia. 1986. *Women's Work Interruptions*. Ottawa: Ministry of Supply and Services.

Rooke, Patricia, and R.L. Schnell. 1982. "Guttersnipes and Charity Children: 19th Century Child Rescue in the Atlantic Provinces," in P. Rooke and R.L. Shnell, eds, *Studies in Childhood History: A Canadian Perspective*. Calgary: Detselig.

Rosenthal, Marguerite O. 1990. "Sweden: Promise and Paradox," in Gertrude Schaffner Goldberg and Eleanor Kremen, eds, *The Feminization of Poverty: Only in America?* New York: Praeger.

Ross, David, and Richard Shillington. 1989. *The Canadian Fact Book on Poverty*. Ottawa: Canadian Council on Social Development.

Ross et al. 1994. *The Canadian Fact Book on Poverty*. Ottawa: Canadian Council on Social Development.

Sainath, P. 1996. *Everybody Loves a Good Drought*. London: Review.

Sarlo, Christopher. 1992. *Poverty in Canada*. Vancouver: Fraser Institute.

Simmons, Christina. 1986. "'Helping the Poorer Sisters': The Women of the Jost Mission, Halifax, 1905–1945," in Veronica Strong-Boag and Anita Clair Fellman, eds, *Rethinking Canada: The Promise of Women's History*. Toronto: Copp Clark Pitman.

Spears, John. 1991. "NB Seeks Answer to Childhood Poverty," *Toronto Star*, 31 May, A21.

_____. 1999. "Rent Erodes Tenants' Income, Study Shows," *Toronto Star*, 23 Mar., A6.

Special Senate Committee on Poverty. 1976. *Poverty in Canada*. Ottawa: Ministry of Supply and Services.

Statistics Canada. 1998. "Sources of Income, Earnings and Total Income and Family Income," *The Daily*, Catalogue no. 11-001E, 9 June.

_____. 1999. "Social Indicators," *Canadian Social Trends* (Spring): 27.

Sweet, Lois. 1991a. "Is Welfare Cheating Running Wild?," *Toronto Star*, 2 June, B1, B7.

_____. 1991b. "Jobs Offer Hope as Welfare Cure," *Toronto Star*, 3 June, A15.

Toronto Star. 1998a. "World's Richest Get richer," 29 Apr., E2.

_____. 1998b. "Canada's a Fine Home ... for Some of Us," 10 Sept., A24.

_____. 1998c. "Amnesty Report Slams U.S. Prisons," 7 Oct., A20.

_____. 1999. "Poverty Can't Be Measured Away," 5 Apr., A16.

Vienneau, David. 1991. "Court-Ordered Child Support Often Too Low Report Warns," *Toronto Star*, 4 July, A2.

Waddell, Christopher. 1989. "The Debt: Where Does All the Money Go?," *Globe and Mail*, 8 Apr., D1, D8.

Williamson, Deanna L., and Janet E. Fast. 1998. "Poverty Status, Health Behaviours and Health: Implications for Social Assistance and Health Care Policy," *Canadian Public Policy* 24, 1: 1–22.

Women for Economic Survival. 1984. *Women and Economic Hard Times: A Record*. Victoria: Women for Economic Survival and the University of Victoria.

Wright, Lisa. 1998. "Big Brass Earn Top Dollar," *Toronto Star*, 10 Dec, C3.

Zyblock, Myles, and Zhengxi Lin. 1997. *Trickling Down or Fizzling Out?: Economic Performance, Transfers, Inequality and Low Income*. Ottawa: Statistics Canada.

CHAPTER 24
Introduction to *New Slavery: A Reference Handbook*

KEVIN BALES

Most of us think that slavery ended a long time ago—or that if it does exist, it only happens in poor countries far away. Maybe that is one reason why Hilda Dos Santos stayed in slavery for so long in the well-to-do suburbs outside Washington, D.C., Hilda had worked as a domestic servant in her native Brazil for many years, and when her employers, Rene and Margarida Bonnetti, asked her to move with them to the United States in 1979, she agreed. Once in the United States, the Bonnettis stopped paying Hilda and locked her into a life of slavery. She cleaned the house, did the yardwork, cooked the meals, cared for the pets, and even shoveled snow without gloves, boots, or a coat. Her bed was a mattress in the basement, and she was not allowed to use the showers or bathtubs in the house. Her food was scraps and leftovers, and when Hilda made mistakes in her work, she was beaten. Mrs. Bonnetti once poured hot soup over her face and chest when she didn't like the way it tasted. When a cut on Hilda's leg became infected the Bonnettis refused to provide medical care. A stomach tumor grew to the size of a soccer ball without any help from the Bonnettis; a neighbor finally took her to the hospital. It was there that social workers were alerted to her situation and the law stepped in. She had been in slavery for twenty years.

Hilda Dos Santos is typical of many slaves in the world today—poor, vulnerable people tricked into slavery. Her case demonstrates that slavery is alive and well. If her case was unique it would be shocking enough, but Hilda is one of hundreds, perhaps thousands, of slaves in the United States, and one of millions of slaves in the world. The slavery she suffered is much the same as the old kinds of slavery we learn about in history. It is still about one person controlling another, taking away an individual's free will and abusing and stealing his or her life and livelihood. But slavery today is also different, for slavery has evolved into new—and in some ways more destructive—forms that stretch through our global economy to touch us wherever we are.

＊　　＊　　＊　　＊　　＊

Slavery Defined

Since the abolition of legal slavery in the nineteenth century, the word "slavery" has been used to describe many different things: prostitution, prison labor, even the sale of human organs. More than 300 international slavery treaties have been signed since 1815, but none have defined slavery in exactly the same way. Many definitions of slavery focus on *the legal ownership of one person by another*, since most slavery in the nineteenth century took that form. But it is important to remember that slavery has been part of human history for thousands of years. Some of that time slavery was about legal ownership of people, but at other times it was not.

Before we can define "slavery," we need to recognize the characteristics and conditions that make it what it is. Slavery is a relationship between two people. It is both a social and economic relationship, and like all relationships it has certain characteristics and rules. The key characteristics of slavery are not about ownership but about how people are controlled. The core characteristics of slavery throughout history, whether it was legal or not, is violence. The slave master or slaveholder controls a slave by using or threatening violence. Slavery is about no choices at all, no control over your life, and a constant fear of violence. This is the key to slavery. Violence brings a person into slavery. Many people who become slaves are tricked into it. Many people, following a trail of lies, walk into enslavement, but what keeps them there is violence. Once enslaved, there are all sorts of ways that slaves are held in slavery—sometimes it is the way the slave gives up and gives into slavery, sometimes it is about the personal relationships that develop between slaves and slaveholders—but the essential ingredient is violence.

The second key characteristic of slavery is *loss of free will*; slaves are under the complete control of someone else. There is no other person, authority, or government the slave can turn to for protection. Slaves must do as they are told or they will suffer. The third characteristic is that slavery is normally used to *exploit* someone in some kind of economic activity. No one enslaves another person just to be mean; people are enslaved to make a profit. Most slaveholders see themselves as normal businesspeople.

They have little interest in hurting anyone, in being cruel or torturing people; it is just part of the job. Slavery is about money. If we put these characteristics together we can define slavery in this way: *Slavery is a social and economic relationship in which a person is controlled through violence or its threat, paid nothing, and economically exploited.*

A definition that works for many different types of slavery is important because slavery, like all human relationships, changes over time. The main characteristics of slavery is control through violence, but that can take many forms. The conditions in which slaves live around the world vary enormously. In those few places where old styles of slavery are still practiced, like Mauritania, there are long-term, often lifelong relationships between slave and master. In most countries slavery is more short-term and dangerous.

How Many Slaves?

No one knows how many slaves are in the world. Slavery is illegal in virtually every country, and that means it is usually hidden from view. But if we carefully review all the information available about slaves around the world, we can estimate that there are perhaps 27 million slaves alive today. Where are all these slaves? The biggest part of that 27 million, perhaps 15 to 20 million, is in India, Pakistan, and Nepal. Slavery also is concentrated in Southeast Asia, in Northern and Western Africa, and in parts of South America, but there are some slaves in almost every country in the world, including the United States, Japan, and many European countries. To put it in perspective, today's slave population is greater than the population of Canada and six times greater than the population of Israel.

Slaves tend to be used in simple, nontechnological, traditional work. The largest proportion works in agriculture. Other kinds of work include brick making, mining and quarrying, textiles, leather working, prostitution, gem working and jewelry making, cloth and carpet making, domestic servantry, forest clearing, charcoal making, and working in shops. Much of this work is aimed at local sale and consumption, but slave-made goods filter throughout the global economy. Carpets, fireworks, jewelry, metal goods, steel (made with slave-produced charcoal), and foods like grains, rice, and sugar are imported directly to North America and Europe after being produced using slave labor. In countries where slavery and industry coexist, cheap slave-made goods and food keep factory wages low and help make everything from toys to computers less expensive.

The Nature of Contemporary Slavery

As a human relationship, slavery has changed over time. Of course, slavery remains the same in that one person has complete control of another person, but exactly how that happens changes from time to time and place to place. Slavery today is different from slavery in the past in three important ways. First, slaves today are cheaper than they have ever been. The cost of slaves has fallen to a historical low, and they can be acquired in some parts of the world for as little as $10. Second, the length of time that slaves are held has also fallen. In the past, slavery was usually a lifelong condition; today it is often temporary, lasting just a few years or even months. Third, slavery is globalized. This means that the forms of slavery in different parts of the world are becoming more alike. The way slaves are used and the part they play in the world economy is increasingly similar wherever they are. These changes have come about very quickly, occurring, for the most part, in the past fifty years. What has made these new forms of slavery possible?

How Slavery Changed into Its Modern Form

There are three key factors in the emergence of this new kind of slavery. The first is the *dramatic increase in world population* since World War II, which has increased the supply of potential slaves. In a classic example of "supply and demand," the increase in population has also driven down their price. Since 1945 the world population has tripled from about 2 billion people to over 6 billion. The greatest part of that increase has been in those countries where slavery is most prevalent today. Across Southeast Asia, the Indian subcontinent, Africa, and the Arab countries, the population boom has more than tripled populations and flooded countries with children. Over half the population in some countries is under the age of fifteen. In countries that were already poor, the sheer weight of numbers sometimes overwhelms resources. Especially in those parts of the world where slavery still existed or had been practiced in the past, the population explosion radically increased the number of people who could be enslaved and drove down their price.

The second key factor is *rapid social and economic change*. This has been caused in part by the population explosion, which created global conditions that make new forms of slavery possible. In many developing countries the postcolonial period brought immense wealth to the elite and continued or increased the poverty of the majority of the population. Throughout Africa and Asia, the past fifty years have been scarred by civil war and the wholesale looting of resources by dictators, who were often supported by the powerful nations of Europe and North America. Countries with little to sell on the world market have been put deeply into debt to pay for the weapons the dictators needed to hold on to power. Meanwhile, traditional ways of agricultural life and farming were sacrificed to concentrate on cash crops needed to pay off those foreign debts. As the world economy grew and became more global, it had a profound impact on people in the Third World and the small-scale farming that supported them. The shift from small-scale farming to cash-crop agriculture, the loss of common land shared by all the people in a village, and government policies that pushed down farm income in favor of cheap food for city workers have all helped to bankrupt millions of peasants and drive them from their land. All across the Third World the slums and shantytowns that surround big cities hold millions of these displaced people. They come to the cities in search of jobs but find they are competing for jobs with thousands of other people. With little income and no job security, they are powerless and very vulnerable.

Some national and global policies and trends also threaten these vulnerable displaced people. Although economic modernization may have good effects as well, particularly in improvements to health care and education, the political focus in many developing countries concentrates on economic growth rather than on sustainable livelihoods for the majority of people. So while the rich of the developing world grow richer, the poor have fewer and fewer options, and in the disruption that comes with rapid social change, slavery can become one of those options.

Government corruption is the third key that supports this new form of slavery. Just having large numbers of vulnerable people doesn't automatically make them slaves. In order to turn vulnerable people into slaves on any scale, violence must be used. One of the basic ideas about democratic government is that it should have a monopoly on the means of violence. The military and the police are generally the only ones who can use weapons and commit violence legally. Normally they do so to protect citizens from crime, including criminal or illegal violence. But if anyone in a society can use violence freely for their own ends, without fear of being arrested and locked up, then they can force others into slavery. To do that on any scale requires government corruption, especially police corruption. In some countries the police act as slave catchers, pursuing and punishing escaped slaves. Often police require that people holding slaves pay them weekly for police "protection." For the slave-using businessperson, payments to the police are just a normal part of business. When laws against kidnapping are not enforced, those who have the means of violence (often the police themselves) can harvest slaves.

Old and New Slavery Compared

The population boom, the vulnerability of poor people in the Third World, and government corruption have led to new forms of slavery. For the first time in human history there is an absolute glut of potential slaves. It is a dramatic example of supply and demand. There are so many possible slaves that their value has fallen and fallen. Slaves are now so cheap that they have become cost-effective in many kinds of work. Their value is so low that it has completely changed the way they are

seen and used. Slaves are no longer major investments. This fact has changed the nature of the relationship between slaves and slaveholders. It has also dramatically changed the amount of profit to be made from a slave as well as the length of time a person might be enslaved. And it has made the question of legal ownership less important. When slaves were expensive, it was important to safeguard that investment by having clear and legally documented ownership. Slaves of the past were worth stealing and worth chasing down if they escaped. Today slaves are so cheap that they are not worth securing permanent ownership. The fact that ownership of slaves is now illegal is not really a problem for slaveholders; slaves are disposable.

Disposability means that the new forms of slavery are less permanent. Across the world the length of time a slaves spends in bondage varies enormously. It is simply not profitable to keep slaves when they are not immediately useful. Although most are enslaved for years, some are held for only a few months. In countries where sugarcane is grown, for example, people are often enslaved for a single harvest. Since they are used only for a short time, there is no reason to insure that they survive their enslavement. Although slaves in the American South in the nineteenth century were often horribly treated, there was still a strong incentive to keep them alive as long as possible. Slaves were like valuable livestock; the owner needed to make back his investment. There was also pressure to breed them and produce more slaves, since it was usually cheaper to raise new slaves than to buy adults. Today no slaveholder wants to spend money supporting useless infants.

The key differences between old and new forms of slavery are these:

Old Forms of Slavery	New Forms of Slavery
Legal ownership asserted	Legal ownership avoided
High purchase cost	Very low purchase cost
Low profits	Very high profits
Shortage of potential slaves	Surplus of potential slaves
Long-term relationship	Short-term relationship
Slaves maintained	Slaves disposable
Ethnic differences important	Ethnic differences less important

*   *   *   *   *

The Question of Race

In the new forms of slavery, race means little. Ethnic and racial differences were used in the past to explain and excuse slavery. These differences allowed slaveholders to make up reasons why slavery was acceptable and even benefited the slaves. The *otherness* of the slaves made it easier to use the violence and the cruelty necessary for total control. This otherness could be defined in almost any way—a different religion, or tribe, or skin color, or language, or customs, or economic class. Any of these could be used to separate the slaves from the slaveholders. Maintaining these differences required tremendous investment in some very irrational ideas, and the crazier the justifying idea, the more strongly it was insisted upon. The "Founding Fathers" of the United States of America had to go through moral, linguistic, and political contortions to explain why the "land of the free" only applied to white people.[1] Many of them knew they were lying, that they were betraying their most cherished ideals. They were driven to it because slavery was worth a lot of money to a lot of people in Colonial America. They still went to the trouble of legal and political justification because back then they felt they had to make moral excuses for their economic decisions.

Today the morality of money overrides most others. Most slaveholders feel no need to explain or defend their choice to use slavery. Slavery is a very profitable business, and a good profit is reason enough. Freed of ideas that restrict the status of slave to "other" and of ideas that say you can't enslave your own people, modern slaveholders use other criteria to choose slaves. When you can enslave people from your own country, your costs are low. Slaves in the American South were very expensive, in part due to the fact that the first generation of them had to be shipped thousands of miles from Africa. When you can go to the next town or region for slaves, transport costs fall to a minimum. The question isn't "Are they the right color to be slaves?" but "Are they vulnerable enough to be enslaved?" The criteria of enslavement is not about color, tribe, or religion; it is about weakness, gullibility, and vulnerability.

It is true that in some countries there are ethnic or religious differences between slaves and slaveholders. In Pakistan, for example, many enslaved brick makers are Christians, and the slaveholders are Muslim. In India slave and slaveholder may be of different castes. In Thailand they might come from different regions of the country. But in Pakistan there are Christians who are not slaves, and in India some members of a caste are free while others are enslaved. Their caste or religion simply reflects their vulnerability to enslavement; it doesn't cause it. Only in one country, Mauritania, does the racism of old slavery persist. In Mauritania, black slaves are held by Arab slaveholders and race is a key division, but this is the last and fading survival of old slavery. Of course, some cultures are more divisive than others. Cultural ideas in Japan very strongly separate Japanese people from everyone else, and so enslaved prostitutes in Japan are more likely to be Thai or Philippine women, though they may also be Japanese. The key difference is that Japanese women are not nearly so vulnerable and desperate as Thais or Filipinas. And the Thai women are avail-

able for shipment to Japan because Thais are enslaving Thais. The same pattern occurs in the oil-rich states of Saudi Arabia and Kuwait, where Muslim Arabs might enslave Sri Lankan Hindus, Filipino Christians, or Nigerian Muslims. The common denominator is poverty, not color. Behind every assertion of ethnic difference is the reality of economic disparity. If every left-handed person in the world were made destitute tomorrow, there would soon be slaveholders arguing that slavery was perhaps the best thing for them. Modern slaveholders are color blind, but they are predators acutely perceptive to weakness. Although slavery has been around for thousands of years, these predators are rapidly adapting it to the new global economy.

* * * * *

Examples of Contemporary Slavery

Lives Up in Smoke

In a recent survey over a third of all American high school students said that they used tobacco at least once in the last month. That students should be doing something so stupid is alarming, but what is even worse is that many of them were supporting slavery as they smoked. Almost 300,000 students said that they had been smoking *beedis*, small flavored cigarettes from India. Would they have done so if they knew that most beedis are made by slave children?

In the southern Indian state of Tamil Nadu, outside the big city of Madras, are small towns where millions of beedis are made. On the outskirts of one of these towns lives an eleven-year-old boy named Vikram. He and many of the other children in his town are slaves. When Vikram was nine his younger brother became very ill. His family is very poor, and the only way his parents could buy medicine was to borrow money from a local man. This man controls the production of beedis in their village. This moneylender used the loan as a way to take Vikram into debt bondage. Since Vikram's parents had nothing else to give as collateral, the moneylender said they must pledge Vikram against the debt. His parents' choice was a terrible one: to save the life of their youngest son, they must put their oldest son into bondage. For the moneylender it was business as usual, and he had obtained another slave for just a few dollars. Today none of the work that Vikram does pays off the debt. He is basically the property of the moneylender until his parents can find the money for repayment. Two years after it was first made, the debt has grown with extra charges to about $65.

Vikram works from six in the morning until nine at night, with breaks for breakfast and lunch. Each day he rolls about 1,500 beedi cigarettes by hand. Each beedi is smaller than a normal cigarette, and instead of paper the tobacco is wrapped in a leaf from the kendu tree. Since no glue is used, each beedi must be tied shut with a thread and a tiny knot. Sitting cross-legged on the floor with a tray of tobacco and kendu leaves on his lap, Vikram's hands fly through the motions of wrapping, rolling, and tying the beedis. He has to work very quickly, like a machine, if he is to make the number required of him every day. If he is sick, he still has to work, and if he fails to deliver the full number, his debt will be increased. He can watch the world, or a very small piece of it, from the porch where he sits rolling the beedis, but he cannot be part of it. Some of the local children go off to school in the mornings; he sees them go as he rolls beedi. In the afternoon other children play around the village, and Vikram watches but cannot join in. His childhood has been taken by the moneylender to provide virtually free labor and high profits.

In some ways Vikram's slavery could be worse. At night he is allowed to go home for supper and to sleep with his family. Of course, this is very clever of the moneylender, since it means that he doesn't have to provide food or lodging for his slave. Vikram, like so many modern slaves, was very cheap to buy and is also very cheap to maintain. Until recently a boy in Vikram's position would have little to look forward to except years spent rolling beedis. Many children have had their whole childhood taken by beedi rolling. When they become young adults the moneylender will often turn them to other kinds of work, since their larger hands are not as nimble for rolling beedis. When they finally stop rolling beedis, they are young men with no education and little experience of the world. Their job prospects, if they can get away from the moneylender, are dismal.

Slavery in the City of Lights

In France I interviewed an animated twenty-two-year-old woman, who told me of her life as a slave in Paris:

I was raised by my grandmother in Mali, and when I was still a little girl a woman my family knew came and asked her if she could take me to Paris to care for her children. She told my grandmother that she would put me in school and that I would learn French. But when I came to Paris I was not sent to school, I had to work every day. In their house I did all the work, I cleaned the house, cooked the meals, cared for the children, and washed and fed the baby. Every day I started work before 7 a.m. and finished about 11 p.m.; I never had a day off. My mistress did nothing—she slept late and then watched television or went out.

One day I told her that I wanted to go to school. She replied that she had not brought me to France to go to school but to take care of her children. I was so tired and run down. I had problems with my teeth; sometimes my cheek would swell and the pain would be terrible. Sometimes I had stomachaches, but when I was ill I still had to work. Sometimes when I was in pain I would cry, but my mistress would shout at me.

I slept on the floor in one of the children's bedrooms; my food was their leftovers. I was not allowed to take food from the refrigerator like the children. If I took food she would beat me. She often beat me. She would slap me all the time. She beat me with the broom, with kitchen tools, or whipped me with an electric cable. Sometimes I would bleed. I still have marks on my body.

Once in 1992 I was late going to get the children from school. My mistress and her husband were furious with me and beat and then threw me out on the street. I had nowhere to go, I didn't understand anything, and I wandered on the streets. After some time her husband found me and took me back to their house. Then they beat me again with a wire attached to a broomstick until I lost consciousness.

Sometime later one of the children came and untied me. I lay on the floor where they had left me for several days. The pain was terrible but no one treated my wounds. When I was able to stand I had to start work again, but after this I was always locked in the apartment. They continued to beat me.

Seba was finally freed when a neighbor, after hearing the sounds of abuse and beating, managed to talk to her. Seeing her scars and wounds, the neighbor called the police and the French Committee Against Modern Slavery (CCEM), which brought a case against Seba's abusers and took Seba into care. Medical examinations confirmed she had been tortured. Today Seba is well cared for, living with a volunteer family. She is receiving counseling and learning to read and write. Recovery will take years, but she is a remarkably strong young woman. What amazed me was how far Seba still needs to go. As we talked I realized that though she was twenty-two and intelligent, her understanding of the world was less developed than the average five-year-old's. For example, until she was freed she had little understanding of time—no knowledge of weeks, months, or years. For Seba there was only the endless round of work and sleep. She knew that there were hot days and cold days, but she never learned that the seasons follow a pattern. If she had once known her birthday she had since forgotten it, and she did not know her age. She is baffled by the idea of "choice." Her volunteer family tries to help her make choices, but she still can't grasp the concept. [...]

If Seba's case were unique it would be shocking enough, but Seba is one of perhaps three thousand household slaves in Paris. Nor is this slavery unique to Paris. In London, New York, Zurich, Los Angeles, and across the world children are brutalized as household slaves. And they are just one small group of the world's slaves.

* * * * *

Liberation and Rehabilitation

The human and economic relationships of modern slavery are complex. It would be so much easier to understand and combat slavery if there were very clear good guys and bad guys, if all slaveholders were cruel and all slaves yearned for freedom, if the solution to all slavery were simply to set slaves free. But being free means more than just walking away from bondage. Liberation is a bitter victory if it only leads to starvation and re-enslavement. Freedom is both a mental realization and a physical condition. Ultimately, slaves have to find their own way into true freedom. The physical and psychological dependence they often felt toward their masters can make this a long process. If we expect an abused child to need years of therapy and guidance to overcome trauma, we can hardly expect equally abused slaves to enter society immediately as full citizens. It is true that many ex-slaves are phenomenally resilient, but the worst abused may need a lifetime of care. In the struggle to survive not just slavery but liberation, there is one striking parallel between the old slavery of the United States and the new slavery of today: When slavery came to an end in 1865 the slaves were just dumped; and so it is with slaves today. If slavery is to end, we must learn how ex-slaves can best secure their own freedom.

Liberation brings new problems. A lifetime of dependence cannot be swept away in an instant. A person denied autonomy, who has never had to make choices, can be paralyzed when confronting decisions. If we can learn anything from the lives of freed slaves, it is that liberation is a process, not an event. If we are serious about stopping slavery, we have to be committed to supporting freed slaves in a process that can take years. It means thinking very carefully about what slaves need in order to achieve true freedom. For example, we have to consider how to help slaves as people. What kind of care do slaves and ex-slaves need to attain a sense of free-

dom and personhood? Unfortunately, we know very little about the psychology of slavery or how to help its victims. To end slavery we will have to become experts in repairing the damage slavery brings to both mind and body.

We will also have to become experts in slaves as economic beings. Slaves have few skills. The jobs they do as slaves are not usually worth much on the free market. But if they are freed and can't support themselves, how will they avoid being enslaved again? Small children are dependent on their parents, who often expect them to do simple tasks around the house. Slaves are kept in a state of permanent dependence and are normally prevented from learning all but the most simple tasks. No one would dream of dropping an eight-year-old into the job market to compete for his or her livelihood, but this has happened to thousands of freed slaves. Around the world, only a tiny handful of people work to understand and build new economic routes from slavery to self-sufficiency. The economic process of becoming self-supporting parallels the growth to psychological independence.

From psychology to small-scale economics to large-scale law enforcement, much more research and development is needed. From the little work that has been done, it seems that there are several ways to help people to stay free: helping them to make the psychological adjustment to freedom; giving them access to credit; letting ex-slaves make their own decisions about what work they will do; overcoming corruption in the rehabilitation programs; the presence and oversight of powerful people on the side of ex-slaves; and the greatest of liberators, education.

Notes

Parts of this chapter have been adapted or excerpted from my book *Disposable People: New Slavery in the Global Economy* (Berkeley: University of California Press, 1999) by permission of the publisher.

1 See, for example, Benjamin Quarles, *The Negro in the American Revolution*, 1961; and David Brion Davis, *The Problem of Slavery in the Age of Revolution 1770–1823*, 1975.

References

Genovese, Eugene. *Roll, Jordan, Roll: The World the Slaves Made* (New York: Vintage, 1976).

Greider, William. *One World Ready or Not: The Manic Logic of Global Capitalism* (New York: Simon and Schuster, 1997).

Ransom, Roger L. *Conflict and Compromise: The Political Economy of Slavery, Emancipation, and the American Civil War* (Cambridge: Cambridge University Press, 1989).

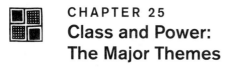

CHAPTER 25

Class and Power: The Major Themes

JOHN PORTER

The Canadian Middle Class Image

One of the most persistent images that Canadians have of their society is that it has no classes. This image becomes translated into the assertion that Canadians are all relatively equal in their possessions, in the amount of money they earn, and in the opportunities which they and their children have to get on in the world. An important element in this image of classlessness is that, with the absence of formal aristocracy and aristocratic institutions, Canada is a society in which equalitarian values have asserted themselves over authoritarian values. Canada, it is thought, shares not only a continent with the United States, but also a democratic ideology which rejects the historical class and power structures of Europe.

Social images are one thing and social realities another. Yet the two are not completely separate. Social images are not entirely fictional characters with only a coincidental likeness to a real society, living or dead. Often the images can be traced to an earlier historical period of the society, its golden age perhaps, which, thanks to the historians, is held up, long after it has been transformed into something else, as a model way of life. As well as their historical sources, images can be traced to their contemporary creators, particularly in the world of the mass media and popular culture. When a society's writers, journalists, editors, and other image-creators are a relatively small and closely linked group, and have more or less the same social background, the images they produce can, because they are consistent, appear to be much more true to life than if their group were larger, less cohesive, and more heterogeneous in composition.

The historical source of the image of a classless Canada is the equality among pioneers in the frontier environment of the last century. In the early part of the present century there was a similar equality of status among those who were settlers in the west, although, as we shall see, these settlers were by no means treated equally. A rural, agricultural, primary producing society is a much less differentiated society than one which has highly concentrated industries in large cities. Equality in the rural society may be much more apparent than real, but the rural environment has been for Canada an important source of the image of equality. Later we shall examine more closely how the historical image has become out of date with the transformation of Canadian society from the rural to the urban type.

Although the historical image of rural equality lingers it has gradually given way in the urban industrial setting to an image of a middle level classlessness in which there is a general uniformity of possessions. For families these possessions include a separate dwelling with an array of electrical equipment, a car, and perhaps a summer cottage. Family members, together or as individuals, engage in a certain amount of ritualistic behaviour in churches and service clubs. Modern advertising has done much to standardize the image of middle class consumption levels and middle class behaviour. Consumers' magazines are devoted to the task of constructing the ideal way of life through articles on childrearing, homemaking, sexual behaviour, health, sports, and hobbies. Often, too, corporations which do not produce family commodities directly will have large advertisements to demonstrate how general social well-being at this middle level is an outcome of their own operations.

That there is neither very rich nor very poor in Canada is an important part of the image. There are no barriers to opportunity. Education is free. Therefore, making use of it is largely a question of personal ambition. Even university education is available to all, except that it may require for some a little more summer work and thrift. There is a view widely held by many university graduates that they, and most other graduates, have worked their way through college. Consequently it is felt anyone else can do the same.

In some superficial respects the image of middle class uniformity may appear plausible. The main values of the society are concerned with the consumption of commodities, and in the so-called affluence that has followed World War II there seem to have been commodities for everybody, except, perhaps, a small group of the permanently poor at the bottom. Credit facilities are available for large numbers of low income families, enabling them, too, to be consumers of commodities over and above the basic necessities of life. The vast array of credit facilities, some of them extraordinarily ingenious, have inequalities built

199

into them, in that the cost of borrowing money varies with the amount already possessed. There are vast differences in the quality of goods bought by the middle income levels and the lower income levels. One commodity, for instance, which low income families can rarely purchase is privacy, particularly the privacy of a house to themselves. It is perhaps the value of privacy and the capacity to afford it which has become the dividing line between the real and the apparent middle class.

If low income families achieve high consumption levels it is usually through having more than one income earner in the household. Often this is the wife and mother, but it may be an older child who has left school, and who is expected to contribute to the family budget. Alternatively, high consumption levels may be achieved at a cost in leisure. Many low income family heads have two jobs, a possibility which has arisen with the shorter working day and the five-day week. This "moonlighting," as it is called in labour circles, tends to offset the progress which has been made in raising the level of wages and reducing the hours of work. There is no way of knowing how extensive "moonlighting" is, except that we know that trade unions denounce it as a practice which tends to take away the gains which have been obtained for workers. For large segments of the population, therefore, a high level of consumption is obtained by means which are alien to a true middle class standard. In a later chapter where we shall examine closely the distribution of income we shall see what a small proportion of Canadian families were able to live a middle class style of life in the middle 1950s, the high tide of post-war affluence.

At the high end of the social class spectrum, also in contrast to the middle level image, are the families of great wealth and influence. They are not perhaps as ostentatious as the very wealthy of other societies, and Canada has no "celebrity world" with which these families must compete for prestige in the way Mills has suggested is important for the very rich in American society.[1]

Almost every large Canadian city has its wealthy and prominent families of several generations. They have their own social life, their children go to private schools, they have their clubs and associations, and they take on the charitable and philanthropic roles which have so long been the "duty" of those of high status. Although this upper class is always being joined by the new rich, it still contributes, as we shall see later, far more than its proportionate share to the elite of big business. The concentration of wealth in the upper classes is indicated by the fact that in Canada in 1955 the top one per cent of income recipients received about 40 per cent of all income from dividends [....]

Images which conflict with the one of middle class equality rarely find expression, partly because the literate middle class is both the producer and the consumer of the image. Even at times in what purports to be serious social analysis, middle class intellectuals project the image of their own class onto the social classes above and below them. There is scarcely any critical analysis of Canadian social life upon which a conflicting image could be based. The idea of class differences has scarcely entered into the stream of Canadian academic writing despite the fact that class differences stand in the way of implementing one of the most important values of western society, that is equality.[2] The fact, which we shall see later, that Canada draws its intellectuals either from abroad or from its own middle class, means that there is almost no one producing a view of the world which reflects the experience of the poor or the underprivileged. It was as though they did not exist. [...]

Closely related to differences in class levels are differences in the exercising of power and decision-making in the society. Often it is thought that once a society becomes an electoral democracy based on universal suffrage power becomes diffused throughout the general population so that everyone participates somehow in the selection of social goals. There is, however, a whole range of institutional resistances to the transfer of power to a democratic political system. [...]

Notes

[1] C.W. Mills, *The Power Elite* (New York, 1956), chap. 4.

[2] Nor does class appear as a theme in Canadian literature. See R.L. McDougall, "The Dodo and the Cruising Auk," *Canadian Literature*, no. 18 (Autumn 1963).

SECTION
4B Gender

CHAPTER 26
The Many Faces of Gender Inequality

AMARTYA SEN

1.

It was more than a century ago, in 1870, that Queen Victoria wrote to Sir Theodore Martin complaining about "this mad, wicked folly of 'Women's Rights.'" The formidable empress certainly did not herself need any protection that the acknowledgement of women's rights might offer. Even at the age of eighty, in 1899, she could write to Arthur James Balfour that "we are not interested in the possibilities of defeat; they do not exist." Yet that is not the way most people's lives go, reduced and defeated as they frequently are by adversities. And within every community, nationality, and class, the burden of hardship often falls disproportionately on women.

The afflicted world in which we live is characterized by a deeply unequal sharing of the burden of adversities between women and men. Gender inequality exists in most parts of the world, from Japan to Morocco, from Uzbekistan to the United States. Yet inequality between women and men is not everywhere the same. It can take many different forms. Gender inequality is not one homogeneous phenomenon, but a collection of disparate and inter-linked problems. I will discuss just a few of the varieties of the disparity between the genders.

Mortality inequality. In some regions in the world, inequality between women and men directly involves matters of life and death, and takes the brutal form of unusually high mortality rates for women and a consequent preponderance of men in the total population, as opposed to the preponderance of women found in societies with little or no gender bias in health care and nutrition. Mortality inequality has been observed and documented extensively in North Africa and in Asia, including China and South Asian nations.

Natality inequality. Given the preference for boys over girls that characterizes many male-dominated societies, gender inequality can manifest itself in the form of parents' wanting a baby to be a boy rather than a girl. There was a time when this could be no more than a wish—a daydream or a nightmare, depending on one's perspective. But with the availability of modern techniques to determine the gender of a fetus, sex-selective abortion has become common in many countries. It is especially prevalent in East Asia, in China and South Korea in particular; but it is found also in Singapore and Taiwan, and it is beginning to emerge as a statistically significant phenomenon in India and in other parts of South Asia as well. This is high-tech sexism.

Basic-facility inequality. Even when demographic characteristics do not show much anti-female bias or any at all, there are other ways in which women can get less than a square deal. Afghanistan may be the only country in the world where the government is keen on actively excluding girls from schooling (the Taliban regime combines this with other features of massive gender inequality); but there are many countries in Asia and Africa, and also in Latin America, where girls have far less opportunity for schooling than do boys. And there are other deficiencies in basic facilities available to women, varying from encouragement to cultivate one's natural talents to fair participation in social functions of the community.

Special-opportunity inequality. Even when there is relatively little difference in basic facilities including schooling, the opportunities for higher education may be far fewer for young women than for young men. Indeed, gender bias in higher education and professional training can be observed even in some of the richest countries in the world, in Europe and North America. Sometimes this type of asymmetry has been based on the superficially innocuous idea that the respective "provinces" of men and women are just different. This thesis has been championed in different forms over the centuries, and it has always enjoyed a great implicit, as well as explicit, following. It was presented with particular directness more than one hundred years before Queen Victoria's complaint about "woman's rights" by the Reverend James Fordyce in his *Sermons to Young Women* (1766), a book that, as Mary Wollstonecraft noted in *A Vindication of the Rights of Woman* (1792), had been "long made a part of woman's library." Fordyce warned the young women to whom his sermons were addressed against "those masculine women that would plead for your sharing any part of their province with us," identifying the province of men as including not only "war," but also "commerce, politics, exercises of strength and dexterity, abstract philosophy and all the abstruser sciences." Such clear-cut beliefs about the province of men and women are now rather rare, but the presence of extensive gender asymmetry can be seen in many areas of education, training, and professional work even in Europe and North America.

Professional inequality. In employment as well as promotion in work and occupation, women often face greater handicaps than men. A country such as Japan may be quite egalitarian in matters of demography or basic facilities, and even to a great extent in higher education, and yet progress to elevated levels of employment and occupation seems to be much more problematic for women than for men. In the English television series *Yes, Minister*, there was an episode in which the Minister, full of reforming zeal, is trying to ascertain from the immovable permanent secretary, Sir Humphrey, how many women are in senior positions in the British civil service. Sir Humphrey says that it is very difficult to give an exact number; it would require a lot of investigation. The Minister is insistent, and wants to know approximately how many women are in these senior positions. To which Sir Humphrey finally replies, "Approximately, none."

Ownership inequality. In many societies, the ownership of property can also be very unequal. Even basic assets such as homes and land may be very asymmetrically shared. The absence of claims to property can not only reduce the voice of women, it can also make it harder for women to enter and to flourish in commercial, economic, and even some social activities. Inequality in property ownership is quite widespread across the world, but its severity can vary with local rules. In India, for example, traditional inheritance laws were heavily weighed in favor of male children (until the legal reforms after independence), but the community of Nairs (a large caste in Kerala) has had matrilineal inheritance for a very long time.

Household inequality. Often there are fundamental inequalities in gender relations within the family or the household. This can take many different forms. Even in cases in which there are no overt signs of anti-female bias in, say, mortality rates, or male preference in births, or in education, or even in promotion to higher executive positions, family arrangements can be quite unequal in terms of sharing the burden of housework and child care. It is quite common in many societies to take for granted that men will naturally work outside the home, whereas women could do so if and only if they could combine such work with various inescapable and unequally shared household duties. This is sometimes called a "division of labor," though women could be forgiven for seeing it as an "accumulation of labor." The reach of this inequality includes not only unequal relations within the family, but also derivative inequalities in employment and recognition in the outside world. Also, the established persistence of this type of "division" or "accumulation" of labor can also have far-reaching effects on the knowledge and the understanding of different types of work in professional circles. In the 1970s, when I first started working on gender inequality, I remember being struck by the fact that the Handbook of Human Nutrition Requirements of the World Health Organization, in presenting "calorie requirements" for different categories of people, chose to classify household work as "sedentary activity," requiring very little deployment of energy. I was not able to determine precisely how this remarkable bit of information had been collected.

2.

It is important to take note of the implications of the varieties of gender inequality. The variations entail that inequality between women and men cannot be confronted and overcome by one all-purpose remedy. Over time, moreover, the same country can move from one type of gender inequality to another. I shall presently argue that there is new evidence that India, my own country, is undergoing just such a transformation at this time. The different forms of gender inequality may also impose adversities on the lives of men and boys, in addition to those of women and girls. In understanding the different aspects of the evil of gender inequality, we have to look beyond the predicament of women and examine the problems created for men as well by the asymmetrical treatment of women. These causal connections can be very significant, and they can vary with the form of gender inequality. Finally, inequalities of different kinds can frequently nourish one another, and we have to be aware of their linkages.

In what follows, a substantial part of my empirical focus will be on two of the most elementary kinds of gender inequality: mortality inequality and natality inequality. I shall be concerned particularly with gender inequality in South Asia, the so-called Indian subcontinent. While I shall separate out the subcontinent for special attention, I must warn against the smugness of thinking that the United States and Western Europe are free from gender bias simply because some of the empirical generalizations that can be made about other regions of the world would not hold in the West. Given the many faces of gender inequality, much depends on which face we look at.

Consider the fact that India, along with Bangladesh, Pakistan, and Sri Lanka, has had female heads of government, which the United States and Japan have not yet had (and do not seem very likely to have in the immediate future, if I am any judge). Indeed, in the case of Bangladesh, where both the prime minister and the lead of the opposition are women, one might begin to wonder whether any man could soon rise to a leadership position there. To take another bit of anecdotal evidence against Western complacence in this matter: I had a vastly larger proportion of tenured women colleagues when I was a professor at Delhi University—as long ago as the 1960s—than I had in the 1990s at Harvard University or presently have at Trinity College, Cambridge. And another example, of a more personal kind: when I was searching, a few years ago, for an early formulation of the contrast between the instrumental importance of wealth and the intrinsic value of human life, I found such a view in the words of Maitreyee, a woman intellectual depicted in the Upanishads, which date from the eight century B.C.E. The classic formulation of this distinction, of course, would come about four centuries later, in Aristotle's *Nicomacheon Ethics*; but it is interesting that the first sharp formulation of the value of living should have come from a woman thinker in a society that has not yet—three thousand years later—been able to overcome the mortality differential between women and men. In the scale of mortality inequality, India is close to the bottom of the league in gender disparity, along with Pakistan and Bangladesh; and natality inequality is also beginning to rear its ugly head very firmly and very fast in the subcontinent in our own day.

In the bulk of the subcontinent, with only a few exceptions (such as Sri Lanka and the state of Kerala in India), female mortality rates are very significantly higher than what could be expected given the mortality patterns of men (in the respective age groups). This type of gender inequality need not entail any conscious homicide, and it would be a mistake to try to explain this large phenomenon by invoking the cases of female infanticide that are reported from China or India: those are truly dreadful events, but they are relatively rare. The mortality disadvantage of women works, rather, mainly through the widespread neglect of health, nutrition and other interests of women that influence their survival.

It is sometimes presumed that there are more women than men in the world, since such a preponderance is well known to be the case in Europe and North America, which have an average female-to-male ratio of 1.05 or so (that is, about 105 women to 100 men). Yet women do not outnumber men in the world as a whole. Indeed, there are only about 98 women per 100 men on the globe. This "shortfall" of women is most acute in Asia and North Africa. The number of females per 100 males in the total population is 97 in Egypt and Iran, 95 in Bangladesh and Turkey, 94 in China, 93 in India and Pakistan, and 84 in Saudi Arabia (though the last ratio is considerably reduced by the presence of male migrant workers from elsewhere in Asia).

It has been widely observed that given similar health care and nutrition, women tend typically to have lower age-specific mortality rates than men. Indeed, even female fetuses tend to have a lower probability of miscarriage than male fetuses. Everywhere in the world, more male babies are born than female babies (and an even higher proportion of male fetuses are conceived compared with female fetuses); but throughout their respective lives the proportion of males goes on falling as we move to higher and higher age groups, due to typically greater male mortality rates. The excess of females over males in the populations of Europe and North America comes about as a result of this greater survival chance of females in different age groups.

In many parts of the world, however, women receive less attention and health care than do men, and girls in particular often receive very much less support than boys. As a result of this gender bias, the mortality rates of females often exceed those of males in these countries. The concept of the "missing women" was devised to give some idea of the enormity of the phenomenon of women's adversity in mortality by focusing on the women who are simply not there, owing to mortality rates that are unusually high compared with male mortality rates. The basic idea is to find some rough and ready way to understand the quantitative difference between the actual number of women that we could expect to see if the gender pattern of mortality were similar there to the patterns in other regions of the world that do not demonstrate a significant bias against women in health care and other attentions relevant for survival.

We may take the ratio of women to men in sub-Saharan Africa as the standard, since there is relatively little bias against women in health care, social status, and mortality rates there, even though the absolute numbers are quite dreadful for both men and women. When estimating the size of the phenomenon of "missing women" in the mid-1980s, I used the prevailing female-male ratio in sub-Saharan Africa, around 1,022, as the standard. For example, with India's female-male ratio of 0.93, there is a total difference of 9 percent (of the male population) between that ratio and the sub-Saharan standard used for comparison. In 1986, this yielded a figure of 37 million missing women. Using the same sub-Saharan standard, China had 44 million missing women; and it became evident that, for the world as a whole, the magnitude of the gender shortfall easily exceeded 100 million. Other standards and other methods may also be used: Ansley Coale and Stephan Klasen have arrived at somewhat different numbers, but invariably very large ones. (Klasen's total number is about 80 million missing women.) So gender bias in mortality takes an astonishingly heavy toll.

How can this be reversed? Some economic models have tended to relate the neglect of women to the lack of economic empowerment of women. Ester Boserup, an early feminist economist, in her classic book *Women's Role in Economic Development*, published in 1970, discussed how the status and the standing of women are enhanced by economic independence (such as gainful employment). Others have tried to link the neglect of girls to the higher economic returns for the family from boys compared with girls. I believe that the former line of reasoning, which takes fuller note of social considerations that take us beyond any hard-headed calculation of relative returns from rearing girls vis-à-vis boys, is broader and more promising; but no matter which interpretation is taken, women's gainful employment, especially in more rewarding occupations, clearly does play a role in improving the life prospects of women and girls. So, too, does women's literacy. And there are other factors that can be seen as adding to the standing and to the voice of women in family decisions.

The experience of the state of Kerala in India is instructive in this matter. Kerala provides a sharp contrast with many other parts of the country in having little or no gender bias in mortality. The life expectancy of Kerala women at birth is above 76 (compared with 70 for men), and even more remarkably, the female-male ratio of Kerala's population is 1.06 according to the 2001 census, much the same as Europe or North America. Kerala has a population of 30 million, so it is an example that involves a fair number of people. The causal variables related to women's empowerment can be seen as playing a role here, since Kerala has a very high level of women's literacy (nearly universal for the younger age groups), and also much more access for women to well-paid and well-respected jobs.

One of the other influences of women's empowerment, a decline in fertility, is also observed in Kerala, where the fertility rate has fallen very fast (much faster, incidentally, than in China, despite Chinese coercive measures in birth control). The fertility rate in Kerala is 1.7 (roughly interpretable as an average of 1.7 children per couple), and it is one of the lowest in the developing world—about the same as in Britain and in France, and much lower than in the United States. We can see in these observations the general influence of women's education and empowerment.

Yet we must also take note of other special features of Kerala as well, including female ownership of property for an influential part of the Hindu population (the Nairs); openness to, and interaction with, the outside world (Christians form about the one-fifth of the population and have been in Kerala much longer—since the fourth century—than they have been in, say, Britain, not to mention the very old community of Jews in Kerala); and activist left-wing politics with a particularly egalitarian commitment, which has tended to focus strongly on issues of equality (not only between classes and castes, but also between women and men). While these influences may work in the same way as the impact of female education and employment in reducing mortality inequality, they can have different roles in dealing with other problems, particularly the problem of natality inequality.

3.

The problem of gender bias in life and death has been much discussed, but there are other issues of gender inequality that are sorely in need of greater investigation. I will note four substantial phenomena that happen to be quite widely observed in South Asia.

There is, first, the problem of the undernourishment of girls as compared with boys. At the time of birth, girls are obviously no more nutritionally deprived than boys, but this situation changes as society's unequal treatment takes over from the non-discrimination of nature. There has been plenty of aggregative evidence on this for quite some time now; but it has been accompanied by some anthropological skepticism about the appropriateness of using aggregate statistics with pooled data from different regions to interpret the behavior of individual families. Still, there have also been more detailed and concretely local studies on this subject, and they confirm the picture that emerges on the basis of aggregate statistics. One case study from India, which I myself undertook in 1983 along with Sunil Sengupta, involved weighing every child in two large villages. The time pattern that emerged from this study, which concentrated particularly on weight-for-age as the chosen indicator of nutritional level for children under five, showed clearly how an initial neonatal condition of broad nutritional symmetry turns gradually into a situation of significant female disadvantage. The local investigations tend to confirm rather than contradict the picture that emerges from aggregate statistics.

In interpreting the causal process that leads to this female disadvantage, it is important to emphasize that the lower level of nourishment of girls may not relate directly to their being underfed as compared with boys. Often enough, the differences may arise more from the neglect of health care of girls compared with what boys receive. Indeed, there is some direct information about comparative medical neglect of girls vis-à-vis boys in South Asia. When I studied, with Jocelyn Kynch, admissions data from two large public hospitals in Bombay, it was very striking to find clear evidence that the admitted girls were typically more ill than the boys, suggesting that a girl has to be more stricken and more ill before she is taken to the hospital. Undernourishment may well result from a greater incidence of illness, which can adversely affect both the absorption of nutrients and the performance of bodily functions.

There is, secondly, a high incidence of maternal undernourishment in South Asia. Indeed, in this part of the world, maternal undernutrition is much more common than in most other regions. Comparisons of body mass index (BMI), which is essentially a measure of weight for height, bring this out clearly enough, as do statistics of such consequential characteristics as the incidence of anemia.

Thirdly, there is the problem of the prevalence of low birth weight. In South Asia, as many as 21 percent of children are born clinically underweight (by accepted medical standards), more than in any other substantial region in the world. The predicament of being low in weight in childhood seems often enough to begin at birth in the case of South Asian children. In terms of weight for age, around 40 to 60 percent of the children in South Asia are undernourished, compared with 20 to 40 percent undernourishment even in sub-Saharan Africa. The children start deprived and stay deprived. Finally, there is also a higher incidence of cardiovascular diseases. Generally, South Asia stands out as having more cardiovascular diseases than any other part of the Third World. Even when other countries, such as China, show a greater prevalence of the standard predisposing conditions to such illness, the subcontinental population seems to have more heart problems than these other countries.

It is not difficult to see that the first three of these problems are very likely connected causally. The neglect of the care of girls and women, and the underlying gender bias that their experience reflects, would tend to yield more maternal undernourishment; and this in turn would tend to yield more fetal deprivation and distress, and underweight babies, and child undernourishment. But what about the higher incidence of cardiovascular diseases among South Asian adults? In interpreting this phenomenon, we can draw on the pioneering work of a British medical team led by D.J.P. Barker. Based on English data, Barker has shown that low birth weight is closely associated with the higher incidence, many decades later, of several adult diseases, including hypertension, glucose intolerance, and other cardiovascular hazards.

The robustness of the statistical connections and the causal mechanisms involved in the retardation of intra-uterine growth can be further investigated, but as matters stand the medical evidence that Barker has produced linking the two phenomena offers the possibility of proposing a causal relation between the different empirical observations of the harsh fate of girls and women in South Asia and the phenomenon of high incidence of cardiovascular diseases in South Asia. This strongly suggests a causal pattern that goes from the nutritional neglect of women to maternal undernourishment, and thence to fetal growth retardation and underweight babies, and thence to greater incidence of cardiovascular afflictions much later in adult life (along with the phenomenon of undernourished children in the shorter run). In sum: what begins as a neglect of the interests of women ends up causing adversities in the health and the survival of all, even at an advanced age.

These biological connections illustrate a more general point: gender inequality can hurt the interests of men as well as women. Indeed, men suffer far more from cardiovascular diseases than do women. Given the uniquely critical role of women in the reproductive process, it would be hard to imagine that the deprivation to which women are subjected would not have some adverse impact on the lives of all people—men as well as women, adults as well as children—who are "born of a woman," as the Book of Job says. It would appear that the extensive penalties of neglecting the welfare of women rebound on men with a vengeance.

But there are also other connections between the disadvantage of women and the general condition of society—non-biological connections—that operate through women's conscious agency. The expansion of women's capabilities not only enhances women's own freedom and well-being, it also has many other effects on the lives of all. An enhancement of women's active agency can contribute substantially to the lives of men as well as women, children as well as adults: many studies have demonstrated that the greater empowerment of women tends to reduce child neglect and mortality to decrease fertility and overcrowding, and more generally to broaden social concern and care.

These examples can be supplemented by considering the functioning of women in other areas, including in the fields of economics and politics. Substantial linkages between women's agency and social achievements have been noted in many different countries. There is plenty of evidence that whenever social and economic arrangements depart from the standard practice of male ownership, women can seize business and economic initiative with much success. It is also clear that the result of women's participation in economic life is not merely to generate income for women, but also to provide many other social benefits that derive from their enhanced status and independence. The remarkable success of organizations such as the Grameen Bank and BRAC (Bangladesh Rural Advancement Committee) in Bangladesh is a good example of this, and there is some evidence that the high-profile presence of women in social and political life in that country has drawn substantial support from women's economic involvement and from a changed image of the role of women.

The Reverend Fordyces of the world may disapprove of "those masculine women" straying into men's "province," but the character of modern Bangladesh reflects in many different and salutary ways the increasing agency of women. The precipitate fall of the total fertility rate in Bangladesh from 6.1 to 3.0 in the course of two decades (perhaps the fastest such decline in the world) is clearly related to the changed economic and social roles of women, along with increases in family-planning facilities. There have also been cultural influences leading to a re-thinking of the nature of the family as Alaka Basu and Sajeda Amin have shown recently in *Population and Development Review*. Changes can also be observed in parts of India where women's empowerment has expanded, with more literacy and greater economic and social involvements outside the home.

4.

There is something to cheer in the developments that I have been discussing and there is considerable evidence of a weakened hold of gender disparity in several fields in the subcontinent; but the news is not, alas, all good. There is also evidence of a movement in the contrary direction, at least with regard to natality inequality. This has been brought out sharply by the early results of the 2001 decennial national census in India, the results of which are still being tabulated and analyzed. Early results indicate that even though the overall female-male ratio has improved slightly for the country as a whole (with a corresponding reduction of the proportion of "missing women"), the female-male ratio of the population under age six has fallen from 94.5 girls per 100 boys in 1991 to 92.7 girls per 100 boys in 2001. While there has been no such decline in some parts of the country (most notably Kerala), it has fallen very sharply in Punjab, Haryana, Gujarat, and Maharashtra, which are among the richer Indian states.

Taking together all the evidence that exists, it is clear that this change reflects not a rise in female child mortality, but a fall in female birth vis-à-vis male births; and it is almost certainly connected with the increased availability and the greater use of gender determination of fetuses. Fearing that sex-selective abortion might occur in India, the Indian parliament some years ago banned the use of sex determination techniques for fetuses, except as a by-product of other necessary medical investigation. But it appears that the enforcement of this law has been comprehensively neglected. When questioned about the matter by Celia Dugger, the energetic correspondent of *The New York Times*, the police cited difficulties in achieving successful prosecution owing to the reluctance of mothers to give evidence of the use of such techniques.

I do not believe that this need be an insurmountable difficulty (other types of evidence can in fact be used for prosecution), but the reluctance of the mothers to give evidence brings out perhaps the most disturbing aspect of this natality inequality. I refer to the "son preference" that many Indian mothers themselves seem to harbor. This form of gender inequality cannot be removed, at least in the short run, by the enhancement of women's empowerment and agency, since that agency is itself an integral part of the cause of natality inequality.

Policy initiatives have to take adequate note of the fact that the pattern of gender inequality seems to be shifting in India, right at this time, from mortality inequality (the female life expectancy at birth has now become significantly higher than male life expectancy) to natality inequality. And, worse, there is clear evidence that the traditional routes of combating gender inequality, such as the use of public policy to influence female education and female economic participation, may not on their own, serve as a path to the eradication of natality inequality. A sharp pointer in that direction comes from the countries in East Asia that have high levels of female education and economic participation.

Compared with the biologically common ratio across the world of 95 girls being born per 100 boys, Singapore and Taiwan have 92 girls, South Korea only 88, and China a mere 86—their achievements in female empowerment notwithstanding. In fact, South Korea's overall female-male ratio for children is also a meager 88 girls per 100 boys. In comparison, the Indian ratio of 92.7 girls per 100 boys (though lower than its previous figure of 94.5) looks far less unfavorable.

Still, there are reasons for concern. For a start, these may be early days, and it has to be asked whether with the spread of sex-selective abortion India may catch up with—and perhaps even go beyond—Korea and China. Moreover, even now there are substantial variations within India, and the all-India average hides the fact that there are states in India where the female-male ratio for children is very much lower than the Indian average.

Even though sex-selective abortion is to some extent being used in most regions in India, there seems to be something of a social and cultural divide across India, splitting the country in two, in terms of the extent of the practice and the underlying bias against female children. Since more boys are born than girls everywhere in the world, even without sex-specific abortion, we can use as a classificatory benchmark the female-male ratio among children in advanced industrial countries. The female-male ratio among children for the zero-to-five age group is 94.8 in German, 95.0 in the United Kingdom, and 95.7 in the United States. And perhaps we can sensibly pick the German ratio of 94.8 as the cut-off point below which we should suspect anti-female intervention.

The use of this dividing line produces a remarkable geographical split in India, in the states in the north and the west, the female-male ratio of children is uniformly below the benchmark figure, led by Punjab, Haryana, Delhi, and Gujarat (with ratios between 79.8 and 87.8), and also including the states of Himachal Pradesh, Madhya Pradesh, Rajasthan, Uttar Pradesh, Maharashtra, Jammu and Kashmir, and Bihar. The states in the east and south, by contrast, tend to have female-male ratios that are above the benchmark line of 94.8 girls per 100 boys, such as Kerala, Andhra Pradesh, West Bengal, and Assam (each between 96.3 and 96.6), and also including Orissa, Karnataka, and the northeastern states to the east of Bangladesh.

Aside from the tiny states of Dadra and Nagar Haveli (with less than 250,000 people), which have a high female-male ratio among children despite being in the west, the one substantial exception to this adjoining division is Tamil Nadu, where the female-male ratio is just below 94—higher than the ratio of any state in the deficit list, but still just below the cut-off line (94.8) used for the partitioning. But the astonishing finding is not that one particular state is a marginal misfit. It is that the vast majority of the Indian states fall firmly into two contiguous halves, classified broadly into the north and the west on one side and the south and the east on the other. Indeed, every state in the north and the west (with the slight exception of tiny Dadra and Nagar Haveli) has strictly lower female-male ratios of children than every state in the east and the south (even Tamil Nadu fits into this classification). This is quite remarkable.

The pattern of female-male ratio of children produces a much sharper regional classification than does the female-male ratio of mortality of children, even though the two are also strongly correlated. The female-male ratio in child mortality varies, at one end, from 0.91 in West Bengal and 0.93 in Kerala, in the eastern and southern group, to 1.30 at the other end, in Punjab, Haryana, and Uttar Pradesh (with high ratios also in Gujarat, Bihar, and Rajasthan), in the northern and western group.

The pattern of contrast does not have any obvious

economic explanation. The states with anti-female bias include rich states (Punjab and Haryana) as well as poor states (Madhya Pradesh and Uttar Pradesh), fast-growing states (Gujarat and Maharashtra) as well as states that are growth failures (Bihar and Uttar Pradesh). Also, the incidence of sex-specific abortions cannot be explained by the availability of medical resources for determining the sex of the fetus: Kerala and West Bengal in the non-deficit list have at least as many medical facilities as do the deficit states of Madhya Pradesh, Haryana, or Rajasthan. If the provision for sex-selective abortion is infrequent in Kerala of West Bengal, it is because of a low demand for those specific services, rather than any great barrier on the side of supply.

This suggests that we must inquire beyond economic resources or material prosperity or GNP grown into broad cultural and social influences. There are a variety of influences to be considered here, and the linking of these demographic features with the subject matter of social anthropology and cultural studies would certainly be very much worth doing. There is also some possible connection with politics. It has been noted in other contexts that the states in the north and the west of India generally have given much more room to religion-based sectarian politics than has the east or the south, where religion-centered parties have had very little success. Of the 197 members of the present Indian parliament from the Bharatiya Janata Party (BJP) and Shiva Sena, which represent to a great extent the forces of Hindu nationalism, as many as 169 were elected from the north and the west. While it would be important to keep a close watch on the trend of sex-selective abortion everywhere in India, the fact that there are sharp divisions related to culture and politics may suggest lines of probing investigation as well as remedial action.

Gender inequality, then, has many distinct and dissimilar faces. In overcoming some of its worst manifestations, especially in mortality rates, the cultivation of women's empowerment and agency, through such means as women's education and gainful employment, has proved very effective. But in dealing with the new form of gender inequality, the injustice relating to natality, there is a need to go beyond the question of the agency of women and to look for a more critical assessment of received values. When anti-female bias in behavior (such as sex-specific abortion) reflects the hold of traditional masculinist values from which mothers themselves may not be immune, what is needed is not just freedom of action but also freedom of thought—the freedom to question and to scrutinize inherited beliefs and traditional priorities. Informed critical agency is important in combating inequality of every kind, and gender inequality is no exception.

CHAPTER 27

Gender and Power:
Society, the Person, and Sexual Politics

R.W. CONNELL

The central argument can be put in a few paragraphs. There is an ordering of versions of femininity and masculinity at the level of the whole society, in some ways analogous to the patterns of face-to-face relationship within institutions. The possibilities of variation, of course, are vastly greater. The sheer complexity of relationships involving millions of people guarantees that ethnic differences and generational differences as well as class patterns come into play. But in key respects the organization of gender on the very large scale must be more skeletal and simplified than the human relationships in face-to-face milieux. The forms of femininity and masculinity constituted at this level are stylized and impoverished. Their interrelation is centred on a single structural fact, the global dominance of men over women.

This structural fact provides the main basis for relationships among men that define a hegemonic form of masculinity in the society as a whole. "Hegemonic masculinity" is always constructed in relation to various subordinated masculinities as well as in relation to women. The interplay between different forms of masculinity is an important part of how a patriarchal social order works.

There is no femininity that is hegemonic in the sense that the dominant form of masculinity is hegemonic among men. [...]

At the level of mass social relations, however, forms of femininity are defined clearly enough. It is the global subordination of women to men that provides an essential basis for differentiation. One form is defined around compliance with this subordination and is oriented to accommodating the interests and desires of men. I will call this "emphasized femininity." Others are defined centrally by strategies of resistance or forms of non-compliance. Others again are defined by complex strategic combinations of compliance, resistance and co-operation. The interplay among them is a major part of the dynamics of change in the gender order as a whole.

In the concept of hegemonic masculinity, "hegemony" means (as in Gramsci's analyses of class relations in Italy from which the term is borrowed) a social ascendancy achieved in a play of social forces that extends beyond contests of brute power into the organization of private life and cultural processes. Ascendancy of one group of men over another achieved at the point of a gun, or by the threat of unemployment, is not hegemony. Ascendancy which is embedded in religious doctrine and practice, mass media content, wage structures, the design of housing, welfare/taxation policies and so forth, is.

Two common misunderstandings of the concept should be cleared up immediately. First, though "hegemony" does not refer to ascendancy based on force, it is not incompatible with ascendancy based on force. Indeed it is common for the two to go together. Physical or economic violence backs up a dominant cultural pattern (for example beating up "perverts"), or ideologies justify the holders of physical power ("law and order"). The connection between hegemonic masculinity and patriarchal violence is close, though not simple.

Second, "hegemony" does not mean total cultural dominance, the obliteration of alternatives. It means ascendancy achieved within a balance of forces, that is, a state of play. Other patterns and groups are subordinated rather than eliminated. If we do not recognize this it would be impossible to account for the everyday contestation that actually occurs in social life, let alone for historical changes in definitions of gender patterns on the grand scale.

Hegemonic masculinity, then, is very different from the notion of a general "male sex role" [....] First, the cultural ideal (or ideals) of masculinity need not correspond at all closely to the actual personalities of the majority of men. Indeed the winning of hegemony often involves the creation of models of masculinity which are quite specifically fantasy figures, such as the film characters played by Humphrey Bogart, John Wayne and Sylvester Stallone. Or real models may be publicized who are so remote from everyday achievement that they have the effect of an unattainable ideal, like the Australian Rules footballer Ron Barassi or the boxer Muhammed Ali.

As we move from face-to-face settings to structures involving millions of people, the easily symbolized aspects of interaction become more prominent. Hegemonic masculinity is very public. In a society of mass communications it is tempting to think that it exists only as publicity. Hence the focus on media images and media discussions of masculinity in the "Books About Men" of the 1970s and 1980s, from Warren Farrell's *The Liberated Man* to Barbara Ehrenreich's *The Hearts of Men*.

To focus on the media images alone would be a mistake. They need not correspond to the actual characters of the men who hold most social power—in contemporary societies the corporate and state elites. Indeed a ruling class may allow a good deal of sexual dissent. A minor but dramatic instance is the tolerance for homosexuality that the British diplomat Guy Burgess could assume from other men of his class during his career as a Soviet spy. The public face of hegemonic masculinity is not necessarily what powerful men are, but what sustains their power and what large numbers of men are motivated to support. The notion of "hegemony" generally implies a large measure of consent. Few men are Bogarts or Stallones, many collaborate in sustaining those images.

There are various reasons for complicity, and a thorough study of them would go far to illuminate the whole system of sexual politics. Fantasy gratification is one—nicely satirized in Woody Allen's Bogart take-off, *Play It Again, Sam*. Displaced aggression might be another—and the popularity of very violent movies from *Dirty Harry* to *Rambo* suggest that a great deal of this is floating around. But it seems likely that the major reason is that most men benefit from the subordination of women, and hegemonic masculinity is the cultural expression of this ascendancy.

This needs careful formulation. It does not imply that hegemonic masculinity means being particularly nasty to women. Women may feel as oppressed by non-hegemonic masculinities, may even find the hegemonic pattern more familiar and manageable. There is likely to be a kind of "fit" between hegemonic masculinity and emphasized femininity. What it does imply is the maintenance of practices that institutionalize men's dominance over women. In this sense hegemonic masculinity must embody a successful collective strategy in relation to women. Given the complexity of gender relations no simple or uniform strategy is possible: a "mix" is necessary. So hegemonic masculinity can contain at the same time, quite consistently, openings towards domesticity and openings towards violence, towards misogyny and towards heterosexual attraction.

Hegemonic masculinity is constructed in relation to women and to subordinated masculinities. These other masculinities need not be as clearly defined—indeed, achieving hegemony may consist precisely in preventing alternatives gaining cultural definition and recognition as alternatives, confining them to ghettos, to privacy, to unconsciousness.

The most important feature of contemporary hegemonic masculinity is that it is heterosexual, being closely connected to the institution of marriage; and a key form of subordinated masculinity is homosexual. This subordination involves both direct interactions and a kind of ideological warfare. Some of the interactions [include] police and legal harassment, street violence, economic discrimination. These transactions are tied together by the contempt for homosexuality and homosexual men that is part of the ideological package of hegemonic masculinity. The AIDS scare has been marked less by sympathy for gays as its main victims than by hostility to them as the bearers of a new threat. The key point of media concern is whether the "gay plague" will spread to "innocent," i.e., straight, victims.

In other cases of subordinated masculinity the condition is temporary. Cynthia Cockburn's splendid study of printing workers in London portrays a version of hegemonic masculinity that involved ascendancy over young men as well as over women. The workers recalled their apprenticeships in terms of drudgery and humiliation, a ritual of induction into trade and masculinity at the same time. But once they were in, they were "brothers."

Several general points about masculinity also apply to the analysis of femininity at the mass level. These patterns too are historical: relationships change, new forms of femininity emerge and others disappear. The ideological representations of femininity draw on, but do not necessarily correspond to, actual femininities as they are lived. What most women support is not necessarily what they are.

*　　*　　*　　*　　*

CHAPTER 28
Gender Trouble

JUDITH BUTLER

* * * * *

The terms *queens, butches, femmes, girls,* even the parodic reappropriation of *dyke, queer,* and *fag* redeploy and destabilize the categories of sex and the originally derogatory categories for homosexual identity. All of these terms might be understood as symptomatic of "the straight mind," modes of identifying with the oppressor's version of the identity of the oppressed. On the other hand, *lesbian* has surely been partially reclaimed from its historical meanings, and parodic categories serve the purposes of denaturalizing sex itself. When the neighborhood gay restaurant closes for vacation, the owners put out a sign, explaining that "she's overworked and needs a rest." This very gay appropriation of the feminine works to multiply possible sites of application of the term, to reveal the arbitrary relation between the signifier and the signified, and to destabilize and mobilize the sign. Is this a colonizing "appropriation" of the feminine? My sense is no. That accusation assumes that the feminine belongs to women, an assumption surely suspect.

Within lesbian contexts, the "identification" with masculinity that appears as butch identity is not a simple assimilation of lesbianism back into the terms of heterosexuality. As one lesbian femme explained, she likes her boys to be girls, meaning that "being a girl" contextualizes and resignifies "masculinity" in a butch identity. As a result, that masculinity, if that it can be called, is always brought into relief against a culturally intelligible "female body." It is precisely this dissonant juxtaposition and the sexual tension that its transgression generates that constitute the object of desire. In other words, the object [and clearly, there is not just one] of lesbian-femme desire is neither some decontextualized female body nor a discrete yet superimposed masculine identity, but the destabilization of both terms as they come into erotic interplay. Similarly, some heterosexual or bisexual women may well prefer that the relation of "figure" to "ground" work in the opposite direction— that is, they may prefer that their girls be boys. In that case, the perception of "feminine" identity would be juxtaposed on the "male body" as ground, but both

terms would, through the juxtaposition, lose their internal stability and distinctness from each other. Clearly, this way of thinking about gendered exchanges of desire admits of much greater complexity, for the play of masculine and feminine, as well as the inversion of ground to figure can constitute a highly complex and structured production of desire. Significantly, both the sexed body as "ground" and the butch or femme identity as "figure" can shift, invert, and create erotic havoc of various sorts. Neither can lay claim to "the real," although either can qualify as an object of belief, depending on the dynamic of the sexual exchange. The idea that butch and femme are in some sense "replicas" or "copies" of heterosexual exchange underestimates the erotic significance of these identities as internally dissonant and complex in their resignification of the hegemonic categories by which they are enabled. Lesbian femmes may recall the heterosexual scene, as it were, but also displace it at the same time. In both butch and femme identities, the very notion of an original or natural identity is put into question; indeed, it is precisely that question as it is embodied in these identities that becomes one source of their erotic significance.

* * * * *

The notion of an original or primary gender identity is often parodied within the cultural practices of drag, cross-dressing, and the sexual stylization of butch/femme identities. Within feminist theory, such parodic identities have been understood to be either degrading to women, in the case of drag and cross-dressing, or an uncritical appropriation of sex-role stereotyping from within the practice of heterosexuality, especially in the case of butch/femme lesbian identities. But the relation between the "imitation" and the "original" is, I think, more complicated than that critique generally allows. Moreover, it gives us a clue to the way in which the relationship between primary identification—that is, the original meanings accorded to gender—and subsequent gender experience might be reframed. The performance of drag plays upon the distinction between the anatomy of the performer and the gender that is being performed.

But we are actually in the presence of three contingent dimensions of significant corporeality: anatomical sex, gender identity, and gender performance. If the anatomy of the performer is already distinct from the gender of the performer, and both of those are distinct from the gender of the performance, then the performance suggests a dissonance not only between sex and performance, but sex and gender, and gender and performance. As much as drag creates a unified picture of "woman" (what its critics often oppose), it also reveals the distinctness of those aspects of gendered experience which are falsely naturalized as a unity through the regulatory fiction of heterosexual coherence. *In imitating gender, drag implicitly reveals the imitative structure of gender itself—as well as its contingency.* Indeed, part of the pleasure, the giddiness of the performance is in the recognition of a radical contingency in the relation between sex and gender in the face of cultural configurations of causal unities that are regularly assumed to be natural and necessary. In the place of the law of heterosexual coherence, we see sex and gender denaturalized by means of a performance which avows their distinctness and dramatizes the cultural mechanism of their fabricated unity.

The notion of gender parody defended here does not assume that there is an original which such parodic identities imitate. Indeed, the parody is *of* the very notion of an original; just as the psychoanalytic notion of gender identification is constituted by a fantasy of a fantasy, the transfiguration of an Other who is always already a "figure" in that double sense, so gender parody reveals that the original identity after which gender fashions itself is an imitation without an origin. To be more precise, it is a production which, in effect—that is, in its effect—postures as an imitation. This perpetual displacement constitutes a fluidity of identities that suggests an openness to resignification and recontextualization; parodic proliferation deprives hegemonic culture and its critics of the claim to naturalized or essentialist gender identities. Although the gender meanings taken up in these parodic styles are clearly part of hegemonic, misogynist culture, they are nevertheless denaturalized and mobilized through their parodic recontextualization. As imitations which effectively displace the meaning of the original, they imitate the myth of originality itself. In the place of an original identification which serves as a determining cause, gender identity might be reconceived as a personal/cultural history of received meanings subject to a set of imitative practices which refer laterally to other imitations and which, jointly, construct the illusion of a primary and interior gendered self or parody the mechanism of that construction.

* * * * *

CHAPTER 29
Skater Girlhood and Emphasized Femininity: "You Can't Land an Ollie Properly in Heels"

DEIRDRE M. KELLY, SHAUNA POMERANTZ, AND DAWN CURRIE

Introduction

What sociologist R.W. Connell has called "emphasized femininity" is very much in evidence in North American high schools in the early twenty-first century. By "emphasized femininity," Connell refers to the form of femininity, defined at "the level of mass social relations," that is based on women's "compliance" with their subordination to men and "oriented to accommodating the interests and desires of men" (1987, p. 183). Connell used the term "emphasized femininity" to contrast with what he called "hegemonic masculinity," which is "constructed in relation to women and to subordinated masculinities" and ascendant over all of these (1987, p. 186). Emphasized femininity, as the earlier empirical work of Connell and his colleagues in Australia had shown, is the most culturally valued form of femininity, albeit not necessarily the most prevalent pattern among high school girls (Connell *et al.*, 1982).

* * * * *

Nevertheless, some girls resist emphasized femininity, either wholly or in part. We heard girls in our study defining themselves as "alternative" to that dominant form of femininity, for example, through their participation in skateboarding and skateboarding culture (discussed later in the article). That skateboarding and emphasized femininity are in tension with each other is captured by Tori, a hardcore skater. Tori's friend and co-interviewee, Priscilla (aged 14), had just announced that her mother had a "big problem" with the fact that her daughter preferred more androgynous, baggy clothes to dresses and skirts. Explained Priscilla, "She'll go out and buy me shoes, but they'll have the heels on them. I cannot stand the heels." Tori (aged 16) responded:

I can skate in a heel. I have done it, and it hurts. You can't land an ollie properly in heels, but I have done it.

An ollie, the basis of most other skateboarding tricks, consists of a girl smacking down the end of her board, moving her foot forward to bring the board up into the air, then landing with her feet equally apart in the middle of the board. The high-heeled shoe remains a common and powerful symbol of emphasized femininity. That Tori claimed to have skated in a heel possibly hints at a desire to be attractive to boys in conventional terms, in the emphasized vulnerability evoked by a girl wearing heels. At the same time, Tori noted the near impossibility of skating well (landing an ollie) while wearing heels. Tori's declaration that she had managed this particular feat of athleticism despite wearing heels speaks volumes about the physical and emotional energy that girls must invest in fashioning their identities.

The purpose of this article is to explore what it means to be a skater girl, particularly in relation to emphasized femininity. Skater girlhood can be seen as part of a larger category, alternative girlhood. By alternative girlhood, we mean the range of ways that girls consciously position themselves against what they perceive as the mainstream in general and against conventional forms of femininity in particular. Alternative girls in our wider study named themselves as "alternative." They engaged in a variety of activities (e.g., creating animé—Japanese-style animation—web sites featuring their own drawings and fictional writing), displayed styles (e.g., Goth) or expressed tastes (e.g., for punk music) that they perceived as avant-garde or linked to an underground or alternative culture.[1] Skater girlhood, in particular, is also part of the larger skateboarding culture. For the purpose of the analysis that follows, it is important to bear in mind that skater girlhood is always in the process of formation but never fully formed; that is, it is a site of negotiation infused, in turn, by other dynamic discourses such as punk rock, Goth and hip hop.[2]

How do girls come to be seen as skaters, particularly in and around school and among their same-age peers? What do girls say, do, wear, believe, value and know that allows them to see themselves and be seen by others as skaters? What do they not say, do and so on? These factors "combine" in ways that "can get one recognized as a certain 'kind of person'" (Gee, 2001, p. 110)—that is, as a skater girl. These ways of being are what we mean by discourse. Claiming such a label, particularly one that, as we will show, is oppositional to emphasized femininity, is an example of what some feminist poststructuralists have theorized as agency (see Davies, 1991; Pomerantz *et al.*, 2004).

In answering these questions and exploring the skater girl discourse, we draw upon interviews with 20 girls recruited for the study because they identified to some degree with skater girlhood. The skater girls ranged in age from 13- to 16-years. At the time of the interview, two were 13, seven were 14, eight were 15, and three were 16. Eleven were White (European Canadian), four were Chinese Canadian, three were of mixed racial/ethnic identity, and two were Aboriginal. (In Canada the term "Aboriginal" includes both First Nations peoples as well as the Métis, that is, persons of both Native and European ancestry.) Based on information the girls provided about their parents' occupations and educational backgrounds and their current living arrangements, 15 came from middle-class families and five from working-class families. One identified as bisexual, and the other 19 implied or stated that they were heterosexual. Sixteen of the girls lived in Vancouver, British Columbia, and of those eight attended public school in an upper middle-class neighborhood, six attended public schools in working-class neighborhoods, one attended a private girls' school and one attended a Catholic school. The remaining four attended public schools in suburbs of Vancouver. Eighteen of the girls had never left school, while two girls had each been out of school for a total of one year and were one grade behind as a result.

Pomerantz conducted the semi-structured, hour-long interviews. By design, most of the interviews were with pairs of friends, recruited in public places like community centres and skate parks or by personal referral. Sixteen of the girls were initially interviewed in pairs, while four girls were interviewed individually. In addition, Pomerantz did follow-up interviews with six girls, either in pairs or alone, for an overall total of 16 interviews. In a manner similar to that described by Hollway and Jefferson (2000), we encouraged participants to tell stories. Each of the 20 participants chose her pseudonym and received a complimentary movie pass.

The skater girls in our study participated to different degrees in skateboarding culture. We discerned three broad categories. The "hardcore" or "serious skaters," such as Tori, referred to themselves as skaters, frequented skate parks, had mastered a number of tricks, and knew how to assemble their own board. The "skaters" (the biggest category), such as Priscilla, liked the "lifestyle" but skated more infrequently, and they had usually mastered only the basics, although some knew a few tricks. The "skater affiliates," such as Gracie, Sandy or Amanda (all aged 15), identified as, or were known as, skaters mainly because of their friendships with other skaters, an affinity for skater culture, or both.

* * * * *

We offer here, therefore, a more detailed descriptive analysis of how the girls came to be seen as skaters, and

in the process, we point to the contradictions or tensions within skater girl discourse, such as emphasizing being one's self while adhering to the emerging norms of skater girlhood. We then discuss the difference social class made in how girls at different schools took up skater discourse and how one group of middle-class girls, "in-betweeners," defied easy labels to forge a positive identity for themselves. In their strategic play within and among discourses, we think we discerned an alternative girlhood in the process of gaining cultural definition.

Becoming Skater Girls

The girls came to be seen—both by themselves as well as their friends and peers—as skaters by: expressing particular beliefs, values and feelings; using a skateboard and demonstrating technical knowledge about skateboarding; displaying physical risk-taking and enduring bodily pain; dressing in certain ways; using skater and other in-group slang; avoiding behavior associated with emphasized or dominant femininity; and engaging in activities closely allied with skater culture, such as listening to alternative or punk rock music. Because we know of no empirical studies of skater girls,[3] in this section we explore these facets of their identity construction in some depth. As will become clear, the ways girls came to be seen as skaters often meant an embrace of skater culture's masculine norms (cf. Leblanc, 1999, on punk girls).

Fun, Adventure, Confidence and Nonconformity

According to the girls in our study, skateboarding symbolizes fun (acting "loud and crazy"), adventure (meaning, in particular, a willingness to try new things or take a risk), confidence and nonconformity. They valued the image of skateboarding as fun and daring, and this image prompted them to try it. Having once tried skateboarding, regardless of how much they actually practiced, most of the girls came to realize, as Zoey (aged 15) put it, "Hey, we're the only girl skaters around here!" As they gained in skill at skating, they gained in confidence. Even when she felt her own sense of confidence wavering, Pete, aged 15, said that other kids at school saw her as confident "because of the skateboarding thing." At the same time, they became more aware of their nonconformity as girls within the male-dominated skater culture, which is already associated with other forms of rebellion (see Beal, 1995, 1996; Willard, 1998; Borden, 2001; Peralta, 2001).

Every skater girl participant said she valued being "different." Other words used to convey the value placed on nonconformity included: "alternative," "unique," not "normal," "weird," "an original," "freaky," "creative," "artistic" and "standing out" from the crowd and what is considered "trendy."[4] Many different styles of skateboarding exist and all are accepted (Beal, 1996). Tori spoke for many of the girls interviewed when she stated, "I feel it's more important to be who you are, and not what people want you to be." More specifically, girls liked proving through their skateboarding that they were or could be physically strong and brave.

While all of the skater girls seemed to enjoy challenging dominant stereotypes associated with being a girl, they were more divided about skateboarding's more general image of rebellion. Among other things, skateboarding has been associated with nonconformity to: (a) prevailing mores against drug use (the "pothead" stereotype); (b) prevailing mores supporting respect for private property (the "punk" or "hooligan" stereotype);5 (c) the dominant work ethic (the "slacker" stereotype); and (d) capitalist consumer culture (the "laid back" and "underground" stereotype). We return to this point later in the article.

Technical Knowledge: A Board of Her Own

"Believe it or not," explained Tori, "[skateboarding] is a hell of a lot harder than it looks." Beginning skateboarders have to learn to balance and move forward before they can advance to even the most basic tricks. Most girls reported learning the basics in relatively private spaces, like driveways and streets near home. As some became more technically proficient, they ventured into public places, like skate parks, which brought them into contact with other skaters who were often older, better, and male. Because "it's not too common" to be a girl skater, explained Grover (aged 15), "the guys are like, 'What are you doing?'" "Like invading their space or something," added Onyx (aged 14). In a subsequent interview, Grover noted that she and her friend Zoey avoided the park when they practiced because the "guys" there were "rude" to them; these guys felt "threatened … because girls are doing *their* sport."

Madeline (aged 16) reported a similar (in her words) "intimidating" "boy/girl issue" at the skate parks:

The guys don't think you're so good, and if there's a lot of people there, like I don't like to go, because you feel that you're getting in their way. I mean, even if you're trying to get better, if you can't do certain things, they'll automatically think that you're really bad.

Later in the interview, however, when asked if she had ever "stood up" for herself "as a girl," Madeline recounted a triumphant moment at the skate park:

This one guy came up to me. He's like, "Oh, girls can't skate." I'm like, "What?!" And like yeah, so I showed him like all my tricks, and he's like, "Oh, wow, that's pretty cool."

Other skater girls reported that they were more watched or scrutinized and more quickly "judged" than boys. "The image is that guys, they screw up or whatever, it doesn't matter," according to Kate (aged 15). "If girls do something really stupid and they fall or whatever, it's like *oh, my God*, looked down upon."

The most serious skaters in our study also took obvious pride in knowing how to assemble their own skateboard as well as maintain it. Several questioned the motives of girls who did not display technical competence or technical knowledge of skateboarding. "I actually go around and look for other skater chicks," said Tori, "and it's like really hard. I've found quite a few chicks who carry the boards [and] quite a few chicks who can't use them." In a similar vein, Madeline said, "I've seen a couple of girls that have skateboards that go to skater parks to look at guys. It kind of bugs me." In short, skater girls drew on the technical competence symbolized by skateboarding to challenge the socially constructed feminine stereotypes of physical, mechanical and technical helplessness.

The Risks: "Face Plants" and "Road Rash"

To get better at skateboarding necessarily involves physical risk-taking. As Michelle (aged 13) succinctly put it, "*Everybody* falls." "First, you've got to get the balance," explained Tori:

And then you've got to be fearless as shit, because 24/7 … you're riding along cement. When you fall, it hurts. It doesn't just hurt a little bit—it hurts a lot. But in order to learn these tricks, you fall down a lot.

A number of skater girls speculated that the fear of falling and getting hurt was an important factor preventing more girls from taking up skateboarding. Indeed, some of the less serious skaters in our study admitted that they disliked falling. For example, Emily and Amanda (both aged 15 and interviewed together), said they "respected" the "guy" skaters as "more risk taking." According to Amanda, "They don't care if they get bruises and stuff. They'll be like, 'Yeah, cuts!'" Emily added that she was "trying" to develop the same attitude, "but most of the time when I fall, I'm like, 'Oh, I don't want to do it anymore!'"

Conversely, the girls who practiced skateboarding a lot reported being less afraid. Pete enjoyed the adrenaline "rush," and Zoey added:

The first time I wiped out I was just like, "Whoa!" I fell really hard, I was like, "Aahh," kind of, and then I just wanted to do it again, because it was like, "Wow!"

Kate (aged 15) described her "face plant" the first time she skateboarded:

She [Christine, aged 16, and co-interviewee] lives on a really, really steep hill. And I decided that I was going to go down it [laughs]. And it was really steep and [had] bumpy spots and everything, and I didn't make it very far, and I jumped off the board, and I like slid on my hip and my eye and I got like a black eye and everything.

Later in the interview, Kate noted that Christine had "freaked out" over Kate's accident, but "I'm back on there still doing like weird stuff." Like Kate, Lexi (aged 14) evinced stoicism about her inevitable injuries:

I'm not very good, but if I get scraped, I'm not going to whine and bitch about it. I'm just going to go, "Oh, damn. OK."

"Road rash" seemed to be a badge of honor for Tori and Priscilla, who were visibly scraped and bruised at the time of the interview. "I've got permanent road rash scar on my hip," explained Tori.

You know when they're about to put traffic lights up, they put the counters on the road? I didn't see it. I thought it was a shadow, and I hit it. And I just went poof, flying, and I had road rash all down the side of my face.

The skater girls' toughness and relative lack of concern about bruises, scrapes and scars provide a sharp contrast with dominant images of femininity.

Skater Style: Casual, Comfortable and Not "Slutty"

Across the 20 girls whom we interviewed, a fairly wide variety of styles and attitudes toward dress were in evidence. Nevertheless, taken as a whole, the girls liked the casual, comfortable (baggy) look of skater clothes, and many were quick to contrast skater style with what they disliked: "revealing," brand-name attire that they associated with a certain type of popular, "boy-hunting" girl. As Zoey explained:

A lot of the skater clothes aren't slutty, so that's really cool…. That really tight stuff—those can get really annoying after awhile, and you can't do anything on a board in it.

According to Grover, "bun girls" (her group's name for girls who displayed an emphasized femininity) wear "tanks tops four seasons a year…. They base a lot upon their looks and what they think the guys will like." "They're not really their own person," added Onyx.

Some of the skater girls were clear that, through their style, they wanted to "be their own person," to "stand out" (e.g., by wearing all orange or safety pins as earrings) or to be "funky" (e.g., by dying their hair blue or wearing an "explosive shirt"). But they were equally clear that their primary purpose was not to attract the attention of boys, but rather to make a statement about their individuality and difference. In seeming protest of corporate consumerism, a number of skater girls said they shopped at Value Village and other second-hand

clothing stores, and Tori said she designed her own clothes as a hobby. Pete noted about her friendship circle:

I think we're kind of the different, kind of alternate, creative group, because we're always making up our own clothes and trends.

Rather than "making up" a trend of their own, skater girls Grenn and Lexi (both aged 14 and perhaps the most working-class of the participants) asserted that they were following "no fashion trend at all" and that this defined them as "weird" in the eyes of their more affluent, "preppy" peers.

Of course, in recent years the skater style has become popular, thus complicating the discussion of what is "trendy" and increasing the cost of skater clothes. This development angered a number of the girls, particularly the most hardcore skaters. Kate and Christine spoke derisively of "little posers" who wore skater clothes but did not really skate. Madeline said it "bugged" her that some girls at her school bought expensive stuff that they did not really "need." For example, they wore skate shoes that "aren't really great for skating; they're just kind of poser brands." (Bettie, 2003, analyzes these types of competing "claims to authenticity" as displaced class antagonism; see especially p. 127.)

The increasing popularity of skater style affected the hardcore yet working-class skater girls like Tori the most strongly.

It bugs me 'cause you see all these preppy little kids and they are going and buying skate shoes and skate clothing, which makes the price go up for people like us who depend on that. Like my shoes have the biggest ollie hole in them, like you have no idea!

Tori went on to explain that she used to be able to replace her shoes for $30, but now the "cheapest shoe" cost her $120. Pointing to her skate shoe, she explained:

This piece in here gets thrashed the most because when you ollie, it rubs up against your board. So you want nice plastic in here and you want the lips to be up high, and in order to get that, you have to pay [a lot].

To recap, girls participated in skater culture by wearing the casual, comfortable clothes that allowed them to move with ease on their skateboards. Their dress contrasted sharply with the attire favored by a certain type of popular girl across a number of different school settings: tight, expensive designer jeans or skirts, "really tight tank tops" and lots of makeup. As Zoey declared, her friendship group was "totally the opposite" of girls who dress "sexy" to "attract guys," and her co-interviewee, Pete, agreed:

Dressing sexy kind of, in my perspective, attracts the wrong type of guys for me. I'm not into those guys … that are attracted to sex appeal only [and not the brain].

At the same time, some skater girls expressed concern that skater style had become a "cool" commodity.

One way for girls to expand the meaning of femininity is to use the resources of what has been a male-dominated youth culture to make those norms and values their own. So far, we have seen that through skateboarding girls appropriated the traditionally masculine traits of physical strength and bravery, technical competence, physical risk-taking and stoicism, as well as non-sexualized androgyny (read: masculine dress style). Another way that skater girls defined an alternative femininity was against other girls and women whom they perceived as embodying emphasized femininity. They did this through in-group language, by avoiding behavior they associated with dominant femininity, and by participating in the politics of distinction (or rejection of an undiscerning mainstream culture; see Thornton, 1995) that characterizes skater culture.

Skater and In-Group Slang

Using skater slang was another way girls came to be seen as skaters. Some used jargon to describe the skateboard or skateboarding tricks. Others used slang associated with hip hop or skater culture more generally. Different groups of friends developed inside jokes, invented funny names for each other, and made up words that were, as Gracie (aged 15) put it, "fun and fun to use." Their speech enacted fun, a value seen to be at the heart of skateboarding and skater culture.

Nowhere was this more evident than among the self-named "Park friends," which included Gracie, Sandy, Zoey, Pete, Onyx and Grover. They created the term "snorkomdorfs" (later variations included "s–and–dorf" and "snork–and–dork") as a fun word to call each other, and they contrasted it with their term for the girls at their schools whom they perceived as ultra-feminine, "the bun girls." At one time, those girls liked to wear their hair in a bun, and although that fad had since passed, the Park friends continued to use the term "bun girls" to refer to the more "ditzy" girls. Snorkomdorf, according to Pete and Zoey, meant "dorky and corny" and "weird." Grover noted that "it replaces using ... swear words and mean words that could actually be hurtful." Onyx agreed, adding, "Yeah, we make fun of each other for fun, too." By contrast, they said the bun girls, particularly "bun girls with attitude," were "mean to each other." "They'll swear at each other, and it's almost like they have no respect for each other."

By using terms like "snorkomdorf" the Park friends could also gauge the reactions of outsiders to their use of slang and decide whether they would "want to make friends" with them. Explained Grover:

If they're kind of like, "Snorkomdorf? What do you mean?!", [then we assume] they're kind of more close minded to things and less likely to just let loose and just have fun, you know?

The Park friends also created the word "glutty" (meaning "guy slut") to voice their critique of the sexual double standard and the term "skank monkey"[6] ("the male equivalent of a bun girl") to extend their critique of the superficiality of the popular crowd at school. Grover elaborated:

... [skank monkeys] think they're so great, and they care so much about their looks, and everything has to be *perfect*.

Disassociation from Emphasized Femininity

The girls in the skater study, without exception, said they tried to avoid behavior they associated with a certain type, referred to, variously, as "bun girls," "ditzy girls," "teeny boppers," "preppy girls," "girly girls" and "poppy girls." The various names highlighted different types of behavior generally frowned upon by the skater girls: flirting with boys, spending too much time and money making themselves "pretty," "living their life for a guy" (as Pete put it), worrying about what the cool or popular kids thought, being hurtful as they tried to achieve or maintain social standing and listening to pop music. As has been documented in studies of other youth cultures, the skater girls constructed a homogeneous mainstream group against which they positioned themselves in order to further define their own sense of self (see Thornton, 1995; Leblanc, 1999; Hodkinson, 2002; Bettie, 2003).

Skater "Culture" or "Lifestyle"

Another way that girls in our study came to be seen as skaters was by engaging in activities closely allied with skater culture. Madeline, from a White, middle-class family, provided an interesting map of skater culture at her large, urban high school, located in a working-class, multiethnic neighborhood:

There's [three] different kinds of groups.... There's more like the hip hop group, and there's like the Goth, and there's people kind of in the middle, who aren't ... all bugged out [bugged out means they wear really, really big pants and they listen to hip hop music] and people who aren't total Goth.... I'm kind of in the middle of both of them.... I have friends that are Goth and I have friends that are really into hip hop and stuff like that.

Madeline's group, the middle group, was into "punk" and wore "hoodies" and pants.

Although it is difficult to generalize about the participants, most girls identified with alternative rock, punk or metal music—music that is loud, edgy, irreverent and often rebellious or anti-corporate. As Jessica (a 13-year-old skater affiliate) noted, pop stars sing mainly about "love and relationships," whereas alternative bands write songs that "have meaning" and are "worth hearing." The lyrics are "about them growing up or them having trouble with friends, not liking school or dropping out." Two girls, Tori and Grenn, had been in, or planned to form, punk rock groups, and the band names indicate the tone of critique ("Gadfly") and rebellion ("Normal," so named because "We're all the opposite of normal"). Grenn had a poster of singer-songwriter Avril Lavigne, a self-described "skater punk," prominently displayed in her bedroom. Notwithstanding disputes about Lavigne's authenticity as a skater, her themes—such as the importance of being oneself amidst the pressures to conform—certainly echo what many skater girls said in their interviews. (Lavigne has publicly criticized pop singer Britney Spears for "using sex to sell music"; see Halpin, 2003, p. 103.)

Constraints of Male-Dominated Gender Relations within Skater Culture

Skater culture, with its emphasis on individual self-expression and nonconformity, afforded skater girls room to develop a critique of, and distance from, emphasized femininity. Yet the male-dominated gender relations within skater culture seemed also to constrain them. Because our study is based mainly on interviews, we have to rely primarily on the girls' descriptions of their relations with skater boys. The spirit of cooperation and participation (versus competition) that is felt by (mainly male) skaters to distinguish their activity from traditional sports (see Beal, 1995, 1996) was in some evidence. A number of skater girls in our study mentioned first learning to skateboard from boys or men, often family members or friends. The younger brother of one of Grover's girlfriends taught her. Gouge learned from her cousin's boyfriend. Emily learned from, and was encouraged by, skater boys at her school. Michelle followed her older brother into skating. Madeline practiced at skater parks with her male cousin.

Nevertheless, as was described earlier, skater girls reported feeling scrutinized and judged more quickly and harshly by some skater boys. As well, some skater boys used technical language and superior mechanical knowledge as an exclusionary strategy to mystify skateboarding and make girls feel less than true skaters. Skater girls regularly had to confront sexist assumptions about girls being unable to skate or as not having (or "choosing" not to have) what it takes to skate. Skater girls were ignored, accused of merely wanting to boy-watch, insulted, and otherwise made to feel like outsiders in male-dominated skate parks. (In another paper, we provide a detailed analysis of one such skate park incident and how the girls successfully challenged the boys' dominance; see Pomerantz et al., 2004).

* * * * *

"In-betweeners": "Carving" and "Grinding"[7] within and among Discourses

Tori spoke of "skater culture" with a more oppositional, working-class inflection than most. Perhaps in solidarity with male skaters, Tori resisted her friend Priscilla's attempts to generalize about, and criticize, male behavior. For example, in response to Priscilla's complaint about being propositioned by older men and being "gawked at," Tori replied, "Chicks are as bad as guys for sitting there and turning people into meat [sexual objects]." At one level, Tori can be seen as rejecting an essentialist view of gender identity, yet at another level, she can be seen as blocking an exploration of gender and enforced heterosexuality as structuring processes. Drawing on a fierce individualism evident in skater discourse generally, Tori argued that guy skaters "don't mean to discriminate" against girls, but there are just not many girls willing to endure the physical pain involved in learning to skateboard. She did not report feeling "intimidated" by guys, the way other skater girls did. Tori drew an analogy between her experience as one of the few girl skaters and being "the only chick in this power mechanics class." She took obvious delight in being the first one to assemble her car engine, despite teasing from the boys ("In their face"). Not surprisingly, then, Tori did not identify with what she saw as the more "extreme" strand of feminism that she equated with the impossible goal of "equality" for "everybody." She did "believe" in the strand that she felt encouraged girls to take "pride in who you are and what you are."

Skateboarding has long been male dominated, and the culture that has sprung up around it has not been immune to patriarchal influences. Our impression is that the more hardcore skater girls like Tori seem to identify with skater culture, the less likely they are to perceive sexism operating at anything but an individual level. We do not think it a coincidence that Tori was the lone girl in the skater study to refer to herself (without irony) as a "skater chick." Complementary explanations of Tori's downplaying of sexism are suggested by the ethnographic work of Leblanc and Bettie. Like the punk girls in Leblanc's study, Tori may have internalized the "masculinist" norms of skater culture, colluding with these norms rather than resisting them, for fear of being expelled from the skateboarding subculture (1999, chapter 4). Like some of the White, working-class girls in Bettie's study, Tori may have perceived skater boys (however patriarchal some may have appeared to others) as allies:

… against adults and peers at school who are oppressively judgmental and adults at home who are unaffectionate at best and abusive at worst. (Bettie, 2003, p. 113)

By contrast, other girls (in our study at least, all middle to upper middle class) appeared to use skater girl discourse as a way of distancing themselves from the sexism evident in skater culture as well as emphasized femininity. These girls deployed skater discourse to counter the potentially stigmatizing or limiting effects of other discourses (and vice versa) as well as to name an alternative, potentially more powerful way of being. Appropriating some skater terms, we argue that these girls "carved" among multiple discourses and "grinded" (exploited contradictions) within discourses. Following terminology suggested by Zoey, we call this set of carving and grinding girls "in-betweeners."

Zoey said she and the Park friends at Midtown moved "in between" the "studying group" and the skateboarders. This was how they attempted to resolve the dilemma of avoiding the "mean" set of popular skaters, while remaining distinct from the "nice" students who focused more exclusively on academics, yet who got labeled as "geeks" by the popular crowd. Zoey acknowledged that as skater girls, she and her friends were "respected." They could be seen as fun loving and open-minded, yet, because they were girls and good students, they avoided the stereotypes associated with boy skaters, that is, as "into drugs," "punky" and "tough."

In addition, the Park friends (subconsciously?) seized on a contradiction within skater discourse in a way that seemed to generate goodwill among their peers toward them. Skater culture tends to deride pop music and mass consumerism, while simultaneously valuing individuality and authenticity. The Park friends felt relatively free to select what they liked from mainstream or popular culture, and they turned their eclectic taste (in music, clothing style) into a mark of their individuality. Zoey, for example, said:

There's some pop music that we like and we're not—like around skaters—we can tell them that we don't really care, even if they don't think that's cool.

Added Pete, "Yeah, like I'm not afraid to say that I like N'Sync [a popular boy vocal group]." They made it clear that they were not necessarily, as Sandy put it, "trying to be rebellious" or "anti-mainstream," although Pete said she did "rebel" against "close-mindedness."

We find evidence in the story of Pete's planned, public pratfall that the Park friends' strategy had proved successful. Pete had decided to run for Grade 10 representative to the student council against a popular "bun girl" (also Chinese-Canadian). "It was only the two of us," explained Pete, "so I thought, 'I *want* to beat her.'" In order to underscore her promise to be "fun," Pete planned to trip "purposely" on the way to the podium to give her campaign speech. "I even practiced tripping" ahead of time. Picking up the story, Zoey said, "And so she [Pete] trips, she falls, and got up and said, 'Supah star'" [super star], in imitation of a character that Molly Shannon developed in a recurring *Saturday night live* skit. "Everyone was hooting," said Pete. "Especially us in the back," added Zoey. Through such actions, these skater girls, who partially identified with the "studying group" at their school, avoided the label of "geek" (and

related labels such as "nerd," "brain" and "keener"). Pete and her friends took pleasure in the fact that Pete got voted onto student council.

The Park friends were, by no means, the only examples of in-betweeners. Madeline (White and middle class), a serious skater attending an inner-city school, mentioned:

I know so many people from different groups [academic students, French Immersion students, the Asian "fashionable group" and the skaters] that I can basically go in to any group and ... hang around.

Being a skater girl helped to offset the "smart student" stigma of having received the top academic achievement award at her school for two years running.

Sara (aged 14, White and middle class), a skater affiliate, said her friends called her "the chameleon," because she had the ability to move easily between different groups at school:

I can just hang out with the poppy people and be really ditzy and like "ah hah hah," and then I can hang out with the intellectual people and be very like deep and "blah blah blah," and hang out with the skaters and be a moron.... I like breaking out of myself and just exploring the different characteristics of myself, and so that's how it helps me to go from group to group, right?

Developing the discursive repertoire to recognize and enact several distinct ways of being, based on interaction with others in particular contexts, no doubt depends on a certain material privilege (i.e., economic and cultural resources from home) yet may also suggest some important lessons for rethinking girls' agency and power (see Pomerantz et al., 2004, for a related discussion). More ethnographic research is needed on girls who perceive an ability to move successfully between social groups at school.[8]

Conclusion

Collectively, the 20 girls in our skater study attended nine different high schools in Vancouver and its environs. Without exception, the girls attending each of these schools identified a discourse of femininity that we have called, following Connell (1987), emphasized femininity. Viewed as a discourse, there is no expectation that the concept of femininity "define[s] a determinate and unitary phenomenon"; rather, femininity as discourse focuses our analytic attention on the "ongoing, evolving, unfolding social organization of the actual practices of actual individuals" (Smith, 1988, pp. 37, 38). At this particular moment, in a particular locale, certain girls (known variously as the "bun girls," the "poppy girls," the "preppy girls" or the "girly girls") were seen to spend their time shopping for fashionable, sexy clothing; applying makeup; flirting with boys; and talking about fashion and popular music. While the skater girls certainly articulated these as stereotypes of emphasized femininity, there appeared to be some truth to the stereotypes, judging from the interviews in our wider study with self-described "Popular" girls (see Currie et al., 2003) and other empirical work (Eder et al., 1995; Merton, 1997; Bettis & Adams, 2003). These activities helped to organize the popular girls' lives, shape their friendships with each other, inform their individual and group identities, and influence their relations with other girls as well as boys, both inside and outside of school.

Against this, we found that skater girls saw themselves as participating in an "alternative" girlhood, an alternative that was, in some sense, oppositional to emphasized femininity. Becoming skater girls involved the work and play of producing themselves in relation to alternative images found, for example, among peers at school, at skate parks, on the streets, in songs and music videos, in skater magazines (online and in print) and so on. The alternative authority of skater girl discourse gave the girls in our study room to maneuver within and against the culturally valued discourse of emphasized femininity.

Skater girlhood, as we have shown, is not without its contradictions or tensions: expressing one's unique personal style while adhering to particular group norms; disavowing fashion and popularity even as skateboarding itself was becoming more expensive and "trendy"; and valuing an easygoing demeanor while distancing oneself from "posers." We also found that social class made a difference in how girls at different schools took up skater discourse. Working-class girls in class-divided schools resonated to the anti-mainstream, yet fiercely individualist messages of hardcore skater culture, which may have made them less receptive to feminist discourses that emphasize institutional-level gender inequality. In contrast, middle-class girls in a variety of schools, particularly a group we have called the "in-betweeners," appeared to engage in skater girl discourse as a way of gaining distance from both the sexism evident in skater culture and emphasized femininity.

Our study of skater girlhood is exploratory and our findings tentative. Nevertheless, we detected in the narratives of the skater girls, particularly the "in-betweeners," the capacity (at least implicitly) to recognize multiple, competing discourses, including the dominant discourse of emphasized femininity. They provided examples of carving among these multiple discourses, playing one off against another, as well as of grinding or finding, and using to their advantage, contradictions within any one discourse. The skater girls were exercising agency, in the sense developed by Bronwyn Davies:

Agency is never freedom from discursive constitution of self but the capacity to recognise that constitution and to resist, subvert and change the discourses themselves through which one is being constituted. It is the freedom to recognise multiple readings such that no discursive practice, or positioning within it by powerful others, can capture and control one's identity. (1991, p. 51)

To the extent that skater girlhood is in opposition to emphasized femininity, we find within it at least an implicit critique of the form of femininity "oriented to accommodating the interests and desires of men" (Connell, 1987, p. 183). In this vein, educators might work with young people to promote what Davies (1997) has called:

Critical social literacy, [which] involves the development of a playful ability to move between and amongst discourses, to move in and out of them, to mix them, to break their spell when necessary. (p. 29)

We leave the last word to Sara, the 14-year-old skater affiliate, who bemoaned the "many" unspoken "rules" to being a girl today.

That's why I like being alternative, because you can break so many more rules. If you hang out with the cliques and the mainstreamers and the pop kids, there's so many more rules that you have to follow. And if you don't follow [them] … you're no longer cool, and they start rumors about you.

Notes

1 *Alternative culture* is an umbrella term for various non-mainstream styles (Hodkinson, 2002, p. 56). In the realm of music, the term *alternative* is used to signify difference from (or refusal to conform to) the mainstream in a wide variety of genres (e.g., rock, country, rap, folk). Alternative bands bend the rules, either from inside or outside of a musical tradition; they sometimes fuse together elements of different categories of music. They do not cater to mainstream sensibilities. Because major corporate recording companies want to market their artists to as wide an audience as possible, alternative musicians are more often represented by independent ("indie") labels.

2 The various youth cultures (punk, Goth, hip hop) that cross-fertilize with skater culture should not be seen as clearly bounded and distinctive from one another. With this caveat in mind, punk refers to a genre of rock music and an antiauthoritarian subculture that has been associated with White working-class youth in Great Britain.

It dates to the mid-1970s and such British bands as the Sex Pistols and the Clash. Style-wise, punk is associated with shaved heads and spiked haircuts, dog collars (spiked leather necklaces), piercing and military attire (e.g., heavy boots and leather jackets). A DYI ("do it yourself"), anti-mass culture ethic and aesthetic also characterize the subculture (see Leblanc, 1999).

Goth is an offshoot of punk, associated with the darker themes of punk music developed by Siouxsie and the Banshees in the late 1970s. Fashion-wise, goths commonly display black hair and clothes; horror-style makeup (white facial foundation, black eyeliner, and dark lipstick for both women and men); and symbols of death (e.g., crucifixes). Subcultural themes include "horror, death, misery and gender ambiguity" (Hodkinson, 2002, p. 61).

Hip hop names the culture surrounding rap music, including break dancing, graffiti-spraying, and disc-jockeying. Hip hop is linked with urban Black youth culture in the US and messages of rebellion and alienation. Fashion-wise, hip hop has been associated with baggy jeans, gold jewelry, baseball caps, and certain designer brands like Tommy Hilfiger (see Rose, 1994; Spiegler, 1996; Kitwana, 2002).

3 In a recent review of research on youth cultures, Bucholtz (2002) remarks that "ethnographic research on many aspects of youth cultural practice is often surprisingly scarce" (p. 526).

4 Further evidence that skateboarding is coded as "creative": The City of Vancouver recently legalized skateboarding on city streets in an effort to cultivate innovation. A city planner noted, "If we want to attract the creative people, we have to accept that they are somewhat on the edge and want to do different things" (quoted in Anderson, 2003).

5 Architects in downtown Vancouver have begun to design buildings and public spaces to discourage skateboarders from "trespassing" and to "protect property and landscaping." One property manager

noted, "It's a constant battle. This building's on a web site as one of the recommended places to skateboard" (Bellett, 2003, p. G2).

6 According to the High Definition Dictionary, "skank" means a promiscuous person, especially one who transmits sexual diseases, as well as an undesirable, irresponsible or dishonest person or free-loader. See www.hdd.rox.com.

7 "Carving" means to make a long, curving arc while skateboard-ing; "grinding" refers to skateboarding tricks where the hanger/s of the truck (the part of the skateboard that connects the deck with the wheels and allows the board to turn) grind along the edge of an obstacle.

8 Bettie (2003) noted, in her ethnography of working-class girls in a small-town high school in California, that "Many students who believed they were unusual in their ability to cross groups were in fact not as widely accepted as they thought by the groups they crossed into" (p. 110).

References

Anderson, C. (2003) Urban warrior: Some biz owners don't share LOVE: Prefer no skateboarding downtown—at all, *Philadelphia Daily News*, 15 September. Available online at: www.philly.com/mld/dailynews/news/columnists/6774732.htm (accessed 30 September 2003).

Beal, B. (1995) Disqualifying the official: An exploration of social resistance through the subculture of skateboarding, *Sociology of Sport Journal*, 12, 252–267.

Beal, B. (1996) Alternative masculinity and its effects on gender relations in the subculture of skateboarding, *Journal of Sport Behavior*, 19(3), 204–220.

Bellett, G. (2003) Skateboarders have forever changed look of the city, *Vancouver Sun*, 4 October, G1-2.

Bettie, J. (2003) *Women without class: Girls, race, and identity* (Berkeley, University of California Press).

Bettis, P.J. & Adams, N.G. (2003) The power of the preps and a cheerleading equity policy, *Sociology of Education*, 76, 128–142.

Borden, I. (2001) *Skateboarding, space and the city: Architecture and the body* (Oxford, Berg).

Bucholtz, M. (2002) Youth and cultural practice, *Annual Review of Anthropology*, 31, 525–552.

Connell, R.W. (1987) *Gender and power* (Stanford, Stanford University Press).

Connell, R.W., Ashenden, D.J., Kessler, S. & Dowsett, G.W. (1982) *Making the difference: Schools, families and social division* (Sydney, Allen & Unwin).

Currie, D., Kelly, D.M. & Pomerantz, S. (2003) "I'm going to crush you like a bug": Understanding girls' aggression, manuscript submitted for publication.

Davies, B. (1991) The concept of agency: a feminist post-structuralist analysis, *Social Analysis*, 30, 42–53.

Davies, B. (1997) Constructing and deconstructing masculinities through critical literacy, *Gender and Education*, 9(1), 9–30.

Eder, D., with Evans, C.A., Therine, C., & Parker, S. (1995) *School talk: Gender and adolescent culture* (New Brunswick, NJ, Rutgers University Press).

Gee, J.P. (2001) Identity as an analytic lens for research in education, *Review of Research in Education*, 25, 99–125.

Halpin, M. (2003) Go Avril!, *Seventeen*, January, 100–103.

Hodkinson, P. (2002) *Goth: Identity, style and subculture* (Oxford, Berg).

Hollway, W. & Jefferson, T. (2000) *Doing qualitative research differently: Free association, narrative and the interview method* (London, Sage).

Kitwana, B. (2002) *The hip hop generation: Young blacks and the crisis in African-American culture* (New York, Basic Civitas).

Leblanc, L. (1999) *Pretty in punk: Girls' gender resistance in a boys' subculture* (New Brunswick, Rutgers University Press).

Merton, D.E. (1997) The meaning of meanness: popularity, competition, and conflict among junior high school girls, *Sociology of Education*, 70(3), 175–191.

Peralta, S. (2001) *Dogtown and Z-boys* (Culver City, Sony Pictures Classics).

Pomerantz, S., Currie, D.H. & Kelly, D.M. (2004) Sk8er girls: Skateboards, girlhood, and feminism in motion, *Women's Studies International Forum*, 27, 547–557.

Rose, T. (1994) *Black noise: Rap music and black culture in contemporary America* (Hanover, NH, University Press of New England).

Smith, D.E. (1988) Femininity as discourse, in: L.G. Roman, L.K. Christian-Smith, with E. Ellsworth (Eds) *Becoming feminine: The politics of popular culture* (London, Falmer Press).

Spiegler, M. (1996) Marketing street culture: Bringing hip-hop style to the mainstream, *American Demographics*, 18, 28–34.

Thornton, S. (1995) *Club cultures: Music, media and subcultural capital* (Cambridge, Polity Press).

Willard, M.N. (1998) Seance, tricknowledgy, skateboarding, and the space of youth, in: J. Austin & M.N. Willard (Eds) *Generations of youth: Youth cultures and history in twentieth-century America* (New York, New York University Press).

CHAPTER 30
Emerging Realities and Old Problems

GRACE-EDWARD GALABUZI

Canada's Economy and Changing Population across the Millennium Divide

Canada's population has become more ethnically and racially diverse in the late 20th and early 21st century. This follows key changes in the 1960s to an otherwise historically Eurocentric immigration policy. This Eurocentric bias was part of a nation-building project that traces its roots to Canada's original imaginary as a White-settler colony. This imaginary was sketched out in the early colonial contact with the Aboriginal nations, and continued through the period of colonization right into Confederation. But that picture's veracity was always suspect; in fact, Canada has always had a multi-cultural, multi-racial character. The "White nation" myth was achieved through a state-sponsored campaign of social exclusion of Aboriginal peoples and racialized groups throughout Canada's history.

The tension between myth and reality was suppressed for as long as the population profile could sustain the concept of Canada as a White nation. Immigration policy staunchly defended the socially constructed notion of Canada's character by encouraging and even recruiting European immigrants, while turning away formerly enslaved African Americans or Caribbeans, Middle-Easterners, Latin Americans, South Asians, and South East Asians. But that is fast changing and the raw nerves of the project are beginning to fray. Canada's population growth is now disproportionately dependent on immigration from source countries with racialized populations.

This reversal of earlier trends and policies assuring near-exclusive European or White immigration has less to do with political choice, and more with population pressures in Canada, global immigration trends and the process of globalization.[1] Yet debates on Canada's immigration policy continue to labour under a White-settler colony imaginary, betraying a persistent hostile sentiment towards racialized group settlement in Canada.[2]

The percentage of racialized groups in the Canadian population, under 4% in 1971, grew to 9.4% by 1991, then 11.2% by 1996, and had reached 13.4% by 2001.

The immigrant population accounted for 18.4% of the Canadian population in 2001. Both racialized groups and immigrants are projected to rise to 20% and 25% respectively by 2015. Outside of Australia, this is the highest proportion of immigrants in any population, higher than the 9% in the United States. In a number of major Canadian urban centres, racialized group members and recent immigrants now make up majorities in the population.

The trend is more likely to grow than recede. In fact, in the most recent census period, 1996–2001, while the general population grew by 3.9%, the racialized population grew by a remarkable 24.6%. Between 1996 and 2001, the male racialized proportion of the labour force grew by 28.7% (compared to 5.5% of total working male population) and the female racialized working group population grew by 32.3% (compared to 9.0% of the total working female population).

While the growth was highest in Ontario (28%), it was significant in British Columbia (26.6%), Alberta (22.5%), New Brunswick (18%), Quebec (14.7%), and Manitoba (12.6%) among others, only falling in Prince Edward Island (–22%).

According to the 2001 Census, the largest number of racialized group members were to be found in Ontario (2,153,045), making up 19% of the population of Canada's largest province. That share is projected to rise to 25% by 2015. British Columbia had the highest proportion of racialized group members (836,445) in its population at 22%.

Much of that growth can be attributed to immigration, with significant increases from Asia and the Middle East, and some growth in Africa and Latin America as source areas too. Given Canada's continued reliance on immigration for population growth and labour-market needs, and the escalating process of globalization, these trends are likely to persist and even intensify.

Canada's racialized population is mainly concentrated in urban centres, with nearly three quarters (73%) living in Canada's three largest cities in 2001 and accounting for major proportions of the populations of

221

those municipalities—Toronto (43%), Vancouver (49%), and Montreal (23%). Other municipalities with significant racialized populations include Calgary (18%); Edmonton (15%); Markham, Ontario (56%); and Richmond, B.C. (59%) (Statistics Canada, 2003).

While 68% of Canada's racialized group members are immigrants, a significant proportion, 32%, are Canadian-born. The size of the racialized population will continue to be an important consideration for public policy because it is concentrated in urban Canada, which, in the early 20th century, is the engine of Canada's economy.

Immigrants and Urban Canada

[...] Racialized groups now represent a key source of human resources for the Canadian labour market. Already, according to Human Resources and Skills Development Canada (HRSDC), 70% of net new entrants into the labour force are immigrants, 75% of whom are racialized. By 2011, over 100% of net new entrants will come from this group. Resolving the issue of racial discrimination will be critical to their integration into the Canadian labour market and to the continued success of the Canadian economy (HRDC, 2002). According to a Conference Board of Canada study, while racialized groups averaged less than 11% of the labour force between 1992 and 2000, they accounted for 0.3% of real gross domestic product growth (GDP). That contrasts with the remaining 89% of the labour force, which contributed 0.6%. This disproportionately large contribution to GDP growth is likely to grow over the 2002–2016 period as the contribution of the rest of the population falls. However, this productive capacity was not rewarded as the average wages for racialized groups over that period remained 14.5% lower than those of other Canadians. The Board report concludes that in monetary terms, over the period 1992 to 2016, racialized groups will contribute $80.9 billion in real GDP growth.[3]

The complex dynamics of population change are interwoven with the organization of the Canadian economy. Canada's economy has historically created social class hierarchies, which emphasize divisions such as gender and race. While race is a social construct based principally on superficial differences in physical appearance, it has always been an important part of Canada's population-economy complex. From early European attempts to take control of the land, resources, and trade from the First Nations, which involved restricting their economic participation, to the selective importation of African American, Asian, and Caribbean labour, and the more recent casualization of racialized immigrant labour, race has been and continues to be a major factor in determining access to economic opportunity in Canada. Late 20th-century intensification of racial segregation in the labour market is located within the context of the neo-liberal restructuring of the global economy. The shift toward neo-liberal forms of governance and labour market deregulation aimed at flexible labour

deployment is calculated to achieve maximum exploitation of labour. Because of persistent historical structures of systemic discrimination, the growing dominance of flexible work arrangements in this liberalized environment, facilitated by the state deregulation of the labour market and the reversal of state anti-discriminatory policies and programs, has disproportionately impacted racialized groups.

Moreover, the cumulative impact of those processes suggests a redefining of other social hierarchies and social structures in Canadian society. The process of racial segmentation, underway in the Canadian labour market during this neo-liberal era, represents an intensification of the racialization of the process of class formation, as suggested by key structural patterns of income differentials, occupational concentration, and sectoral segregation in the Canadian labour market.[4] Racial segmentation in the labour market then leads to such social outcomes as differential access to housing, neighbourhood selection, contact with the criminal justice system, health risks, and political participation. The result is a deepening of the racialization of poverty and related conditions such as the racial segregation of low-income neighbourhoods, and the intensification of social exclusion for Canada's urban-based racialized group communities. These processes are central to the emergence of what Li (1998) has referred to as a social hierarchy of race, and what we refer to as the *colour-coded vertical mosaic*.[5] But while the racialization of class formation furthers the oppression of racialized groups by intensifying their social exclusion, it also makes it possible to engage in a racially conscious class-based struggle and workplace-based politics of resistance in response to the neo-liberal political project. Ironically, the racializing of the division of labour may serve to undermine the neo-liberal project by mobilizing racialized workers in solidaristic formations based in workplaces where they predominate, but share with other non-racialized workings, and by tapping into their shared experience of class-based social exclusion. The contradictions of the late 20th- and early 21st-century capitalist accumulation make possible a process of class formation rooted both in the common experience of precarious wage relations and in the cultural experience of racialization.[6]

Canada's Population Changes Driven by Labour Needs

As a resource-rich and labour-poor country, Canada has historically met its labour shortages by encouraging immigration, but within the framework of an assimilation policy aimed at maintaining a "White society." Hence the official categories of "desirables" and "undesirables" that dominated immigration policy until recently. The demands of an expanding economy and the slowing of interest in migration to Canada by different groups of Europeans led to a decision to remove the legal restrictions against non-European immigration in the 1960s. Even so, administrative restrictions continued to be enforced, demanding that only those with government designated "essential skills" qualify ahead of family members seeking reunification, as was previously practiced. Refugees had often cracked this carefully constructed shield, but those fissures were closed with a new stringent refugee determination system that ensured that a clear majority of applicants were denied asylum and either deported or descended into a non-status limbo. These measures, largely enacted as the source countries for immigrants became predominantly countries in the Global South, served to manage the flow of immigrants so as not to threaten the Eurocentric nature of the country.

The outcome of the policies is a gender and racially stratified social profile, as manifested in the Canadian labour market today. From a gender standpoint, not only did racialized women face the racial structures in the workplace and society, but also they were incorporated into the "pink ghettos" where women are disproportionately represented. Beyond being imported into the lower ranks of the health-care sector, the textile and garment industry, the service sector and clerical ghettos, and disproportionately subjected to precarious forms of employment, many female immigrants from the global South were forced to apply as domestic workers, although many had professional and other qualifications.7

[...] [T]he developments in the late 20th century and the related insights into the racialized nature of social hierarchies in Canada essentially update John Porter's concept of vertical mosaic based on the social stratification of Canadian society in the 1960s (Porter, 1965).8 The idea of an ethnically defined Canadian vertical mosaic has lost some of its explanatory value and been updated by a racially distinct vertical mosaic on the grounds that while the association between ethnicity and inequality has weakened, the role played by race in stratifying Canadian society has increased. These changes justify references to a colour-coded vertical mosaic (Herberg, 1990; Lian and Matthews, 1998; Li, 1998). [...] The growth of the racialized population makes the characterization more compelling than in years past. [...]

Shifts in Canada's Immigration Policy

Canada's immigration policy shifted in the 1960s towards a more racially liberal skills-based points system that attracted many newcomers from outside Europe. Immigrants from the South with a broad range of skills arrived, only to face barriers to access in employment—as documented by a Royal Commission report in the early 1980s—or to be slotted into low-end job ghettos, as other research shows. The immigration data show that the increased numbers of skilled immigrants from the South have not experienced economic success comparable to that of European immigrants or Canadians of

European heritage. Instead, in a departure from earlier patterns of immigrant economic performance, the lag in economic attainment has become a permanent income gap between racialized communities and the rest of the population. In a pattern that coincides with the influx of racialized immigrant groups, and seems to be holding both during and after the recession years of the late 1970s, 1980s, and early 1990s, immigrant economic performance has grown progressively worse over the last quarter century. So while Canada's population is becoming more racially diverse, the country's history of differential treatment of non-European peoples limits the life chances of racialized groups in a manner not experienced by previous waves of immigrants, who also came to seek a better life.

Racialized Immigration, Neo-racism and Competitive Racism

As we noted above, the political, economic and social destabilization brought about by the processes of global restructuring, together with the growing inequality between the North and the South, have had a profound impact on the nature of population flows around the world. While the population movement during periods of colonialism were from North to South in order to establish settler colonies and to entrench structures of colonialism, the new movements are in reverse. Largely but not exclusively, they are movements of poor people from the South to the North. These "immigrants" come to seek both asylum and a better way of life. They are 138 million migrants, including part of the over 5 million documented refugees running from political conflict and economic displacement, and the many more millions who are internally displaced and cannot afford the means to make the trips North.9 However, the influx of newcomers, combined with the unequal articulations of capitalist development, which force them into conditions of disadvantage, has created what is now called "South in the North"—communities and neighbourhoods whose conditions are more like those in the South than those generally found in the North. This phenomenon is characterized by the racialization of neighbourhoods, and in some cases, cities and regions.

These developments emerge within the framework of existing racialized social structures, prompting new forms of response within the host societies. Immigration has become one of the most contentious public policy areas. What has come to be known as *neo-racism* is said to explain the anti-immigrant discourses and policy actions of people in the North in response to the new migration unleashed by globalization's displacement of entire communities. Neo-racism represents a particular construction of race at the historical moment of 21st-century globalization. Like all other forms of racism, it utilizes the social construction of racial categories to demand limits on the numbers of certain racial groups allowed into the country and on racial mixing. Neo-racism's dominant theme is the insurmountability of cultural differences. It concentrates on the harmful that can come out of abolishing borders, and on the incompatibility of social traditions and lifestyles. In an ironic twist, it uses the very defence of difference to justify its cultural segregationist position.[10]

* * * * *

Canada's Political Economy and the Racialized Growing Economic Gap

There is mounting evidence that the bouts of economic restructuring Canada has endured in the last two decades have intensified processes of racialization and feminization in the labour markets, leading to increased economic, social, and political inequality and immiseration of vulnerable populations of women, men, and children. The patterns of intensified inequality suggest that racialized groups, immigrants, refugees, and women have borne the brunt of economic restructuring and austerity. Global economic restructuring has not only encouraged the informalization of economies and the emergence of "precarious work"—temporary, part-time, contract, and casual work with low pay, no benefits, no job security, and poor working conditions—but also exacerbated previous fissures of racial and gender inequality based on systemic discrimination. A growing body of Canadian studies suggests that flexible work arrangements, facilitated by the state-mediated processes of deregulation and re-regulation of the labour market, have particularly disadvantaged racialized groups, and especially racialized women. Adding to the problem are persistent discriminatory labour-market structures. The consequences are increased segmentation of the labour market along racial lines, the racialization of poverty, the racialization and segregation of low-income neighbourhoods, and intensified social exclusion.

Central to this phenomenon is the global restructuring that is taking place in Canada's economy and changing the nature of work on offer. This restructuring is disproportionately impacting racialized group members. The intensification of flexible accumulation on a global scale has created an increasingly transnational division of labour and unleashed new migrations trends that may partly explain Canada's increased absorption of new immigrants. But it has also ushered in a growing informalization of the economy, "normalizing" the shift to non-standard forms of work through labour market deregulation, as previously peripheral forms of work become increasingly dominant.[11] The disproportionate participation of racialized groups in these forms of work is an important part of their declining social economic status. While the racialization of production is obviously not new, recent patterns and size of migration from the South to the North, which reverse the colonial North-South patterns that ushered in industrial capitalism, have combined with persistent structures of systemic discrim-

ination to disproportionately relegate racialized groups to non-standard forms of work.[12]

Accentuating the consequences of the flexible accumulation, informalization, and South-North migration discussed above, is a shift towards neo-liberal forms of governance that has dismantled the key elements of the Welfare state in the North and many of its social protection mechanisms. This has increased intra-working-class tensions and competition for decent employment, which have unleashed expressions of overt racism. Some refer to these expressions of racism as "competitive racism within capitalist economies."[13] In this instance, racism arises out of competition brought on by the deregulation of work arrangements, which drives down wages and increases levels of exploitation and vulnerability. As we noted before, for racialized groups, this intensification of oppression ironically opens the door to a class-based yet racially conscious struggle against the articulations of global capitalism.

Given the nature of economic restructuring, the normalization of non-standard forms of work is central to understanding the present-day racialization of class formation, especially in Canada's urban areas. The racialization of class formation is an outcome of the impact of historical processes of flexible accumulation identified with capitalist restructuring on a global scale on Canada's labour market in the late 20th and early 21st centuries. It also reproduces pre-existing racial discriminatory structures in the labour market directed at racialized populations for the purposes of subsidizing global capital. The labour of racialized group members is devalued, with added significance because of their increased numbers in Canada's urban areas. The process of intensified exploitation is manifest even during a period of relative prosperity in Canada, and as we account in this book, between 1996 and 2001, the gap between rich and poor became not only wider, but also increasingly racialized.

While historically, the majority of immigrants have achieved some degree of economic success in the Canadian labour market, many immigrants started with wages and salaries lower than those of comparable Canadian-born workers. But as the length of residence in Canada increased, their earnings approached, and sometimes exceeded, those of Canadian-born workers. However, as we will see below, recent trends raise questions about this analysis of immigrants' economic integration. Since the beginning of the 1980s, immigrants' earnings have stalled and are no longer converging with comparable Canadian-born workers' (DeVoretz, 1995; Ley and Smith, 1997; Reitz and Sklar, 1997). National data show evidence of racialized workers, many of whom have arrived since 1980, stuck disproportionately at the bottom of the economic ladder in terms of income, employment, and access to high-paying sectors and jobs (Ornstein, 2000; Galabuzi, 2001; Lian and Matthews, 1998; Reitz, 1998; Smith and Jackson, 2002).

The Emergence of Precarious Work and the Racialization of the Labour Market

The neo-liberal global economic restructuring has left a mark on Canada's labour market, one felt intensely by racialized groups. This restructuring represents a qualitative shift in the way work is organized in Canada. Broad (2000) has suggested that five interrelated structural transformations have combined to create the conditions for the emergence of precarious work as a major feature of Canadian labour markets. These include the globalization of capitalist production, the emergence of the neo-liberal state, flexible production, the rise of the service economy, and the increased re-entry of women into the economy.[14] For our purposes, these combine with the phenomenon of increased flow of immigrants from the South to Canada's urban areas to create the conditions under which racial segmentation of the labour market is becoming normalized. For those concerned about the everyday life conditions of working people, it is clear that these processes, coupled with the dismantling of the Canadian welfare state, have created key deficits in social reproduction that help explain the racialization of poverty, which we will discuss in detail below. Cutbacks in social program spending, cuts to income transfers to individuals and families, a shift to the workfare program, deregulation, the lowering of employment standards and other forms of labour legislation have had a deleterious effect. Compounding this is the fact that the state has also retreated from anti-discriminatory policies and programs. The devaluation of racialized labour and the increased supply of low-end labour have allowed for greater employer latitude and have given currency to demands for Canadian experience, to rejection of skills gained in other countries, and to other forms of employment discrimination.[15]

Precarious work has become a major feature of the Canadian labour market at the beginning of the 21st century. By the end of the 1990s, a far greater proportion of people were either on contract, self-employed, or doing temporary work than at the beginning of the decade. While the form of work is not new, the levels depart from previous decades. Growth in full-time employment accounted for only 18% of new job growth between 1989 and 1998, compared to 58% during the preceding decade. Meanwhile, self-employment accounted for 58%, compared to 18% in the 1980s.[16]

The dramatic increase in temporary, contract, part-time, piece work, and self-employment has had a dramatic impact on racialized group members, especially racialized women. Not only do disproportionate numbers of racialized group members depend on precarious work, but also the work is largely unregulated, involving long hours and low pay. The effect is an intensification of work, with many either working longer hours or working multiple jobs. Many of the workers in the service sector and light manufacturing industries increasingly find themselves on temporary contracts from Employment Service Agencies, which pay them a fraction of what they earn in the jobs to which they are assigned, and hold them to those contracts even when their employers require their services permanently.

In material terms, the disproportionate concentration of racialized populations in part-time, temporary, and home work—particularly for racialized women—leads to their overrepresentation in substandard and increasingly segregated housing, along with higher mental and other health risks, tensions between communities, and contact with the criminal justice system. There is heightened *social exclusion* of whole segments of racialized groups, some of which have resorted to internecine violence.

Employment Income and Racialized Groups

A series of studies done in the late 1990s by economist Armine Yalnizyan for the Toronto-based Centre for Social Justice, titled *Growing Gap*, show that while the Canadian economy was growing faster in the late 1990s than at any time over the last 25 years, Canadian incomes were becoming more unequal. There is a generalized growing gap between the top 10% income earners and the rest of the population.[17] The gap between Canada's racialized groups and other Canadians has also grown and become sustained in double digits. What we show here is that the income inequality in Canada is also increasingly along racial lines. This represents just one dimension of the socio-economic exclusion of racialized groups, which is manifested in their labour-market experiences of higher unemployment; overrepresentation in low-end occupations and low-income sectors; and underrepresentation in managerial, professional, and high-income occupations and sectors. The process of economic exclusion has had broader effects such as higher poverty rates, lower civic and political participation, higher health risks, lower quality housing, intensified segregation of neighbourhoods, and more contact with the criminal justice system. It is important to note that these effects are not limited to immigrants or "newcomers," but are also experienced by many racialized group members who have either lived in Canada for extended periods of time or were born in the country.

Analysis of a special run of Survey of Labour and Income Dynamics (SLID) data for the CSJ Foundation for the period 1996–2001 show a sustained double-digit gap between the incomes of racialized group members and other Canadians. This being a period of relative prosperity, suggests that the market-based approach to dealing with racial inequality has clearly failed. Based on individual earnings, racialized Canadians in 1996 earned a pre-tax average of $19,227, while non-racialized Canadians made $25,069, or 23% more. The median income (showing half earning more and half earning less) gap at 29% ($13,648 to $19,111) suggests an even more profound inequality. The gap grew in 1997 as the racialized group average pre-tax income increase of $19,558 did not keep pace with the $25,938 earned by other Canadians; the gap is 25%. The median before-tax income again betrays deeper inequality, with racialized earnings declining to $13,413, while others saw a modest increase to $19,602. The median income gap also grew from 1996 to 1997 to 32%. The growing economy improved the income position of racialized group members in 1998, but the gap did not diminish substantially over the three-year period. Data show an average before-tax income for racialized groups of $20,626, which accounted for 76% of the $27,174 the rest of the population earned, for a gap of 24%. The median racialized income increased to $14,507, compared to $20,517, leaving the gap at 28%.[18]

The tax effect was marginal in terms of closing the gap. The average after-tax income of the racialized groups in 1996 was $16,053, compared to $20,129 for other Canadians, a 20% gap. After-tax incomes grew for both groups in 1997 to $16,438, or 79% of the $20,793 for other Canadians, figures still showing a marginal growing gap. But while the median after-tax income for 1996 was $12,991 for racialized groups, compared to $16,922 for other Canadians, a gap of 23%, that gap grew in 1997 to 26% as racialized group members took home less at $12,895, while other Canadians increased their earnings to $17,320. In 1998, taking the tax effect into consideration, racialized groups earned an after-tax average of $17,376, i.e., 80% of the $21,694 for the rest of the population. The median racialized after-tax income was $13,561, compared to $18,146, for a still-high gap of 25%.[19]

In essence, analysis of the employment income data for this period "economic boom" period (1996–98) shows a growing gap that marginally levelled off in 1998, leaving a high income gap that, if one looks at median incomes for the three years, is as high as 32%.

The situation did improve as there was a delayed benefit for racialized groups from the economic gains of the late 1990s. However, the gap remained double digit, and the time lag in acquiring the benefit suggests that structures exist that impede the allocation of rewards to certain groups in society.

During the period 1991–2001, racialized groups experienced a median after-tax income gap of 13.3% ($18,138 to $15,909), and an average after-tax income gap of 12.2% ($23,023 to $20,627). The gap is highest among male youth (average after-tax income gap 42.3% and median after-tax income gap 38.7%), as well as those with less than high school education (median after-tax income gap 20.6%) and those over 65 years (average income gap of 28% and median income gap of 21%).[20]

The gap was evident among those with higher education as well as among those with less than high school education, as was the time lag between non-racialized and racialized populations seeing the rewards of the improved economy.

Racialized Groups and Unequal Access to the Workplace

Numerous studies discuss the issue of unequal access to the workplace for racialized groups.[21] This is an important factor in explaining the double-digit racialized income gap. The employment gap between racialized groups and other Canadians dramatically demonstrates this unequal access to work opportunities. The unemployment rate in 1991 was 16%, compared to 11% for the general population.[22] The data show that the levels of unemployment were much higher among specific racialized groups, including women and youths. The 1995 rate for racialized women was 15.3%, compared to 13.2% for racialized men, 9.4% for other women and 9.9% for other men.[23]

In 1991, the participation rate for the non-racialized group adult population was 78%, compared to 70.5% of the racialized adult population. The participation gap grew in 1996, with the participation rate for the non-racialized group adult population dropping to 75%, compared to 66% of the racialized adult population. While the participation rate for the total population improved to 80% in 2001, racialized participation rates lagged at 66%. Unemployment rate differentials were also evident, with the total population at 6.7% in 2001, and the racialized rate about twice as high at 12.6%. In 1996, unemployment rates were also higher among specific racialized groups, including women, youths, and those without post-secondary education; this difference levelled off in 2001, except among recent immigrants. The data show a relationship between systemic discrimination in access to employment and overrepresentation in low-income sectors and low-paying occupations, despite comparable educational levels. For many racialized group members, educational attainment has not translated into comparable compensation, labour-market access, or workplace mobility. Immigrants (68% of the racialized group) face structural barriers to recognizing their skills, demands for Canadian experience, denial by provincially regulated licensing bodies of accreditation for those with trade and professional qualifications, and the general devaluation of their skills. These factors in part account for immigrants' inability to translate qualifications—key to their selection in the immigration process—into comparable employment and compensation.

Both newcomers and other racialized group members experience differential treatment in the labour market. Consequently, the impact of systemic racial discrimination is crucial to understanding the emergence of the racialized income and employment gap. In most cases, this experience is shared by Canadian-born members of the groups.[24] The data show that immigrant members of racialized groups have more in common, in terms of unemployment and low income, with Canadian-born racialized group members than with immigrants from Europe arriving in the same period. In fact, the income gap between European immigrants and other immigrants is also growing; this suggests differential access to economic opportunity due to discriminatory structures in the labour market.

The impact of systemic discrimination in employment has been identified by a major Royal Commission and by numerous studies conducted in the 1980s and 1990s. This research prompted some government policy responses, including federal employment equity legislation in 1986. Annual reports under the federal legislation show a continuing pattern of discrimination in employment both in the federal public service and in federally regulated sectors such as banking, telecommunications, and broadcasting.[25]

The Racialization of Poverty

According to 1995 Statistics Canada data, 35.6% of members of racialized groups lived under the poverty line, compared to 17.6% in the general Canadian population; the rate of poverty is thus twice as high.[26] In 1996, the rate of poverty among racialized group members in Canada's urban centres was 37.6%, compared to 20.9% for the rest of the population.[27] While we are not able to disaggregate the data further, the picture is even worse when one looks at particular racialized groups. Research has indicated that such is the case with racialized women, single-parent groups and certain ethno-racial groups.[28] Other research—based on SLID special run data for the CSJ Foundation—which looks at after-tax family income shows that in 1998, some 19% of racialized community families lived in poverty, compared to 10.4% of other Canadians, i.e., almost double the poverty rate.[29]

Poverty rates were particularly high among recent immigrants, signalling the failure to translate internationally obtained skills into equivalent compensation. During the past two decades, low-income rates have increased among successive groups of newly arrived immigrants. In 1980, 24.6% of immigrants who had arrived during the previous five-year period lived below the poverty line. By 1990, the low-income rate among recent immigrants had increased to 31.3%. After peaking at 47.0% in 1995, the rate fell back to 35.8% in 2000. In 1995, four out of every ten racialized immigrants who held less than a high school education were among the poorest 20% in the country.[30] Between 1980 and 2000, the full-time employment earnings of recent male immigrants fell 7% (from $40,600 to $37,900). This compares with a rise of 7% for the Canadian-born cohort ($45,600 to $48,600). Among the university-educated the drop was deeper (13%—$55,300 to $48,300, versus $69,100 to $76,000). The full-time employment earnings of recent female immigrants rose, but less than other female full-time earnings ($23,800 to $26,800 versus $28,800 to $34,400; $32,700 to $34,700, versus $45,200 to $50,000).[31]

According to 1995 Statistics Canada data, 35.6% of members of racialized groups lived below the poverty line. The developments described above point directly to a process of racialization of poverty. Key social and economic indicators like income, levels of unemployment, and sectoral participation patterns offer some insights into how economic globalization and the persistent legacy of racism have resulted in the growing patterns of low incomes among the racialized groups, income inequality between racialized group members and other Canadians, and the deterioration of the standard of housing available to racialized group members. Today, racialized group families are twice as likely to be poor as are other Canadian families. In some urban areas and among some groups of racialized group members, the rate is three to four times. The situation is particularly adverse with single-parent families, most of which are led by women.[32]

In urban centres like Toronto, Vancouver, Montreal, and Calgary, where racialized group populations are statistically significant, the normalization of racially segmented labour markets has an impact beyond the racialization of poverty. Racialized groups face other social patterns such as sustained school drop-out rates; the racialization of the penal system; the criminalization of the young, especially African Canadians; and the racial segregation of urban low-income neighbourhoods. These conditions have created a deepening social marginalization unprecedented in modern Canadian society. This is seen, for example, in a number of low-income neighbourhoods in Toronto where African Canadians are disproportionately represented as tenants of poorly maintained public and substandard private housing. In these neighbourhoods, the process of immiseration, desperation, hopelessness, and disempowerment has resulted in a level of violence that has claimed many young lives and threatens to spiral out of control.[33]

The experience of poverty has many implications for the lifechances of an individuals, families, or groups. Low incomes cut into basic-needs budgets, dooming many racialized people to substandard and increasingly segregated housing, poor-quality diets, reliance on food banks, and a decline in health status. Poverty imposes learning difficulties for the young; social and psychological pressures within the family; increased mental and other health risks. It also imposes an array of symptoms of social exclusion, including increased contact with the criminal justice system, and an inability to participate fully in the civic and social life of the community or to exercise democratic rights such as voting and advocacy.

Why Conventional Explanations for Racial Inequality Don't Measure Up

Conventional explanations for the gap in the economic performance of racialized groups—the income gap, the gap in employment levels, overrepresentation in low-paid occupations, underrepresentation in high-income occupations and sectors, and disproportionate exposure to precarious work—tend to focus on three factors: recent immigration, lack of Canadian experience, and educational attainment differentials. It is commonly argued that, because of these three, recent immigrants initially lag behind other Canadians, but are able to catch up over time.

However, the experience of the last 25 years is one of sustained low relative economic performance for racialized immigrant groups. Both educational attainment and human capital data for immigrants after the 1970s, when the majority of immigrants to Canada were racialized, do not support the "low immigrant quality" contention. A number of recent studies refute the myth that the lower "human capital quality" of racialized job seekers and/or workers explains these differential experiences in the labour market. While Canadian experience should matter less and less in a globalized economy, it is often noted that in Canada's major urban centres, far too many cab drivers have professional and advanced degrees. Why are people who have previously enjoyed such high levels of success excluded from reasonable access to the labour market?

Racialized immigrant groups are increasingly better educated, yet they face longer immigration lag periods and relegation into casual and temporary work; Canadian-born group members are experiencing similar patterns in the labour market. Moreover, the gap in economic performance between racialized and non-racialized immigrants is growing, with an income gap of 28% over the period 1991–95. The persistence of systemic discrimination, including the use of immigrant status as a proxy for "low human capital," conditions the patterns of underemployment of a labour force with above-average education. Even when dealing with segments not as highly qualified for labour-market participation (as is often said of some refugee populations, for instance), there are unjustifiable levels of overrepresentation in low-income sectors and occupations, casual, contract, temporary, and piecemeal work.[34] These are better explained by differential access to the labour market, which in turn leads to the growing gap in economic performance, and the incidence of poverty along racial lines.

* * * * *

Social Inequality: An Issue of Public Concern

Social inequality is both a social justice and an economic issue. It is also an issue of public and political concern because inequality leads to group tensions and social instability in society. Studies from around the world, as well as some recent Canadian studies, show that the most unequal societies are also the most unstable. The higher the level of inequality, the higher is the probability of violence and disorder within society. Inequality does in fact matter.

Health and well-being are heavily influenced by the distribution of economic resources, prestige, and social position. Studies show that quality of life appears to be lower in unequal societies, as such societies suffer illness-generating conditions. Socio-economic inequality is one of the most powerful influences on health and mortality rates. The greater the income differences within populations, the greater the health risks. There are risks arising from the conditions of work to which low-income earners are subjected, so that the disproportionate participation of groups in that type of work leads to greater exposure to health risks. This is clearly the case with racialized groups, especially women involved in garment work, domestic work, industrial cleaning, etc. The gender and racial stratification of the labour market definitely has implications for health and well-being.[35]

North American studies show that reducing income disparity decreases mortality rates. Other data show that income inequality is related to other social breakdowns, such as the amount of homicide and violent crime.[36] A final observation relating to income distribution is that cities with greater inequality are less socially cohesive. The challenge of social harmony is likely greater if the inequality is along racial lines.

* * * * *

Notes

[1] However, the change in immigration policy in the 1960s coincided with the Canadian government's enactment of the Bill of Rights and Canada's prominent role in the creation of the international human rights regime, developments that probably had some impact on the immigration policy debates at the time.

[2] An Ekos/*Toronto Star* poll conducted in June 2000 found that 30% of those surveyed believed that there were too many immigrants of colour in Canada. See also, P. Li, *Destination Canada: Immigration Debates and Issues* (2003); D. Palmer, "Determinants of Canadian Attitudes Towards Immigration: More Than Just Racism?" *Canadian Journal of Behavioural Sciences* 28 (1996): 180–92. The Ekos/*Toronto Star* poll results reflect this sentiment, as does some of the discourse on immigration. Both the discourse and public attitudes have had an impact on Canadian immigration policy, leading to key changes aimed at stricter selection rules and dramatically lower refugee admission rates.

[3] Conference Board of Canada, "Making a Visible Difference: The Contributions of Visible Minorities to Canadian Economic Growth," *Economic Performance and Trends* (April, 2004).

[4] See Creese (1999); Das Gupta (1996); de Wolff (2000); Galabuzi (2001); Hiebert (1997).

[5] The idea of a colour-coded vertical mosaic updates John Porter's concept of an ethnically defined vertical mosaic based on the social stratification of Canadian society in the 1960s (Porter, 1965). It suggests the emergence of a racially defined stratification of Canadian society, with a hierarchical social structure where racialized groups are located at the bottom and non-racialized groups at the top. In this formulation, race is said to be a determinant of access to opportunities in a variety of sectors of life, including income (and protection against poverty), employment, health care, political participation, neighbourhood selection, and, in general, a group's life chances. While not fully formed, the various indica-

tors of social economic status [...] suggest a resonance with such a hierarchical ordering of Canadian society. [...]

6 See G. Galabuzi, "Racializing the Division of Labour: Neo-liberal Restructuring and the Economic Segregation of Canada's Racialized Groups," in *Challenging the Market: The Struggle to Regulate Work and Income*, edited by J. Stanford and L. Vosko (Montreal: McGill-Queens University Press, 2004), 175–204; P. Daenzer, *Regulating Class Privilege: Immigrant Servants in Canada, 1940–1990s* (Toronto: Canadian Scholars' Press, 1993).

7 T. Das Gupta, "The Political Economy of Gender, Race and Class: Looking at South Asian Immigrant Women in Canada," *Canadian Ethnic Studies* XXVL no. 1 (1994): 59–73; D. Brand, "Black Women and Work: The Impact of Racially Constructed Gender Roles on the Sexual Division of Labour," *Fireweed* 25 (1987): 35.

8 Porter's concept of a vertical mosaic differentiated the dominant or privileged social status of what he called the Charter class—the English and the French—from that of groups that had immigrated after the establishment of the modern Canadian nation. These were a range of ethnic groups mostly from Northern, Eastern, and Southern Europe, as well as racialized groups. The concept of the mosaic refers also to the power relations that maintained that status. More recently, though, some of the then-underprivileged groups have been able to acquire "white" status, making the analysis less compelling.

9 H. Zlotnik, "Trends of International Migration Since 1965: What Existing Data Reveal," *International Migration* 37, no. 1 (1999).

10 E. Balibar, "Is There a Neo-racism," in *Race, Nation, Class: Ambiguous Identities*, edited by E. Balibar and I. Wallerstein (London: Verso, 1991).

11 J. Stanford, "Discipline, Insecurity and Productivity: The Economics behind Labour Market Flexibility," in *Remaking Canada's Social Policy: Social Security in the Late 1990s*, 130–150, edited by J. Pulkingham and G. Ternowetsky (Halifax: Fernwood Publishing, 1996). Stanford argues that there has been a "substantial weakening of a whole range of institutional and social controls over labour market outcomes." The result is the proliferation of non-standard forms of work.

12 A. Jackson and D. Robinson, *Falling Back: The State of Working Canada 2000* (Ottawa: Canadian Centre for Policy Alternatives, 2000); Vosko (2000); de Wolff (2000); Fox and Sugiman (Autumn, 1999): 59–84; Ornstein (2000); Galabuzi (2001).

13 B.S. Bolaria and P. Li (eds.), *Racial Oppression in Canada* (Toronto: Garamond Press, 1988); V. Satzewich (ed.), *Racism and Social Inequality in Canada: Concepts, Controversies and Strategies of Resistance* (Toronto: Thompson Publishing, 1998); R. Miles, *Racism* (London: Routledge, 1989).

14 D. Broad, *Hollow Work, Hollow Society: Globalization and the Casual Labour Problem in Canada* (Halifax, N.S.: Fernwood Publishing, 2000).

15 S. McBride and J. Shields, *Dismantling a Nation: The Transition to Corporate Rule in Canada* (Halifax: Fernwood, 2000).

16 G. Picot and A. Heisz, *The Performance of the 1990s Canadian Labour Market*, Paper no. 148 (Ottawa: Statistics Canada, April, 2000).

17 A. Yalnyzian, *The Growing Gap* (Toronto: Centre for Social Justice, 1998).

18 Based on a special run of Statistics Canada's *Survey of Labour and Income Dynamics (SLID)*, 1996, 1997, 1998, 1999, 2000, for the Centre for Social Justice.

19 Ibid.

20 Statistics Canada, Income Statistics Division, Survey of Labour and Labour and Income Dynamics, "Custom Tables, 1999–2002." See C. Teelucksingh and G. Galabuzi, *Working Precariously: The Impact of Race and Immigrants Status on Employment Opportunities and Outcomes in Canada* (Centre for Social Justice/Canadian Race Relation Foundation, 2005).

21 The list of reports and studies dealing with racial inequality in employment runs from the 1981 study by J. Reitz, L. Calzavara,

and D. Dasko, *Ethnic Inequality and Segregation in Jobs* (Centre for Urban and Community Studies, University of Toronto, 1981) through to that of the Canadian Parliamentary Taskforce on the Participation of Visible Minorities in Canada titled *Equality Now* (1984); also, the Abella Commission report *Equality in Employment* (1985), the Henry and Ginsberg reports *Who Gets the Job* and *No Discrimination Here* (1985); the Urban Alliance on Race Relations and Social Planning Council of Metro Toronto report *A Time for Change* (1990), and the most recent Federal government's *Taskforce on the Participation of Visible Minorities in the Federal Public Service* (2000). These, and many more, all conclude that racial discrimination was pervasive in Canada's employment systems. Further, that, as Judge Abella remarked, "Strong measures were needed to remedy the impact of discriminatory attitudes and behaviour."

22 R. Dibbs and T. Leesti, "Survey of Labour and Income Dynamics: Visible Minorities and Aboriginal Peoples," Statistics Canada, 1995.

23 J. Chard, J. Badets, and L. Howatson-Leo, "Women in Visible Minorities, in Women in Canada: A Gender-Based Statistical Report," Statistics Canada, Ottawa, 2000.

24 Some exceptions exist, though. Japanese Canadians are often cited as one. For comparison, according to 1996 Census data, two out of every three Japanese-Canadians (44,000) are Canadian born, while the ratio among African-Canadians is two out of every five African-Canadians (241,000). That is closer to the racialized group average of 68% (immigrants) to 32% (Canadian born).

25 Various Annual Reports, *Employment Equity Act*; See also Federal Taskforce on the Participation of Visible Minorities in the Federal Public Service, 2000.

26 Statistics Canada, "1996 Census: Sources of Income, Earnings," *The Daily* (May 12, 1998).

27 K. Lee, *Urban Poverty in Canada* (Ottawa: Canadian Council on Social Development, 2000).

28 Ornstein (2000).

29 R. Dibbs and T. Leesti, *Survey of Labour and Income Dynamics: Visible Minorities and Aboriginal Peoples* (Ottawa: Statistics Canada, 1995).

30 A. Jackson, "Poverty and Immigration" *Perception* 24, no. 4 (Spring, 2001).

31 Statistics Canada, "Low-Income Rates among Immigrants, 1980–2000," *The Daily* (June 19, 2003).

32 Ornstein (2000).

33 J.D. Hulchanski, "Immigrants and Access to Housing: How Welcome Are Newcomers to Canada?" *Proceedings of the Second National Conference, Seminar on Housing and Neighbourhoods* (Montreal, November 23–26, 1997):263; S. Novak, J. Darden, J.D. Hulchanski, A.-M. Seguin, "Housing Discrimination in Canada: What Do We Know about It?" *University of Toronto Research Bulletin* #1 (2002), Centre for Urban and Community Research; K. Dion, "Immigrants' Perceptions of Housing Discrimination in Toronto: The Housing New Canadians Project," *Journal of Social Issues* 57 (2001): 523–539.

34 J. Anderson and J. Lynam, "The Meaning of Work for Immigrant Women in the Lower Echelons of the Canadian Labour Force," *Canadian Ethnic Studies* XIX, no. 2 (1987): 67–90; Vosko (2000); T. Das Gupta, *Racism and Paid Work* (Toronto: Garamond Press, 1996).

35 L.Yanz, B. Jeffcott, D. Ladd, and J. Atlin, *Policy Options to Improve Standards for Women Garment Workers in Canada and Internationally* (Ottawa: Status of Women, Canada, 1999); Vosko (2000); Das Gupta (1996); R. Sennett and J. Cobb, *The Hidden Injuries of Class* (New York: Knopf, 1973).

36 R. Wilkinson, *Unhealthy Societies: The Afflictions of Inequality* (New York: Routledge, 1996); G.B. Rodger, "Income and Inequality as Determinants of Mortality: An International Cross-Section Analysis," *Population Studies* 33 (1979): 343–351; J. Bartley,

"Ethnic Inequality and the Rate of Homicide," *Social Forces* 69 (1990): 53–70; J. Blau and P. Blau, "The Costs of Inequality: Metropolitan Structure and Violent Crime," *American Sociological Review* 47 (1982): 114–129; A. Glyn and D. Miliband,

"Introduction," in *Paying for Inequality: The Costs of Social Injustice*, edited by A. Glyn and D. Miliband (London: Rivers Oram Press, 1994).

Bibliography

Abella, R. *Equality Now: Report of the Commission on Equality in Employment.* Ottawa: Supply and Services Canada, 1984.

Anderson, J., and M. Lynam. "The Meaning of Work for Immigrant Women in the Lower Echelons of the Canadian Labour Force." *Canadian Ethnic Studies* 19, no.2 (1987): 67–90.

Balibar, E. "Is There a Neo-Racism?" In *Race, Nation, Class: Ambiguous Identities*, edited by E. Balibar and I. Wallerstein. London: Verso, 1991.

Bartley, J. "Ethnic Inequality and the Rate of Homicide." *Social Forces* 69 (1990): 53–70.

Blau, J., and P. Blau. "The Costs of Inequality: Metropolitan Structure and Violent Crime." *American Sociological Review* 47 (1982): 114–129.

Bolaria, B.S., and P. Li. *Racial Oppression in Canada.* Toronto: Garamond Press, 1985.

Brand, D. "Black Women and Work: The Impact of Racially Constructed Gender Roles on the Sexual Division of Labour." *Fireweed* 25 (1987).

Broad, D. *Hollow Work, Hollow Society? Globalization and the Casual Labour Problem in Canada.* Halifax: Fernwood, 2000.

Chard, J., J. Bagets, and L. Howatson-Leo. "Immigrant Women," *Women in Canada, 2000: A Gender-Based Statistical Report.* Ottawa: Statistics Canada, 2000.

Conference Board of Canada. *Making a Visible Difference: The Contributions of Visible Minorities to Canadian Economic Growth.* Ottawa: Economic Performance and Trends, April 2004.

Creese, G. *Contracting Masculinity: Gender, Class, and Race in a White-Collar Union.* Toronto: Oxford University Press Canada, 1999.

Daenzer, P. 1993. *Regulating Class Privilege: Immigrant Servants in Canada, 1940–1990s.* Toronto: Canadian Scholars Press.

Das Gupta, T. "Political Economy of Gender, Race and Class: Looking at South Asian Immigrant Women in Canada." *Canadian Ethnic Studies* 26, no. 1 (1994): 59–73.

Das Gupta, T. *Racism and Paid Work.* Toronto: Garamond Press, 1996.

DeVoretz, D.J. (ed.). *Diminishing Returns: The Economics of Canada's Recent Immigration Policy.* Toronto: CD Howe Institute, 1995.

de Wolff, A. 2000. *Breaking the Myth of Flexible Work: Contingent Work in Toronto.* Toronto: Contingent Worker's Project.

Dibbs, R., and T. Leesti. *Survey of Labour and Income Dynamics: Visible Minorities and Aboriginal Peoples.* Ottawa: Statistics Canada, 1995.

Dion, K. "Immigrants' Perception of Housing Discrimination in Toronto: The Housing New Canadians Project." *Journal of Social Issues* 57 (2001): 523–539.

Fox, B., and P. Sugiman. "Flexible Work, Flexible Workers: The Restructuring of Clerical Work in a Large Telecommunications Company." *Studies in Political Economy* 60 (Autumn 1999): 59–84.

Galabuzi, G. *Canada's Creeping Economic Apartheid: The Economic Segregation and Social Marginalization of Racialized Groups.* Toronto: CJS Foundation and Research and Education, 2001.

Galabuzi, G. "Racializing the Division of Labour: Neo-liberal Restructuring and the Economic Segregation of Canada's Racialized Groups." In *Challenging the Market: The Struggle to Regulate Work and Income*, edited b J. Stanford and L. Vosko, 175–204. Montreal/Kingston: McGIll-Queen's University Press, 2004.

Glyn, A., and D. Miliband (eds.). *Paying for Inequality: The Costs of Social Injustice.* London: Rivers Oram Press, 1994.

Government of Canada. *Report of the Taskforce on the Participation of Visible Minorities in the Federal Public Service, 2000: Embracing Change in the Federal Public Service.* Ottawa: Supply and Services Canada, 2000.

Henry, F., and E. Ginsberg. *Who Gets the Job: A Test of Racial Discrimination in Employment.* Toronto: Urban Alliance on Race Relations/Social Planning Council of Metro Toronto, 1985.

Herberg, E. "The Ethno-racial Socio-Economic Hierarchy in Canada: Theory and Analysis if the New Vertical Mosaic." *International Journal of Comparative Sociology* 31, no. 3–4 (1990): 206–221.

Hiebert, D. "The Colour of Work: Labour Market Segregation in Montreal, Toronto, and Vancouver, 1991." Working Paper No. 97-02. Burnaby: Simon Fraser University, Centre of Excellence, Research on Immigration and Integration in the Metropolis, 1997.

Hulchanski, J.D. *Immigrants and Access to Housing: How Welcome Are Newcomers to Canada?* Proceedings of the 2nd National Conference, Seminar on Housing and Neighbourhoods. Montreal, 1997.

Human Resources and Skills Development Canada. *Knowledge Matters: Canada's Innovation Strategy* (February, 2002). www.hrdc.gc.ca/stratpol/sl-ca/doc/summary.shtml

Human Resources Development Canada. *Knowledge Matters: Skills and Learning for Canadians—Canada's Innovation Strategy.* Ottawa: HRDC, 2002. http://www.hrdc-drch.gc.ca/sp-ps/sl-ca/doc/summary.shtml

Jackson, A. "Poverty and Racism." *Perception* 24, no. 4 (2001): 6–7.

Jackson, A., and D. Robinson. *Falling Back: The State of Working Canada 2000*. Ottawa: Canadian Centre for Policy Alternatives, 2000.

Ley, D. and H. Smith. "Immigration and Poverty in Canadian Cities, 1971–1991." *Canadian Journal of Regional Science* 20, no. 1–2 (1997): 29–48.

Li, P. "The Market Value and Social Value of Race." In *Racism and Social Inequality in Canada: Concepts, Controversies and Strategies of Resistance*, edited by V. Satzewich. Toronto: Thomson Educational Publishing, 1998.

Li, P. 2003. *Destination Canada: Immigration Debates and Issues*. Toronto: Wall and Thompson.

Lian, J., and D. Matthews. "Does a Vertical Mosaic Really Exist? Ethnicity and Income in Canada, 1991." *Canadian Review of Sociology and Anthropology* 35, no. 4 (1998): 461–481.

McBride, S., and J. Shields. *Dismantling a Nation: The Transition to Corporate Rule in Canada*. Halifax: Fernwood, 2000.

Miles, R. *Racism*. London: Routledge, 1989.

Novak, S., J. Darden, J. Hulchanski, and A.-M. Seguin. *Housing Discrimination in Canada: What do we Know about it?* University of Toronto Research Bulletin no. 1 (2002).

Ornstein, M. *Ethno-racial Inequality in the City of Toronto: An Analysis of the 1996 Census*. Toronto: City of Toronto, 2000. http://ceris.metrpolis.net

Palmer, D. "Determinants of Canadian Attitudes towards Immigration: More Than Just Racism?" *Canadian Journal of Behavioural Sciences* 28 (1996): 190–192.

Picot, G., and A. Heisz. *The Performance of the 1990s Canadian Labour Market*. Paper 148. Ottawa: Statistics Canada, 2000.

Porter, J. *The Vertical Mosaic: An Analysis of Social Class and Power in Canada*. Toronto: University of Toronto Press, 1965.

Reitz, J., and M. Sklar. "Culture, Race and the Economic Assimilation of Immigrants." *Sociological Forum* 12, no. 2 (1997): 233–277.

Reitz, J., L. Calzavara, and D. Dasko. *Ethnic Inequality and Segregation in Jobs*. Toronto: Centre for Urban and Community Studies, University of Toronto, 1981.

Reitz, J.G. *Warmth of the Welcome: The Social Causes of Economic Success for Immigrants in Different Nations and Cities*. Boulder, CO: Westview Press, 1998.

Rodger, G.B. "Income and Inequality as Determinants of Mortality: An International Cross-Section Analysis." *Population Studies* 33 (1979): 343–351.

Satzewich, V. *Racism and Social Inequality in Canada: Concepts, Controversies and Strategies of Resistance*. Toronto: Thomson Publishing, 1998.

Sennett, R., and J. Cobb. *The Hidden Injuries of Class*. New York: Knopf, 1973.

Smith, E., and A. Jackson. *Does a Rising Tide Lift All Boats? The Labour Market Experiences and Incomes of Recent Immigrants, 1995 to 1998*. Ottawa: CCSD 2002.

Stanford, J. "Discipline, Insecurity and Productivity: The Economics Behind Labour Market Flexibility." In *Remaking Canada's Social Policy: Social Security in the late 1990s*. edited by J. Pulkingham and G. Ternowetsky. Halifax: Fernwood, 1996.

Statistics Canada. "1996 Census: Sources of Income and Earnings." *The Daily*, February 17, 1998.

Statistics Canada. "Longitudinal Survey of Immigrants to Canada, 2001." *The Daily*, September 4, 2003.

Teelucksingh, C., and G. Galabuzi. *Working Precariously: The Impact of Race and Immigrants' Status on Employment Opportunities and Outcomes in Canada*. Toronto: Centre for Social Justice and the Canadian Race Relations Foundation, 2005.

Vosco, L. *Temporary Work: The Gendered Rise of Precarious Employment Relationship*. Toronto: University of Toronto Press, 2000.

Wilkinson, R. *Unhealthy Societies: The Afflictions of Inequality*. New York: Routledge, 1996.

Yalnizyan, A. *The Growing Gap: A Report on Growing Inequality between the Rich and Poor in Canada*. Toronto: Centre for Social Justice, 1998.

Yanz, L., B. Jeffcoat, D. Ladd, and J. Altin. *Policy Options to Improve Standards for Women Garment Workers in Canada and Internationally*. Toronto: Maquila Solidarity Network/Status of Women Canada, 1999.

Zlotnik, H. "Trends of International Migration since 1965: What Existing Data Reveal." *International Migration* 37, no. 1 (1999): 21–61.

CHAPTER 31

"Canadian" as an Ethnic Category: Implications for Multiculturalism and National Unity

RHODA E. HOWARD-HASSMANN

In a world of increasing ethnic fragmentation and nationalism, Canada is a social experiment that other countries view with some astonishment. Canada is populated by persons who come themselves, or whose ancestors come, from hundreds of different ethnic groups. Yet they coexist in what seems in many other countries remarkable harmony. Even more extraordinary from the point of view of outsiders, Canada has a paradoxical policy of multiculturalism which, far from promoting divisions among Canadians, seems to promote their integration.

To explain this paradox, this paper addresses the question of identity among English-speaking, non-aboriginal Canadians. It argues that there is such a thing as an ethnic Canadian identity. Frequently, biological ancestry is confused with social ethnicity, so that everyone's "true" identity is presumed to be rooted somewhere else. Yet most people who are born in Canada, or who immigrate to Canada at young ages, become ethnic Canadians. The application to English-Canadians of standard sociological theory about the characteristics and creation of ethnicity is rarely done, yet it reveals Canadian ethnicity. The government policy of multiculturalism permits—even encourages—Canadians to retain aspects of their ancestral ethnic heritage, yet it does not undo the tendency of most people living in Canada to become ethnic Canadians.

Part of the debate about multiculturalism pits illiberal against liberal multiculturalists. Illiberal multiculturalists argue for stronger identification of Canadians with ancestral ethnic groups. By contrast, Canada's present public policy of liberal multiculturalism encourages private, individual choices of identity. Paradoxically, this liberal policy also encourages identification with a Canadian nation. The more members of minorities are encouraged to retain their ancestral identities, the more welcome they feel in Canada, and the more they identify with Canada and with Canadian citizenship, both vital to Canadian unity. But if, as some illiberal critics argue should occur, multiculturalism were diverted to promote identification with ancestral ethnicities at the expense of social assimilation into Canadian ethnicity, the net result would be to reduce identification with Canada.

Social Ethnicity, Biological Ancestry

In early 1996, Lucien Bouchard shocked many people in the "rest of Canada" by stating that unlike Quebec, Canada was not a real country (Seguin 1996, p. A4). Canada, it seemed, had no sense of coherence and unity, and Canadians (other than Québécois) were just a mishmash of individuals from all over the place. Bouchard was wrong. English-Canadians, like Québécois, are an ethnic group; like Québécois, they form a nation as well as living within a state. By English-Canadian is meant Canadians, other than indigenous peoples, who normally speak English, rather than French, in the public realm. (Indigenous peoples are not included as English-Canadians because they are the original inhabitants of the country with their own original languages, and they are covered in law by their own sets of rights, separate from the policy of multiculturalism.)

As this paper will argue, there is such a thing as an ethnic Canadian. But both public policy and much academic analysis conspire to prevent Canadians from recognizing this by insisting that their "ethnic" identity must be that of their ancestors. This occurs in public policy via the failure, until very recently, to recognize "Canadian" as an ethnic category. At the same time, among some academics, as discussed below, Canadianness is viewed as a covert means of promoting immigrants' assimilation, at the expense of their cultural heritage.

Social scientists frequently confuse ethnicity with ancestry. Then, wishing to promote the multiculturalism which is so much a part of prevailing Canadian ideology, they propose public policies based on people's ancestries. Evelyn Kallen asserts that Canada should become a multilingual as well as a multicultural society; all children should be taught in their "ethnic languages" (1990, p. 178). Kallen believes that all privileging of French and English as the founding (non-aboriginal) languages of Canada should end. No assimilative policies should exist: the Canadian government should do as much as it possibly can to assure that immigrants to Canada retain their ancestral language and culture. Yet in 1996, 84 percent of people living in Canada listed English or French as their sole mother tongue or one of their mother tongues (calculated from Statistics Canada

1998b), and only 1.7 percent of the population claimed to speak neither English nor French (calculated from Statistics Canada 1998a).

In Kallen's reading, the policy of multiculturalism means that the government must encourage citizens to define their ethnicity as that of their ancestors. The government must preserve the ancestral languages, customs, and religions of immigrants. No matter how long an individual or her family has lived in Canada, her ethnicity is still that of her ancestors who never left the "old country." Moreover, such ancestry always can be identified and is always unitary; there is no room in Kallen's analysis for the products of mixed marriages with multiple ethnic ancestries. Yet in 1996, 10,224,500 Canadians, or 36 percent of the population, reported that they had mixed ethnic ancestries (calculated from Statistics Canada 1998c).

The 1991 Citizens' Forum on Canada's Future revealed a strong sense of Canadianness. Overall, the commissioners of the forum wrote, "participants told us that reminding us of our different origins is less useful in building a united country than emphasizing the things we have in common." As one group from Richmond, BC stated: "We are generally in favour of celebrating our cultural heritage.... However, we must remain Canadian first.... We must have a strong core" (Spicer 1991, p. 85). Yet Abu-Laban and Stasiulis, writing in *Canadian Public Policy*, were strongly critical of the Citizen's Forum, claiming that "what is being favoured in this report is for multiculturalism to serve as a device for immigrant integration" (1992, p. 370).

There is, among these academics, a notion of ethnicity as a fixed, concrete entity. Ethnicity cannot be changed; you are what your ancestors were. Yet many students of ethnicity argue that it is a social creation. Ethnicity is not a "thing" outside and immune from human action and perception; it is "a process by which individuals either identify themselves as being different from others or belonging to a different group or are identified as different by others" (Isajiw 1985, p. 9). Max Weber defined ethnic groups as "human groups that entertain a subjective belief in their common descent"; ethnic membership, according to Weber, was a "presumed identity" (1978, p. 389). There is no such thing as a fixed primordial group: there are only socially constructed groups, sometimes so constructed by ethnic entrepreneurs for reasons of self-promotion rather than preservation of a romanticized ethnic heritage (Amit-Talai 1996; Burnet 1987, p. 74).

To posit ethnicity as a static entity derived from one's ancestors is to ignore socialization. Socialization is the process by which individual members of the human species learn to be human beings, to be members of society. Socialization occurs in the home, but it also occurs in peer relationships, in the schoolyard, via the media, and via the larger world. Yet in the Canadian discussion of multiculturalism, socialization frequently has become forced assimilation, seemingly a racist practice denying to immigrants the right to maintain their own culture. The changes in identity that happen to any immigrant to Canada, and the Canadian identity that any immigrant's child born in Canada absorbs, are viewed as enemies of the immutable, "natural" ancestral ethnicity that immigrants and their children ought to exemplify (on this, see also DiSanto 1989, p. 147).

There are many advantages to the Canadian policy of multiculturalism: most important is that non-European and/or non-Christian immigrants receive a strong message that they are welcome in this predominantly white, predominantly Christian country. But these advantages should not be allowed to obscure that, as this paper argues, there are also ethnic Canadians in Canada. The complexity of social roles and identities in modern Canadian life creates a new type of individual, not closely tied to his ancestral origins.

By encouraging individuals to think of themselves, and identify themselves, in terms of their ancestral ethnicity, public policy may render it difficult to instill a sense of Canadian identity in the population at large. As Weinfeld stated, "support for the image of Canada as an ethnic mosaic is facilitated when census data reify arbitrarily assigned census categories" (1981, p. 91). If, on the other hand, people living in Canada are permitted to be Canadians in public policy and official ideology, the result is likely to be a thickening of the sense of citizenship, and a consequent strengthening of the sense of nationhood.

Liberal versus Illiberal Multiculturalism

In a discussion of educational policies in the US, K. Anthony Appiah distinguishes between liberal and illiberal multiculturalism. Liberal multicultural education allows each child "to negotiate the creation of his or her own individual identity, using ... collective [racial, ethnic, etc.] identities as one (but only one) of the resources" available to him or her; illiberal multicultural education "wants to force children to live within separate spheres defined by the common culture of their race, religion or ethnicity" (1997, p. 34). Liberal multiculturalism, that is, makes racial or ethnic identity a choice; illiberal multiculturalism categorizes people and obliges them to live within those categories. The individual takes precedence over the group in liberal multiculturalism; in illiberal multiculturalism, the group takes precedence.

Academics such as Kallen and Abu-Laban and Stasiulis, are illiberal multiculturalists. Kallen wants all children to remain within their ancestral collectivities, with state-supported multilingual education dedicated to this goal; Abu-Laban and Stasiulis also want the state to recognize the fixed, unchanging ethnic identity of all Canadians. For these scholars, multiculturalism as a policy must ensure that individuals identify themselves as members of their ancestors' ethnicities. They believe in the idea of fixed, primordial groups.

But for liberal multiculturalists, multiculturalism is a resource of which citizens may or may not avail themselves, as they see fit. It is not a policy to which citizens must conform, in part because there are no fixed, primordial groups. Official Canadian multiculturalism is liberal, reflecting Canada's overall liberal political democracy. Section 27 of Canada's *Charter of Rights and Freedoms* (1982) states explicitly: "This Charter shall be interpreted in a manner consistent with the preservation and enhancement of the multicultural heritage of Canadians." Following this, the Canadian *Multiculturalism Act* (Bill C-23, 1988) notes in its preamble "the importance of preserving and enhancing the multicultural heritage of Canadians." It also proclaims (in s. 3, b) that "multiculturalism is a fundamental characteristic of the Canadian heritage and identity." The Act makes clear the government's intention not merely to recognize the multicultural origins of Canadians, but to maintain and foster their various cultural heritages by engaging in policies that enhance the diversity of Canada's culture, such as disbursement of funds to groups promoting their ancestral languages and arts. This includes policies to "facilitate the acquisition, retention and use of all languages that contribute to the multicultural heritage of Canada" (s. 5, 1, f). Thus the government encourages Canadians not only to retain languages they may speak already, but also to repossess or adopt languages that they and several generations of ancestors may never have spoken. Canadians do so, however, on an entirely voluntary basis: the groups they "belong" to cannot oblige them to preserve or repossess their ancestral languages.

This official commitment to a culture of racial and ethnic diversity is less than 30 years old. For it to become absorbed as part of the underlying cultural belief system of most Canadians requires constant promotion by the state and by educational institutions. This effort seems to have had some effect—public opinion polls indicate less racism and fear of strangers in Canada in the late twentieth century than 30 years ago. For example, in 1968 53 percent of Canadians polled answered "disagree" to the question: "Do you agree/disagree with a marriage between whites and non-whites?" (Gallup Report 1968). But in 1991 only 15 percent of Canadians agreed that "It is a bad idea for people of different races to marry" (Angus Reid Group 1991). Yet even if racism has declined substantially in Canada, memories of past discrimination fester and demand recognition. Here too, the federal government has taken action, for example, by agreeing in 1988 to pay compensation to the entire community of Canadians of Japanese ancestry who had been stripped of their property and interned as enemy aliens (some despite Canadian citizenship) during World War II (Griffin 1992).

By compensating groups for discrimination that they themselves or their ancestors suffered, the Canadian government makes a symbolic gesture that reaffirms Canadian values. The liberal values enshrined in Canada's *Charter of Rights and Freedoms* symbolize a change from religio-ethnic exclusivity to religio-ethnic openness. Racist expressions and assertions of religious superiority are excluded from the realm of acceptable public discourse, as the application of hate speech laws demonstrates (Jones 1998, pp. 205–11). The prescribed political culture at the end of the twentieth century assumes that all ethnic affiliations are equally valuable.

But this political culture rests on the assumption that in the final analysis, religion and ethnicity are private matters. Life in Canada is characterized by choice. Regardless of race (used here in the sense of phenotypical variety), ethnicity or religion, one is supposed to be able to choose one's occupation, to be fully mobile, to work and live wherever one can afford. One is supposed to be free to choose friends and a spouse from any background, religion or race. Religion, ethnic or cultural affiliation, indeed choice of language used in private, are matters of official public indifference; the groups that practise different religions, promote cultural or ethnic memberships, or speak unofficial languages are private groups. It is not the business of the government to ensure the preservation or influence of such private groups. The government can only encourage their preservation when their individual members indicate their desire for its assistance.

Nevertheless, in the interests of acknowledging the diverse origins of Canadians, the state supports some aspects of multiculturalism. "Heritage" language programs provide public funds for children to learn the language of their immediate or even more remote ancestors. But again, no child is obliged to attend such a program, and children who are not members of the ethnic group identified with the language are free to enrol in the class if their parents wish. Language usage is part of the private sphere. Anyone in Canada is permitted to speak whatever language she wishes in private conversation. Each individual Canadian can choose to identify herself as a member of her ancestral community or to withdraw from that community and stress other aspects of identity, such as occupation. Public multiculturalism is thus a liberal multiculturalism, posited on the preservation of private identity. And indeed, despite the academic and social movements of identity politics that have dominated much discussion of multiculturalism in the 1980s and 1990s, early evidence suggests that members of minorities in Canada preferred that the multiculturalism policy take this approach; "members of ethnic groups do not want to be 'locked in' by ethnic boundaries" (Breton 1986, p. 54).

Ethnicity: English Canadian

The current buzzword for multiculturalism, tolerance, and racial harmony is "diversity." Diversity must be not only protected but also promoted, many multiculturalist activists believe. Yet while diversity does shower a host of blessings onto Canada, nevertheless national unity requires a Canadian community with a common, shared understanding of identity in all citizens. Such a community is based on common experiences in Canada and a common set of fundamental principles. Citizenship in Canada, as in any other country, must have more meaning than merely legal rights; it must imply shared ways of living, shared values, and loyalty to the country. Without a deep sense of shared citizenship, an emotional attachment of Canadians to the country and to each other, little except common material goals will hold Canada's inhabitants together.

A country will be more closely knit if it shares a special sense of common life; if it is indeed a national community, not merely a collection of individuals sharing the common legal status of citizen. Communities are often thought to require common ethnic (actually ancestral) origins. But in Canada, there are fewer and fewer commonalities of historic ancestral origin. Immigration patterns and intermarriage create a mélange of citizens, many with four or more ethnic ancestries. At the same time, official policy requires that a community be created voluntarily by people from myriad different ancestral groups. Community in Canada is not supposed to, and cannot, require ethnic, religious or other types of ascriptive conformity.

To many citizens, community is also an ideal that can remedy the individualism that seems to afflict modern Western society. There is a general concern that modernity has produced aggregates of individuals plagued by angst, anomie, and malaise who are incapable of exercising responsibility to their families and the wider society (see e.g., Bibby 1990). One recent result of urban angst has been a social movement toward preoccupation with one's ancestral identity. Tightly knit communities of recent immigrants, often centred around a temple, mosque or church, seem to have retained the sense of community that native-born Canadians have foolishly lost in the pursuit of material prosperity (Frideres 1993, 65). Thus, many individuals are returning to their religious, national, and ancestral "roots," frequently several generations removed. As in the United States, these ancestral roots endow their fictive Canadian descendants with a symbolic sense of difference from the North American mainstream (Gans 1979; Breton 1986).

In part, this preoccupation with roots enhances equality, as it signifies the passing of the social domination of the anglo-Protestant elite. For example, Canadians of Eastern European origin who 50 years ago might have changed their names to something sounding more English now feel little or no pressure to do so. In part, however, this new preoccupation with ethnic identity is a manifestation of a social fiction. Yearning to be different, to somehow escape the social malaise of urban life, Canadians seek identity in symbolic adoptions of ancestral ethnicity. "Small differences" of dress, food or ritual behaviour are cultivated as symbolic indicators of uniqueness, in a pattern identified decades ago by Weber (1978, p. 388). But this social movement toward recognition of ancestral difference obscures the reality, argued in this paper, that there is such a thing as an English-Canadian ethnicity.

Community is possible in heterogeneous societies. It is not a community of ascriptive assignment to particular ethnic, religious or ancestral groups; it is a community of diversity, heterodoxy, and individual choice. To a significant extent, Canadians have in the last three decades accommodated themselves to the increasing diversity of their society. They have, in fact, created a new ethnic group, the ethnic English-Canadian. The ethnic English-Canadian is not necessarily a possessor of English or even British ancestry. Mainstream Canadian culture has long since ceased to be "English": even the language bears differences in Canada and the United Kingdom, and English immigrants to Canada frequently find the country, its customs, and linguistic usages strange (Greenhill 1994, p. 33). The ethnic English-Canadian is a new social creation.

Ethnicity is not a static entity; it is not a marker of what one intractably *is*. Ethnicity is a form of cultural practice. It is created and recreated by the perceptions and actions of individuals in society. In part, a sense of ethnicity is located in obvious social markers such as territory, language, religion, and ancestry. But ethnicity is also a complex of cultural behaviours that people have in common. Ethnicity is located in shared customs, beliefs, rituals, norms, and social conventions.

Two important characteristics of English Canadians are their territory, Canada, and their language, English. Territory gives individuals a mental map of the world and a sense of how space, time, and topography interact. Even if one has never travelled, as a Canadian one has a sense of expanse, of the flatness of the Prairies and the enormity of the Arctic; this sense is inculcated in school geography lessons and national news and weather reports. Canada, for Canadians, is the centre of the world.

Likewise, English is the public language of social intercourse. English is the vibrant, dynamic language of technical change, modern slang, and the arts. In the public world, language evolves; together, groups of English-speakers create a language that reflects the changing world around them. By contrast, the private non-English maternal language of the home that some Canadians speak may well be dated and outmoded, not having a living public world with which to keep up.

While territory and language are usually accepted as markers of ethnicity elsewhere in the world, they are often ignored in the discussion of what makes a Canadian. Only characteristics brought to Canada by immigrants, not characteristics acquired by virtue of immigration, are deemed relevant to the discussion of Canadian ethnicity. If one speaks English and one's ancestors did not, that is an indication that one has had to give up one's ethnic identity to live in Canada, even if one's nearer ancestors have been speaking English in Canada for several generations. One is similarly expected to have a fictive sense of place, an attachment to a homeland one has never seen, rather than to view Canada as one's homeland.

Another common shared characteristic of Canadians is religion. In the 1991 census 83.4 percent of Canadians identified themselves as Christians (calculated from Statistics Canada 1993). Given the weakness of Christian practice in Canada, the divisions among Christians, and the tendency of some Christian churches to be identified with different ancestral groups, this commonality is little more than an overarching belief system (on actual religious practice, see Bibby 1993). It does, however, provide most Canadians with common festive days, and a common belief in Sunday as an appropriate day of rest.

Again, religion is seen as a standard mark of ethnicity in the rest of the world, yet in Canada it is often thought that to point out that there is a common religious heritage, experienced by the vast majority of the population, is to undermine the multiculturalist premise of diversity. Yet many Canadians whose ancestors lived in parts of the world outside Europe are also Christian: there are Christians in Canada of Indian, Korean, Chinese, and African ancestry. This is because in a liberal country such as Canada, religion—like culture in general—is not merely a matter of ancestral identity, it is a matter of choice.

Another overarching commonality of Canadian life is that in 1996 about 87 percent of Canadians were of European ancestry (calculated from Statistics Canada 1998c, d). Again, many analysts hesitate to point out this obvious fact, assuming that an observation of statistical frequency might be taken to be an observation about the ideal Canadian. But when we observe other parts of the world, "racial" homogeneity, whether African, Indian or Chinese, immediately strikes us as a marker of ethnicity. Nevertheless, common European ancestry is neither sufficient nor necessary to create a Canadian community. In Europe itself, divisions such as language and type of Christianity sharply distinguish one group from another. And as the proportion of Canadians not of European ancestry—or of mixed European and other ancestries—increases, the "racial" identification of Canadians changes to an identification with broader Canadian culture. In Canada, the sharpness of diverse ancestral origins is blurred easily among those who are either born in the country or immigrate at an early age. This is because ethnicity is active and malleable.

Ethnicity evolves, shifts, and changes partly as a consequence of structural factors. An important structural factor in Canada has been the generational upward mobility that characterized almost all European immigrant groups during Canada's long period of settlement. Immigrants wishing to rise in the social scale knew that adoption of dominant Canadian customs would advance their opportunities. Some changed religions, or adopted more "Canadian" forms of Christianity such as membership in the Anglican or United churches (Bibby 1993, pp. 25–27). Most encouraged their children to learn and speak English, many going so far as to abandon their original language even within the home. Immigrant children attended Canadian schools, where they learned not only the English language but also Canadian rules, customs, and values. They met people not "of their own kind" whom they later frequently married (Reitz and Breton 1994, p. 52).

Among those favouring illiberal multiculturalism, immigrants' adoption of the English language or Christian religion indicates the "racist" (perhaps better "ethnicist") biases of the Anglo-Canadian elite. Certainly such biases existed. But choice also impelled immigrants. Life in Europe, like life in many parts of Asia, Africa, and Central and South America now, was hard and dangerous. Political democracy was unknown in most of the countries producing Canada's early waves of non-British immigrants. Parents who migrated often wished to shed their pasts, literally to change their children into the new breed of free, educated Canadians. Parents did suffer as their children abandoned their customs and churches and brought home previously unthinkable marriage partners. But this does not mean that immigrants abjured all change, that had it been possible they would have transported their entire cultures lock, stock, and barrel to the new world. A new Canadian ethnicity was adopted and created by immigrants, whose ancestral identifications were but one aspect of their sense of self in the new society.

Although Canada's economy is no longer as expansionist as it was during the decades of high European immigration, more recent immigrants from Asia, Africa, and Central and South America do find much economic opportunity, both for themselves and their children. Many also enjoy political democracy for the first time in their lives. In Canada, an orderly, hard-working, law-abiding life can bring security and comfort; this is a luxury in many other parts of the world where property can be arbitrarily confiscated, unemployment rates reach 30 or 40 percent, and political police can incarcerate and torture citizens at will. Canadian multicultural norms of religious tolerance are also attractive to many immigrants, who can equally take advantage of that tolerance by rejecting or by re-embracing their ancestral religions. If the price of this freedom and security is loss of language and strange sons and daughters-in-law, it is a price that for many is well worth paying.

This does not mean that becoming Canadian is a smooth, painless process for immigrants. Particular actions, such as religious worship, participation in ceremonial occasions, courtship rituals, and types of food preferred, are often taken in Canada as the most important markers of one's ethnic identity. These actions—Weber's small differences—do differentiate groups of Canadians from each other. How and on what occasions a family serves food to outsiders, how one welcomes a new child into the world, and how one mourns one's dead are all important aspects of one's life. Feeling uncomfortable with "Canadian" social norms, recent immigrants may well prefer to socialize with one another, to ignore the public world of Canadianness in favour of the private world of familiarity (See e.g., Hoffman 1989).

Nevertheless, as Howard Brotz pointed out, most of these customs are merely "private or social differences in ethnic tastes" (1980, p. 41). As he explained, with the exception of aboriginal Canadians "there are no ethnic differences in Canada about the desirability of the bourgeois-democratic way of life" (ibid.) Moodley makes the same point: "few immigrants choose to exchange attractive individualism, North American style, for the sake of cultural sentimentalities" (1983, p. 322).

To be English-Canadian, then, is to have an ethnic identity. Someone speaking English as a first language, or as the public language outside the home, is an English-Canadian. An English-Canadian may be of any ethnic or racial background; he may have Ukrainian or Ghanaian rather than British-Protestant ancestry. While the parents' sense of place may be Ukraine or Ghana, the English-Canadian's sense of place will be his immediate environment, the town or city that he knows well enough to get around—the personal map of schools, shops, offices, relatives, and friends (Fischer 1982). His personal life history will have taken place in Canada, not abroad. Though he may eat foods different from other Canadians and worship at a mosque or a temple rather than a church, he will have attended the same schools, learned the same Canadian history and geography, and been present at the same lessons in family studies and sex education.

An English-Canadian is likely to share many of her customs, desires and ambitions with people of dissimilar ethnic or even racial ancestry. Her class position will be an important marker of cultural behaviour. In the occupational sphere, everyone in Canada behaves in much the same way; choice depends significantly on education. Consumer choices are also much the same among groups with different ancestors. Canadians of all ancestral backgrounds favour one-family houses, and purchase cars and labour-saving household appliances.

Ethnicity is also characterized by common norms and values. Among the most important of these norms and values in Canada are the very principles of multiculturalism that the ideological elite now strives to implant in all Canadians via the educational system and state publicity, and which are absorbed (at least in part) by anyone whose education is primarily in Canada. To be Canadian, increasingly, is in state ideology and public practice to be a multiculturalist: multiculturalism is a key Canadian value.

This is not to deny that racial, religious, and ethnic prejudices still exist in Canada. They do, and they affect how Canadians think of themselves. To be of Ghanaian ancestry, for example, is to be vulnerable to racism, whereas to be of Ukrainian is not. To bear non-European phenotypical features or speak with a heavy non-Canadian accent is always to be vulnerable to inquiries regarding where one is "from." Those perceived to be part of the "multicultural (minority) communities" may find that some of their fellow citizens do not accord them the status of "real" Canadian, although this implicit

hierarchy of Canadianness long precedes the establishment of the policy of multiculturalism. And discrimination does affect the employment opportunities of some ethnic and racial groups (Henry and Ginzberg 1993; Reitz 1993; but for differences among non-European groups, showing that some earn above the average for British-Canadians, see Winn 1985). Yet incidents of racism are not sufficient in and of themselves to convince citizens of non-European descent that they are not Canadians. For example, of 19 civic leaders in Hamilton, Ontario of non-aboriginal, non-European descent interviewed in 1996–97, only one said racism made her feel an outsider in Canada: all the others expressed a strong sentiment that they were Canadian (Howard 1998).

That Canadians themselves recognize their ethnicity is evident in their willingness to identify themselves as "Canadian" when given the chance. In a national survey conducted in 1991, 89 percent of respondents "identified with being a Canadian," while only 6 percent did not. When told that they could choose only one answer to indicate their identity, 63 percent chose Canadian. Most tellingly, only 13 percent of those born in Canada identified themselves primarily by their "ethnic origin" (i.e., their ancestry), while among those born outside Canada, only 33 percent so identified themselves (Angus Reid Group 1991, pp. 3–4).

On the 1991 national census, only 2.8 percent of respondents wrote in that they were Canadian (in the box marked "other"). Yet prior to that census, Statistics Canada had conducted a series of mini-polls and focus groups that suggested that large numbers of people chose "Canadian" as their full or partial ethnic identification when that option was presented to them. In one experiment the total of those choosing full or partial Canadian identification was 53 percent, although in others it was 30 or 35 percent. Wanting information about ancestral, not social, ethnicity, Statistics Canada did not include Canadian as a specific ethnic option on the 1991 census, leaving individuals to figure out for themselves that it was an ethnic category (Pryor et al. 1992; for other studies showing the tendency of respondents to identify as ethnic Canadians see Mackie and Brinkerhoff 1984; Roberts and Clifton 1982).

By 1996 Statistics Canada had decided to include "Canadian" as an example of an ethnic group in its census form. As a result, 18.7 percent of the population reported Canadian as their sole ethnic origin. Another 12.2 percent reported mixed origins that included Canadian, for a total of 30.9 percent reporting to be fully or partially Canadian in an ethnic sense (calculated from Statistics Canada 1998c). In recognizing Canadian as an ethnic category, Statistics Canada has opened the possibility of a stronger sense of Canadian identity. It remains for the government to follow suit, to encourage citizens' ethnic identification with Canada at the same time as it continues to pursue its policy of liberal multiculturalism.

Liberal Multiculturalism and Canadian Unity

In 1994 the Montreal novelist Neil Bissoondath created a stir by publishing a book criticizing multiculturalism.

> I would venture that a Canadian of Italian descent and a Canadian of Pakistani descent are likely to have more in common with one another than with Italians or Pakistanis ... Such commonality is not possible, however, if a racial vision leads the way.... [M]ulticulturalism has failed us. In eradicating the centre, in evoking uncertainty as to what and who is a Canadian, it has diminished all sense of Canadian values, of what is a Canadian (Bissoondath 1994, p. 71).

Originally from Trinidad, and possessing extremely remote Indian/Hindu ancestral background, Bissoondath may be read as an immigrant pleading to be recognized as an ethnic Canadian. His behaviour, he says, is Canadian, like the behaviour of many other immigrants, no matter what their ethnic or racial background. He lives in Canada, not Trinidad; he lives in the present, not the mythical Hindu past of his distant Indian ancestors. It is one thing to recognize the interesting and valued cultural backgrounds of the many immigrants to Canada: it is another to force those backgrounds on them as their sole ethnic identity.

Bissoondath seems to be afraid of the illiberal multiculturalism—forcing individuals to stay in their ancestral boxes—that he thinks is the dominant ideological trend in Canadian discussion. This is a fear also expressed by Reginald W. Bibby in his provocatively titled *Mosaic Madness*: "Since the 1960s ... [Canada] has been leading the world in advocating freedom through pluralism and relativism ... trying to be a multinational society, enshrining coexistence and tolerance. The preliminary results are beginning to appear. The news is not that good" (1990, p. 3).

Bibby confuses multiculturalism with multinationalism, a policy which, if it did exist, might indeed fracture the Canadian nation, as Bibby believes is happening (ibid., p. 96). For critics such as Bibby and Bissoondath, multiculturalism is an illiberal policy which promotes individuals' and families' preoccupations with ancestral identity to such an extent that it undermines the sense of community necessary to shared citizenship in Canada. But this is a false fear. The official multiculturalism policy in Canada to date is liberal, and as such, it promotes the integration of immigrants into the dominant society. It does not promote multinationalism; rather, by incorporating immigrants and non-whites into the Canadian mainstream as equals whose ancestral cultures are symbolically valued, it promotes Canadianness.

This democratic and egalitarian approach to all religions, languages, and customs promotes Canadian inclusivity. Multiculturalism "normalizes" a wide range of customs and makes the enjoyment of such customs part of what it means to be a Canadian. It paradoxically universalizes specificity; all Canadians are expected to have and to enjoy a specific ethno-cultural ancestral identity as well as their universal Canadian identity. To be Canadian now, in the dominant ideology, is to revel in the exciting international flavour of the society. Far from threatening it, as they might have been perceived to do in the past, recent immigrants vivify Canadian culture.

For the state to symbolically recognize the varied cultural origins of Canadians, as Canada's multiculturalism policy does, is to acknowledge that individuals have identities other than mere citizen. Liberal multiculturalism acknowledges the social need for difference, for smaller, more close-knit communities separated from the Canadian mainstream. But it does not mandate such difference. In contrast, to stretch multiculturalism to the point at which it becomes an illiberal principle, as academics such as Kallen and Abu-Laban and Stasiulis suggest, would force Canadians into ethnic groups and ignore the fundamental individualism of Canadians' cultural choices.

Abu-Laban and Stasiulis want group identities to take precedence over individual ones: "At best," they state of Canada's policy of multiculturalism, "what is left is a discourse emphasizing individual as opposed to group rights through the subsumption of the pluralist notion of multiculturalism under the individualist notion of citizenship" (1992, p. 372). In an earlier article Peter made a similar comment, criticizing multiculturalism for promoting ethnicity as a sort of cultural festival, while actually advocating "societal mobility of the ethnic individual while retarding the advancement of ethnic groups" (1981, p. 65).

But the Canadian multicultural policy is indeed predicated on individual citizenship, not on group rights. Citizenship requires a "thick" sense of belonging: individual citizens of a country must feel that they have ties to other members. As Fierlbeck notes, "Too strong an emphasis upon cultural identity discourages identification with those who are clearly different from oneself" (1996, p. 20). An illiberal multiculturalism policy that forgets or ignores the many commonalities of citizenship—such as regionalism, professional affiliation, personal interests, or intermarriage—that emerge from identities other than religion, culture, and ethnicity would undermine individual citizens' connectedness with other Canadians and their sense of belonging to Canada. Canada's multiculturalism policy does not protect the rights of groups. It protects individuals' rights to enact or preserve ancestral cultures, as they see fit, without any obligation whatsoever to the groups to which they may be perceived to belong.

The danger of moving from a liberal policy of individual rights to an illiberal one of group rights underlies much of the recent concern with multiculturalism in both the US and Canada; Schlesinger, for example, worries about a cult of ethnicity whose "underlying philosophy is that America is not a nation of individuals at all but a nation of groups ... and that division into ethnic communities establishes the basic structure of American society"

(1992, p. 16). This is the attitude reflected in Bannerji's (1997) argument that race and ethnicity are such salient aspects of the identity of all Canadians that there is in effect no difference in the way minorities were treated in 1920 and the way they were treated in the mid-1990s. Relying in part on her own experience as an adult immigrant, Bannerji implies that it is impossible for an individual not of European descent to feel Canadian.

Such a feeling is common, though certainly not universal, among first-generation adult immigrants (Howard 1998). But as much empirical evidence shows (Reitz and Breton 1994), the salience of ethnicity declines drastically among second- and third-generation immigrants (that is, Canadians with immigrant parents or grandparents), who normally feel a sense of connection to others in the country who have ethnically different ancestors. Even many first-generation immigrants feel such a connection, especially those who are already professionals prior to coming to Canada, who speak English before arrival, and who have a generally cosmopolitan outlook (Moodley 1983). A public policy that encourages liberal multiculturalism can simultaneously encourage identification with ancestral culture and a sense of connection with other Canadians.

The danger of a policy of illiberal multiculturalism, as Appiah suggests and as Bibby and Bissoondath fear, is that ethnic and racial essentialism could replace the complex, diverse identities of individual Canadians that enable them routinely to form ties with those who do not share their religious, ethnic or racial background. In the short term, a policy of illiberal multiculturalism might result in more social recognition of, and more pride in, a minority religion such as Islam, or a non-white race. But in the long run, the result might well be a fragmentation of society and a closing in of the different groups. Differentiated ethnic and national groups would coexist uneasily in a shared public space. This would be the result of the type of multiculturalism that Kallen and Abu-Laban and Stasiulis advocate.

But in fact, this warning about illiberal multiculturalism is presently a warning about a false danger. The Canadian public policy of multiculturalism remains—and ought to remain—liberal, rooted in individual citizens' choices; academic and activist advocacy of illiberal group-oriented policies has had no effect on government in this regard. And social behaviour reflects the appropriateness of government policy. Immigrants and their children do become ethnic Canadians.

Paradoxically, liberal protection of cultural "uniqueness" promotes a universal sense of citizenship. Immigrants' "strong affiliation with their new country seems to be based in large part on its willingness not just to tolerate but to welcome cultural difference" (Kymlicka and Norman 1995, p. 307). Members of minorities and new Canadians feel more valued than previously; as such, they find it easier, and more to their liking, to become Canadians. Canadians exist: there is a Canadian identity in which all Canadians, regardless of ethnic

ancestry, can share. Identity is a state of mind; to think of oneself as Canadian is to be Canadian. Public policy needs to promote this Canadianness, which increases citizens' loyalty to each other and the nation as a whole. A loyal Canadian will not question the nation "as a project" (MacIntyre 1995, p. 221): the entity Canada is something of which a person feels part and to which he or she is bound.

At its best, nationhood is based on a sense of commonality among all legal citizens; at its worst, on an exclusivist sense that only people of certain ethnic, racial, or religious background can be citizens. In part via its policy of multiculturalism, Canada has progressed beyond a notion of citizenship based on exclusion of the "Other." But it has not yet created a strong sense of citizenship based on common experience in, and loyalty to, the country of Canada. Yet Canada is increasingly composed not of strangers from different parts of the world and different cultural backgrounds, but of people who share not only the flat, thin legal state of citizenship, but also the complex, thickening state of fictive kinship that underlies the sense of nationhood.

The policy of illiberal multiculturalism suggested by Kallen and Abu-Laban and Stasiulis (and more broadly by those who adhere to the social movement of the politics of identity) would reduce Canadians' sense of citizenship and nationhood. National unity, a sense of identification with the country at large and with fellow citizens, would be undermined by a public policy that fears to acknowledge that people who live in Canada for any length of time become ethnic Canadians. The trick is in the balance. Ethnic ancestry and actual personal culture are both valued forms of identity. But they are not the only forms. Personal life experience, personal connection with others in the land of one's birth or adoption, is also a form of identity. Individual immigrants frequently insist that they are Canadians. They value their citizenship papers and their new sense of belonging: their sense of Canadianness thickens as they and their descendants stay in Canada (Howard 1998). Canadian public policy can easily acknowledge and strengthen that thickened identity without undermining liberal multiculturalism.

The more important issue, though, is not the sense of identity adopted by recent immigrants: it is the sense of identity of all Canadians. Whether Quebec separates or not, Canadians in the rest of Canada will need a stronger identity in the twenty-first century than they presently have. A public policy that stresses difference and diversity, but forgets also to stress sameness and similarity, will make it more difficult for such an identity to coalesce. *Pace* Bouchard, English-Canada is a nation, but it is a hidden nation, not yet revealed to itself. One step in preserving and strengthening the nation of English-Canada is to recognize that there is such a thing as Canadian ethnicity. The other step is to preserve the policy of multiculturalism as it now exists; that is, to preserve liberal multiculturalism and not adopt its illiberal variant.

References

Abu-Laban, Y. and D. Stasiulis (1992), "Ethnic Pluralism under Siege: Popular and Partisan Opposition to Multiculturalism," *Canadian Public Policy/Analyse de Politiques* 18(4):365–86.

Amit-Talai, V. (1996), "The Minority Circuit: Identity Politics and the Professionalization of Ethnic Activism," in *Re-situating Identities: The Politics of Race, Ethnicity and Culture*, ed. V. Amit-Talai and C. Knowles (Peterborough: Broadview Press), pp. 89–114.

Angus Reid Group (1991), *Multiculturalism and Canadians*, Attitude Study 1991-National Survey Report submitted to Multiculturalism and Citizenship Canada.

Appiah, K.A. (1997), "The Multiculturalist Misunderstanding," *New York Review of Books* 44(15):30–36.

Bannerji, H. (1997), "Geography Lessons: On Being an Insider/Outsider to the Canadian Nation," in *Dangerous Territories: Struggles for Difference and Equality in Education*, ed. L.G. Roman and L. Eyre (New York: Routledge).

Bibby, R.W. (1990), *Mosaic Madness: Pluralism without a Cause* (Toronto: Stoddart).

——— (1993), *Unknown Gods: The Ongoing Story of Religion in Canada* (Toronto: Stoddart).

Bissoondath, N. (1994), *Selling Illusions: The Cult of Multiculturalism in Canada* (Toronto: Penguin).

Breton, R. (1986), "Multiculturalism and Canadian Nation-Building," in *The Politics of Gender, Ethnicity and Language in Canada*, ed. A. Cairns and C. Williams (Toronto: University of Toronto Press), pp. 27–66.

Brotz, H. (1980), "Multiculturalism in Canada: A Muddle," *Canadian Public Policy/Analyse de Politiques* 6(1):41–46.

Burnet, J. (1987), "Multiculturalism in Canada," in *Ethnic Canada: Identities and Inequalities*, ed. L. Driedger (Toronto: Copp Clark Pitman), pp. 65–79.

DiSanto, J.E. (1989), "Nonhyphenated Canadians—Where Are You?" in *Multiculturalism and Intergroup Relations*, ed. J.S. Frideres (Westport, CT: Greenwood Press), pp. 141–48.

Fierlbeck, K. (1996), "The Ambivalent Potential of Cultural Identity," *Canadian Journal of Political Science* 29(1):3–22.

Fischer, C.S. (1982), *To Dwell among Friends: Personal Networks in Town and City* (Chicago: University of Chicago Press).

Frideres, J.S. (1993), "Changing Dimensions of Ethnicity in Canada," in *Deconstructing a Nation: Immigration, Multiculturalism and Racism in '90s Canada*, ed. V. Satzewich (Halifax: Fernwood Publishing), pp. 47–67.

Gallup Report (1968), "Canadians Express Disapproval of Marriages between White and Non-white," 11 September.

Gans, H. J. (1979), "Symbolic Ethnicity: The Future of Ethnic Groups and Cultures in America," *Ethnic and Racial Studies* 2(1):1–20.

Greenhill, P. (1994), *Ethnicity in the Mainstream: Three Studies of English Canadian Culture in Ontario* (Montreal and Kingston: McGill-Queen's University Press).

Griffin, K. (1992), "Ottawa Redress Total Climbs to $365 Million," *Vancouver Sun*, 24 February, p. B4.

Henry, F. and E. Ginzberg (1993), "Racial Discrimination in Employment," in *Social Inequality in Canada: Patterns, Problems, Policies*, ed. J. Curtis, E. Grabb and N. Guppy, 2d ed. (Scarborough: Prentice-Hall Canada), pp. 353–60.

Hoffman, E. (1989), *Lost in Translation: A Life in a New Language* (New York: Penguin).

Howard, R.E. (1998), "Being Canadian: Citizenship in Canada," *Citizenship Studies* 2(1):133–52.

Isajiw, W.W. (1985), "Definitions of Ethnicity," in *Ethnicity and Ethnic Relations in Canada*, ed. R.M. Bienvenue and J.E. Goldstein (Toronto: Butterworth), pp. 5–17.

Jones, T.D. (1998), *Human Rights: Group Defamation, Freedom of Expression and the Law of Nations* (Boston: Martinus Nijhoff).

Kallen, E. (1990), "Multiculturalism: The Not-So-Impossible Dream," in *Human Rights in Canada: Into the 1990s and Beyond*, ed. R.I. Cholewinski (Ottawa: Human Rights Research and Education Centre, University of Ottawa), pp. 165–81.

Kymlicka, W. and W. Norman (1995), "Return of the Citizen: A Survey of Recent Work on Citizenship Theory," in *Theorizing Citizenship*, ed. R. Beiner (Albany: State University of New York Press), pp. 283–322.

Mackie, M. and M.B. Brinkerhoff (1984), "Measuring Ethnic Salience," *Canadian Ethnic Studies* 16(1):114–31.

MacIntyre, A. (1995), "Is Patriotism a Virtue?" in *Theorizing Citizenship*, ed. R. Beiner (Albany: State University of New York Press), pp. 209–28.

Moodley, K. (1983), "Canadian Multiculturalism as Ideology," *Ethnic and Racial Studies* 6(3):320–31.

Peter, K. (1981), "The Myth of Multiculturalism and Other Political Fables," in *Ethnicity, Power and Politics in Canada*, Vol. 13, ed. J. Dahlie and T. Fernando (Toronto: Methuen), pp. 56–67.

Pryor, E.T. *et al.* (1992), "Measuring Ethnicity: Is 'Canadian' an Evolving Ethnic Category?" *Ethnic and Racial Studies* 15(2):214–35.

Reitz, J.G. (1993), "Statistics on Racial Discrimination in Canada," *Policy Options* (March):32–36.

Reitz, J.G. and R. Breton (1994), *The Illusion of Difference: Realities of Ethnicity in Canada and the United States* (Toronto: C.D. Howe Institute).

Roberts, L.W. and R.A. Clifton (1982), "Exploring the Ideology of Canadian Multiculturalism," *Canadian Public Policy/Analyse de Politiques* 8(2):88–94.

Schlesinger, A.M., Jr. (1992), *The Disuniting of America: Reflections on a Multicultural Society* (New York: W.W. Norton).

Seguin, R. (1996), "Cabinet Edgy as Bouchard Takes over," *The Globe and Mail*, 29 January, p. A4.

Spicer, K. (Chairman) (1991), *Citizen's Forum on Canada's Future: Report to the People and Government of Canada* (Ottawa: Supply and Services Canada).

Statistics Canada (1991), *Census of Canada 1991: The Nation-Knowledge of Languages* (Ottawa: Statistics Canada).

———— (1993), *Census of Canada: Religions in Canada* (Ottawa: Industry, Science and Technology Canada).

———— (1998a), *1996 Census: Population by Knowledge of Official Languages, Showing Age Groups, for Canada, Provinces and Territories.* http://www.statcan.ca/english/census96/dec2/off.htm.

———— (1998b), *1996 Census: Population by Mother Tongue, Showing Age Groups, for Canada, Provinces and Territories.* http://www.statcan.ca/english/census96/dec2/mother.htm.

———— (1998c), *1996 Census: Total Population by Ethnic Origin.* http://www.statcan.ca/english/census96/feb17/eo2can.htm.

———— (1998d), *Total Population by Visible Minority Population for Canada, 1996 Census.* http://www.statcan.ca/english/census96/feb17/vmcan.htm.

Weber, M. (1978), *Economy and Society*, ed. G. Roth and C. Wittich (Los Angeles: University of California Press).

Weinfeld, M. (1981), "Myth and Reality in the Canadian Mosaic: 'Affective Ethnicity'," *Canadian Ethnic Studies* 13(3):80–100.

Winn, C. (1985), "Affirmative Action and Visible Minorities: Eight Premises in Quest of Evidence," *Canadian Public Policy/Analyse de Politiques* 11(4):684–700.

CHAPTER 32

Heroes or Villains?; and Stereotyping as a Signifying Practice

STUART HALL

Heroes or Villains?

Look, first, at the magazine cover on this page. It is a picture of the Men's 100 metres final at the 1988 Olympics, which appeared on the cover of the Olympics Special of the *Sunday Times* colour magazine. It shows the black Canadian sprinter Ben Johnson winning in record time from Carl Lewis and Linford Christie: five superb athletes in action, at the peak of their physical prowess. All of them men and—perhaps, now, you will notice consciously for the first time—all of them black!

"Heroes and Villains" cover of *The Sunday Times Magazine*, October 9, 1988

ACTIVITY 1

How do you "read" the picture—what is it saying? In Barthes' terms, what is its "myth"—its underlying message? One possible message relates to their racial identity. These athletes are all from a racially defined group—one often discriminated against precisely on the grounds of their "race" and colour, whom we are more accustomed to see depicted in the news as the victims or "losers" in terms of achievement. Yet here they are, winning!

In terms of difference, then, a positive message: a triumphant moment, a cause for celebration. Why, then, does the caption say, "Heroes and villains"? Who do you think is the hero, who the villain?

Even if you don't follow athletics, the answer isn't difficult to discover. Ostensibly about the Olympics, the photo is in fact a trailer for the magazine's lead story about the growing menace of drug-taking in international athletics—what inside is called "The Chemical Olympics." Ben Johnson, you may recall, was found to have taken drugs to enhance his performance. He was disqualified, the gold medal being awarded to Carl Lewis, and Johnson was expelled from world athletics in disgrace. The story suggests that all athletes—black or white—are potentially "heroes" and "villains." But in this image, Ben Johnson personifies this split in a particular way. He is *both* "hero" and "villain." He encapsulates the extreme alternatives of heroism and villainy in world athletics in one black body.

There are several points to make about the way the representation of "race" and "otherness" is working in this photo. First, […] think [about] Barthes' […] idea of "myth." This photo functions at the level of "myth." There is a literal, denotative level of meaning: This is a picture of the 100 metres final and the figure in front is Ben Johnson. Then there is the more connotative or thematic meaning: the drug story. And within that, there is the sub-theme of "race" and "difference." Already, this tells us something important about how "myth" works. The image is a very powerful one, as visual images often are. But its meaning is highly ambiguous. It can carry more than one meaning. If you didn't know the context, you might be tempted to read this as a moment of unqualified triumph. And you wouldn't be wrong since this, too, is a perfectly acceptable meaning to take from the image. But, as the caption suggests, it is not produced here as an image of unqualified triumph. So, the same photo can carry several, quite different, sometimes diametrically opposite meanings. It can be a picture of disgrace or of triumph, or both. Many meanings, we might say, are potential within the photo. But there is no one, true meaning. Meaning "floats." It cannot be finally fixed. However, attempting to fix it is the work of a representational practice, which intervenes in the many potential meanings of an image in an attempt to privilege one.

So, rather than a right or wrong meaning, what we need to ask is, "Which of the many meanings in this image does the magazine mean to privilege?" Which is the *preferred meaning*? Ben Johnson is the key element here because he is both an amazing athlete, winner and record-breaker, *and* the athlete who was publicly disgraced because of drug-taking. So, as it turns out, the preferred meaning is *both* heroism and villainy. It wants to say something paradoxical like, "In the moment of the hero's triumph, there is also villainy and moral defeat. In part, we know this is the preferred meaning that the magazine wants the photo to convey because this is the meaning that is singled out in the caption, HEROES AND VILLAINS. Roland Barthes (1977) argues that, frequently, it is the caption that selects one out of the many possible meanings from the image, and *anchors* it with words. The "meaning" of the photograph, then, does not lie exclusively in the image, but in the conjunction of image *and* text. Two discourses—the discourse of written language and the discourse of photography—are required to produce and "fix" the meaning (see Hall, 1972).

As we have suggested, this photo can also be read, connotatively, in terms of what it has to say about race. Here, the message could be, black people shown being good at something, winning *at last!* But in the light of the "preferred meaning," hasn't the meaning with respect to race and otherness changed as well? Isn't it more something like, even when black people are shown at the summit of their achievement, they often fail to carry it off? This having-it-both-ways is important because, as I hope to show you, people who are in any way significantly different from the majority "them" rather than "us"—are frequently exposed to this binary form of representation. They seem to be represented through sharply opposed, polarized, binary extremes: good/bad, civilized/primitive, ugly/excessively attractive, repelling-because-different/compelling-because-strange-and-exotic. And they are often required to be *both things at the same time!* We will return to these split figures or tropes of representation in a moment.

But first, let us look at another, similar news photo, this time from another record-breaking 100 metres final. It shows Linford Christie, subsequently captain of the British Olympics squad, at the peak of his career, having just won the race of a lifetime. The picture captures his elation at the moment of his lap of honour. He is holding

Linford Christie, holding a Union Jack, having won the men's 100 metres Olympic gold medal [Barcelona 1992]

ACTIVITY 2

Which of the following statements, in your view, comes closest to expressing the "message" of the image?
  (a) This is the greatest moment of my life! A triumph for me, Linford Christie.
  (b) This is a moment of triumph for me and a celebration for black people everywhere!
  (c) This is a moment of triumph and celebration for the British Olympic team and the British people!
  (d) This is a moment of triumph and celebration for black people *and* the British Olympic team. It shows that you can be "black" *and* "British"!

the Union Jack. In the light of the earlier discussion, how do you "read" this photograph? What is it saying about race and cultural identity?

There is, of course, no right or wrong answer to the question. The image carries many meanings, all equally plausible. What is important is the fact that this image both shows an event (denotation) and carries a message or meaning (connotation). Barthes would call it a "meta-message" or *myth* about race, colour, and otherness. We can't help reading images of this kind as saying something, not just about the people or the occasion, but about their otherness, their difference. *"Difference" has been marked.*

How it is then interpreted is a constant and recurring preoccupation in the representation of people who are racially and ethnically different from the majority population. Difference signifies. It "speaks."

In a later interview, discussing his forthcoming retirement from international sport, Christie commented on the question of his cultural identity—here he feels he "belongs" *(The Sunday Independent*, November 11, 1995). He has very fond memories of Jamaica, he said, where he was born and lived until the age of seven. But "I've lived here [in the U.K.] for 28 [years]. I can't be anything other than British" (p. 18). Of course, it isn't as simple as that. Christie is perfectly well aware that most definitions of Britishness assume that the person who belongs is white. It is much harder for black people, wherever they were born, to be accepted as British. In 1995, the cricket magazine *Wisden* had to pay libel damages to black athletes for saying that they couldn't be expected to display the same loyalty and commitment to winning for England because they are black. So Christie knows that every image is also being read in terms of this broader question of cultural belongingness and difference.

Indeed, he made his remarks in the context of the negative publicity to which he has been exposed in some sections of the British tabloid press, a good deal of which hinges on a vulgar, unstated but widely recognized "joke" at his expense: namely, that the tight-fitting Lycra shorts that he wears are said to reveal the size and shape of his genitals. This was the detail on which *The Sun* focused on the morning after he won an Olympic gold medal. Christie has been subject to continuous teasing in the tabloid press about the prominence and size of his "lunchbox"—a euphemism that some have taken so literally that, he revealed, he has been approached by a firm wanting to market its lunchboxes around his image! Linford Christie has observed the following about these innuendoes: "I felt humiliated ... My first instinct was that it was racist. There we are, stereotyping a black man. I can take a good joke. But it happened the day after I won the greatest accolade an athlete can win ... I don't want to go through life being known for what I've got in my shorts. I'm a serious person ..." (p. 15).

ACTIVITY 3

What is going on here? Is this just a joke in bad taste, or does it have a deeper meaning? What do sexuality and gender have to do with images of black men and women? Why did the black French writer from Martinique, Frantz Fanon, say that white people seem to be obsessed with the sexuality of black people?

It is the subject of a widespread fantasy, Fanon says, which fixates the black man at the level of the genitals. "One is no longer aware of the Negro, but only of a penis; the Negro is eclipsed. He is turned into a penis" (Fanon, 1986/1952, p. 170).

Stereotyping as a Signifying Practice

Before we pursue this argument, however, we need to reflect further on how this racialized regime of representation actually works. Essentially, this involves examining more deeply the set of representational practices known as *stereotyping*. So far, we have considered the essentializing, reductionist, and naturalizing effects of stereotyping. Stereotyping reduces people to a few simple, essential characteristics that are represented as fixed by nature. Here, we examine four further aspects: (a) the construction of otherness and exclusion; (b) stereotyping and power; (c) the role of fantasy; and (d) fetishism.

Stereotyping as a signifying practice is central to the representation of racial difference. But what is a stereotype? How does it actually work? In his essay on stereotyping, Richard Dyer (1977) makes an important distinction between *typing* and *stereotyping*. He argues that, without the use of *types*, it would be difficult, if not impossible, to make sense of the world. We understand the world by referring individual objects, people, or events in our heads to the general classificatory schemes into which—according to our culture—they fit. Thus we decode a flat object on legs on which we place things as a "table." We may never have seen that kind of table before, but we have a general concept or category of table in our heads, into which we fit the particular objects we perceive or encounter. In other words, we understand the particular in terms of its type. We deploy what Alfred Schutz called *typifications*. In this sense, typing is essential to the production of meaning [....]

Richard Dyer argues that we are always making sense of things in terms of some wider categories. Thus, for example, we come to "know" something about a person by thinking of the *roles* that he or she performs: Is he/she a parent, a child, a worker, a lover, a boss, or an old age pensioner? We assign him/her to the *membership* of different groups, according to class, gender, age group, nationality, race, linguistic group, sexual preference, and so on. We order him/her in terms of *personality type*—is he/she a happy, serious, depressed, scatterbrained, overactive kind of person? Our picture of whom the person "is" is built up out of the information we accumulate from positioning him/her within these different orders of typification. In broad terms, then, "a *type* is any simple, vivid, memorable, easily grasped and widely recognized characterization in which a few traits are foregrounded and change or 'development' is kept to a minimum" (Dyer, 1977, p. 28).

What, then, is the difference between a type and a stereotype? *Stereotypes* get hold of the few "simple, vivid, memorable, easily grasped and widely recognized" characteristics about a person, *reduce* everything about the person to those traits, *exaggerate* and *simplify* them, and *fix* them without change or development to eternity. This is the process we described earlier. So the first point is that *stereotyping reduces, essentializes, naturalizes, and fixes difference.*

Secondly, *stereotyping deploys a strategy of "splitting."* It divides the normal and the acceptable from the abnormal and the unacceptable. It then excludes or expels everything that does not fit, that is different. Dyer argues that "a system of social- and stereo-types refers to what is, as it were, within and beyond the pale of normalcy [i.e., behaviour that is accepted as 'normal' in any culture]. Types are instances which indicate those who live by the rules of society (social types) and those who the rules are designed to exclude (stereotypes). For this reason, stereotypes are also more rigid than social types .... [B]oundaries ... must be clearly delineated and so stereotypes, one of the mechanisms of boundary maintenance, are characteristically fixed, clear-cut, unalterable" (p. 29). So, another feature of stereotyping is its practice of closure and exclusion. *It symbolically fixes boundaries, and excludes everything that does not belong.*

Stereotyping, in other words, is part of the maintenance of social and symbolic order. It sets up a symbolic frontier between the normal and the deviant, the normal and the pathological, the acceptable and the unacceptable, what belongs and what does not or is other, between insiders and outsiders, Us and Them. It facilitates the binding or bonding together of all of Us who are "normal" into one imagined community; and it sends into symbolic exile all of Them—the others—who are in some way different, —beyond the pale. Mary Douglas (1966), for example, argued that whatever is "out of place" is considered polluted, dangerous, taboo. Negative feelings cluster around it. It must be symbolically excluded if the purity of the culture is to be restored. The feminist theorist, Julia Kristeva (1982), calls such expelled or excluded groups "abjected" (from the Latin meaning, literally, "thrown out").

The third point is that *stereotyping tends to occur where there are gross inequalities of power.* Power is usually directed against the subordinate or excluded group. One aspect of this power, according to Dyer, is *ethnocentrism*—"the application of the norms of one's own culture to that of others" (Brown, 1965, p. 183). Again, remember Derrida's argument that, between binary oppositions like Us/Them, "we are not dealing with—peaceful coexistence—but rather with a violent hierarchy. One of the two terms governs ... the other or has the upper hand" (1972, p. 41).

In short, stereotyping is what Foucault called a "power/knowledge" sort of game. It classifies people according to a norm and constructs the excluded as other. Interestingly, it is also what Gramsci would have called an aspect of the struggle for hegemony. As Dyer observes, "The establishment of normalcy (i.e., what is accepted as 'normal') through social- and stereo-types is one aspect of the habit of ruling groups—to attempt to fashion the whole of society according to their own world view, value system, sensibility and ideology. So right is this world view for the ruling groups that they make it appear (as it does appear to them) as 'natural' and 'inevitable'—and for everyone—and, in so far as they succeed, they establish their hegemony" (Dyer, 1977, p. 30). Hegemony is a form of power based on leadership by a group in many fields of activity at once, so its ascendancy commands widespread consent and appears natural and inevitable.

Representation, Difference, and Power

Within stereotyping, then, we have established a connection between representation, difference, and power. However, we need to probe the nature of this *power* more fully. We often think of power in terms of direct physical coercion or constraint. However, we have also spoken, for example, of power *in representation*; power to mark, assign, and classify; of *symbolic* power; of *ritualized* expulsion. Power, it seems, has to be understood here, not only in terms of economic exploitation and physical coercion, but also in broader cultural or symbolic terms, including the power to represent someone or something in a certain way—within a certain regime of representation. It includes the exercise of *symbolic power* through representational practices. Stereotyping is a key element in this exercise of symbolic violence.

In his study of how Europe constructed a stereotypical image of the Orient, Edward Said argues that, far from simply reflecting what the countries of the Near East were actually like, Orientalism was the *discourse* "by which European culture was able to manage—and even produce—the Orient politically, sociologically, militarily, ideologically, scientifically and imaginatively during the post-Enlightenment period." Within the framework of Western hegemony over the Orient, he says, there emerged a new object of knowledge, "a complex Orient suitable for study in the academy, for display in the museum, for reconstruction in the colonial office, for theoretical illustration in anthropological, biological, linguistic, racial and historical theses about mankind and the universe, for instances of economic and sociological theories of development, revolution, cultural personalities, national or religious character" (pp. 7–8). This form of power is closely connected with knowledge, or with the practices of what Foucault called "power/ knowledge."

Said's discussion of Orientalism closely parallels Foucault's power/knowledge argument: a *discourse* produces, through different practices of *representation* (scholarship, exhibition, literature, painting, etc.), a form of *racialized knowledge of the Other* (Orientalism) deeply implicated in the operations of *power* (imperialism). Interestingly, however, Said goes on to define power in ways that emphasize the similarities between Foucault and Gramsci's idea of *hegemony*:

In any society not totalitarian, then, certain cultural forms predominate over others; the form of this cultural leadership is what Gramsci has identified as *hegemony*, an indispensable concept for any understanding of cultural

Edwin Long, *The Babylonian Marriage Market*, 1882

ACTIVITY 4

For an example of Orientalism in visual representation, look at the reproduction of a very popular painting, *The Babylonian Marriage Market* by Edwin Long. Not only does the image produce a certain way of knowing the Orient—as the mysterious, exotic, and eroticized Orient; but also, the women who are being sold into marriage are arranged, right to left, in ascending order of whiteness. The final figure approximates most closely to the Western ideal, the norm; her clear complexion accentuated by the light reflected on her face from a mirror.

life in the industrial West. It is hegemony, or rather the result of cultural hegemony at work, that gives Orientalism its durability and its strength—Orientalism is never far from—the idea of Europe, a collective notion identifying "us" Europeans as against all "those" non-Europeans, and indeed it can be argued that the major component in European culture is precisely what made that culture hegemonic both in and outside Europe: the idea of European identity as a superior one in comparison with all the non-European peoples and cultures. There is in addition the hegemony of European ideas about the Orient, themselves reiterating European superiority over Oriental backwardness, usually overriding the possibility that a more independent thinker—may have had different views on the matter. (Said, 1978, p. 7)

[...] [Also,] *power* [is introduced] into questions of representation. Power—always operates in conditions of unequal relations. Gramsci, of course, would have stressed "between classes," whereas Foucault always refused to identify *any* specific subject or subject-group

as the source of power, which, he said, operates at a local, tactical level. These are important differences between these two theorists of power.

However, there are also some important similarities. For Gramsci, as for Foucault, power also involves knowledge, representation, ideas, cultural leadership and authority, as well as economic constraint and physical coercion. Both would have agreed that power cannot be captured by thinking exclusively in terms of force or coercion: Power also seduces, solicits, induces, wins consent. It cannot be thought of in terms of one group having a monopoly of power, simply radiating power *downwards* on a subordinate group by an exercise of simple domination from above. It includes the dominant *and* the dominated within its circuits. As Homi Bhabha has remarked, apropos Said, "it is difficult to conceive—subjectification as a placing *within* Orientalist or colonial discourse for the dominated subject without the dominant being strategically placed within it too" (Bhabha, 1986a, p. 158). Power not only constrains and prevents: it is also productive. It produces new discourses, new kinds of knowledge (e.g., Orientalism), new objects of knowledge (the Orient), it shapes new practices (colonization) and institutions (colonial government). It operates at a micro-level—Foucault's micro-physics of power—as well as in terms of wider strategies. And, for both theorists, power is to be found everywhere. As Foucault insists, power circulates.

The circularity of power is especially important in the context of representation. The argument is that everyone—the powerful and the powerless—is caught up, *though not on equal terms*, in power's circulation. No one—neither its apparent victims nor its agents—can stand wholly outside its field of operation [....]

References

Barthes, R. (1977). Rhetoric of the image. In *Image-music-text*, Glasgow: Fontana.

Bhabha, H. (1986a). The Other question. In *Literature, politics and theory*, London: Methuen.

Brown, R. (1965). *Social psychology*, London/New York: Macmillan.

Christie, L. (1988, October). *Sunday Times Magazine*, p. 15.

Derrida, J. (1972). *Positions*, Chicago: University of Chicago Press.

Douglas, M. (1966). *Purity and danger*, London: Routledge & Kegan Paul.

Dyer, R. (ed.) (1977). *Gays and film*, London: British Film Institute.

Fanon, F. (1986 [1952]). *Black skin, white masks*. London: Pluto Press.

Hall, S. (1972). Determinations of news photographs. In *Working papers in cultural studies no. 3*, Birmingham: University of Birmingham.

Kristeva, J. (1982). *Powers of horror*, New York: Columbia University Press.

Said, E. (1978). *Orientalism*, Harmondsworth: Penguin.

4D Age

CHAPTER 33
Health Care in an Aging Society: Issues, Controversies, and Challenges for the Future

KAREN R. GRANT

Introduction

[...] Although being old and being sick are not equivalent, there is a general impression that older Canadians suffer inordinately from declining health, and consequently utilize health services more than other segments of the population. To many, the crisis in medicare is associated with a growing aged population. In this chapter, we explore trends in population aging, as well as the factors that contribute to the greying of Canadian society. In addition, students will learn about the relationship between health and aging, with a particular emphasis on the health service implications of chronic disease and declining health among Canadian seniors. [...]

I am not mad, only old. I make this statement to give me courage ... I am in a concentration camp for the old, a place where people dump their parents or relatives exactly as though it were an ash can ... I have to hang on to every scrap of information I have to keep my sanity, and it is for that purpose that I am keeping a journal. Then if I forget things later, I can always go back and read them here.

I call it *The Book of the Dead*. By the time I finish it I shall be dead. I want to be ready, to have gathered everything together and sorted it out, as if I were preparing for a great final journey. I intend to make myself whole here in this Hell. It is the thing that is set before me to do. So, in a way, this path inward and back into the past is like a map, a map of my world. If I can draw it accurately, I shall know where I am. (Sarton 1973)

So begins the journal of 76-year-old Caro Spencer who, following a heart attack, finds herself sent off by her family to a home for the aged. Her journal reveals the despair and degradation, the loneliness and helplessness of an elderly woman. Her experience is not uncommon in our contemporary society.

Although there has been a progressive aging of the Canadian population over the past century, it is only in the last few decades that this phenomenon has attracted much attention from academics and the popular press.

A voluminous research literature has been amassed and it is now commonplace to see headlines decrying the problems of a growing elderly population. We hear of "geriatric bed blockers" inappropriately occupying acute-care hospital beds as they await transfer to long-term care institutions. This practice contributes to lengthy queues for people in need of acute care in Canadian hospitals. We hear of elders making extensive use of healthcare and social services, thus placing undue economic (and other) burdens on our welfare state institutions. Expressed in terms of an *old age dependency ratio*, we are left with the impression that elders are not making a "real" contribution to society, but instead are exacting a burden on the rest of society. We hear of drug dependency and *iatrogenesis* experienced by elders because of the numerous prescription medications they receive. And so on.

To a considerable degree, aging has become a social problem (Macintyre 1977), or what C. Wright Mills called a public issue (1959). For Mills, using a "sociological imagination" involves the ability to transcend a problem's personal, individual qualities, so that a particular phenomenon can be understood within the larger social and historical milieux. In this way, private troubles (such as growing old) are no longer private matters at all, but rather public issues that involve the entire array of social institutions and values of a society.

This chapter is devoted to a consideration of the very public and social nature of population aging, and the response of the health-care system to a changing demographic profile in this country. Throughout, the objective is to reinforce the point that population aging highlights many of the contradictions and conflicts within the health-care system and within society at large. Consequently, it is argued that to see aging as the private trouble of individuals is misguided and problematic.

* * * * *

Table 33.1: **Number and Percentage of Population Aged 65 and Older, Canada, 1891–1991**

Year	Number of persons aged 65+	Percentage of population
1891	218 790	4.5
1901	271 201	5.0
1911	335 315	4.7
1921	420 244	4.8
1931	576 076	5.6
1941	767 815	6.7
1951	1 086 237	7.8
1961	1 391 154	7.6
1971	1 744 405	8.1
1981	2 360 975	9.7
1986	2 697 580	10.7
1991	3 200 000	12.0

Sources: N.L. Chappell, L.A. Strain, and A.A. Blandford, *Aging and Health Care: A Social Perspective* (Toronto: Holt, Rinehart and Winston, 1986), 19; Statistics Canada, Age, Sex and Marital Status, Cat. no. 93-310 (Ottawa: Minister of Supply and Services, 1992).

A Demographic Profile of Canada's Elderly

In recent years, a good deal has been written about the aging of the Canadian population. Demographers and gerontologists have described what amounts to a "seniors boom" (Stone and Fletcher 1986), which is having a profound effect on the cultural and economic institutions of Canadian society. The best-selling book *Boom, Bust and Echo* (Foot 1996) wants of the economic and social consequences of the aging "baby boom" generation. It is not too much of an exaggeration to say that Canada is "greying." According to the United Nations, a population is considered "aged" when persons 65 years and older constitute more than 7 per cent of the population (McDaniel 1986). With about 12 per cent of our population over the age of 65, Canada qualifies as an aged nation.

Canada's population is in a state of transition. Just a century ago, Canada's population pyramid was heavily weighted toward the younger ages, with elders constituting only a relatively small fraction of the total population. More recently, however, the pyramid's shape has changed. Younger people (sometimes called Generation X) are fewer in number, and there is an increase in older age groups, most notably persons in their middle years (i.e., baby boomers). As shown in Table 33.1, the number of seniors in Canada has increased steadily over the past century. Whereas in 1891 elders accounted for only 4.5 per cent of the total Canadian population, in 1991 nearly 12 per cent of the population was 65 years or older (Statistics Canada 1992). Based on current projections, it is estimated that persons 65 years or older will constitute nearly one-quarter of the population by 2011. By 2031, 9.2 million Canadians will be 65 years or older,

compared with the current 3.7 million Canadians in the same age group (Denton and Spencer 1996).

A similar characterization can be made for other industrialized nations, such as the United States, where more than 11 per cent of the population was 65 or older in 1981 (Institute for Philosophy and Public Policy 1988; Brody, Brock, and Williams 1987; Dorney 1983; Stone and Fletcher 1988). Some European countries have somewhat larger elderly populations; for example, in 1981, approximately 15 per cent of Britons and 16.5 per cent of Swedes were 65 and older (McDaniel, 1986). By contrast, countries in the developing world do not have large numbers of elders. To be sure, the differences in the demographic make-up of any society are tied very much to social and economic conditions; in the developing world, conditions are not always conducive to a long life.

What has just been described is something demographers call population or demographic aging. Demographic aging refers to the progressive aging of a population (as opposed to the aging of individuals). There are several reasons underlying the phenomenon of demographic aging in Canada and other industrialized nations (McDaniel 1986; Stone and Fletcher 1986). First of all, improvements in health care (a subject to which we will return later in this chapter) have led to significant decline in mortality over the past century, which has contributed to the aging of Canada's population. It is important to note, however, that reduced mortality and increased longevity owe much more to improvements in sanitation, personal hygiene, and living standards than to specific medical measures per se (McKeown 1979; McKinlay et al. 1983). This is not to suggest that doctors have made no contribution—only that public health measures have had a more significant impact on declines in mortality.

This having been said, the effects of improved health care on population aging really are limited, since it is the young and not the old who have benefited most (McDaniel 1986). Medicine has been most effective in dealing with acute conditions, which are more likely to affect younger members of society. In the past century, prophylactic measures have been developed to control or eliminate most infectious diseases. The same is not true for chronic conditions, which more commonly affect older members of the population. Though some medical measures allow for the extension of human life, McDaniel (1986) suggests that there is a ceiling to the biological life span that medicine has not appreciably altered. McKinlay et al. (1983) also indicate that where medical measures have lengthened life, they have often produced more years of disabled life, a very high cost indeed.

The second major factor contributing to population aging is immigration. Canada's relatively open immigration policy has brought a steady influx of mostly young immigrants from various parts of the world over the past century. In the first half of this century, the wave of immigration was from Eastern and Western European countries. More recently a substantial proportion of immigrants are coming to Canada from countries in Southeast Asia, the Indian subcontinent, and Latin America. The earlier immigrants to Canada are now among the elderly, while the more recent immigrants "contribute to the relative youthfulness of the country and ... stave off aging of the population" (McDaniel 1986).

The third, and most important, factor responsible for population aging is the decline in fertility. While the effects of declining fertility are obvious in terms of family size and composition (i.e., the average number of children per family is still less than two), its effects on population aging are not as readily apparent. Yet the reduced fertility of Canadians in the past century has meant that while the absolute number of elders in a population may not have increased, the fact that younger age groups are relatively smaller automatically increases the proportional size of the elderly segment of the population. Gee (cited in McDaniel 1986) puts this rather succinctly: "Population aging is an unplanned by-product of planned parenthood."

With the aging of Canada's population has come the realization that not all individuals have an equal likelihood of surviving to advanced age. We have already noted the differences in life expectancy between developed and developing countries. A similar differential exists within Canada. [...] Proportionally the greatest numbers of elders are found in Saskatchewan, Manitoba, and Prince Edward Island, while in the Northwest and Yukon Territories, elders make up only a small fraction of the total population. Aboriginal persons, many of whom live in Canada's territories (as well as on reserves and in large cities), represent a much smaller proportion of persons aged 65 and over when compared with all other Canadians. In 1986, for example, approximately

10 per cent of the Canadian population was 65 or older, while only 4 per cent of aboriginal Canadians were 65 or older (National Advisory Council on Aging 1993). Poverty and deprivation, as well as living in rural and remote areas with limited access to health services, no doubt contribute to the poorer health and shorter life expectancy of aboriginal Canadians.

If we look at the age composition of the elderly population, here too, we find important variation. Elder Canadians are getting older. Recent evidence from Statistics Canada indicates that the proportion of seniors 65 years and older increased 17.5 per cent between 1986 and 1991. Between 1981 and 1991, the number of Canadians 85 years and older jumped 31 per cent, from 194,000 to 283,000 (National Advisory Council on Aging 1993). The growth rates of the aged have continued to increase over the past century. [...] Demographers project that the rate of population growth for all elders will decline somewhat at the start of the next century, but that this will be followed by an increase in the number of elders around 2030.

One of the more interesting sources of variation among Canada's elderly has to do with gender. Put rather succinctly, aging is a women's issue (Dulude 1978; Nett 1982; Estes, Gerard, and Clarke 1984; Reinharz 1986; Russell 1987; McDaniel 1988, 1989), since women are disproportionately represented among the elderly. This gender imbalance became most apparent in the 1950s. [...] Currently, nearly 60 per cent of seniors are women. The imbalance of the sexes owes much to the greater longevity of females and the higher rates of mortality among males, topics to be considered shortly.

The importance of gender differences in longevity is seen in terms of the sex ratio. In Canada in 1991, for every 100 men aged 65 years or older, there were 138 women. The ratio becomes even more lopsided among the old—for every 100 men aged 85 years or older, there were 200 women (National Advisory Council on Aging 1993). The consequences of this imbalance are profound in terms of health and social policy, as well as at a more personal level. For example, widowhood is "an expectable life event" for most women, particularly elderly women (Martin Matthews 1987) and it has been estimated that most women who marry can expect to live ten years as widows. In 1991, 28 per cent of women 65 years and older were widowed, while 82 per cent of women aged 90 and older were widowed. Among seniors, 13 per cent of men (as compared with 47 per cent of women) were widowed in 1991 (National Advisory Council on Aging 1993). The potential adverse effects of widowhood have been well documented (see, for example, Lopata 1987). Beyond this, the large numbers of elderly women who may or may not have sources of support (because of a loss of spouse or peers) means that community and other institutional supports need to be found for this segment of the elderly population.

Another variable that is often considered when describing the elderly is their socio-economic situation. It is commonplace to hear of elders barely eking out a living on their pension monies. For many elders in Canada, the loss of financial security is a part of growing old. It has been estimated that most elders can expect their incomes to drop by about half at retirement. While the economic situation of elders has improved substantially as a result of government and private pension plans instituted in the post-Second World War era, a risk of poverty remains for large numbers of elderly persons, particularly women. Dulude has noted that "to be old and female is the best combination to ensure being poor in Canada ... to be old and a widow is an even better one" (1978).

* * * * *

Elders' primary sources of income include Old Age Security, the Guaranteed Income Supplement, and the Canada (and Quebec) Pension Plans. In addition to these programs, various provinces have created programs and tax subsidies for elders. Together, all public programs account for about half of elders' incomes (National Council of Welfare 1984). For many elders, the public monies they receive are augmented by private pensions funded through payroll deductions. As noted by the National Council of Welfare, however, "the failings of private pension plans are glaring: most working Canadians are not covered by them (especially lower wage earners and workers in the private sector) and the minority who do belong typically receive meagre pensions that are not adequately protected against inflation" (1984). And, it should be added, most private plans do not benefit women since few of today's elderly women were employed outside the home; consequently, they stand a much greater chance of finding themselves in poverty in their "golden years."

* * * * *

Demographic differences are among the most salient variables that influence health and well-being, but there are other variable among Canadian seniors, including urban or rural residence, education levels, marital status, and living arrangements (see Chappell, Strain, and Blandford 1986; Novak 1988; Centre on Aging 1996). It is important to note how heterogeneous the elderly are as a group. Indeed, the demographic make-up of elders often parallels the demographic make-up of the rest of society.

Typically, we tend to lump all persons with a particular attribute together, and make assumptions based upon various stereotypes. This tendency applies to elders just as it does to other identifiable social groups (e.g., women, aboriginal people, or people with disabilities). While stereotypes can tell us something about the attributes of such groups, more often than not, truths, half-truths, and outright lies are mixed into the stereotypes that we develop. When these stereotypes misinform, they have the potential to cause divisions and conflicts

between people. On this basis, a growing number of researchers reject the stereotypes of deprivation, isolation, and loss that so commonly described seniors even a decade ago. In their most vile form, these stereotypes lead to a form of bigotry described by Robert Butler as ageism (1969, 1980). Ageism is a form of prejudice against elders that "reflects a deep-seated uneasiness on the part of the young and middle-aged—a revulsion to and distaste for growing old, disease, disability; and fear of powerlessness, 'uselessness,' and death" (Butler 1969). Based on many unfounded myths, ageism often has the result of making seniors feel stigmatized and devalued, and may exacerbate the difficult conditions that can be associated with growing old (Dorney 1983). As we shall almost surely all grow old some day, it is time to rid ourselves of these misconceptions. It is also time to enhance our understanding of the aging process and its implications for society and its institutions. Perhaps one of the institutions most affected by population aging is the health-care system, to which we will now turn.

A Brief Look at Canada's Health-Care Program

In recent years, Canada's health-care system has come under increasing scrutiny and criticism. Seldom a day goes by without a headline in one newspaper or another claiming that the health-care system is in a state of crisis. Long queues for surgery and specialist care, bed closures, shortages of nurses and doctors, and striking health-care workers are now commonplace. Yet despite these concerns, Canada's health-care system and medicare program are viewed around the world as exemplary. Indeed, few Canadians today can remember a time when medicare did not exist, and most Canadians could not imagine life without medicare.

Comprehensive, universal, government-funded health insurance, or medicare, has been in place for more than 25 years.

* * * * *

Funding for the program came through taxation, and the government initially agreed to share the costs of health care on a fifty-fifty basis with the provinces, provided that each provincial plan met five requirements:

1. accessibility (reasonable access should be guaranteed to all Canadians);
2. comprehensiveness (all necessary medical services should be guaranteed, without dollar limit, and should be available solely on the basis of medical need);
3. universality (all Canadians should be eligible for coverage on uniform terms and conditions);
4. portability (benefits should be transferable from province to province); and
5. administration by a public non-profit agency or commission.

Beginning in 1977, as a result of the implementation of the Established Programs Financing Act (EPF), the formula for sharing costs was changed. In part, this change was introduced by the federal government as a cost-saving mechanism. Following the introduction of medicare, the governments of Canada (particularly the federal government) found the costs of this program difficult to bear. By the mid-1970s, approximately 7 to 7.5 per cent of the Gross National Product (GNP) was being allocated to health care. In order to put a ceiling on this expense, the federal government introduced the EPF, which tied federal contributions to the size of the population and the growth in the GNP. Rather than providing dollar-for-dollar funding, the federal government provided each province with a block of funds (transfer payments) to be used by the provinces in support of health services, education, and social assistance. By the mid-1980s, it was estimated that the changes brought about by the EPF had reduced federal contributions to medicare from 50 per cent to approximately 38 per cent (Barber 1989).

The EPF, for all intents and purposes, ushered in the progressive erosion of medicare in Canada.

* * * * *

The latest wrinkle in federal-provincial funding of health care has been the creation of the Canada Health and Social Transfer (CHST). The CHST was introduced by the Chrétien government in 1996–97 to replace the EPF and the Canadian Assistance Plan. The CHST provides federal funding as a combination of cash contributions and tax points. It is intended to reduce federal contributions to social spending in health, education, and social assistance, and that is exactly what is happening. According to Kent (1997), "all that is left of federal involvement ... is a relatively small block grant arbitrarily fixed by Ottawa without reference to the health and social costs incurred by the provinces." The current federal contribution toward health, education, and social assistance is $12.5 billion, which represents approximately 15 per cent of the costs of these programs. As a result, provincial treasuries bear a sizable proportion of the remaining costs (in 1994–95, the provinces spent $79 billion). In 1996, expenditures for health care alone in Canada amounted to $75.2 billion or $2,510 per capita, representing 9.5 per cent of the GNP.

There is understandable resentment on the part of the provincial governments about how the funding of medicare has evolved over time. Lured into the creation of a universal, comprehensive public health-care system, the provinces now find themselves bearing considerable costs for an increasingly expensive, technology-intensive health system. The federal government (beginning with Trudeau and continuing with Mulroney and Chrétien) has gradually and substantially reduced its contributions to medicare and other social spending, all the while insisting that "national standards" must be maintained by the provinces. The federal government threatens that departures from the founding principles of medicare—most notably, the prohibition against extra-billing and user fees that create barriers to accessibility—will result in even further reductions in the federal contributions to medicare. Court challenges to federal penalties have been waged in a number of provinces in recent years. According to some critics, the federal government has lost the moral authority to insist that the provinces steadfastly uphold the principles of medicare when its contribution has become so meagre. Health Canada (1997) reports that the actual federal contribution to health expenditures in 1996 was a mere 3.5 per cent of the total, with the remainder paid for through provincial funding (64.4 per cent), private expenditures (30.1 per cent), municipal funding (1.0 per cent), and workers' compensation (0.8 per cent).

* * * * *

Most observers believe that the reduction in federal contributions to medicare has imperilled the system to a considerable degree. But it is also true that several provincial governments have opted to reduce their contributions to the health system. They have initiated major system restructuring, contending that there is too much fat in the system or that resources are being used inefficiently (Armstrong and Armstrong 1996). Under the rubric of "health reform," provincial governments have downsized the health-care system, reducing the number of hospital beds, laying off nursing and other health-care workers, limiting the number of services that are insured and restricting access to others.

* * * * *

The increasing costs of health care today coupled with the changing disease (mostly chronic) and demographic (increasingly older) profiles of the country heighten concerns about medicare's future. This "sacred trust" is under attack. Efforts by the federal government to privatize Crown corporations raise the spectre that medicare may someday be privatized as well, returning Canada to a system not unlike that of the United States. The establishment of private clinics and hospitals in various provinces is the thin edge of a wedge. How government fiscal and free-trade policies like NAFTA and the Multilateral Agreement on Investment (MAI) will affect medicare and other social programs is not entirely clear at this time.

* * * * *

Even the most ardent supporter of medicare would readily acknowledge that the system is not beyond criticism or the need for some types of reform. For example, services, facilities, and personnel continue to be maldistributed among urban, rural, and remote areas of the country. Physicians and hospitals are primarily found in urban centres, as are research and teaching facilities, because it is not feasible to locate facilities in all areas, particularly those that are sparsely populated. Even within cities, not everyone has equal access to the same quality medical care. Various groups, differentiated on the basis of age, sex, race, and socio-economic status, have different susceptibilities to disease and disability; they also experience differential access to quality health services. This problem is best summarized by what Julian Tudor Hart called "the inverse care law": "the availability of good medical care tends to vary inversely with the need for it in the population served" (1971 cf. Grant 1988).

*   *   *   *   *

While medical care is a crucial component of the health delivery system, the needs of many Canadians, and of elders in particular, cannot be met by medical services alone. More medical care does not in itself lead to better health. That the formal system of health care must be augmented by informal and community-based care has been realized for a long time, but only now are governments looking to develop a social care infrastructure based in the community. The development of community-based alternatives to institutional care is highly desirable in that they allow people to be more independent by remaining in their homes and neighbourhoods where familiar social supports are more readily available. At the same time, the off-loading of caring work from professional health-care workers to unpaid caregivers in the home has fallen disproportionately on women, often at a cost to their own health and well-being. A recent study reported that most caregivers experienced some disruption in their lives, and 27 per cent of women caregivers indicated that their health had been affected by their caring work (Cranswick 1997).

Programs providing social care have yet to receive the kind of funding that medicare has, or they have been considered add-ons with varying services, eligibility requirements, and user fees (Schwenger 1987). Furthermore, while federal legislation more ore less guarantees that all Canadians shall have access to medical services, no such guarantees exist with respect to community services. The decentralized nature of health and social programs for the elderly makes assurances of equal access problematic (Chappell, Strain, and Blandford 1986; Chappell 1987, 1988; Statistics Canada 1986).

There is indeed a cost crisis in Canada's medicare program. On the one hand, more money is spent on health care today than ever before, but on the other hand, almost everywhere one turns, the system appears to be underfunded. This contradiction plagues the Canadian health-care system, but how we might effect a desirable solution to the cost crisis remains a matter of considerable debate.

*   *   *   *   *

A Health Profile of Canada's Elderly

As Canadian society has aged, much attention has focussed on the health consequences of this demographic shift. Inasmuch as declining health is often associated with aging (Longino and Soldo 1987), a great deal of attention is directed to the association between sickness and the aging process. Recent evidence suggests that the health and life expectancy of elders is improving, and at a quicker pace than for other age groups (Guralnik and Kaplan 1989; Brody 1989; Ulysse 1997). [...] Health can be assessed in a number of ways, the most common of which use life expectancy, mortality, and morbidity statistics. In the past century, dramatic increases in life expectancy have been achieved in Canada and other industrialized countries. [...] [A] male born in 1986 could expect to live about 73 years, while a female could expect to live to the ripe old age of 80. In the period between 1931 and 1986, the net gains in expected years of life for males and females were, respectively, 13.04 and 17.63 years. [...] Longevity has increased for both sexes, although for women the increases have been more substantial.

The leading causes of death for Canadian seniors—heart disease, cancer, and stroke—mirror those for all Canadians. Diseases of the circulatory system are the number one killer of both men and women, with the rates elevated for persons 65 years and older (Centre on Aging 1996). There is an important difference, however, as to when the risk of heart disease becomes elevated—while men are more likely to be struck down by a heart attack in their mid-years (beginning around age 35), women are at greater risk in their post-menopausal years (beginning around 55). This difference is attributed to the protective effects of estrogen on women.

Based on 1986 data, the second leading cause of death for elderly men is lung cancer, while for elderly women it is stroke. Prostate cancer ranks sixth as a leading cause of death among elderly men, and breast cancer ranks fifth among women (Ulysse 1997). Cancer incidence has risen steadily in recent years, although for persons diagnosed with many forms of cancer, early detection and better treatment have meant improved survival rates. According to the National Advisory Council on Aging (1993), roughly two-thirds of all cancer deaths occur among individuals aged 65 and older.

*   *   *   *   *

It is commonly assumed that being old means being sick. Today, however, there is much evidence to suggest that many seniors are living longer healthier lives (Foot 1996; Ulysse 1997; Macleod and Associates 1997). Both men and women participating in the 1991 Manitoba Study of Health and Aging tended to rate their health as "pretty good" or "very good," although those over 85 became more likely to state that their health was "not too good" (Centre on Aging 1996).

At the same time, epidemiological evidence indicates that there is a much greater likelihood of chronic conditions and various forms of functional limitation occurring in the later stages of the life cycle. Data from the Canada Health Survey and the National Population Health Survey indicate a significantly higher prevalence of chronic health problems among elders than among younger persons. Acute illnesses are less common among elders than other age groups; however, they may be more debilitating for older persons (Verbrugge 1985).

While the mortality and life expectancy data clearly favour women, measures of morbidity do not. Put succinctly, the research evidence suggests that "women get sicker, but men die quicker" (Grant 1989). Women report a greater prevalence of most chronic health problems at all ages including at age 65 and over (Statistics Canada 1981; Federal, Provincial, and Territorial Advisory Committee on Population Health 1996). In the Manitoba Study of Health and Aging, women tended to report more chronic health problems than men, the only exceptions being hearing and memory loss. Common health problems reported by Manitoba seniors included arthritis/rheumatism, trouble with feet or ankles, high blood pressure, ear trouble/hearing loss, eye trouble not relieved by glasses, heart/circulation problems, stomach troubles, memory loss, trouble with nerves, and chest problems (Centre on Aging 1996). American data based on self-reports and physical examinations show a similar pattern (Verbrugge 1985, 1986; Wingard 1984).

*   *   *   *   *

One problem that is more common among older women than men is osteoporosis (brittle bones), which is believed to affect approximately 25 per cent of post-menopausal women (National Advisory Council on Aging 1993). According to Ulysse (1997), most cases of hospitalization related to osteoporosis involve women; in fact, osteoporosis—associated with hip fractures, fractures to the wrist and spine, and accidental falls—is the second leading cause of hospitalization for elderly women. The cost of hip replacement surgery is considerable ($400 million in 1990), and is expected to increase in the future. Yet, for those whose functional capacity is restored, the benefits to their quality of life are incalculable.

Another health problem affecting elders is Alzheimer's disease, which ranks as the tenth leading cause of death in Canada. The prevalence of dementias increases with age (Ulysse 1997), but while some forms of dementia may occur throughout life, Alzheimer's disease commonly occurs among elders. The 1991–92 Canadian Study of Health and Aging estimated an age-standardized rate of Alzheimer's disease of 51 per 1,000 persons aged 65 years and over, and an age-standardized rate of all types of dementia of 80 per 1,000 persons aged 65 years and older. Both the Canadian and Manitoba Studies of Health and Aging report higher rates of all dementias and Alzheimer's disease among women

(Centre on Aging 1996). The National Advisory Council on Aging (1993) estimates that by the year 2006, 324,000 seniors will suffer some form of dementia, representing a 71 per cent increase since 1991.

Based on data from the Canada Health Survey (Statistics Canada 1981), physical functioning declines with age. This study found that less than 10 per cent of persons under 65 had any limitations on their usual activities, while almost 40 per cent of those aged 65 and older were limited in their activity to some degree. Furthermore, approximately the same proportion of males as females experienced partial or total activity limitation at all ages, including the older age brackets. Women, however, reported more disability days—time taken off from their usual activities as a result of poor health. This latter finding was true at all ages, elders included. [...] Overall, 14 per cent of Canadians aged 15 and over reported at least one disability day during the two-week period prior to the survey. Reported disability days increased considerably after age 64, to 17 per cent among those aged 65 to 74, and to 24 per cent among those aged 75 years and over. A higher proportion of females reported disability in all age groups. The largest difference was in the age group of 75 years and over—28 per cent for females and only 18 per cent for males. Reporting on the Health and Activity Limitation Surveys in 1986 and 1991, Raina, Dukeshire, and Lindsay (1997) found that approximately 40 per cent of seniors had at least one disability. Mobility and agility disabilities—by far the most common types of disabilities—are more commonly experienced by elderly women, as are seeing disabilities. Hearing and speaking disabilities are more common among elderly men.

What can we conclude about the health of Canadian seniors? First, being old and being sick are *not* synonymous. While some elders may experience impairment with advancing years, this is not the lot of everyone. Health seems to diminish with age, but other variables—gender, class, and income level—also influence susceptibility to poorer health, and the degree of impairment one experiences (Ulysse 1997). Let us now consider how elders use health care and how well their needs are being met by the formal system of care.

Health Care and Aging in Canada

"The elderly who receive medical care receive more of it than the young" (Barer et al. 1987). The jury is still out on how much seniors cost the Canadian healthcare system. Still, it is widely believed that seniors do use health services more than individuals in other age groups, and that their use of health services intensifies as they get older and sicker. The proportion of health expenditures devoted to the care of seniors is variously estimated to be as low as 20 per cent or as high as 50 per cent of spending (National Advisory Council on Aging 1996).

According to an examination of late 1970s Manitoba health statistics by Roos, Shapiro, and Roos (1984), persons 65 years and older (9 per cent of the total population in 1977) consumed 43 per cent of all acute hospital days. In 1978, these researchers found that seniors consumed 36 per cent of all short-stay hospital days. Persons 70 to 85 years of age consumed three times as many hospital days as those under 60; those 85 years or older consumed ten times as many as those under 60 (cf. Shapiro and Roos 1986; Shapiro and Tate 1985). On this basis, the study concluded that hospital use increases with age, and that a small segment of the elderly population (and of the population as a whole) accounts for a large proportion of utilization of the system.

But this evidence from the 1970s is a less than complete account of the relationship between age and health-care use. In 1994–95, Manitoba seniors (who constituted just over 13 per cent of the population) received approximately 28 per cent of all medical services provided and accounted for almost 32 per cent of all hospitalizations (Centre on Aging 1996). Individuals in the under-45 age group (who constituted nearly 68 per cent of the population), however, received 49 per cent of medical services and accounted for 53 per cent of all hospitalizations. The average length of a hospital stay for those under 45 was 4.2 days, while for seniors between 65 and 74 it was 12.6 days, and for seniors 75 years and older it was 20.1 days in hospital. These differences reflect the nature and severity of disease typically affecting different age groups—younger people are likely to suffer from short-term acute conditions, whereas older people may require longer periods of hospital-based treatment for conditions such as coronary artery disease or cancer.

A recent Saskatchewan study by the National Advisory Council on Aging found that seniors also use doctors' services more than those in other age groups. "In 1987, a physician was consulted 21 times by men 65 and over and 23 times by women 65 and over; in comparison, men and women aged 45 to 64 used a doctor's services 11 times and 14 times, respectively" (1996 Vignette #31).

It has been estimated (based on 1981 census data) that 7.5 per cent of persons aged 65 and older and 35.6 per cent of persons aged 85 and older reside in long-term care institutions (residential treatment centres, nursing homes, personal care homes, etc.) (Forbes, Jackson, and Kraus 1987). Studies suggest that there has been a steady increase in long-term institutionalization over the past several decades, particularly for the very old.

These data confirm the observation that some segments of the elderly population are more likely to be hospitalized, and for longer periods of time, and that some seniors make more extensive use of health services than those in younger age groups. These data also tell us that our health-care system has a very strong institutional focus. Chappell (1988) suggests that the very name medicare underscores the medical emphasis of Canada's health-care system. Although relatively few elders are institutionalized, this type of care is labour- and technology-intensive: the conditions inpatients may suffer are often chronic and may cause functional impairments. Hospital and other institutional care, whether for frail elders or others, is expensive, consuming approximately half of every health dollar in Canada (Chappell, Strain, and Blandford 1986; Evans 1984; Centre on Aging 1996).

Whether elders are best served by acute-care or long-term care facilities is a separate issue. Sociologists have long decried the adverse consequences of institutional life, which include fostering "learned helplessness," "institutionalism," and so on (cf. Goffman 1961; Gubrium 1975). Numerous critics have suggested that there are plenty of people in Canadian hospitals who don't belong there and that Canadians are kept in hospitals too long (Evans 1984). Can a system that stresses reactive acute care adequately deal with individuals who suffer from chronic conditions, which require a more holistic, social, and health (as opposed to medical) focus?

About a decade ago, researchers began turning their attention to the problems that occurred when acute-care beds in general hospitals were being blocked by elderly persons who were awaiting placement in long-term care facilities (Marshall 1987). These "geriatric bed blockers" were seen as difficult to place in long-term care facilities, and family members stood accused of being reluctant to provide supportive services to frail elders about to be discharged. Marshall (1987) suggested an alternative explanation for this phenomenon—that the reimbursement system in Canada's medicare program promotes delayed discharges because it does not consider the level or severity of care. Hospitals are reimbursed for acute-care beds even if they are occupied by a chronic-care patient. In a general hospital, a patient awaiting discharge is a relatively "cheap" patient, but in a long-term care facility, that same patient (who might require several hours of intensive nursing care) is an "expensive" patient. It requires no advanced degree in economics or managerial science to figure out why frail elders are occupying acute-care beds!

The reluctance of families to take their frail elderly relatives home probably has much to do with the negative connotations of nursing homes that have been cultivated over the past few decades. Forbes, Jackson, and Krause (1987), among others, have suggested that the manner in which Canada's medicare program evolved may also help to explain why an institutional focus remains and why families prefer hospital to nursing-home care. Hospital services, they point out, were insured first, only later to be followed by medical services and some community/home services.

The issue of "geriatric bed blockers" has not gone away. In the winter of 1998, journalists across the country reported on the swelling of hospital emergency rooms (and emergency-room hallways!) with sick people, many of whom were seniors. A particularly difficult flu season was blamed for this inundation. However, critics of provincial health ministries accused the governments of having made so many deep cuts to the system that it was hemorrhaging, leaving too few long-term care beds, too many people being discharged from hospital too soon, and too few nurses to take care of patients.

It is difficult to make broad generalizations about the relationship between age and the use of health services. Roos, Shapiro, and Roos (1984), McKinlay (1972), and Grant (1984) suggest that utilization is influenced by numerous factors, including the attributes of patients and physicians, and the settings in which medicine is practised. Keeping this in mind, Roos, Shapiro, and Roos note that "although the elderly initiate most ambulatory physician visits, the physician largely determines whether an individual will be admitted to a hospital" (1984). Charges, then, that elders make disproportionate use of the health system should be tempered by some understanding of the reasons for various types of utilization, and the sources of the decision making. Roos, Shapiro, and Roos suggest that "a preoccupation with the influence that increasing numbers of elderly will have on the health-care system should not mask the potentially even greater impact that the increasing physician supply in North America is likely to have on health expenditures during the next decade" (1984).

This latter point is significant because, in many ways, it hints that the elderly have become the scapegoats for the funding crisis in medicare today. The prospect of population aging sends chills down the spines of health ministers! Branch, Sager, and Meyers (1987) describe long-term care policy in the United States as being "mired in trench warfare," and population aging as a "demographic time bomb." Elders' omnipresence in long-term facilities and in increasing numbers of beds in acute-care hospitals makes them easy targets. More reasoned scrutiny of

Canadian medicine and medicare would suggest that population aging is not so much the problem. In fact, according to the National Advisory Council on Aging:

Population aging contributes to rising health-care costs, but less so than other factors. In the Organization of Economic Cooperation and Development (OECD) community, which includes Canada, population aging was estimated to account for 22 per cent of the growth in health-care costs between 1960 and 1988. The remaining 78 per cent of growth in health-care costs was attributed to factors such as inflation, the growth of the Gross National Product (GNP), and to political and professional choices (1996 Vignette #25).

* * * * *

Conclusions

At the outset of this chapter, it was noted that aging is best viewed as a public issue, rather than a private trouble. Routinely, the social nature of aging and the consequences of the aging process are forgotten or ignored. The experience of growing old can be seen either as a trial or as just another stage of life. In either case, living to a good old age has become a matter of personal responsibility in this society.

* * * * *

References

Barber, J. 1989. "Sick to Death," *Maclean's* 13 February: 32–5.

Barer, M.L., R.G. Evans, C. Hertzman, and J. Lomas. 1987. "Aging and Health Care Utilization: New Evidence on Old Fallacies," *Social Science and Medicine* 24: 851–62.

Basen, M.A. 1977. "The Elderly and Drugs: Problem Overview and Program Strategy," *Public Health Reports* 92: 43–8.

Becker, M.H., ed. 1974. *The Health Belief Model and Personal Health Behavior.* Thorofare, NJ: Charles B. Slack.

Branch, L.G., A. Sager, and A.R. Meyers. 1987. "Long-Term Care in the United States: A Study in Trench Warfare," in R.A. Ward and S.S. Tobin, eds, *Health in Aging: Sociological Issues and Policy Directions.* New York: Springer: 215–32.

Brody, J.A. 1989. "Toward Quantifying the Health of the Elderly," *American Journal of Public Health* 79: 685–6.

Brody, J.A., D.B. Brock, and T.F. Williams. 1987. "Trends in the Health of the Elderly Population," *Annual Review of Public Health* 8: 211–34.

Centre on Aging. 1996. *Manitoba Fact Book on Aging.* Winnipeg: University of Manitoba.

Chappell, N.L. 1987. "The Interface among Three Systems of Care: Self, Informal and Formal," in R.A. Ward and S.S. Tobin, eds, *Health in Aging: Sociological Issues and Policy*

Directions. New York: Springer: 159–79.

———. 1988. "Long-Term Care in Canada" in E. Rathbone-McCuan and B. Havens, eds, *North American Elders: United States and Canadian Perspectives.* New York: Greenwood Press: 73–88.

Chappell, N.L., L.A. Strain, and A.A. Blandford. 1986. *Aging and Health Care: A Social Perspective.* Toronto: Holt, Rinehart and Winston.

Cranswick, K. 1997. "Canada's Caregivers," *Canadian Social Trends* (winter). Ottawa: Statistics Canada.

Denton, F.T. and B.G. Spencer. 1996. "Population Aging and the Maintenance of Social Support Systems," IESOP Research Paper No. 9, McMaster University.

Dorney, R.P. 1983. "Old Age and Long-Term Care in the U.S.A.," unpublished manuscript, Department of Sociology, Boston University.

Dulude, L. 1978. *Women and Aging: A Report on the Rest of Our Lives.* Ottawa: Canadian Advisory on the Status of Women.

Estes, C.L., L.E. Gerard, and A. Clarke. 1984. "Women and the Economics of Aging," *International Journal of Health Services* 14: 55–68.

Evans, R.G. 1984. *Strained Mercy: The Economics of Canadian Health Care*. Toronto: Butterworths.

Federal, Provincial, and Territorial Advisory Committee on Population Health. 1996. *Report on the Health of Canadians*. <http://www.hc-sc.gc.ca/hppb/nhrdp/healthof-canadians/cont-e.htm>.

Foot, D.K. with D. Stoffman. 1996. *Boom, Bust and Echo*. Toronto: Macfarlane Walter and Ross.

Forbes, W.F., J.A. Jackson, and A.S. Kraus. 1987. *Institutionalization of the Elderly in Canada*. Toronto: Butterworths.

Garnick, D.W. and T. Short. 1985. *Utilization of Hospital Inpatient Services by Elderly Americans*. Hospital Studies Program, Hospital Cost Utilization Project Research Note 6. Washington, DC: US Department of Health and Human Services (PHS Pub. No. 85–3351).

Goffman, E. 1961. *Asylums*. New York: Anchor Books.

Grant, K.R. 1984. "Clnical Decision-Making as Social Triage: The Influence of Non-biomedical Factors on Physician Behavior," unpublished manuscript, Department of Sociology, Boston University.

———. 1988. "The Inverse Care Law in Canada: Differential Access under Universal Free Health Insurance," in B.S. Bolaria and H.D. Dickinson, eds, *Sociology of Health Care in Canada*. Toronto: Harcourt Brace Jovanovich: 118–34.

———. 1989. *Lifestyle, Gender and Health: An Examination of the Canada Health Survey*. Unpublished Doctoral Dissertation, Department of Sociology, Boston University.

Gubrium, J. 1975. *Living and Dying at Murray Manor*. New York: St Martin's Press.

Guralnik, J.M. and G.A. Kaplan. 1989. "Predictors of Healthy Aging: Prospective Evidence from the Alameda County Study," *American Journal of Public Health* 79: 703–8.

Health Canada. 1997. *Canada's Health System*. <http://www.hcsc.gc.ca/datapcb/datahesa/hlthsys/Ehlthsys.htm>.

Institute for Philosophy and Public Policy. 1988. "The Graying of America," *Report of the Institute for Philosophy and Public Policy* 8: 1–5.

Kandrack, M-A., K.R. Grant, and A. Segall. 1991. "Gender Differences in Health Related Behaviour: Some Unanswered Questions," *Social Science and Medicine* 32: 579–90.

Kent, T. 1997. "Medicare: How to Keep and Improve It, Especially for Children." <http://www.cyberplus.ca/-caledon/ful183.htm.>.

Longino, C.F. Jr. and B.J. Soldo. 1987. "The Graying of America: Implications of Life Extension for Quality of Life," in R.A. Ward and S.S. Tobin, eds, *Health in Aging: Sociological Issues and Policy Directions*. New York: Springer: 58–85.

Lopata, H.Z., ed. 1987. *Widows, Volume II: North America*. Durham, NC: Duke University Press.

McDaniel, S.A. 1986. *Canada's Aging Population*. Toronto: Butterworths.

———. 1988. "Getting Older and Better: Women and Gender Assumptions in Canada's Aging Society," *Feminist Perspectives* 11, Canadian Research Institute for the Advancement of Women.

———. 1989. "An Aging Canada: Sandwich and Caregiver Dilemmas," *Perspectives: Journal of Gerontological Nursing Association* 12, no. 2: 15–18.

Macintyre, S. 1977. "Old Age as a Social Problem: Historical Notes on the English Experience," in R. Dingwall, C. Heath, M. Reid, and M. Stacey, eds, *Health Care and Health Knowledge*. London: Croom Helm, 41–63.

McKeown, T. 1979. *The Role of Medicine: Dream, Mirage or Nemesis?* Oxford: Basil Blackwell.

McKinlay, J.B. 1972. "Some Approaches and Problems in the Study of the Use of Services: An Overview," *Journal of Health and Social Behavior* 13: 115.

McKinlay, J.B., S.M. McKinlay, S.E. Jennings, and K.R. Grant. 1983. "Mortality, Morbidity, and the Inverse Care Law," in A.L. Greer and S. Greer, eds, *Cities and Sickness: Health Care in Urban America*. Beverly Hills, CA: Sage: 99–138.

Macleod, L., and Associates. 1997. *Toward Health—Aging Communities: A Population Health Approach*. Ottawa: Division of Aging and Seniors, Health Canada.

Marshall, V.M. 1987. "Older Patients in Acute-Care Hospital Setting," in R.A. Ward and S.S. Tobin, eds, *Health in Aging: Sociological Issues and Policy Directions*. New York: Springer: 194–208.

Martin Matthews, A. 1987. "Widowhood as an Expectable Life Event," in V.M. Marshall, ed., *Aging in Canada: Social Perspectives*, 2nd edn. Toronto: Fitzhenry and Whiteside: 343–66.

Mills, C.W. 1959. *The Sociological Imagination*. New York: Oxford University Press.

National Advisory Council on Aging. 1993. *Aging Vignettes #1–#20*. Ottawa: National Advisory Council on Aging.

———. 1996. *Aging Vignettes #21–#33*. Ottawa: National Advisory Council on Aging.

National Council of Welfare. 1984. *Sixty-Five and Older: A Report of the National Council of Welfare on the Incomes of the Aged*. Ottawa: Minister of Supply and Services.

National Forum on Health. 1997. *Canada Health Action: Building on the Legacy*, 2 vols. Ottawa: Minister of Public Works and Government Services.

Nett, M., ed. 1982. "Women as Elders," *Resources for Feminist Research* 11 (Special Issue).

Norland, J.A. 1994. *Profil des personnes âgées au Canada*. Ottawa: Minister of Public Works and Government Services. Cat. No. 96-312F.

Novak, M. 1988. *Aging and Society: A Canadian Perspective*. Toronto: Nelson Canada.

Raina, P., S. Dukeshire, and J. Lindsay 1997. "Prevalence, Risk Factors, and Primary Causes of Disability among Canadian Seniors: An Analysis of the 1986 and 1991 Health and Activity Limitation Surveys," IESOP Research Paper No. 11, McMaster University.

Reinharz, S. 1986. "Friends or Foes: Gerontological and Feminist Theory," *Women's Studies International Forum* 9: 503–14.

Roos, N.P., E. Shapiro, and L.L. Roos. 1984. "Aging and the Demand for Health Services," *The Gerontologist* 24: 31–6.

Russell, C. 1987. "Ageing as a Feminist Issue," *Women's Studies International Forum* 10: 125–32.

Sandelowski, M. 1981. *Women, Health, and Choice.* Englewood Cliffs, NJ: Prentice-Hall.

Sarton, M. 1973. *As We Are Now.* New York: W.W. Norton.

Schwenger, C.W. 1987. "Formal Health Care for the Elderly in Canada," in V.M. Marshall, ed., *Aging in Canada: Social Perspectives*, 2nd edn. Toronto: Fitzhenry and Whiteside: 505–19.

Shapiro, E. and N.P. Roos. 1986. "High Users of Hospital Days," *Canadian Journal on Aging* 5: 165–74.

Shapiro, E. and R.B. Tate. 1985. "Predictors of Long-Term Care Facility Use among the Elderly," *Canadian Journal on Aging* 4: 11–19.

Statistics Canada. 1981. *The Health of Canadians: Report of the Canada Health Survey.* Ottawa: Minister of Supply and Services.

———. 1986. *Age, Sex, and Marital Status.* Ottawa: Minister of Supply and Services. Cat. No. 93-101-1986. Table 1–13.

———. 1987. *Health and Social Support, 1985.* No. 1. Ottawa: Minister of Supply and Services. Cat. No. 11-612.

———. 1988. *Canada Year Book 1988.* Ottawa: Minister of Supply and Services.

———. 1990. *Canada Year Book 1990.* Ottawa: Minister of Supply and Services.

———. 1992. *Age, Sex, and Marital Status.* Ottawa: Minister of Supply and Services. Cat. No. 93-101-1992. Table 1–13.

Stone, L.O. and S. Fletcher. 1986. *The Seniors Boom: Dramatic Increases in Longevity and Prospects for Better Health.* Ottawa: Minister of Supply and Services.

———. 1988. "Demographic Variations in North America," in E. Rathbone-McCuan and B. Havens, eds, *North American Elders: United States and Canadian Perspectives.* New York: Greenwood Press: 9–36.

Tudor Hart, J. 1971. "The Inverse Care Law," *The Lancet* 1: 405–12.

Urquhart, M.C. and K.A.H. Buckley, eds. 1983. *Historical Statistics of Canada*, 2nd edn. Ottawa: Statistics Canada.

Verbrugge, L.M. 1985. "An Epidemiological Profile of Older Women," in M.R. Haug and A.B. Ford, eds, *The Physical and Mental Health of Aged Women.* New York: Springer: 41–64.

———. 1986. "From Sneezes to Adieux: Stages of Health for American Men and Women," *Social Science and Medicine* 22: 1195–212.

Wingard, D.L. 1984. "The Sex Differential in Morbidity, Mortality and Lifestyle," *Annual Review of Public Health* 5: 433–58.

SECTION 4E

Sexuality

CHAPTER 34

The Trouble with Normal:
Postwar Youth and the Making of Heterosexuality

MARY LOUISE ADAMS

Pause of a moment to consider what the boy or girl of today is confronted with: countless novels filled with immortality, profanity, and a profound belief in nothing—most of them, hailed as masterpieces by reviewers who don't know a sentence from a group of words; radio programs that in the main get laughs by scoffing at what were once considered sterling virtues; movies that glorify rudeness, riches, power, animal passion, and drinking; a world that cheerfully squanders billions on liquor, cars, tobacco, gambling, sports, chewing gum, and sleeping tablets [...]

This postwar version of "the world's going to hell in a handbasket" was penned by the principal of Toronto's Palmerston Avenue Public School in 1948 .... [yet] Present-day sexual conservatives like to remember the 1950s as a lost era of family values and solid, "traditional" morals. In contemporary sexual politics, the 1950s are the standard against which some conservatives measure changes in the organization of sexuality. The mores of that decade sit as a kind of benchmark, a symbol of how far North Americans have travelled since morality was "as it should be," with clear gender roles in every household and heterosexual conjugal monogamy as the primary form of sexual partnership.[1] That this portrait is an idealized version of fifties norms does not decrease its effectiveness in contributing to present-day anxieties about changing sexual behaviours and identities. A study of the late 1940s and 1950s makes apparent the ideological underpinnings of the nostalgia that currently runs counter to the gains made by feminists, gay men, and lesbians over the past two decades [....]

During the postwar years, young people were the targets of a range of formal and informal sex-education materials through which mainstream sexual norms were both reproduced and constituted. But the importance of young people to sexual discourses did not lie solely in their position as targets of knowledge; they were also important to the construction of that knowledge. Assumptions about the corruptibility of young people, about their need for protection from moral harm, and

about their role as representatives of the future helped to set boundaries for how sexuality in a general sense, could be understood [....]

The notion of discourse I use here is a Foucauldian one and refers to organized systems of knowledge that make possible what can be spoken about and how one may speak about it. At their most fundamental level, these "systems" are about the production of meaning, a process that is not without its material effects. Discourses, according to Foucault, "crystallize into institutions, they inform individual behaviour, they act as grids for the perception and evaluation of things."[2] They are not, as some have suggested, unrelated to the material aspects of our world. Indeed, material factors—printing presses, institutional resources, money—are what allow certain discourses to become more powerful than others. The task of discourse analysis is to determine which discourses are operating when and how and in what configurations. What possibilities for the construction of meaning arise through their circulation? In analyzing discourses one investigates the various processes—language and social practices—which make possible the statement of the "truths" that order our social world—for instance, the claim that heterosexuality is the most (or, in some versions the only) natural form of sexual expression. The intent is not to prove the veracity of such claims or their alternatives, but to understand how it is that they have come to be made.

Heterosexuality as Subject of Investigation

Heterosexuality is not natural, just common—T-shirt slogan, 1993

In the late 1800s, sexologists across Europe and North America compiled vast lists of strange and unusual sexual "types" and sexual behaviours. These ranged from various forms of bestiality and sado-masochism to auto-eroticism, fetishism, and a wide array of what were assumed to be neurotic distortions of the "sex instinct." Given this history, it is interesting that out of all these possibilities, the most profound sexual-social division in present-day western culture is the one between straight and gay, although the divide between homo- and heterosexualities is perhaps more a linguistic construction than a reflection of the sociosexual landscape. Clunky and inefficient in an analytic sense, this divide works politically to obscure the diversity of experience and allegiance among those who participate in same-sex sexual activity—a diversity that makes it impossible to construct a firm boundary around the proper subject matter of specifically lesbian and gay or specifically heterosexual research. As long as homosexualities and heterosexualities are dichotomized, it is difficult to understand either side of the dichotomy without also considering its so-called opposite. As an analytic category, sexuality—like race, like gender, like class—is relational. There can be no homosexuality without a heterosexuality from which to differentiate it. Thus, it makes sense for those of us interested in the social meanings of the former to engage in research on the latter.

As a means of categorizing and regulating particular types of behaviour and people, both homo- and heterosexuality are relative latecomers to everyday discourse. The term "homosexuality" was coined in 1868 by German sodomy-law reformer Karl Maria Kertbeny. In his usage, the term referred not to sexual object choice, as it does now, but to gender inversion, that is to effeminacy exhibited by men and masculine demeanour exhibited by women.[3] According to gay historian Jonathan Ned Katz, in his important book *The Invention of Heterosexuality*, this new category of homosexuality was initially counterposed not to heterosexuality, which did not yet exist as either a word or a concept, but to a narrowly defined reproductive sexuality. Katz says that it wasn't until 1880 that Kertbeny's new word "heterosexuality" went public—in a published defence of homosexuality (Katz, 1990, p. 54). Twelve years later, an American doctor named James Kiernan used the new term to refer to those who were sexually inclined towards both sexes (p. 19). A 1901 medical dictionary, cited by Katz, gave a more narrow definition: "Abnormal or perverted appetite toward the opposite sex" (p. 85).

The equation of heterosexuality with perversion reflected the centrality of reproduction to pre-twentieth-century sexual systems. It was not until the beginning of this century that the criteria for classifying sexual behaviours shifted from their reproductive to their erotic possibilities. Katz argues that the emergence of the homosexual/heterosexual opposition was part of this shift away from reproductive norms and towards what he calls a "different-sex erotic norm" (p. 81). The work of Viennese sexologist Richard von Krafft-Ebing helped to crystallize this binary as well as the notion of heterosexuality as a non-pathological predisposition to different-sex erotic feelings and behaviour. In his book *Psychopathia Sexualis*, which first appeared in English in 1893, the erot-

ically normal heterosexual is counterposed to the abnormal homosexual, thus setting the groundwork for the hierarchical organization of sexuality that we continue to face today.[4]

It took some time, however, for the homosexual/heterosexual binarism to be widely adopted as a form of classifying erotic attraction. George Chauncey argues that in male working-class communities in New York City, for instance, "homosexual behaviour per se became the primary basis for the labelling and self-identification of men as 'queer' only around the middle of the twentieth century." Prior to that time, "queerness" had been attributed to a man's inability to fit into normative gender roles, not to the sex of the people he chose to have sex with. Thus, masculine men who had sex with effeminate men—"fairies"—had not been considered to be abnormal or homosexual. It wasn't until the 1930s, 1940s, and 1950s, says Chauncey, that "the now-conventional division of men into 'homosexuals' and 'heterosexuals,' based on the sex of their sexual partners, replace[d] the division of men into 'fairies' and 'normal men,'" a distinction that had been based on their display of accepted gender attributes. For white, middle-class men in New York, the importance of erotic inclination and the division between homo- and heterosexuality had become a way of normality two generations earlier (Chauncey, 1994, p. 13).

Chauncey says that the increasing importance of heterosexuality to the middle class reflected the reorganization of gender relations in the early part of the twentieth century. New corporate forms of work, the growing participation of women in the public sphere, and perceptions that modern life was "softening" the male character had led to a crisis of middle-class masculinity. Widespread fear of effeminacy—crystallized around the public image of the fairy—translated into a fear of homosexuality, thereby making heterosexuality a route for the demonstration of manliness. Exclusive erotic desire for women came to be a mark of being a man, while gender identify and sexual identity came to be an inseparable pair (pp. 111–127; see also White, 1993).

This coupling of gender and sexual identities helped to transform the place of sex in North American cultures. Victorian discourses about the need for sexual control and about women's sexual passivity and passionlessness were, increasingly, being questioned by young women and men and by political and sexual radicals. Christina Simmons says that by the 1920s in the United States, the "predominant tone" about sex was one of "liberal reform" (Simmons, 1989, p. 160). Simmons writes that the "new" thinkers argued for less distance between husband and wife, especially in terms of sex. They claimed that "denying sexual urges made marriage itself less stable"; hence they argued for companionate marriages based on emotional intimacy and sexual satisfaction for both women and men (p. 162). This became the model of heterosexuality in the 1920s and 1930s, although, as Simmons makes clear, it did not go uncontested by those, especially women, who felt that the new sexualized marriages diminished female power. In previous middle-class arrangements, women had held a moral power that enabled them to determine the shape of their sexual relationships. In companionate marriages, women's role became a responsive one. Women were counselled to follow men's sexual lead; to withdraw from sex was to threaten the marriage, to treat a husband unfairly. Sex was the glue that was to hold these marriages together. Gender-based roles under male control were the prescription for making sex work. Heterosexuality itself became synonymous with gender hierarchy.

By the 1940s, companionate forms of heterosexual marriage had achieved dominance as the way of organizing erotic, emotional, and reproductive life. The "revival of domesticity" after the war helped to entrench the strict gender dichotomies that held up these forms of marriage, while efforts to control extramarital sex contributed to their sexualization, a process that was seen as one route to family harmony and domestic stability. The increasing influence of psychoanalytic theories in the postwar period also meant that heterosexuality was not simply a means of organizing relationships between women and men; rather, it came to be seen as essential to the expression of "maturity," and it determined one s ability to make claims on normality, that most important of postwar social classifications.

It was not until the postwar period that the process of developing a proper heterosexual identity came to be understood as something that took place before marriage. Not only was teenage sexuality acknowledged—in dozens of advice books and magazine articles on petting and necking—but it was watched and nurtured and guided in socially appropriate directions by sex educators, concerned parents, various civic bodies, and voluntary organizations. Following Freud, heterosexual development was seen as a fragile process, one open to corruption. Adult heterosexuality was not taken to be an inevitability; it was an achievement, a marker of safe passage through adolescence.

What I want to stress in sketching how the notion of heterosexuality developed is both its only recent emergence as an articulated concept and the fact that it has, over the last 100 years, changed considerably as an idea and a practice. As an important sexual category that is too often taken for granted, it requires historical and sociological investigation. Such scrutiny is especially important in light of present-day popular wisdom about so-called family values, in which nothing is seen as more natural and universal than heterosexuality and the nuclear families many people build around it.

To say that homo- and heterosexuality are only recent concepts is, of course, not to say that people in earlier eras did not engage in activities which today we would think of as homo- or heterosexual. Nor is it to suggest that forms of sexual expression were not, previously, subjected to processes and differentiation and regulation. The point is that over the course of several decades, sexual desire and behaviours came to be seen in a new light, as central to identity, as keys to the personality of the individual, and, most importantly for this study, to his or her claim on normality.

In this study, the trouble with normal is its taken-for-grantedness and its power as a regulatory sexual category. In the 1940s and 1950s, the difference between definitions of normal and abnormal sexuality operated as a profound space of social marginalization and exclusion. As a powerful organizer of everyday life, the imperative to be normal limited possibility in peoples lives; certainly it limited the forms of sexual expression and identity available to them [....]

[....] To argue that sexuality is socially constructed, that it changes across time and place, is not to say that we experience it that way. Certainly, as Foucault and others have pointed out, people in western cultures have not done so over the last two centuries during which sexological, medical, and psychoanalytic discourses have all, in various ways, come to place sexuality at the centre of our personal identities. To say that sexuality is socially constructed is not to say that it is not real right now, in the late 1990s, that it is a trivial force in our lives, or that it is easily changed. Rather, it is to suggest the importance of questioning the way we think about sexuality, how it is organized and regulated. Why is it that we categorize ourselves and others by our sexual behaviours and identities? Why has sexuality come to be so "personal"? Why is it assumed to hold the key to our development as individuals?

For Foucault, sexual discourses are conduits through which power gains access to human bodies and where it is expressed by them at the most fundamental level: "When I think of the mechanics of power, I think of its capillary form of existence, of the extent to which power seeps into the very grain of individuals, reaches right into their bodies, permeates their gestures, their posture, what they say, how they learn to live and work with other people" (cited by Martin, 1988, p. 6). This particular understanding of the relationship between sexuality and power and the framing of power as something which operates within and through the individual is immensely important to contemporary notions of sexuality as one of the primary defining features of the individual [....]

As a concept, normalization draws our attention to discourses and practices that produce subjects who are "normal," who live "normality," and, most importantly, who find it hard to imagine anything different. These discourses and practices work to delineate possible forms of expression, sexual or otherwise, as legitimate, while others are left to exist beyond the limits of acceptability. As Cathy Urwin describes it, normalization operates as a type of deviance-prevention mechanism (Steedman, Urwin & Walkerdine, 1985, p. 165). Individuals are encouraged, through a variety of discursive and institutional practices, to meet normative standards, and they come to desire the rewards that meeting those standards makes possible. In this way individuals become self-regulating. While repressive mechanisms may be tied to this process, as in the criminalization of homosexual behaviours in the 1950s, their effects are far outweighed by the power of the original "encouragement."

What makes normalization such an effective exercise of power is the way it operates at the level of the individual, the way, as Foucault says, it uses its subjects. As a form of social regulation, normalization defines and limits the choices that are available to us. Julian Henriques and colleagues write that norms form the "conditions of [our] desire" (Henriques et al., 1984, p. 218). The point is not that we simply try to meet social norms, it's that we *want* to. In the 1950s, this tendency to conformity was lauded and derided by social critics; many thought it was one of the defining features of the period (See Reisman, 1991).

While there is definitely a relationship between social norms and various scientific and professional constructions of "normality," these two categories are not entirely synonymous. Norms are not always based on what's normal. Normal, as Ian Hacking points out, can refer simply to what's usual or typical, a definition which may approximate the norm or may not.5 To simplify Hacking's argument, the notion of normal as what is usual comes from medicine where, in the 1820s, it evolved as an empirical category counterposed to be pathological. In this sense "normal" was descriptive; however, it also had a positive value, as in "healthy." This normal/pathological opposition eventually moved from medical fields to sociological and political ones. As social systems were perceived to be in an unhealthy state, normal conditions were what these systems had deviated from—normal conditions were seen as "the good ones." Here, normal does match "the norm" in the sense of how "things ought to be."6

Both of these senses of the word—normal as description, normal as desirable— differ from more recent connotations of normality as a statistical category. In this usage, normal is not necessarily desirable; it is "mediocre," as Hacking puts it, following Francis Galton. Normal is the point from which we deviate, for better or worse. It is perhaps not a coincidence that "the normal curve," the bell curve, was developed in 1893, at the same time that sexologists were detailing and defining the "normal" sexual type known as heterosexuality.7 While these two modes of determining normality were different, they both helped contribute to notions of its importance as a social marker, a means of measuring difference.

It is when this measure of difference goes to work through moral discourses that it becomes a norm, a regulatory standard of behaviour, an expression of disciplinary power. In detailing the competing means of defining normal, Hacking makes clear that this progression is not inevitable. Nevertheless, what I want to suggest here is that sexual and moral discourses were so tightly connected in the post-Second World War period that definitions of "normal sexuality"—as defined, for instance, in sex education manuals, in films for teenagers, or in magazine articles—and social/sexual norms and the moral

discourses through which they are produced. It's for this reason that Alfred Kinsey, in his statistical studies of sexual behaviours, tried to avoid using "normal" as a category. In the present study, the relationship between definitions of normality and social norms is often a circular one.

Historical sociologists Philip Corrigan and Derek Sayer identify the power of the norm and the process of normalization as an important aspect of what they call moral regulation—the social and political project of rendering "natural" the perspectives and ideologies of hegemonic interests (Corrigan & Sayer, 1985, p. 4). Their idea of moral regulation shares certain features with the forms of disciplinary power, the self-regulatory processes described by Foucault in *The History of Sexuality* and elsewhere (Foucault, 1981, p. 116. See also Foucault, 1979). Like Foucault, Corrigan and Sayer are concerned with the ways that discourses come to work through us so that we become not only easily regulated, but self-regulating. But Corrigan and Sayer, more than Foucault, tend to focus on the fact that only certain discourses seem to gain this power. There are powerful and less powerful discourses, a distinction that has much to do with the material relationships within which they are grounded. The effects of even the "positive," "productive" exercise of power are related to material circumstances through, for instance, the means by which discourses are circulated, whether that be printed materials, television and radio broadcasts, public school lessons, or any of a multitude of other means. Such attention to the inequities in the distribution of power is crucial to an analysis of sexuality, where the realities of subordination and domination are longstanding and impossible to ignore.

Corrigan and Sayer suggest that moral regulation works by limiting the forms of expression available to us—in part, by masking difference under an illusion of social unity. It homogenizes. What we take to be "normal" are, for the most part, representations of dominant interests. Moral regulation helps establish dominant modes of being as not only legitimate, but desirable. Thus, as individuals, we become embedded in and embrace the very processes which restrict possibility in our lives and which diminish our abilities to make sense of ourselves and the world around us. If, for instance, heterosexuality is revered and validated while same-sex sex is punishable by law, by social ostracism, or by its definition as abnormal, it can be difficult for young people who feel they are homosexual to reconcile their sexual and social desires. Fears of punishment, or of not fitting in, can inhibit their ability to express themselves in a manner of their own choosing. It's in this most insidious way that moral regulation limits the number of acceptable or possible social identities that we can take on, all the while making this situation of reduced opportunity appear natural.

It is because the various procedures and regulatory techniques of normalization are directed towards the formation of appropriate kinds of persons that discussions of moral regulation, and the normalization that accomplishes it, are by necessity discussions about subjectivity and about the construction of social subjects. Here, subjectivity is to be understood as both the conscious and unconscious aspects of the individual. It refers to the way we understand who we are in the world and how we take our place in it. We make this knowledge "ours," not through the revelations of our "true selves," but via our negotiations through and within discourse—regulated systems of what can be expressed or said. Our discursive attachments let us bring meaning to the world around us and to our place within it. They offer us subject positions through which we come to understand who and what we are. Our location at the confluence of a variety of discourses makes possible the range of ways we have of expressing ourselves, as well as the meanings we assign to our expressions. It makes it possible to resist what some have called "discourse-determinism."

The production of subjectivity is an ongoing and contested process, not something that occurs once and for all. In terms of the marginalization of homosexualities, for instance, we need to question how such a process of differentiation is accomplished, and how difference comes to be known (and respected or resisted) by people on either side of it. How is "queerness," for instance, positioned by the discourses and practices which contribute to dominant heterosexual norms? The point is, as Richard Johnston writes, that subjectivities—even the most normal and heterosexual ones—are "produced and not given and are therefore the objects of inquiry, not the premises or starting points" (Johnston, Winter 1986/1987, p. 23). [I explore] some of the conditions of possibility within postwar sexual subjectivities were produced. What were the systems of sexual meaning available to adults and teenagers, through which identity could be expressed and understood? While I talk very little about the subjectivities of specific individuals, I am interested in the different subject positions produced in and made available by various discursive formations, in the way discourses position both those who speak through them and those of whom they speak. It is through the negotiation of multiple, often contradictory subject positions that subjectivity is produced. In this light, it is the "preconditions" of subjectivity that I am concerned with here. How were specific subject positions—the juvenile delinquent, the pervert, the nice girl, the sissy, the promiscuous teen—organized through discourse? What was their relationship to the "normal heterosexual"?

In my research I looked at a variety of sites through which the postwar social-sexual order was constructed and maintained: schools, courtrooms, social-work agencies, municipal bureaucracies, popular advice literature, and mainstream social comment [....] As a concept, heterosexuality was not yet sixty years old as the Second World War ended. Still, it has already evolved considerably: from a category of deviant sexual behaviour, to a classification of sexual object choice, to the basis of successful marriages, to a marker of the maturity and ability to conform that were critical to social reckoning

at mid-century. Moreover, between the 1920s and the 1940s, definitions of heterosexuality came to encompass notions about proper gender roles, about the nature of sexualized relationships between women and men, and about the emotional and psychic development of individuals. Indeed, by the late 1940s, the meanings of heterosexuality had expanded to such an extent that its hegemonic position in Canadian culture—as represented by the number of Canadians marrying and starting families—was read as a marker of national stability.

Clearly, heterosexuality is not reducible to any type of natural or biological essence. Neither is it a simple matter of sexual attraction between women and men, nor of the particular forms of sexual behaviour women and men might engage in with each other. Heterosexuality is a discursively constituted social category that organizes relations not only between women and men, but also between those who fit definitions of heterosexuality and those who do not, and between adults and youth. Heterosexuality also helps to constitute relations of class, ethnicity, and race. It is frequently made meaningful by way of non-sexual discourses, and, in turn, these discourses are themselves sexualized.

The ability to lay claim to a definition of normality was a crucial marker of postwar social belonging. To be marked as sexually "abnormal" in any way was to throw into question the possibility of achieving or maintaining status as an adult, as a "responsible citizen," as a valued contributor to the social whole. Normal sexuality, as constructed in postwar advice books, films, magazines, and sex-education curricula, in legal, medical, psychological, and popular discourses, was invariably the preserve of married, monogamous, adult heterosexual couples who produced children, and of the adolescent girls and boys who were preparing themselves to fit into that model. That young people could "prepare for" or be prepared for normal sexuality is a central aspect of postwar sexual discourses. With the rise of developmental psychology, so-called normal sexuality was understood to be an emotional and psychic achievement. While this process played itself out on biological terrain, biology alone was not enough to guarantee one's normalness. Hence the tremendous impulse, expressed by many adults, to intervene in teenage sexual development.

Teens were assumed, in many senses, to be works-in-progress, malleable and easily influenced—characteristics that many adults thought could facilitate their turning into either delinquents or model, sexually responsible citizens. As a group, therefore, teens were often the targets of an "ideal" sexual knowledge intended to guide them towards maturity. Youth were portrayed in popular media and sex education materials as the "parents of the future," a formulation which brought teen sexual development to social prominence and aligned it with the development of society as a whole. Given this, it is not surprising that teenagers were frequently the ground over which the boundaries of normative sexuality were negotiated and reinforced. But young people were not simply the targets of sexual knowledge. Notions about their moral and physical capacities also helped to constitute sexual discourse in a more general sense. The desire to "protect" youth and the future they were assumed to represent helped to constitute sexual discourse in a more general sense. The desire to "protect" youth and the future they were assumed to represent helped to motivate broad-ranging initiatives of moral and sexual regulation that took adults and young people as their objects. Common-sense ideas about the nature of adolescent sexual and moral development contributed to the setting of limits on how and where sexuality could be expressed or represented, and by whom. Some adults saw teenagers as being under the control of their blossoming sex drives. These adults wanted to set limits on public discussions of sexuality because they feared such discussions would set teens off in an orgy of experimentation. Other adults were less concerned about the impulses of puberty and the exigencies of hormones than they were about teenagers' moral immaturity. They worried that boys and girls faced with sexual information or images could be unable to distinguish right from wrong and thus, "innocently," might engage in questionable activities. In both perspectives, notions of sexuality as potentially dangerous, destabilizing, and morally charged combined with ideas about the nature of puberty and adolescent development to curtail public discussion of sex—as we saw in previous chapters in debates over both sex education and indecent literature.

As a concept, "youth" was part of what made postwar sexual discourses work. Regulatory efforts that were promised as a means of "protecting the children" carried a certain moral weight that both justified their existence and increased the likelihood of their success. In this framework, images and discussions of juvenile delinquency operated as the possible fate of young people who were left "unprotected." While delinquency had many social meanings in the postwar years, it was routinely invoked as a sexual category, as the consequence of the moral corruption of youth, or of youthful sexuality run amok.

In either case, fears about delinquency contributed to calls for regulation that would control the sexual activities of young people and efforts that would steer teenage morality in the right direction.

The centrality of youth in postwar sexual discourses was a product of the particular social conditions of the era. After six years of war and the decade-long Depression that had preceded them, Canadians were not always trusting of what the future might bring. They worried about the rise of the cold war and expressed fears about the fragility of the nascent peace and prosperity. At the same time, people revelled in the allied victory over fascism and demonstrated a heightened faith in democracy. Technological change and the increasing availability of consumer goods put "modern life" within the reach of large segments of the Canadian population. These contradictory aspects of postwar life combined to orient Canadians in a profound way towards home, family, and stability. Nuclear families would help protect Canadians against the insecurities of the age. They would also provide the base for the growing consumer economy and for the democracy that was promoted as the route to victory in the cold war. Families were understood to be the primary stabilizing influence on both individuals and the nation as a whole.

In this context, postwar youth, as the "parents of the future," would prove critical to Canada's success or failure in the modern age. As a collectivity, youth were represented in popular discourses as a product of both wartime disruptions and modern prosperity. The social progress of adolescents was read by many as an indication of the shape society would take in the future. While the "youth problem" was taken up as a sign of social disarray, the confidence of "modern" teens was seen as a sign of postwar progress. Issues of sexuality could determine which of these images was prominent or appropriate at any given time for particular groups of young people. Were they behaving "normally" or not? If teenagers were normal—that is, if they met the social norms through which sexual normality was constituted—popular discourses suggested that the future would be normal too.

Notes

1 Stephanie Coontz gives an excellent account of this kind of "nostalgia" in her book, *The Way We Never Were*.

2 For discussions of discourse, see the following by Foucault: *Power/Knowledge*; *The History of Sexuality*; *Questions of Methods* and *The Subject and Power*. The following texts have also been useful: Belsey, *Critical Practice*; Weedon, *Feminist Practice and Postindustrialist Theory*; Henriques et al., *Changing the Subject*.

3 For discussions of the linguistic and political emergence of the homosexual, see: Weeks, *Coming Out: Homosexual Politics in Britain, from the Nineteenth Century to the Present*; Foucault, *The*

History of Sexuality, vol. 1; and Jonathan Ned Katz, *Gay/Lesbian Almanac*.

4 Krafft-Ebing, *Psychopathia Sexualis* (numerous editions; English translations are generally of the 12th, revised edition, originally published in the United States in 1906).

5 Hacking, "Normal." Thanks to Ian Hacking for sharing his notes with me and thanks, too, to James Heap for bringing the paper to my attention.

6 Ibid., 13.

7 Thanks to James Heap for pointing this out to me.

References

Belsey, Catherine. *Critical Practice*. New York: Routledge, 1980.

Chauncey, George. "From Sexual Inversion to Homosexuality: The Changing Medical Conceptualization of Female 'Deviance.'" In Kathy Peiss and Christine Simmons, eds. *Passion and Power*, 87–117. Philadelphia: Temple University Press, 1989.

_____. *Gay New York: Gender, Urban Culture and the Making of the Gay Male World, 1890–1940*. New York: Basic Books, 1994.

Coontz, Stephanie. *The Way We Never Were: American Families and the Nostalgia Trap*. New York: Basic Books, 1992.

Corrigan, Philip, and Derek Sayer. *The Great Arch: English State Formation as Cultural Revolution*. Oxford: Blackwell, 1985.

Foucault, Michel. *The History of Sexuality*, Vol. I. Translated by Robert Hurley. New York: Pelican, 1981.

_____. *Power/Knowledge*. Edited by C. Gordon. New York: Pantheon, 1980.

_____. "Questions of Method: An Interview with Michel Foucault." *Ideology and Consciousness* 8 (1981): 3–14.

_____. "The Subject and Power." *Critical Inquiry* 8 (1982): 777–95.

Hacking, Ian. "Normal." A discussion paper prepared for the "Modes of Thought" Workshop, Toronto, Sept. 1993.

Henriques, Julian, Wendy Hollway, Cathy Urwin, Couze Venn, and Valerie Walkerdine. *Changing the Subject: Psychology, Social Regulation and Subjectivity*. London: Methuen, 1984.

Johnstone, Richard. "What Is Cultural Studies Anyway?" *Anglistica* 26, nos. 1, 2 (1983): 1–81.

Katz, Jonathan Ned. *Gay/Lesbian Almanac*. New York: Harper and Row, 1983.

_____. "The Invention of Heterosexuality." *Socialist Review* 20, no. 1 (1990): 7–34.

_____. *The Invention of Heterosexuality*. New York: Dutton, 1995.

Krafft-Ebing, Richard von. *Psychopathia Sexualis*. New York: Paperback Library, 1965 (originally published 1892).

Martin, Bibby. "Feminism, Criticism and Foucault." In Irene Diamond and Lee Quinby, eds., *Feminism and Foucault: Reflections on Resistance*. Boston: Northeastern University Press, 1988.

Reisman, David. *The Lonely Crowd*. New Haven: Yale University Press, 1950.

"Reject Junction Club's Bid for Mixed Splash Parties." *Globe and Mail*, 18 Jan. 1949.

Resources for Feminist Research. "Confronting Heterosexuality," a special issue. Vol. 19, nos. 3, 4 (1991).

Simmons, Christina. "Modern Sexuality and the Myth of Victorian Repression." In Kathy Peiss and Christina Simmons, eds., *Passion and Power*, 157–77. Philadelphia: Temple University Press, 1989.

Steedman, Carolyn, Cathy Urwin, and Valerie Walkerdine, eds. *Language, Gender and Childhood*. London: Routledge and Kegan Paul, 1985.

Weedon, Chris. *Feminist Practice and Poststructuralist Theory*. Oxford: Blackwell, 1987.

Weeks, Jeffrey. *Coming Out: Homosexual Politics in Britain, from the Nineteenth Century to the Present*. London: Quartet, 1977.

White, Kevin. *The First Sexual Revolution: The Emergence of Male Heterosexuality in Modern America*. New York: New York University Press, 1993.

CHAPTER 35

Gays and Lesbians of the First Nations

SUSAN BEAVER

This article is dedicated to all those who have gone before us to the spirit world and to all our Grandmothers, without whom we would not be here physically or culturally.

Generations before the Europeans invaded Turtle Island our Grandmothers and Grandfathers, our ancestors, lived, breathed, held ceremonies and governed themselves according to the complex demands and gifts of the land, our Mother. It was, and continues to be, a life rooted in respect, spirituality and a little bit of humour.

Before the Europeans invaded Turtle Island there lived the Berdache, the cross-dressers and the two-spirited people, in a respected and vital place in the societies of the ancestors. "Two-spirited" is a positive, traditional term that we prefer to call ourselves. What heterosexual people achieve spiritually in marriage, the union of two beings, we achieve by simply being ourselves. Creator made all beings spiritual beings but Creator gifted some of us to carry two spirits—male and female. Before the invaders we were the healers or medicine people, the visionaries and the blessed. For 500 years the colonizers have been trying to stamp out the First Nations people. And we have survived. Our cultures, languages, land, governments and children have all been the subject of attack. One of the first things the Europeans used to justify our inherent inferiority to their ways, and subsequently most viciously attack, was the two-spirited people. And we have survived.

Today we come together after a long, hard road on which we still travel. Our strength lies in our collective heritage as First Nations people. Like First Nations people everywhere, we are still feeling the effects of colonization. Some of us can't speak our language, some were raised as Roman Catholics and others stolen outright from their people. We come together with our varying degrees of knowledge and hope both to learn as well as share. We learn what it is that makes us unique as Nations and as individuals. We come together as social creatures (witness our tea and bannock get togethers) to forge stronger links. We learn of similarities as First Nations people and our differences as men and women. We come together as educators: GLFN's "Aboriginal Women and AIDS" community forum. We have gone out into our own communities and talked about what it is to be two-spirited, to be HIV+, to risk rejection by our family and community. We speak of acceptance and respect.

Like many communities, we have been infected and affected by AIDS. Our response has been that only Native people can talk to Native people about our sexuality, our lives and our futures with any understanding or success. This is very much in line with principles of self-determination for Aboriginal people. Our response has taken us to high school classrooms, reserves, to our own leaders and to nurses. We ask you, the reader, to take time at this point to honour and remember the ones already taken by AIDS.

As First Nations people and as two-spirited people we struggle to maintain our circle in a society that does not value the First People of this land. It is our intention as an organization to strengthen our cultures and reclaim our place in society. It is also our intention to laugh at ourselves and at life, the entire journey. Ny-weh/Meegwetch.

CHAPTER 36
Beyond Image Content: Examining Transsexuals' Access to the Media

VIVIANE NAMASTE

They cannot represent themselves, they must be represented. Their representative must at the same time appear as their master, as an authority over them, as an unlimited governmental power that protects them against the other classes and sends them rain and sunshine from above. The political influence of the small-holding peasants, therefore, finds its final expression in the executive power subordinating society to itself.[1]

—Karl Marx

In recent years, English-speaking contexts have witnessed a proliferation of images and representations with transsexual or transvestite content. These documents take different forms, from films such as *Priscilla, Queen of the Desert, All About My Mother, Ma Vie en Rose,* and *Boys Don't Cry,* to academic studies such as *Gender Trouble* and *Female Masculinity,* to popular books such as *Stone Butch Blues, Gender Outlaw,* and *Read My Lips.*[2] Photography has also played an important role in recent years, notably with the works of Del LaGrace Volcano, Loren Cameron, and Dean Kotula.[3]

This explosion of images related to transsexuals and transvestites has encouraged everyone to talk about gender. Whether it be on the talk-show circuit or in the university classroom, everyone is fascinated with, in the words of Marjorie Garber, "looking at" transsexuals and transvestites.[4]

Now, the reasons for such "looking at" may differ. The American host Maury Povitch, for example, may present a talk show purely for entertainment purposes: audience members and the spectators at home are invited to "guess" if the guests are biologically male or female. American humanities-based academics like Garber and Butler, however, are fond of putting images of transsexuals and transvestites alongside their readings of French theory. They are primarily motivated by their institutional location: they are less interested in understanding the everyday lived experience of transsexuals and transvestites, and deeply invested in making their theoretical point. Butler, for instance, makes casual references to

drag queens on stage in order to make broad claims about the sex/gender system. In this view, transsexuals and transvestites are a pawn of knowledge, propped up on display only to be erased in the complicated fabric of their struggles. And activists like Cameron and Kotula want to make transsexuals visible for a different reason altogether. They want to offer the crucial information about transsexualism and sex change to other transsexuals and those who support them. They take photographs to make visible the erasure of transsexual men in culture.

Now, with all this talk about transsexuals and transvestites, it is perhaps especially difficult to think about some of the images of the people we do *not* see. Furthermore, in such a context it becomes increasingly challenging to make adequate sense of the conditions that govern what gets put on display. That is the subject of this paper. I want to explore some of the institutional ways in which transsexuals and transvestites can be represented (whether that representation be proffered by a non-transsexual or a transsexual individual). I will consider how it is that certain kinds of speech about transsexuals are not allowed, while others can only occur in select contexts. Let me put it another way: everyone else is talking about transsexual and transvestites, limiting their discussion to image content. I shift the focus by looking at the institutional elements of representation. Having examined some of the institutional workings of the media—unwritten codes and norms that determine what gets said, how it is articulated, and where it is distributed—it is possible to situate the truly radical and groundbreaking contributions of the Counting Past 2 Festival (CP2). CP2 is a festival in Toronto that allows transsexual and transgender artists to speak on their own terms.

Transsexuals experience many difficulties in gaining access to the media on their own terms. There are a variety of ways in which this refusal functions, and I will elaborate on each of them in the substance of this paper.

Outright Refusal of Access

One of the reasons the public does not see images of transsexuals and transvestites is that there has been an outright refusal to disseminate the artistic work they produce. Now, this refusal can happen in both explicit and implicit ways, and I offer an example of each case.

An explicit refusal can be witnessed in the early distribution of the documentary film *Gendertroublemakers*.[5] *Gendertroublemakers* is a short documentary in which two male-to-female transsexuals, who are lovers, interview each other about their experiences trying to live as gay men in urban gay communities. The documentary is groundbreaking in many ways, notably in denouncing the cult of masculinity within urban gay culture, and in offering a positive portrayal of transsexual sexuality on screen. Yet when the video-makers submitted the work to lesbian and gay film festivals, it was flatly rejected. It is important to situate this historically. At the time (a mere decade ago), transsexuals and transvestites were not the next big thing—the biggest fad—on the lips of the gender theorists and the political activists. The innovative nature of this video, then, is all the more remarkable given the epoch of its creation. In the case of Toronto, the video was submitted to and rejected by the Inside Out Lesbian & Gay Film & Video Festival. Yet significantly, the festival organized a night dedicated to transsexual and transvestite film, entitled "gender bending." The program referred to drag queens, chicks with dicks, and transsexuals as "sexual anomalies" [*sic*]. This reference sparked local activists to form TAC—Trans Activist Committee. TAC protested the event, handing out posters that proclaimed NO TO THE GERALDO APPROACH! TRANSEXUALS ARE NOT YOUR ENTERTAINMENT![6]

The refusal to screen *Gendertroublemakers* is particularly significant, then, given the Festival's organizing of the "gender bending" film night. Indeed, while there was space for representation of transsexuals within a framework of the aberrant and the monstrous, Festival organizers chose not to select a video in which two male-to-female transsexual lovers represented themselves and their experience.

Yet the refusal of access to the media for transsexuals can also be more subtle. In many instances, media representatives simply do not listen to the voices of transsexuals. My own experience as a coordinator of a community-based transsexual health project illustrates this implicit exclusion. In the fall of 1999, the *Montréal Mirror*, an alternative weekly newspaper proud of its leftist reputation and "cutting edge" journalism, printed a review of the film *Boys Don't Cry*. The film recounts the story of female-to-male transsexual Brandon Teena, a man raped and murdered in Nebraska shortly after the discovery that he was biologically female. Here is a film that speaks about the harsh realities of living as a transsexual man in this culture. Yet the "leftist" reviewer does not make a link to the local community-based project for transsexuals. Subsequent to this review, I wrote a letter to the editor that let readers know about the existence of our health project, which had been actively providing services at the time for six months. Fortunately, this letter to the editor was published.[7]

Continued and Prolonged Dismissal of Transsexuals Who Contact the Media

That there is a general denial of transsexual access to the media (whether alternative or mainstream) is clear. What is perhaps less obvious, however, is that this dismissal occurs despite the tenacious efforts of transsexual activists to have their voices heard in these forums. Some examples illustrate that the problems transsexuals encounter accessing the media are of a systemic nature.

The organizing of the Counting Past 2 festival offers relevant information in this regard. In its first year, festival organizer Mirha-Soleil Ross sent out press releases, faxes, and telephone calls to all the major mainstream and lesbian/gay media in and around the greater Toronto area. This dissemination was broad, including mainstream newspapers such as the *Toronto Star* and the *Globe and Mail*, as well as alternative publications like *Eye* and *Now Magazine*. Local television stations were also contacted. Incredibly, CP2 received only one mention in the Arts section of the *Globe and Mail*.[8] This absence is surely remarkable: here was a brand-new festival showcasing the work produced by transsexual and transvestite film, video, and performance artists. The 1997 festival actually featured Canadian artists prominently, with four of the five shorts screened having been produced by Canadians. Why is it, then, that publications dedicated to an alternative viewpoint—whether it be a lesbian/gay/queer perspective of *Xtra!* or the left-leaning criticism of *Now Magazine*—decide not to publish a few words on this subject? From the perspective of an institutional analysis, what is important to underline is not only that this exclusion happens, but also that it occurs despite the repeated efforts of activists like Ross to gain a voice for transsexuals in the mass media.

A second example of exclusion of transsexuals from the media comes from my own organizing experience. When I began work as the coordinator of a community-based transsexual health project in Montréal, I faxed out press releases to the local media. Since the project was new, I wanted transsexuals to know about it, and needed the media in this regard. Following up the press releases with phone calls, I spoke with the editor of *Voir*, a weekly cultural publication that includes articles on current social and political affairs. I was told that there was a possibility for an article on the health care needs of transsexuals, but that it was not an immediate priority for the paper. Three months later, the paper published a special issue on "*L'identité sexuelle en question*" (Gender identity in question), with no mention of our local group.[9] The subsequent letter to the editor that I wrote, which pointed out this significant absence, was also not printed.

These examples inform us that the exclusion of transsexual voices from the media needs to be situated as a result of more than prejudice or disinterest on the part of certain editors or journalists. We need to understand such issues systematically, which is to say in relation to questions of power and control over access to representation. Within this context, the persistent and invisible work of transsexual activists goes unrecognized: faxes and press releases ignored, phone calls not returned, vague commitments without appropriate follow-up, letters of protest and correction unacknowledged and unpublished. Once we examine the sheer volume of energies transsexuals have invested in their efforts to gain access to the media, we must simultaneously understand that their institutional exclusion from self-representation occurs in the most persistent and pernicious manner.

Representation to Satisfy the Curiosity of the Non-transsexual Viewer

The examples of *Gendertroublemakers* and a film review of *Boys Don't Cry* tell us something about the denial of access to the media for transsexuals. Yet these cases also inform us about some of the implicit ways in which representations about transsexuals are permitted to circulate. In the beginning of this paper, I stated that everyone was talking about transsexuals and transvestites, but that people were not necessarily saying the same things. The cases presented here provide clear evidence that, in an institutional sense, non-transsexual individuals have the first and final word on the matter. This can be witnessed through the programming committee of the Inside Out film festival, which prevented transsexuals from speaking about their own lives and struggles at the very moment in which it organized a program on transsexuals! It is also evidenced in the case of the *Boys Don't Cry* review. My letter to the editor began from the premise that readers interested in the film would need to know about the existence of our project. Transsexuals who were isolated and without information or support would well appreciate learning of a pertinent resource. Yet the editor of the paper judged that this need—that of transsexuals—was not important enough to warrant inclusion in his review. In this light, although the film review deplored the violence against Teena, the practices of the paper sent a different message. The film reviewer and the editor didn't seem to imagine that transsexuals would see the film, or read the review, and that they would need additional information and resources. Only the realities of the non-transsexual individual matter. In both instances, we can see that the representation of transsexuals does not occur first and foremost with the lives and experiences of transsexuals in mind. Moreover, in many instances the activist energies and protests of transsexuals—demanding the right to self-representation—go unrecognized and ignored. In this light, the representation of transsexuals occurs primarily to satisfy the curiosity of the non-transsexual viewer.

The two situations described above also illustrate the circular loop of the two mechanisms of exclusion (outright refusal of access, and representation to satisfy the curiosity of the non-transsexual viewer). Images of transsexuals are displayed to pique the curiosity of the non-transsexual. And if transsexuals organize themselves to protest this staging, to demand that they articulate their own concerns, they are unable to disseminate their message through the media (alternative or otherwise). This situation allows non-transsexuals to continue to present transsexual realities. And since no one objects(!), the situation goes on and on, ad infinitum.

The Autobiographical Imperative

An important limit to contain transsexual self-representation is the autobiographical imperative, a logical result of the previous limit in which non-transsexuals have the final word on transsexual lives. Transsexuals may be allowed to speak, but only insofar as they offer their personal autobiographies, and only as long as they respond to the questions posed by a non-transsexual interviewer.[10] Another example from my work as a project coordinator of a community-based transsexual health project drives this point home.

I was approached by the French-language Radio Canada television program *Enjeux*. *Enjeux* has a reputation of being serious journalism, dealing with contemporary social and political issues in a sensitive, thought-provoking, and in-depth manner. It is akin to the American program *20/20*, or the English-Canadian *Witness*. (Indeed, the final program produced by Radio Canada on transsexuals also aired on *Witness* on the English airwaves of CBC.) This is no sensationalized show just for the ratings, then, no *Métier Policier* here. *Enjeux* is serious investigative reporting.

Journalists for the program telephoned me in my role as project coordinator in order to contact transsexuals to be interviewed for the show they were planning on the subject. Given the high profile of the show, I asked to meet with them to learn more about their request and to provide them with some relevant information on the situation of transsexuals in Québec.

Having had some experience with the media and the silencing of transsexual voices (the situation with *Voir*), I made it clear to the journalists and producers that my participation—even in a preliminary interview so they could gather information—was conditional on publishing the phone number of the community group I coordinated. As I had been at the time of the *Mirror* experience, I was conscious that transsexuals all over Québec (and elsewhere) would watch the show, and they would need information, resources, and support immediately. I was assured that the contact information would be communicated.

Our meeting was most pleasant, and I spent a great deal of time situating the lives of transsexuals in Québec within their proper judicial, political, and economic contexts. For instance, I explained how sex-reassignment surgery was not paid for through provincial health insurance. I outlined how the law with respect to the change of name and the change of sex in Québec states that transsexuals can only change their names after they have had a genital operation. This situation causes incredible stress and hardship for people, and prevents them from adequately integrating into Québec society. At the medical clinic or the hospital, transsexuals are often ridiculed or stared at incredulously because of their unchanged papers, while getting a job or going to school are remote possibilities indeed. And because of this legal situation, many transsexuals live in extreme poverty, with all that entails: inadequate nutrition and substandard housing. We spoke about these issues in great length, and I provided them with appropriate documentation.[11] I stated quite clearly that it was important to address these issues in the show, since they determine how transsexuals in Québec live and since they constitute the fabric of our daily lives.

The journalists were most interested in the possibility of conducting a formal interview with me for their show. Yet they limited their questions to those about my personal history. How long had I lived as a woman? When did I have my surgery? Was I happy with the results? How did my family accept my transformation? I informed the journalists and producers that I was not interested in telling my personal story. I did specify, however, that I was open to granting an interview as an expert in the field: I laid out my credentials, with several research projects on transsexual health care, many years of community experience in the field, and (at that time) a book contract. Perhaps not surprisingly, however, the journalists continued to try to persuade me to accept the terms of an autobiography. I was so articulate, they noted. (How shocking that people can change sex and still maintain their linguistic capabilities! Imagine how impressed the journalists would have been if we had spoken in English; I was, after all, conversing with them in French, my second language!)

The situation made me both uncomfortable and angry. I carefully pointed out that they were reducing me to only a transsexual. Were they to do a show on vaginal cancer and interview community health activists in the field, they would not demand that the women health activists speak of their own personal vaginas. Yet transsexuals are not accorded the same respect: we can only tell our stories and respond to their questions. We cannot be positioned as experts in the field, and we cannot set the agenda for discussion.

Since I did not agree to the terms of autobiography set out by the *Enjeux* team, the journalists did not interview me. Sadly, they also neglected to include in the broadcast the contact information for the community group I coordinated, despite their assurances to do so and their stated understanding of the needs of transsexual viewers. The interviewees chosen for the Enjeux show—a male-to-female Canadian soldier transitioning in mid-life, a male-to-female police officer transitioning after retirement, and an American female-to-male transsexual—all pre-empted a critical analysis of health care and universal access to services for transsexuals. The

soldier was able to have her surgery paid for through the military, since they have an internal policy that guarantees the provision of health services available to the Canadian population at large. Since some provinces pay for sex-reassignment surgery (though not Québec), this individual did not have to pay for surgery. The police officer, from Ontario, was planning to pay for surgery privately, as did the FTM from the United States. In all of these instances, then, the issue of privatization of health care for transsexuals remained unaddressed. This absence underlines the severe limitations of an autobiographical framework. An exclusive focus on the *what* and the *why* of transsexuality ("Can you orgasm?" "How did your family take the news?") forecloses a critical analysis of the institutional, economic, and political contexts in which sex change occurs.

The autobiographical imperative requires that transsexuals tell our stories of sex change on demand, that we speak about our bodies, our sexualities, our desires, our genitals, and our deep pain at the whim of a curious non-transsexual person. It requires that we recount all this—whether in a public café, in a university classroom, or on the set of a television studio—on command. And by extension it ensures that we will not have the time, space, or authorization to address the underlying political and institutional issues that make our lives so difficult: the legal context of name change, or the administrative policies governing the universal health insurance of sex change surgery and other services related to transsexualism. The autobiographical imperative is a natural progression of a social relation in which non-transsexuals determine when and where transsexuals can speak.

Professional Transsexuals Only, Please

My experience with the *Enjeux* show provokes a reflection on the kinds of transsexual people often portrayed in the mass media, notably within print and television. There are several common characteristics of the individuals profiled. (I am speaking here in generalities, recognizing of course that exceptions are possible and do exist.) In the first instance, most of the transsexuals are male-to-female. Furthermore, they are usually at the beginning of their transition: it is extraordinarily rare for us to see a documentary in mainstream media about a transsexual woman who has lived as a woman for 25 years. Most of the interviewees are white, and they almost always have some professional career. Finally, they have generally begun their transition late in life, somewhere in their forties or fifties. The case from *Enjeux* illustrates well this portrait: two MTFs are portrayed, one a soldier in the Canadian army and the other a police officer.

While these individuals certainly are able to speak about their own experiences of transition, they are not necessarily able to speak about the process of sex change for younger transsexuals, or for those who are poor. And it seems to me important to question the generalizability of these women, the fact that through the media they stand in for all transsexual people. This point was made most clear to me in my meetings with the staff of *Enjeux*. In seeking my assistance to contact potential interviewees, the journalists and producers informed me that it was important to find someone who was well-spoken and articulate, who would present the issues well on air. I raised the question of the inclusion of prostitutes. Since most transsexual youth work as prostitutes, and since most of these individuals are from ethnocultural communities, I felt it important that the research team work to have a diversity of transsexual experiences included in the show. The idea was not well received; they justified their position by explaining that they wanted to offer education on transsexuals to the everyday viewer ("Monsieur et Madame Tout le Monde"), and that if the individuals presented had stable jobs, this would facilitate acceptance.

Sadly, this discourse is often repeated within transsexual communities, as when non-prostitute transsexuals lament the fact that there is an implicit link between transsexuality and prostitution. Such individuals happily accept invitations from the media with the argument that they are going to show everyone that transsexuals are "normal."[12] How sad that the hatred of prostitutes has been so internalized by these people that they do not see prostitutes, transsexual or otherwise, as "normal." The justification of the *Enjeux* team for the exclusion of prostitutes raises some important questions. Are we to accept transsexuals based on their jobs and professional status? Do poor people have the right to change sex? Furthermore, given problems transsexuals experience in changing their papers before sex change surgery, and the subsequent difficulties in finding employment, what does it mean when there is a systematic silencing of the people who live in the margins of society as a direct result of these policies? Does the critical journalist not have a moral and an ethical obligation to discuss the very social policies and institutional practices that force transsexuals into abject poverty and profound social isolation?

Professional and middle-class norms determine not only what transsexuals can say and in what spaces. They also confer the right to speak to those transsexuals who will abide by the codes of a middle-class discourse. These codes, then, proclaim who has the right to speak. In this light, the behind-the-scenes decisions of the *Enjeux* team tell us a great deal about the professional and class biases of the mainstream media. The media want nice, middle-class professionals to speak about the marginal transsexual position, presumably so that the imagined middle-class viewers at home will identify with them. Such a position is offensive both to poor transsexuals and to the viewers of programs like *Enjeux* who do not share middle-class values.

Herein lies the ultimate irony: non-transsexual people working in the media make calculated decisions about which transsexuals can speak, what they can say, and when they can say it.

"We Love Transsexuals ... Especially the Lesbian and Gay Ones!"

Transsexuals are further limited in gaining access to the media to the extent that they do not present themselves in a lesbian/gay discourse. Indeed, careful reflection on the transsexuals who do manage to distribute their work and ideas widely in English-speaking contexts reveals that they almost all advocate an alliance between lesbian/gay and transsexual/transvestite communities. Consider, for example, the work of Leslie Feinberg, Kate Bornstein, or Riki Ann Wilchins. All of these authors are cited and discussed within lesbian/gay activist and academic circles. Their names come up again and again in conference presentations, community-based education workshops, and on the syllabi of college and university courses dealing with issues of sexuality and gender. All three elaborate at great length on the value of a coalition between lesbians/gays and the transsexual/transvestite movement.

Now, the issue here is not that they propose a coalition. The matter at hand, rather, is that these three writers come to stand in for an entire transsexual community. This representation is further ironic when we consider that most transsexuals do not want to have any formal association with the lesbian/gay communities. (I make this statement based on my observations within transsexual communities for 10 years, as well as extensive research on the health care needs of transsexual and transvestites.) Yet the position of transsexuals who want no association with the lesbian/gay communities is never heard in most English-speaking discussions of transsexual ("transgendered") identity and politics. The situation is a curious contradiction. It is claimed that there is a coalition to be made amongst transsexuals and the lesbian/gay movement, and the evidence cited to support the position is the words of the transsexuals who advocate this program and who designate themselves as representatives of the transsexual community. We must ask: why is this so? And how did it come to be that the knowledge we have of transsexuals is so circular? Margaret Deidre O'Hartigan, in an insightful and damning critique of the relations between lesbians and transsexuals, offers an important contribution in this regard. O'Hartigan goes beyond talking about these political issues in the abstract. She provides an analysis of some of the unseen institutional relations that determine who gets to speak in public forums on transsexual issues. O'Hartigan says,

> Leslie Feinberg, Kate Bornstein, and Riki Anne Wilchins all share the same lesbian publicist—Gail Leondar—and are repeatedly booked by Leondar for paid speaking engagements before lesbian audiences.
>
> Imagine the righteous anger amongst Blacks if mainstream, white-owned media proclaimed as "leaders" a handful of collaborators publicized by a white PR firm while ignoring true Black leaders like Jesse Jackson and Louis Farrakhan.

That is the situation occurring with the proclamation by the lesbian press that Feinberg, Bornstein, and Wilchins are transsexual leaders.[13]

O'Hartigan's intervention is so worthwhile because she rips us out of the abstract world of political utopias and plunges us into the seen but unnoticed workings of institutions. She exposes how the infrastructure of lesbian organizing serves to propel the visibility of lesbian-identified transsexuals. Within these institutional relations, transsexuals who do not adopt the party line (when it comes to the relations between lesbian/gay and transsexual communities) cannot speak.[14]

O'Hartigan's point is confirmed in considering the reception of the work of female-to-male transsexual Max Wolf Valerio. Valerio is well known within English-speaking transsexual communities. He was featured in Monica Treut's film *Female Misbehaviors*, in Loren Cameron's book *Body Alchemy*, and in the documentary about FTMs *You Don't Know Dick*. Despite this wide exposure, a lesbian reception of Valerio frequently misunderstands his life. Valerio is often portrayed as a "controversial" figure within the transsexual scene, notably in reinforcing sexist stereotypes of men and masculinity. In an open e-mail and fax sent to supporters and allies on the issue of transsexuality, Mirha-Soleil Ross outlines this attitude:

The idea that transsexuals (and especially transsexual men) are reinforcing sex/gender stereotypes is one of the most damaging piece of propaganda we are dealing with on a regular basis in our relationship with non-transsexuals lesbians and gays here in Toronto.... I recently gave a course for the Queer Exchange (a series of courses of lesbian/gay/bi/transsexual/transgender interest) about transsexual/transgender activism and that was one of the major issues that came up. During one of the seminars, I presented *You Don't Know Dick*. Several of the non-transsexual participants (many of whom were lesbian-identified) said they found the men [in the film] to be very sexist and misogynist. The non-transsexual women were particularly disturbed when transsexual men talked about the effects of testosterone on their sex drive and the way they see and live in the world. I also showed the film *Max* (an excerpt of *Female Misbehaviors*) by Monika Treut featuring Max Wolf Valerio who also appears in *You Don't Know Dick*. I had Max on speakerphone live from San Francisco for a question/answer/discussion period afterward. There is a moment in Monika's film where he is goofing around pretending to shadow-box in the air. So one participant asked if he was forced into or manipulated into performing that scene and if not, why he needed to reproduce such stereotypically masculinist behaviours. Max responded that he was not "forced" into it and that interestingly, if he had performed the same scene when living as a woman and a lesbian, he would have been held as a heroine, breaking gender stereotypes.... He also said, "Now that I have transitioned, what do you want me to do? Start knitting?"[15]

This particular reception of Valerio tells us a great deal about the accommodation of transsexuals within lesbian and gay communities. As long as transsexuals present ourselves with the language, gestures, clothes, and political-speak familiar and comfortable to English-speaking lesbian and gay activists, we are accepted. We may even be celebrated, as the lesbian enthusiasm over Leslie Feinberg attests. But if we dare to present ourselves as we are—if those darned FTMs have the audacity to beat up the air like that, if those MTFs have the temerity to wear perfume to the conference, even when they know it's a scent-free event—our gestures, clothing, "experience," political commitment, and thoughts are sure to be questioned.

Within English-speaking contexts, transsexuals are silenced to the extent that we do not speak the language of lesbian/gay politics.

CP2: An Intervention in the Institutional Dimensions of Art and Culture

The innovative and groundbreaking nature of Counting Past 2 needs to be situated in relation to the institutional exclusion of transsexuals from self-representation as outlined above. Indeed, CP2 offers much more than a variety of images of transsexual and transvestites in all our diversity. More important, CP2 intervenes in the ways in which a silencing of transsexuals is institutionally organized. In this regard, the festival offers an important contribution not only to transsexual politics, but also to the politics of art and culture more generally. Given this contribution, it is useful to briefly examine the different ways in which CP2 intervenes in the six forms of institutional exclusion outlined above.

The very organization of the CP2 festival is a direct result of the first two institutional relations identified: outright refusal of access and a continued dismissal of transsexuals who contact the media. The festival offers a forum in which transsexuals and transvestites can articulate their own lives and bodies on their own terms. In encourages people to submit creative cultural and political work, even if it does not follow the "accepted" aesthetic or production standards of the artistic world. Numerous examples from the festivals throughout the years offer compelling evidence of the importance of this strategy. CP2 has presented many student films, as well as videos produced by people who are not film- or video-makers. Some of it is not very polished on a technical level. Some of it is rough: the sound is a bit off, the editing was done on two VCRs and it shows, or the camera is out of focus. CP2 accepts this kind of work as a way to encourage transsexuals to represent themselves. Were the festival to impose professional standards of the art world on all its submission entries, the result would be one that excludes most transsexual voices. The third manner in which transsexuals are silenced has been characterized as representations that satisfy the curiosity of the non-transsexual viewer.

CP2 offers an important departure from this framework, by creating a social context in which transsexuality is assumed. In this regard, transsexuals are not bound to respond to the questions posed by a non-transsexual journalist. They can create work that asks and answers the questions they deem relevant for their lives.

CP2 also challenges the autobiographical imperative. To be sure, the festival provides an occasion for transsexuals to recount their personal narratives. Yet interestingly, much of the work departs from this perspective. In several instances, transsexuals have used the opportunity created by CP2 to question the very terms and conditions of the autobiographical imperative. In its first year (1997), for instance, activist Xanthra Phillippa MacKay presented an audio performance that questioned the representation of transsexuals on talk shows. On the level of content, MacKay's piece provided incisive critique of the stereotypical ways in which talk shows frame transsexual lives. And on the level of form, MacKay's piece offered a brilliant critique of the autobiographical imperative: here was an audio piece about the visual representation of transsexuals! Transsexuals were nowhere to be seen. That is, of course, precisely the point MacKay wanted the listeners to understand. Aside from questioning how the autobiographical imperative functions, CP2 allows transsexuals to just simply bypass their personal stories. Indeed, it is possible to see work created by a transsexual whose subject matter has nothing whatsoever to do with transsexuality! How refreshing.

CP2 also intervenes in the requirement that professional transsexuals offer the only public face of transsexual and transvestites. The festival's flexibility with regard to film and video style ensures that more than professional artists get to have their say. Moreover, CP2 has since 1998 incorporated a cabaret evening into its festivities. This forum has allowed for the participation of broad and diverse segments of the transsexual and transvestite communities, notably people of colour and prostitutes. The cabaret has featured spoken-work artists, dancers, performance artists, drag kings, drag queens, and female impersonators. Interestingly, the cabaret showcases a much more ethnically diverse group of people than that comprising the filmmakers, who are predominantly white. In the past, for instance, Mister Cool presented an energetic Soca dance from Trinidad, while Maury Mariana delighted participants with a flamenco dance.

Importantly, the cabaret also creates a context in which transsexual prostitutes are both comfortable and willing to participate. Within the local Toronto transsexual community, there is a great deal of crossover between prostitutes and show queens. In some instances, these are the same people: an individual who sometimes does female impersonation shows, and sometimes works as a prostitute. In other cases, the link is one of physical space: the prostitutes work out of a bar, and so come to know the female impersonators. And in still other contexts, the prostitutes and the female impersonators

are friends, socializing both inside and outside of transsexual/transvestite spaces such as bars. What all of this means, in the concrete terms of transsexual/transvestite community and politics, is that it is important to create a context in which transsexual prostitutes are at ease. By involving some show queens in the cabaret, and by having it in a bar, CP2 organizes itself to ensure the active participation of transsexual and transvestite prostitutes. Whereas the media and many non-prostitute transsexuals work to exclude transsexual prostitutes, CP2 allows them to be full and active participants in the festivities. CP2 isn't a designated "scent-free" event, because the organizers know that prostitutes like to wear perfume and hair spray. And they reapply all night long! CP2 teaches us that "inclusivity" and attention to "diversity" is more complicated than a formula learned in a self-designated feminist activist arena.[16]

Finally, CP2 challenges the assumption, taken for granted in most English-speaking contexts, that transsexuals automatically endorse a coalition with lesbians and gays and that they express themselves in these terms. The choice of invited guests is insightful in this light. CP2 has brought in a variety of transsexual individuals to promote their ideas and their work, including Max Valerio. Now, the festival certainly would have been able to garner more media attention if it had invited Leslie Feinberg, Riki Ann Wilchins, or even well-known San Francisco FTM activist James Green. Yet CP2 has refused such an easy solution, and instead has invited people who do not necessarily endorse a coalition with lesbians and gays. Invited guest Valerio, for instance, read from a section of his upcoming work when he presented at the festival in 1998. Among other material, Valerio read from a very charged segment that speaks about the powerful, almost uncontrollable, effects of testosterone on his sex drive and his daily life. He writes about feeling an uncontrollable, biological urge to rape. Valerio's work is challenging. He offers no easy solutions, and asks us to think. He doesn't provide a succinct recipe, or a passionate speech to motivate his listeners. He confronts us with the very raw material of our lives as transsexuals: we know, experientially, what it is to have testosterone rage through our bodies, to feel out of control, to want to do anything just to get off. It's not an argument that sits easily with feminists. And it's not one you will hear articulated by Leslie Feinberg or Kate Bornstein.

The choice of Valerio as a featured guest, then, challenges the requirement that transsexuals present ourselves in terms acceptable to English-speaking lesbians and gays.

Conclusion

I have examined here some of the different ways in which transsexuals are prevented from representing themselves. Through some case studies and examples, I have presented a great deal of behind-the-scenes information that explains who gets to speak on behalf of transsexuals, in which contexts, and at which times. It is important to examine all of this unseen work, because it has such a tremendous impact on what kinds of speech are permitted to circulate.

The CP2 festival is so important given the general silencing of transsexual voices in the mainstream and alternative media. It is a festival, to be sure, with images about transsexuals. And it is also a festival with images about transsexuals created by transsexuals. As such, CP2 intervenes in the actual institutional relations that determine what kinds of images get created, seen, and discussed. CP2 provides an engaging opportunity for an institutional analysis of culture.

At the beginning of this paper, I stated that everyone is talking about transsexuals. CP2 is crucial in this regard. More than just allowing us to note a recent visibility of transsexuals, CP2 asks us to think through the conditions that have rendered transsexuals invisible.

Notes

1 Karl Marx, *The Eighteenth Brumaire of Louis Bonaparte* (Moscow: Progess Publishers, 1972): 106.

2 Judith Butler, *Gender Trouble: Feminism and the Subversion of Identity* (New York: Routledge, 1990); Judith Halberstam, *Female Masculinity* (Durham, NC: Duke University Press, 1998); Leslie Feinberg, *Stone Butch Blues* (Ithaca, NY: Firebrand, 1993); Kate Bornstein, *Gender Outlaw: On Men, Women, and the Rest of Us* (New York: Routledge, 1994); Riki Ann Wilchins, *Read My Lips: Sexual Subversion and the End of Gender* (Ithaca, NY: Firebrand Books, 1997).

3 Del LaGrace Volcano and Judith Halberstam, *The Drag King Book* (London: Serpent's Tail, 1999); Loren Cameron, *Body Alchemy* (San Francisco: Cleis Press, 1996); Dean Kotula, *The Phallus Palace: Female to Male Transsexuals* (Boston: Alyson, 2002).

4 Marjorie Garber, *Vested Interests: Cross-Dressing and Cultural Anxiety* (New York: Routledge, 1993), *passim*.

5 Jeanne B. and Xanthra Phillippa, *Gendertroublemakers*, documentary (Toronto, 1993).

6 This video did screen in Toronto, as part of a panel at the conference Queer Sites: Bodies at Work, Bodies at Play, May 1993. The screening was organized in collaboration with the Inside Out film festival. However, it is important to point out that when the video was presented to the festival screening committee, it was rejected. Only when different organizers (the Conference Committee) created a forum was the video publicly distributed in Toronto.

7 *Montréal Mirror* January 6, 2000.

8 *The Globe and Mail* Thursday, September 11, 1997.

9 *Voir* 16, September 22, 1999:8–12.

10 For a compelling analysis of the ways in which media interviews contain public representations of the private, pre-empting any political representation of the private, see Friederike Herrman, *Medien, Privatheit und Geschlecht: Bisexualität in Daily Talks* (Opladen: Leske und Budrich, 2002).

11 For more on the juridical dimensions of name change in Québec, see Viviane Namaste, *Invisible Lives: The Erasure of Transsexual and Transgendered People* (Chicago: University of Chicago Press, 2000).

12 An exposure of the discrimination against prostitutes within transsexual communities is available in Monica Forrester, Jamie-Lee Hamilton, Viviane Namaste, and Mirha-Soleil Ross, "Statement for Social Service Agencies and Transsexual/Transgendered Organizations on Service Delivery to Transsexual and Transvestite Prostitutes," *ConStellation* 7.1 (Spring 2002): 22–25. This statement is reprinted as chapter 6 of this book.

13 Margaret Deirdre O'Hartigan, *Our Bodies, Your Lies: The Lesbian Colonization of Transsexualism* (Portland, Oregon: 1997). A copy of O'Hartigan's pamphlet can be obtained by writing her c/o P.O. Box 82447, Portland, Oregon, 97282, USA.

14 For more on the ways in which transsexuals must present themselves within the terms of lesbian and gay politics, see my *Invisible Lives: The Erasure of Transsexual and Transgendered People* (Chicago: University of Chicago Press, 2000): especially pp. 60–9.

15 Mirha-Soleil Ross, open letter, April 7, 1998.

16 Lessons from non-prostitute feminists working with prostitutes are instructive here. In the organization of a conference on prostitution, designed to bring together both prostitutes and feminists, the organizers met regularly for planning meetings. However, the meeting was held in a smoke-free house: a compromise was reached wherein one room was designated for non-smokers. All of the prostitutes were smokers, and so much of the concrete organizing was accomplished in that room.

Here, politics that are friendly to non-smokers exclude, de facto, most prostitutes. See Laurie Bell, *Good Girls/Bad Girls: Feminists and Other Sex Trade Workers Face to Face* (Toronto: Women's Press, 1987): "Introduction," 13–14. Jeanne B. and Xanthra Phillippa, *Gendertroublemakers* (Toronto, 1993).

Rethinking Section 4:
ISSUES OF INEQUALITY

Critical Thinking Questions

Section 4A: Social Class

Ann Duffy and Nancy Mandell

1. Although poverty is often thought of as a personal problem, it is a social problem with societal roots. In what ways is poverty routinely explained as a personal failing and how would you counter this argument?
2. Why is the face of poverty in Canada overwhelmingly female? Why are so many children poor?

Kevin Bales

1. If most slavery is no longer predominantly rooted in racist ideologies, how can we explain its existence and persistence?
2. What is the relationship between global capitalism and slavery?
3. How do consumers "benefit" from slavery? How might you challenge slave labour?

John Porter

1. What factors account for the image that Canada is a class-less, or a primarily middle-class society?
2. What is the relationship between class, power and decision-making authority in Canadian society?

Section 4B: Gender

Amartya Sen

1. What are some of the long-term consequences of gender inequality?
2. Various forms of gender inequality exist around the world. What accounts for the relative gender equality in Kerala? What kinds of remedies does the Kerala experience suggest for gender inequality?

R.W. Connell

1. How do rigid notions of patriarchal masculinity harm men as well as women?
2. Why is masculinity hegemonic and femininity emphasized?

Judith Butler

1. What is the connection between nature and sex?
2. What is meant by the binary logic of gender?
3. How are gender identities parodied in cultural practices? Discuss some examples. According to Butler, what is the connection between gender and sex?

Deirdre Kelly, Shauna Pomerantz, and Dawn Currie

1. What is meant by the term "emphasized femininity"? How do the authors take up this concept in relation to skater girlhood?
2. The authors discuss the process of becoming skater girls. What are the key aspects/concepts of this transition?
3. The authors discuss skater culture in terms of its slang and style. Give some examples of this culture and discuss gender dominance and barriers.
4. How did the girls experience contradictions and tensions within their "alternative" girlhood?

Section 4C: Ethnicity and Race

Grace-Edward Galabuzi

1. In immigration, who are the "undesirables" and "desirables"? Be specific. How is making this categorization problematic and what are its implications for immigration policy?

2. Discuss some of the structural barriers limiting racialized groups from achieving economic prosperity. How are they linked to a neo-liberal and capitalist agenda? What are the implications of such barriers?
3. Do the media play a role in the sustaining of racialized stereotypes, especially pertaining to immigration? If so, how? Is this problematic?

Rhoda Howard-Hassman

1. Discuss the differences between illiberal and liberal multiculturalists. How is it apparent, as the author suggests, that Canada aligns with liberal multiculturalism?
2. How are private versus public lines blurred by policies of multiculturalism? Is this problematic? If so, how?
3. Discuss the significance of "community" in terms of identity formation and multiculturalism?

Stuart Hall

1. Discuss racialized knowledge using a symbolic interactionist perspective. In your experience, how does the media sustain and perpetuate racist, sexist, and class-based stereotypes? What two discourses are in play when we see a picture with a caption?
2. What is the relationship between image and myth?
3. Dyer (1977) argues that we need stereotypes in order to make sense of the world. Do you agree or disagree? With reference to the seven forms of stereotyping listed in the article, discuss how stereotyping leads to discrimination and inequality.

Section 4D: Age

Karen Grant

1. How do differences in gender, class, and age affect aging and health care in Canada?
2. Why does the author argue that the stresses on the health care system are not caused by a growing aged population?

Section 4E: Sexuality

Mary Louise Adams

1. How is heterosexuality constructed? How does the media produce and perpetuate an ideology of heterosexuality?
2. What is the relationship between heterosexuality and the reorganization of gender relations in the early 20th century?
3. How can "normalization" be used as an effective exercise of power? Who has the ability to lay claim to "normalcy"?

Susan Beaver

1. What are the some of the effects of colonization on the people of the First Nations?

Viviane Namaste

1. What are some of the images of transsexuals you can think of from recent media? How would you argue they have been represented by mainstream media?
2. What accounts for the misrepresentation or lack of representation of transsexuals according to Namaste?
3. In addition to the CP2 festival, what are other means to generate and circulate positive images of transsexuals?

Glossary Terms

Section 4A: Social Class

Ann Duffy and Nancy Mandell

feminization of poverty: Refers to the trend indicating that women, regardless of age, have higher poverty rates than men.

LICO: Based on family spending and family size, low-income cut-offs (LICOs) represent a measure employed by Statistics Canada. The LICO indicates a cut-off point below which Canadians are considered to be living on low income.

Kevin Bales

disposability: The ease with which a person can be gotten rid of.

exploitation: Exploitation refers to the consumption and use of a person's labour for profit. Where labourers receive wages, exploitation follows Marx's logic of capitalism. Labourers are not paid in the case of slavery, hence the experience of exploitation is tied to a lack of free will.

otherness: Characteristic of being "different" from the dominant group. Is part of the process of "othering," which is carried out by the dominant group in order to justify violence and/or subordination.

slavery: Slavery is a social and economic relationship in which a person is controlled through violence or its threat, paid nothing, and economically exploited.

Section 4B: Gender

Amartya Sen

basic-facility inequality: Inadequate access to personal support and to participation in social and educational structures for girls and women.

household inequality: Inequality in gender relations within households, which translates into unequal bargaining power across society.

mortality inequality: Unusually high rates of mortality for women and thus a preponderance of men in the population.

natality inequality: Preference for male children, which can result in sex-selected abortions.

ownership inequality: Inequality in access to the ownership of goods and assets.

professional inequality: Inequality in employment and promotion for women.

special opportunity inequality: Inadequate access to higher education and training for women.

R.W. Connell

emphasized femininity: A form of femininity defined at the level of mass social relations, which is based on women's compliance with their subordination to men and oriented to accommodating the interests and desires of men. Emphasized femininity is not hegemonic to the same extent that masculinity is.

hegemonic masculinity: A dominant form of masculinity that is more or less recognized and internalized by men and women.

Judith Butler

imitation: In the act of "doing" and "performing" gender, you are imitating a gender identity.

parody: Original meanings accorded to gender are parodied in a performance of an alternative gender identity. Examples: drag, cross-dressing, sexual stylization of butch/femme identities.

primary/original gender identity: The assumption that there is one original gender and a singular gender identity, often the biological sex assigned at birth.

Deirdre Kelly, Shauna Pomerantz, and Dawn Currie

alternative femininity: A femininity that is different from the dominant form of femininity.

alternative girlhood: Ranges of ways that girls consciously position themselves against what they perceive as the mainstream in general and against conventional forms of femininity in particular.

discourse: A way of thinking, a way of organizing thoughts about an issue.

emphasized femininity: A form of femininity defined at the level of mass social relations, which is based on women's compliance with their subordination to men and oriented to accommodating the interests and desires of men.

Section 4C: Race and Ethnicity

Grace-Edward Galabuzi

immigrant: Has been redefined in both Europe and North America to refer to non-Whites (namely Africans, Caribbeans, East Asians, South Asians, and Latin Americans) regardless of whether they are actually immigrants or born in the particular country in question.

precarious work: A recent trend in employment relationships stemming from a neo-liberal social and economic model; precarious work tends to be temporary, part-time, contract, and/or casual work with low pay, no benefits, no job security, and poor working conditions.

"White nation": a mythical perception of Canada achieved through a state-sponsored campaign of social exclusion of Aboriginal peoples and racialized groups throughout history.

Rhoda Howard-Hassman

ethnicity: A form of cultural practice where ethnicity becomes rooted in behaviours that people share (customs, beliefs, rituals, norms, and social conventions); not a static entity, but is active and malleable.

illiberal multiculturalism: Argues for strong identification with ancestral ethnic groups; people are categorized, and are obliged to live by these categorizations; groups take precedence over the individual.

liberal multiculturalism: Encourages private and individual choices of identity; race or ethnic identity is a choice; the individual takes precedence over groups.

socialization: The process through which an individual learns to be a member of society. Sites of socialization include, but are not limited to, relationships with peers, familial interaction, education system, religion, the media, etc.

Stuart Hall

discourse: Ideas that operate as a set of rules that guide behaviour.

stereotype: Refers to rigid views about how members of various groups act, regardless of whether or not they really act in that way. Stereotyping is a negative and harmful practice that reduces a group of people to a few, simple, essential characteristics.

symbolic power: The assigning, classification, and marking of a person or group through representation.

Section 4D: Age

Karen Grant

Ageism: A form of discrimination by younger people against older people, or vice versa.

Section 4E: Sexuality

Mary Louise Adams

dichotomy: Contrast between two ideas or forces. Adams refers to the creation of a dichotomy between heterosexuality and homosexuality. Dichotomies usually involve the elevation of one element and the submersion of the other.

normalization: The process of making a practice appear "natural" and taken for granted. Normalization is an exercise of power that regulates and defines what is acceptable in a given society at a given time.

Susan Beaver

two-spirited: Refers to bisexual individuals.

Viviane Namaste

autobiographical imperative: Non-transsexuals have the final word on transsexuals' lives; it requires that transsexuals tell their stories of sex changes on demand, that they speak out about their bodies, sexualities, desires, genitals, and pain.

FTM: Female to male.

MTF: Male to female.

Relevant Web sites

http://socialjustice.org

The Centre for Social Justice is an advocacy organization seeking to strengthen the struggle for social justice. The site offers links to publications and media releases.

http://www.canadiansocialresearch.net/poverty.htm

A site offering definitions of absolute and relative poverty. Includes explanations of how these are calculated. The site also provides links to articles examining poverty in Canada.

http://www.pch.gc.ca/multi/index_e.cfm

A Canadian government site that discusses multicultural initiatives in Canada. Heritage Canada's mandate is to promote the creation, dissemination, and preservation of diverse Canadian cultural works, stories, and symbols.

http://fatty.law.cornell.edu/topics/civil_rights.html

This Web site explains American civil rights and offers links to the United States constitution (portions that discuss race) as well as court cases that involve civil rights issues.

http://www.gender.org/

This site is run by a gender education and advocacy group. The site seeks to educate and advocate for those who encounter gender-based oppression.

http://www.gendertalk.com

A site that presents news information as well as first-person accounts that challenge traditional conceptions of gender.

http://www.hrdc-drhc.gc.ca/menu/seniors.shtml

A Government of Canada site that offers information for seniors on retirement issues.

http://www.sppd.gc.ca

This site is the Canadian seniors' social policies and programs database. Visitors can link to federal, provincial, and territorial governments. The site also provides links to articles discussing new social policies.

http://www.ejhs.org/

Electronic journal of human sexuality published by the Institute for Advanced Study of Human Sexuality.

http://www.fsw.ucalgary.ca/ramsay/gay-lesbian-bisexual/3b-transgender-resources.htm

A gay, lesbian, bisexual, transgender, and queer information site; a comprehensive resource site.

Further Reading

Armstrong, Pat, and Hugh Armstrong. (1994). *The Double Ghetto: Canadian Women and Their Segregated Work.* Toronto: McClelland & Stewart.
An important study of inequalities of gender in Canada.

Butler, Judith. (1990). *Gender Trouble: Feminism and the Subversion of Identity.* New York: Routledge.
Deconstructs femininity and masculinity, and asserts that neither is authentic and thus gender is a performance.

Calliste, Agnes, George Dei, and Jean Belkhir. (1995). "Canadian Perspectives on Anti-racism and Race, Gender, and Class." *Race, Gender, and Class*, 2(3), pp. 5–10.
Puts forward the case that anti-racist education must include an examination of the economic, political, social, and ideological process that structures racism in Canadian society.

Cheal, David (ed.). (2002). *Aging and Demographic Change in a Canadian Context*. Toronto: University of Toronto Press.

An edited collection that considers various aspects of age and aging in Canada, including work and family, language and leisure.

Cheal, David, and Karen Kampen. (1998). "Poor and Dependent Seniors in Canada." *Aging and Society*, 18(2), pp. 147–166.

A recent study that finds that seniors experience high levels of poverty and that senior women are most at risk.

Galabuzi, Grace-Edward. (2006). *Canada's Economic Apartheid: The Social Exclusion of Racialized Groups in the New Century*. Toronto: Canadian Scholars' Press Inc.

This original volume calls attention to the growing racialization of the gap between rich and poor. It challenges some common myths about the economic performance of Canada's racialized communities, and examines the role of historical patterns of systemic racial discrimination as essential in understanding the persistent overrepresentation of racialized groups in low-paying occupations.

Goldie, Terry. (2001). *In a Queer Country: Gay and Lesbian Studies in the Canadian Context*. Vancouver: Arsenal Pulp Press.

A collection of articles pertaining to sexual and cultural diversity in Canada.

Henry, Frances, Carol Tator, Winston Mattis, and Tim Rees. (1998). *The Colour of Democracy: Racism in Canadian Society*. Toronto: Nelson.

Illustrates how racism is embedded in the politics and practices of the Canadian government and in education, the media, employment, and the justice system.

Kazemipur, Adulmohammad, and Shivas Halli. (2001). "The Changing Colour of Poverty in Canada." *Canadian Review of Sociology and Anthropology*, 38(2), pp. 217–239.

Using recent census data, the authors find that immigrants are overrepresented among those living in poverty in Canada.

Nelson, Adie, and Barrie Robinson. (2002). *Gender in Canada*, 2nd ed. Toronto: Prentice Hall.

An accessible Canadian text introducing key elements of the sociology of gender.

Porter, John. (1965). *The Vertical Mosaic: An Analysis of Social Class and Power in Canada*. Toronto: University of Toronto Press.

A pivotal Canadian study examining class, ethnicity, and power in Canada.

Raphael, Dennis. (2007). *Poverty and Policy in Canada: Implications for Health and Quality of Life*. Toronto: Canadian Scholars' Press Inc.

Offers a unique, interdisciplinary perspective on poverty and its importance to the health and quality of life of Canadians. Central issues include the definitions of poverty; the causes of poverty; the health and social implications of poverty for individuals, communities, and society as a whole; and the means of addressing its incidence and mitigating its effects.

SECTION 5

Crime, Moral Regulation, and Social Justice

The Readings

This section represents a snapshot of the overlapping areas of crime, moral regulation, and social justice. The pieces chosen for this section all highlight the degree to which the state is firmly implicated in people's daily lives. Gary Kinsman traces the moral regulation of gay and lesbian sexualities. He points to the national security campaigns of the 1950s and 1960s in Cold War Canada. Through these campaigns, heterosexuality was normalized while gay and lesbian sexualities were rendered "immoral," "risky," and "deviant." Kinsman argues that these historical anti-queer constructions shape current social practices of discrimination against those who take up sexualities that challenge heterosexual hegemony (lesbians, gay men, bisexuals, and transgendered people).

Next, Elizabeth Sheehy discusses legal responses to violence against women in Canada. She recognizes that all legislation and policy that asserts that women have the right to be free of men's violence has been developed because of the efforts of the women's movement in Canada. Nonetheless, violence against women is still a significant social problem in Canada. Like the readings in the section on inequality, Sheehy argues that women cannot be free from men's violence until all women's equality in Canada is achieved.

Lastly, Little and Morrison's piece on "Pecker Detectors" explores the "spouse-in-the-house" rule and Ontario welfare policy. Margaret Hillyard Little and Ian Morrison utilize a moral regulation framework to understand the relationship between instances of "economic need" and "moral worthiness." The implications of amendments made in 1995 are explored. Little and Morrison argue that single mothers are faced with constant surveillance of moral worthiness, which affects all women's abilities to enjoy full and equal citizenship in Ontario, Canada.

CHAPTER 37

National Security as Moral Regulation: Making the Normal and the Deviant in the Security Campaigns against Gay Men and Lesbians

GARY KINSMAN

This article focuses on the moral regulation organized through the anti-homosexual national security campaigns in the 1950s and 1960s in Cold War Canada. Moral regulation can be seen as the social institutions, discourses, and practices making the normal, and the moral; normalizing and naturalizing only certain ways of living. A crucial part of the national security campaigns was the making of heterosexuality as the moral, national, safe, and normal sexuality while gay and lesbian sexualities were made into the "immoral," "risky," and "deviant" sexualities that were thrown outside the fabric of the "nation." This marking of queer sexualities as "suspect" and "risky" has a legacy in our historical present[1] continuing to shape social practices of discrimination against lesbians, gay men, bisexuals, and transgendered people who do not fit into the dominant two-gender system. I use queer to reclaim and neutralize a term of abuse directed against us, as a broader term than lesbian and gay, and as a place from which to challenge heterosexual hegemony—the social practices, discourses, and ideologies constructing heterosexuality as the only "natural," and "normal" sexuality.

During the 1950s and 1960s, hundreds if not thousands of homosexuals and suspected homosexuals lost their jobs in the public service and the military, as the RCMP collected the names of close to 9,000 suspected lesbians and gay men by 1967–1968 in the Ottawa area (Directorate of Security and Intelligence Annual Report, 1967–1968). Pressuring gay men to inform on other homosexuals, hundreds were interrogated, and many were followed, photographed, and spied upon. Later we will hear from some of these men. The Canadian government even funded research into the detection of homosexuality known as the "fruit machine" for more than four years.[2] Homosexuals were portrayed in this Cold War national security discourse as suffering from a "character weakness" or "moral failing" that would make us vulnerable to blackmail and compromise by foreign agents and therefore into "security risks." Although these national security campaigns lessened in intensity in much of the public service in the 1970s and 1980s, they continued at a high rate of intensity in the RCMP and military into the late 1980s and for the military the early 1990s.

To this day closeted homosexuals can be denied security clearances with the argument that they have something to hide and therefore are vulnerable to blackmail and are a "security risk."[3]

The Moralization and Normalization of Sexuality

Mary Douglas, in her anthropological work, shows how social and moral notions of purity, pollution, and taboo have often been built on the social relations of physiological reproduction and erotic practices. These symbols have played an important part in organizing social boundaries and in providing a sense of social and moral order in an often chaotic and conflicted world, "Ideas about separating, purifying, demarcating, and punishing transgressions have as their main function to impose system on an inherently untidy experience. It is only be exaggerating the difference between within and without, above and below, male and female, that a semblance of order is created" (Douglas, 1979, p. 4).

Douglas argues that, "nothing is more essentially transmitted by a social process of learning than sexual behaviour and this of course is closely related to morality" (Douglas, 1973, p. 93). Reproductive and sexual norms and taboos produce a "natural" order around which life comes to be organized. This natural order depends on boundaries separating the normal from the ambiguous. Any challenge to these boundaries by "deviant" behaviour leads to the mobilization of social fear and anxiety. This moral order therefore depends on the marginalization of anomalies and firm social boundaries demarcated by "natural" markers that are rigorously policed.

Moral regulation is made up of a broad range of social discourses, institutions, ideologies, and practices. Ideologies are the ruling ideas in a society that are usually just taken-for-granted as "common-sense."[4] Moral regulation covers a much broader terrain than that of "the sexual," including non-sexual practices such as alcohol, drug-use, gambling, and crime. At the same time eroticism and sexual activity has been a key area for moral regulation, often informing the moral regulation of seemingly non-sexual activities. Sexual regulation includes the various practices, ideologies, and institutions that define and regulate our sexual lives. More recently, as I mention later, there has been a limited moral de-regulation of queer sexualities as new less moral forms of sexual regulation have emerged to contain queer sexualities while at the same time buttressing heterosexual hegemony.

The making of the moral and the immoral—the right and wrong ways to live— which often in the west has its roots in absolutist church ideologies, has especially been applied to the body and its pleasures over the last two centuries. New secular, or non-church-based, disciplinary knowledges like medicine, psychiatry, and psychology, came to build on earlier church-based prohibitions and came to transform and shift moral/immoral distinctions on a new secular and "scientific" basis. The new terrain of sexuality came to be defined in the 19th century as an essential "instinct" or drive that defined people's activities and began to become the "truth" of people's beings. This new concept of sexuality emerged through the opening up of new social spaces outside the family realm and the household economy through the development of capitalist social relations. The new disciplinary knowledges and forms of sexual policing developed in response to the emergence of forms of "sexual deviance" in these social spaces. Sexual policing is the social policing of this new terrain of "sexuality," focusing on the regulation of "deviant" sexualities through the extension of the Criminal Code and police activity into new areas of sexual activity. It includes expansion of the policing of the "sexual" through growing police and criminal justice systems and other social agencies. Forms of sexual resistance were generated by groups of people actively seizing these new social spaces in order to meet their erotic needs. The response to these new forms of policing and new forms of "scientific" knowledge was the emergence of forms of sexual difference and oppositional erotic cultures that would eventually be called homosexual, gay, and lesbian.

Through this process of struggle and social transformation, the sexual became a highly moralized terrain. The Criminal Code sections referring to sex-related offences in Canada were referred to as "offences against morality," until they were moved into a new section called "Sexual Offences" in the 1950s. This moralization of the "sexual" continued even after there was a shift away from moral conservatism—an approach that argues that there is only one "right" sexuality, that is often religiously based, and generally argues for a rather repressive approach to erotic activity outside marriage—towards a more liberal policy of sexual regulation focused on public/private distinctions in the 1960s. In this liberal strategy there was still a common public morality which prohibited the public affirmation of queer sexualities, and the limited private "moral" space provided for homosexual sex was clearly subordinated to this public morality. This was also the terrain of the making of heterosexuality as "normal" in the 1950s and 1960s. If we think of the struggles over the "moral" and the "normal" of the last forty years, key to this has been

struggles over sex education; birth control, abortion and reproductive rights; lesbian and gay rights; prostitution; pornography; and AIDS/HIV.

In the late nineteenth and twentieth centuries heterosexuality was associated with the natural, the normal, the clean, the healthy, and the pure; homosexuality was in contrast the dangerous, the impure, the unnatural, the sick, and the abnormal [....] In this chapter, I focus on how homosexuality was made into a moral problem through the national security campaigns. This was built on top of earlier moral constructions of homosexuality and heterosexuality. One extract from right-wing discourse shows this mobilization against queers because we were seen to transgress sexual, class, political, and other social boundaries. R.C. Waldeck in *The International Homosexual Conspiracy* published in 1960 gives us a taste of this discourse.

Homosexual officials are a peril for us in the present struggle between West and East: members of one conspiracy are prone to join another ... many homosexuals from being enemies of society in general become enemies of capitalism in particular. Without being necessarily Marxist they serve the ends of the Communist International in the name of their rebellion against the prejudices, standards, ideals of the "bourgeois" world. Another reason for the homosexual-Communist alliance is the instability and passion for intrigue for intrigue's sake, which is inherent in the homosexual personality. A third reason is the social promiscuity within the homosexual minority and the fusion of its effects between upper class and proletarian corruption. (1981, p. 13)

We get a clear sense of the "homosexual personality" characteristics, which are perceived to be a problem, and also the association constructed with Marxism and its challenge to capitalism. The challenging of erotic and social boundaries is equated with challenging class and political boundaries. The construction of homosexuality as a moral and political problem has been closely related to its construction as a "deviant" sexuality. Deviance constructs groups like homosexuals as different, other, and "abnormal." A key strategy of disciplinary power and power/knowledge relations, as Michel Foucault has pointed out, is normalization. For Foucault forms of power are expressed through the claims to knowledge of doctors, psychiatrists, and other "experts" and knowledge is always bound up with power relations. Normalization leads to the making normal of only some practices and ways of living and the making of others as pathological, abnormal, and deviant. The pathological strategy constructs some ways of living as physiological or mental sickness or illness. The normalization of sexuality has involved forms of policing and criminalization as well as psychiatric, psychological, and sociological forms of disciplinary knowledge. For instance, mainstream sociological notions of the "normal" and the "deviant," often resting on statistical regimes of the "norm," have played an important part in strategies of normalization. Even critical approaches to deviancy studies by not taking up the social standpoints of those labelled as "deviants" can end up participating in normalizing practices by suggesting there really is something that is "deviant" about these groups of people. Deviancy is an administrative collecting category grouping together different social practices with very different social characteristics so they can all be addressed together as "deviant." [...] Administrative knowledge is designed for state and professional agencies, and for corporations to rule over, classify, manage, and administer the lives of people in this society.

Central to this making of the normal and the deviant, as already suggested, have been questions of sexuality and sexual identification. The paradigmatic examples of "deviance" have been homosexuality and prostitution. This has been part of the relational normalization of heterosexuality and the "deviantization" of homosexuality. This historical and social process not only marginalizes the "deviant" homosexual on the social periphery it also places the "normal" heterosexual at the social centre. The national security campaigns against queers are a key part of this social and historical project.

"I Have Undergone an Experience Which Has Destroyed the Efforts of My Life to Date"

I begin exploring the moralization and normalization work of the national security campaigns against queers with a quote from a gay man whose life was very detrimentally affected by the campaigns. I contrast this with the national security campaign's ideology that mandated this campaign against queers.

The following quote from a first-hand account written by Harold in the early 1960s tells of his experiences of being purged from the Canadian Navy in the late 1950s and the impact of this in his life.[5]

> Until recently I was a trusted, respected citizen. I held a position of responsibility and had spent years working hard in what I believed—and still do—was a worthwhile, if not highly remunerative organization. Then one day, the culmination of months of severe mental stress, I was dismissed .... Quite unnecessarily, I feel, I have undergone an experience which has destroyed the efforts of my life to date ... I have been deprived of two basic human needs—a reason for living and a degree of self-confidence .... At an age when I had commenced to reap the benefit of years of conscientious and highly commended effort I have been removed from my position and world because, very belatedly, it seems, my superiors discovered I am a homosexual. ("Harold, Case Study," 1960–1961)

This quote brings into view the rupture, or line of fault [...] between Harold's lived social experiences and

the security regime practices which made him into a security problem with the "solution" of forcing his resignation from the Navy. In starting here I start a critical investigation of the social organization of the national security campaign from the social standpoint of the oppressed in relation to national security. The world of national security looks very different if we start from the social experiences of those most detrimentally affected as opposed to the RCMP agents or state officials directly involved in organizing queers as a "national security threat." Harold's experiences were shaped both through security regime practices that defined homosexuals as threats to "national security" because of their "character weakness" and the policies of the Canadian military which called for the "disposal" of all "sex deviates" found in the military, which pre-dated and helped to shape these security campaigns.

I contrast this first-hand account of the destruction of Harold's career and life with the national security construction of the homosexual "problem." This construction of homosexuality made homosexuality into a moral/ethical problem as well as a security problem—and in some ways a security problem because of these "immoral" characteristics,

> ... sexual abnormalities appear to be the favourite target of hostile intelligence agencies, and of these homosexuality is most often used .... The nature of homosexuality appears to adapt itself to this kind of exploitation. By exercising fairly simple precautions, homosexuals are usually able to keep their habits hidden from those who are not specifically seeking them out. Further, homosexuals often appear to believe that the accepted ethical code, which governs normal human relationships does not apply to them .... The case of the homosexual is particularly difficult for a number of reasons. From the small amount of information we have been able to obtain about homosexual behaviour generally, certain characteristics appear to stand out—instability, willing self-deceit, defiance towards society, a tendency to surround oneself with persons of similar propensities, regardless of other considerations—none of which inspire the confidence one would hope to have in persons required to fill positions of trust and responsibility. (Wall, 1959, pp. 12–13)

This quote comes from a 1959 Canadian Security Panel memorandum. The Security Panel was the interdepartmental committee that coordinated the national security efforts of various agencies and institutions within Canadian state formation. In this security text, homosexuals were constructed as a security problem because of their characteristics which included "weaknesses," "unreliability" and "unethical" and "immoral" characteristics. These constructions were built on psychiatric knowledge that regarded homosexuals as "psychopathic personalities" who were unable to tell the difference between right and wrong or to control their sexual impulses, and this linked to national security concerns regarding moral and character weakness. This conceptualization of the "deficiencies" of the homosexual character is one of the central ways that the practices of moral regulation enter into the national security campaigns against gay men and lesbians. While not always being overtly and explicitly moral in character, moral regulation is carried forward through the active work of the concept of "character weakness" in the discourse and practices of the national security regime. We also see here that homosexuals are constructed as distinct from the "normal." We begin to see that what led to the end of Harold's career was the mobilization of moral regulation through the national security campaigns.

Critically Interrogating National Security

To explore the social organization of this security campaign, I use two major theoretical/methodological approaches. The first is Dorothy Smith's marxist feminist sociological contributions of a sociology for women and the oppressed; text-mediated social organization; and her alternative way of doing sociology called institutional ethnography [....] Dorothy Smith uses the social and historical materialist approach developed by Karl Marx, adapted for feminism, as a critical method of analysis to examine the relation between the oppression of women and the social relations of capitalism. Her method is to disclose the social practices of people, while resisting the profound social processes of reification that transform social relations between people into relations between things in a capitalist society.

I start this inquiry from the social standpoints of those who were most directly affected by these national security campaigns. From these standpoints we can critically interrogate and analyze the national security campaigns against queers and can disclose their social organization from a vantage point that allows us to move beyond the ideological limitations of national security discourse.

The social relations and practices of the national security campaigns are organized, mobilized, and mediated through the documents of the national security regime and other official texts. These texts are used by people in the national security regime to co-ordinate their work of defining and doing surveillance work on "national security risks." Using Smith's approach, I read the national security texts as active texts used to organize the campaigns against gay men and lesbians. These national security texts and their conceptual framings of queers as "national security risks" suffering from a "character weakness" were used to mandate and co-ordinate the purging of queers and spying upon gay men and lesbians.

Smith's alternative way of doing sociology—institutional ethnography—allows me to turn the insights of ethnographic analysis (how cultures and forms of social organization work) to critically interrogate the institutional relations of the national security regime from the standpoints of queers in order to explicate how they organized problems in the everyday/everynight lives of gay men and lesbians. Institutional ethnography involves a critical analysis of the ideological organization of the national security campaigns including that of national security itself. This is a broader notion of work that allows us to grasp the concerted activities going into the social organization of the national security campaigns and the resistance and accommodation to it; and the ways in which the national security campaigns are hooked up to the broader social relations of the criminalization and social stigmatization of homosexuality and the national security policies of the USA, Canada, and England. The national security regime is accomplished by people active in a number of different institutional locations. This regime can be seen as being made up of a number of intersecting and coordinated social relations. First, this research is based on interviews with more than 30 people who were purged, transferred, or forced into informing on others. These interviews begin to interrogate the broader institutional relations through which this security campaign was organized as well as critical textual analysis of national security discourse from a grounded social analysis developed from the accounts of those most directly affected.

Second, I use analysis derived from the work of Michel Foucault to explore the organization of the security regime as a concrete and grounded form of power/knowledge relation based on social surveillance, normalization, and disciplinary power. While Foucault's work has major insights and is especially useful in critically addressing the technologies and strategies of social surveillance and normalization, it also has some significant limitations given its tendency towards discourse reductionism and determinism. While Foucault believes that power is everywhere, he never locates power as the social accomplishments of people in the historical and social contexts in which we live. In my use of Foucault's insights, I try to always read discourse and power as social accomplishments. What has been produced socially can also be transformed collectively by the people ourselves. Foucault's work on governmentality, which focuses on how power operates around and across public/private boundaries and on practices of self-formation, is also useful for this investigation. While national security has a lot to do with self-formation and self-surveillance and it involves the collaboration of groups outside state relations, it is also a very state-focused practice.

National Security and Moral Regulation

The social organization of the security regime in Canada is an under-documented and under-theorized area in Canadian history and sociology, especially as it relates to sexual and moral regulation. Here I focus on the moral dimensions of the work of the security regime, while noting this work is only one of its central features. In specifying more precisely the moral character of national security we also begin to see the shifting strategies of moral regulation across time and space.

"National security" rests on the construction of the nation and the national interest. The very construction of the nation and its subjects, and state formation more generally, is an intensely moral project. It is a project of moral regulation and normalization—the construction of moral subjects and "citizens." The constructions of nation and national security are ideological productions and cannot be simply assumed or taken-for-granted. We always have to ask, which nation and whose security is being defined and defended? On the one hand, the unitary or totalizing construction of the "nation" of Canada codes Canadians with particular social characteristics, including racial characteristics painting Canada as "white" and in this context as "normally" and "morally" heterosexual. At the very same time, the very real social differences of sexuality, class, gender, race, ethnicity, age, ability, language, and nation, especially regarding Quebec and the First Nations which are subsumed under this "unitary" Canadianness, can also be polarized out, individualized, or otherized as "threats" to the nation, as homosexuals were in Canada in the 1950s, 1960s, and 1970s. There is a dialectic here between the unitary classification of "Canadian" and the very real social differences people live in their lives in relation to sexuality, class, race, gender, and other social relations.

The ideological construction of nation and national security includes some as being moral/normal Canadians, while at the every same time, excluding others like queers as immoral/deviants. The construction of national security is defined in particular by the "interests" of the "nation," including capitalist social relations, national defense concerns, and the inter-state alliances in which the Canadian state was involved. To define someone as a "national security risk" was also a moral evaluation, a way of denying them citizenship and civil rights and a way of "cutting" them out of "normal" social interaction. Homosexuals were thereby cut out of or excluded from the national social fabric, defined as breaking the boundaries of public morality, and therefore were able to be entered into the investigation and surveillance relations mandated in national security discourse.

"National security risks," especially those claimed to be suffering from a "character weakness" or moral failing, were constructed as immoral subjects that made them unreliable and suspect. They supposedly had something to hide and therefore were vulnerable to compromise and blackmail [....]

One important aspect of the security campaign was an attempt to construct moral/normal subjects who would not jeopardize "national security." This was to be constructed in part, through actual social surveillance and perhaps more significantly as in the Foucaultian image of the Panopticon (Jeremy Bentham's ideal model for a prison in which prisoners could be under constant surveillance) through the constant threat or possibility of being watched and monitored by the security police. [...] This was a project of attempted self-surveillance and self-governance which had a certain effectiveness in forcing people into the living of a double life and the relations of the closet, but at the same time as we will see, this could not prevent non-cooperation and resistance to the national security campaigns. Living a double life is a survival strategy when a person performs themselves in the "public" world of work as heterosexual and is only "gay" or "lesbian" in more "private" gay or lesbian circles. The social relations of the closet is produced through criminalization, social stigmatization, and the national security campaigns themselves which often forced people to live in the closet performing themselves as heterosexual in the work world and many other aspects of their lives as well. They were generally not visible as gay or lesbian to any other people around them.

The national security regime was organized through two key conceptual practices. First, it was organized and mandated through "national security" itself which defined this against the "other"—against socialists, trade unionists, immigrants, peace activists, gay men and lesbians, student activists, and the black community in Nova Scotia in the late 60s, among many others. Second, on top of this construction of national security, lesbians and gay men were inscribed into the conceptualization of "character weakness." The classification of "character weakness" was an administrative collecting category grouping together a series of unrelated practices that could include excessive drinking, gambling, adultery, and homosexuality. At the same time, this classification became increasingly homosexualized in Canadian national security discourse and practice by the late 1950s. Basically, character weakness came to equal homosexual.

I talked to Fred, who worked in the Character Weakness subdivision of the RCMP's Directorate of Security and Intelligence in Ottawa in the late 1960s. Close to 90 percent of his work, he said, was dealing with homosexuals [October 21, 1994]. The clear implication was that homosexuals raised moral, character, and security questions that most heterosexuals did not. This focus on homosexuals was not simply a mistake or an aberration as some have suggested, or the result of homophobic prejudices among some in the security regime. Nor is it to imply that homosexuals were not the real threat, while other people were. For this last formulation retains national security discourse. Rather I want to draw attention to a particular social construction of national security, which produces lesbians and gays as a threat to the "nation-state."

This [article] focuses mostly on the social experiences of gay men, since men were more present in security positions during these years and gay men were more visibly constructed as a social danger. However, it is important to also stress that these security campaigns did have major impacts in the lives of women and lesbians.[6] [...]

*　　*　　*　　*　　*

The Social Relations of Interrogation and Blackmail: "Which Is the Greater Treason ... Treason to Your Country or Treason to Your Friends?"

Once gay men and lesbians were designated as "national security risks" suffering from a "character weakness" and following security surveillance confirmation that they were a "confirmed homosexual" through a number of identifications from gay informants or surveillance work individual gay and lesbian members of the public service and the military could be held in the social relations of interrogation (Kinsman, 2000). In a 1994 interview, Harold, whom we have already met, told me that the RCMP was much more heavy-handed than Naval Intelligence during interrogations [February 21, 1994]. This was related to their different mandates and the division of labour developed between them. The RCMP bore major responsibility for the national security campaigns while the responsibility of Naval Intelligence was organized differently and related far more to the policies of the military including the "disposal" of homosexuals.

According to Harold the RCMP would ask over and over again for the names of homosexuals and they would tape the interrogations. Harold also said the two officers interrogating him would make statements like "'Look you've got to know something for god's sake tell us, tell us. We won't hurt anybody but tell us come on tell us.' [bangs on table] Boy you have no idea of how I hated them" [February 21, 1994].

In his written account written shortly after he was forced out of the Navy Harold described the interrogation.

> This particular agency [the RCMP] does not operate with kid gloves ... It is true that to state the terms used by these agents were, mildly expressed, forceful but the method of attack was decidedly clever .... I was told that persons of my caliber are so much easier to handle than "drug store cowboys." To my enquiry why, the answer was that I was an individual of responsibility, integrity, and background as could readily understand the terrible import of the question, "Which is the greater treason ... treason to your country or treason to your friends?" Or, "A person like yourself must realize what a serious disservice you may do your country by withholding the names of people we must ensure are never exposed to treasonous blackmail." ... All they wanted was that I should talk, give names and suspicions. ("Harold, Case Study," 1960–1961)

There is a construction here of a divergence of loyalty to gay friends versus loyalty to the country in which loyalty to the nation is constructed as the most significant and privileged. In contrast loyalty to his homosexual friends was constructed as disloyalty or risk to

national security. Loyalty to his friends meant he was a traitor to Canada. [...]

Inverting the Problem of Blackmail

The RCMP interrogations were oriented around "security" concerns and "blackmail," as Harold's text suggests,

> They were, of course, applying a form of blackmail very difficult to resist. It contained an appeal to patriotism and reason, the pseudo-flattery of apparent recognition of integrity and a thinly veiled threat ... "we are not concerning ourselves, right now, with the criminal aspects of the situation." ... To my sickened dismay, even the success I had achieved in keeping my professional and personal lives strictly separated was turned against me. I was told I MUST know quite a "ring" of homosexuals in professional circles and my statement that I did not was immediately and emphatically rejected as a lie .... ("Harold, Case Study," 1960–1961)

Harold made an important reversal here of the security argument that homosexuals were vulnerable to blackmail from Soviet agents to viewing the RCMP itself as trying to "blackmail" him. They used him being gay and living a "double life" to try to "blackmail" him into doing what he did not want to do. In response Harold attempted to develop an alternative ethical form of resistance that refused to allow his statements to be turned against his friends. Implicitly this begins to develop an ethical position that challenges national security by placing loyalty to one's friends and other gay men above the interests of "national security." There was also the threat from the RCMP officers that they might be able to lay criminal charges against him given that RCMP work is also organized through the Criminal Code and at this time all homosexual acts were criminalized.

This view of the RCMP, police or military authorities as the blackmailers resonates with other accounts we have heard and read from gay men and lesbians who had experienced surveillance and interrogation. Harold stated that he was "only ever blackmailed by the RCMP" [Feb. 20, 1995]. Axel Otto Olson, then living in Toronto, was one of the few "non-expert" witnesses to give testimony before the Commission investigating the criminal law relating to Criminal Sexual Psychopaths which led to the extension of the criminalization of homosexual acts and individuals (Kinsman, 1996). Criminal Sexual Psychopath legislation, which I come back to later, had been expanded to include all homosexual activities as possible "triggering" offences which made it possible for conviction for a consensual homosexual offence to lead to an indefinite sentence. In his 1956 testimony to the Commission, Olson detailed a series of blackmail attempts against himself and other men which followed accusations of homosexuality that were carried out by "certain police officers, court officials, and members of religious youth organizations." Like other gay men during these years, he located the very real problems of blackmail that they faced in the laws criminalizing homosexuality, in police actions, and in social practices stigmatizing homosexuality. He described being falsely charged with having sex with boys and being dragged to the police station and through the courts in Montreal where he was kept in jail for several weeks. The government he said was investigating and blackmailing men in the civil service. It was "almost impossible to teach school," said Olson, "because if you are friendly with the pupils you run the risk of being accused of being homosexual or a sex deviate." As he stated, "I don't believe the sex deviate ... is the main problem." In his view the blackmailers were the "most serious problem." This was also an important inversion of the hegemonic discourse that permeated state policy and the social "common-sense" put in place through the criminalization of homosexuality, through the psychiatric/psychological construction of homosexuality as a mental illness, and the mainstream media coverage of "sex deviation" that then existed.

Harold and Olson were in different ways reversing the focus of the national security campaign, and turning back the accusation of "blackmail" against the RCMP and the police. This is part of the development of an ethics of resistance, which begins by turning the practices of ruling moral regulation on its head. The early gay rights position argued that it was only because of laws criminalizing homosexual sex that such blackmail was possible. Early gay activist Jim Egan felt that the security campaigns ignored the fact that the only reason they were possibly subject to blackmail was because of the laws that made the whole thing illegal. And if they had issued a directive to every commanding officer [or person in charge of a government department] that he was to inform his men [sic] that if they were approached by a foreign agent that they could report the matter to their commanding officer who would guarantee them absolute immunity and they could have cooperated in trapping foreign agents. Instead of that they thought the solution was the wholesale firing of anyone who was or was suspected of being gay [Jan. 5, 1998]. Yvette, a woman who was purged from the military in the 1950s for being a lesbian stated that, "They say that being a lesbian or a homosexual puts you as a target for blackmail. Well, if it were legitimized, it would no longer be, there would be no blackmail."7

The national security campaigns against queers, along with the criminalization of homosexual sexual activities, were an important part of the putting in place of the social relations of the closet and living a double life, as mentioned earlier. The national security regime was both aware of the social relations of the closet and the consequent need for secrecy and invisibility on the part of gay men and lesbians as we saw earlier when a memo for the Security Panel read, "By exercising fairly simple precautions, homosexuals are usually able to keep their habits hidden from those who are not specifically seeking them out" (Wall, 1959, p. 12). The national security regime themselves made use of and intensified the social space of the closet to organize their national security campaigns. While the early gay movement was beginning to call for the repeal of anti-gay laws and social stigmas as a way of getting rid of blackmail concerns, the RCMP and national security discourse by simply accepting this as a "natural" and not a social and historical construction positioned the need for secrecy and invisibility as inherent in the homosexual character. They did not locate this as a response to specific social and historical conditions, including the national security campaigns themselves. Judging from the documents we have been able to read no one on the Security Panel suggested that there was a need to repeal the laws criminalizing homosexuality to begin to alleviate the problems of blackmail facing many gay men and lesbians.

The Mediated Character of National Security

The national security campaign against queers did not exist independently. It had a mediated or mutually constructed character also being organized and shaped through the criminalization of homosexuality. This was especially the case for the RCMP whose work was also organized through the Criminal Code that then mandated the criminalization of all homosexual sexual practices. But this also occurred through many other social practices and policies stigmatizing homosexuality and constructing heterosexual hegemony. The national security campaigns against queers were thereby tied into other regulatory strategies then being deployed against gay men and lesbians. In the 1950s and into the 1960s, homosexuality was being constructed as a social, sexual, national, and moral danger. The national security campaigns against queers were also organized in relation to the campaigns against the left and the various ways in which the national security campaigns impacted on race, gender, class, and other social relations. Lois, for instance, describes how she was caught up in the security campaigns in the 1950s because she had a sexual relationship with a left-wing woman who was married to a member of the Communist Party of the U.S. As a result, Lois' household in Ottawa was placed under surveillance and her husband was forced to resign from a position with the Department of National Defence. [...] Here national security surveillance against leftists and against lesbians was brought together. Queers and heterosexuals never simply live their lives as queers or "straights" but always in relation to race, gender, class, ability, age, and other social relations. The oppression of queers is also organized through class, gender, and racial relations.

The 1950s and into the 1960s was a period of the extension of the criminalization of male homosexual activities with the incorporation of consensual homosexual offences (such as "gross indecency" and "buggery") as triggering offences into Criminal Sexual Psychopath and later Dangerous Sexual Offender sentencing procedures, as mentioned earlier. This rested on the linking together of criminal and psychiatric regulation, since psychiatric testimony was required to inscribe these individuals into these legal classifications. Once convicted of a homosexual offence a sentencing hearing could be held. If the psychiatric testimony confirmed the individual to be a sexual psychopath or dangerous sexual offender (for instance that he was likely to engage in further homosexual activity) then he could be sentenced under these provisions to indefinite detention. As George Smith pointed out, the organization of the sexual policing of gay men's lives has been textually mediated through the classifications of the Criminal Code, which mobilize the police to criminalize sexual activities between men (Smith, 1988).

There was also a prohibition on membership of lesbians and gay men in the military and the RCMP. In the military there had been prohibitions against those classified as having "psychopathic personalities with abnormal sexuality" during the years of World War II. There were military directives mandating the disposal of "sex deviates" (Kinsman, 1996). In part, this was organized through the mobilization within military and paramilitary state institutions of the organizing ideology of the heterosexual masculinity, of "fighting men" and its integral relation to nation-state building and national security. Gay men were not seen as the disciplined fighting men who should be in these institutions and sex between men was seen as disruptive of military discipline and hierarchy. Lesbians were also seen as a particular threat to the "proper femininity" of women within the military (Berube & D'Emilio, 1984; Meyer, 1992, 1996). These strategies, along with the hegemony of psychological and psychiatric theories of homosexual causation, sociological theories of "deviance," and the unfounded association of gay men with "child molestation" were part of a broader construction of the normalization of heterosexuality during these years, which was constructed relationally in response to various queer "threats."

By the 1960s in Canada, there was an uneven shift in official regulatory strategy towards a liberal public/private strategy of sexual regulation. The 1957 British Wolfenden Report on homosexuality and prostitution articulated a new strategy of sexual and moral regulation oriented around public/private and adult/youth distinctions. This conceptual framework was developed at a level of abstraction that allowed it to be applied to a number of sexual and moral related terrains, especially female prostitution and male homosexuality. This established a limited realm of "private" morality (basically behind bedroom doors) which was not always to be directly regulated by the criminal law. In this narrow space, homosexual acts were to become a personal moral question and homosexual acts between two consenting adults were to be decriminalized. At the same time, a much more expansive terrain of "public" morality was to lead to a clamping down on

"public" expressions of homosexual eroticism and female prostitution. In relation to homosexual acts, those in "private" and those involving two individuals aged 21 and over ("adults") were to be decriminalized. Those in "public" or those involving anyone under 21 ("youth") were to continue to be highly policed. A very strong heterosexist "public" morality continued. This Wolfenden approach, which was enacted in Canada in 1969, led to only a partial decriminalization of homosexual acts. Heterosexual hegemony was held in place while it was at the same time modified and shifted. This liberal strategy gained cogency, establishing a certain resiliency in the face of the growing inability of moral conservative strategies of regulation to handle sexual and moral contradictions in the face of dramatic transformations in sex and gender and other social relations in the postwar years. Early gay activists in Canada in the 1960s like the Association for Social Knowledge tried to use the Wolfenden approach to open up a space for criminal law reform and popular education. This space was narrowed when the 1969 reform took place which reduced the popular education around homosexuality these groups were undertaking to questions of whether homosexual sex was in private or in public.

When implemented in Canada, the Wolfenden approach was linked to a sickness conceptualization of homosexuality. Supporters of this approach argued that homosexuals who engaged in acts with only one other consenting adult in "private" were no longer criminals but were sick. Rather than being locked away in jail they should be under a doctor's or a therapist's care (Kinsman, 1996). The passage of the 1969 reform did nothing in the short term to lessen the national security campaigns against gay men and lesbians. Even though the national security campaign was shaped by the total criminalization of homosexual activity it was not dependent on it. Even when some homosexual acts were decriminalized these homosexuals could still be considered to be suffering from a "character weakness," which meant they had something to hide and therefore they were still vulnerable to compromise and were "risks" to national security.

Resistance and Ethics

The security campaign encountered difficulties in the 1960s from the non-cooperation of the gay informants they relied on for information in identifying homosexuals. As we will see this resistance had a social and ethical basis to it. In 1962 to 1963 the RCMP reported that,

During the past fiscal year the homosexual screening program ... was hindered by the lack of cooperation on the part of homosexuals approached as sources. Persons of this type, who had hitherto been our most consistent and productive informers, have exhibited an increasing reluctance to identify their homosexual friends and associates ....(Directorate of Security and Intelligence Annual Report, 1962–1963, p. 19)

These people began to engage in practices similar to that reported by Harold earlier in this chapter. They began to place loyalty to their gay friends and lovers above those of Canadian "security" interests and the RCMP. In 1963–64 the *Annual Report of the Security Service* reported,

> During the year the investigation to identify homosexuals employed in or by the Federal Government resulted in initial interviews with twenty-one homosexuals, four of whom proved to be uncooperative, and re-interviews with twenty-two previously cooperative homosexuals, seven of whom declined to extend further cooperation. (p. 30)

They seem rather frustrated at encountering this growing opposition. They constructed a distinction between "cooperative" and "un-cooperative" homosexuals to try to deal with this situation of growing non-cooperation. This was related to the process of constructing the RCMP/informant relation and the rating of the usefulness of homosexual informants. Clearly with the growth of forms of resistance and non-cooperation, previously cooperative homosexuals were moving into the uncooperative classification. This was an important dividing line for RCMP work and only those homosexuals designated to be "cooperative" would be helpful in producing the "confirmed" homosexuals the RCMP was after.

The other side of this "lack of cooperation" is in part described by David [May 12, 1994]. David was not a civil servant but was involved in gay networks in Ottawa in the 1960s. David's involvement in the security investigations began when a friend gave the RCMP his name during a park sweep. David was interrogated by the RCMP, he was followed, and his place was searched.

A gay RCMP officer who was later cashiered had earlier given David some advice on what to do if he was interrogated that he found quite useful. His account gives us a clear sense of awareness of the security campaign in the networks he participated in from about 1964 on. David describes two situations that I report here. The first regards men with cameras taking pictures of gay men in the Lord Elgin Hotel, and the second the response of a group of young gays to being pulled in by the RCMP.

David reported that gay men who hung out in the tavern in the basement of the Lord Elgin, which had become a gay meeting spot before the early 1960s, encountered police-organized surveillance. As David described this situation,

> we even knew occasionally that there was somebody in some police force or some investigator who would be sitting in a bar .... As a matter of fact, when my RCMP friend was about to be cashiered from the RCMP he was shown pictures that had been taken in the bar—that is the tavern downstairs in the Lord Elgin Hotel—of everybody and you could see the vantage point at which the person had been sitting behind a newspaper and taking pictures. He said there were pictures of everybody includ-

ing myself sitting there having a drink ... The thing is you could even tell where the person had been sitting from the views of the walls and the people who were there and he was asked to name all the people at the various tables.

This is one way the RCMP collected information on homosexuals and part of the relations of surveillance it organized. What is most remarkable, however, is how David then described the response of the men in the bar to this surveillance.

> We always said that when you saw someone with a newspaper held up in front of their face ... that somebody would take out something like a wallet and do this sort of thing [like snapping a photo] and then of course everyone would then point over to the person you see and of course I'm sure that the person hiding behind the newspaper knew that he had been found out ....

David's account gives us a glimpse of non-cooperation and resistance to the security investigations as well as a resistance strategy of exposing and mocking the security campaign. During our discussion David also described a group of young gay men who were detained by the RCMP.

> One group of about seven friends all got pulled in .... All were asked to give names. They all said "I know the following people" and gave the names of the other six. And the next person would give the names of the other six. All they [the RCMP] did was get that one circle of names.

David described how these young men thought they had outwitted the RCMP since they had only given information to them that they already had and had not revealed the names of any other gays. By giving them some names this also meant they would be released. We also get a clear sense from this story of how the "cooperation" that the RCMP did manage to get was sometimes produced.

Michael, a civilian employee of the military and then a non-civil servant who was interrogated by the RCMP in the 1960s, stated that the advice in the gay networks he was familiar with was to say nothing to the RCMP about people's names or identities and "if anybody did give anything they were ostracized." There was a clear ethical position of not giving names in the gay networks of which he was part. If this position was violated, a response was organized against the person who had violated the ethical code within the gay networks of the day. Michael also reported that when he was left alone in the interrogation room with one RCMP officer that officer said,

> "Is it true that you are a homosexual?" and I said "yes!" And he looked at me and I said, "Is it true that you ride side saddle?" and he laughed and that almost ended the

interview. I mean, my intent was there, don't bother me any more, because I began to get the impression that it was a witch hunt. It was a real witch hunt. [July 15, 1994]

These stories of elementary resistance are very informative in beginning to flesh out the social organization of the "non-cooperation" mentioned in the RCMP texts. The response in the Lord Elgin suggested that people went beyond exposing the officer; they were able to turn the tables on him so to speak. It also was a way of making fun of him and the security and police campaigns, using humour and camp as a way to survive. Camp sensibility and humour, which plays with elements of incongruity and theatricality and at times the glorification of female stars, is a cultural form produced by gay men to manage and negotiate the contradictions between our particular experiences of the world as gays and the institutionalized heterosexuality that hegemonizes social relations. It can provide a creative way of dealing with social stigma—a way of fully embracing it, thereby neutralizing it and making it laughable. A crucial part of this cultural formation is to denaturalize normality and heterosexuality by making fun of it. As David says "I think that the way people coped with the whole situation of surveillance and harassment and so on was basically to make the best of it. And turn it as much as possible into a humorous situation ..." [May 12, 1994]. People had enough of a sense of themselves and the expanding queer networks and community formation they participated in to engage in these collective and individual acts of defiance. The social basis for this non-cooperation and resistance was the expanding social spaces queers came to occupy in the 1960s and the expansion of queer networks, community formation, solidarity, and queer talk, within and around these spaces.

In contrast to the attempt within ruling moral regulation to portray homosexuality as a moral problem and a national security risk, what we see here is that moral regulation becomes a contested terrain with some gay men and lesbians challenging the basis of this campaign by refusing to give the names of other homosexuals. In developing an ethics of resistance they placed their erotic, emotional, and social ties to their friends and other homosexuals, and their loyalty to other queers, above the interests of "national security." The ethics developed within these gay networks had a very different character to it than the moral regulation driving the national security campaigns. I choose the expression ethics of resistance deliberately here since ethics has a rather different connotation than morals and morality.

Ruling forms of moral regulation—or "morality from above"—tends to rely on moral rules that are portrayed ideologically as being absolute, law-like, and ahistorical. The conceptualization of "character weakness" for instance views unreliability and subversion as inherent in the homosexual character. The ethics of resistance developed "from below" by Harold, David, and others

in contrast has much more of an affective, erotic, contextual, social, and historical character, as well as being more clearly self-made by the oppressed themselves in resistance to ruling forms of regulation. [...]

*   *   *   *   *

What we need is not a new morality or moral code but an ethics of resistance and social transformation that provides us with a basis for discussion and guidelines for practice that allows us to resist ruling forms of moral and social regulation and can clarify how we as individuals and as communities can make decisions that lead us towards more democratic control over our own lives, and which undermine oppression and inequality. In the early resistance to the national security campaigns by gay men and lesbians in Canada we see the generation of an ethics of resistance that allowed some gay men and lesbians to place their ties to other queers above the needs of "national security." This provided a basis for them to refuse to cooperate with the security police.

Summary: National Security as Moral Regulation and Normalization and Its Current Relevance

In summing up this investigation, I draw some conclusions about the relation between national security and strategies of moral regulation and normalization. First of all from this investigation we can clearly see the "moral" character of the construction of the "nation" and state formation—of Canada and Canadianness. The conceptualizations of "national security," "security risk," and "character weakness" rely on notions of moral character that participate in constantly constructing the moral and the immoral and the normal/deviant. In this sense national security is moral regulation and national security is an important strategy of normalization. Second, the national security campaigns played an important part in constructing homosexuality as against the nation—as "immoral," "risky," and "abnormal" while at the very same time constructing heterosexuality as moral, safe and normal—as the national sexuality. This was a central aspect of the Canadian Cold war and the national security campaigns in Canadian state and social formation. National security was therefore an important part of sexual regulation more generally during these years and was also closely related to the management of gender relations.

These anti-queer national security practices have also shaped our historical present. They have had a lasting and active impact in constructing lesbians and gays as immoral, as deviant, as risks, as a danger, as being unreliable workers, and in the organization of employment discrimination and the construction of the social relations of the closet which still shape and constrain many of our lives in the present. The national security campaigns against queers are not yet over and other targets have also been selected for national security surveillance.

The moral regulation and normalization of the national security campaigns also became a contested terrain, with some gay men and lesbians able to engage in acts of non-cooperation and resistance. Even within major social constraints and prior to the development of gay and lesbian movements, some gay men and lesbians were able to engage in limited acts of resistance and were able to generate an ethics of resistance that disputed the logic of the national security campaigns. Viewing moral regulation as a contested terrain and seeing how resistance takes on ethical forms give us insights and resources for our continuing struggles against oppression in the present.

Most recently Canadian state agencies have produced the anti-capitalist globalization or global justice movement (Cockburn, St. Clair, & Seluka, 2000; Klein, 2000; McNally, 2002) from the protests against the Asia Pacific Economic Cooperation (APEC) meetings in Vancouver in 1997 to the protests against the Free Trade Area of the Americas (FTAA) in Quebec City in April 2001, to the protests against the meetings of the G8 countries in 2002, as threats to "national security." This has mandated forms of police repression and violence against protestors from pepper spray, tear gas, and plastic and rubber bullets. Here "national security" gets defined by the international trade and investment agreements into which the Canadian state enters. In relation to the protests against the FTAA, the focus has been especially against "anarchists" by the Canadian Security and Intelligence Service (CSIS—which took over security work from the discredited RCMP in the 1980s), state officials, and much of the mainstream media. In part this is done by associating the global justice movement with "violence" even though it is state agencies directing police repression against demonstrators and inflicting institutional and social violence against poor people around the world. In response, a new ethics of resistance based in civil disobedience and direct action that places responsibility to oppressed and poor people, people in "third world" countries, to the environment, and to more direct forms of democracy above those of loyalty to the Canadian state, has emerged. We have a lot to learn from the struggles of the past in dislodging these contemporary forms of national security and in challenging the moral regulation and normalization strategies that would read global justice protestors out of the national social fabric as "deviant" and "immoral."

Notes

1 This term is used by Jeffrey Weeks in *Sexuality and Its Discontents*, London: Routledge and Kegan Paul, pp. 5–10.

2 The label "fruit machine" came from RCMP officers who were to be members of the "normal" (read heterosexual) control group for this study. Such was the concern that psychology had the ability to reveal what one did not know about oneself, or that the investigative process was itself defective, these officers feared that even though they were recruited into the research as "normals" they would be found out to be "fruits." [...]

3 A Canadian Security and Intelligence (CSIS) spokesperson reiterated this position in 1998. See Brian K. Smith, CBC Radio, 1998. Also see Jeff Sallot, "The Spy Masters' Talent Hunt Goes Public" (1999, June 22). *The Globe and Mail*, pp. A1, A14.

This moral order therefore depends on the marginalization of anomalies and firm social boundaries demarcated by "natural" markers that are rigorously policed

4 "Ideology refers to all forms of knowledge that are divorced from their conditions of production (their grounds)." Roslyn Wallach Bologh (1979). *Dialectical Phenomenology: Marx's Method* (p. 19). Boston: Northeastern University Press. On ideology also see the work of Dorothy E. Smith and Himani Bannerji.

5 Throughout this chapter I use pseudonyms for the people I have interviewed to protect their anonymity. Square brackets at the end of interview extracts are the date the interview took place.

6 At the same time this does not entail that lesbians were less oppressed than gay men. Lesbians were less visible than gay men and had less social space because of the general denial of the social and economic autonomy of women from men and the specific social denial of lesbianism in the construction of heterosexual hegemony.

7 This account comes from the preliminary research interviews conducted for the film *Forbidden Love* (NFB, 1993). I thank Lynne Fernie and Aerlyn Weissman for their permission to use this account for this research.

References

Bannerji, H. (2000). *The dark side of the nation: Essays on multiculturalism, nationalism and gender.* Toronto: Canadian Scholars' Press.

Berube, A., & D'Emilio, J. (1984). The military and lesbians during the McCarthy years. *Signs 9, 4.*

Bologh, Roslyn Wallach. (1979). *Dialectical phenomenology: Marx's method.* Boston: Northeastern University Press.

Cockburn, Alexander, St. Clair, Jeffrey, & Seluka, Alan. (2000). *5 days that shook the world, Seattle and beyond.* London: Verso.

Directorate of Security and Intelligence Annual Report. (1962–1963). Ottawa: RCMP.

Directorate of Security and Intelligence Annual Report. (1963–1964). Ottawa: RCMP.

Directorate of Security and Intelligence Annual Report. (1967–1968). Ottawa: RCMP.

Douglas, Mary. (1973). *Natural Symbols*. New York: Penguin.

Foucault, M. (1979). *Discipline and punish: The birth of the prison*. New York: Pantheon.

Foucault, M. (1980). *Power/Knowledge*. In C. Gordon (Ed.). New York: Pantheon.

Foucault, M. (2000). *Power: Essential works of Foucault, Volume Three*. Faubion, New York: The New Press.

Kinsman, G. (1996). *The regulation of desire: Homo and hetero sexualities* (2nd ed.). Montreal: Black Rose Books.

Kinsman, G. (1996, August). "Responsibility" as a strategy of governance: Regulating people living with AIDS and lesbians and gay men in Ontario. *Economy and Society 25*, 3, 393–409.

Kinsman, G. (2000). Constructing gay men and lesbians as national security risks, 1950–1970. In G. Kinsman, D. Buse, & M. Stedman (Eds.), *Whose national security? Canadian state surveillance and the creation of enemies* (pp. 143–153). Toronto: Between the Lines.

Klein, Naomi. (2000). *No logo: Taking aim at the brand name bullies*. Toronto: Alfred A. Knopf.

McNally, D. (2002). *Another world is possible: Globalization and anti-capitalism*. Winnipeg: Arbeiter Ring Publishing.

McNally, D. (2001, Summer). Mass protests in Quebec City: From anti-globalization to anti-capitalism. *New Politics*, pp. 21–25.

McNally, D. (2002). *Another world is possible: Globalization and anti-capitalism*. Winnipeg: Arbeiter Ring Publishing.

Meyer, Lisa. (1992). Creating G.I. Jane: The regulation of sexuality and sexual behaviour in the Women's Army Corps during World War II. *Feminist Studies* 18, No. 3, pp. 581–661.

Meyer, Lisa. (1996). *Creating GI Jane: Sexuality and power in the Women's Army Corps during World War II*. New York: Columbia University Press.

Smith, D.E. (1987). *The everyday world as problematic: Toward a feminist sociology*. Toronto: University of Toronto Press.

Smith, D.E. (1990). K is mentally ill. In D.E. Smith (Ed.), *Texts, facts, and femininity: Exploring the relations of ruling*. London and New York: Routledge Press.

Smith, G. (1988). Policing the gay community: An inquiry into textually mediated social relations. *International Journal of the Sociology of Law 16*, 163–183.

Waldeck, R.C. (1960, September 29). The international homosexual conspiracy. Human Events, reprinted in *New York Native* (1981, September 21/October 4), 13.

Wall, D.F. (1959, May 12). Security cases involving character weakness, with special reference to the problem of homosexuality. Memorandum to the security panel, p. 12.

CHAPTER 38

Legal Responses to Violence against Women in Canada

ELIZABETH A. SHEEHY

Any history of the development and changes in the law as it relates to women and male violence is also a chronicle of the history of the women's movement and its relationship to law [....] All of the legislation and policy that recognizes women's rights to be free of male violence has been put in place because of the political strength and persistence of the women's movement in our country. While this movement has always articulated women's issues and rights in the context of equality, the repatriation of Canada's constitution in 1982 from Great Britain (*Constitution Act*), and specifically, the enshrinement of women's equality rights in ss.15 and 28 of the *Canadian Charter of Rights and Freedoms*, for the first time created a specific legal tool by which to advance these claims.

In spite of our many legal advances, violence against women has not subsided in Canada because women's vulnerability to male violence and our ability to harness law are inextricably linked to women's social, economic, and political position in Canada, in relation to those who hold power. Thus, while law is an important tool in advancing women's equality rights, law alone cannot end this violence until all women's equality is fully realized.

Before I commence, I would like to define my terms. First, when I speak of feminists or the women's movement in Canada, I am speaking of women who accept and recognize the existence of women's subordination economically, socially, and politically, and who have a commitment to engage in struggle of one sort or another, to change women's inequality. This movement is aimed at achieving equality for all women, and recognizes that women do not experience uniformly the benefits or disadvantages of sex, but rather are differentially affected by white supremacy, class privilege, the heterosexual presumption, and the "norms" of ability.

Second, when I speak of women's equality, I am referring to the idea of substantive equality. This difference between formal and substantive equality is that while formal equality merely insists on equality of treatment (and only to the extent that the decision-maker agrees that the two groups are similarly situated), substantive equality looks to the end result [....] Are women and men in a given society equal recipients of the benefits and burdens of that society? Among women, are we equally credible when we speak in the justice system? Are we equally free of violent assault? Sometimes, the most productive route to substantive equality will be to use formal equality or equal treatment as a tool; at other times, the specific conditions of women's lives, including, for example, the threat and impact of male violence, or the racialized abuse experienced by African Canadian women, will require very particular rules or practices to move us toward equality.

Third, when I speak of law, I am using the term broadly, to refer to the law as drafted by legislators, as interpreted by judges in the common law or by jurors as finders of fact in trials, and as implemented by those who enforce the law and wield a great deal of discretion, such as police and prosecutors. Thus the women's movement has recognized that the achievement of reforms in statutes or even in constitution does not guarantee that those laws will become a lived reality, for police can refuse to take reports or can discredit women's accounts of violence; prosecutors can decide which cases to pursue, based on their perhaps discriminatory beliefs or on their prediction that the case will fail in court due to the discriminatory beliefs of others; judges can effectively nullify a law through narrow interpretations, through the creation of common law defences that uphold male supremacy, [...] through the use of constitutional doctrines, through rulings on the evidence, and through instructions to the jury; and even if a conviction is imposed, a judge can undermine its symbolism by imposing a sentence that makes a mockery of the conviction [....] Because of all of these ways that law works, women's advocates must be prepared for a long-term process of both political struggle and legal engagement.

Women's Legal History

In the nineteenth century, as part of the ongoing process of colonization, England imposed British common law, including criminal law, on the inhabitants of what is now called Canada. Criminal law, in this context, must be linked to other forms of law that confer legal status, rights, and obligations, given that criminal law acts as an enforcement mechanism for many legal relations and values.

From the Middle Ages through to the mid-nineteenth century, women in England experienced a massive curtailment of their role in public life, through the exclusion of women from the church, the destruction of hereditary offices for government and their replacement by appointed office, and the growth of the universities and professions, through which women's occupations in the public sphere were superseded by male control (Atkins and Hoggett; Sachs and Wilson). Judges played a major part in this process, by creating the common law doctrine of women's "legal disabilities": women and children were declared to be the legal property of their fathers, and girls, once married, became the legal property of their husbands. Women did not have separate legal identity from their fathers or husbands, such that they were severely restricted in their ability to accumulate property and wealth, to assert control over their children and their own destiny, and to protect or claim their own physical integrity. Women's lack of legal status had public law implications as well: women could not vote in elections, participate in government or make policy, enter the professions, including law, or generally participate in public life (Sachs and Wilson).

These limits on women's legal status were reflected in the criminal law's stance on violence against women such as British law did not prohibit violence against women, but rather, at best, regulated its "excesses." Thus, the British law as stated by Bacon in the mid-eighteenth century was that "The husband hath, by law, power and dominion over his wife, and may keep her by force within the bounds of duty, and may beat her, but not in a violent manner" (qtd. in Strange 295). As a member of our Supreme Court, Justice Wilson stated:

[T]he law historically sanctioned the abuse of women within marriage as an aspect of the husband's ownership of his wife and his "right" to chastise her. One need only recall the centuries-old law that a man is entitled to beat his wife with a stick "no thicker than his thumb." (R. v. Lavallee, 872)

Similarly, rape was criminal only to the extent that either a father or a husband held a proprietary interest in the woman's sexuality: it was a crime against the father if the girl was chaste and unmarried; it was a crime against the husband if she was monogamous and married (Clark and Lewis).

Thus, in 1892 Canada's first Criminal Code only punished rape if it was committed by a man other than the woman's husband; penetration had to prove non-consent, usually by proving violent resistance by the girl or woman. Rape was also adjudicated according to three common law rules that were unique to this offence: a rule permitting the evidence that a woman had reported the offence "at the earliest reasonable opportunity" to rebut a presumption that the complaint was false; the

use of women's past sexual history evidence to demonstrate their lack of credibility; and the requirement that the jury be warned that it is dangerous to convict based solely upon the uncorroborated testimony of a woman or child [....]

Assault upon a woman could be prosecuted in the 1892 Code as any other assault. An offence of indecent assault against a wife occasioning actual bodily harm was enacted in 1909 (Boyle) and remained in the Criminal Code until 1960 (McLeod, 1989). It was punishable by two years imprisonment, which was then extremely low in comparison to punishments of execution and life imprisonment for many other offences.

Wife murder could be punished by the law prohibiting murder, but it was in no way parallel to husband murder, which was in law a form of "petit treason" (Gavigan). Additionally, numerous practices and doctrines made it difficult to say that wife murder was outright prohibited. The defence of provocation, for example, reduced murder to manslaughter on the basis that someone engorged by "passion" has lost self-control, and should thereby be treated more leniently by the criminal law. Of course women's behaviour, whether it be by infidelity, insubordination, or by desertion, was (and arguably still is) more easily characterized as provocative from the standpoint of the male legislators who enacted, the male police who enforced, and the male judges and jurors who interpreted the law [....]

Some women would have had access to remedies in civil law for rape, seduction, or breach of promise to marry, although these remedies depended on access to money to pursue them, were interpreted as essentially aimed at compensating fathers and husbands for lost value in the sexual property of women, and were given generous interpretations for only chaste and "deserving" women (Backhouse, 1986).

First-Wave Feminism

At the same time that this Criminal Code was adopted in Canada marking women's social subordination by its narrow prohibitions, the first wave of the feminist movement was already well underway, as women in the United Kingdom, Europe, the United States, and Canada fought for the extension of the promise of liberal democratic rights to them (Mossman). Women variously made important gains in the political and legislative arenas, after long and arduous campaigns, for example, reversing women's common law disabilities with respect to holding and dispensing of property and concluding valid contracts by legislation as early as 1872 in Ontario and achieving the right to vote in federal elections, for non-Aboriginal women, in 1918 (see Altschul and Carron; Abell).

In spite of these and many other gains, including the admission, by special legislation in 1892, to the bar of Canada's first woman lawyer in 1897 (Backhouse, 1985), the judges of the common law countries for 60 years resisted and denied women's claims to be recognized as "persons" entitled to participate fully in public life, including the practice of law. So it was that rather than lead the way in advancing women's equality, and rather than even reflecting women's changing social position, the judges, almost to a man, in countless cases, acted as "dogged defenders of male supremacy" (Sachs and Wilson, 48).

At long last, in 1929, the Privy Council decided the famous "Persons" (*Edwards v. A.G. Canada*) case in women's favour, ruling that in the absence of evidence of parliamentary intent to the contrary, women should be presumed included within the legal understanding of "persons." This case constituted a sudden and dramatic reversal of six decades of legal precedent. It cannot be explained internally, but only by reference to the context of the changes that had already been wrought in the legal landscape, by legislation, through the women's movement (see Mossman; Sachs and Wilson).

Second-Wave Feminism

Although once the public sphere was opened to women and the theoretical possibility was created of women as lawyers, legislators, and judges exerting a more direct influence on the law regulating male violence against women, the formal equality of opportunity models did not yield immediate results in terms of women's access to law. While our first women magistrate was appointed as early as 1916 (Harvey), it was not until 1926 that most provinces admitted women to the practice of law, and Quebec did not do so until 1941. Women were not permitted to sit as jurors in Manitoba until 1952, and until 1971 in Quebec (Harvey). By the 1950s, only four per cent of Ontario law students were women (Hagan and Kay, 11) and by 1971, women were still greatly underrepresented in the profession at a rate of 38:1 (Hagan and Kay).

In 1970, when the Royal Commission on the Status of Women was appointed to inquire into the steps that should be taken by the federal government to ensure equal opportunities for women, violence against women was conceptualized as a formal equality issue. The Commission focused on the unfairness in the *Criminal Code* of limiting criminal responsibility for sexual offences to men as perpetrators, of not protecting boys and men from sexual offences, and of the different rules for rape depending on the female's age, marital status, and moral character (Royal Commission on the Status of Women).

Although these criticisms were rendered deeper and more complicated by the work of the women's movement in providing services for women who had been raped (crisis centers) and for women who were fleeing violent men (women's shelters), the law reforms subsequently passed in 1982 [...] essentially used the model of formal equality employed by the Royal Commission. The new offences were gender neutral such that assaults on boys and men are punishable, as are assaults commit-

ted by women upon males. Sexual assault became a three-tiered offence, with higher sentence ceilings as the offence involves more violence and/or injury. The structure parallels that used for non-sexual assault, implying the only difference is the sexual nature of the attack. The offence can be committed by a husband against a wife; it need not include penetration; and many of the evidentiary rules unique to rape were abolished in the *Criminal Code*. Finally, a number of specific reforms have been legislated that create new evidentiary rules for the testimony of children and abolish some of the common law rules for dealing with their evidence (Boyle).

In the area of wife assault, while one of its earliest forms had been sex-specific, a similar pattern of second-wave feminism to law reform can be discerned. An undifferentiated offence of a common assault was in the *Code* from 1960 on, but it was usually dealt with in the family rather than criminal law courts (Bonnycastle and Rigakos) and was often treated as a private matter, requiring the woman to initiate and carry the prosecution, rather than the public prosecutor. The women's movement attempted to introduce formal equality by forcing police, prosecutors, and judges to deal with wife assault as they would any other life-threatening harm. However, the demands made by the women's movement have tended to be translated by the state in punitive terms rather than as a way to protect women's lives and safety (Currie).

For example, in 1982, the Attorney General for Ontario wrote to prosecutors urging them to encourage police to lay charges of assault rather than leaving the burden of prosecution to individual women. He also suggested to prosecutors that such assaults be considered more serious than stranger assaults because "the victims are in a captive position socially or economically and accordingly the likelihood of a recurrence is far more substantial." In 1984 the same office designated resources to appoint 50 Crowns to deal with domestic assault matters. In 1982, the federal Solicitor General wrote to police chiefs across the country, urging them to aggressively charge in cases of spouse assault, and in 1983 guidelines were created for the RCMP and police and prosecutors in the Yukon and N.W.T. (McLeod, 1989).

Some jurisdictions drafted guidelines requiring that charges be laid by police as a matter of course, to avoid discriminatory exercise of discretion (Ontario Provincial Police). Other jurisdictions adopted "no drop" guidelines for prosecutors, to curb their discretion such that they must continue with a prosecution and do not have the discretion to desist, even when the woman expresses a desire to withdraw the charges (Manitoba Department of Justice) [....]

At the same time, women in Canada became engaged in another political and legal struggle with respect to women's equality. When the government proposed to repatriate (or bring home) Canada's constitution and to attach a new bill of rights that would constitute the supreme law of the country permitting the courts to declare contrary legislation inoperative, women were not included in the negotiations over the terms of the new constitution, nor were their interests or analyses represented in the specific proposals. Women's groups across the country fought successfully for a voice in the drafting process (Hosek), and worked hard to give as full a scope as was possible to a concept of substantive, not mere formal, equality in the language of the new *Charter*, now sections 15 and 28.

With the passage of the equality guarantees in the *Charter*, feminists inside and outside of law began to reconfigure their ideas about equality and to conceptualize violence as both an expression of women's inequality and a barrier to substantive equality. That women's struggle for equality and freedom from violence was a long-term one was painfully illustrated by a notorious exchange in the House of Commons in 1982 when women Parliamentarians attempted to put the issue and statistics of wife battering on the legislative agenda and the House erupted in prolonged laughter and general derision (Bonnycastle and Rigakos). Although the next two days in the House saw resolutions and apologies by the male members, the obstacles to simple law reform as a strategy to end violence against women were illuminated rather clearly.

Third-Wave Feminism

The achievements of the second wave of feminists and the guarantee of at least formal equality under the *Charter* have permitted the third wave of feminists to bring critical analysis and new understandings of equality to the issue of the legal treatment of violence against women.

As of the 1980s, women constituted 50 per cent of students in Ontario law schools; as of 1991, the ratio of men to women in the profession in Ontario was 2.63:1 (Hagan and Kay). Women have marked achievements in law, including three women jurists who have sat or sit at the highest level of court in Canada, [...] two of whom have explicitly articulated feminist visions of law. At the level of government, in 1992 the Federal/Provincial/Territorial Attorney Generals made a public commitment to promoting gender equality within the criminal law, and stated that "legal theory, common law and statute law must be developed equally from both male and female perspectives." Three prominent women judges have been appointed to head very important public inquiries into the treatment of women in the legal profession, federally sentenced women offenders, and women convicted of killing alleged violent mates (see Wilson; Arbour; Ratushny). In 1995, Status of Women Canada released its "Gender Plan" outlining the commitment of the federal government to adopting policy that advances women's equality (Status of Women Canada); in 1996, the Department of Justice appointed a Senior Advisor on Gender Equality who is to ensure that women's equality issues are integrated into all of the work, policy, litigation, and legislation of the department (Bernier). As well, between 1993 and 1997, the Department of Justice invested in ongoing consultations with the women's movement on violence against women.

What kinds of new insights and legal strategies around violence against women has the third wave brought us in Canada? Again I will deal with sexual assault and wife assault in turn. Both areas of law reform have revealed to us the serious limitations of a formal equality model.

First, our experience with sexual assault indicates that the mere change in language has not shifted the underlying operative understandings of "rape." For example, although the new laws are broader in terms of definitions of prohibited conduct and protected groups of women, those who enforce and interpret these laws may still hold and wield the same beliefs and values that more explicitly underpinned the old laws. Feminist researchers such as Lorenne Clark and Debra Lewis had previously demonstrated that although the former legislation did not explicitly endorse the notion that women should be protected under the law against rape only to the extent that they constituted the sexual property of individual fathers or husbands, this was in fact the way that the law was interpreted by police, by Crown attorneys, and by judges. Many feminists assert that the new reforms have not disrupted these beliefs or the practices in which they manifested. For example, even ten years after the reforms, crisis centre workers reported that the legislative restrictions on women's sexual history were simply ignored by defence, Crown attorneys, and judges in sexual assault trials (Sheehy, 1991). Feminist researchers found that the former understandings of "real rape" still underlay investigative and prosecutorial decisions, such that stereotypes continued to play a significant role (Muzychka) and the "unfounding" rate for sexual assault remains incongruously high (Roberts).

Second, the neutrality in the language describing the offence has been criticized, as it tends to hide the gendered nature of sexual assault, erroneously conveying the notion that "equality" has been achieved by suggesting that the law now recognizes that men can be raped too, and women can be sexually violent. Of course the gendered statistics have not changed in this regard, [...] but we may have lost a critical and shared social understanding of the meaning of rape for women (Cohen and Backhouse). For example, in one case, the issue of whether touching a woman's breast amounted to a sexual assault had to be litigated all the way to the highest court in the country, because lower court judges took the gender neutral approach literally, reasoning that breasts were secondary sex characteristics, like men's beards, and that since touching a man's beard was not a sexual assault, touching a woman's breast was likewise not a sexual assault [....]

Finally, women have discovered that the *Charter*, in the hands of the same judiciary, can be used once again to doggedly defend men's rights at the expense of women's security. Thus, using the *Charter* as a weapon, a significant feature of the law, a non-discretionary ban on women's sexual history evidence in all but four fairly narrow situations, was declared unconstitutional by the Supreme Court because it allegedly violated men's rights to fair trials (*R. v. Seaboyer; R. v. Gayme*). Women's equality rights were barely mentioned by the judges, so irrelevant were they seen to be by the Supreme Court of Canada. This put women in Canada back by almost two decades, and raised serious questions about whether the *Charter* would be used to roll back women's democratic gains (see Sheehy, 1991).

The response of the Canadian public, and of course the women's movement, was one of disbelief and outrage with the decision of the Supreme Court. Such an outcry was raised that the Minister of Justice initiated a law reform process that ultimately was led by the women's movement and its lawyers. Feminists determined that any new law needed to name women's equality and women's rights as the legal and constitutional basis for the reform; that women's interests and perspectives needed to be incorporated into the law; that women's experiences of racism, disabilityism, and lesbophobia needed to be recognized in crafting the law; that the law had to be drafted so to specifically challenge the underlying beliefs about women and rape; and that mechanisms to check discretion had to be built into the law [....]

The newest sexual assault law was passed in 1992 (*An Act to Amend the Criminal Code*, 1992). The preamble to the law sets out women's *Charter* rights as the impetus for the law, and specifies the particular problems that it is meant to solve as an interpretive aid for the judiciary. The law now defines consent as "voluntary agreement to engage in the activity," rather than leaving it to the judges, and specifies situations in which there can be no consent in law, such as where consent is expressed by a third party, where the woman was incapable of consenting, and where her agreement was achieved through reliance upon a position of trust or authority over the woman. It creates a new process and set of criteria by which to limit when sexual history evidence is admissible, and sets out certain prohibited uses of this evidence. Finally, it imposes a new and significant limit on men's defence of "mistaken belief" regarding consent, by requiring that men take "reasonable steps" to ascertain consent.

This law is only just beginning to receive judicial interpretations at the higher levels of court, so it is difficult to assess at this early point its impact (see Sheehy, 1996). It is also being challenged again under the *Charter* by men (*R. v. Darrach*); it remains to be seen whether the statements of legislative purpose will inspire the judges to pay deference to the democratic process and uphold the law.

In 1994, the justices of the Supreme Court again used the *Charter* to widen men's immunity from criminal liability for sexual and other violence against women by recognizing a new defence of "extreme intoxication" (*R. v. Daviault*). Again, feminist criticism and the women's movement's outrage reached the public demand (Sheehy,

1995a), and the Department of Justice, in consultation with women's groups, amended the *Criminal Code* in response (*An Act to amend the Criminal Code*, 1995; Sheehy, 1995b).

In the meantime, another defence strategy has flourished, that of demanding access to women's personal records so as to dig for information that can be used to contradict her statements or to undermine her credibility (see MacCrimmon). Unfortunately, our Supreme Court has once more upheld men's rights at the expense of women's, based on the *Charter* (*R. v. O'Connor; R. v. Carosella*). Once more, a hue and cry has been raised, and broadly-based consultation within the women's movement and with the Department of Justice ensued. The result is another new law, Bill C-46 (*An Act to Amend the Criminal Code*, 1997), which puts limits on disclosure of women's records, creates the legal possibility of women having standing in court to defend their interests in the criminal process, and again frames the law in legal and constitutional terms pursuant to women's equality rights. This law is also under attack using the *Charter*, and it remains to be seen whether this democratic gain by the women's movement will be obliterated by the Supreme Court (*R. v. Mills*).

The difficulties with the specific legal strategies around wife assault have been identified by both researchers and the women's movement. First, gender neutral offences and policies have furthered the criminalization of women. Thus we see new practices of counter-charging women such that women who resist the violence of their mates or who fight back can be charged as well [....] By way of further example, our *Criminal Code* s.753 creates a process by which a prosecutor can apply to have an offender convicted of a "serious personal injury offence" declared dangerous offender such that the sentence will be an indeterminate one. Although sex offenders have been incarcerated under this section, it had never, until 1996 (*R. v. Currie*), been used to deal with persistently violent men who threatened and terrorized their former mates. However, it had been used, on two notorious occasions to declare young women who primarily posed a danger to themselves as "dangerous offenders." [...]

Second, the resistance of police, prosecutors, and judges continues to shape women's responses to criminal law (see Rigakos), and police failure to implement in any consistent fashion the various "zero tolerance" policies remains problematic. Third, mediation and diversion have been used to take these cases out of the criminal law system; [...] while the women's movement has not insisted on increased punitive sentencing in response to wife battering, it has viewed the adjudication of criminal responsibility to be critical. Finally, as long as women's external realities of poverty and male violence persist, criminal law intervention may carry more risk than benefit for women. Thus, numbers of women have refused criminal justice intervention because the costs to women and sometimes to their mates and children, have been too high (Martin and Mosher). For example, some prosecutors and judges have proceeded with contempt charges against women who refuse to testify; some women have experienced retaliatory violence from their mates; and others have experienced abuse from the state (Snider, 1998). New sentencing laws such as Bill C-41 [...] that require judges to consider specific aggravating factors such as abuse of a position of trust and responsibility and the fact that the offence was committed against the offenders' spouse or child, may do little to address these structural issues because sentencing is inherently focused on the individual.

One of the more controversial responses to violence against women is a new substantive criminal offence, called criminal harassment "stalking." The impetus for this offence came not from the women's movement but from the federal government, following the lead of many states in the United States, and conceptualizing, drafting, and passing the new law in a record time of eight months (Cairns Way). Women's groups did not deny the significance and dangerousness of the behaviour of men, usually former partners, who terrorize women, but voiced many concerns: why create a new law when the old ones (assault, peace bonds) are not enforced? Women's groups participated reluctantly, tentatively, and ultimately unsuccessfully in the reform, attempting to shape a law that at least would not increase women's inequality. The problems with the law are many, including the imagery and examples that informed it, which were of the dangerous "stranger," not the angry ex-husband or former boyfriend; the use of gender neutrality in its drafting, such that women who are trying to collect child support from their mates have been charged with stalking; and the use of traditional understandings of legal culpability such that only a man who consciously intends to create fear in the mind of the woman can be found guilty (Cairns Way).

In contrast, a substantive equality model, which would take account of the inequalities in which women currently find themselves and would be directed at ending the violence rather than reinforcing it, excusing it, or further isolating the woman, has been sought by the women's movement. The succeeding interventions were more formal and directive. For example, some police departments created protocols for dealing with violence against women, to ensure professional, prompt, and safety-conscious responses by police to calls from women asking for emergency assistance (British Columbia Ministry of the Attorney General). In several provinces, new initiatives are underway that attempt to create altogether new ways of dealing with wife assault, de-emphasizing the criminal law approach and focusing on stopping male violence. In Manitoba a new family violence court has been created, which speeds the process of prosecuting these offences, but also has developed specialized sentencing practices that are arguably more attuned to ending violence (mandatory counseling for male batterers is a regular feature of over 50 per cent of the sentences) and to ensuring the safety of the women

(Ursel and Brickey). In Saskatchewan new legislation was proclaimed in 1995 that creates an interdisciplinary approach to wife assault (Turner): it provides for emergency intervention orders (EMOs), victim assistance orders (VAOs), and warrants of entry. EMOs can cover a range of actions including exclusive possession of the matrimonial home, removal of the offender by police, and restraining orders. VAOs can provide monetary aid, temporary possession of property, restraining orders, and their breach can result in a criminal conviction.

The notion of substantive equality has also brought with it the idea that women need access to the resources of the state if they are to challenge violence perpetrated against them and to defend their equality rights. Thus, two Ontario legal clinics have created policies whereby they provide legal services to women only, in the context of cases involving wife assault, as a way of meeting women's greatly undeserved legal needs and avoiding conflicts of interests (Carey). This practice has been challenged by defence lawyers, but ultimately was upheld by the body governing the practice of law in Ontario. In the context of legal aid, women have sometimes succeeded in seeking funding to hire their own lawyers in the criminal process, given that Crown attorneys cannot and do not always act as their advocates.

Finally, legal responses to violence against women have been created outside of criminal law as well. The women's movement has created and sustained a support system of crisis centers and shelters, feminist models of counseling and support, and public education campaigns around the issues of male violence of women. Numerous initiatives have been put in place across the country. The federal government and provinces have enacted human rights codes and tribunals to adjudicate wrongs including sex discrimination, which has been held to include sexual harassment against women (*Brooks v. Canada Safeway Ltd.*). This behaviour may be verbal, but some claims pursued are actually cases of sexual assault that have taken place in the workplace. The consequences of a human rights claim may be an order to apologize to and/or compensate a woman, or some other order aimed at rehabilitating the wrongdoer; if the claim is settled by the board without adjudication, however, any public educative value is lost as the terms are not disclosed publicly. The human rights models in place in Canada have proven to be profoundly inadequate (Faraday; Young); however, there is currently tremendous energy being invested in the revisioning of these schemes so as to capitalize on and deal with issues of group rights and wrongs and their potential to provide justice to persons who cannot, for many reasons, pursue litigation in the criminal or civil courts.

The provinces have also created criminal injuries compensation legislation and boards, to provide some monetary compensation for those injured by the criminal acts of others. These schemes do not do much to address violence against women in a direct way, since the proceedings are not public, the decisions are not published, and the offender is not punished (the money comes out of an allocated fund) (see Sheehy, 1994). However, since many women who do not pursue criminal prosecution may seek compensation, these claims can provide much more public information about the extent and consequences of male violence, for example, the sexual abuse of children. As many more women have sought compensation under these schemes, the response of the legal system has been to close this avenue down by: informing the alleged offender of his right to appear and contest the issue of whether a crime occurred; reducing compensation to the extent that the crime victim was at "fault" by invoking woman-blaming beliefs; [...] imposing stricter proof requirements upon the claimants; and limiting the kinds of financial losses for which such women can claim.

In all provinces and territories, women can also sue their assailants in civil law for assault and battery; they can sue police in negligence for failing to enforce the law in a sex discriminatory way, in violation of women's equality rights under the *Charter* (*Jane Doe v. Metropolitan Toronto Police*); and they can sue institutions that failed to protect them, such as Children's Aid Societies (Sheehy, 1994). In all of these cases, some benefits in combating violence against women are possible through public education and resultant changes to institutional practices of law enforcement. Certain other law reforms need to be put in place, however, including longer time limits within which women can decide whether to pursue a civil suit, especially when childhood sexual abuse is the wrong, access to legal aid to pursue these cases, and judicial education, among other reforms.

Many provinces also have disciplinary boards that hear complaints of sexual assault against professionals such as doctors (Rodgers). Some law societies have begun to define professional behaviour and misbehaviour by reference to sex discrimination and sexual harassment (Certosimo). A few judges have been held to account publicly for both their "private" behaviour (e.g. convictions for wife assault) ("Judge convicted of assaulting wife") and for their courtroom behaviour, including sexual harassment of women lawyers, inappropriate and biased statements about women, and voiced opinions on violence against women. Most have been reprimanded at best, many have been exonerated and their remarks "explained," but some have been disciplined more severely and have been removed from the bench. [...]

Conclusion

Violence against women must be conceptualized as an issue of substantive equality, and it will be crucially important to clarify and articulate that understanding as a long-term goal. Clarity about this goal should help steer away from legal responses that frame women as passive "victims," or that feed the "law and order" agenda. A women's movement that is vital and independent of government is critical to this task. Drawing upon the knowledge generated by the women's movement, we must draft legislation that presumes women's inequality, acknowledges context, and challenges power relations and beliefs, such that public debate and social change become possible.

A government committed to ending violence against women will take its leadership and advice from the women's movement since that is where it will find the expertise and the political commitment to women's equality. We must, simultaneously, de-emphasize law as the solution, and support the women's movement; which continues to put the pressure on the state and thereby creates the political conditions for further engagement with law.

We need new standards for judging our lawyers and judges as professionals, including questions of impartiality and bias, in light of their commitment to advancing equality rights and their behaviour in the prosecution and defence of male violence against women.

The placement of feminists in law as lawyers and policy makers is also crucial to provide inside expertise as well on legal strategies and responses, as is the inclusion of women within government itself. Such women must be present in such numbers as to permit the pooling of ideas and experience and to withstand the inevitable backlash.

Mechanisms of enforcement need to be considered, giving women access to power to insist that law be followed. Statutory reviews of the operation of new legislation should be enacted as part of the statute, so as to permit ongoing monitoring and to provide women's groups with the tools with which to pursue further reform. Our hopes for our future include publicly available and enforceable guidelines for police, Crowns, and judges; legal standing for women in criminal proceedings apart from the prosecutor; access to money to hire our own lawyers; and the power to choose to avoid law altogether.

References

Abell, J. *Bringing It All Back Home: Feminist Struggle, Feminist Theory and Feminist Engagement With Law. The Case of Wife Battering.* LL.M. Thesis. Osgoode Hall Law School, 1991.

An Act to Amend the Criminal Code (production of records in criminal proceedings), S.C. 1997, c. 30.

An Act to Amend the Criminal Code, S.C. 1995, c. 22.

An Act to Amend the Criminal Code (self-induced intoxication). S.C. 1995, c. 32.

An Act to Amend the Criminal Code, S.C. 1992, c. 38.

Altschul, S., and C. Carron. "Chronology of Some Legal Landmarks in the History of Canadian Women." *McGill Law Journal* 21 (1975): 476–494.

Arbour, The Honourable Louise, Commissioner. *Commission of Inquiry into Certain Events at the Prison fir Women in Kingston.* Ottawa: Public Works and Government Services, 1996.

Atkins, S., and B. Hoggett. *Women and the Law.* Oxford: Basil Blackwell, 1984.

Backhouse, C. "The Tort of Seduction: Fathers and Daughters in Nineteenth-Century Canada." *Dalhousie Law Journal* 10 (1986): 45–80.

Backhouse, C. "'To Open the Way for Others of My Sex': Clara Brett Martin's, Career as Canada's First Woman Lawyer." *Canadian Journal of Women and the Law* 1.1 (1985): 1–41.

Backhouse, C. "Nineteenth-Century Canadian Rape Law 1800–1892." *Essays in the History of Canadian Law, Vol. II.* Ed. D. Flaherty. Toronto: The Osgoode Society, 1983. 200–247.

Bernier, C. "Bringing a Feminist Analysis to the Department of Justice." On file at the University of Toronto Law Library, 1996.

Bonnycastle, K., and G. Rigakos. "The 'Truth' About Battered Women as Contested Terrain." *Unsettling Truths: Battered Women, Policy, Politics, and Contemporary Research in Canada.* Eds. K. Bonnycastle and G. Rigakos. Vancouver: Collective Press, 1998. 10–20.

Bourrie, M. "Disgraced Judge Resigns Before Impeachment." *Law Times* 30 September–6 October 1996: 1.

Boyd, S., and E. Sheehy, "Feminism and the Law in Canada: Overview." *Law and Society: A Critical Perspective.* Eds. T.C. Caputo, M. Kennedy, C.E. Reasons, and A. Brannigan. Toronto: Harcourt, Brace, Jovanovich, 1989. 255–270.

Boyle, C. *Sexual Assault.* Toronto: Carswells, 1984.

British Columbia Ministry of the Attorney General. *Policy on the Criminal Justice System Response to Violence against Women and Children. Violence against Women in Relationships Policy.* Victoria: British Columbia Ministry of the Attorney General, 1996.

Brooks v. *Canada Safeway Ltd.,* [1989] 1 S.C.R. 1219.

Busby, K. "Discriminatory Uses of Personal Records in Sexual Violence Cases." *Canadian Journal of Women and the Law* 9.1 (1997): 148–177.

Cairns Way, R. "The Criminalization of Stalking: An Exercise in Media Manipulation and Political Opportunism." *McGill Law Journal* 39 (1994): 379–400.

Canadian Charter of Rights and Freedoms, Part I of the *Constitution Act, 1982,* being Schedule B to the *Canada Act 1982* (U.K.), 1982, c. 11.

Carey, R. "Useless (UOSLAS) v. The Bar: The Struggle of the Ottawa Student Clinic to Represent Battered Women." *Journal of Law and Society* 8 (1992): 54–81.

Certosimo, M. "A Conflict Is a Conflict Is a Conflict: Fiduciary Duty and Lawyer-Client Sexual Relations" *Dalhouise Law Journal* 16 (1993): 448–470.

Clark, L., and D. Lewis. *Rape: The Price of Coercive Sexuality.* Toronto: Women's Press, 1977.

Cohen, L., and C. Backhouse. "De-sexualizing Rape: Dissenting View on the Proposed Rape Amendments." *Canadian Woman Studies/les cahiers de la femme* 2.4 (1980): 99–103.

Constitution Act, 1982, being Schedule B to the *Canada Act 1982* (U.K.), 1982, c. 11.

"Controversial Judge Resigns." *The [Toronto] Globe and Mail* 28 February 1998: A10.

Côté, Andree. *Violence against Women and Criminal Law Reform: Recommendations for an Egalitarian Reform of the Criminal Law.* Ottawa: Action Ontarienne contre la violence faite aux femmes, 1995.

Criminal Law Amendment Act, S.C. 1980-81-82, c. 125.

Currie, D. "The Criminalization of Violence against Women: Feminist Demands and Patriarchal Accommodation." *Unsettling Truths. Battered Women, Policy, Politics, and Contemporary Research in Canada.* Eds. K. Bonnycastle and G. Rigakos. Vancouver: Collective Press, 1998. 41–51.

Dawson Brettel, T. "Legal Structures: A Feminist Critique of Sexual Assault Law Reform." *Resources for Feminist Research* 14 (1985): 40–43.

Edwards, S. "Male Violence against Women: Excusatory and Explanatory Ideologies in Law and Society." *Gender, Sex and the Law.* Ed. S. Edwards. London: Croon Helm, 1985. 183–218.

Edwards v. *A. G. Canada,* [1930] A.C.124 (P.C.).

Faraday, F. "Dealing with Sexual Harassment in the Workplace: The Promise and Limitations of Human Rights Discourse." *Osgoode Hall Law Journal* 32 (1994): 33–63.

Federal/Provincial/Territorial Working Group of Attorney Generals. *Gender Equality in the Canadian Justice System.* Ottawa: Department of Justice, 1992.

Gavigan, S. "Petit Treason in Eighteenth-Century England: Women's Inequality Before the Law." *Canadian Journal of Women and the Law* 3.2 (1989–90): 335–374.

Hagan, J., and F. Kay. *Gender in Practice. A Study of Lawyers' Lives.* Oxford: Oxford University Press, 1995.

Harvey, C. "Women in Law in Canada." *Manitoba Law Journal* 4 (1970): 9–38.

Hosek, C. "Women and Constitutional Process." *And No One Cheered.* Eds. K. Banting and R. Simeon. Toronto: Agincourt, 1983. 280–300.

Jane Doe v. *Metropolitan Toronto Police* (1998), 39 O.R. (3d) 487 (C.A.).

"Judge Convicted of Assaulting Wife." *Ottawa Citizen* (31 May 1989) A5.

Kershaw, A., and M. Lasovich. *Rock-a-Bye Baby. A Death Behind Bars.* Toronto: McClelland & Stewart, 1991.

MacCrimmon, M. "Trial by Ordeal." *Canadian Criminal Law Review* 1 (1996): 31–56.

"Man Gets Day's Probation in Rape of Ex-Girlfriend." *Globe and Mail* 21 June 1990: A1.

Manitoba Department of Justice. *Directive of the Attorney General and Solicitor General Regarding Spousal Assault.* Winnipeg: Manitoba Department of Justice, 1992.

Martin, D., and J. Mosher. "Unkept Promises: Experiences of Immigrant Women with the Neo-Criminalization of Wife Abuse." *Canadian Journal of Women and the Law* 3.1 (1995): 3–44.

McIntyre, S "Redefining Reformism: The Consultations that Shaped Bill C-49." *Confronting Sexual Assault. A Decade of Legal and Social Change*. Eds. J. Roberts and R. Mohr. Toronto: University of Toronto Press, 1994. 293–327.

McLeod, L. "Policy Decisions and Prosecutorial Dilemmas: The Unanticipated Consequences of Good Intentions." *Wife Assault and the Canadian Criminal Justice System*. Eds. M. Valverde, L. McLeod, and K. Johnson. Toronto: Centre of Criminology, 1993.

McLeod, L. *Wife Battering and the Web of Hope: Progress, Dilemmas and Visions of Prevention*. Ottawa: National Clearinghouse on Family Violence, 1989.

Mossman, M. J. "Feminism and Legal Method: The Difference It Makes." *Australian Journal of Law and Society* 30 (1986): 30–52.

Muzychka, M. *Beyond Reasonable Doubt: The Influence of Victim Stereotypes and Social Biases on Police Response to Women's Complaints of Sexual Assault*. St. John's, Newfoundland: Provincial Advisory Council on the Status of Women, 1991.

Ontario Provincial Police, *Police Standards Manual 0217.00. Police Response to Wife Assault*. Toronto: Ontario Provincial Police, 1994.

R. v. Carosella, [1997] 1 S.C.R. 80.

R. v. Chase, (1987), 37 C.C.C. (3d) 97 (S.C.C.).

R. v. Chase (1984), 55 N.B.R. 97 (C.A.).

R. v. Currie (1996), 26 O.R. (3d) 444 (C.A.).

R v. Darrach(1998), 38 O.R. (3d) 1 (C.A.).

R. v. Daviault, [1994] 3 S.C.R. 63.

R. v. Lavallee, [1990] 1 S.C.R. 852.

R. v. Mills, [1997] A.J. No. 891 (Q.B.), on appeal to the Supreme Court of Canada.

R. v. O'Connor, [1995] 4 S.C.R. 411.

R. v. O'Leary (14 February 1989), (Ont. Prov. Ct.) [unreported].

R. v. Osolin, [1993] 4 S.C.R. 595 at 669.

R. v. Seaboyer, R. v. Gayme, [1991] 2 S.C.R. 577.

Ratushny, Lynn. *Self Defence Review: Final Report*. Ottawa: Minister of Justice and Solicitor General of Canada, 1997.

Re Attorney General for Ontario and Criminal Injuries Compensation Board et al; Re Jane Doe and Criminal Injuries Compensation Board, (1995), 22 O.R. (3d) 129 (Gen. Div.).

Renke, W. "Case Comment: Lisa Neve: Dangerous Offender." *Alberta Law Review* 33 (1995): 650–676.

Rigakos, G. "The Politics of Protection: Battered Women, Protection Orders, and Police Subculture." *Women, Policy, Politics, and Contemporary Research in Canada*. Eds. K. Bonnycastle and G. Rigakos. Vancouver: Collective Press, 1998. 82–92.

Roberts, J. "Sexual Assault in Canada: Recent Statistical Trends." *Queen's Law Journal* 21 (1996): 395–421.

Rodgers, S. "Health Care Providers and Sexual Assault: Feminist Law Reform?" *Canadian Journal of Women and the Law* 8.1 (1995): 159–189.

Royal Commission on the Status of Women. *Report of the Royal Commission on the Status of Women*. Ottawa: Queen's Printer, 1970.

Sachs, A., and J. H. Wilson. *Sexism and the Law: A Study of Male Beliefs and Judicial Bias*. Oxford: Martin Roberston and Co., 1978.

Sheehy, E. "Legalizing Justice for All Women: Canadian Women's Struggle for Democratic Rape Law Reforms." *Feminist Law Journal* 6 (1996): 87–113.

Sheehy, E. *The Intoxication Defence in Canada: Why Women Should Care*. Ottawa: Canadian Advisory Council on the Status of Women, 1995a.

Sheehy, E. *A Brief on Bill C-72*. Ottawa: National Association of Women and the Law, 1995b.

Sheehy, E. "Compensation for Women Who Have Been Raped." *Confronting Sexual Assault. A Decade of Legal and Social Change*. Eds. J. Roberts and R. Mohr. Toronto: University of Toronto Press, 1994. 205–241.

Sheehy, E. "Feminist Argumentation Before the Supreme Court of Canada in *R. v. Seaboyer, R. v. Gayme:* The Sound of One Hand Clapping" *Melbourne University Law Review* 18 (1991): 450–468.

Shrofel, S. "Equality Rights and Law Reform in Saskatchewan: An Analysis of the Charter Compliance Process." *Canadian Journal of Women and the Law* 1.1 (1985): 108–118.

Snider, L "Struggles for Social Justice: Criminalization and Alternatives." *Unsettling Truths, Battered Women, Policy, Politics, and Contemporary Research in Canada*. Eds. K. Bonnycastle and G. Rigakos. Vancouver: Collective Press, 1998. 145–154.

Status of Women Canada. *Setting the Stage for the Next Century: The Federal Plan for Gender Equality*. Ottawa: Status of Women Canada, 1995.

Strange, C. "Historical Perspectives on Wife Assault." *Wife Assault and the Canadian Criminal Justice System*. Eds. M. Valverde, L. MacLeod, and K. Johnson. Toronto: Centre of Criminology, 1993. 293–304.

Stubbs, J. "'Communitarian' Conferencing and Violence against Women: A Cautionary Note." *Wife Assault and the Canadian Criminal Justice System*. Eds. M. Valverde, L. MacLeod, and K. Johnson. Toronto: Centre of Criminology, 1993. 260–289.

Turner, J. "Saskatchewan Responds to Family Violence: *The Victims of Domestic Violence Act, 1995.*" *Wife Assault and the Canadian Criminal Justice System*. Eds. M. Valverde, L. MacLeod, and K. Johnson. Toronto: Centre of Criminology, 1993. 183–197.

Ursel, J., and S. Brickey. "The Potential of Legal Reform Reconsidered: A Case Study of the Manitoba Zero Tolerance Policy on Family Violence." *Post-Critical Criminology*. Ed. T. O'Reilly-Fleming. Scarborough: Prentice Hall, 1996. 56–77.

Wiegers, W. "Compensation for Wife Abuse: Empowering Victims?" *University of British Columbia Law Review* 28 (1994): 247–307.

Wilson, The Honourable Bertha, Commissioner. *Touchstones for Change: Equality, Diversity and Accountability. The Report on Gender Equality in the Legal Profession*. Ottawa: Canadian Bar Association, 1993.

Young, D. *The Handling of Race Discrimination Complaints at the Ontario Human Rights Commission*. Toronto: unpublished, 1992.

CHAPTER 39
"The Pecker Detectors Are Back": Regulation of the Family Form in Ontario Welfare Policy

MARGARET HILLYARD LITTLE AND IAN MORRISON

[T]here is some continuity in the gendered content of today's discussion of welfare and that of eighty years ago. Then and now one dominating concern is a fear that "proper" families would be destabilized by the provision of incentives to single motherhood—whether through marital breakup or out-of-wedlock births—a fear which reveals not far below the surface a view that proper families must be enforced precisely because they do not always come "naturally" and are not always inherently desirable.[1]

—Linda Gordon

In 1940 Gladys Walker, a single mother, had her Mothers' Allowance cheque cancelled after the welfare worker made several surprise visits to her home. The welfare worker wrote:

I was mystified by a "boy friend" who was in the house when I called and stayed right through the time I was there and had many suggestions as to *why* the allowance should be granted. I didn't like his manner at all—he was decidedly too much at home. I asked Mrs. Walker if he boarded there—"No, just a *close friend*." Mrs. Walker seemed most anxious to secure the allowance at once as she needed some new clothes for a *special occasion*. I thought the *close friend* would likely be there for life when the occasion occurred....[2]

The occasion that was on the welfare worker's mind was probably marriage. In the fall of 1995 Bonnie Nye, whose boyfriend was in jail, moved to Prescott, Ontario. She was desperate for a place to live and could not find one within her welfare budget. In October, on her boyfriend's suggestion, she moved in with his best friend, Jerome Arthurs. She filled out a spouse-in-the-house questionnaire and provided other evidence that she and Jerome were co-residents and not a couple. In December she waited and waited for the welfare cheque to arrive but it never did. Instead, she discovered that she had been cut off welfare because a neighbour had made an

anonymous phone call to the welfare office and said that Bonnie's co-resident was actually her boyfriend and that they were living common-law.[3]

These are two very different eras in the administration of Ontario Mothers' Allowance (OMA).[4] Yet, in both cases these single mothers lost their welfare cheques because it was assumed that they had an intimate relationship with a man. How do we understand the state's need to police the social and sexual lives of single mothers? To what extent has this policy changed over time in its regulation of single mothers' relationships? This paper will attempt to explain how the state determines who is and who is not worthy of Mothers' Allowance based on a mother's associations with men—and how this regulation has been contested by those subject to it. Following a brief historical examination of the policy's determination of moral worthiness, we will pay particular attention to a 1995 change to the definition of "spouse" in the social assistance system that has meant a return to the practice of intense surveillance of poor mothers' relationships and contacts with men, after an eight-year period in which the state withdrew somewhat—although never entirely—from this scrutiny. Those who police these relationships have been nicknamed the "Pecker Detectors."[5]

In the eyes of low-income single mothers, the Pecker Detectors are back and with a vengeance. The 1995 changes have had a dramatic effect on how the social assistance system constructs the experience of poverty for low-income mothers. Its immediate impact was to disqualify from assistance thousands of women who had been receiving assistance as "single" mothers prior to October 1995. For others, the new rule has intensified the scrutiny of their personal lives. It sharply restricts their financial and social autonomy by forcing them to apply for public assistance as members of "couples" with men who are not their spouses for any other legal purposes, regardless of their own understanding of the nature of their relationships and regardless of their wishes to remain financially independent of these men.

Although the definition of "spouse" in social assistance regulations is gender neutral on its face, its impact is felt disproportionately by low-income mothers seeking assistance as sole-support parents. The welfare system is an immanent presence in the lives of most single mothers. In 1995, 61.7 per cent of all sole-support parent families in Ontario received social assistance.[6] The vast majority of these families—over 90 per cent—were headed by women. Many of those who are not on assistance live at similar income levels from low wage and precarious employment, "in the shadow" of the welfare system. Movement back and forth between welfare and work is common for sole-support mothers. The welfare system reaches far in defining the parameters of these mothers' contacts with men.

Viewing Social Assistance through the Lens of Moral Regulation

The history of how the welfare system has treated the definition of "family" and poor women's relationships with men clearly reflects the entanglement of the issues of economic need and moral worthiness. Throughout the history of this policy the state has always been concerned about how to provide aid to single mothers and yet ensure that the policy did not promote this "deviant family form." Moral worthiness has always been a concern for the provision of any kind of social assistance, but the moral test has always been gendered. Poor relief for the destitute employable man has always depended upon demonstrated willingness to work at any available job.[7] Poor relief for destitute mothers depended upon compliance with standards of behaviour judged in relation to women's (idealized) role in the traditional heterosexual nuclear family. This family model assumed that the man was the sole breadwinner with an economically dependent wife and children. Assistance was provided to women with children outside such relationships only where they conformed adequately to this family model especially, for the purposes of this paper, in respect to sexual behaviour. Historically, the granting of sexual access by a single mother to a man disentitled her to further state assistance.

The persistence of intense scrutiny of welfare recipients' moral worthiness has not been adequately explored by most welfare scholars. Generally, moral concerns regarding the poor are associated with charity work prior to the twentieth century. Many assume that this type of moral scrutiny withered with the emergence of the welfare state.[8] But the history of OMA suggests that moral questions continue to dominate some areas of welfare legislation. By highlighting the moral investigative processes of a policy one is better able to understand the complex and interdependent relationship between the regulator and the regulated.[9]

Traditional welfare studies have not adequately addressed this relationship. Social control scholars tend to grant the regulators absolute power and focus attention on those who are regulated. But moral regulation students argue that this process is more one of preserving and shaping, rather than suppressing.[10] They suggest

that there is a relationship developed over time between the regulator and the regulated that must be explored.[11] In sum, moral regulation provides us with another lens under which to examine the complexities of welfare policy. This model cannot *explain* the conditions observed but it can help to highlight relationships and regulations that many take for granted. In doing so moral regulation presents welfare state scholars with an important tool with which we can better understand the cultural activities of the state and other social agencies.

* * * * *

Who Is a Spouse?

From 1987 to 1995, the definition of spouse for people who were not married or did not have children together was easy to administer. The presence of a co-resident of either sex was taken into account in determining a recipient's allowance,[12] but the nature of the relationship was ignored for three years.[13] The 1995 amendment purports to replace this "arbitrary" line with what the government has called a "functional" definition. But in the absence of marriage, what is a couple? The state faces an increasingly intractable dilemma here. The ideological force of "family"—particularly the traditional, i.e., heterosexual nuclear family—remains powerful, but has been problematized and complicated by awareness and varying degrees of acceptance of diversity within the umbrella of "family."

The welfare system now operates in a profoundly different social context than that which existed through most of the history of Mothers' Allowance. Historically, most women became single mothers as widows and remained so permanently. Today, both the cause and the duration of episodes of single motherhood have dramatically changed. The breakdown of marriage or a common-law relationship now accounts for almost 60 per cent of all single motherhood. A smaller but increasing percentage of single mother families are formed by women giving birth without a male partner at the time of conception, who decide to raise the child alone. Single motherhood tends now to be a temporary rather than a permanent condition, as it was in earlier times. Most single mothers will eventually form part of a new heterosexual family unit[14] and a growing number will do so more than once.[15] Over 90 per cent of women who are single at the time of giving birth later form a heterosexual partnership, most within three or four years.[16] The relationships that single mothers come from or enter into may or may not ever involve marriage. Unmarried cohabitation has become increasingly common as a prelude to or a substitute for marriage. The percentage of self-identified couples who cohabit rather than marry increased from 5.6 per cent in 1981 to 9.9 per cent in 1991;[17] close to a third of all adults have cohabited at least once.[18] Younger adults are far more likely to cohabit than older adults, although cohabitation is increasingly common at all age groups.[19] Well over half of all couples under age 24 are living "common law."

The economic role of women in families has also changed dramatically. Most mothers now have paid employment of some kind outside the home. Almost all modest and low-income families need this income to maintain their living standards. Indeed, one of the government's real concerns about the three-year rule during the recession was not that women got benefits while living with men who were supporting them, but rather with the number of "couples" where the woman received sole-support parent benefits while living with a man receiving welfare as a single person, with a combined income greater than they would have received as a couple on assistance.

One telling indicator of the complexity of the social and political concerns underlying the 1995 amendments is that both proponents and opponents of the changes support their positions with appeals to principles of equity. As stated by Social Services Minister Janet Ecker,

Couples who live together and have a spousal relationship should be treated the same as married couples when they apply for welfare. The income of both individuals must be taken into account when deciding if they are eligible for welfare.... The old rule was simply not fair. It meant that one member of a common law couple could receive welfare for three years while living with a spouse who might have a good income. Married couples could not.[20]

On the surface, the man in the house rule has now entirely abandoned any overt concern with sexual morality *per se* (although we argue below that this is not really so). At a more fundamental level, though, the moral underpinnings of the rule remain the same: the "normal" economic unit of society, at least for the purposes of state aid and poor relief, is the family. And not just any family, but the heterosexual nuclear family, the "married couple" and their children. For welfare purposes, couples (unlike any other people who live together such as friends, siblings, other relatives) are conclusively deemed to operate as an economic unit. The welfare system assumes for this grouping alone that all income and assets of each partner are fully shared and equally available to each other.[21] Providing state support to a poor mother who is or appears to be living as part of a couple is to privilege her in relation to women who live with "husbands." The concern with welfare as a moral hazard for the behaviour of women has changed little from the first days of Mothers' Allowance.

The problem with the government's claim of equity is that it begs the question. To treat "common-law" couples like married couples, one must first be able to say what defines a married couple,[22] but the only irreducible common characteristic of married couples is that they are married. The Ontario government itself has admitted that:

While most spouses have a sexual relationship, some are celibate. While many spouses have children with each other, one or both of them may have had children with different partners, or may have had none. Where there are children, both spouses are normally involved in parenting, but sometimes only one or neither is involved. Spouses normally share the same residence, but they may live in different residences for a short or long term period. Family members are generally positively emotionally involved with each other, but may be negatively involved or not involved at all. Personal service interactions range from everyone in the family rendering personal services to all others, to one person providing service to others, or to no one providing services to anyone. Economic co-operation can refer to a wide variety of possible relationships, either monied or non-monied (e.g., child care). It ranges from one family member being largely responsible for the support of all family members as well as for performing financially valuable but unpaid work, to a family in which all members are totally economically independent.[23]

The fundamental paradox of the new definition, then, is that it can only claim to be treating common-law couples the same as married couples by ignoring the profound ambiguity in the very areas it has chosen to make the comparisons. Married couples—and those people defined as spouses in clauses (a) to (c) of the definition—either have voluntarily chosen to pool finances or have a mutual support obligation imposed by law. People who fall within clause (d) have no legal support obligation to each other. Some may indeed view themselves as an economic unit, but others strongly object to this. Although the government has argued vigorously that the 1995 changes replaced an "arbitrary" rule with a "functional" definition of what it means to be a couple, in fact its functional definition can only operate by deliberately ignoring this divergence. Unlike any other two unrelated people who live together, a social assistance recipient is not free to define her economic relationship with an opposite sex co-resident, including the freedom to enjoy a social relationship without financial dependency.

The imperative of the welfare system, then, is not to treat women living with men as couples because they share identical characteristics (even if such a test could be devised, which it could not). Indeed, when pressed on its rationale, the government admits as much:

Economic interdependence cannot depend exclusively on a statement of intention to support. It is often difficult to know whether one intends to support in the absence of a necessity to do so. This necessity does not arise as long as social assistance is available.[24]

The man in the house rule no longer assumes that female dependency in male-female relationships is normal and no longer expressly demands chastity in behaviour, but the fundamental principle remains much the same.

State aid will not be given to single mothers and their children if she *appears* to have granted sexual access to a man in a relationship which the state—not the woman—decides is spousal. The welfare system still assigns women to "couple" relationships based on an expressly heterosexual[25] (and implicitly sexual) model. Women seeking benefits for themselves and their children lose the autonomy to define the conditions of their relationships with men that all other women in society can exercise.

What does the new definition mean in practice? Before we turn to look at the systemic impact of the 1995 changes and the ongoing consequences for low-income mothers, it will be useful to look at how the spousal definition is actually applied. To understand what it means in the lives of those affected, it is necessary to look at how the welfare system deals with the presence—or the alleged presence—of an opposite sex co-resident in the home of a woman claiming sole-support parent benefits.

Who Does the Laundry? The "Spouse in the House" Questionnaire

Under clause (d), opposite sex co-residents are deemed to be spouses unless they can satisfy a welfare worker that they are not. The main tool for making this assessment is an exhaustive questionnaire that involves some 80 questions, covering almost every imaginable aspect of the recipient's living situation. The economic relationship between a single mother and a male boarder is particularly scrutinized. Training material for welfare workers suggest that all arrangements in which common expenses are shared will be considered a spousal relationship under the new rule. Caseworkers are explicitly directed to assess whether such items as televisions, cars, furniture or telephones are used jointly by co-residents, and to take such sharing as evidence of financial interdependence.[26] It is interesting to note that other financial criteria in regards to this policy are quite explicit. The act clearly states how much a single mother can earn, the amount of assets she can have and how much her car can be worth. Yet, when it comes to financial arrangements within a household the criteria are quite vague. There is no stated dollar figure or percentage of household expenses that can be shared without repercussions.

Social and familial interdependence is also assessed through this questionnaire. Some of the questions asked in this regard include the following:

14. Do you and your co-resident have common friends?
15b. Do other people invite the two of you over together?
18. Do you and your co-resident spend spare time at home together?
22a. Do you and your co-resident attend holiday celebrations together (e.g., Christmas, Thanksgiving dinners, birthdays)? Does (s)he buy holiday presents?
24a. How do you and your co-resident divide the household chores? (e.g., mowing the lawn, shovelling snow, raking leaves, repairs, laundry, housework?)
24b. Does your co-resident ever do your laundry (or the children's)?
27. Who takes care of you and your co-resident when either of you are ill?

There are also numerous questions to determine the relationship between the co-resident and the single mother's children. They include:

30a. Do you ask your co-resident for advice regarding the children?
32. Does your co-resident impose discipline or corrective action on your children?
35a. Does your co-resident attend your children's birthday parties?

Community members are engaged both directly and indirectly in the assessment of the nature of the relationship. The opinions of landlords, neighbours, teachers, policy, charity workers and ex-husbands are often considered by workers in deciding how to characterize a relationship with a co-resident. These opinions are also implicitly mirrored in the questionnaire, in which applicants or recipients are asked:

13. Do people think of you as a couple?
16. Are you known as a couple by public agencies or service (e.g., Children's Aid Society, the police, bank, school, doctors, recreational activities?)

These questions clearly encourage a single mother to be concerned about how all those around her interpret her relationships, while reflecting the continued role of the community in the moral scrutiny of those seeking welfare assistance.

Despite policy guidelines and the length and complexity of the questionnaire, we would argue that in the end the real function of the questionnaire is to provide a veneer of "objectivity" over a process that is profoundly subjective. Most of the questions are ambiguous, equally compatible with a traditional "spousal" relationship and with behaviour that any two people living together might display. There are no right or wrong answers, no combination or sum that necessarily defines the relationship as spousal or otherwise. Nor, as shown above, could there be: after all, what exactly *does* it signify if a man does or does not help with the laundry? The "interpretation" of the answers depends on an already-existing concept of what a "couple" is and how the person being investigated fits the welfare worker's conceptions.

* * * * *

Back to the Future: Living in the Shadow of the Man in the House Rule

Serious as the immediate impact of the rule changes was for those women who were living with men and receiving sole-support parent benefits in October 1995, the first wave of terminations is over. A new set of questions is now emerging for low-income mothers on welfare now or who may enter the system in the future. What does the man in the house rule mean for their lives and their options as they negotiate the welfare system?

First, social assistance recipients have lost the right to test a potential relationship by living together on a trial basis. The three-year rule permitted women the opportunity to attempt new relationships without immediately losing all financial independence. Women interviewed who used this amendment consistently stated how this reduced their anxiety and provided them with a breathing space to assess the relationship adequately.[27] This is a special concern for women who have been abused in previous relationships, a common situation for single mothers on social assistance.[28] Women who have been abused are often especially cautious about making an unreserved commitment to a new relationship. Some of those affected by the 1995 changes testified that they would never have commenced cohabitation if it had meant losing Mothers' Allowance.[29]

Second, single mothers' freedom to choose to share accommodation even with a roommate is seriously compromised, as Bonnie Nye's story shows. There are many reasons why recipients may want to make this choice: friendship and emotional support, financial assistance with shelter costs, physical security. Although in theory the man in the house rule does not prevent this, in practice the 1995 amendments have made such arrangements almost impossibly difficult. Someone trying to set up a household with a person of the opposite sex must face the task of convincing a welfare worker that the relationship is not spousal—and must convince the potential room-mate to go through the determination process. Even if a welfare worker is convinced that the relationship is not spousal, under ministry policy the issue is to be revisited annually.

Finally, but perhaps most profoundly, the 1995 amendments along with the Harris government's changes to welfare administration mean a new era in policing the lives of recipients. Much of the energy of the welfare system is devoted not to determining the nature of the relationship between a recipient and her roommate, but to finding out whether a man is there at all. Historically, these surveillance practices were the main focus of complaints about the intrusive and oppressive nature of the rule. These concerns diminished during the period 1987 to 1995 although they did not disappear.[30] With the 1995 changes and the increasing emphasis of the system on "fraud" detection, investigations to determine the presence of a man in the house have once again become an important presence in recipients' lives.

Investigations of an alleged man in the house can be triggered many ways: random home visits by welfare workers, suspicious computer cross-referencing, observations recounted to the welfare office by neighbours, family members, employers, landlords or other "concerned citizens," retaliatory denunciations by former spouses or boyfriends seeking revenge through harassment, etc. Both the initial reports and the investigations often involve the participation of community members, who are sought out by welfare investigators for questioning. Community surveillance and anonymous reporting of welfare recipients is actively encouraged by the Ontario government. The 1995 "anti-fraud" initiatives included a highly publicized welfare "snitch line" with a 1-800 number. While there are no data available on the use of this Ontario fraud line a similar province-wide telephone service in Manitoba revealed that the majority of the callers complained about single mothers and their associations with men.[31] Of the cases reported to the snitch line where action was taken, by far the largest category (42 per cent) was "spouse not declared" (although it is also important to note that the vast majority of calls to the snitch line either were not even investigated or revealed no fraud or error upon investigation).[32]

Disproving a false allegation of co-residency can be very difficult. Policy guidelines and court and tribunal decisions give some indication of the kinds of evidence that may lead to an assumption of an unreported spouse. Welfare workers are directed to consider, amongst other evidence:[33]

- statement from the landlord that the person lives in the applicant's or participant's dwelling or is listed on the lease;
- driver's licence history;
- car registration;
- employment records;
- credit checks;
- self-declared common residency;
- registry office records;
- voters' lists or enumeration; and
- telephone directory (common phone number).

Items from this list may seem like obvious grounds for suspicion, but in practice these "facts" may be far more ambiguous than appears at first sight. Indeed, there is a hidden but powerful class bias in this list. For example, the combination of low welfare rates and widespread discrimination from landlords makes it extremely difficult for a single mother to find decent and affordable accommodation. Many single mothers have a male friend or even an ex-partner view apartments with them and even co-sign leases or rental agreements or utilities contracts, although they have no intention of living there. Conversely, many recipients, who may have more stable lives than low-income men, allow friends, boyfriends or ex-partners to use their addresses and telephone numbers as contact points for employers or others (and sometimes to escape unwanted attention from creditors or others). In some cases women have deliberately led others to believe that they are residing with a partner for protection, for purposes of family law or because of intense cultural pressures against separation. In many cases women have no control over the conduct of abusive partners or ex-partners, who may use their addresses without their knowledge or against their wishes. In short, while documentary evidence of shared addresses and similar indicators may result from the presence of an unreported coresident, this may also represent a survival strategy or even a situation over which the recipient has no control.[34] Moreover, the rule also creates a dilemma for women who do have a current boyfriend. The formal rules of the system no longer prohibit sexual activity but there are no rules as to how often a man may visit or stay over without triggering an investigation and possible disqualification.[35]

For single mothers who have separated, the welfare system may also discourage contact with an ex-spouse, even if this may be to the advantage of the recipient and her children. In a companion amendment to the 1995 change to the definition of spouse, a new rule was added to the regulations providing that even someone living alone would be ineligible if a welfare worker concluded that there was a "reasonable prospect of reconciliation" with a former spouse. Thus, frequent visits by an ex-spouse to see children or provide assistance may trigger an investigation into possible co-residence, but even if this is not established, it may lead to disqualification because a welfare worker has decided that there is a possibility of reconciliation.

Termination of benefits on the basis of a false assumption that a man is present is obviously a very serious matter; however, the allegation of unreported co-residence alone may have serious consequences, even if the recipient is later cleared. The investigation alone can be damaging. Many recipients hide their status from neighbours, employers and even family members. Many do not even tell their own children, either from shame or from a well-founded fear of encountering discrimination and hostility. An investigation will usually reveal the status of the recipient to those questioned, who may be neighbours, landlords, employers or almost anyone else. This is one of the most pervasive fears for many recipients.[36]

Conclusion

The 1995 amendments have had an enormous impact on the lives of poor single mothers. First, single mothers have experienced a new heightened level of moral scrutiny and surveillance. While single mothers on welfare have always experienced intrusive moral investigation into their lives, this scrutiny waned somewhat during the 1970s and early 1980s. Today, the administration of this amendment, alone, signifies a renewed and intensive level of investigation into the moral behaviour of single mothers. This scrutiny is not merely carried out by welfare administrators. Numerous community members are also

highly involved in the determination of the spousal status of single mothers on welfare. And in fact, the government has taken measures to encourage the community to be more involved in this determination. Indeed, this amendment ensures a role for both government and community versions of the "Pecker Detector."

Second, this amendment has increased the dissonance between welfare regulations and the reality of single mothers' lives. Low-income single mothers rely upon male friends to break the isolation of poverty, provide role models for their children and to help them obtain decent housing. This "help" from a man can now be defined as evidence of a spousal relationship. Also, this paper demonstrates that fewer families live according to the traditional heterosexual nuclear family model which this spousal amendment reinforces. Low-income single mothers are forced to live according to a familial model that is increasingly outdated.

Finally, this spousal amendment discourages the creation of new familial units. It has always been the explicit or implicit goal of this policy to be a stop-gap for single mothers until they found another male bread-winner and formed a new family. Yet, this spousal amendment clearly discourages ex-male partners or male friends from associating too frequently with a female welfare recipient. The goal of the policy is contradictory at best.

All of this suggests that low-income single mothers have become a target for moral scrutiny and blame in the 1990s. The Harris government has encouraged both its paid workers and the community to intensify their surveillance of single mothers and to ensure that these mothers lead isolated and stigmatized lives. This not only impacts single mothers on welfare but it affects all women. Condemning single mothers to abject poverty and moral scrutiny deters other women from leaving unhappy or abusive relationships. Therefore this policy amendment impedes the ability of all women to become full and equal citizens in Ontario society.

Epilogue

Shortly after it was enacted, a legal challenge to the 1995 amendments was commenced in Ontario on behalf of four women who lost sole-support parent benefits as a result of the changes. Much of the material on which this paper is based is drawn from the evidence and testimony led by both sides in that case. In August 1998 a panel of the Ontario Social Assistance Review Board ruled that clause (d) of the definition as enacted in 1995 was inconsistent with the Canadian Charter of Rights and Freedoms. The board held that the definition violated the right to equality protected under section 15 of the Charter, because it discriminated against sole-support parents on social assistance vis-à-vis all other sole-support parents in Ontario; the board held further that the rule violated rights to privacy and personal autonomy under section 7 of the Charter. The board ordered benefits reinstated to the four appellants.

Response to the ruling was, predictably, polarized along lines that are familiar to all students of the rule's history. One newspaper columnist accused the Social Assistance Review Board of "social engineering" and demanded that the government appeal the decision as a "moral imperative" for the sake of children, claiming that the rule placed children at risk in unstable (unmarried) relationships and discourages partners from marrying.[37] Anti-poverty activists and community legal workers, on the other hand, saw the ruling as a victory for single mothers and hoped that the decision would permit low-income women more freedom in their living arrangements and personal lives.

This is far from the final word on the spouse in the house rule. The Ontario government filed an appeal to the SARB decision almost immediately. There are several levels of possible appeal remaining, including the eventual possibility of an appeal to the Supreme Court of Canada. How far the case will actually be appealed— and what will happen if the courts ultimately affirm the board's decision—cannot be predicted at this point. In the meantime, the new definition remains in effect and the spouse in the house rule continues to regulate the lives of poor women.[38] What can be safely predicted is that the issue will remain contentious—and poor women's behaviour and life choices will continue to be scrutinized and moralized. As long as the state chooses to distinguish between "single" mothers and "couples" in providing support to women with children, a line must be drawn between the groups. Where this line should be drawn, however, and the important consequences that flow from this choice, remains an inescapable dilemma of social assistance policy in a social order that refuses to value women's caregiving work in and of itself.

* * * * *

Notes

1 Linda Gordon, *Pitied But Not Entitled: Single Mothers and the History of Welfare 1890–1935* (New York: The Free Press, 1994) 34.

2 D.B. Weldon Library, Western Regional Collection, London, Ontario, Mothers' Allowance Case Files, London, Ontario, "Letter from Investigator to Local Mothers' Allowance Board, 27 August 1940." Gladys Walker is a pseudonym used to protect the anonymity of this applicant and to meet the terms under which access to case records were granted.

3 "Affidavit of Bonnie Nye," in *Re Sandra Elizabeth Falkiner et al. and Ontario*, Ontario Court of Justice (Divisional Court), File #310-95, (hereafter, "Falkiner Record"). The Falkiner case involves a legal challenge to the 1995 regulation changes, based on the Canadian Charter of Rights and Freedom. The case is still under appeal at the time of writing. Much of the information in this paper is taken from the many volumes of evidence filed by both sides in this case.

4 Mothers' Allowance was the original name of this programme. As discussed below, the *Ontario Mothers' Allowance Act* was repealed in 1968 and the programme name has changed twice since then; however, the name "Mothers' Allowance" is still in common popular usage.

5 Brenda Thompson made the nickname infamous in her book, *A Survival Guide for Single Mothers on Welfare in Nova Scotia* (Halifax: Dalhousie Public Interest Research Group, 1990). Some Ontario low-income mothers interviewed by Margaret Little have used the same term.

6 Affidavit of Kevin Costante, *Falkiner Record*, Exhibit 12, "Sole-Support Parents on Assistance as Percent of Lone Parents," Ministry of Community and Social Services (MCSS). All references to social assistance statistics in this paper are from MCSS sources unless otherwise noted. The number of sole-support parents on assistance has dropped since 1995; however, as of August 1998 there were still 150,000 sole-support parents receiving assistance in Ontario. As of the 1996 census, there were approximately 355,000 female-headed lone-parent families in Ontario.

7 See generally James Struthers, *The Limits of Affluence: Welfare in Ontario, 1920–1970* (University of Toronto Press, Toronto, 1994).

8 Questions of morality and welfare have not been adequately addressed in the Canadian welfare state literature. Liberal scholars such as Guest and Splane have argued that charity-style social programmes involved in moral investigation were replaced by a rights-based welfare system. The majority of Canadian welfare state scholars have focussed on questions of federalism (Banting), production (Finkel, Swartz) or the relationship between production and reproduction (Dickinson and Russell, Ursel) and virtually ignored moral concerns. While several articles in *The "Benevolent" State* and the title itself speak to the punitive nature of public and private welfare programs they do not directly address the question of morality (i.e., Struthers, Mitchinson, Schnell and Taylor): Alan Moscovitch and Jim Albert, *The "Benevolent State": The Growth of Welfare In Canada*, (Toronto: Garamond, 1987). And see Dennis Guest, *The Emergence of Social Security in Canada*, 3rd ed. (Vancouver: University of British Columbia, 1997) 54–56, 63. See: Richard Splane, *Social Welfare in Ontario* (Toronto: University of Toronto Press, Toronto 1965); Keith Banting, *The Welfare State and Canadian Federalism* (Kingston: McGill-Queen's University Press, 1982); Alvin Finkel, "Origins of the Welfare State in Canada," *The Canadian State*. Ed. Leo Panitch (Toronto: University of Toronto Press, 1977) 344–72; Donald Swartz, "The Politics of Reform: Conflict and Accommodation in Canadian Health Policy," *The Canadian State*, 311–43; James Dickinson and Bob Russell, eds., *Family, Economy and State: The Social Reproduction Process under Capitalism* (Toronto: Garamond, 1987); Jane Ursel, Private Lives, *Public Policy: 100 Years of State Intervention in the Family* (Toronto: Women's Press, 1992).

9 For further discussion of moral regulation see: Phillip Corrigan and Derek Sayer, *The Great Arch: English State Formation as Cultural Revolution* (London: Basil Blackwell, 1985); Mariana Valverde, *The Age of Light, Soap and Water: Moral Reform in English Canada, 1885–1925* (Toronto: University of Toronto Press,

1991) ("The Age of Light"); and Margaret Little, "No Car, No Radio, No Liquor Permit": *The Moral Regulation of Single Mothers in Ontario, 1920–1997* (Toronto: Oxford University Press, 1998) "Introduction."

10 Valverde, *The Age of Light* 39.

11 Althusserian philosophy lacks an adequate appreciation of the possibilities of agency, but it does attempt to explore the relationship between regulator and regulated. Through "hailing" or "interpellation" Althusser believes a person becomes defined by the regulations s/he applies or adheres to. See: Louis Althusser, "Ideology and Ideological State Apparatuses," *Lenin and Philosophy and Other Essays* (London: New Left Books, 1971).

12 It is not commonly understood that whenever another adult was present in the residence of a social assistance recipient, a deduction was made from the allowance. Welfare regulations simply assumed that the co-resident was paying a prescribed portion of the rent (whether or not this was actually the case).

13 Disputes could and did arise at the end of three years as to whether the co-resident was a "spouse"; however, these were relatively infrequent. In most cases, after three years the nature of the relationship and the evidence as to the nature of the relationship was fairly clear. A more common dispute during this period was whether an admitted "spouse," a husband or the father of the recipient's children, had returned to the home.

14 The likelihood of remarriage increases progressively with younger age cohorts: 60 per cent of all women born between 1951 and 1960 who have married and divorced have subsequently remarried: Statistics Canada *Family over the Life Course*, Ottawa, Canada, 1995. "Remarriage" is, of course, an underinclusive category. The few longitudinal studies of single mothers on social assistance also show that most eventually form new partnerships.

15 According to a study based on the 1990 General Social Survey, the number of children who have experienced multiple changes in family composition (including periods of living with a lone parent) is rising. Growing numbers by age cohort will have experienced two or even three successive two-adult families, usually with intervening periods in a single-parent family. See: Nicole Marcil-Gratton, "Growing up with a Single Parent, A Transitional Experience? Some Demographic Measurements," *Single-Parent Families: Perspectives on Research and Policy*, eds. Joe Hudson and Burt Galaway (Toronto: Thompson Educational Publishing 1993) 73–90.

16 Marcil-Gratton 85.

17 Statistics Canada, *Families in Canada*, Catalogue No. 96-307 E, Chart 2.1.

18 "Common Law: A Growing Alternative," *Canadian Social Trends* 18 (Winter 1991).

19 Ibid.

20 Ontario, Ministry of Community and Social Services News Release (4 September 1998), "Ontario Appeals Social Assistance Review Board's Decision on the Definition of Spouse."

21 Under welfare regulations, the income and assets of all members of the "benefit unit" (i.e., family) are lumped together to determine eligibility: Ontario Regulation 134/98 (Ontario Works) s. 38, s. 48.

22 It may be noted that although the term "common-law couple" is in common usage this is not a legal term of art and there is no such status in Ontario law. In fact, the term is invariably used by the Ontario government in relation to the 1995 changes because it obscures the very issue: whether people who are not spouses for any other legal purpose should be treated as a "couple" for welfare purposes.

23 Affidavit of Susannah Wilson, expert witness for the province of Ontario, *Falkiner Record*. Remarkably, this proposition was advanced to support the government's argument that it was possible to administer a functional test to determine whether a relationship was spousal.

24 Affidavit of Kevin Costante, *Falkiner Record*, paragraph 66. This statement was made as part of the government's formal legal defence to the constitutional challenge to the 1995 changes.

25 The restriction of the spousal definition to opposite-sex couples is interesting. There is no reason why same-sex couples should not be included, in light of the public rationales advanced for the definition in the first place; however, "legitimizing" same-sex couples in this context would obviously have had radical implications in other legal contexts which the Harris government, still fighting in the courts against the recognition of same-sex relationships, was not prepared to face.

26 Ontario, MCSS, *Ontario Works Policy Directives* (1 June 1998) Directive 14.0, Determining Coresidency. (These directives incorporate earlier policies sent to welfare workers at the time of the 1995 changes.)

27 Little, *No Car, No Radio, No Liquor Permit* Chapter 6.

28 The prevalence of violence in the lives of low-income single mothers is not often fully acknowledged. Almost half of all Canadian women have been seriously assaulted and the statistics are even higher for low-income women: K. Rodgers, "Wife Assault: The Findings of a National Survey," *Juristat* 14.9 (1994), reporting on the 1993 Statistics Canada's *Violence against Women Survey*. In one study of 114 young (age 13–26) mothers in Metro Toronto (almost all on social assistance), one third were being abused by a current partner and one third had been abused by their first partner during pregnancy: Robert Fulton et al. *Young Mothers in Metro Toronto* (Toronto: Young Mothers Resource Group, 1993) 28. There is also extensive research evidence in the United States that consistently confirms high levels of histories of abuse and violence amongst single mothers in welfare programs.

29 All four of the appellants in the *Falkiner* Charter challenge were single mothers who had been the victims of serious violence and abuse in previous relationships, in some cases lasting for years. All testified that this was an important reason why they were not prepared to sacrifice financial independence immediately upon co-residence: Affidavits of SF, DS, CC, CJ-P, *Falkiner Record*.

30 From 1987 to 1995 allegations of an unreported spouse in the house usually arose with respect to men who were spouses under clauses (b) or (c) of the definition, that is, an ex-husband or the father of a recipient's child(ren). Also, under the three-year rule women were still obliged to report the presence of a coresident, as this still affected the calculation of an allowance.

31 Based on interviews conducted by Margaret Little with community legal workers in Winnipeg, Manitoba, 1994–1995. For more information, see: Margaret Little, "He Said, She Said: The Role of Gossip in Determining Eligibility for Ontario Mothers' Allowance," Paper presented to the Canadian Historical Association, Brock University, St. Catharines, 31 May 1996.

32 See Ontario, MCSS, *Social Assistance Fraud Control Report*, 13 November 1997. For a brief discussion of the ideology of snitch

lines and a critical assessment of this report, see also Morrison, "Ontario Works" 32–33.

33 Ministry of Community and Social Services, *Ontario Works Policy Directives*, Directive 14.0, "Determining Co-residency."

34 None of these situations are uncommon. Numerous examples of terminations based on this kind of evidence which were subsequently reversed can be found in decisions of the Social Assistance Review Board: e.g., see SARB Decision No. L-06-09-18; Decision No. J-07-04-17R; Decision No. K-06-24-18; Decision No. P-12-13-01; Decision No. N-07-14-39; Decision No. Q-04-19-37; Decision No. Q-04-23-13; Decision No. K-06-26-01; Decision No. M-04-23-26; Decision No. J-02-25-06; Decision No. L-06-09-18; Decision No. L-10-28-20; Decision No. M-11-28-47; Decision No. K-11-21-34. From the collection of the Clinic Resource Office, Ontario Legal Aid Plan.

35 It is MCSS policy that recipients will not be given any specific rules as to how often a "boyfriend" may visit.

36 The situation under the new *Ontario Works Act* may be even worse. The OWA gives welfare investigators special powers, exceeding those of the police in some respects. Under new regulations, they can now enter any place other than a dwelling place without a warrant and demand information or records to investigate an allegation of an unreported spouse, and can order any third party to answer questions on pain of prosecution if they refuse: Ontario Regulation 134/98, section 65.

37 Christina Blizzard, "Turning back the welfare clock," *Toronto Sun* 15 September 1998.

38 A decision by an administrative tribunal such as the Social Assistance Review Board does not change the law. Only a ruling by a court will have that effect. Moreover, when the *Ontario Works Act* came into force in the summer of 1998, the Social Assistance Review Board was replaced by a new appeals body called the Social Benefits Tribunal. Unlike the SARB, the SBT does not have the power to rule on constitutional questions—a jurisdiction specifically excluded by the new legislation. In theory, women affected by the rule under the new legislation could start new court applications to challenge the application of the new definition. In practice, the burden of bringing such an application is so enormous that no one has done so and it is not likely that this will happen while an appeal is outstanding.

Rethinking Section 5:

CRIME, MORAL REGULATION, AND SOCIAL JUSTICE

Critical Thinking Questions

Gary Kinsman

1. How are "normal" and "deviant" constructed? Think of examples from the media of how sexual behaviour is morally regulated.
2. Discuss the relationship between national security and strategies of moral regulation and normalization.
3. How have anti-queer national practices shaped our historical present?

Elizabeth A. Sheehy

1. Despite many legal advances, violence against women is still a significant social problem. Why might this be? Discuss the aspects of the judicial system that can hinder justice and perpetuate inequality. Can laws change the behaviour of those who are violent?
2. Discuss the difference and implications of formal and substantive equality.
3. What does the author mean when she argues that "drawing upon the knowledge generated by the women's movement, we must draft legislation that presumes women's inequality, acknowledges context, and challenges power relations and beliefs"?

Margaret Little and Ian Morrison

1. What stereotypes do you (we as a society) have about those who are recipients of welfare? What stereotypes do you (we) have of single mothers? Are these stereotypes accurate?
2. How are the government and other various social organizations involved in processes that create and perpetuate moral regulation?
3. How have the Ontario welfare policies changed? How have these changes affected single mothers?
4. Discuss welfare, poverty, and the inability to find paid work from both a Marxist and a functionalist perspective.

Glossary Terms

Gary Kinsman

discourse: Ideas that operate as a set of rules that guide behaviour.

hegemony: The saturation of a particular society by a system of values, attitudes, beliefs, and morality that is pro status quo.

normalization: A process of making a practice appear "natural" and "taken for granted." Normalization is an exercise of power that regulates and defines what is acceptable in a given society at a given time.

Elizabeth A. Sheehy

formal equality: Equality of treatment (between men and women).

substantive equality: Looks at the end result: Are women and men equal recipients of benefits and burdens in a given society?

Margaret Little and Ian Morrison

ideological family: The notion of a "traditional" heterosexual nuclear family.

moral regulation: Government and social organizations create and maintain a moral order, a set of rules and regulations that outline what is "moral" and what is "immoral."

OMA: Ontario Mother's Allowance

Relevant Web sites

http://www.canada.justice.gc.ca/en/ps/rs/

The research and statistics division of the Department of Justice Canada. The site offers research and statistics on criminal justice issues.

http://www.statcan.ca/english/Pgdb/justic.htm

Canadian statistics on justice and crime collected by Statistics Canada.

http://www.homeoffice.gov.uk/justice/index.html

The "Justice and Victims" site for England and Wales. Provides information about victims of crime, court and legal processes, sentencing and justice, prisons and probation.

http://www.chebucto.ns.ca/CommunitySupport/YSJ/ysj.html

A Web site developed by the Youth for Social Justice Network. Its purpose is to increase people's understanding of social justice issues such as sexism, ageism, racism, heterosexism, and so forth.

http://uk.geocities.com/balihar_sanghera/cmemorality.html

This site examines the moral regulation of new technologies and discusses the regulation of pornography and homosexuality.

http://www.jpp.org

This is a prisoner-written journal. The purpose of the journal is to integrate experiential accounts of incarceration with academic arguments and to offer insight into the current state of carceral institutions.

http://www.graffiti.org

Graffiti art from around the world. "We do not advocate breaking the law, but we think art belongs in public spaces and that more legal walls should be made available for this fascinating art form."

http://www.sentencingproject.org

The Sentencing Project, incorporated in 1986, has become a national leader in the development of alternative sentencing programs and in research and advocacy on criminal justice policy. Here you will find links to their publications.

http://www.prevention.gc.ca/index.html

This is a French and English Web site run by the government of Canada. "The National Crime Prevention Strategy aims to reduce crime and victimization by tackling crime before it happens."

http://www.caveat.org

CAVEAT is a non-profit charitable group working for safety, peace, and justice. It provides publications, news, and other related resources.

Further Reading

Adams, Mary Louise. (1997). *The Trouble with Normal: Postwar Youth and the Making of Heterosexuality.* Toronto: University of Toronto Press.
A historical examination of the construction of heterosexuality as a "normal" sexuality.

Carrington, Peter. (2001). "Population Aging and Crime in Canada, 2000–2041." *Canadian Journal of Criminology,* 43, pp. 331–356.
Explores how an aging Canadian population alters crime rates and rates of criminal victimization.

Duffy, Ann, and Rina Cohen. (2001). "Violence against Women: The Struggle Persists." In Nancy Mandell (ed.), *Feminist Issues: Race, Class, and Sexuality*, pp. 134–165. Toronto: Prentice-Hall.
The authors discuss how violence permeates women's daily lives.

Foucault, Michel. (1977). *Discipline and Punish: The Birth of the Prison.* New York: Pantheon.
An influential analysis of the development of the prison.

Foucault, Michel. (1978). *The History of Sexuality*. New York: Pantheon.
An influential account of power and sexuality.

Kinsman, Gary. (1996). *The Regulation of Desire: Homo and Hetero Sexualities*. Montreal: Black Rose Books.
Explores the social forces that organize and maintain lesbian and gay oppression.

Little, Margaret Hillyard. (1998). *No Car, No Radio, No Liquor Permit: The Moral Regulation of Single Mothers in Ontario 1920–1997*. Toronto: Oxford University Press.
Utilizing government records, newspapers, magazines, and interviews, Little illuminates changes and continuities in support programs for poor single mothers.

Ouimet, Marc. (1999). "Crime in Canada and in the United States: A Comparative Analysis." *Canadian Review of Sociology and Anthropology, 36*(3), pp. 389–408.
Examines the idea that Canadians are relatively crimeless when compared to their southern neighbours.

Poutanen, Mary Ann. (1999). "The Homeless, the Whore, the Drunkard, and the Disorderly: Contours of Female Vagrancy in the Montreal Courts, 1810–1842." In K. McPherson, C. Morgan, and N. Forestall (eds.), *Gendered Pasts: Historical Essays in Femininity and Masculinity in Canada*, pp. 29–47. Toronto: Oxford University Press.
Explores the socio-historical context of law.

Ursel, Jane. 1992. *Private Lives, Public Policy: 100 Years of State Intervention in the Family*. Toronto: Women's Press.
A historical feminist analysis of the relationship between family and state, focusing on changes in family, labour, and welfare law.

SECTION

6 Population, Globalization, and the New World Order

The Readings

The final section of the book takes on current issues pertaining to population, modernity, and the "clash of civilizations." The articles in this section represent interventions from some of the foremost thinkers on key challenges and dilemmas of the 21st century.

Amartya Sen's critical intervention into the population debate challenges narrow and archaic understandings of the causes of, and potential interventions into, global population growth. He debunks a series of myths about the "world population problem," highlighting the often racist, anti-poor, anti-women, and anti-redistribution sentiments that usually accompany population panics. He is critical of North America and Europe's gross overconsumption and calls for a reintroduction of political and economic analysis into the population debate.

Edward Said provides a scathing critique of the simplistic "West versus Islam" thesis that has dominated policy and political thinking for the last decade. He reflects on the perils of simplistic approaches to culture and conflict. Said asserts that battle lines drawn from reductionist positions of good versus evil misunderstand that solutions will come only when we approach zealotry and extremism in all its forms in terms of justice, reason, and power.

CHAPTER 40

Population:
Delusion and Reality

AMARTYA SEN

1.

Few issues today are as divisive as what is called the "world population problem." With the approach this autumn of the International Conference of Population and Development in Cairo, organized by the United Nations, these divisions among experts are receiving enormous attention and generating considerable heat. There is a danger that in the confrontation between apocalyptic pessimism, on the one hand, and a dismissive smugness, on the other, a genuine understanding of the nature of the population problem may be lost.[1]

Visions of impending doom have been increasingly aired in recent years, often presenting the population problem as a "bomb" that has been planted and is about to "go off." These catastrophic images have encouraged a tendency to search for emergency solutions, which treat the people involved not as reasonable beings, allies facing a common problem, but as impulsive and uncontrolled sources of great social harm, in need of strong discipline.

Such views have received serious attention in public discussions, not just in sensational headlines in the popular press, but also in seriously argued and widely read books. One of the most influential examples was Paul Ehrlich's *The Population Bomb*, the first three sections of which were headed "Too Many People," "Too Little Food," and "A Dying Planet."[2] A more recent example of a chilling diagnosis of imminent calamity is Garrett Hardin's *Living within Limits*.[3] The arguments on which these pessimistic visions are based deserve serious scrutiny.

If the propensity to foresee impending disaster from overpopulation is strong in some circles, so is the tendency, in others, to dismiss all worries about population size. Just as alarmism builds on the recognition of a real problem and then magnifies it, complacency may also start off from a reasonable belief about the history of population problems and fail to see how they may have changed by now. It is often pointed out, for example, that the world has coped well enough with fast increases in population in the past, even though alarmists had expected otherwise. Malthus anticipated terrible disasters resulting from population growth and a consequent imbalance in "the proportion between the natural increase of population and food."[4] At a time when there were fewer than a billion people, he was quite convinced that "the period when the number of men surpass their means of subsistence has long since arrived." However, since Malthus first published his famous *Essay on Population* in 1798, the world population has grown nearly six times larger, while food output and consumption per person are considerably higher now, and there has been an unprecedented increase both in life expectancies and in general living standards.[5]

The fact that Malthus was mistaken in his diagnosis as well as his prognosis 200 years ago does not, however, indicate that contemporary fears about population growth must be similarly erroneous. The increase in the world population has vastly accelerated over the last century. It took the world population millions of years to reach the first billion, then 123 years to get to the second, 33 years to the third, 14 years to the fourth, 13 years to the fifth billion, with the sixth billion to come, according to one UN projection, in another 11 years.[6] During the last decade, between 1980 and 1990, the number of people on earth grew by about 923 million, an increase nearly the size of the total world population in Malthus's time. Whatever may be the proper response to alarmism about the future, complacency based on past success is no response at all.

Immigration and Population

One current worry concerns the regional distribution of the increase in world population, about 90 percent of which is taking place in the developing countries. The percentage rate of population growth is fastest in Africa—3.1 percent per year over the last decade. But most of the large increases in population occur in regions other than Africa. The largest absolute increases in numbers are taking place in Asia, which is where most of the world's poorer people live, even though the rate of increase in population has been slowing significantly there. Of the worldwide increase of 923 million people in the 1980s, well over half occurred in Asia—517 million in fact (including 146 million in China and 166 million in India).

Beyond concerns about the well-being of these poor countries themselves, a more self-regarding worry causes panic in the richer countries of the world and has much to do with the current anxiety in the West about the "world population problem." This is founded on the belief that destitution caused by fast population growth in the Third World is responsible for the severe pressure to emigrate to the developed countries of Europe and North America. In this view, people impoverished by overpopulation in the "South" flee to the "North." Some have claimed to find empirical support for this thesis in the fact that pressure to emigrate from the South has accelerated in recent decades, along with a rapid increase in the population there.

There are two distinct questions here: first, how great a threat of intolerable immigration pressure does the North face from the South, and second, is that pressure closely related to population growth in the South, rather than to other social and economic factors? There are reasons to doubt that population growth is the major force behind migratory pressures, and I shall concentrate here on that question. But I should note in passing that immigration is now severely controlled in Europe and North America, and insofar as Europe is concerned, most of the current immigrants from the Third World are not "primary" immigrants but dependent relatives—mainly spouses and young children—of those who had come and settled earlier. The United States remains relatively more open to fresh immigration, but the requirements of "labour certification" as a necessary part of the immigration procedure tend to guarantee that the new entrants are relatively better educated and more skilled. There are, however, sizable flows of illegal immigrants, especially to the United States and, to a lesser extent, to southern Europe, though the numbers are hard to estimate.

What causes the current pressures to emigrate? The "job-worthy" people who get through the immigration process are hardly to be seen as impoverished and destitute migrants created by the sheer pressure of population. Even the illegal immigrants who manage to evade the rigours of border control are typically not starving wretches but those who can make use of work prospects in the North.

The explanation for the increased migratory pressure over the decades owes more to the dynamism of international capitalism than to just the growing size of the population of the Third World countries. The immigrants have allies in potential employers, and this applies as much to illegal farm labourers in California as to the legally authorized "guest workers" in automobile factories in Germany. The economic incentive to emigrate to the North from the poorer Southern economies may well depend on differences in real income. But this gap is very large anyway, and even if it is presumed that population growth in the South is increasing the disparity with the North—a thesis I shall presently consider—it seems unlikely that this incentive would significantly change if the Northern income level were, say, 20 times that of the Southern as opposed to 25 times.

The growing demand for immigration to the North from the South is related to the "shrinking" of the world (through revolutions in communication and transport), reduction in economic obstacles to labour movements (despite the increase in political barriers), and the growing reach and absorptive power of international capitalism (even as domestic politics in the North has turned more inward-looking and nationalistic). To try to explain the increase in immigration pressure by the growth rate of total population in the Third World is to close one's eyes to the deep changes that have occurred—and are occurring—in the world in which we live, and the rapid internationalization of its cultures and economies that accompanies these changes.

Fears of Being Engulfed

A closely related issue concerns what is perceived as a growing "imbalance" in the division of the world population, with a rapidly rising share belonging to the Third World. That fear translates into worries of various kinds in the North, especially the sense of being overrun by the South. Many Northerners fear being engulfed by people from Asia and Africa, whose share of the world population increased from 63.7 percent in 1950 to 71.2 percent by 1990, and is expected, according to the estimates of the United Nations, to rise to 78.5 percent by 2050.

It is easy to understand the fears of relatively well-off people at the thought of being surrounded by a fast-growing and increasingly impoverished Southern population. As I shall argue, the thesis of growing impoverishment does not stand up to much scrutiny; but it is important to address first the psychologically tense issue of racial balance in the world (even though racial composition as a consideration has only as much importance as we choose to give it). Here it is worth recollecting that the Third World is right now going through the same kind of demographic shift—a rapid expansion of population for a temporary but long stretch—that Europe and North America experienced during their industrial revolution. In 1650 the share of Asia and Africa in the world population is estimated to have been 78.4 percent, and it stayed around there even in 1750.[7] With the industrial revolution, the share of Asia and Africa diminished because of the rapid rise of population in Europe and North America; for example, during the nineteenth century while the inhabitants of Asia and Africa grew by about 4 percent per decade or less, the population of "the area of European settlement" grew by around 10 percent every decade.

Even now the combined share of Asia and Africa (71.2 percent) is considerably below what its share was in 1650 or 1750. If the United Nations' prediction that this share will rise to 78.5 percent by 2050 comes true, then the Asians and the Africans would return to being proportionately almost exactly as numerous as they were before the European industrial revolution. There is, of course, nothing sacrosanct about the distributions of population in the past; but the sense of a growing "imbalance" in the world, based only on recent trends, ignores history and implicitly presumes that the expansion of Europeans earlier on was natural, whereas the same process happening now to other populations unnaturally disturbs the "balance."

Collaboration versus Override

Other worries involving the relation of population growth to food supplies, income levels, and the environment reflect more serious matters.[8]

Before I take up those questions, a brief comment on the distinction between two rival approaches to dealing with the population problem may be useful. One involves voluntary choice and a collaborative solution, and the other overrides voluntarism through legal or economic coercion.

Alarmist views of impending crises tend to produce a willingness to consider forceful measures for coercing people to have fewer children in the Third World. Imposing birth control on unwilling people is no longer rejected as readily as it was until quite recently, and some activists have pointed to the ambiguities that exist in determining what is or is not "coercion."[9] Those who are willing to consider—or at least not fully reject—programs that would use some measure of force to reduce population growth often point to the success of China's "one-child policy" in cutting down the national birth rate. Force can also take an indirect form, as when economic opportunities are changed so radically by government regulations that people are left with very little choice except to behave in ways the government would approve. In China's case, the government may refuse to offer housing to families with too many children—thus penalizing the children as well as the dissenting adults.

In India the policy of compulsory birth control that was initiated during the "emergency period" declared by Mrs Gandhi in the 1970s was decisively rejected by the voters in the general election in which it—along with civil rights—was a major issue. Even so, some public health clinics in the northern states (such as Uttar Pradesh) insist, in practice, on sterilization before providing normal medical attention to women and men beyond a certain age. The pressures to move in that direction seem to be strong, and they are reinforced by the rhetoric of "the population bomb."

I shall call this general approach the "override" view, since the family's personal decisions are overridden by some agency outside the family—typically by the government of the country in question (whether or not it has been pressed to do so by "outside" agencies, such as international organizations and pressure groups). In fact, overriding is not limited to an explicit use of legal coercion or economic compulsion, since people's own choices can also be effectively overridden by simply not offering them the opportunities for jobs or welfare that they can expect to get from a responsible government. Override can take many different forms and can be of varying intensity (with the Chinese "one-child policy" being something of an extreme case of a more general approach).

A central issue here is the increasingly vocal demand by some activists concerned with population growth that the highest "priority" should be given in Third World countries to family planning over other public commitments. This demand goes much beyond supporting family planning as a part of development. In fact, proposals for shifting international aid away from development in general to family planning in particular have lately been increasingly frequent. Such policies fit into the general approach of "override" as well, since they try to rely on manipulating people's choices through offering them only some opportunities (the means of family planning) while denying others, no matter what they would have themselves preferred. Insofar as they would have the effect of reducing health care and educational services, such shifts in public commitments will not only add to the misery of human lives, they may also have, I shall argue, exactly the opposite effect on family planning than the one intended, since education and health care have a significant part in the voluntary reduction of the birth rate.

The "override" approach contrasts with another, the "collaborative" approach, that relies not on legal or economic restrictions but on rational decisions of women and men, based on expanded choices and enhanced security, and encouraged by open dialogue and extensive public discussions. The difference between the two approaches does not lie in government's activism in the first case as opposed to passivity in the second. Even if solutions are sought through the decisions and actions of people themselves, the chance to take reasoned decisions with more knowledge and a greater sense of personal security can be increased by public policies, for example, through expanding educational facilities, health care, and economic well-being, along with providing better access to family planning. The central political and ethical issue concerning the "override" approach does not lie in its insistence on the need for public policy but in the ways it significantly reduces the choices open to parents.

The Malthus-Condorcet Debate

Thomas Robert Malthus forcefully argued for a version of the "override" view. In fact, it was precisely this preference that distinguished Malthus from Condorcet, the eighteenth-century French mathematician and social scientist from whom Malthus had actually derived the analysis of how population could outgrow the means of living. The debate between Condorcet and Malthus in some ways marks the origin of the distinction between the "collaborative" and the "override" approaches, which still compete for attention.[10]

In his *Essay on Population*, published in 1798, Malthus quoted—extensively and with approval—Condorcet's discussion, in 1795, of the possibility of overpopulation. However, true to the Enlightenment tradition, Condorcet was confident that this problem would be solved by reasoned human action: through increases in productivity, through better conservation and prevention of waste, and through education (especially female education), which would contribute to reducing the birth rate.[11] Voluntary family planning would be encouraged, in Condorcet's analysis, by increased understanding that if people "have a duty toward those who are not yet born, that duty is not to give them existence but to give them happiness." They would see the value of limiting family size "rather than foolishly ... encumber the world with useless and wretched beings."[12]

Even though Malthus borrowed from Condorcet his diagnosis of the possibility of overpopulation, he refused to accept Condorcet's solution. Indeed, Malthus's essay on population was partly a criticism of Condorcet's Enlightenment reasoning, and even the full tide of Malthus's famous essay specifically mentioned Condorcet. Malthus argued that

> there is no reason whatever to suppose that anything beside the difficulty of procuring in adequate plenty the necessaries of life should either indispose this greater number of persons to marry early, or disable them from rearing in health the largest families.[13]

Malthus thus opposed public relief of poverty: he saw the "poor laws" in particular as contributing greatly to population growth.[14]

Malthus was not sure that any public policy would work, and whether "overriding" would in fact be possible: "The perpetual tendency in the race of man to increase beyond the means of subsistence is one of the great general laws of animated nature which we can have no reason to expect will change."[15] But insofar as any solution would be possible, it could not come from voluntary decisions of the people involved, or acting from a position of strength and economic security. It must come from overriding their preferences through the compulsions of economic necessity, since their poverty was the only thing that could "indispose this greater number of persons to marry early, or disable them from rearing in health the largest families."

Development and Increased Choice

The distinction between the "collaborative" approach and the "override" approach thus tends to correspond closely to the contrast between, on the one hand, treating economic and social development as the way to solve the population problem and, on the other, expecting little from development and using, instead, legal and economic pressures to reduce birth rates. Among recent writers, those such as Gerard Piel,[16] who have persuasively emphasized our ability to solve problems through reasoned decisions and actions, have tended—like

Condorcet—to find the solution of the population problem in economic and social development. They advocate a broadly collaborative approach, in which governments and citizens would together produce economic and social conditions favouring slower population growth. In contrast, those who have been thoroughly skeptical of reasoned human action to limit population growth have tended to go in the direction of "override" in one form or another, rather than concentrate on development and voluntarism.

Has development, in fact, done much to reduce population growth? There can be little doubt that economic and social development, in general, has been associated with major reductions in birth rates and the emergence of smaller families as the norm. This is a pattern that was, of course, clearly observed in Europe and North America as they underwent industrialization, but that experience has been repeated in many other parts of the world.

In particular, conditions of economic security and affluence, wider availability of contraceptive methods, expansion of education (particularly female education), and lower mortality rates have had—and are currently having—quite substantial effects in reducing birth rates in different parts of the world.[17] The rate of world population growth is certainly declining, and even over the last two decades its percentage growth rate has fallen from 2.2 percent per year between 1970 and 1980 to 1.7 percent between 1980 and 1992. This rate is expected to go steadily down until the size of the world's population becomes nearly stationary.[18]

There are important regional differences in demographic behaviour; for example, the population growth rate in India peaked at 2.2 percent a year (in the 1970s) and has since started to diminish, whereas most Latin American countries peaked at much higher rates before coming down sharply, while many countries in Africa currently have growth rates between 3 and 4 percent, with an average for sub-Saharan Africa of 3.1 percent. Similarly, the different factors have varied in their respective influence from region to region. But there can be little dispute that economic and social development tends to reduce fertility rates. The regions of the Third World that lag most in achieving economic and social development, such as many countries in Africa, are, in general, also the ones that have failed to reduce birth rates significantly. Malthus's fear that economic and social development could only encourage people to have more children has certainly proved to be radically wrong, and so have all the painful policy implications drawn from it.

This raises the following question: in view of the clear connection between development and lower fertility, why isn't the dispute over how to deal with population growth fully resolved already? Why don't we reinterpret the population problem simply as a problem of underdevelopment and seek a solution by encouraging economic and social development (even if we reject the over-simple slogan "development is the most reliable contraceptive")?

In the long run, this may indeed be exactly the right approach. The problem is more complex, however, because a "contraceptive" that is "reliable" in the long run may not act fast enough to meet the present threat. Even though development may dependably work to stabilize population if it is given enough time, there may not be, it is argued, time enough to give. The death rate often falls very fast with more widely available health care, better sanitation, and improved nutrition, while the birth rate may fall rather slowly. Much growth of population may meanwhile occur.

This is exactly the point at which apocalyptic prophecies add force to the "override" view. One claim, then, that needs examination is that the world is facing an imminent crisis, one so urgent that development is just too slow a process to deal with it. We must try right now, the argument goes, to cut down population growth by drastic and forceful means if necessary. The second claim that also needs scrutiny is the actual feasibility of adequately reducing population growth through these drastic means, without fostering social and economic development.

2.
Population and Income

It is sometimes argued that signs of an imminent crisis can be found in the growing impoverishment of the South, with falling income per capita accompanying high population growth. In general, there is little evidence for this. As a matter of fact, the average population of "low-income" countries (as defined by the World Bank) has been not only enjoying a rising gross national product (GNP) per head, but a growth rate of GNP per capita (3.9 percent per year for 1980–92) that is much faster than those for the "high-income" countries (2.4 percent) and for the "middle-income" ones (0 percent).[19]

The growth of per capita GNP of the population of low-income countries would have been even higher had it not been for the negative growth rates of many countries in sub-Saharan Africa, one region in which a number of countries have been experiencing economic decline. But the main culprit causing this state of affairs is the terrible failure of economic production in sub-Saharan Africa (connected particularly with political disruption, including wars and military rule), rather than population growth, which is only a subsidiary factor. Sub-Saharan Africa does have high population growth, but its economic stagnation has contributed much more to the fall in its per capita income.

With its average population growth rate of 3.1 percent per year, had sub-Saharan Africa suddenly matched China's low population growth of 1.4 percent (the lowest among the low-income countries), it would have gained roughly 1.7 percent in per capita GNP growth. The real income per person would still have fallen, even with that minimal population growth, for many countries in the region. The growth of GNP per capita is minus 1.9 percent for Ethiopia, minus 1.8 percent for Togo, minus 3.6 percent for Mozambique, minus 4.3 percent for Niger, minus 4.7 percent for Ivory Coast, not to mention Somalia, Sudan, and Angola, where the political disruption has been so serious that no reliable GNP estimates even exist. A lower population growth rate could have reduced the magnitude of the fall in per capita GNP, but the main roots of Africa's economic decline lie elsewhere. The complex political factors underlying the troubles of Africa include, among other things, the subversion of democracy and the rise of combative military rulers, often encouraged by the cold war (with Africa providing "client states"—from Somalia and Ethiopia to Angola and Zaire—for the superpowers, particularly from the 1960s onward). The explanation of sub-Saharan Africa's problems has to be sought in these political troubles, which affect economic stability, agricultural and industrial incentives, public health arrangements, and social services—even family planning and population policy.[20]

There is indeed a very powerful case for reducing the rate of growth of population in Africa, but this problem cannot be dissociated from the rest of the continent's woes. Sub-Saharan Africa lags behind other developing regions in economic security, in health care, in life expectancy, in basic education, and in political and economic stability. It should be no great surprise that it lags behind in family planning as well. To dissociate the task of population control from the politics and economics of Africa would be a great mistake and would seriously mislead public policy.

Population and Food

Malthus's exact thesis cannot, however, be disputed by quoting statistics of income per capita, for he was concerned specifically with food supply per capita, and he had concentrated on "the proportion between the natural increase of population and food." Many modern commentators, including Paul Ehrlich and Garrett Hardin, have said much about this, too. When Ehrlich says, in his *Population Bomb*, "too little food," he does not mean "too little income," but specifically a growth shortage of food.

Is population beginning to outrun food production? Even though such an impression is often given in public discussions, there is, in fact, no serious evidence that this is happening. While there are some year-to-year fluctuations in the growth of food output (typically inducing, whenever things slacken a bit, some excited remarks by those who anticipate impending doom), the worldwide trend of food output per person has been firmly upward. Not only over the two centuries since Malthus's time, but also during recent decades, the rise in food output has been significantly and consistently outpacing the expansion of world population.[21]

But the total food supply in the world as a whole is not the only issue. What about the regional distribution of food? If it were to turn out that the rising ratio of food to population is mainly caused by increased production

Table 40.1: Indices of Food Production Per Capita

	1979–81 Base Period	1991–93
World	100	103
Europe	100	102
North America	100	95
Africa	100	94
Asia	100	122
including		
India	100	123
China	100	139

Source: FAO Quarterly Bulletin of Statistics, Food and agriculture Organization of the United Nations.

in richer countries (for example, if it appeared that U.S. wheat output was feeding the Third World, in which much of the population expansion is taking place), then the neo-Malthusian fears about "too many people" and "too little food" may have some plausibility. Is that what is happening?

In fact, with one substantial exception, exactly the opposite is true. The largest increases in the production of food—not just in the aggregate but also per person—are actually taking place in the Third World, particularly in the region that is having the largest absolute increases in the world population, that is, in Asia. The many millions of people who are added to the populations of India and China may be constantly cited by the terrorized—and terrorizing—advocates of the apocalyptic view, but it is precisely in these countries that the most rapid rates of growth in food output per capita are to be observed. For example, between the three-year averages of 1979–81 and 1991–93, food production per head in the world moved up by 3 percent, while it went up by only 2 percent in Europe and went down by nearly 5 percent in North America. In contrast, per capita food production jumped up by 22 percent in Asia generally, including 23 percent in India and 39 percent in China[22] (see Table 40.1).

During the same period, however, food production per capita went down by 6 percent in Africa, and even the absolute size of food output fell in some countries (such as Malawi and Somalia). Of course, many countries in the world—from Syria, Italy, and Sweden to Botswana in Africa—have had declining food production per head without experiencing hunger or starvation, since their economies have prospered and grown; when the means are available, food can be easily bought in the international market if it is necessary to do so. For many countries in sub-Saharan Africa the problem arises from the fact that the decline in food production is an integral part of the story of overall economic decline, which I have discussed earlier.

Difficulties of food production in sub-Saharan Africa, like other problems of the national economy, are not only linked to wars, dictatorships, and political chaos.

In addition, there is some evidence that climatic shifts have had unfavourable effects on parts of that continent. While some of the climatic problems may be caused partly by increases in human settlement and environmental neglect, that neglect is not unrelated to the political and economic chaos that has characterized sub-Saharan Africa during the last few decades. The food problem of Africa must be seen as one part of a wider political and economic problem of the region.[23]

The Price of Food

To return to "the balance between food and population," the rising food production per capita in the world as a whole, and in the Third World in general, contradicts some of the pessimism that characterized the gloomy predictions of the past. Prophecies of imminent disaster during the last few decades have not proved any more accurate than Malthus's prognostication nearly two hundred years ago. As for new prophecies of doom, they cannot, of course, be contradicted until the future arrives. There was no way of refuting the theses of W. Paddock and P. Paddock's popular book *Famine—1975!* published in 1968, which predicted terrible cataclysm for the world as a whole by 1975 (writing off India, in particular, as a basket case), until 1975 actually arrived. The new prophets have learned not to attach specific dates to the crises they foresee, and past failures do not seem to have reduced the popular appetite for this creative genre.

However, after noting the rather dismal forecasting record of doomsayers, we must also accept the general methodological point that present trends in output do not necessarily tell us much about the prospects of further expansion in the future. It could, for example, be argued that maintaining growth in food production may require proportionately increasing investments of capital, drawing them away from other kinds of production. This would tend to make food progressively more expensive if there are "diminishing returns" in shifting resources from other fields into food production. And, ultimately, further expansion of food production may become so expensive that it would be hard to maintain the trend of increasing food production without reducing other outputs drastically.

But is food production really getting more and more expensive? There is, in fact, no evidence for that conclusion either. In fact, quite the contrary. Not only is food generally much cheaper to buy today, in constant dollars, than it was in Malthus's time, but it also has become cheaper during recent decades. As a matter of fact, there have been increasing complaints among food exporters, especially in the Third World, that food prices have fallen in relation to other commodities. For example, in 1992 a United Nations report recorded a 38 percent fall in the relative prices of "basic foods" over the last decade.[24] This is entirely in line with the trend, during the last three decades, toward declining relative prices of particular food items, in relation to the prices of manufactured goods. The World Bank's adjusted estimates of the prices of particular food crops, between 1953–55 and 1983–85, show similarly steep declines for such staples as rice (42 percent), wheat (57 percent), sorghum (39 percent), and maize (37 percent).[25]

Not only is food getting less expensive, but we also have to bear in mind that the current increase in food production (substantial and well ahead of population growth, as it is) is itself being kept in check by the difficulties in selling food profitably, as the relative prices of food have fallen. Those neo-Malthusians who concede that food production is now growing faster than population often point out that it is growing "only a little faster than population," and they are inclined to interpret this as evidence that we are reaching the limits of what we can produce to keep pace with population growth.

But that is surely the wrong conclusion to draw in view of the falling relative prices of food, and the current difficulties in selling food, since it ignores the effects of economic incentives that govern production. When we take into account the persistent cheapening of food prices, we have good grounds to suggest that food output is being held back by a lack of effective demand in the market. The imaginary crisis in food production, contradicted as it is by the upward trends of total and regional food output per head, is thus further debunked by an analysis of the economic incentives to produce more food.

Deprived Lives and Slums

I have examined the alleged "food problem" associated with population growth in some detail because it has received so much attention both in the traditional Malthusian literature and in the recent writings of neo-Malthusians. In concentrating on his claim that growing populations would not have enough food, Malthus differed from Condorcet's broader presentation of the population question. Condorcet's own emphasis was on the possibility of "a continual diminution of happiness" as a result of population growth, a diminution that could occur in many different ways—not just through the deprivation of food, but through a decline in living conditions generally. That more extensive worry can remain even when Malthus's analysis of the food supply is rejected.

Indeed, average income and food production per head can go on increasing even as the wretchedly deprived living conditions of particular sections of the population get worse, as they have in many parts of the Third World. The living conditions of backward regions and deprived classes can decline even when a country's economic growth is very rapid on the average. Brazil during the 1960s and 1970s provided an extreme example of this. The sense that there are just "too many people" around often arises from seeing the desperate lives of people in the large and rapidly growing urban slums—*bidonvilles*—in poor countries, sobering reminders that we should not take too much comfort from aggregate statistics of economic progress.

But in an essay addressed mainly to the population problem, what we have to ask is not whether things are just fine in the Third World (they obviously are not), but whether population growth is the root cause of the deprivations that people suffer. The question is whether the particular instances of deep poverty we observe derive mainly from population growth rather than from other factors that lead to unshared prosperity and persistent and possibly growing inequality. The tendency to see in population growth an explanation for every calamity that afflicts poor people is now fairly well established in some circles, and the message that gets transmitted constantly is the opposite of the old picture postcard: "Wish you weren't here."

To see in population growth the main reason for the growth of overcrowded and very poor slums in large cities, for example, is not empirically convincing. It does not help to explain why the slums of Calcutta and Bombay have grown worse at a faster rate than those of Karachi and Islamabad (India's population growth rate is 2.1 percent per year, Pakistan's 3.1), or why Jakarta has deteriorated faster than Ankara or Istanbul (Indonesian population growth is 1.8 percent, Turkey's 2.3), or why the slums of Mexico City have become worse more rapidly than those of San Jose (Mexico's population growth rate is 2.0, Costa Rica's 2.8), or why Harlem can seem more and more deprived when compared with the poorer districts of Singapore (U.S. population growth rate is 1.0, Singapore's is 1.8). Many causal factors affect the degree of deprivation in particular parts of a country—rural as well as urban—and to try to see them all as resulting from overpopulation is the negation of social analysis.

This is not to deny that population growth may well have an effect on deprivation, but only to insist that any investigation of the effects of population growth must be part of the analysis of economic and political processes, including the effects of other variables. It is the isolationist view of population growth that should be rejected.

Threats to the Environment

In his concern about "a continual diminution of happiness" from population growth, Condorcet was a pioneer in considering the possibility that natural raw materials might be used up, thereby making living conditions worse. In his characteristically rationalist solution, which relied partly on voluntary and reasoned measures to reduce the birth rate, Condorcet also envisaged the development of less improvident technology: "The manufacture of articles will be achieved with less wastage in raw materials and will make better use of them."[26]

The effects of a growing population on the environment could be a good deal more serious than the food problems that have received so much attention in the literature inspired by Malthus. If the environment is damaged by population pressures, this obviously affects the kind of life we lead, and the possibilities of a "diminution in happiness" can be quite considerable. In dealing with this problem, we have to distinguish once again between the long and the short run. The short-run picture tends to be dominated by the fact that the per capita consumption of food, fuel, and other goods by people in Third World countries is often relatively low, consequently the impact of population growth in these countries is not, in relative terms, so damaging to the global environment. But the problems of the local environment can, of course, be serious in many developing economies. They vary from the "neighbourhood pollution" created by unregulated industries to the pressure of denser populations on rural resources such as fields and woods.[27] (The Indian authorities had to close down several factories in and around Agra, since the facade of the Taj Mahal was turning pale as a result of chemical pollution from local factories.) But it remains true that one additional American typically has a larger negative impact on the ozone layer, global warmth, and other elements of the earth's environment than dozens of Indians and Zimbabweans put together. Those who argue for the immediate need for forceful population control in the Third World to preserve the global environment must first recognize this elementary fact.

This does not imply, as is sometimes suggested, that as far as the global environment is concerned, population growth in the Third World is nothing to worry about. The long-run impact on the global environment of population growth in the developing countries can be expected to be large. As the Indians and Zimbabweans develop economically, they too will consume a great deal more, and they will pose, in the future, a threat to the earth's environment similar to that of people in the rich countries today. The long-run threat of population to the environment is a real one.

3.
Women's Deprivation and Power

Since reducing the birth rate can be slow, this and other long-run problems should be addressed right now. Solutions will no doubt have to be found in the two directions to which, as it happens, Condorcet pointed: (1) developing new technology and new behaviour patterns that would waste little and pollute less, and (2) fostering social and economic changes that would gradually bring down the growth rate of population.

On reducing birth rates, Condorcet's own solution not only included enhancing economic opportunity and security, but also stressed the importance of education, particularly female education. A better-educated population could have a more informed discussion of the kind of life we have reason to value; in particular it would reject the drudgery of a life of continuous child bearing and rearing that is routinely forced on many Third World women. That drudgery, in some ways, is the most immediately adverse consequence of high fertility rates.

Central to reducing birth rates, then, is a close connection between women's well-being and their power to make their own decisions and bring about changes in the fertility pattern. Women in many Third World countries are deprived by high birth frequency of the freedom to do other things in life, not to mention the medical dangers of repeated pregnancy and high maternal mortality, which are both characteristic of many developing countries. It is thus not surprising that reductions in birth rates have been typically associated with improvement of women's status and their ability to make their voices heard—often the result of expanded opportunities for schooling and political activity.[28]

There is nothing particularly exotic about declines in the birth rate occurring through a process of voluntary rational assessment, of which Condorcet spoke. It is what people do when they have some basic education, know about family planning methods and have access to them, do not readily accept a life of persistent drudgery, and are not deeply anxious about their economic security. It is also what they do when they are not forced by high infant and child mortality rates to be so worried that no child will survive to support them in their old age that they try to have many children. In country after country the birth rate has come down with more female education, the reduction of mortality rates, the expansion of economic means and security, and greater public discussion of ways of living.

Development versus Coercion

There is little doubt that this process of social and economic change will over time cut down the birth rate. Indeed the growth rate of world population is already firmly declining—it came down from 2.2 percent in the 1970s to 1.7 percent between 1980 and 1992. Had imminent cataclysm been threatening, we might have had good reason to reject such gradual progress and consider more drastic means of population control, as some have advocated. But that apocalyptic view is empirically baseless. There is no imminent emergency that calls for a breathless response. What is called for is systematic support for people's own decisions to reduce family size through expanding education and health care, and through economic and social development.

It is often asked where the money needed for expanding education, health care, and so on would be found. Education, health services, and many other means of improving the quality of life are typically highly labour-intensive and are thus relatively inexpensive in poor countries (because of low wages).[29] While poor countries have less money to spend, they also need less money to provide these services. For this reason many poor countries have indeed been able to expand educational and health services widely without waiting to become prosperous through the process of economic growth. Sri Lanka, Costa Rica, Indonesia, and Thailand are good examples, and there are many others. While the impact of these social services on the quality and length of life has been much studied, they are also major means of reducing the birth rate.

By contrast with such open and voluntary developments, coercive methods, such as the "one-child policy" in some regions, have been tried in China, particularly since the reforms of 1979. Many commentators have pointed out that by 1992 the Chinese birth rate had fallen to 19 per 1000, compared with 29 per 1000 in India, and 37 per 1000 for the average of poor countries other than China and India. China's total fertility rate (reflecting the number of children born per woman) is now at "the replacement level" of 2.0, compared with India's 3.6 and the weighted average of 4.9 for low-income countries other than China and India.[30] Hasn't China shown the way to "solve" the population problem in other developing countries as well?

4.
China's Population Policies

The difficulties with this "solution" are of several kinds. First, if freedom is valued at all, the lack of freedom associated with this approach must be seen to be a social loss in itself. The importance of reproductive freedom has been persuasively emphasized by women's groups throughout the world.[31]

The loss of freedom is often dismissed on the grounds that, because of cultural differences, authoritarian policies that would not be tolerated in the West are acceptable to Asians. While we often hear references to "despotic" Oriental traditions, such arguments are not more convincing than a claim that compulsion in the West is justified by the traditions of the Spanish Inquisition or of the Nazi concentration camps. Frequent references are also made to the emphasis on discipline in the "Confucian tradition"; but that is not the only tradition in the "East," nor is it easy to assess the implications of that tradition for modern Asia (even if we were able to show that discipline is more important for Confucius than it is for, say, Plato or Saint Augustine).

Only a democratic expression of opinion could reveal whether citizens would find a compulsory system acceptable. While such a test has not occurred in China, one did in fact take place in India during "the emergency period" in the 1970s, when Indira Gandhi's government imposed compulsory birth control and suspended various legal freedoms. In the general elections that followed, the politicians favouring the policy of coercion were overwhelmingly defeated. Furthermore, family planning experts in India have observed how the briefly applied programs of compulsory sterilization tended to discredit voluntary birth control programs generally, since people became deeply suspicious of the entire movement to control fertility.

Second, apart from the fundamental issue of whether people are willing to accept compulsory birth control, its specific consequences must also be considered. Insofar as coercion is effective, it works by making people do things they would not freely do. The social consequences of such compulsion, including the ways in which an unwilling population tends to react when it is coerced, can be appalling. For example, the demands of a "one-child family" can lead to the neglect—or worse—of a second child, thereby increasing the infant mortality rate. Moreover, in a country with a strong preference for male children—a preference shared by China and many other countries in Asia and North Africa—a policy of allowing only one child per family can easily lead to the fatal neglect of a female child. There is much evidence that this is fairly widespread in China, with very adverse effects on infant mortality rates. There are reports that female children have been severely neglected as well as suggestions that female infanticide occurs with considerable frequency. Such consequences are hard to tolerate morally, and perhaps politically also, in the long run.

Third, what is also not clear is exactly how much additional reduction in the birth rate has been achieved through these coercive methods. Many of China's longstanding social and economic programs have been valuable in reducing fertility, including those that have expanded education for women as well as men, made health care more generally available, provided more job opportunities for women, and stimulated rapid economic growth. These factors would themselves have reduced the birth rates, and it is not clear how much "extra lowering" of fertility rates has been achieved in China through compulsion.

For example, we can determine whether many of the countries that match (or outmatch) China in life expectancy, female literacy rates, and female participation in the labour force actually have a higher fertility rate than China. Of all the countries in the world for which data are given in the World Development Report 1994, there are only three such countries: Jamaica (2.7), Thailand (2.2), and Sweden (2.1)—and the fertility rates of two of these are close to China's (2.0). Thus the additional contribution of coercion to reducing fertility in China is by no means clear, since compulsion was superimposed on a society that was already reducing its birth rate and in which education and jobs outside the home were available to large numbers of women. In some regions of China, the compulsory program needed little enforcement, whereas in other—more backward—regions, it had to be applied with much severity, with terrible consequences in infant mortality and discrimination against female children. While China may get too much credit for its authoritarian measures, it gets far too little credit for the other, more collaborative and participatory, policies it has followed, which have themselves helped to cut down the birth rate.

China and India

A useful contrast can be drawn between China and India, the two most populous countries in the world. If we look only at the national averages, it is easy to see that China with its low fertility rate of 2.0 has achieved much more than India has with its average fertility rate of 3.6. To what extent this contrast can be attributed to the effectiveness of the coercive policies used in China is not clear, since we would expect the fertility rate to be much lower in China in view of its higher percentage of female literacy (almost twice as high), higher life expectancy (almost ten years more), larger female involvement (by three-quarters) in the labour force, and so on. But India is a country of great diversity, whose different states have very unequal achievements in literacy, health care, and economic and social development. Most states in India are far behind the Chinese provinces in educational achievement (with the exception of Tibet, which has the lowest literacy rate of any Chinese or Indian state), and the same applies to other factors that affect fertility. However, the state of Kerala in southern India provides an interesting comparison with China, since it too has high levels of basic education, health care, and so on. Kerala is a state within a country, but with its 29 million people, it is larger than most countries in the world (including Canada). Kerala's birth rate of 18 per 1000 is actually lower than China's 19 per 1000, and its fertility rate is 1.8 for 1991, compared with China's 2.0 for 1992. These low rates have been achieved without any state coercion.[32]

The roots of Kerala's success are to be found in the kinds of social progress Condorcet hoped for, including, among others, a high female literacy rate (86 percent, which is substantially higher than China's 68 percent). The rural literacy rate is in fact higher in Kerala—for women as well as men—than in every single province in China. Male and female life expectancies at birth in China are respectively 67 and 71 years; the provisional 1991 figures for men and women in Kerala are 71 and 74 years. Women have been active in Kerala's economic and political life for a long time. A high proportion do skilled and semi-skilled work, and a large number have taken part in educational movements.[33] It is perhaps of symbolic importance that the first public pronouncement of the need for widespread elementary education in any part of India was made in 1817 by Rani Gouri Parvathi Bai, the young queen of the princely state of Travancore, which makes up a substantial part of modern Kerala. For a long time, public discussions in Kerala have centred on women's rights and the undesirability of couples marrying when very young.

This political process has been voluntary and collaborative, rather than coercive, and the adverse reactions that have been observed in China, such as infant mortality, have not occurred in Kerala. Kerala's low fertility rate has been achieved along with an infant mortality rate of 16.5 per 1000 live births (17 for boys and 16 for girls), compared with China's 31 (28 for boys and 33 for girls). And as a result of greater gender equality in Kerala, women have not suffered from higher mortality rates than men in Kerala, as they have in China. Even the ratio of females to males in the total population in Kerala (above 1.03) is quite close to that of the current ratios in Europe and America (reflecting the usual pattern of lower female mortality whenever women and men receive similar care). By contrast, the average female-to-male ratio in China is 0.94 and in India as a whole 0.93.[34] Anyone drawn to the Chinese experience of compulsory birth control must take note of these facts.

The temptation to use the "override" approach arises at least partly from impatience with the allegedly slow process of fertility reduction through collaborative, rather than coercive, attempts. Yet Kerala's birth rate has fallen from 44 per 1000 in the 1950s to 18 by 1991—not a sluggish decline. Nor is Kerala unique in this respect. Other societies, such as those of Sri Lanka, South Korea, and Thailand, which have relied on expanding education and reducing mortality rates—instead of on coercion—have also achieved sharp declines in fertility and birth rates.

It is also interesting to compare the time required for reducing fertility in China with that in the two states in India, Kerala and Tamil Nadu, which have done most to encourage voluntary and collaborative reduction in birth rates (even though Tamil Nadu is well behind Kerala in each respect).[35] Table 40.2 shows the fertility rates both in 1979, when the one-child policy and related programs were introduced in China, and in 1991. Despite China's one-child policy and other coercive measures, its fertility rate seems to have fallen much less sharply than those of Kerala and Tamil Nadu. The "override" view is very hard to defend on the basis of the Chinese experience, the only systematic and sustained attempt to impose such a policy that has so far been made.

Family Planning

Even those who do not advocate legal or economic coercion sometimes suggest a variant of the "override" approach—the view, which has been getting increasing support, that the highest priority should be given simply to family planning, even if this means diverting resources from education and health care as well as other activities associated with development. We often hear claims

Table 40.2: **Fertility Rates in China, Kerala, and Tamil Nadu**

	1979	1991
China	2.8	2.0
Kerala	3.0	1.8
Tamil Nadu	3.5	2.2

Sources: For China, Xizhe Peng, *Demographic Transition in China* (New York: Oxford University Press, 1991), Li Chengrui, *A Study of China's Population* (Beijing: Foreign Language Press, 1992), and *World Development Report, 1994* (New York: Oxford University Press, 1996). For India, *Sample Registration System, 1979–80* (New Delhi: Ministry of Home Affairs, 1982) and *Sample Registration System: Fertility and Mortality Indicators, 1991* (New Delhi: Ministry of Home Affairs, 1993).

that enormous declines in birth rates have been accomplished through making family planning services available, without waiting for improvements in education and health care.

The experience of Bangladesh is sometimes cited as an example of such success. Indeed, even though the female literacy rate in Bangladesh is only around 22 percent and life expectancy at birth no higher than 55 years, fertility rates have been substantially reduced there through the greater availability of family planning services, including counselling.[36] We have to examine carefully what lessons can, in fact, be drawn from this evidence.

First, it is certainly significant that Bangladesh has been able to cut its fertility rate from 7.0 to 4.5 during the short period between 1975 and 1990, an achievement that discredits the view that people will not voluntarily embrace family planning in the poorest countries. But we have to ask further whether family-planning efforts may themselves be sufficient to make fertility come down to really low levels, without providing for female education and the other features of a fuller collaborative approach. The fertility rate of 4.5 in Bangladesh is still quite high—considerably higher than even India's average rate of 3.6. To begin stabilizing the population, the fertility rates would have to come down closer to the "replacement level" of 2.0, as has happened in Kerala and Tamil Nadu, and in many other places outside the Indian subcontinent. Female education and the other social developments connected with lowering the birth rate would still be much needed.

Contrasts between the records of Indian states offer some substantial lessons here. While Kerala and, to a smaller extent, Tamil Nadu have surged ahead in achieving radically reduced fertility rates, other states in India in the so-called "northern heartland" (such as Uttar Pradesh, Bihar, Madhya Pradesh, and Rajasthan) have very low levels of education, especially female education, and of general health care (often combined with pressure on the poor to accept birth control measures, including sterilization, as a qualifying condition for medical attention and other public services). These states all have high fertility rates—between 4.4 and 5.1. The regional contrasts within India strongly argue for the collaborative approach, including active and educated participation of women.

The threat of an impending population crisis tempts many international observers to suggest that priority be given to family planning arrangements in the Third World countries over other commitments such as education and health care, a redirection of public efforts that is often recommended by policy makers and at international conferences. Not only will this shift have negative effects on people's well-being and reduce their freedoms, it can also be self-defeating if the goal is to stabilize population.

The appeal of such slogans as "family planning first" rests partly on misconceptions about what is needed to reduce fertility rates, but also on mistaken beliefs about the excessive costs of social development, including education and health care. As has been discussed, both these activities are highly labour-intensive, and thus relatively inexpensive even in very poor economies. In fact, Kerala, India's star performer in expanding education and reducing both death rates and birth rates, is among the poorer Indian states. Its domestically produced income is quite low—lower indeed in per capita terms than even the Indian average—even if this is somewhat deceptive, for the greatest expansion of Kerala's earnings derives from citizens who work outside the state. Kerala's ability to finance adequately both educational expansion and health coverage depends on both activities being labour-intensive; they can be made available even in a low-income economy when there is the political will to use them. Despite its economic backwardness, an issue that Kerala will undoubtedly have to address before long (perhaps by reducing bureaucratic controls over agriculture and industry, which have stagnated), its level of social development has been remarkable, and that has turned out to be crucial in reducing fertility rates. Kerala's fertility rate of 1.8 not only compares well with China's 2.0, but also with the United States' and Sweden's 2.1, Canada's 1.9, and Britain's and France's 1.8.

The population problem is serious, certainly, but neither because of "the proportion between the natural increase in population and food" nor because of some impending apocalypse. There are reasons for worry about the long-term effects of population growth on the environment; and there are strong reasons for concern about the adverse effects of high birth rates on the quality of life, especially of women. With greater opportunities for education (especially female education), reduction of mortality rates (especially of children), improvement in economic security (especially in old age), and greater participation of women in employment and in political action, fast reductions in birth rates can be expected to result through the decisions and actions of those whose lives depend on them.

This is happening right now in many parts of the world, and the result has been a considerable slowing down of world population growth. The best way of dealing with the population problem is to help to spread

these processes elsewhere. In contrast, the emergency mentality based on false beliefs in imminent cataclysms leads to breathless responses that are deeply counterproductive, preventing the development of rational and sustainable family planning. Coercive policies of forced birth control involve terrible social sacrifices, and there is little evidence that they are more effective in reducing birth rates than serious programs of collaborative action.

Notes

[1] This chapter draws on a lecture by Amartya Sen arranged by the "Eminent Citizens Committee for Cairo '94" at the United Nations in New York on April 18, 1994, and also on research supported by the National Science Foundation.

[2] Paul Ehrlich, *The Population Bomb* (New York: Ballantine, 1968). More recently Paul Ehrlich and Anne H. Ehrlich have written *The Population Explosion* (New York: Simon and Schuster, 1990).

[3] Garrett Hardin, *Living within Limits* (New York: Oxford University Press, 1993).

[4] Thomas Robert Malthus, *Essay on the Principle of Population As It Affects the Future Improvement of Society with Remarks on the Speculation of Mr. Godwin, M. Condorcet, and Other Writers* (London: J. Johnson, 1798), chapter 8; in the Penguin classics edition, *An Essay on the Principle of Population* (Harmondsworth, UK: Penguin, 1982), p. 123.

[5] See Simon Kuznets, Modern Economic Growth (New Haven, CT: Yale University Press, 1966).

[6] Note by the Secretary-General of the United Nations to the Preparatory Committee for the International Conference on Population and Development, Third Session, A/Conf.171/ PC/5, February 18, 1994, p. 30.

[7] Philip Morris Hauser's estimates are presented in the National Academy of Sciences publication *Rapid Population Growth: Consequences and Policy Implications*, Vol. 1 (Baltimore, MD: Johns Hopkins University Press, 1971). See also Kuznets, *Modern Economic Growth*, chapter 2.

[8] For an important collection of papers on these and related issues, see Sir Francis Graham-Smith, F.R.S., ed., *Population—The Complex Reality: A Report of the Population Summit of the World's Scientific Academies*, issued by the Royal Society and published in the United States by North American Press Golden, Colorado. See also D. Gale Johnson and Ronald D. Lee, eds., *Population Growth and Economic Development, Issues and Evidence* (Madison: University of Wisconsin Press, 1987).

[9] Hardin, *Living within Limits*, 274.

[10] Paul Kennedy, who has discussed important problems in the distinctly "social" aspects of population growth, has pointed out that this debate "has, in one form or another, been with us since then," and "it is even more pertinent today than when Malthus composed his Essay," in *Preparing for the Twenty-First Century* (New York: Random House, 1993), pp. 5–6.

[11] On the importance of "Enlightenment" traditions in Condorcet's thinking, see Emma Rothschild, "Condorcet and the Conflict of Values," forthcoming in *The Historical Journal*.

[12] Marie Jean Antoine Nicholas de Caritat Marquis de Condorcet's *Esquisse d'un Tableau Historique des Progrès de l'Esprit Humain, Xe Epoque* (1795). English translation by June Barraclough, *Sketch for a Historical Picture of the Progress of the Human Mind*, with an introduction by Stuart Hampshire (London: Weidenfeld and Nicolson, 1955), pp. 187–92.

[13] T.R. Malthus, *A Summary View of the Principle of Population* (London: John Murray, 1830); in the Penguin classics edition (Harmondsworth, UK: Penguin, 1982), p. 243; emphasis added.

[14] On practical policies, including criticism of poverty relief and charitable hospitals, advocated for Britain by Malthus and his followers, see William St. Clair, *The Godwins and the Shelleys: A Biography of a Family* (New York: Norton, 1989).

[15] Malthus, *Essay on the Principle of Population*, chapter 17; in the Penguin classics edition, *An Essay of the Principle of Population*, pp. 198–99. Malthus showed some signs of weakening in this belief as he grew older.

[16] Gerard Piel, *Only One World: Our Own to Make and to Keep* (New York: Freeman, 1992).

[17] For discussions of these empirical connections, see R.A. Easterlin, ed., *Population and Economic Change in Developing Countries* (Chicago: University of Chicago Press, 1980); T.P. Schultz, *Economics of Population* (London: Addison-Wesley, 1981); J.C. Caldwell, *Theory of Fertility Decline* (New York: Academic Press, 1982); E. King and M.A. Hill, eds., *Women's Education in Developing Countries* (Baltimore, MD: Johns Hopkins University Press, 1992); Nancy Birdsall, "Economic Approaches to Population Growth," in *The Handbook of Development Economics*, H.B. Chenery and T.N. Srinivasan, eds. (Amsterdam: North Holland, 1988); Robert Cassen et al., *Population and Development: Old Debates, New Conclusions* (New Brunswick, NJ: Overseas Development Council/ Transaction Publisher, 1994).

[18] World Bank, *World Development Report 1994* (New York: Oxford University Press, 1994), Table 25, pp. 210–11.

[19] World Bank, *World Development Report 1994*, Table 2.

[20] These issues are discussed in Jean Dreze and Amartya Sen, *Hunger and Public Action* (New York: Oxford University Press, 1989), and the three volumes edited by them, *The Political Economy of Hunger* (New York: Oxford University Press, 1990), and also in Amartya Sen, "Economic Regress: Concepts and Features," in *Proceedings of the World Bank Annual Conference on Development Economics 1993* (Washington, DC: World Bank, 1994).

[21] This is confirmed by, among other statistics, the food production figures regularly presented by the United Nations Food and

Agricultural Organization (see the *FAO Quarterly Bulletin of Statistics*, and also the *FAO Monthly Bulletins*).

[22] For a more detailed picture and references to data sources, see Amartya Sen, "Population and Reasoned Agency: Food, Fertility and Economic Development," in *Population, Economic Development, and the Environment*, Kerstin Lindahl-Kiessling and Hans Landberg, eds. (New York: Oxford University Press, 1994); see also the other contributions in this volume. The data presented here have been slightly updated from later publications of the FAO.

[23] On this see Amartya Sen, *Poverty and Famines* (New York: Oxford University Press, 1981).

[24] See UNCTAD VIII, *Analytical Report by the UNCTAD Secretariat to the Conference* (New York: United Nations, 1992), Table V-S, p. 235. The period covered is between 1979–81 and 1988–90. These figures and related ones are discussed in greater detail in Amartya Sen, "Population and Reasoned Agency."

[25] World Bank, *Price Prospects for Major Primary Commodities, Vol. II* (Washington, DC: World Bank, March 1993), Annex Tables 6, 12, and 18.

[26] Condorcet, *Esquisse d'un Tableau Historique des Progrès de l'Esprit Humain*; in the 1968 reprint, p. 187.

[27] The importance of "local" environmental issues is stressed and particularly explored by Partha Dasgupta in *An Inquiry into Well-Being and Destitution* (New York: Oxford University Press, 1993).

[28] In a forthcoming monograph by Jean Dreze and Amartya Sen called *India: Economic Development and Opportunity* (New York: Oxford University Press, 1995), they discuss the importance of women's political agency in rectifying some of the more serious lapses in Indian economic and social performance—not just pertaining to the deprivation of women themselves.

[29] See Dreze and Sen, *Hunger and Public Action*, which also investigates the remarkable success of some poor countries in providing widespread educational and health services.

[30] World Bank, *World Development Report 1994*, p. 212; and *Sample Registration System: Fertility and Mortality Indicators 1991* (New Delhi: Ministry of Home Affairs, 1993).

[31] See the discussions, and the literature cited, in Gita Sen, Adrienne German, and Lincoln Chen, eds., *Population Policies Reconsidered: Health, Empowerment, and Rights* (London: Harvard Center for Population and Development Studies/International Women's Health Coalition, 1994).

[32] On the actual processes involved, see T.N. Krishnan, "Demographic Transition in Kerala: Facts and Factors," in *Economic and Political Weekly*, Vol. 11 (1976), and P.N. Mari Bhat and S.I. Rajan, "Demographic Transition in Kerala Revisited," in *Economic and Political Weekly*, Vol. 25 (1990).

[33] See, for example, Robin Jeffrey, "Culture and Governments: How Women Made Kerala Literate," in *Pacific Affairs*, Vol. 60 (1987).

[34] On this see Amartya Sen, "More Than 100 Million Women Are Missing," *New York Review of Books*, December 20, 1990; Ansley J. Coale, "Excess Female Mortality and the Balance of the Sexes: An Estimate of the Number of 'Missing Females,'" *Population and Development Review*, No. 17 (1991); Amartya Sen, "Missing Women," *British Medical Journal*, No. 304 (March 1992); Stephan Klasen, "'Missing Women' Reconsidered," *World Development*, Vol. 22 (1994).

[35] Tamil Nadu has benefited from an active and efficient voluntary program of family planning, but these efforts have been helped by favourable social conditions as well, such as a high literacy rate (the second highest among the sixteen major states), a high rate of female participation in work outside the home (the third highest), a relatively low infant mortality rate (the third lowest), and a traditionally higher age of marriage. See also T.V. Antony, "The Family Planning Programme—Lessons from Tamil Nadu's Experience," *Indian Journal of Social Science*, Vol. 5 (1992).

[36] World Bank and Population Reference Bureau, *Success in a Challenging Environment: Fertility Decline in Bangladesh* (Washington, DC: World Bank, 1993).

CHAPTER 41
The Clash of Ignorance

Edward W. Said

Samuel Huntington's article "The Clash of Civilizations?" appeared in the Summer 1993 issue of *Foreign Affairs*, where it immediately attracted a surprising amount of attention and reaction. Because the article was intended to supply Americans with an original thesis about "a new phase" in world politics after the end of the cold war, Huntington's terms of argument seemed compellingly large, bold, even visionary. He very clearly had his eye on rivals in the policy-making ranks, theorists such as Francis Fukuyama and his "end of history" ideas, as well as the legions who had celebrated the onset of globalism, tribalism and the dissipation of the state. But they, he allowed, had understood only some aspects of this new period. He was about to announce the "crucial, indeed a central, aspect" of what "global politics is likely to be in the coming years." Unhesitatingly he pressed on:

"It is my hypothesis that the fundamental source of conflict in this new world will not be primarily ideological or primarily economic. The great divisions among humankind and the dominating source of conflict will be cultural. Nation states will remain the most powerful actors in world affairs, but the principal conflicts of global politics will occur between nations and groups of different civilizations. The clash of civilizations will dominate global politics. The fault lines between civilizations will be the battle lines of the future."

Most of the argument in the pages that followed relied on a vague notion of something Huntington called "civilization identity" and "the interactions among seven or eight [*sic*] major civilizations," of which the conflict between two of them, Islam and the West, gets the lion's share of his attention. In this belligerent kind of thought, he relies heavily on a 1990 article by the veteran Orientalist Bernard Lewis, whose ideological colors are manifest in its title, "The Roots of Muslim Rage." In both articles, the personification of enormous entities called "the West" and "Islam" is recklessly affirmed, as if hugely complicated matters like identity and culture existed in a cartoonlike world where Popeye and Bluto bash each other mercilessly, with one always more virtuous pugilist getting the upper hand over his adversary. Certainly neither Huntington nor Lewis has much time

to spare for the internal dynamics and plurality of every civilization, or for the fact that the major contest in most modern cultures concerns the definition or interpretation of each culture, or for the unattractive possibility that a great deal of demagogy and downright ignorance is involved in presuming to speak for a whole religion or civilization. No, the West is the West, and Islam Islam.

The challenge for Western policy-makers, says Huntington, is to make sure that the West gets stronger and fends off all the others, Islam in particular. More troubling is Huntington's assumption that his perspective, which is to survey the entire world from a perch outside all ordinary attachments and hidden loyalties, is the correct one, as if everyone else were scurrying around looking for the answers that he has already found. In fact, Huntington is an ideologist, someone who wants to make "civilizations" and "identities" into what they are not: shut-down, sealed-off entities that have been purged of the myriad currents and countercurrents that animate human history, and that over centuries have made it possible for that history not only to contain wars of religion and imperial conquest but also to be one of exchange, cross-fertilization and sharing. This far less visible history is ignored in the rush to highlight the ludicrously compressed and constricted warfare that "the clash of civilizations" argues is the reality. When he published his book by the same title in 1996, Huntington tried to give his argument a little more subtlety and many, many more footnotes; all he did, however, was confuse himself and demonstrate what a clumsy writer and inelegant thinker he was.

The basic paradigm of West versus the rest (the cold war opposition reformulated) remained untouched, and this is what has persisted, often insidiously and implicitly, in discussion since the terrible events of September 11. The carefully planned and horrendous, pathologically motivated suicide attack and mass slaughter by a small group of deranged militants has been turned into proof of Huntington's thesis. Instead of seeing it for what it is—the capture of big ideas (I use the word loosely) by a tiny band of crazed fanatics for criminal purposes—international luminaries from former Pakistani Prime Minister Benazir Bhutto to Italian Prime Minister Silvio

Berlusconi have pontificated about Islam's troubles, and in the latter's case have used Huntington's ideas to rant on about the West's superiority, how "we" have Mozart and Michelangelo and they don't. (Berlusconi has since made a halfhearted apology for his insult to "Islam.")

But why not instead see parallels, admittedly less spectacular in their destructiveness, for Osama bin Laden and his followers in cults like the Branch Davidians or the disciples of the Rev. Jim Jones at Guyana or the Japanese Aum Shinrikyo? Even the normally sober British weekly *The Economist*, in its issue of September 22–28, can't resist reaching for the vast generalization, praising Huntington extravagantly for his "cruel and sweeping, but nonetheless acute" observations about Islam. "Today," the journal says with unseemly solemnity, Huntington writes that "the world's billion or so Muslims are 'convinced of the superiority of their culture, and obsessed with the inferiority of their power.'" Did he canvas 100 Indonesians, 200 Moroccans, 500 Egyptians and fifty Bosnians? Even if he did, what sort of sample is that?

Uncountable are the editorials in every American and European newspaper and magazine of note adding to this vocabulary of gigantism and apocalypse, each use of which is plainly designed not to edify but to inflame the reader's indignant passion as a member of the "West," and what we need to do. Churchillian rhetoric is used inappropriately by self-appointed combatants in the West's, and especially America's, war against its haters, despoilers, destroyers, with scant attention to complex histories that defy such reductiveness and have seeped from one territory into another, in the process overriding the boundaries that are supposed to separate us all into divided armed camps.

This is the problem with unedifying labels like Islam and the West: They mislead and confuse the mind, which is trying to make sense of a disorderly reality that won't be pigeonholed or strapped down as easily as all that. I remember interrupting a man who, after a lecture I had given at a West Bank university in 1994, rose from the audience and started to attack my ideas as "Western," as opposed to the strict Islamic ones he espoused. "Why are you wearing a suit and tie?" was the first retort that came to mind. "They're Western too." He sat down with an embarrassed smile on his face, but I recalled the incident when information on the September 11 terrorists started to come in: how they had mastered all the technical details required to inflict their homicidal evil on the World Trade Center, the Pentagon and the aircraft they had commandeered. Where does one draw the line between "Western" technology and, as Berlusconi declared, "Islam's" inability to be a part of "modernity"?

One cannot easily do so, of course. How finally inadequate are the labels, generalizations and cultural assertions. At some level, for instance, primitive passions and sophisticated know-how converge in ways that give the lie to a fortified boundary not only between "West" and "Islam" but also between past and present, us and them,

to say nothing of the very concepts of identity and nationality about which there is unending disagreement and debate. A unilateral decision made to draw lines in the sand, to undertake crusades, to oppose their evil with our good, to extirpate terrorism and, in Paul Wolfowitz's nihilistic vocabulary, to end nations entirely, doesn't make the supposed entities any easier to see; rather, it speaks to how much simpler it is to make bellicose statements for the purpose of mobilizing collective passions than to reflect, examine, sort out what it is we are dealing with in reality, the interconnectedness of innumerable lives, "ours" as well as "theirs."

In a remarkable series of three articles published between January and March 1999 in *Dawn*, Pakistan's most respected weekly, the late Eqbal Ahmad, writing for a Muslim audience, analyzed what he called the roots of the religious right, coming down very harshly on the mutilations of Islam by absolutists and fanatical tyrants whose obsession with regulating personal behavior promotes "an Islamic order reduced to a penal code, stripped of its humanism, aesthetics, intellectual quests, and spiritual devotion." And this "entails an absolute assertion of one, generally de-contextualized, aspect of religion and a total disregard of another. The phenomenon distorts religion, debases tradition, and twists the political process wherever it unfolds." As a timely instance of this debasement, Ahmad proceeds first to present the rich, complex, pluralist meaning of the word *jihad* and then goes on to show that in the word's current confinement to indiscriminate war against presumed enemies, it is impossible "to recognize the Islamic—religion, society, culture, history or politics—as lived and experienced by Muslims through the ages." The modern Islamists, Ahmad concludes, are "concerned with power, not with the soul; with the mobilization of people for political purposes rather than with sharing and alleviating their sufferings and aspirations. Theirs is a very limited and time-bound political agenda." What has made matters worse is that similar distortions and zealotry occur in the "Jewish" and "Christian" universes of discourse.

It was Conrad, more powerfully than any of his readers at the end of the nineteenth century could have imagined, who understood that the distinctions between civilized London and "the heart of darkness" quickly collapsed in extreme situations, and that the heights of European civilization could instantaneously fall into the most barbarous practices without preparation or transition. And it was Conrad also, in *The Secret Agent* (1907), who described terrorism's affinity for abstractions like "pure science" (and by extension for "Islam" or "the West"), as well as the terrorist's ultimate moral degradation.

For there are closer ties between apparently warring civilizations than most of us would like to believe; both Freud and Nietzsche showed how the traffic across carefully maintained, even policed boundaries moves with often terrifying ease. But then such fluid ideas, full of ambiguity and skepticism about notions that we hold on to, scarcely furnish us with suitable, practical guidelines for situations such as the one we face now. Hence the altogether more reassuring battle orders (a crusade, good versus evil, freedom against fear, etc.) drawn out of Huntington's alleged opposition between Islam and the West, from which official discourse drew its vocabulary in the first days after the September 11 attacks. There's since been a noticeable de-escalation in that discourse, but to judge from the steady amount of hate speech and actions, plus reports of law enforcement efforts directed against Arabs, Muslims and Indians all over the country, the paradigm stays on.

One further reason for its persistence is the increased presence of Muslims all over Europe and the United States. Think of the populations today of France, Italy, Germany, Spain, Britain, America, even Sweden, and you must concede that Islam is no longer on the fringes of the West but at its center. But what is so threatening about that presence? Buried in the collective culture are memories of the first great Arab-Islamic conquests, which began in the seventh century and which, as the celebrated Belgian historian Henri Pirenne wrote in his landmark book *Mohammed and Charlemagne* (1939), shattered once and for all the ancient unity of the Mediterranean, destroyed the Christian-Roman synthesis and gave rise to a new civilization dominated by northern powers (Germany and Carolingian France) whose mission, he seemed to be saying, is to resume defense of the "West" against its historical-cultural enemies. What Pirenne left out, alas, is that in the creation of this new line of defense the West drew on the humanism, science, philosophy, sociology and historiography of Islam, which had already interposed itself between Charlemagne's world and classical antiquity. Islam is inside from the start, as even Dante, great enemy of Mohammed, had to concede when he placed the Prophet at the very heart of his *Inferno*.

Then there is the persisting legacy of monotheism itself, the Abrahamic religions, as Louis Massignon aptly called them. Beginning with Judaism and Christianity, each is a successor haunted by what came before; for Muslims, Islam fulfills and ends the line of prophecy. There is still no decent history or demystification of the many-sided contest among these three followers—not one of them by any means a monolithic, unified camp— of the most jealous of all gods, even though the bloody modern convergence on Palestine furnishes a rich secular instance of what has been so tragically irreconcilable about them. Not surprisingly, then, Muslims and Christians speak readily of crusades and *jihads*, both of them eliding the Judaic presence with often sublime insouciance. Such an agenda, says Eqbal Ahmad, is "very reassuring to the men and women who are stranded in the middle of the ford, between the deep waters of tradition and modernity."

But we are all swimming in those waters, Westerners and Muslims and others alike. And since the waters are part of the ocean of history, trying to plow or divide them with barriers is futile. These are tense times, but it is better to think in terms of powerful and powerless communities, the secular politics of reason and ignorance, and universal principles of justice and injustice, than to wander off in search of vast abstractions that may give momentary satisfaction but little self-knowledge or informed analysis. "The Clash of Civilizations" thesis is a gimmick like "The War of the Worlds," better for reinforcing defensive self-pride than for critical understanding of the bewildering interdependence of our time.

Rethinking Section 6:
POPULATION, GLOBALIZATION, AND THE NEW WORLD ORDER

Critical Thinking Questions

Amartya Sen

1. Discuss the anxiety and perceived threats concerning the "world population problem." What are the common misconceptions, and what are the real reasons that explain why the "population problem" is a serious concern?
2. Given that there is a connection between socio-economic development and major reduction in birth rates, why have we not resolved the question of how to deal with the world's population growth? Can population control be discussed in isolation and removed from a discussion of global politics and economics?
3. Given that there is not a food shortage in the world, nor is food becoming more expensive, why do so many people die of hunger every day?

Edward Said

1. What is the nation state?
2. How do the media influence our perceptions of the nation?
3. Who gets constructed as the "other"?
4. Is the principle of universal justice practised? Give support for your argument.

Glossary Terms

Amartya Sen

collaborative versus override approach: A collaborative approach relies on rational decisions of men and women based on choices and security and an open dialogue. An override approach involves compulsory legal and state control, often in the form of mandatory birth control.

Malthus: Thomas Malthus developed a theory of population in the late 1700s, which argued that a check on the rate of population growth was desirable.

Edward Said

Jihad: According to Said, the meaning of *jihad* has been distorted by fundamentalists; refers to militant fundamentalism, and is *not* a referent to Islam or indeed any religion, as militant fundamentalism is found in all groups the world over.

Relevant Web sites

http://www.nologo.com

A site containing a selection of writings by Naomi Klein discussing globalization and social justice issues.

http://maquilasolidarity.org

Run by the Maquila Solidarity Network (a Canadian organization), this site explores the working condition of factories in the maquiladoras with the aim to improve conditions and wages.

http://www.canadiansocialresearch.net/global.htm

Links to resources about the G8, human rights, and the North American Free Trade Agreement (NAFTA).

http://www.worldbank.com

The site of the World Bank wherein their mission is stated: "to fight poverty and improve the living conditions of people in the developing world."

http://www.whirledbank.org

This is a spoof site of the World Bank.

http://www.globalresearch.ca

Articles by writers, scholars, and activists committed to fighting globalization and the new world order.

http://www.globalisationguide.org

A site put together by the Australian Apec Study Centre. It attempts to answer basic questions about globalization. It also provides links to other sites dedicated to globalization.

http://www.southcentre.org

The South Centre is an organization representing countries from the "South" of the world. The site contains speeches and articles related to globalization.

http://www.wtowatch.org

This site keeps a watch on the World Trade Organization. It is a critical site on trade and globalization matters.

http://www.ssrc.org/sept11/essays/globalization.htm

Several essays discussing globalization and the new world order post–September 11.

Further Reading

Amin, Samir. (2000). *Capitalism in the Age of Globalization: The Management of Contemporary Society.* London: Zed Books.
An emphatic rejection of globalization in its current form, this book offers insight into the content and consequences of trade and economic restructuring in the world today.

Bantjes, Rod. (2007). *Social Movements in a Global Context: Canadian Perspectives.* Toronto: Canadian Scholars' Press Inc.
Global social movements: The focus of this original book is on interpreting the resurgence in popular protest to a growing audience of university students.

Barlow, Maude, and Tony Clarke. (2001). *Global Showdown: How the New Activists Are Fighting Global Corporate Rule.* Toronto: Stoddart.
An examination of resistance to the globalization process and its transfer of wealth to high-income nations.

Bové, José, and François Dufour. (2001). *The World Is Not for Sale: Farmers against Junk Food.* London: Verso.
Interviews with two French farmers who were imprisoned for protesting against large agribusiness practices.

Carroll, William (ed.). (1997). *Organizing Dissent: Contemporary Social Movement in Theory and Practice.* Toronto: Garamond.
A survey of Canadian literature on, and case studies about, social movements.

Chossudovsky, Michel. (1998). *The Globalisation of Poverty: Impacts of IMF and World Bank Reforms.* London: Zed Books.
An incisive examination of the increased polarization of wealth and inequality that have stemmed from neo-liberal economic reforms.

Clarkson, Stephen. (2002). *Uncle Sam and Us: Globalization, Neoconservatism, and the Canadian State.* Toronto: University of Toronto Press.
A thorough analysis of transformations in the Canadian state arising from the forces of globalization.

Huntington, Samuel. (1993). "The Clash of Civilizations?" *Foreign Affairs, 72*(3), pp. 22–49.
A highly debated article pertaining to globalization, development, and resistance.

Klein, Naomi. (2000). *No Logo: Taking Aim at the Brand Bullies*. Toronto: Vintage.
Klein's path-breaking book on the history of superbrands and their control over the global economy.

Sassen, Saskia. (1998). *Globalization and Its Discontents: Essays on the New Mobility of People and Money*. New York: The New Press.
This text considers gender, migration, technology, and the dynamics of inequality.

Urmetzer, Peter. (2003). *From Free Trade to Forced Trade: Canada in the Global Economy*. Toronto: Penguin.
An analysis of the debates surrounding free trade in Canada.

Copyright Acknowledgements